Governance, Corruption, & Economic Performance

George T. Abed
Sanjeev Gupta
Editors

International Monetary Fund
Washington, D.C. 2002

© 2002 International Monetary Fund

Production: IMF Graphics Section
Cover design and charts: Sanaa Elaroussi
Typesetting: Alicia Etchebarne-Bourdin

Cataloging-in-Publication Data

Governance, corruption, and economic performance / editors, George T. Abed, Sanjeev Gupta—Washington, D.C.: International Monetary Fund, [2002].
   p. cm.

   Includes bibliographical references.
   ISBN 1-58906-116-0

   1. Political corruption—Economic aspects. 2. Political corruption—Economic aspects—Developing countries. 3. International Monetary Fund. I. Abed, George T. II. Gupta, Sanjeev. III. International Monetary Fund.

JF1081.G67 2002

Price: US$37.50

Address orders to:
International Monetary Fund, Publication Services
700 19th Street, N.W., Washington, D.C., 20431, U.S.A.
Tel.: (202) 623-7430   Telefax: (202) 623-7201
E-mail: publications@imf.org
Internet: http://www.imf.org

Contents

Foreword		vii
Acknowledgments		ix
Contributors		xi
1	The Economics of Corruption: An Overview *George T. Abed and Sanjeev Gupta*	1

Part I   Causes and Consequences of Corruption

2	Corruption Around the World: Causes, Consequences, Scope, and Cures *Vito Tanzi*	19
3	Bureaucratic Corruption and the Rate of Temptation: Do Wages in the Civil Service Affect Corruption and by How Much? *Caroline Van Rijckeghem and Beatrice Weder*	59
4	Controlling Fiscal Corruption *Sheetal K. Chand and Karl O. Moene*	89
5	A Game Theoretic Analysis of Corruption in Bureaucracies *Era Dabla-Norris*	111
6	Institutionalized Corruption and the Kleptocratic State *Joshua Charap and Christian Harm*	135

Contents

7 Does Mother Nature Corrupt? Natural Resources, Corruption, and Economic Growth   159
Carlos Leite and Jens Weidmann

8 Corruption, Growth, and Public Finances   197
Vito Tanzi and Hamid R. Davoodi

Part II Corruption and Government Expenditures

9 Corruption and the Composition of Government Expenditure   225
Paolo Mauro

10 Corruption and the Provision of Health Care and Education Services   245
Sanjeev Gupta, Hamid R. Davoodi, and Erwin R. Tiongson

11 Corruption, Public Investment, and Growth   280
Vito Tanzi and Hamid R. Davoodi

12 Corruption and Military Spending   300
Sanjeev Gupta, Luiz de Mello, and Raju Sharan

13 Fiscal Decentralization and Governance: A Cross-Country Analysis   333
Luiz de Mello and Matias Barenstein

Part III Corruption and Taxes

14 Tax Revenue in Sub-Saharan Africa: Effects of Economic Policies and Corruption   369
Dhaneshwar Ghura

15 Corruption, Extortion and Evasion   396
Jean Hindriks, Michael Keen, and Abhinay Muthoo

Part IV Corruption, Income Distribution, and Poverty

16 Production, Rent Seeking, and Wealth Distribution   439
Era Dabla-Norris and Paul Wade

17 Does Corruption Affect Income Inequality and Poverty?   458
Sanjeev Gupta, Hamid R. Davoodi, and Rosa Alonso-Terme

Contents

Part V Corruption and Transition Economies

18 Corruption, Structural Reforms, and Economic
    Performance in the Transition Economies   489
    George T. Abed and Hamid R. Davoodi

19 Improving Governance and Fighting Corruption in
    the Baltic and CIS Countries: The Role of the IMF   538
    Thomas Wolf and Emine Gürgen

The following symbols have been used throughout this volume:

... to indicate that data are not available;

—   to indicate that the figure is zero or less than half the final digit shown, or that the item does not exist;

–   between years or months (for example, 2000–01 or January–June) to indicate the years or months covered, including the beginning and ending years or months;

/   between years (for example, 2000/01) to indicate a fiscal (financial) year.

"Billion" means a thousand million.

Minor discrepancies between constituent figures and totals are due to rounding.

The term "country," as used in this volume, does not in all cases refer to a territorial entity that is a state as understood by international law and practice; the term also covers some territorial entities that are not states, but for which statistical data are maintained and provided internationally on a separate and independent basis.

Foreword

For some time now, the IMF has recognized the important role of good governance in influencing economic performance. The IMF's role in this area is founded on its mandate to promote macroeconomic stability and sustained noninflationary growth in member countries. Poor governance and widespread corruption cut into government revenues and lead to wasteful spending, thereby weakening the macroeconomic position of a country. Corruption also impinges on the effectiveness of the state, and erodes the confidence of the public in its institutions and policies. It is against this background that the IMF is actively promoting good governance in member countries through enhanced surveillance; the promulgation of standards and codes of good practice in the fiscal, monetary, and statistical areas; technical assistance to strengthen institutional capacity; and specific measures to address particular instances of poor governance and corruption in IMF-supported programs. While the IMF provides member countries with the know-how and the tools, the main responsibility for tackling these problems resides with the countries themselves.

The increased involvement of the IMF in governance issues has been facilitated by the growing consensus in the economics profession and in the international community at large on the adverse effects of corruption on economic performance. Recent empirical research, including that presented in this volume, documents the detrimental impact of corruption on economic growth, inflation, public finances, investment, poverty, and the provision of social services. In particular, studies demonstrate how weak and poorly run institutions fall prey to vested interests which, in effect "capture the state" and then use their

Foreword

power to preserve monopolies and extract rent, hinder competition, and inhibit economic reform. Corruption is equally damaging when those in positions of authority exploit their public trust to achieve personal gain. Such practices not only impose additional taxes on the economy, they also undermine the rule of law, which is essential to the proper functioning of a market economy.

In such situations, governments must be prepared to challenge vested interests and root out corruption. They need to foster transparency in the management of public funds and in the legal and regulatory frameworks, and must establish competent and impartial courts of law, trustworthy law enforcement agencies, and better trained, properly paid civil servants and judges. The global consensus on the importance of good governance can be effective only on the basis of the increased willingness and commitment of authorities to foster a transparent and accountable system of government at the national level. The IMF has always been ready to work with member countries to identify ways to reduce the risks of mismanagement and corruption in its areas of expertise. A case in point is the heavily indebted poor countries, where the IMF is working closely with the World Bank and national governments to ensure that additional spending, facilitated by the recently launched initiative to reduce their debt burdens, is channeled into programs that reduce poverty. This requires that concerted efforts be made to strengthen institutional reforms, especially in the areas of public expenditure management.

I welcome the publication of this volume. It has consolidated research by IMF staff on the impact of corruption and poor governance on macroeconomic performance. I hope that it will stimulate further research and wider discussion on this vitally important topic, both within and outside the IMF.

Horst Köhler
Managing Director
International Monetary Fund

Acknowledgments

This volume is a product of the collective effort of many individuals. In particular, we are grateful to the contributing authors for their papers. Most papers were originally issued as IMF Working Papers and the revised versions of some these papers were published in journals and other volumes. Thanks are due to Edward Elgar Publishing, Elsevier Science, Ltd., North-Holland Publishing Co., Routledge, and Springer for allowing us to reprint these articles.

Staff of the Fiscal Affairs Department's Expenditure Policy Division provided valuable assistance. We are particularly grateful to Hamid Davoodi, Luiz de Mello, Shamit Chakravarti, Erwin Tiongson, and Meike Gretemann for their assistance and advice in compiling this volume. Special thanks are due to Suzanne Alavi, who managed the correspondence with authors and publishers and prepared the volume for publication. Esha Ray of the IMF's External Relations Department edited the manuscript and coordinated production.

The views expressed are those of the authors and do not necessarily reflect those of the IMF.

George T. Abed
Sanjeev Gupta
Editors

Contributors

George T. Abed	Director, Middle East Department, IMF
Rosa Alonso-Terme	Economist, Office of the Vice President, Economic Policy and Poverty Reduction, World Bank; formerly Economist, Fiscal Affairs Department, IMF
Matias Barenstein	Department of Economics, University of California at Berkeley
Sheetal K. Chand	Professor of Economics, University of Oslo, Oslo, Norway; formerly Advisor, Fiscal Affairs Department, IMF
Joshua Charap	Senior Economist, European I Department, IMF
Era Dabla-Norris	Economist, IMF Institute, IMF
Hamid R. Davoodi	Economist, Fiscal Affairs Department, IMF
Luiz de Mello	Senior Economist, Fiscal Affairs Department, IMF
Dhaneshwar Ghura	Deputy Division Chief, African Department, IMF
Sanjeev Gupta	Assistant Director, Fiscal Affairs Department, IMF
Emine Gürgen	Formerly Assistant to the Director, European II Department, IMF

Contributors

Christian Harm	Professor of International Business, University of Münster, Münster, Germany
Jean Hindriks	Assistant Professor of Economics, CORE, Université Catholique de Louvain, Louvain-la-Neuve, Belgium
Michael Keen	Advisor, Fiscal Affairs Department, IMF
Carlos Leite	Economist, African Department, IMF
Paolo Mauro	Economist, Research Department, IMF
Karl O. Moene	Professor of Economics, Department of Economics, University of Oslo, Oslo, Norway
Abhinay Muthoo	Professor of Economics, University of Essex, Colchester, United Kingdom
Raju Sharan	Deputy Controller General of Accounts, Government of India, New Delhi, India
Vito Tanzi	Undersecretary of State at the Ministry of Economy and Finance, Rome, Italy; formerly Director, Fiscal Affairs Department, IMF
Erwin R. Tiongson	Senior Research Officer, Fiscal Affairs Department, IMF
Paul Wade	Senior Economist, IMF Institute, IMF
Beatrice Weder	Professor of Economics, University of Mainz, Mainz, Germany
Jens Weidmann	Secretary General, German Council of Economic Experts, Bonn, Germany
Thomas Wolf	Assistant Director, European II Department, IMF
Caroline van Rijckeghem	Professor of Economics, Faculty of Arts and Social Sciences, Sabanci University Campus, Istanbul, Turkey; formerly Economist, Research Department, IMF

1

The Economics of Corruption: An Overview

George T. Abed and Sanjeev Gupta

I. Introduction

Until the 1980s, scholarly research on corruption was largely confined to the fields of sociology, political science, history, public administration, and criminal law. Since then, economists have also turned their interest to this topic, largely on account of its increasingly evident link to economic performance. Much of the early research[1] focused on weaknesses in public institutions and distortions in economic policies that gave rise to rent seeking by public officials and the incubation of corrupt practices. It also highlighted some positive effects of corruption, which were discounted in the subsequent literature.

Since the early 1990s, there has been a virtual explosion of academic writing on the economics of corruption. The initial thrust for this work came from the transformation of the socialist economies of the

---

[1]See Bhagwati (1982); Becker (1968); Buchanan, Tollison, and Tullock (1980); Klitgaard (1984 and 1988); Krueger (1974 and 1993); Murphy, Shleifer, and Vishny (1993); and Rose-Ackerman (1975 and 1978).

former Soviet Union,[2] awareness of the costs of corruption in both developed as well as developing countries, and the construction of indicators of corruption that could be used in empirical studies. The flood of writings has continued unabated.[3] As noted below, and as is clear from the contents of this volume, a considerable part of this research activity took place at the IMF and the World Bank. There are several reasons for the burgeoning interest of Bretton Woods institutions, and the economics profession in general, in this topic.

One factor is the accelerating trend of globalization and world economic integration. Together with an associated drive for economic liberalization, notably in the area of international trade, globalization has increased the pressure on countries to be more transparent and accountable in the management of their economies. More to the point, it created incentives for policymakers to reform policies and institutions for countries to benefit from the rising international flows of capital, technology, and information. While the countries most eager to exploit the widening opportunities were initially the larger emerging economies, other developing countries also sought to access markets and attract investment flows in the new environment.

Data on the size and composition of international capital movements in the 1990s underscore this point. Since the mid-1990s, the composition of capital flows to emerging and developing countries began to shift markedly in favor of the private sector, with multinational corporations, and financial markets more generally, dominating the field and eclipsing the role of official transfers. Thus, while at the start of the decade private capital flows to developing countries were about the same as official transfers, about $50 billion each, by mid-1997 (on the eve of the Asian financial crisis) the former had grown to about six times the size of the latter. Not surprisingly, private capital flows to developing countries declined in the wake of the financial crises of the late 1990s, but they remained at levels that are a multiple of official transfers.

The importance of this development to growing interest in the economics of corruption is compelling, if at first not so obvious. Official flows to developing countries had been motivated, since the early postwar period, by the exigencies of the Cold War and the desire by the su-

---

[2]For example, Shleifer and Vishny (1993).
[3]Bardhan (1997).

perpowers and their allies to maintain political influence in various strategic areas of the globe. The strict criteria of economic performance and commitment to reform played only a minor role, if at all, in the distribution of bilateral official aid. In this environment, the pressure to reform was absent or minimal in many developing countries. A number of countries operated their economies under the protection of high tariffs and pervasive state intervention with only a minimum of transparency and accountability. However, they suffered neither the displeasure of aid givers nor the retribution of the markets, whose influence was too small to matter anyhow. Moreover, many countries were governed by regimes that, to say the least, did not adhere to the strictures of good governance, and most bilateral (and to some extent multilateral) donors and creditors often refrained from asking too many questions. The economics profession, with notable exceptions, lacking the requisite information or the will to challenge the prevailing political order, went on to other pursuits.

With the end of the Cold War, the breakup of the former Soviet Union, and the consequent unwinding of regional conflicts, many developing countries lost their privileged position in the global geopolitical game and were suddenly exposed to the more exacting requirements of market discipline. In the increasingly globalized and private-sector-driven world of the 1990s, developing countries (including the newly industrialized countries of Asia and the transition economies of Central and Eastern Europe) found themselves in a highly competitive environment where financial flows were now driven, above all, by expected rates of return on investment. Sound macroeconomic policies, a healthy regulatory environment, more transparent and accountable public institutions, and protection of property and investor's rights became essential prerequisites for attracting foreign direct investment and for accessing financial markets at reasonable terms.

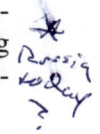

The breakup of the former Soviet Union also brought on one of the most profound and far-reaching transformations of the twentieth century. The disintegration of the command structures in the old regimes triggered some of the most chaotic economic, political, and social changes in modern history. Absence of the rule of law and accountable systems of governance led to rent seeking, corruption, and outright thievery. While some governments, notably in Eastern Europe, quickly found their bearings and developed the institutional and policy frameworks needed for the operation of markets, others took much longer. In the meantime, professional economists could not help but be struck by the importance of sound policies and institutions for better performance in the newly created market economies. This "discovery" triggered a wave of research on rent seeking, the role of the state, governance, and corruption. While the awakened interest of researchers in corruption in the transition economies was somewhat distinct from that which focused on developing countries, the two developments were not entirely unrelated. Indeed, both had their provenance in the end of the Cold War and the shift in the risk/reward calculus from one based on geopolitics to one based on hard, economic criteria.

Another factor underlying the rising importance of transparency in government operations is the spread of democratic practices in the late 1980s and throughout the decade of the 1990s.[4] In Central and South America, generally open elections for top officials and representative assemblies were held in virtually all countries, while in Africa the spread of presidential and parliamentary elections was also notable. Although not necessarily immune to corruption, electoral democracies have been found to foster a vigilant civil society, increased government accountability, and a higher degree of transparency.[5]

Growing availability of data "measuring" corruption further stimulated the empirical research on its economic effects. During the 1980s, new statistical surveys of households, enterprises, public officials, and others became available to researchers. This led to the construction of summary governance indicators, such as the indices of "perception of corruption" that were then widely used in the empirical analysis.

II. International Organizations

Another factor that heightened interest in the economics of corruption, and more generally the promotion of good governance, is the growing role of the international financial institutions (IFIs) as well as trade and regulatory organizations in defining international standards as a basis for transparent policy formulation and implementation. Stimulated in

---

[4]Between 1987 and 2000, the number of electoral democracies rose from 69 to 120, representing 63 percent of the world's states (Freedom House, various issues). This roster is based on a stringent standard; elected national authorities must be drawn from free and fair elections.

[5]See, for example, Freedom House (2000) and Treisman (2000).

large part by the desire to prevent the occurrence of global financial crises, such as those of Mexico, East Asia, and Russia in the middle and late 1990s, the IFIs took a number of initiatives to promote greater transparency and accountability in member countries. These initiatives were reinforced by the promulgation of codes and standards embodying good international practice in economic management and by newly created obligations for countries to widely disseminate statistical information on fiscal, monetary, and financial developments in a timely manner. In this regard, the IMF has taken the lead in work on standards and codes in the fiscal and statistical areas and jointly with the World Bank and the Bank for International Settlements on the promotion of standards and codes in the monetary and banking area (see below).

Moreover, the World Bank has recently adopted a framework for addressing corruption as a development issue, in the context of assistance it provides to member countries. The framework has the following components: (1) preventing fraud and corruption in Bank-financed projects by improving procurement and financial management policies related to the implementation of projects; (2) helping countries in their efforts to eliminate corruption; (3) taking corruption more explicitly into account in the formulation of country assistance strategies; and (4) adding voice and support to the international efforts to reduce corruption, including by collaborating with regional development institutions on anticorruption measures.

Interest in research on corruption and governance in IFIs was also stimulated by concern that public spending and aid were not having the desired impact on poverty and social outcomes. Questions have been raised on the extent to which budgetary allocations for unproductive programs or inefficiencies in public spending are attributable to corrupt practices. In fact, as the present volume demonstrates, these issues have received special attention from IFIs.

III. Nongovernmental Organizations

Other players on the international scene also became interested in more transparent and accountable conduct of economic management. Nongovernmental organizations (NGOs) and other organs of civil society, including the media, showed greater interest in the economics of corruption and in the conduct of officials entrusted with the management of public funds. A variety of motives spurred this awakened interest.

The Economics of Corruption: An Overview

For the media, the demise of the once overarching ideological confrontation of the Cold War created room for a wider coverage of economic news. Economic prosperity in a number of countries and regions became headline news (Japan and Europe in the 1980s, the United States, the Asian tigers, and peripheral Europe in the 1990s), stimulated by the technology and information revolution, fascinated large portions of the globe and made for good copy in the press. The growing reach of the Internet spread the news of economic success, as well as of economic failure. In the midst of all of this activity, stories of corruption and malfeasance fed the curiosity of a global audience and brought questions of good governance and economic performance to the forefront of academic and policy debate.

Other interested parties incorporated the problems of corruption into their agendas for yet different reasons. NGOs in industrial countries took up the cause of monitoring aid spending of their own governments, while seeking to enhance the capacity of the recipient countries to use such aid more effectively. This enterprise invariably involved the NGOs in questions of transparency and accountability of the donors (and the institutions through which they channel the bulk of their aid funds), and in the drive for instituting good governance and anticorruption safeguards in recipient countries. In time, many NGOs were brought into the deliberations of the IFIs on questions of debt relief and its use, development assistance, and governance.

Other NGOs took up the fight against corruption directly. Foremost among them is Transparency International (TI), established by a former World Bank staff member. It has grown to be a visible presence on the world economic scene, pressing its campaign in global forums (such as the biennial International Conference on Corruption) and through chapters in an increasing number of countries. TI's annual publication of country rankings on a "corruption perception index" is a major event and is widely noted by the countries so ranked, by academics and policymakers, and, above all, by financial markets.

Other organizations that have expanded their coverage of country assessments to include important indicators of transparency, accountability, and good governance are the Political Risk Services Group, which publishes the *International Country Risk Guides*; the Switzerland-based International Institute for Management Development, which publishes the *World Competitiveness Report*; and other credit-rating agencies. The International Chamber of Commerce has also added its voice and influence to combat corruption in international transactions through revised Rules of Conduct on Extortion and Bribery in International Business Transactions and through the creation of standing committees of business executives, lawyers, and academics to mobilize support for adherence to the new rules.

IV. Multilateral Action

Since the passage of the U.S. Foreign Corrupt Practices Act in 1977, pressure on the international community has been mounting for multilateral action not only to specifically outlaw the bribery of foreign public officials but also to take measures to fight corruption in general. One of the more far-reaching efforts in this regard is that of the Organization for Economic Cooperation and Development (OECD), which, beginning in 1994, sought to end the tax deductibility of bribes and to criminalize the bribing of foreign officials. In a landmark decision taken at its ministerial meeting in May 1997, the OECD Council adopted recommendations of a working group on a Revised Recommendation on Combating Bribery in International Business Transactions. Compared with earlier recommendations, the Revised Recommendation was far more concrete and prescriptive, covering broad areas related to the conduct of international business and establishing a mechanism for monitoring implementation. The adoption of a Convention on Combating Bribery of Foreign Officials in International Business Transactions obligated signatory states, all 30 OECD members plus a growing number of nonmembers, to make bribery a crime under their laws.

In December 1996, the United Nations (UN) General Assembly adopted a Declaration Against Corruption and Bribery in International Commercial Transactions, as recommended by the UN Economic and Social Council. Although not legally binding, the declaration's wording on criminalizing foreign bribery and ending its tax deductibility signifies broad political agreement in the international community on this matter.

In May 1997, the European Commission (EC) issued a Communication to the Council and the European Parliament on a Union Policy against corruption. This communication sets out the EC's comprehensive policy on corruption inside the European Union as well as regarding relations with nonmember countries.

V. The Role of the IMF

The IMF has paid increasing attention to the importance of good governance in member countries in support of macroeconomic stability and noninflationary sustainable growth, the promotion of which is central to its mandate. This recognition is reflected in the IMF's three core activities: surveillance of economic policies of member countries, financial support for adjustment programs, and technical assistance to strengthen economic and financial management. The IMF's Interim Committee—now the International Monetary and Financial Committee—stressed the importance of good governance for macroeconomic policies in its meetings in September 1996 and September 1997.

The IMF is contributing to strengthening governance in member countries through various means. The first is by *supporting economic policies and structural reforms* that limit the scope for ad hoc decision making, for rent seeking, and for preferential treatment of individuals or organizations. This approach is founded on the IMF's mandate to promote macroeconomic stability, and limits its role to those aspects of governance that could have a significant macroeconomic impact. A Guidance Note for IMF staff, for example, calls for

- A more comprehensive treatment of governance issues in the IMF's core activities and policy advice.
- A more proactive approach in advocating policies and development of institutions that promote governance.
- An evenhanded treatment of governance issues in all member countries.
- Enhanced collaboration with other multilateral institutions, in particular the World Bank and other IFIs such as the regional development banks, to make better use of complementary areas of expertise.

What forms have governance issues taken in IMF policy advice? In general, the IMF has required greater transparency and accountability in the management of public funds, including strengthening revenue administration, enhancing the financial accountability of state enterprises, monitoring the use of public resources for poverty reduction (part of the enhanced Heavily Indebted Poor Countries (HIPC) Initiative), consolidating extrabudgetary funds into the budget, enhancing transparency of tax and tariff systems, reinforcing central bank independence, strengthening prudential bank supervision, and improving the quality and timeliness of economic and financial statistics. Where issues of poor governance may have affected macroeconomic performance, the IMF has also urged member countries to address specific instances of poor governance and corruption (e.g., illegal logging in Cambodia following evidence published by Global Witness and fraud in government accounts reported by the Attorney-General in Kenya), and has recently strengthened policies to safeguard the use of IMF resources with regard to misreporting of information to the IMF. These measures have led to inquiries directed at central bank actions in Russia, Ukraine, and Indonesia.

In its approach to governance, the IMF has increasingly taken a proactive role along with the World Bank, stressing the importance of country ownership of policies for improving governance. Prevention is the centerpiece of the IMF's governance strategy. According to the strategy, participation in initiatives to strengthen governance, including the adoption of standards and codes, is voluntary. Furthermore, the strategy recognizes the importance of timely and well-targeted technical assistance to help alleviate constraints on institutional capacity.

The second principal means through which the IMF is contributing to strengthening governance in member countries is by *promoting transparency* in financial transactions in the government budget, the central bank, and the public sector at large. This is being done by developing standards and codes of best practices. They include

- Data dissemination standards. These standards guide member countries in the dissemination of their economic and financial data to the public, and consists of two tiers:

  — Special Data Dissemination Standard (SDDS). Established in March 1996 for those members that have, or that might seek, access to international capital markets.

  — General Data Dissemination System (GDDS). Established in December 1997, it applies to all member countries and guides them in the dissemination of comprehensive, timely, and reliable economic, financial, and socio-demographic statistics to the public.

- The Code of Good Practices on Fiscal Transparency, which was adopted in 1998 and updated in March 2001. Adoption of this code is voluntary, and diversity across countries is fully recognized.

One of the key objectives of the code is to promote open budget preparation, execution, and reporting.

- Reports on the Observance of Standards and Codes (ROSCs), adopted in 1999. These reports summarize the extent to which countries observe certain internationally recognized standards in the areas of direct operational concerns to the IMF. Numerous ROSC modules have been published on the IMF's external website.
- The Code of Good Practices on Transparency in Monetary and Financial Policies, adopted in 1999. Good governance calls for central banks and financial agencies to be accountable, particularly where the monetary and financial authorities are granted a high degree of autonomy.

The IMF also adopted Financial System Stability Assessments (FSSAs) and the Financial Sector Assessment Program (FSAP) in 1999. These instruments help countries assess vulnerabilities in the financial sector and identify the needs for corrective action. FSAPs, jointly conducted with the World Bank, have led to FSSAs, which become part of the IMF's core responsibility of surveillance. The IMF plans to conduct 24 FSAPs every year over the next couple of years. The IMF has also adopted, in collaboration with the Financial Stability Forum and the World Bank, experimental modalities for its approach to financial sector practices in offshore centers concerning financial system abuse, financial crime, and money laundering.

Since April 2001, the IMF has strengthened its efforts to counter money laundering, as well as terrorism financing. Together with other financial institutions, it has a key role in preventing the abuse of financial systems as well as protecting and enhancing the integrity of the international financial system. In this regard, IMF and World Bank staffs have prepared a draft methodology to assess a country's compliance with certain standards, and this methodology is being applied to several pilot cases. Anti-money-laundering concerns are being included in IMF's surveillance and other operational activities when they are relevant from a macroeconomic perspective.

Third, the IMF contributes to improved governance in member countries by helping them through *technical assistance* to strengthen their capacities for effective public resource management, as well as the design and implementation of economic policies. The focus of IMF technical assistance has been on areas in which the IMF has a comparative advantage—strengthening public expenditure management, tax administration, banking systems, foreign exchange, and on improving the quality and timeliness of data. Since 1997, the IMF has developed new forms of technical assistance that attempt to ascertain the extent to which countries are complying with the above-noted standards and codes.

In recognition of a close nexus between weak public expenditure management systems and poor governance, both the IMF and the World Bank have initiated additional work in the area of public expenditure management in heavily indebted poor countries. The objective is to help strengthen the link between debt relief and poverty reduction and make government budgets more pro-poor. There is recognition that citizens and governments in donor countries need assurances that debt relief and other financial assistance are devoted to poverty reduction. Citizens and legislatures in recipient countries also need assurances that these resources are being used for the purpose intended, to strengthen country ownership of the poverty-reduction strategy.

VI. The Focus of This Volume

The fourth principal means through which the IMF is contributing to strengthening governance in member countries is through *policy research*. The IMF has thus contributed to the growing awareness of the causes, consequences, and remedies for fighting corruption. The empirical research has highlighted the impact of corruption on economic growth, public finances, poverty, income inequality, provision of social services, and the causes of corruption and anticorruption strategies. Many studies have been carried out by IMF staff since the mid-1990s. This volume compiles most of these studies, with the objective of contributing to the ongoing debate on the role of good governance in promoting growth and reducing poverty. As discussed above, the empirical research in this area has been facilitated by the efforts of IFIs and others to collect and construct indicators of governance in recent years.

In Chapter 2, Tanzi discusses issues related to the causes, consequences, and scope of corruption and possible corrective actions. The phenomenon of corruption affects many countries and is a source of disillusionment among the population of some transition economies and developing countries. Corruption cannot be substantially reduced without modifying the way governments operate, and in this sense, the fight against corruption is linked with the reform of the state. Thus, a multipronged strategy is needed, including reducing excessive and complex regulations and reforming the civil service.

How critical is the role of civil service salaries in curbing corruption? In Chapter 3, Van Rijckeghem and Weder find that an increase in civil service salaries in relation to those paid in the manufacturing sector has a favorable impact on the corruption index. Civil service wages are also highly correlated with measures of rule of law and quality of bureaucracy. A related issue is whether government officials responsible for fiscal management of a country should be paid bonuses, particularly when public sector wage levels are relatively low. Chand and Moene examine a country case in Chapter 4 and analyze the circumstances under which bonus payments to tax officers can promote less corrupt outcomes. They further contend that this strategy is not sufficient: corruption at higher levels of government also needs to be contained—a strategy that would entail reforming the role of the state as suggested by Tanzi (Chapter 2).

In Chapter 5, Dabla-Norris argues that there is an optimal level of corruption, reflecting self-interested behavior of different players in a society. And because governments in some countries lack an effective monitoring mechanism, it may be optimal for them to pay lower wages to their employees—a policy recommendation that is contrary to the one contained in the study by Van Rijckeghem and Weder (see Chapter 3). Typically, most developing countries have a bloated civil service, and a corruption-reducing higher wage for all government employees is not sustainable from a fiscal perspective. This implies that the issue of a higher wage for government workers should be an integral part of a comprehensive civil service reform.

Charap and Harm (Chapter 6) contend that corruption is endogenous to political structures and helps maintain an "equilibrium" among different population groups. Elimination of corruption in such instances could then destabilize existing political systems and lead to anarchy, rather than enhancing economic efficiency. Under these conditions, a comprehensive reform of the civil service could be implemented only if a "ruler" gains stability from benevolence, rather than patronage. If the survival of the regime is threatened, this reform program is likely to be rejected.

In Chapter 7, Leite and Weidmann identify availability of natural resources as another factor that creates opportunities for corruption. Their statistical results show that capital- (labor-)intensive natural resource industries tend to induce a higher (lower) level of corruption, other things being equal.

Corruption lowers growth through limiting development of small and medium-sized enterprises, and has serious implications for a country's public finances. This is the subject of Chapter 8 by Tanzi and Davoodi. Because entrepreneurs have to devote their scarce time to bribing officials, the growth-promoting benefit of small and medium-sized enterprises is not fully realized. As a result, they estimate that due to this misuse of resources, economic growth is lowered by 0.4 percentage point for a sample of countries.

Understandably, the link between corruption and public finances is of special interest to the IMF in the conduct of its core mandate. The studies carried out at the IMF show that both expenditure and revenue sides of the budget are affected by corruption and rent-seeking behavior. By using cross-section data, Mauro (Chapter 9) shows that corruption is negatively associated with government expenditure on education. An increase in corruption by one unit (on a scale of 0 to 10) lowers the ratio of public spending on education by 0.2 percentage point of GDP. Corruption, therefore, could lead to a suboptimal composition of government expenditure. The reason for this result is that education programs are less prone to rent seeking.

The adverse impact of corruption is not confined to inappropriate expenditure allocations. Gupta, Davoodi, and Tiongson (Chapter 10) show that a high level of corruption has adverse consequences for a country's child and infant mortality rates, percent of low-birthweight babies in total births, and dropout rates in primary schools. For example, an increase in corruption by one unit (on a scale of 0 to 10) raises the child mortality rate on average by 1.1 to 2.7 deaths per 1,000 live births. These results are consistent with predictions stemming from theoretical models and service delivery surveys. An important implication of the results is that improvements in health and education outcomes do not necessarily require higher public spending.

In Chapter 11, Tanzi and Davoodi provide further evidence on how corruption distorts the composition of public expenditure. It leads to allocations in favor of less-productive investment projects and against nonwage operations and maintenance expenditures, such as books and medicines, which reduce the quality and productivity of existing infrastructure. Corruption also reduces government revenue needed to finance productive spending.

There are other types of public spending that are affected by corruption as well. Gupta, de Mello, and Sharan (Chapter 12) show that corruption is associated with higher military spending as a share of both GDP and total government spending, as well as with arms procurement in relation to GDP and total government spending. Military spending is a monopoly of the state, and contracts are often drawn in secrecy and under considerable discretionary power of the authorities. The results from the study suggest that defense spending can be considered for constructing governance indicators.

A considerable amount of public spending takes places at subnational levels in a number of countries, and the share of this spending is increasing. De Mello and Barenstein (Chapter 13) find that governance can be enhanced through the decentralization of expenditure functions to subnational governments. The higher the share of subnational spending in total government expenditures, the stronger the positive association between decentralization and governance. The relationship between decentralization and poor governance also depends on how subnational expenditures are financed—the higher the share of nontax revenues in total revenues as well as grants and transfers from higher levels of government in total expenditure, the stronger the association between decentralization and corruption.

Studies have also focused on the revenue side of the budget. In Chapter 14, Ghura contends on the basis of data for sub-Saharan African countries that the level of corruption also influences the tax revenue-to-GDP ratio. Lower revenues, in turn, have an impact on the ability of the government to finance critical poverty-allocation programs. For a given tax regime and rate structure, measures taken to curb corruption can be expected to raise tax revenues.

Collecting taxes while minimizing evasion and corruption remains a challenging policy problem. Hindriks, Keen, and Muthoo (Chapter 15) find that the distributional implications of evasion and corruption are unambiguously regressive under most tax collection schemes, and that collecting progressive taxes without inducing evasion or corruption may require that inspectors be paid commissions, with the cost of this policy potentially creating a trade-off between equity and efficiency. Inducing honesty in the collection of taxes therefore carries a cost. Hindriks, Keen, and Muthoo thus support the results of Van Rijckeghem and Weder (Chapter 3) as well as Chand and Moene (Chapter 4).

Poor governance also affects a country's income distribution and poverty. Dabla-Norris and Wade (Chapter 16) present a model to explain why the relatively wealthy choose rent-seeking activities such as employment in the government bureaucracy, army, and police rather than engaging in productive and entrepreneurial activities. Given imperfect capital markets, and lump-sum entry fees associated with rent seeking, those who are relatively wealthy to begin with tend to engage in rent seeking to protect their wealth from expropriation.

Gupta, Davoodi, and Alonso-Terme (Chapter 17) provide evidence of significant adverse distributional effects of corruption. They find that high and rising corruption is associated with higher income inequality and poverty. A worsening of the corruption index of a country by one standard deviation increases the Gini coefficient by 11 points, and one standard deviation increase in the growth of corruption reduces income growth of the poor by 4.7 percentage points a year.

The issue of governance has assumed increasing importance in transition economies in recent years. In Chapter 18, Abed and Davoodi conclude that corruption is mostly, but not entirely, a symptom of underlying policy distortions and weak economic institutions in transition economies. They argue that reform of the state—as noted by Tanzi in Chapter 2—is critical for reducing corruption and enhancing economic performance in transition economies. Increasing the reliance on market-based pricing and creating a sound regulatory environment should help in lowering corruption. Abed and Davoodi also provide evidence to show that structural reforms in these economies can help lower the scope for corruption, a point reiterated by Wolf and Gürgen (Chapter 19), who examine the indirect role played by the IMF in combating corruption in the Baltic and Commonwealth of Independent States countries through its policies for promoting structural reforms. The IMF's emphasis on deregulation, liberalization, privatization, and its technical assistance aimed at strengthening the budgetary process and institution building, help improve economic governance and reduce opportunities for rent-seeking behavior.

References

Bardhan, Pranab, 1997, "Corruption and Development: A Review of Issues," *Journal of Economic Literature*, Vol. 35 (September), pp. 1320–46.

Becker, Gary S., 1968, "Crime and Punishment: An Economic Approach," *Journal of Political Economy*, Vol. 76 (March/April), pp. 169–217.

Bhagwati, Jagdish N., 1982, "Directly Unproductive, Profit-Seeking (DUP) Activities," *Journal of Political Economy* Vol. 90 (October), pp. 988–1002.

Buchanan, James M., Robert D. Tollison, and Gordon Tullock, eds., 1980, *Toward a Theory of the Rent-Seeking Society* (College Station, Texas: Texas A & M University Press).

Freedom House, *Freedom in the World: The Annual Survey of Political Rights and Civil Liberties* (New York: Freedom House, various issues).

———, 2000, Nations in Transit (New York: Freedom House).

Klitgaard, Robert E., 1984, "Managing the Fight Against Corruption: A Case Study," *Public Administration and Development*, Vol. 4 (January/March), pp. 77–98.

———, 1988, *Controlling Corruption* (Berkeley: University of California Press).

Krueger, Anne O., 1974, "The Political Economy of the Rent-Seeking Society," *American Economic Review*, Vol. 64 (June), pp. 291–303.

———, 1993, "Virtuous and Vicious Circles in Economic Development," *American Economic Review, Papers and Proceedings*, Vol. 83 (May), pp. 351–55.

Mauro, Paolo, 1995, "Corruption and Growth," *Quarterly Journal of Economics*, Vol. 110 (August), pp. 681–712.

Murphy, Kevin, Andrei Shleifer, and Robert Vishny, 1993, "Why Is Rent-Seeking So Costly to Growth" *American Economic Review, Papers and Proceedings*, Vol. 83 (May), pp. 409–14.

Rose-Ackerman, Susan, 1975, "The Economics of Corruption," *Journal of Public Economics*, Vol. 4, No. 2 (February), pp. 187–203.

———, 1978, *Corruption: A Study in Political Economy* (New York: Academic Press).

Shleifer, Andrei, and Robert Vishny, 1993, "Corruption," *Quarterly Journal of Economics*, Vol. 108 (August), pp. 599–617.

Tanzi, Vito, 1995, "Corruption: Arm's Length Relationships and Markets," in *The Economics of Organised Crime*, ed. by Gianluca Fiorentini and Sam Peltram (Cambridge, England; Cambridge University Press).

Treisman, Daniel, 2000, "The Causes of Corruption: A Cross-National Study," *Journal of Public Economics*, Vol. 76, No. 3 (June), pp. 399–457.

Part I

Causes and Consequences of Corruption

2

Corruption Around the World: Causes, Consequences, Scope, and Cures

Vito Tanzi

I. The Growth of Corruption

In recent years, and especially in the 1990s, a phenomenon broadly referred to as corruption has attracted a great deal of attention. In countries developed and developing, large or small, market-oriented or otherwise, governments have fallen because of accusations of corruption, prominent politicians (including presidents of countries and prime ministers) have lost their official positions, and, in some cases, whole political classes have been replaced. For examples, see Johnston (1997).

Corruption is not a new phenomenon. Two thousand years ago, Kautilya, the prime minister of an Indian kingdom, had already written a book, *Arthashastra,* discussing it. Seven centuries ago, Dante placed bribers in the deepest parts of Hell, reflecting the medieval distaste for corrupt behavior. Shakespeare gave corruption a prominent

---

Reprinted from *IMF Staff Papers*, Vol. 45 (December 1998), pp. 559–94. The author thanks Hamid Davoodi and Shing-Jin Wei for their comments.

role in some of his plays; and the American Constitution made bribery and treason the two explicitly mentioned crimes that could justify the impeachment of a U.S. president.[1] However, the degree of attention paid to corruption in recent years is unprecedented. For example, in its end-of-year editorial on December 31, 1995, *The Financial Times* characterized 1995 as the year of corruption. The following three years could have earned the same title. The writing of books on corruption has become a growth industry in various countries.

The degree of attention now paid to corruption leads naturally to the question of why. Why so much attention now? Is it because there is more corruption than in the past? Or is it because more attention is being paid to a phenomenon that had always existed but had been largely, though not completely, ignored? The answer is not obvious, and there are no reliable statistics that would make possible a definitive answer.

Several arguments can be advanced that suggest that corruption is simply attracting more attention now than in the past.

First, the end of the Cold War has stopped the political hypocrisy that had made the decision makers in some industrial countries ignore the political corruption that existed in particular countries, such as Zaïre (now the Democratic Republic of the Congo). As long as the latter were in the right political camp, there was a tendency to overlook obvious cases of high-level corruption.

Second, perhaps because of lack of information, or reluctance to talk about it by those familiar with these countries, there was also a tendency not to focus on corruption in the centrally planned economies.[2] It is now widely known that centrally planned economies, such as the Soviet Union, or those imitating them through highly regimented economic activities, such as Nicaragua and Tanzania, experienced a great deal of corrupt practices. However, these practices were either ignored or not widely reported at the time. Donor countries also tended to play down this problem in countries that they assisted financially, even in the face of misuse or misappropriation of foreign aid.

---

[1]See Noonan, Jr. *(1984)* for a very interesting historical overview of corruption in different societies.

[2]However, much information was available on the corruption in centrally planned economies. See, for example, Simis (1982), Galasi and Gertesi (1987), Grossman (1982), and Remnick (1994).

Third, the increase in recent years in the number of countries with democratic governments and free and active media has created an environment in which discussion of corruption is no longer a taboo. In some countries, such as Russia, the media has responded with a vengeance to this newly acquired freedom.[3] In some other countries, political changes have increased the reporting of cases of corruption. See Davigo (1998).

Fourth, in all its ramifications, globalization has brought individuals from countries with little corruption into frequent contact with those from countries where corruption is endemic. These contacts have increased the international attention paid to corruption, especially when some companies believed that they were cut out of some contracts because the winning company had paid a bribe.

Fifth, a growing role has been played by nongovernmental organizations, such as Transparency International, in publicizing the problems of corruption and in trying to create anticorruption movements in many countries. Recently the international financial institutions, such as the IMF and the World Bank, and other international organizations have been playing a growing role in the anticorruption movement. In addition, empirical studies of corruption have contributed to a greater awareness of the economic costs of this problem.

Sixth, the greater reliance on the market for economic decisions and the increased need to be competitive have created an environment in which the pursuit of efficiency has acquired greater importance and distortions attributed to corruption attract more attention.

Finally, the role played by the United States, especially through its influence in some international institutions, has been important. American policymakers have argued that American exporters have lost out in foreign deals because they have not been allowed by law to pay bribes to foreign officials. For American companies, the payment of bribes to foreign officials is a criminal act, and, of course, the bribes paid cannot be deducted as costs for tax purposes.[4] This has not been the case in other OECD countries, although recently, under the spon-

---

[3] An attempt by the author of this paper to create a corruption index on the basis of newspaper stories reported by the Internet found that for some countries these Internet entries amount to tens of thousands.

[4] See, for example, the remarks by (then) Secretary of Commerce, Michael Kantor, to the Detroit Economic Club (July 25, 1996) in which he stated that since 1994 American companies had lost international contracts worth $45 billion because of bribes paid by foreign contractors to the officials of foreign countries. See also Hines, Jr. (1995).

sorship of the OECD, the situation has started to change. In several other countries, bribing a foreign official was not illegal and bribes paid could be considered a deductible business cost.

A case can also be made that the increased attention now paid to corruption reflects the growth of that phenomenon in recent decades, a growth that culminated in a peak in corruption activities in the 1990s. Let me briefly consider a few arguments that support this alternative hypothesis.

Recent studies have shown the extent to which the role of the government in the economy has grown in recent decades.[5] The environment that prevailed in these years brought about (1) a large increase in the level of taxation in many countries; (2) a large increase in the level of public spending; and (3) probably, though not statistically ascertainable, a large increase in regulations and controls on economic activities on the part of governments. In recent decades, in a significant number of countries, many economic operations or activities have required various kinds of permits or authorizations on the part of, often, several public offices. This gave the bureaucrats charged with giving the authorizations the opportunity to request bribes or to accept offered bribes.

I would hypothesize that the impact that high taxes, a high level of spending, and new regulations have on acts of corruption is not immediate but, rather, a function of time, given the established norms of behavior.[6] In a country with traditionally well-functioning and honest bureaucracy, the *short-term impact* of a larger government role on public officials will be limited. For some time, public officials will not be asked to perform corrupt acts and will reject bribery attempts, and they will not initiate such acts. In countries without such tradition, the more invasive role of government, played through higher taxes, higher public spending, and, especially, more widespread regulations, would have a more immediate impact on the behavior of civil servants and on corruption. This will be particularly true if fiscal policy suffers from lack of transparency in policymaking, fiscal reporting, and the assignment of responsibilities to public institutions. See Kopits and Craig (1998) and Tanzi (1998).

However, with the passing of time, and with increasing frequency, some government officials would be approached by bribers and asked to bend rules or even to break laws to obtain a government benefit or

---

[5]See, for example, Tanzi and Schuknecht (1997).

[6]These norms of behavior may be different between countries and are likely to change only slowly over time.

to avoid a government-imposed cost. Some will respond and will get compensation from the bribers for their actions. Others may start emulating them. The process is likely to be cumulative over time and resemble the spreading of a contagious disease. Acts of corruption that might have appeared shocking earlier will begin to look less shocking, and may even begin to be tolerated. The government may respond to this situation not by punishing the officials who bend or break the rules, but by reducing wages on the assumption that officials are getting extra compensation.[7] It is easy to see where this process could lead to if not checked.

Two other factors may have had an impact on corruption in recent years: the growth of international trade and business and the economic changes that have taken place in many countries and especially in the economies in transition.

The growth of international trade and business has created many situations in which the payment of bribes (often euphemistically called "commissions") may be highly beneficial to the companies that pay them by giving them access to profitable contracts over competitors. Large bribes have been reported to have been paid to get foreign contracts or to get privileged access to markets or to particular benefits such as tax incentives. *Le Monde* of March 17, 1995, reported that the bribes paid abroad by French companies in 1994 had been estimated at F 10 billion in a confidential government report. *World Business* of March 4, 1996, reported that the bribes paid abroad by German companies had been estimated to exceed US$3 billion a year.[8] These were not the only countries in which companies had paid bribes to foreign officials. Some experts have estimated that as much as 15 percent of the total money spent for weapons acquisition may be "commissions" that fill somebody's pockets. Here, again, contagion is important. When the economic operators of some countries begin to pay bribes, they put pressure on those from other countries to do the same. The cost of not doing so is lost contracts, as Kantor argued.

Among the economic changes that have taken place in recent years, privatization has been most closely linked with corruption. There is no question that public or state enterprises have been a major source of corruption and especially of political corruption because they have occa-

---

[7]This has actually happened in some countries vis-à-vis public employees working in particular areas such as customs administration.

[8]Reported in Galtung (1997).

sionally been used to finance the activities of political parties and to provide jobs to the clienteles of particular political groups. This was clearly the case in Italy, before tangentopoli,[9] and in many Latin American countries. Privatization of nonnatural monopolies is necessary to reduce this form of corruption because it eliminates an instrument often used especially in political corruption. Unfortunately, the process of privatizing public or state enterprises has itself created situations whereby some individuals (ministers, high political officials) have the discretion to make the basic decisions while others (managers and other insiders) have information not available to outsiders so that they can use privatization to benefit themselves. These problems have been observed and reported in all regions of the world, but the abuses appear to have been particularly significant in the transition economies.[10] In the latter, terms such as asset stripping and *nomenklatura* privatization have been used to describe the abuses associated with the transfer of state enterprises to private ownership. In these countries some individuals have become enormously rich because of these abuses. Two examples from the Russian experience come to mind. In the privatization of large monopolies, such as Gazprom, many close to the corridors of power received highly valuable shares at very low prices. And the "loans-for-share" scheme made some banks shareholders of enterprises by extending loans to the firms. These developments have made many Russian citizens highly skeptical about the virtues of a market economy.

Thus, several arguments lead to the conclusion that the current interest in corruption probably reflects an increase in the scope of the phenomenon over the years and not just a greater awareness of an age-old problem.

II. The Definition of Corruption

Corruption has been defined in many different ways, each lacking in some aspect. A few years ago, the question of definition absorbed a large proportion of the time spent on discussions of corruption at conferences and meetings. However, like an elephant, while it may be dif-

---

[9]See Nordio (1997). Carlo Nordio was one of the leading judges in the Italian fight against political corruption. "Tangentopoli" or "bribe city" is the term that was given to the Italian corruption scandal that shook Italy.
[10]See Kaufmann and Siegelbaum (1996) and Goldman (1997). For a review of the Latin American experience, see Manzetti and Blake (1997).

ficult to describe, corruption is generally not difficult to recognize when observed. In most cases, different observers would agree on whether a particular behavior connotes corruption. Unfortunately, the behavior is often difficult to observe because acts of corruption do not typically take place in broad daylight.

The most popular and simplest definition of corruption is that it is *the abuse of public power for private benefit.* This is the definition used by the World Bank.[11] From this definition it should not be concluded that corruption cannot exist within private sector activities. Especially in large private enterprises, this phenomenon clearly exists, as for example in procurement or even in hiring. It also exists in private activities regulated by the government.[12] Sometimes, the abuse of public power is not necessarily for one's private benefit but for the benefit of one's party, class, tribe, friends, family, and so on. In fact, in many countries some of the proceeds of corruption go to finance the activities of the political parties.

Not all acts of corruption result in the payment of bribes. For example, a public employee who claims to be sick but goes on vacation is abusing his public position for personal use. Thus, he is engaging in an act of corruption even though no bribe is paid. Or the president of a country who has an airport built in his small hometown is also engaging in an act of corruption that does not involve the payment of a bribe.[13]

It is important to distinguish bribes from gifts. In many instances, bribes can be disguised as gifts. A bribe implies reciprocity while a gift should not.[14] However, even though the distinction is fundamental, it is at times difficult to make.[15] At what point does a gift become a bribe? Does the distinction depend on the size of the gift? What about cultural differences that can explain different sizes of gifts? What if a large gift is not given to the person who provides the favor but to a relative of that person? Does the distinction depend on whether the gift is given

---

[11]A more neutral definition is that corruption is the intentional noncompliance with arm's-length relationship aimed at deriving some advantage from this behavior for oneself or for related individuals. See Tanzi (1995a). For other definitions, see Theobald (1990).

[12]For example, when a taxi driver charges the passenger more than the regulated price or when a doctor in a hospital charges for services not rendered.

[13]It becomes difficult to draw a distinction between some forms of rent seeking and corruption. See Krueger (1974).

[14]In practice, those who give gifts may expect some form of payment for them—for example, we expect love or good behavior from our children when we give them gifts—but the recipients of the gifts do not have an obligation to reciprocate.

[15]For an elaboration of some of these points, see Tanzi (1995a).

in broad daylight, for everyone to see, or privately? Clearly, the identification of a bribe is not always simple.

Acts of corruption can be classified in different categories. Corruption can be

- bureaucratic (or "petty") or political (or "grand"); for example, corruption by the bureaucracy or by the political leadership;
- cost-reducing (to the briber) or benefit-enhancing;
- briber-initiated or bribee-initiated;
- coercive or collusive;
- centralized or decentralized;
- predictable or arbitrary; and
- involving cash payments or not.

Undoubtedly, other classifications could be added to this list.

III. Factors Contributing Directly to Corruption

Corruption is generally connected with the activities of the state and especially with the monopoly and discretionary power of the state. Therefore, as Gary Becker, Nobel Laureate in economics, pointed out in one of his *Business Week* columns, if we abolish the state, we abolish corruption. But, of course, quite apart from the fact that corruption can exist in the private sector, a civilized society cannot function without a state, and in modern, advanced societies, the state must have many functions. The Becker argument seems to collide with the reality that some of the least corrupt countries in the world, such as Canada, Denmark, Finland, the Netherlands, and Sweden, have some of the largest public sectors, measured as shares of tax revenue or public spending in gross domestic product. Thus, the solution to the problem of corruption may not be as simple as just reducing the level of taxation or public spending. Rather, the way the state operates and carries out its functions is far more important than the size of public sector activity measured in the traditional way.[16] Particular aspects of govern-

---

[16]The state can exercise its role through various instruments. Some of these lend themselves more easily to acts of corruption. See Tanzi (1995a). For an empirical analysis that links market structure and rents to the level of corruption, see Ades and Di Tella (forthcoming).

mental activities create a fertile ground for corruption. Let us look at this issue in more detail.

Regulations and Authorizations

In many countries, and especially in developing countries, the role of the state is often carried out through the use of numerous rules or regulations. In these countries licenses, permits, and authorizations of various sorts are required to engage in many activities. Opening a shop and keeping it open, borrowing money, investing, driving a car, owning a car, building a house, engaging in foreign trade, obtaining foreign exchange, getting a passport, going abroad, and so on require specific documents or authorizations. Often several government offices must be contacted to authorize the activity.

The existence of these regulations and authorizations gives a kind of monopoly power to the officials who must authorize or inspect the activities. These officials may refuse the authorizations or may simply sit on a decision for months or even years. Thus, they can use their public power to extract bribes from those who need the authorizations or permits. In India, for example, the expression "licence raj" referred to the individual who sold permits needed to engage in many forms of economic activities. In some countries, some individuals become middlemen or facilitators for obtaining these permits. The fact that in some cases the regulations are nontransparent or are not even publicly available and that an authorization can be obtained only from a specific office or individual—that is, there is no competition in the granting of these authorizations—gives the bureaucrats a great amount of power and a good opportunity to extract bribes.[17]

The existence of these regulations generates the need for frequent contacts between citizens and bureaucrats. It also requires an enormous amount of time to be spent by the citizens in acquiring these permits and in dealing with public officials. Surveys from different countries and especially from developing and transition countries indicate that much of the time of the managers of enterprises, and especially of

---

[17]Some economists have argued that this kind of corruption can be eliminated by setting up several offices all authorized to provide the authorizations or permits. This would remove the monopoly power from the bureaucrats. See Shleifer and Vishny (1993). Unfortunately, the setting up of several offices may be costly. In some cases, particular activities (say, yearly inspections of cars) can be privatized.

small enterprises, is spent dealing with public bureaucracies. This time that is taken away from managing the enterprises can be reduced through the payment of bribes.

Taxation

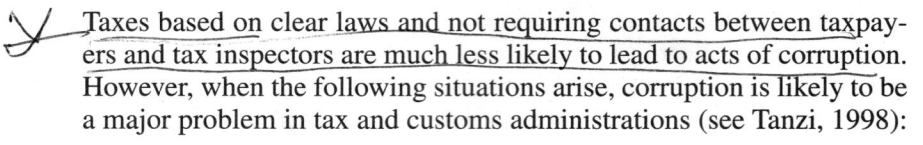

Taxes based on clear laws and not requiring contacts between taxpayers and tax inspectors are much less likely to lead to acts of corruption. However, when the following situations arise, corruption is likely to be a major problem in tax and customs administrations (see Tanzi, 1998):

- the laws are difficult to understand and can be interpreted differently so that taxpayers need assistance in complying with them;
- the payment of taxes requires frequent contacts between taxpayers and tax administrators;
- the wages of the tax administrators are low;
- acts of corruption on the part of the tax administrators are ignored, not easily discovered, or when discovered penalized only mildly;
- the administrative procedures (e.g., the criteria for the selection of taxpayers for audits) lack transparency and are not closely monitored within the tax or customs administrations;
- tax administrators have discretion over important decisions, such as those related to the provision of tax incentives, determination of tax liabilities, selection of audits, litigations, and so on; and
- more broadly, the controls from the state (the principal) on the agents charged with carrying out its functions are weak.[18]

In some countries, at one time, corruption became so endemic in the tax administration (e.g., Peru and Uganda) that the government decided to close down the existing administrations and to replace them by new ones. In several countries, customs administrations have been very corrupt, leading to the jailing of the director of customs and in several cases resulting in the replacement of the domestic customs organizations with the services of foreign companies engaged in pre-shipment inspections.

---

[18]In cases of political corruption, those who represent the state (president, prime minister, ministers) or their close relatives may use the tax and customs administrations to pursue rent seeking and corrupt practices.

Reports from several countries indicate that the number of applicants for poorly paid jobs in administering taxes or in customs has been unusually large, pointing to the possibility that applicants know these jobs create opportunities for extra incomes.[19]

Spending Decisions

Corruption can also affect public expenditure. Corruption related to the provision by the government of goods at below-market prices is discussed below, but I will now discuss other aspects of public expenditure.

Investment projects have lent themselves to frequent acts of high-level corruption. Because of the discretion that some high-level public officials have over decisions regarding public investment projects, this type of public spending can become much distorted, both in size and in composition, by corruption.[20] Public projects have, at times, been carried out specifically to provide opportunities to some individuals or some political groups to get "commissions" from those who are chosen to execute the projects. This has reduced the productivity of such expenditure and has resulted in projects that would not have been justified on objective criteria of investment selection such as cost-benefit analysis.

Procurement spending, that is, the purchase of goods and services on the part of the government, is another area affected by corruption. To reduce corruption possibilities, some countries have developed complex and costly procedures that may have reduced corruption at the cost of sharply increasing the prices at which some goods are purchased.[21]

Extrabudgetary accounts are common in many countries. Some of them have legitimacy and are set up for specific purposes (pension funds, road funds, etc.). Others are set up to reduce the political and administrative controls that are more likely to accompany spending that goes through the budget. In some countries, the money received from foreign aid or from the sale of natural resources such as oil and tin is channeled toward special accounts that tend to be less transparent and

---

[19]There have even been reports that in some countries these jobs can be bought.
[20]See Tanzi and Davoodi (1997).
[21]The notorious US$600 hammers bought by the Pentagon could be explained by such procedures.

less controlled than the money channeled through the budget. Some of this money may go into illegitimate uses or pockets.[22]

In all these areas, lack of transparency and of effective institutional controls are the main factors leading to corruption.

Provision for Goods and Services at Below-Market Prices

In most countries, the government engages in the provision of goods, services, and resources at below-market prices—for example, foreign exchange, credit, electricity, water, public housing, some rationed goods, access to educational and health facilities, access to public land, and so on. Even access to some forms of pensions, such as those for disability, fall into this category because the individuals who get them have paid less in contributions to the pension funds over time than the pension they get once their disability status is approved. In some countries, disability pensions have been a fertile ground for corruption. In others, some individuals benefited enormously when they were able to get access to large amounts of credit or foreign exchange at below-market prices.

Sometimes, because of limited supply, rationing or queuing becomes unavoidable. Excess demand is created and decisions have to be made to apportion the limited supply. These decisions are often made by public employees. Those who want these goods (the users) would be willing to pay a bribe to get access (or a higher access) to what the government is providing. It is thus not surprising that in all the areas mentioned above, cases of corruption have been reported.

Other Discretionary Decisions

Besides the areas mentioned above, in many countries some public officials find themselves in positions where they have discretion over important decisions; in these situations, corruption, including high-level or political corruption, can play a major role. The most important of these discretionary decisions are as follows:

- provision of tax incentives against income taxes, value-added taxes, and foreign trade taxes, which may be worth millions of dol-

---

[22]Because of the variation of the price of commodities even within a day, it may be difficult to ascertain at which price a transaction takes place. Some of the difference between the actual price and the declared price may be channeled into foreign accounts.

lars in terms of the present value of reduced future liabilities to those who benefit from them;[23]

- decisions as to the particular use of private land (zoning laws) that determine whether the same piece of land can be used only for agriculture, and thus have low market value, or for high-rise buildings, and thus be very expensive;
- decisions as to the use of government-owned land, for example, for logging purposes, which may also be worth a lot to the recipients. Major cases of corruption related to permissions to cut trees from publicly owned forests, or to exploit lands for their mineral wealth, have been reported in several countries;
- decisions that authorize major foreign investments, often undertaken in connection with domestic interests, which often provide the privileged investors with monopoly power;
- decisions related to the sale of public sector assets, including the right to extract natural resources;
- decisions on the privatization of state-owned enterprises and on the conditions attached to that process, such as the degree of regulation of the industry; and
- decisions providing monopoly power to particular export, import, or domestic activities.

Decisions such as those described above are often worth a lot to individuals or enterprises. It is natural that attempts will be made by some of them to get favorable decisions, in some cases by paying bribes and in other cases by simply exploiting close personal relations with public officials. The bribes may be paid to public officials whose salaries may be very low and whose "temptation price" may be far less than the value of the potential benefit from a favorable decision to the bribers.

Financing of Parties

Some time before the tangentopoli scandal exploded in Italy, Minister Martelli, an important member of the socialist party, candidly admit-

---

[23]In some countries these incentives have been provided outside the normal legal process, by high-level public officials, to favored individuals.

ted in a speech that the Italian political parties had on their payrolls a small army of employees. The salaries for these employees had to be paid. He implied that the needed money had to come from somewhere. Minister Martelli had put his finger on a major problem for democracies—the need to finance the activities, including the electoral campaigns, of the political parties.[24] When public money is not available for the activities of the political parties, enormous pressures will build up to generate funds. The recent controversy concerning political donations in the United States is an example of this problem. As Susan Rose-Ackerman (1997, p. 40) has put it: "Democracy gives citizens a role in choosing their political leaders. Thus corrupt elected officials can be voted out of office. But democracy is not necessarily a cure for corruption."

IV. Indirect Causes of Corruption

Besides the factors that promote corruption directly, discussed in the previous section, other factors can contribute to corruption indirectly. Some of these are discussed briefly in this section.

Quality of the Bureaucracy

The quality of the bureaucracy varies greatly among countries. In some, public sector jobs give a lot of prestige and status; in others, much less so. Many factors contribute to that quality. Many years ago Max Weber (1947), the outstanding German sociologist, described what should be the characteristics of an *ideal* bureaucracy. He was aware that most bureaucracies are not ideal. Tradition and the effect that it has on the pride that individuals have in working for the government may explain why, all things being equal, some bureaucracies are much more efficient and much less vulnerable to corruption than others.[25] Rauch and Evans (1997) have gathered information on the de-

---

[24]One of the leading judges of *mani pulite* (clean hands), the investigation in the Italian corruption scandal, has recently described the arrangements among the parties to share the proceeds from corruption. See Nordio (1997). On the issue of political corruption, see also Cazzola (1988); Johnston (1997); and Ferrero and Brosio (1997).

[25]See von Klimo (1997). Von Klimo compares the public conception of an inefficient and corrupt public administration in nineteenth century Italy with the "myth of absolute efficiency and incorruptibility" enjoyed by the administration of the Prussian state.

gree to which civil servants' recruitment and promotions are merit based for 35 developing countries. Their results indicate that the less recruitment and promotion are based on merit, the higher is the extent of corruption.

Absence of politically motivated hiring, patronage, and nepotism, and clear rules on promotions and hiring, in addition to some of the factors discussed separately below, all contribute to the quality of a bureaucracy. The incentive structure plus tradition go a long way toward explaining why some bureaucracies are much less corrupt than others.[26]

Level of Public Sector Wages

Over the years many observers have speculated that the wages paid to civil servants are important in determining the degree of corruption. For example, Assar Lindbeck (1998) attributes the low corruption in Sweden in this century partly to the fact that at the turn of the century, high-level administrators earned 12–15 times the salary of an average industrial worker. One can speculate that there may be corruption due to greed and corruption due to need. In Figure 1, CC' represents the trade-off between the level of corruption and the level of wages. The higher the wage level, the lower is corruption. Assume that OR represents a level of wage consistent with the minimum required by the family of a public employee for a decent living. It can be assumed that OA is corruption due to greed, while corruption beyond OA would be due to need. Figure 1 also implies that, regardless of the wage level, some public officials will be corrupt perhaps because of their own psychological or moral makeup, or because some of the bribes offered may be too large for some officials to resist. Thus, it implies, realistically, that not all officials respond in the same way to the same incentives. In theoretical jargon, agents are heterogeneous.

The relationship between wage level and corruption index has been tested empirically by Van Rijckeghem and Weder (1997). See also Haque and Sahay (1996). With the use of cross-sectional data, they have been able to support the common intuition by finding a statistically significant relationship between corruption and wage levels, similar to that shown by the CC' curve in Figure 1. They have speculated that while an increase in the wage level is likely to reduce corruption,

---

[26]In some countries, public sector hiring has had the reduction of unemployment as its main objective, rather than improving the quality of the public administration.

Figure 1. Wage Level Corruption Trade-Off

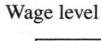

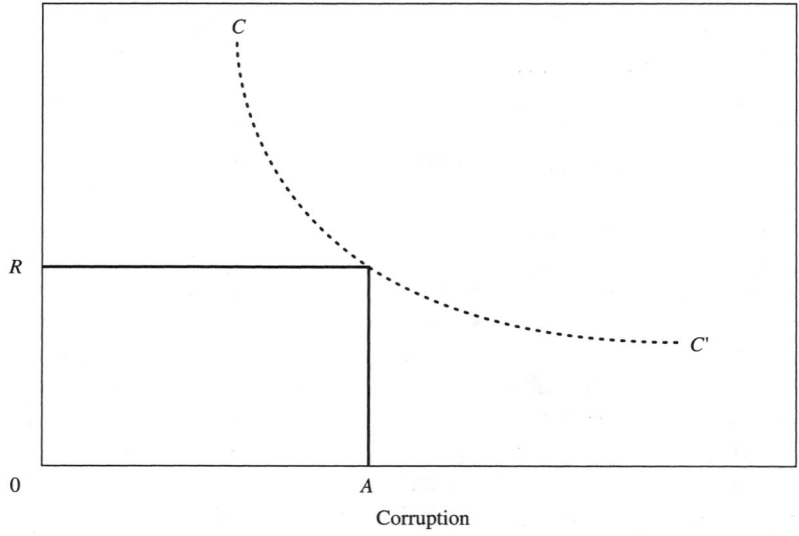

[Figure: Graph with "Wage level" on vertical axis and "Corruption" on horizontal axis. A curve labeled C at the top descends to C' at the right. Point R is on the wage axis, point A is on the corruption axis, forming a rectangle to the curve.]

a very large increase would be necessary to reduce it to minimal levels. In other words, the fight against corruption, pursued exclusively on the basis of wage increases, can be very costly to the budget of a country and can achieve only part of the objective. Furthermore, as argued above, even at high wages some individuals may continue to engage in corrupt practices.

In recent years, several countries (Argentina, Peru, etc.) have attempted to reduce corruption in particularly sensitive areas, such as customs and tax administrations, by increasing the level of salaries for the public employees in these areas.[27] These countries have also increased salary differentials to be able to retain and attract more able, productive, and honest individuals. Over the years, Singapore has pursued a wage policy aimed at reducing the temptation for public offi-

---

[27]In Peru, the wage structure in the tax administration became similar to that of the central bank and thus somewhat higher than the wage structure of the civil service. Also, an incentive system was introduced that assigned to the tax administration (SUNAT) a share of the tax revenue. The average age of the employees of the tax administration fell dramatically.

cials to engage in acts of corruption. Reportedly, the salaries of ministers and other high-level officials in Singapore are among the highest in the world.[28]

There has been some speculation in the theoretical economic literature that high wages may reduce the number of corrupt acts, while they may lead to demands for higher bribes on the part of those who continue to be corrupt. The reason is that high wages raise the opportunity cost of losing one's job, while they do not eliminate the greed on the part of some officials. Thus, while the number of corrupt acts is reduced, the total amount of corruption money paid may not necessarily fall.

Penalty Systems

Following Gary Becker's (1968) classical analysis of crime prevention, given the probability that the perpetrator of a crime would be caught, the penalty imposed plays an important role in determining the probability that criminal or illegal acts would take place.[29] In theory, all things being equal, corruption could be reduced by increasing the penalties on those who get caught. This analysis implies that the penalty structure existing in a country is an important factor in determining the extent of corruption in that country. But once again, at least theoretically, higher penalties may reduce the *number* of acts of corruption, but they may lead to demands for higher bribes on the corrupt acts that still take place.

In the real world, relatively few people are punished for acts of corruption, in spite of the extent of the phenomenon. Furthermore, with the exception of a few countries, there seems to be a wide gap between the penalties specified in the laws and regulations and the penalties that are effectively imposed.[30] Generally, effective penalties tend to be more lenient than the statutory ones. The administrative procedures followed before a public employee is punished for acts of corruption

---

[28] A common belief is that in situations of low wages but high possibilities of corruption, less honest individuals will be attracted to the civil service.

[29] For an econometric application of Becker's theory to the Netherlands, see van Tulden and van der Torre (1997).

[30] China has recently gone as far as applying the death penalty on some individuals accused of corruption. However, many acts of corruption still go unpunished, so that uncertainty prevails on the treatment of individuals accused of corruption. This may lead to the perception that penalties are applied selectively or arbitrarily.

are slow and cumbersome. Often legal, political, or administrative impediments prevent the full or quick application of the penalties. Due process and the need to provide incontrovertible evidence are major hurdles. The potential accusers are often reluctant to come forward and to spend the time and effort to go through the full process required to punish someone. Also, when corruption is widespread, the costs to the accusers in terms of social capital, such as lost friends, can be high.[31] Furthermore, the judges who will impose the penalties may themselves be accessible to corruption or may have political biases, so that they may be bought by the accused or may put obstacles to the proceedings. All these factors limit the role that penalties actually play in many countries, especially when corruption is partly politically motivated. This attitude brings a toleration for small acts of corruption that can in time encourage bigger acts.[32]

Institutional Controls

The other important ingredient in Gary Becker's analysis is the probability that those who commit crimes would be caught. This leads to the role of institutional controls. The existence of these controls reflects to a large extent the attitude of the political body toward this problem. Generally, the most effective controls are those that exist *inside institutions*. This is really the first line of defense. Honest and effective supervisors, good auditing offices, and clear rules on ethical behavior should be able to discourage or discover corrupt activities. Good and transparent procedures should make it easier for these offices to exercise their controls. Supervisors should be able to monitor the activities of their subordinates and they should themselves be held accountable for acts of corruption in their offices that go unpunished. These characteristics vary from country to country. In some, these checks are almost nonexistent, so that corruption is mostly discovered by chance or through the reporting by outsiders, including the media. In this connection, the role of a free press in controlling corruption cannot be exaggerated. See Brunetti and Weder (1998).

---

[31]Even in countries with relatively little corruption, so-called whistle blowers do not seem to have an easy time.

[32]Reluctance to apply harsh penalties may also be due to concerns that the penalties might be applied selectively, to political opponents.

Several countries and regions, including Singapore, Hong Kong SAR, Uganda, Argentina, and others, have created anticorruption commissions or ethics offices expressly charged with the responsibility of following reports on corruption or reducing corruption through the requirement on the part of public officials to report their wealth and in other ways.[33] To be effective, these offices must have independence from the political establishment, ample resources, and personnel of the highest integrity. They must also have the power to enforce penalties, or, at least, have others, including the judiciary, enforce the penalties. Unfortunately, in some countries these offices are required to report confidentially to the president or the prime minister of the country rather than, say, openly to the legislative body. This reduces their effectiveness and politicizes the process. In other countries, these commissions do not have the power to impose penalties and their reports may not have any following by other institutions.

Transparency of Rules, Laws, and Processes

In many countries, the lack of transparency in rules, laws, and processes creates a fertile ground for corruption. Rules are often confusing, the documents specifying them are not publicly available, and, at times, the rules are changed without properly publicized announcements. Laws or regulations are written in a way that only trained lawyers can understand and they are often conceptually opaque about important aspects, thus leaving grounds for different interpretations. Processes or procedures on policy matters and other actions, for example, competitions for public projects, are equally opaque, so that at times it is difficult to understand or to determine the process that was followed before a decision was reached. This makes it difficult to determine whether corruption has played a role in some important decisions.

Some countries—for example, New Zealand—have made great efforts in recent years to bring more transparency to all the accounts and actions of the government. The IMF has recently issued a code on fiscal transparency for its member countries that, if followed, would have the effect of reducing corruption.

---

[33]For the experience of Uganda in the fight against corruption, see Ruzindana (1997) and Langseth and Stapenhurst (1997).

Examples by the Leadership

A final contributing factor is the example provided by the leadership. When the top political leaders do not provide the right example, either because they engage in acts of corruption or, as is more often the case, because they condone such acts on the part of relatives, friends, or political associates, it cannot be expected that the employees in the public administration will behave differently. The same argument applies within particular institutions such as tax administration, customs, and public enterprises. These institutions cannot be expected to be corruption free if their heads do not provide the best examples of honesty.

In some countries, the leadership has been somewhat indifferent to this problem. In an African country, a president refused to fire ministers widely reputed to be corrupt. In an Asian country, a minister who was accused of corruption was simply moved to head another ministry. In a Latin American country, a president who was planning to create an anticorruption commission proposed to appoint as head of this commission an individual widely reported to be corrupt. Examples such as these do not help create the climate for a corruption-free society.

V. Measurement of Corruption

If corruption could be measured, it could probably be eliminated. In fact, conceptually it is not even clear what one would want to measure.[34] Simply measuring bribes paid would ignore many corrupt acts that are not accompanied by the payment of bribes. An attempt to measure acts of corruption rather than the amounts of bribes paid would require counting many relatively unimportant actions and identifying each act—information that is simply not available. While there are no *direct* ways of measuring corruption, there are several indirect ways of getting information about its prevalence in a country or in an institution. Useful information can be obtained from:

- reports on corruption available from published sources including newspapers. The Internet has become a most valuable source.[35] Newspapers such as *Le Monde, The Financial Times*, and *The*

---

[34]One could measure acts of corruption on bribes paid.
[35]For some countries, the Internet reports tens of thousands of entries on the subject of corruption.

New York Times and magazines such as *The Economist* and *The Far Eastern Economic Review* have published many articles on corruption.

- case studies of corrupt agencies such as tax administrations, customs, and police. Unfortunately, while there are many such studies, often the reports are internal and are kept confidential.

- questionnaire-based surveys. These can be related to a specific agency (for example, Peru's or Argentina's tax administration); or to a whole country. These surveys *measure perceptions of corruption rather than corruption per se*. The World Bank has been making use of these surveys in its work in Tanzania, Uganda, India, Ukraine, and other places. It has used these surveys to improve the effectiveness of particular programs such as health care.

Countrywide surveys are available from the following organizations: Global Competitiveness Report (Geneva); Political and Economic Risk Consultancy (Hong Kong SAR); Transparency International (Berlin); and Political Risk Services (Syracuse). The Gallup poll has also conducted a major survey for 44 countries dealing with corruption in particular activities, and the World Bank has conducted a survey for many countries.

The results obtained from these surveys are now widely used by researchers and business people. The best-known of these surveys, the Transparency International index, for example, assesses the perception of corruption on a scale of 0 to 10. Ten refers to a corruption-free country; zero refers to a country where most transactions or relations are tainted by corruption. The variance of these indexes, which reflects how the views are spread among respondents, is also important and has been used by some researchers in their work.[36] People may tend to confuse these indexes with actual measurements of corruption. It is important to keep in mind that the indexes reflect *perceptions and not objective and quantitative measures of actual corruption*. One good feature is that the various indexes available are highly correlated among themselves.

Table 1 shows the indexes for 1995 to 1998 provided by Transparency International. Comparing the 1995 figures with those reported in 1998 for the countries covered in both years indicates that countries

---

[36]See, for example, Wei (1997a) and (1997b).

Table 1. Corruption Perception Index, 1995–98

Country	1995	1996	1997	1998	Rank in 1998	Rank in 1996
Denmark	9.32	9.33	9.94	10.00	1	2
Finland	9.12	9.05	9.48	9.60	2	4
Sweden	8.87	9.08	9.35	9.50	3	3
New Zealand	9.55	9.43	9.23	9.40	4	1
Iceland	. . .	. . .	. . .	9.30	5	. . .
Canada	8.87	8.96	9.10	9.20	6	5
Singapore	9.26	8.80	8.66	9.10	7	7
Norway	8.61	8.87	8.92	9.00	8	6
Netherlands	8.69	8.71	9.03	9.00	9	9
Switzerland	8.76	8.76	8.61	8.90	10	8
United Kingdom	8.57	8.44	8.22	8.70	11	12
Luxembourg	. . .	. . .	8.61	8.70	12	. . .
Australia	8.80	8.60	8.86	8.70	13	10
Ireland	8.57	8.45	8.28	8.20	14	11
Germany	8.14	8.27	8.23	7.90	15	13
Hong Kong SAR	7.12	7.01	7.28	7.80	16	18
Austria	7.13	7.59	7.61	7.50	17	16
United States	7.79	7.66	7.61	7.50	18	15
Israel	. . .	7.71	7.97	7.10	19	14
Chile	7.94	6.80	6.05	6.80	20	21
France	7.00	6.96	6.66	6.70	21	19
Portugal	5.56	6.53	6.97	6.50	22	22
Spain	4.35	4.31	5.90	6.10	23	32
Botswana	. . .	. . .	. . .	6.10	24	. . .
Japan	6.72	7.05	6.57	5.80	25	17
Estonia	. . .	. . .	. . .	5.70	26	. . .
Costa Rica	. . .	. . .	6.45	5.60	27	. . .
Belgium	6.85	6.84	5.25	5.40	28	20
Malaysia	5.28	5.32	5.01	5.30	29	26
Taiwan Province of China	5.08	4.98	5.02	5.30	30	29
Namibia	. . .	. . .	. . .	5.30	31	. . .
South Africa	5.62	5.68	4.95	5.20	32	23
Hungary	4.12	4.86	5.18	5.00	33	31
Mauritius	. . .	. . .	. . .	5.00	34	. . .
Tunisia	. . .	. . .	. . .	5.00	35	. . .
Greece	4.04	5.01	5.35	4.90	36	28
Czech Republic	. . .	5.37	5.20	4.80	37	25
Jordan	. . .	4.89	. . .	4.70	38	30
Italy	2.99	3.42	5.03	4.60	39	34
Poland	. . .	5.57	5.08	4.60	40	24

Table 1 *(continued)*

Country	1995	1996	1997	1998	Rank in 1998	Rank in 1996
Peru	...	...	...	4.50	41	...
Uruguay	...	...	4.14	4.30	42	...
Korea	4.29	5.02	4.29	4.20	43	27
Zimbabwe	...	...	...	4.20	44	...
Malawi	...	...	...	4.10	45	...
Brazil	2.70	2.96	3.56	4.00	46	40
Belarus	...	...	...	3.90	47	...
Slovak Republic	...	...	...	3.90	48	...
Jamaica	...	...	...	3.80	49	...
Morocco	...	...	...	3.70	50	...
El Salvador	...	...	...	3.60	51	...
China	2.16	2.43	2.88	3.50	52	50
Zambia	...	...	...	3.50	53	...
Turkey	4.10	3.54	3.21	3.40	54	33
Mexico	3.18	3.30	2.66	3.30	55	38
Philippines	2.77	2.69	3.05	3.30	56	44
Ghana	...	...	...	3.30	57	...
Senegal	...	...	...	3.30	58	...
Côte d'Ivoire	...	...	...	3.10	59	...
Guatemala	...	...	...	3.10	60	...
Argentina	5.24	3.41	2.81	3.00	61	35
Thailand	2.79	3.33	3.06	3.00	62	37
Romania	...	...	3.44	3.00	63	...
Nicaragua	...	...	...	3.00	64	...
Yugoslavia	...	...	...	3.00	65	...
India	2.78	2.63	2.75	2.90	66	46
Egypt	...	2.84	...	2.90	67	41
Bulgaria	...	...	...	2.90	68	...
Bolivia	...	3.40	2.05	2.80	69	36
Ukraine	...	...	...	2.80	70	...
Pakistan	2.25	1.00	2.53	2.70	71	53
Latvia	...	...	...	2.70	72	...
Uganda	...	2.71	...	2.60	73	43
Vietnam	...	...	2.79	2.50	74	...
Kenya	...	2.21	...	2.50	75	52
Russia	...	2.58	2.27	2.40	76	47
Venezuela	2.66	2.50	2.77	2.30	77	48
Ecuador	...	3.19	...	2.30	78	39
Colombia	3.44	2.73	2.23	2.20	79	42
Indonesia	1.94	2.65	2.72	2.00	80	45

Table 1 *(concluded)*

Country	1995	1996	1997	1998	Rank in 1998	Rank in 1996
Nigeria	...	0.69	1.76	1.90	81	54
Tanzania	...	...	...	1.90	82	...
Honduras	...	...	...	1.70	83	...
Paraguay	...	...	...	1.50	84	...
Cameroon	...	2.46	...	1.40	85	49
Bangladesh	...	2.29	...	...	...	51
Memorandum items:						
Number of countries	41	54	52	85		
Average	5.93	5.35	5.67	4.89		
Median	5.62	5.02	5.23	4.20		
Minimum	1.94	0.69	1.76	1.40		
Maximum	9.55	9.43	9.94	10.00		

Source: Transparency International.
Note: Data refer to perception of corruption ranging from 10 (highly clean) to 0 (highly corrupt). Rankings for 1998 and 1996 are based on 1998 and 1996 data, respectively. The data have been rearranged by the author.

tend to hold their positions although some important changes in particular countries are shown. See Figure 2. How closely changes in these indexes reflect real changes within given countries is an important, open question. A single but widely reported case of corruption may easily change perceptions in a given country and in a given year, and lead to an index that may not correctly assess the extent of corruption in that country.

VI. Economic Effects of Corruption

Review of Theoretical Arguments

The recent fairly broad consensus seems to be that corruption is unqualifiably bad. However, in past years, the views on corruption had been more divergent and some economists had even found some redeeming value in it.[37] Until the 1997 financial crisis, some countries

---

[37]Even today a few economists argue that, within well confined circumstances, corruption may promote faster growth. See, for example, Braguinsky (1996).

Figure 2. Corruption Ranking: 1995 vs. 1998
(53 countries)

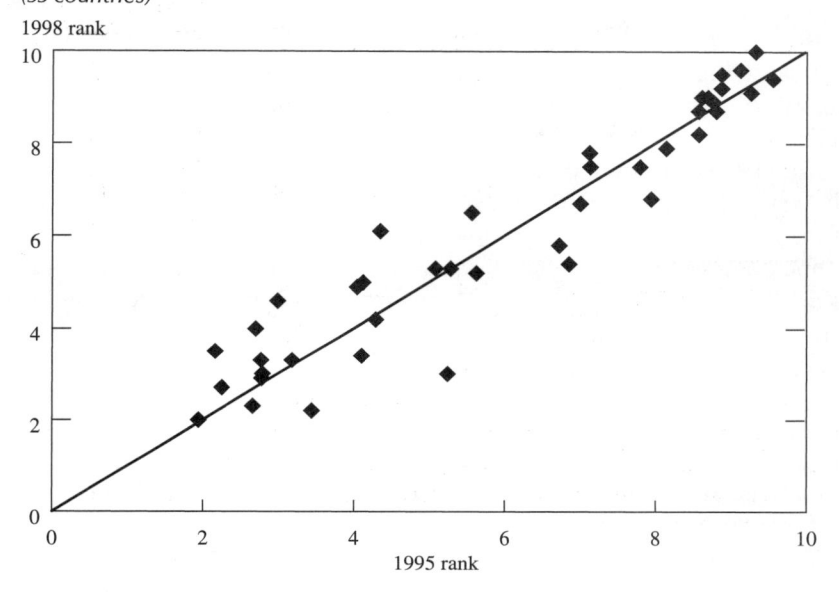

from Southeast Asia seemed to provide support for the view that corruption might promote growth. Indonesia, Thailand, and some other countries were often mentioned as countries growing fast in spite of, or even because of, perceived high levels of corruption. This corruption was associated with a low degree of uncertainty.[38] For Indonesia, it was argued that institutionalizing corruption made it less damaging to economic development than random corruption. One knew where to go and how much to pay for specific services. Some of the arguments in favor of the view that corruption may promote efficiency and even growth are summarized below.[39] This survey is not intended to be exhaustive but just to provide a feel for the relevant literature.

Leff (1964) and Huntington (1968) advanced the view that corruption can be efficiency enhancing because it removes government-imposed rigidities that impede investment and interfere with other economic decisions favorable to growth. Thus, corruption "oils the

---
[38]Since the fall of 1997, some accounts have blamed corruption for the financial crises caused by unproductive investments and high short-term borrowing.

[39]For a review, see Bardhan (1997) and Rose-Ackerman (1997).

mechanism" or "greases the wheel." This reasoning was often used to explain the high rates of growth in some countries of South East Asia.

Beck and Maher (1986) and Lien (1986) have developed models that show that, in bidding competitions, those who are most efficient can afford to offer the highest bribe. Therefore, bribes can promote efficiency by assigning projects to the most efficient firms.

Lui (1985) has argued that time has different values for different individuals, depending on their level of income and the opportunity cost of their time. Those for whom time is most valuable will offer bribes to public officials to be allowed to economize on time by jumping in front of the line, that is, by getting decisions more quickly. Thus, corruption can be efficient because it saves time for those for whom time has the greatest value. In a later paper, Lui (1996) argued that while corruption may improve the allocation of resources in some circumstances, it reduces growth because it provides some individuals the incentive to acquire the kind of human capital that can be used to improve corruption opportunities. This argument is related to those by Baumol (1990) and by Murphy, Shleifer, and Vishny (1991), discussed below.

Corruption can be a useful political glue by allowing politicians to get funds that can be used to hold a country together. The latter outcome may be a necessary condition for growth. See Graziano (1980).

Bribes can supplement low wages. Thus, corruption can allow the government to maintain a lower tax burden, which can favor growth. See Tullock (1996) and Becker and Stigler (1974). The issue here is whether a lower tax burden is more favorable to growth than a lower degree of corruption. This is a classic second-best problem.

The above theoretical arguments, which seemingly favor corruption, can be countered in many ways. First, rigidities and rules are not exogenous and unmovable features of a society; a society is not born with these rigidities. They are created, and, in fact, they may be intentionally created by public officials, to extract bribes. When rules can be used to extract bribes, more rules will be created. Furthermore, these rules are often kept intentionally opaque so that more power will remain on the side of those who enforce them. Knowledge gives power to those who have it.

Second, those who can pay the highest bribes are not necessarily the most economically efficient but rather the most successful at rent seeking. If bribes are seen as investments, those who pay them must consider that they are investments with a high rate of return. Baumol (1990) and Murphy, Shleifer, and Vishny (1991) have advanced related arguments that can be used to argue that, in traditional or corrupt societies, the most able individuals will be diverted, by existing incentives, from pursuing socially productive activities and toward rent-seeking activities. This diversion will impose a high cost for the growth of these countries. If the potentially most socially productive individuals are in scarce supply, as they are assumed to be, the diversion of their talent toward rent-seeking activities and corruption will be particularly damaging to society.

Third, payment of speed money may be an inducement for the bureaucrats to reduce the speed at which most practices are being processed. See Myrdal (1968). Bribes may change the order in which public officials perform the process, say, of providing permits, but they may also slow down the average time for the whole process.

And while corruption and rent seeking may be helpful as political glue or as wage supplements in the short run, they may lead to major problems over the longer run, as shown by the experience of Zaïre under Mobutu.

Qualitative Effects of Corruption on the Economy

Corruption reduces public revenue and increases public spending. It thus contributes to larger fiscal deficits, making it more difficult for the government to run a sound fiscal policy. Corruption is likely to increase income inequality because it allows well-positioned individuals to take advantage of government activities at the cost of the rest of the population.[40] There are strong indications that the changes in income distribution that have occurred in recent years in previously centrally planned economies have partly been the result of corrupt actions such as nomenklatura privatization.

Corruption distorts markets and the allocation of resources for the following reasons, and is therefore likely to reduce economic efficiency and growth.

- It reduces the ability of the government to impose necessary regulatory controls and inspections to correct for market failures. Then the government does not satisfactorily perform its regulatory role

---

[40]For a quantitative analysis that establishes a connection between higher corruption on the one hand and higher income inequality and poverty on the other hand, see Gupta, Davoodi, and Alonso-Terme (1998).

over banks, hospitals, food distribution, transportation activities, financial markets, and so on. When government intervention is motivated by corruption, as for example when the government creates monopolies for private interests, it is likely to add to the existing market failures.

- It distorts incentives. As already mentioned, in a corrupt environment, able individuals allocate their energies to rent seeking and to corrupt practices and not to productive activities. In some cases, the resulting activities have a negative value added.

- It acts as an arbitrary tax (with high welfare costs). Corruption's random nature creates high excess burdens because the cost of searching for those to whom the bribe must be paid must be added to the cost of negotiating and paying the bribe. Also, the contractual obligations secured by the payment of a bribe are more likely to be violated when corruption is decentralized.[41]

- It reduces or distorts the fundamental role of the government in such areas as enforcement of contracts and protection of property rights. When a citizen can buy his or her way out of a commitment or out of a contractual obligation, or when one is prevented from exercising one's property rights because of corruption, this fundamental role of the government is distorted and growth may be negatively affected.

- It reduces the legitimacy of the market economy and perhaps also of democracy. In fact, the criticisms voiced in many countries, especially in transition economies, against democracy and the market economy are motivated by the existence of corruption. Thus, corruption may slow down or even block the movement toward democracy and a market economy.

- Finally, corruption is likely to increase poverty because it reduces the income earning potential of the poor.

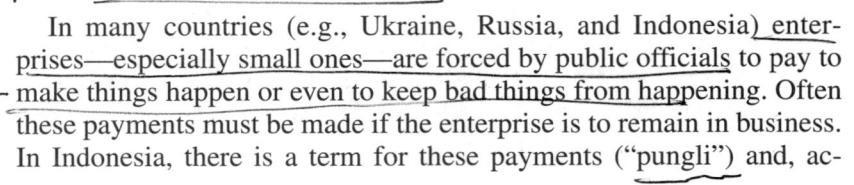

In many countries (e.g., Ukraine, Russia, and Indonesia) enterprises—especially small ones—are forced by public officials to pay to make things happen or even to keep bad things from happening. Often these payments must be made if the enterprise is to remain in business. In Indonesia, there is a term for these payments ("pungli") and, ac-

---

[41]Furthermore, random corruption may also be accompanied by higher penalties if the act of corruption is discovered.

cording to a recent report, these payments may raise the costs of doing business for small activities by as much as 20 percent of total operating costs (see Sjaifudian, 1997). This is equivalent to imposing very high sales taxes on these enterprises. Similar information has been reported for Russia (Shleifer, 1996) and for Ukraine (Kaufmann, 1997), but the problem may be much more widespread.

Cost-increasing corruption is often coercive for small enterprises, especially for emerging enterprises, which are often bullied by bureaucrats and tax inspectors into making substantial payments. Pressures on new enterprises often come from local government officials, who impose high pecuniary costs—some legal and some not—for licenses and authorizations.[42] These officials also impose high costs in terms of the time that the managers of the enterprises must spend to comply with the many requirements imposed on them. The burden of these costs is likely to fall on the small enterprises because they operate in a far more competitive market than large ones, so that they have greater difficulty in passing the costs on to their customers. Since small enterprises are the engine of growth in most countries, obstacles to their creation and growth cause economies to languish, especially in developing countries and increasingly in economies in transition.

Large enterprises can protect themselves more easily from problems of corruption because

- they have specialized departments that can deal with aggressive bureaucrats;
- they can use "facilitators"—individuals skilled at fighting through the jungle of opaque regulations and tax laws;
- their size makes them more immune to the extortion of petty bureaucrats; and
- they can use their political power to influence relevant individuals in the public administration or to pursue rent-seeking activities not available to others. For example, they may use gifts, or bribes camouflaged as political donations, to acquire market power through reduction in competition or to obtain tax incentives, subsidized credit, or other benefits.

---

[42]These small enterprises may be preyed upon by the police, health inspectors, tax inspectors, and the myriad of other individuals presumably representing the government.

Recent reforms, such as trade liberalization, in many countries have removed obstacles to economic growth that had characterized earlier periods. However, these obstacles were imposed mostly by the national governments. They were probably more important for large enterprises, which are more likely to trade abroad and to operate in the whole national territory. These reforms have not done much to reduce the many regulations, controls, opaque taxes, and fees imposed by *local* governments, unions, professional groups, and so on. These are probably the most important obstacles for the small enterprises.

Effects of Corruption on the Economy: Econometric Results

In the past couple of years, several studies, using cross-sectional analysis and the available corruption indexes, have reported important quantitative results on the effects of corruption on economic variables. These results suggest that corruption has a negative impact on the rate of growth of countries. Some, but not all, of these studies are mentioned below.

It has been found that corruption has the following effects.

- It reduces investment and, as a consequence, it reduces the rate of growth. See Mauro (1995). Such reduction in investment is assumed to be caused by the higher costs and by the uncertainty that corruption creates. In this analysis, the reduction in the rate of growth is a direct consequence of the decline in the investment rate. In other words, the analysis is based on a production function that makes growth a function of investment.

- It reduces expenditure on education and health, which does not lend itself easily to corrupt practices on the part of those who make budgetary decisions.[43] See Mauro (1997).

- It increases public investment because public investment projects lend themselves easily to manipulations by high-level officials to get bribes. See Tanzi and Davoodi (1997). Corruption also distorts the effects of industrial policy on investment. See Ades and Di Tella (1997).

---

[43]Of course, this does not mean that there is no corruption in the provision of these services. The provision of health is often distorted by bribes to doctors or other medical personnel to get better or faster service.

- It reduces expenditure for operation and maintenance for reasons similar to those that reduce expenditure for education and health. See Tanzi and Davoodi (1997).
- It reduces the productivity of public investment and of a country's infrastructure. See Tanzi and Davoodi (1997).
- It reduces tax revenue, mainly because of the impact that it has on the tax administration and on customs, thus reducing the ability of the government to carry out needed public expenditure. See Tanzi and Davoodi (1997).
- It reduces foreign direct investment because corruption has the same effect as a tax, and in fact operates as a tax. See Wei (1997a). The less predictable the level of corruption (the higher is its variance), the greater is its impact on foreign direct investment. A higher variance makes corruption behave like an unpredictable and random tax. See Wei (1997b). Thus, increases in corruption and in its unpredictability are equivalent to increases in the tax rate on enterprises. Wei concludes that raising the index of corruption from the Singapore level to the Mexican level is equivalent to increasing the marginal tax rate on enterprises by 20 percentage points.

VII. The Fight Against Corruption and the Role of the State

The many factors that contribute to corruption tend to be more common in poorer countries and in economies in transition than in rich countries. Thus, at some point in time, economic development reduces the level of corruption of a country. However, at similar levels of development, some countries are perceived to have more corruption than others.

Some economies (Singapore, Hong Kong SAR, Portugal) have managed to reduce the incidence of corruption significantly. Lindbeck (1998, p. 3) has pointed out that even in Sweden "corruption flourished . . . in the second half of the 18th century and in the early 19th century." Thus, governments should not be fatalistic or passive about corruption. With well-focused and determined efforts, corruption can be reduced, though not to zero. Trying to eliminate corruption altogether would be too costly, both in terms of resources and in other ways. For example, it may require excessively high public sector wages, major legal or organizational changes, or excessive limitations in civil rights, or very harsh effective penalties. An optimal *theoretical* level would be reached where the marginal social costs of reducing corruption further would be equal to the marginal social benefits from that reduction.[44] Thus, it is realistic to think that the level of corruption will remain above zero in all countries. In fact, probably no country is free of corruption.

Corruption is a complex phenomenon that is almost never explained by a single cause. If it were, the solution would be simple. Of the many factors that influence it, some can be changed more easily than others. Because of the complexity of the phenomenon, the fight against corruption must be pursued on many fronts. It is a fight that cannot be won in months or even in a few years. The greatest mistake that can be made is to rely on a strategy that depends excessively on actions in a single area, such as increasing the salaries of the public sector employees, or increasing penalties, or creating an anticorruption office, and then to expect quick results.

Any realistic strategy must start with an explicit recognition that *there are those who demand acts of corruption* on the part of public sector employees and *there are public employees willing for a price to perform these acts.* There is thus both a demand for and supply of corruption. And as is the case with all demands and supplies, the price plays a major role. Various incentives determine the elasticities of these supply and demand functions. In the basic case, the briber wants something (a reduction in a cost or an increase in a benefit) from the public official and is willing to pay a bribe for it. The official has something to sell (i.e., power) and wants to be compensated for the risk and the effort involved.[45] However, in the background there is the state in the totality of its actions carried out by the many agencies that constitute the public sector. To a large extent it is the state that, through its many policies and actions, creates the environment and incentives that influence those who pay bribes and those who accept or demand them. It is the state that influences the relationship between briber and bribee. See Klitgaard (1988).

---

[44]In practice, of course, these marginal costs and marginal benefits are impossible to measure.

[45]Of course, we are ignoring the cases when corruption is coercive and reflects the pressures of public officials or individuals.

In the ideal bureaucracies described by Max Weber, the public official (as the agent of the state) is the faithful executor of the mandate and instructions that he receives from the state (the principal). The public official is just a conduit, or a direct and legitimate channel for the relationship between the state and the citizen. He would not distort the state-citizen relationship. In this Weberian world, no principal-agent problems would develop. Unfortunately, in the real world, Weberian bureaucracies are rare[46] in part because the actions and the policies of the state are not always transparent and in part because of characteristics of the bureaucracies themselves. The citizens may question the legitimacy of some state actions, attributing them to rent seeking by public officials and not to the pursuit of the public interest. The state may have de facto fractured into several power centers (ministries, public enterprises, independent institutions, subnational governments, and so on), each pursuing somewhat distinct interests. Sometimes the policies of these power centers are not consistent with one another and the instructions that emanate from these public centers are conflicting.[47]

At times the instructions passed on to the agents who will carry out the execution of the policies are not clear because the top policymakers do not have clear ideas or perhaps may not wish their actions to be totally transparent. Total transparency in processes and in policies may imply less power for particular policymakers, in the sense that their discretion in affecting the welfare of particular groups is reduced. Thus, the fight against corruption is not distinct and independent from the reform of the state, because some of the measures to reduce corruption are at the same time measures that change the character of the state. Let us consider a few examples.

It is generally believed that the level of relative wages in the public sector is an important variable in the degree of corruption in a country. Singapore, a country with a good index of corruption and where corruption was much reduced over the years, has some of the highest wages for public employees. Reportedly, its ministers receive the highest salaries in the world. The civil service of Singapore is small and enjoys a high status.

---

[46]They may be approximated only in a few countries such as Denmark, Sweden, New Zealand, Canada, and perhaps a few others.

[47]This is particularly the case of tax officials in some countries with decentralized fiscal systems. In these situations, the officials may be subject to conflicting pressures from the national government and the local governments.

In countries where public sector wages are low with respect to those in the private sector, these wages are often low because public policies have inflated the number of people working for the government. In other words, the governments have traded wage levels against the number of civil servants on their payrolls. The increase in the number of employees has meant lower real wages paid to them. In these situations, it is not realistic or wise to suggest that these countries simply increase real wages without first reducing the size of the civil service. However, for many governments, reducing the number of public employees would run counter to the objectives of their government, or at least would be politically difficult. And many governments believe that unemployment can be reduced through public sector hiring.

The same argument applies to wage differentials. Many governments aim to reduce the spread in their employees' wages. In some countries, the ratio between the highest salaries and the lowest has been reduced to three. This is far less than in the private sector. The effect of this wage compression is that the most qualified and the most honest employees tend to leave the public sector for the private sector. For many governments changing this policy would be contrary to their goals and in many cases would be opposed by the labor unions.

It is generally believed that increasing the penalties for acts of corruption would reduce a country's corruption. However, the imposition of higher penalties could run into problems with employees' associations, with trade unions, with the judiciary system, and so on. Also, there is the danger that an unscrupulous government would use this weapon to go after political opponents. In other words, penalties could be used selectively or, worse, they could be used in connection with fabricated accusations. In democratic societies, penalties are imposed only after what is often a lengthy and costly process. The immediate supervisors of the corrupt officials may be reluctant to carry the brunt of some of the procedural costs (in terms of time lost, damaged friendships, etc.), and may prefer to close their eyes to acts of corruption.

It is generally believed that many acts of corruption are stimulated by the existence of regulations. Some kinds of quasi-fiscal regulations at times substitute for taxing and spending actions. It is useful to point out that some of the countries perceived to be the least corrupt (e.g., Sweden, Denmark, Canada) have some of the highest tax burdens. On the other hand, some of the countries with the highest indexes of corruption (e.g., Nigeria, Pakistan, Bangladesh, China, Venezuela) have some of the lowest tax burdens. In the latter group of countries, quasi-fiscal regulations (i.e., regulations that substitute for taxing and spending) substitute taxes and public expenditures.[48] Thus, to reduce corruption these countries would need to eliminate these quasi-fiscal regulations and, if necessary, replace them with taxing and spending policies. But quasi-fiscal regulations are predominant in these economies and they would have a difficult time in raising the level of taxation substantially. Once again we come to the conclusion that the fight against corruption and the reform of the state are two sides of the same coin.

Tax incentives, especially when they imply discretionary decisions on the part of public officials, create conditions in which corruption develops. A simple recommendation would be to eliminate tax incentives and replace them with tax systems with broad bases and lower rates, as often suggested by tax experts. Unfortunately, the roles that some governments want to play require the use of these incentives.[49] Therefore, once again, the fight against corruption requires a reform in the role of the state.

Corruption often accompanies the provision by the government of goods and services at below-market prices. This often occurs with credit, foreign exchange, the prices of public utility services, public housing, higher education, health services, and so on. The low or zero prices create excess demand and the need to ration the good or service. Rationing always brings corruption. Thus, raising these prices to equilibrium level whenever possible would eliminate or reduce corruption. However, it would also change the role of the state in a way that many governments are not willing to accept.

Many other examples could be provided. However, these are sufficient to make the point that the fight against corruption often cannot proceed independently from the reform of the state. In many ways, it is the same fight. Thus, corruption will be reduced only in those countries where governments are willing to substantially reduce some of their functions.

---

[48]For a discussion of quasi-fiscal regulations and their power to replace taxing and spending, see Tanzi (1995b).

[49]This has been a major issue in economies in transition where governments want to continue to directly influence the activities in some sectors. Thus, the policymakers have found it hard to accept the approach associated with broad-based taxes.

VIII. Concluding Remarks

In this paper I have discussed the phenomenon of corruption, which affects many countries. I have shown the incidence of this phenomenon and the damage that it brings to economies and democracies. When corruption is widespread and especially when it contaminates the actions of the policymakers in democratic, market-oriented economies, it becomes more difficult to argue in favor of such economic and political arrangements.[50] The widespread disillusion among the population of some economies in transition and some developing countries with both market economies and democratic processes is very much caused by the widespread corruption that prevails in these countries and is wrongly attributed to the market economy and the democratic process.

I have also argued that corruption is closely linked to the way governments conduct their affairs in modern societies, and therefore also to the growth of some of the government's activities in the economy. It is unlikely that corruption can be substantially reduced without modifying the way governments operate. The fight against corruption is, thus, intimately linked with the reform of the state.

In any case, any serious strategy to attempt to reduce corruption will need action on at least four fronts:

1. Honest and visible commitment by the leadership to the fight against corruption, for which the leadership must show zero tolerance;
2. Policy changes that reduce the demand for corruption by scaling down regulations and other policies such as tax incentives, and by making those that are retained as transparent and as nondiscretionary as possible;
3. Reducing the supply of corruption by increasing public sector wages, increasing incentives toward honest behavior, and instituting effective controls and penalties on the public servants; and
4. Somehow solving the problem of the financing of political parties.

Societies can do much to reduce the intensity of corruption, but no single action will achieve more than a limited improvement—and some of the necessary actions may require major changes in existing policies.

---

[50]It should be remembered that many dictators or many potential dictators make the fight against corruption one of the reasons why they should be given the reins of a country. Some associate democracy with lack of discipline.

References

Ades, Alberto, and Rafael Di Tella, forthcoming, "Rents, Competition and Corruption," *American Economic Review*.

———, 1997, "National Champions and Corruption: Some Unpleasant Interventionist Arithmetic," *Economic Journal*, Vol. 107 (July), pp. 1023–42.

Bardhan, Pranab, 1997, "Corruption and Development: A Review of Issues," *Journal of Economic Literature*, Vol. 35 (September), pp. 1320–46.

Baumol, William J., 1990, "Entrepreneurship: Productive, Unproductive, and Destructive," *Journal of Political Economy,* Vol. 98 (October) pp. 893–921.

Beck, Paul J., and Michael W. Maher, 1986, "A Comparison of Bribery and Bidding in Thin Markets," *Economics Letters*, Vol. 20, No. 1, pp. 1–5.

Becker, Gary S., 1968, "Crime and Punishment: An Economic Approach," *Journal of Political Economy*, Vol. 76 (March/April), pp. 169–217.

Becker, Gary S., and George J. Stigler, 1974, "Law Enforcement, Malfeasance, and Compensation for Employees," *Journal of Legal Studies* (January), pp. 1–18.

Braguinsky, Serguey, 1996, "Corruption and Schumpeterian Growth in Different Economic Environments," *Contemporary Economic Policy,* Vol. 14 (July), pp. 14–25.

Brunetti, Aymo, and Beatrice Weder, 1998, "A Free Press Is Bad News for Corruption," WWZ Discussion Paper No. 9809 (Basel: Weltwirtschaftswissenschaftliches Zentrum der Universität Basel, April).

Cazzola, Franco, 1988, *Della Corruzione: Fisiologia e Patologia di un Sistema Politico* (Bologna: Il Mulino).

Davigo, Piercamillo, 1998, *La Giubba del Re: Intervista sulla Corruzione* (Rome-Bari: Editori Laterza).

Ferrero, Mario, and Giorgio Brosio, 1997, "Nomenklatura Rule Under Democracy: Solving the Italian Political Puzzle," *Journal of Theoretical Politics*, Vol. 9 (October).

Galasi, Peter, and Gabor Gertesi, 1987, "The Spread of Bribery in a Centrally Planned Economy," *Acta Oeconomica*, Vol. 34 (3–4), pp. 371–89.

Galtung, Frederik, 1997, "Developing Agencies of Restraint in a Climate of Systemic Corruption: The National Integrity System at Work," paper presented at the Third Vienna Dialogue on Democracy, Vienna, June 26–27.

Goldman, Marshall, 1997, "The Pitfalls of Russian Privatization," *Challenge*, Vol. 40 (May–June) pp. 35–49.

Graziano, Luigi, 1980, *Clientelismo e Sistema Politico. Il Caso dell'Italia* (Milan: F. Angeli).

Grossman, Gregory, 1982, "The Second Economy in the USSR," in *The Underground Economy in the United States and Abroad*, ed. by Vito Tanzi (Lexington, Massachusetts: D.C. Heath), pp. 245–70.

Gupta, Sanjeev, Hamid Davoodi, and Rosa Alonso-Terme, 1998, "Does Corruption Affect Income Inequality and Poverty?" IMF Working Paper 98/76 (Washington: International Monetary Fund). [Revised version reproduced as Chapter 17 in this volume—ED.]

Haque, Nadeem Ul, and Ratna Sahay, 1996, "Do Government Wage Cuts Close Budget Deficits? Costs of Corruption," *Staff Papers*, International Monetary Fund, Vol. 43 (December), pp. 754–78.

Hines, James R. Jr., 1995, "Forbidden Payments: Foreign Bribery and American Business After 1977," NBER Working Paper No. 5266 (Cambridge, Massachusetts: National Bureau of Economic Research, September).

Huntington, Samuel P., 1968, *Political Order in Changing Societies* (New Haven, Connecticut: Yale University Press).

Johnston, Michael, 1997, "Public Officials, Private Interests, and Sustainable Democracy: When Politics and Corruption Meet," in *Corruption and the Global Economy*, ed. by Kimberly Ann Elliot (Washington: Institute for International Economics), pp. 61–82.

Kaufmann, Daniel, 1997, "The Missing Pillar of a Growth Strategy for Ukraine: Reforms for Private Sector Development," in *Ukraine: Accelerating the Transition to Market*, ed. by Peter Cornelius and Patrick Lenain (Washington: International Monetary Fund), pp. 234–74.

———, and Paul Siegelbaum, 1996 "Privatization and Corruption in Transition Economies," *Journal of International Affairs*, Vol. 50 (Winter), pp. 419–58.

Klitgaard, Robert E., 1988, *Controlling Corruption* (Berkeley, California: University of California Press).

Kopits, George, and Jon Craig, 1998, "Transparency in Government Operations," IMF Occasional Paper No. 158 (Washington: International Monetary Fund).

Krueger, Anne, 1974, "The Political Economy of the Rent-Seeking Society," *American Economic Review*, Vol. 64 (June), pp. 291–303.

Langseth, Petter, and Rick Stapenhurst, 1997, "National Integrity System: Country Studies," Economic Development Institute Working Paper (Washington: World Bank).

Leff, Nathaniel, 1964, "Economic Development Through Bureaucratic Corruption," *American Behavioral Scientist*, pp. 8–14.

Lien, Da Hsiang Donald, 1986, "A Note on Competitive Bribery Games," *Economics Letters*, Vol. 22, No. 4, pp. 337–41.

Lindbeck, Assar, 1998, "Swedish Lessons for Post-Socialist Countries" (unpublished; Stockholm: University of Stockholm Institute for International Economic Studies).

Lui, Francis T., 1985, "An Equilibrium Queuing Model of Bribery," *Journal of Political Economy*, Vol. 93 (August), pp. 760–81.

———, 1996, "Three Aspects of Corruption," *Contemporary Economic Policy*, Vol. 14 (July), pp. 26–29.

Manzetti, Luigi, and Charles Blake, 1997, "Market Reforms and Corruption in Latin America: New Means for Old Ways," *Review of International Political Economy*, Vol. 3 (Winter), pp. 662–97.

Mauro, Paolo, 1995, "Corruption and Growth," *Quarterly Journal of Economics*, Vol. 110 (August), pp. 681–712.

———, 1997, "The Effects of Corruption on Growth, Investment, and Government Expenditure: A Cross-Country Analysis," in *Corruption in the Global Economy*, ed. by Kimberly Ann Elliott (Washington: Institute for International Economics). [Revised version reproduced as Chapter 9 in this volume—ED.]

Murphy, Kevin M., Andrei Shleifer, and Robert W. Vishny, 1991, "The Allocation of Talent: Implication for Growth," *Quarterly Journal of Economics*, Vol. 106 (May) pp. 503–30.

Myrdal, Gunnar, 1968, *Asian Drama: An Inquiry into the Poverty of Nations* (New York: Twentieth Century Fund).

Nordio, Carlo, 1997, *Giustizia* (Milan: Angelo Gorini e Associati).

Noonan, John T. Jr., 1984, *Bribes* (New York: Macmillan).

Rauch, James E., and Peter B. Evans, 1997, "Bureaucratic Structure and Bureaucratic Performance in Less Developed Countries" (unpublished; San Diego, California and Berkeley, California: University of California at San Diego and University of California at Berkeley).

Remnick, David, 1994, *Lenin's Tomb: The Last Days of the Soviet Empire* (New York: Random House).

Rose-Ackerman, Susan, 1997, "Corruption and Development," paper prepared for the Annual Bank Conference on Development Economics, Washington, April 30 and May 1.

Ruzindana, Augustine, 1997, "The Importance of Leadership in Fighting Corruption in Uganda," in *Corruption in the Global Economy*, ed. by Kimberly Ann Elliott (Washington: Institute for International Economics), pp. 133–46.

Shleifer, Andrei, 1996, "Government in Transition," HIER Discussion Paper No. 1783 (Boston, Massachusetts: Harvard Institute for Economic Research).

———, and Robert W. Vishny, 1993, "Corruption," *Quarterly Journal of Economics*, Vol. 108 (August), pp. 599–617.

Simis, Constantine M., 1982, *USSR: The Corrupt Society. The Secret World of Soviet Communism* (New York: Simon and Schuster).

Sjaifudian, Shetifah, 1997, "Graft and the Small Business," *Far Eastern Economic Review*, October 16, p. 32.

Tanzi, Vito, 1995a, "Corruption, Arm's-Length Relationships, and Markets," in *The Economics of Organised Crime,* ed. by Gianluca Fiorentini and Sam Peltzman (Cambridge, Massachusetts: Cambridge University Press), pp. 161–80.

———, 1995b, "Government Role and the Efficiency of Policy Instruments," IMF Working Paper 95/100 (Washington: International Monetary Fund). Also published in *Public Finance in a Changing World,* ed. by Peter Birch Sørensen (New York: Macmillan), pp. 51–69.

———, 1998, "Corruption and the Budget: Problems and Solutions," in *Economics of Corruption,* ed. by Arvind K. Jain (Boston, Massachusetts: Kluwer Academic Publishers), pp. 111–28.

———, and Hamid Davoodi, 1997, "Corruption, Public Investment, and Growth," IMF Working Paper 97/139 (Washington: International Monetary Fund). [Revised version reproduced as Chapter 11 in this volume—ED.]

Tanzi, Vito, and Ludger Schuknecht, 1997, "Reconsidering the Fiscal Role of Government: The International Perspective," *American Economic Review, Papers and Proceedings,* Vol. 87 (May) pp. 164–68.

Theobald, Robin, 1990, *Corruption, Development, and Underdevelopment* (Durham, North Carolina: Duke University Press).

Tullock, Gordon, 1996, "Corruption Theory and Practice," *Contemporary Economic Policy,* Vol. 14 (July), pp. 6–13.

van Tulden, Frank, and Abraham van der Torre, 1997, "Crime and the Criminal Justice System: An Economic Approach," paper presented at the 53rd Congress of the International Institute of Public Finance, Kyoto, Japan (August).

Van Rijckeghem, Caroline, and Beatrice Weder, 1997, "Corruption and the Rate of Temptation: Do Low Wages in the Civil Service Cause Corruption?" IMF Working Paper 97/73 (Washington: International Monetary Fund). [Revised version reproduced as Chapter 3 in this volume—ED.]

von Klimo, Arpad, 1997, "Fra Stato Centralistico e Periferia. Alti Funzionari Statali in Italia e nella Germania Prussiana dal 1870 al 1914," in *Centralisimo e Federalisimo nel XIX e XX Secolo, Un Confronto tra la Germania e Italia,* ed. by Oliver Janz and Pierangelo Schiero (Bologna: Il Mulino).

Weber, Max, 1947, *The Theory of Social and Economic Organization* (London: The Free Press of Glencoe).

Wei, Shang-Jin, 1997a, "How Taxing Is Corruption on International Investors?" NBER Working Paper No. 6030 (Cambridge, Massachusetts: National Bureau of Economic Research).

———, 1997b, "Why Is Corruption So Much More Taxing Than Tax? Arbitrariness Kills," NBER Working Paper No. 6030 (Cambridge, Massachusetts: National Bureau of Economic Research).

3

Bureaucratic Corruption and the Rate of Temptation: Do Wages in the Civil Service Affect Corruption, and by How Much?

Caroline Van Rijckeghem and Beatrice Weder

> The [Singapore] government believed that an efficient bureaucratic system is one in which the officers are well-paid so the temptation to resort to bribes would be reduced.
>
> (Rahman, 1986, p. 151)

1. Introduction

The importance of adequate remuneration in ensuring an honest civil service is widely recognized in the policy debate.[1] The issue of optimal

---

Reprinted from *Journal of Development Economics*, Caroline Van Rijckeghem and Beatrice Weder, "Bureaucratic corruption and the rate of temptation: do wages in the civil service affect corruption, and by how much?" Vol. 65, pp. 307–331 (2001), with permission from Elsevier Science.

This is a condensed version of an IMF Working Paper (WP/97/73). The views expressed herein are those of the authors and do not necessarily represent those of the International

government pay or its cost-effectiveness has not yet been settled, however, and a number of recent theoretical papers suggest that ensuring an honest civil service may be prohibitively expensive.[2] This paper provides empirical estimates on the magnitude of the effect of civil-service wages on corruption, as a first step toward a cost-benefit analysis of civil-service wage increases.[3]

The models that predict eradication of corruption using wage policy to be expensive are in the spirit of the "shirking model" of Shapiro and Stiglitz (1984) and build on the early work of Becker and Stigler (1974). They assume that civil servants maximize expected income. Corrupt behavior, when detected, is penalized by job loss; hence, high pay constitutes an incentive to be less corrupt. However, when bribe levels are high or the probability of detection and fines low, these models predict that the wage necessary to eliminate corruption is high. Hence, it may be cost-effective for governments to pay "capitulation wages," i.e. wages below reservation wages, that attract only the dishonest, rather than raise wages to the high levels required to deter corruption (Besley and McLaren, 1993).

There are, however, also reasons to expect that corruption can be eliminated at low wage levels. First, bribe levels in much of the civil service, such as in education, may be low, so that corruption may be eliminated at low wage levels even in shirking models. Second, delayed rewards, such as pensions, or the ability to obtain lucrative private-sector jobs after serving in the civil service can be used as an incentive to

---

Monetary Fund. The authors would like to thank Alberto Alesina, Ernst Fehr, Aart Kraay, Nadeem Haque, Paolo Mauro, Susan Rose-Ackerman, Ratna Sahay, Vito Tanzi, three anonymous referees, and participants at seminars at the University of Basel, the LACEA meetings, and Bogazici University for useful suggestions. Manzoor Gill, Philip Polsky, and Stacy Maynes provided excellent research assistance.

[1]See Myrdal (1968), Cariño (1986), Israel (1987), Klitgaard (1989), Tanzi (1994), and Lindauer and Nunberg (1994). There is also an increasing recognition—based on recent research—that net benefits of reducing corruption are positive in terms of investment and growth (see Mauro, 1995, 1998; Wei, 1997; Brunetti et al., 1998).

[2]Notably, Besley and McLaren (1993) and Flatters and McLeod (1995). Some exceptions are Haque and Sahay (1996), who argue that raising wages could be cost-effective by ensuring better human capital in tax administration, and Mookherjee and Png (1995), who conclude that bribes may be less efficient than bonus payments in encouraging effort among law enforcers. See Bardhan (1997) and Rose-Ackerman (1999) for overviews of the corruption literature.

[3]We thank Shanta Devarajan for suggesting cost-benefit analysis of civil-service-pay reform as a topic for research, as opposed to simply documenting the existence of a negative relationship between pay and corruption.

honest behavior, reducing the need to pay high wages during the working life.[4] Third, the probability of detection and punishment of corruption may increase with the wage of civil servants because higher wages (fair treatment of civil servants) lead society to condemn corruption, again imparting greater effectiveness to wage policy.[5]

Finally, civil servants may not be motivated by greed, but may instead willingly forego opportunities for corruption, provided wages meet subsistence levels or are "fair." This view is akin to the "fair wage-effort hypothesis" (Akerlof and Yellen, 1990) and is prevalent among experts on corruption who note a preference for honesty among civil servants.[6,7] Appendix B calibrates a theoretical model of corruption with shirking and the fair-wage hypotheses as special cases. It illustrates that the distinction between the "shirking view" and "fair-wages view" has important quantitative consequences for the strength of the relationship between wages and corruption: under fair-wage models, civil-service wages are an important determinant of corruption, whereas under shirking, civil-service wages may have to be raised to very high levels to eradicate corruption. It also shows that for sufficiently low wages (in conjunction with low bribe levels and or a high probability of detection), fair wages and shirking hypotheses are observationally equivalent.

From the above, it is clear that the effect of civil-service wage policy on corruption is an empirical question. An important obstacle for the empirical examination of the issue is, however, that a panel of data on civil-service wages is not available. We, therefore, assembled a new data set on civil service and manufacturing wages in which we took care to include only data of high quality and good comparability. Based on this data, we find evidence of a statistically and economically significant relationship between relative wages and corruption, in regressions based on country averages. While economically significant, the relationship, nevertheless, implies that a large increase in wages is required to eradicate corruption solely by raising wages, i.e. without accompa-

---

[4]Becker and Stigler (1974).

[5]Tanzi (1994), for example, notes that "unrealistically low wages always invite corruption and, at times, lead society to condone acts of corruption."

[6]See, e.g. Peter N.S. Lee (quoted by Alfiler, 1986, p. 66), who notes that "it is not a question of paying sufficient salary to make a man incorruptible, but rather of not paying salary on which a man is encouraged to be corrupt in order to meet his reasonable commitments." See also Klitgaard (1991).

[7]An additional channel would be that high wages help attract and retain a workforce which includes better, i.e. less corrupt workers.

nying policies to increase transparency and accountability in the civil service or in society as a whole. The relationship between wages and corruption is not found in regressions with country-fixed effects which points to ineffectual wage policy in the short run (we show that the power to reject the null hypothesis of no effect is low, however). Finally, case studies of pay reforms in tax administration suggest the existence of causality running from government wages to corruption.

Two related studies are those of Goel and Rich (1989) for the US and Rauch and Evans (2000) for a sample consisting mostly of developing countries. The research by Goel and Rich, which covers the period 1970–1983, suggests that the proportion of government officials convicted of bribery is negatively related to the difference between government wages and the average income of a private sector group of white-collar professionals (middle grade accountants). Rauch and Evans look into the factors affecting bureaucratic performance. We discuss their results in more detail in the text and use their wage data as an alternate data set when testing the robustness of our results.

The paper proceeds as follows. Section 2 discusses the data and the empirical strategy. Section 3 provides and interprets the panel-data results. It includes a discussion of a number of case studies as well. Section 4 draws out policy implications and concludes. Appendix A provides details on the econometric specification, whereas Appendix B presents a calibration exercise for shirking and fair-wage models, for use as a benchmark in interpreting the empirical results.

2. Empirical Strategy and Description of Data

The empirical estimates aim at testing whether there is a systematic relationship between wages in the civil service and corruption, both across countries and over time. We follow an estimation strategy consistent with the theoretical discussion in the introduction and in Appendix B. Our basic specification is of the following form:

$$\text{CORRUPTION}_i = \alpha + \beta \text{ RELATIVE GOVERNMENT WAGES}_i + \delta \text{ CONTROLS}_i + \epsilon_i$$

where CONTROLS is a vector of variables that may impact on corruption. Theory suggests that such controls should include at least (i) proxies of the probability of detection (through internal or external controls on the bureaucracy); (ii) the penalty rate applied when detection occurs; (iii) the amount of distortions and opportunities for corruption in the economy; and (iv) other factors such as cultural determinants. Our choice of independent variables is detailed further in Van Rijckeghem and Weder (1997).

2.1 Description of Data

Our wage variable of choice is the *ratio of government wages to manufacturing wages*. The manufacturing wage is used as the comparator, as a measure of the opportunity cost which determines whether a worker is tempted to shirk (shirking hypothesis) or feels ill-treated (fair-wage hypothesis). Compared to GDP per capita, which is heavily influenced by the share of agriculture in GDP, the manufacturing sector has the advantage of being relatively comparable across countries in terms of skill-content.[8] The skill-content in the manufacturing sector is probably lower than that in government, so that it should not be considered as a measure of alternatives available to government employees. The aim is only to have a consistent benchmark.[9]

To gain comparable data on wages in the civil service and in manufacturing, we assembled a new data set. The wage data cover 31 developing countries and low-income OECD countries[10] over the period

---

[8] It is only natural, and not an indication of good pay, to have a high government wage relative to GDP per capita in less developed countries, given the predominance of agriculture. Hence, one would not want to use GDP per capita as the comparator.

[9] Data limitations preclude us from capturing certain components of civil-service pay, such as the relative stability of government employment, and deferred benefits, such as pensions. The unemployment rate and education level of civil servants affect the opportunity cost in the shirking model; however, data are not available to permit one to correct the opportunity cost accordingly. Also, benchmarks other than the alternative wage in the private sector may be relevant for corruption behavior in the fair-wage model, but are difficult to capture. These benchmarks could include past wages, wages in civil services abroad, an "adequate" standard of living, etc.

[10] We exclude high-income OECD countries, where relative civil-service wages are low; however, this probably only reflects the high supply of skilled labor, assuming government is the skill-intensive sector (for a theoretical exploration of the link between relative wages in government and development, see Tanzi and Zee, 1995). To decide which sample to use, we ran regressions of relative wages on GDP per capita and secondary education. For a sample which includes all OECD countries, these development indicators have significant negative coefficients. On the other hand, the coefficients are insignificant (and positive) for the more homogeneous sample of developing countries and low-income OECD countries. This suggests that a sample excluding the high-income OECD countries might be appropriate.

1982–1994, gathered from IMF sources, statistical yearbooks, central bank bulletins, and the ILO yearbooks. Care was taken to ensure that only data of relatively high quality and good comparability was included.[11]

There is only one other source of data on relative wages, that of Rauch and Evans (2000), and we use this data in our regressions as well.[12] They conducted a survey with experts in a number of less developed countries that included a question on the level of civil-service wages relative to comparable private sector employment. The correlation coefficient for the period-average relative wage data in our sample and the cross-section data of Rauch and Evans is 0.6.

Data on corruption is available in the form of an index based on surveys by ICRG, a private international investment-risk service. This has become the standard data set used in the empirical growth literature.[13] The variable attempts to capture the extent to which "high government officials are likely to demand special payments" and "illegal payments are generally expected throughout lower levels of government" in the form of "bribes connected with import and export licenses, exchange controls, tax assessment, police protection, or loans."[14] While one could

---

[11]The data must, nevertheless, be interpreted with care as the definitions for government wages are not always comparable across countries. The scope of government also varies across countries and time (for example, after privatization of services formally provided by general government), causing further problems for comparisons. For some countries, the government wage bill was divided by government employment to obtain the average wage, but only if there was a clear indication that the numerator and denominator had the same coverage (i.e. both included or excluded military personnel, casual employees, personnel in semi-autonomous bodies, such as universities and hospitals, whose wage expenditures are often financed through transfers from the central government rather than recorded directly as government wages in the budget). Definitions also differ with respect to inclusion of in-kind benefits (housing, cars, etc.) and allowances. The exact sources of the data are described in detail in IMF Working paper no. 97/73, which can be downloaded at http://www.imf.org.

[12]Schiavo-Campo et al. (1997) provide cross-country data for 1 year for a large sample of countries, but concentrate on government wages relative to GDP per capita, not relative to manufacturing wages.

[13]Published by Political Risk Services in the *International Country Risk Guide* (ICRG), for the period 1982–1995. This data set was assembled by the IRIS Center (University of Maryland) from hard copies of the International Country Risk Guide. The index ranges from 0 to 6 in the original data, with 0 indicating the highest corruption and 6 the lowest. Most of the industrial countries and a few developing countries, such as Singapore, have a value of 6 for the index. For clarity, we redefine the ICRG corruption index, so that an increase in the index indicates worsening corruption (with 0 indicating the lowest level of corruption and 6 the highest).

[14]Knack and Keefer (1995).

question the comprehensiveness of the index as Political Risk Services (various issues) focuses on assessing the business climate for international businesses only, the index is reasonably consistent across countries and time, as it is produced by a single organization, which presumably instructs its country specialists uniformly as to how to rate countries.[15]

As proxies of the probability of detection, we use an index of "quality of the bureaucracy" and an index of the "rule of law" available from the same source.[16] We also proxy for societal pressures using an index of "political rights and civil liberties," a simple average of the index of political rights and the index of civil liberties compiled by Freedom House (various issues) and published in *Freedom in the World*. This index captures factors such as the right to vote, the right to organize political parties, fair elections, meaningful representation by elected representatives, freedom of the press, freedom of assembly and demonstration, an independent judiciary, and the absence of political terror and torture. We also include PPP adjusted per capita GDP and secondary school enrollment (from the Summers-Heston v. 5.6 data set) as proxies for external controls, in general, under the assumption that the higher the social pressures and institutional safeguards against corruption, the higher the general level of income and education.

The penalty rate is probably the instrument governments use most frequently when attempting to combat corruption. In an optimizing model, the penalty rate can directly substitute for wage increases and sufficiently high penalties lead to the eradication of corruption even in the presence of low-detection probabilities. However, cross-country data on statutory penalty rates are not available; therefore, this variable is not included in the empirical analysis.

In addition to these variables, the literature has suggested a number of other determinants of corruption. For instance, in a recent set of papers, Ades and Di Tella (1997, 1999) have shown that the degree of

---

[15]Coplin et al. (1993) describes how country specialists are selected.

[16]Quality of the bureaucracy measures "autonomy from political pressure" and "strength and expertise to govern without drastic changes in policy or interruptions in government services" as well as the existence of an "established mechanism for recruiting and training." Rule of law reflects the degree to which "citizens of a country are willing to accept the established institutions to make and implement laws and adjudicate disputes" and the presence of "sound political institutions, a strong court system, and provisions for an orderly succession of power."

competition and industrial policy have a significant effect on corruption.[17] In their view, this occurs through the rents, which absence of competition and active industrial policies create, by way of more profitable or favored domestic firms, which bureaucrats and politicians then extract. Kaufmann (1997) has found a very strong correlation between bribery to public officials and "regulatory discretion" for a sample consisting mostly of Latin American and Asian countries, using survey responses by businesses. We use the black market premium for foreign exchange as an indicator of the level of distortions in the economy, following common practice in the growth literature.[18] Presumably, economies experiencing exchange controls are subject to a number of other controls generating shortages and providing opportunities for corruption.

In addition to the variables discussed above, corruption is often attributed to purely cultural factors or lack of leadership. For instance, Tanzi (1994) argues that the absence of a culture of arm's-length relationships may lead to corruption becoming ingrained and systemic. Lee (1986, p. 97) suggests that a culture of bureaucratic elitism may lead to a dissociation of civil servants with the rest of society and breed corruption. Alternatively, the level of education of civil servants can be a factor which reduces corruption. Such cultural factors and leadership are inherently difficult to measure; they are not included in the empirical analysis for lack of plausible proxies. Finally, Shleifer and Vishny (1993) suggest that more ethnically diverse countries are prone to a disorganized form of corruption and Mauro (1995) finds evidence of a link between an index of "ethnolinguistic fractionalization" and corruption.[19] We include this variable in our regressions.

---

[17]The degree of competition is measured by an index of market dominance, of the effectiveness of anti-trust regulations, and of political or natural barriers to trade, while industrial policy is measured by indices of the extent to which procurement is open to foreign bidders and of the extent to which all enterprises are treated equally (most data are from the Global Competitiveness Report). We could not include these variables as they were not available for a large number of countries in our sample.

[18]The sources for the black market and the official exchange rate are International Currency Analysis, *World Currency Yearbook* (New York, various issues, December figures) and the IMF's *International Financial Statistics* (Washington, various issues), respectively.

[19]This index measures the probability that two randomly selected persons from a given country do not belong to the same ethnolinguistic group. We would like to thank Paolo Mauro for sharing this data.

2.2 Econometric Issues

Having discussed our choice of variables, we now turn to estimation issues. One important issue here is the choice of estimator. As is well-known, unbiasedness of the OLS, "between" (i.e. regressions based on country means), and "random effects" estimators requires that the independent variables not be correlated with the country-specific effects (often reflecting omitted variables) subsumed in the error term. Even "fixed effects" (i.e. including country dummies) estimation is biased for short panels, in the absence of strict exogeneity (e.g. when the estimating equation is dynamic). The econometrician's solution to these problems is often to first difference the data and estimate a relationship for the first differenced data using instrumental variables.

We are reluctant to apply this procedure here, however, for two reasons. First, our measure of relative wages exhibits very little variation over time. The share of the variation within countries in the total variation in relative wages is 18% for our 31-country sample. Hence, the information content of the data corresponds in large part to the cross-country variation in the data.[20] Estimation based on first differencing (or fixed effects) would, therefore, suffer from low power compared to estimation based on country means or OLS.

Second, the timing with which wage policy and other variables affect corruption could be subject to long lags because of institutional inertia and societal attitudes or uncertainty as to the permanence of the changes. Wage increases might not produce lower corruption contemporaneously, whereas a sustained policy of high civil-service pay could over time produce lower corruption. The lack of variation in the corruption index we use (the coefficient of variation over time averages 0.2 for the countries in our 31-country sample) indeed suggests that corruption may be generated by a moving average process with long lags. If an inappropriate lag structure is specified for the estimating equation, first differencing of the data (or using fixed effects) produces inconsistent estimates of the long-run relationships between the variables. Estimation based on a cross-section or OLS also provides inconsistent results. Estimation based on cross-country means (where the raw data cover a reasonably long time span), on the other hand, provides a consistent estimate of the

---

[20]This applies to most independent variables. The shares of the within-country variation is 13% for the "rule of law," 15% for "quality of the bureaucracy," 18% for "political rights and civil liberties," 2% for real GDP per capita, and 69% for the black market premium.

long-run relationships in the data. That is, the estimate is robust to dynamic mis-specification (Pesaran and Smith, 1995, p. 88).

In view of the issues of power and uncertainty surrounding the correct lag specification, the strategy adopted in this paper is to estimate a number of estimators, including "between" and fixed effects. As we will see, the estimates vary depending on the technique used. This could be a sign of mis-specification, resulting either from a mis-specified lag structure in the fixed effects estimation or from omission of correlated country-fixed effects (variables correlated with wages) in the between estimation. Under the first interpretation, the fixed effects results pertain to the contemporaneous effect of wages on corruption and the "between" results to the long-run relationship between wages and corruption (see Appendix A). Under the second, less benign, interpretation, the significant finding on wages in "between" regressions could be spurious, and the fixed effects estimator would be preferable. It is, however, hard to think of omitted correlated country-fixed effects, as we include a large number of control variables, covering internal and external controls, as well as distortions.[21]

Estimates are derived after weighing the data by a function of the number of observations to correct for heteroscedasticity resulting from using an unbalanced panel (see Appendix A) and "White-correction" of the standard errors to ensure robustness of the standard errors to heteroscedasticity.[22] Only countries with at least five consecutive observations are included in the regression. In our sample, 88% of the countries have seven or more consecutive observations, while 47% of the countries have 10 or more consecutive observations.

A final econometric issue pertains to the direction of causality. Two arguments for reverse causality could be made: (1) corrupt countries

---

[21] Only a few of the relevant variables can not be captured, namely pensions, the size of penalties, cultural factors, and "leadership." Pensions are in theory correlated with relative wages if governments provide delayed rewards in lieu of current ones, under the mechanism identified by Becker and Stigler (1974); however, this mechanism hardly seems relevant in practice in developing countries. The remaining variables do not appear to be related to relative wages a priori and are, therefore, not problematic.

[22] Specifically, correction for heteroscedasticity on account of differing numbers of observations across countries is carried out in three steps. First, between estimation is carried out on the raw data. Second, the squared residuals from this regression are regressed on a constant and the inverse of the number of observations available in a country. Third, the raw data is divided by the square root of the fitted values of the previous regressions (i.e. the estimated country-specific error variances), and between estimation carried out, with White-correction, using this weighted data.

have poor tax collection and, therefore, are constrained to pay less well; and (2) corrupt countries pay less purposefully arguing that civil servants already have incomes from corruption. This issue is difficult to investigate econometrically due to the absence of instruments for civil-service wages that are both highly correlated with wages but uncorrelated with corruption, and can probably be addressed only through case studies.[23]

3. Results

3.1 Regression Analysis

We find a close negative association between relative civil-service wages and corruption across the developing and lower-income OECD countries in our data set. Figure 1 shows the scatterplot of relative wages and corruption. It shows a negative association between the variables, when no other factors are controlled for.

Table 1 presents the results of regressions based on country averages, with different sets of control variables. The relative wage, in a regression with real GDP per capita in PPP terms, is a highly significant explanatory variable (column 1). Real GDP per capita is a comprehensive measure of development, which is positively correlated with law and order, quality of the bureaucracy, civil rights, etc. However, it is not statistically significant in this regression.[24]

Next, we replace real GDP per capita with "law and order" and "quality of the bureaucracy." These are more precise measures of internal and external controls, which affect the probability of detection.

---

[23]Acemoglu and Verdier (2000) suggest another reason why the trade-off between wages and corruption may not be identified: if governments set efficiency wages, they choose just one point on the trade-off schedule, and the trade-off itself cannot be identified. We believe, however, that because of budgetary and political constraints, governments cannot follow optimal pay policy, so that variations in such constraints allow us to trace out the trade-off between wages and corruption. Furthermore, variations in preferences can also help identify the trade-off. One source of such variations is the degree of natural openness in an economy, with more open economies preferring lower corruption because of the presumed high sensitivity of international trade and investment to corruption (Wei, 2000). Evidence presented by Wei indeed suggests that naturally open economies exhibit less corruption. Furthermore, Wei, using our data set, shows that open economies appear to pay higher civil-service wages, presumably in an effort to combat corruption.

[24]This appears to reflect the presence of outliers. When estimated with the technique of least absolute deviations, instead of OLS, real GDP per capita is statistically significant.

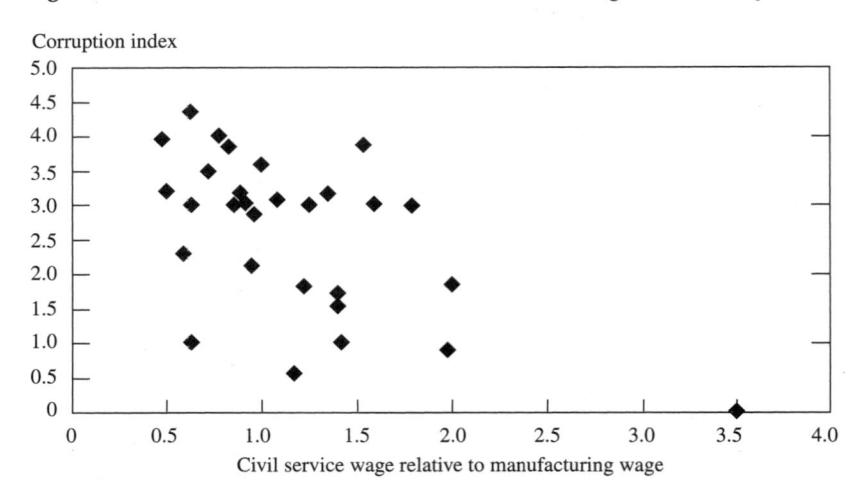

Figure 1. Correlation Between Relative Civil Service Wages and Corruption

Notes: Only countries for which at least five observations are available are included. Corruption index is ICRG index minus 6. Countries include: Argentina, Bolivia, Botswana, China, Colombia, Costa Rica, Egypt, El Salvador, Ghana, Greece, Guatemala, Hong Kong SAR, India, Jordan, Kenya, Korea, Mexico, Morocco, Panama, Peru, Portugal, South Africa, Singapore, Spain, Sri Lanka, Suriname, Thailand, Trinidad and Tobago, Turkey, Uruguay, Zimbabwe.

Relative wages continue to be significant.[25] As for economic significance, the coefficient on relative wages equals 0.5, indicating that a 1-point change in relative wages (say from one to two times the manufacturing wage) leads to a 0.5-point reduction in the corruption index.

We then add a number of variables one at a time to the previous "basic" specification, from a list including real GDP per capita, secondary school enrollment, political rights and civil liberties, an index of ethnographic fractionalization, and the black market premium. The relative wage continues to be statistically or marginally significant when these variables are added.[26]

As an additional test of robustness, we re-estimate the regression in column 2 using the rating for the level of relative wages of higher offi-

---

[25]Note that this is a strong test because the two control variables—rule of law and quality of the bureaucracy—are from the same expert survey as the corruption index and are, therefore, highly correlated, leaving little variation to be explained by relative wages.

[26]Results are not reported and are available upon request. When estimated by the technique of least absolute deviations (LAD), which reduces the role of outliers, the coefficient on the relative wage is always statistically significant.

Table 1. Determinants of Corruption. Regression Based on Country Averages[a, b]

	(1) Parsimonius specification	(2) Basic specification	(3) Rauch-Evans data	(4) Full specification
Constant	6.39 (3.28)	5.14 (18.05)	6.10 (17.42)	8.86 (3.34)
Relative wages	−1.04 (−5.37)	−0.50 (−3.07)	−0.33 (−1.90)[c]	−0.64 (−2.43)
GDP per capita	−0.29 (−1.11)			−0.51 (−1.73)
Secondary schooling				0.01 (0.77)
Law and order		−0.38 (−2.04)	−0.31 (−1.99)	−0.57 (−3.45)
Quality of bureaucracy		−0.24 (−1.93)	−0.54 (−4.09)	−0.07 (−0.59)
Political rights and civil liberties				−0.09 (−0.63)
Ethnographic fractionalization				−0.001 (−0.19)
Black market premium				−0.001 (−0.62)
Korea dummy				1.74 (6.62)
Singapore dummy				0.58 (0.85)
No. of countries[d]	31	31	35	28
Adjusted R^2	0.41	0.66	0.75	0.74

[a] t-Statistics below estimate.

[b] For countries with five or more consecutive observations. Based on weighted least squares, where weights are a function of the number of observations (see text). Standard errors are White-corrected for heteroscedasticity.

[c] When estimated with the method of least absolute deviations to reduce the role of outliers, the t-statistic is 3.6.

[d] Based on developing and low-income OECD countries. Number of countries varies because of availability of the data.

cials in economic agencies contained in the Rauch and Evans (2000) data set.[27] We find a significant or marginally significant relationship for relative wages, the index of law and order and the quality of the bureaucracy for the 35 countries in the Rauch-Evans data set (column 3).[28] The role for relative wages appears somewhat more important than we found earlier. Column 3 indicates that an increase in rating from a "1" to a "4"—or an increase in wages of higher officials in the economic agencies relative to those of private-sector managers from less than 50% to comparable levels—reduces the corruption index by 1 point (3 × 0.33). Thus, the Rauch-Evans data set supports the existence of a significant relationship between civil-service wages and corruption.

Column 4 includes all variables in one regression. In addition to GDP per capita, enrollment rates, rule of law, and quality of the bureaucracy, it also includes the black market premium, "political rights and civil liberties," "ethnolinguistic fractionalization," as well as a dummy variable for Singapore to test whether this outlier influences the results significantly (Singapore has both very low corruption and very high civil-service pay). The black market premium is not significant in this regression (and it has the "wrong" sign), while the Singapore dummy is insignificant.[29] Korea is an outlier in this regression, with higher corruption than expected given its characteristics.[30]

Table 2 gives an impression of the economic significance of our results. It shows the effect of a one standard deviation change on the corruption index, based on the coefficients in the full specification (col-

---

[27]Specifically, Rauch and Evans define the ratings for the salaries of higher officials in economic agencies, compared to those of private sector managers with roughly comparable training and responsibilities, as follows: 1 = less than 50%; 2 = 50–80%; 3 = 80–90%; 4 = comparable; 5 = higher.

[28]When estimated with LAD to reduce the role of outliers, the t-statistic on relative wages is 3.6 rather than 1.9. When real GDP per capita is the control variable, instead of rule of law and quality of the bureaucracy, the t-statistic is 3.0 under LAD. Rauch and Evans (2000) report an insignificant effect of wages on corruption; however, as our regressions show, this appears to reflect the fact that in Rauch-Evans, the dependent variable is defined as a *weighted average* of (ratings for) the *level and trend* in relative wages (rather than just the level of relative wages).

[29]Regressions, which exclude the city-states Singapore and Hong Kong SAR, give almost unchanged results, confirming that the relationship between wages and corruption is not driven by outliers with high wages and low corruption.

[30]Some observers have noted that Korea's civil service could actually be less corrupt than the ICRG index indicates, the relatively high rating for corruption reflecting political corruption, rather than bureaucratic corruption. Without the dummy variable for Korea, the t-statistic on the relative wage variable is still reasonably high, at 1.75.

Table 2. Economic Significance of Results

	Standard deviation[a]	Coefficient in full specification in between regression	Effects of one standard deviation change on corruption index
Corruption index	1.25	...	...
Index of law and order	1.33	−0.57	−0.76
Ratio of civil-service wage to manufacturing wage	0.67	0.64	−0.43
Log of real GDP per capita in constant US$	0.72	−0.51	−0.37
Secondary school enrollment	21.12	−0.01	−0.21
Index of political rights and civil liberties	1.51	0.09	0.14
Index of quality of bureaucracy	1.41	−0.07	−0.10
Black market premium (percent)[b]	287.00	0.0002	0.06
Index of ethnolinguistic fractionalization	28.80	−0.001	−0.03

[a]Pertains to sample for which all variables are available (227 observations).
[b]Pertains to within regression coefficient.

umn 4 in Table 1). We find that the index of rule of law and the relative wage have the largest impact on corruption.

Table 3 turns to the time-series dimension of the data, and reveals no evidence of a within-country effect of wages. It also shows that the high significance of the "rule of law" variable pertains to the cross-country variation in the data. The "quality of the bureaucracy" and the black market premium are significant in the within regressions, though the latter is not economically significant (Table 2). This suggests that higher pay (and/or improved rule of law) does not lead to lower corruption in the short run. However, the power to reject the null hypothesis of no effect is low given the low variance of relative wages (and rule of law) within countries.

Table 4 provides information on the simple correlation between our measure of relative wages and the other independent variables included in the regressions. To the extent that there is an important correlation, it is possible that relative wages also operate through additional channels to reduce corruption. The correlations with the quality of the bu-

Table 3. Determinants of Corruption Index: Within-Country Estimation[a]
For countries with five or more consecutive observations. Standard errors are White-corrected for heteroscedasticity.
Fixed effects are not reported.

Constant	...
Ratio of civil-service wage to manufacturing wage	−0.01
	(−0.48)
Log of real GDP per capita in constant US$	−0.31
	(−0.97)
Secondary enrollment rate	−0.02
	(−2.11)
Index of law and order	0.11
	(1.35)
Index of quality of bureaucracy	−0.39
	(−5.85)
Index of political rights and civil liberties	0.05
	(1.46)
Black market premium (percent)	0.0002
	(3.69)
Number of observations	236
Number of countries	29
Adjusted R^2	0.89

[a] *t*-Statistics below estimate.

reaucracy and the rule of law are of particular interest. These are quite high (48% and 41%, respectively, for the full sample), indicating that relative wages could influence corruption through these channels. This would be consistent with the view that wages have an effect on the tolerance for corruption on the part of the civil service itself, the judiciary, and society at large.

Finally, we test the sensitivity of the results to the presence of omitted variables by conducting Leamer's Extreme Bounds Analysis, i.e. we add a number of "free" regressors (all possible combinations of up to three out of five additional regressors, or 25 combinations) to our basic specification and evaluate the robustness of the results to the inclusion of these variables. The "fixed" variables consist of relative civil-service wages, "law and order," and a dummy variable for Korea (see above). The "free" variables consist of GDP per capita, "quality of the bureaucracy," "political rights and civil liberties," the black market

Table 4. Data Descriptions and Simple Correlations (Number of Observations in Parenthesis)
Data correspond to developing and low-income OECD countries for which five consecutive observations are available.

	Intersection				Full Sample			
			Simple correlation with				Simple correlation with	
Variable	Mean	Standard deviation	Corruption	Relative wages	Mean	Standard deviation	Corruption	Relative wages	Rauch-Evans
Corruption index	2.76 (227)	1.25 (227)	1 (227)		3.13 (897)	1.21 (897)	1 (897)		
Ratio of civil-service wage to manufacturing wage	1.15 (227)	0.67 (227)	−0.47 (227)	1 (227)	1.22 (473)	0.67 (473)	−0.46 (292)	1 (473)	
Log of real GDP per capita in constant US$	8.02 (227)	0.72 (227)	−0.55 (227)	0.43 (227)	7.64 (1684)	0.85 (1684)	−0.36 (686)	0.47 (440)	0.40 (716)
Secondary school enrollment	55.44 (227)	21.12 (227)	−0.34 (227)	0.29 (227)	41.54 (1405)	24.24 (1405)	−0.21 (706)	0.31 (432)	0.20 (596)
Index of law and order	2.81 (227)	1.33 (227)	−0.66 (227)	0.31 (227)	2.74 (907)	1.19 (907)	−0.59 (897)	0.41 (301)	0.34 (450)
Index of quality of bureaucracy	2.64 (227)	1.41 (227)	−0.66 (227)	0.40 (227)	2.69 (907)	1.32 (907)	−0.62 (897)	0.48 (301)	0.35 (450)
Index of political rights and civil liberties	3.46 (227)	1.51 (227)	−0.28 (227)	0.09 (227)	4.42 (1948)	1.77 (1948)	−0.24 (884)	0.08 (473)	0.06 (777)
Index of ethnolinguistic fractionalization	36.85 (227)	28.80 (227)	0.09 (227)	−0.22 (227)	44.51 (1774)	29.62 (1774)	0.23 (854)	−0.22 (437)	−0.23 (801)
Black market premium (percent)	48.40 (227)	287.00 (227)	0.13 (227)	−0.07 (227)	110.93 (144)	1352.45 (144)	−0.07 (615)	−0.11 (433)	0.14 (657)
Memorandum item									
Rauch-Evans, Index of ratio of top civil-service wage to private equivalent					1.74 (801)	0.66 (801)	−0.41 (440)	0.60 (317)	

premium, and a dummy variable for Singapore. We find that zero lies outside of the "extreme bounds," defined as the lowest value of "the estimate minus two standard deviations" (–1.6) and the highest value of "the estimate plus two standard deviations" (–0.1) and conclude that the results are robust to EBA.[31]

To sum up, a robust relationship between corruption and relative civil-service pay appears to exist across countries. The cross-country results are invariant to specification, to the exclusion of the city-states Hong Kong SAR and Singapore, and to the use of an alternate data set. The results are also economically significant. They imply that an increase in civil-service pay from 100% to 200% of the manufacturing wage is associated with an improvement in the corruption index of at least 0.5 points of the index, and more if the indirect effects of wages through the quality of the bureaucracy and rule of law are included.

3.2 Implications for the Shirking vs. Fair-Wage Hypotheses

What light do these results shed on the validity of the shirking vs. fair-wage hypotheses? First, adherence to the shirking view would predict a relatively weak relationship between wages and corruption, as long as the probability of detection of corruption is low and bribe levels are high relative to wages, a situation that appears characteristic of developing countries. As a corollary, wages at which corruption can be eliminated will generally be high under the shirking hypothesis.

The estimated regression equations can be used to calculate the relative wage at which corruption is brought down to the level of the higher-income OECD countries (a corruption index equal to zero). Substitution of the value of zero for the corruption index in our regression result (we use the "full specification" in Table 1) indicates that this value ranges from 2 to 8, depending on the values of the control variables. The upper range is difficult to reconcile with the conceivable level of fair wages, casting doubt on the fair wage-corruption hypothesis. It is, however, important to recall that few countries had high civil-service wages so that the hypothesis that corruption is (close to) zero for that wage range cannot be tested directly; the results rely instead on extrapolation of a linear relationship estimated for low relative wages. And as shown in Appendix B, behavior under the fair-wage hypothesis can "collapse" to that under the shirking hypothesis when

---

[31]Results are not reported and are available upon request.

wages are low if bribe levels are also low and/or the probability of detection and penalties are high.[32]

At the same time, the values of 2–8 are low compared to what one might expect if the shirking hypothesis is in fact is true. In India, some say—though this is not more than a guess and does not apply uniformly to all parts of government—that the probability of detection is 10%, the probability of charges being brought (conditional on detection) is 10%, and the probability of punishment (conditional on charges being brought) is also 10%. This implies an unconditional probability of punishment of 0.1%.[33] India ranks about average in terms of our empirical proxies for internal and external controls.[34] At a probability of detection of 0.1%, the stylized shirking model described in Appendix B predicts that wages would have to be equal to *as much as 19 times* the private sector equivalent under the best of circumstances (i.e. when there is a credible commitment to pay sufficiently high pensions), or much above what our empirical results predict.[35] In sum, the results of this section indicate that neither the shirking nor the fair-wage hypothesis appear to hold in pure form.

3.3 Case Studies on Pay Reform in Tax Administrations

We now address the possibility that the cross-country correlation need not reflect a causal link from government wages to corruption using case studies. As noted above, the fact that corrupt countries tend to have poor budgetary performance and face strong budgetary pressures, or may subscribe to the view that civil servants already earn sufficient income from corruption, may lead them to pay less well.

---

[32]Intuitively, when the targeted income level is unreachable because bribe levels are too low or the probability of detection too high, it is reasonable to expect civil servants to attempt to get as close to their target as possible, which is equivalent to maximizing expected income (i.e. the shirking outcome).

[33]We thank Amitabha Mukherjee for bringing this quote to our attention.

[34]India rates 3.1 on the quality of bureaucracy (compared to 2.8 for the entire sample) and 3.4 for the rule of law (compared to 2.9).

[35]This back-of-the-envelope calculation of the efficiency wage might be an overestimate, as it does not take into account informal punishments, i.e. those not involving formal charges being brought. These punishments would involve (1) stigma; (2) reduced promotion possibilities; and (3) payments to supervisors to avoid punishment. Whether these factors are important or not would depend on how generally accepted corrupt behavior is. When corruption is generally accepted, supervisors turn a blind eye even when they are not corrupt, so that these factors may not come into play.

Evidence from six case studies (Ghana, 1983; Peru, 1991; Uganda, 1992; Zambia, 1994; Kenya, 1995; and Tanzania, 1996) conducted by the authors point to a strong improvement in revenue collection following pay reforms in tax administration.[36] These countries introduced pay reforms in the context of the introduction of independent new revenue authorities and experienced increases in the tax revenue to GDP ratio of up to 3–4% of GDP, amounts that exceed those experienced by other low-income countries engaged in stabilization efforts.

Of course, not all of the increases in the tax ratios can be attributed to pay reforms. Tax rate and base improvements as well as improvements in tax administration are likely to account for part of the improvements in revenues. In order to isolate the impact of pay reforms which went hand in hand with other administrative improvements as well as changes in tax rates and exemptions, we also compared revenue developments with those in low-income countries engaged in an IMF program. The low-income countries with IMF programs are a natural standard for comparison. A study of 21 low-income countries with ESAF programs with the IMF in the late 1980s indicates that these countries experienced improvements of 0.6% of GDP on average in their tax revenues over the course of their (usually 3-year) programs. Of these, 11 experienced improvements of over 1% of GDP.[37] As this improvement in revenues falls much short of the increase in revenues experienced in countries that introduced pay reforms simultaneously with the introduction of independent revenue authorities, this suggests that pay reforms played an important role in generating increased revenues.

4. Policy Implications and Conclusion

Theory is ambiguous in its implications for optimal wage policy. Various mechanisms through which concepts of fairness can affect corruption suggest that the relationship between civil-service wages and cor-

---

[36]Pay of professionals increased from US$50 monthly to US$1,000 after the introduction of an independent revenue authority in Peru (SUNAT). Pay increases were important in the other countries as well, with the exception of Zambia, where pay increases were limited to expatriate staff. See Adamolekum and Jah (1997). In some countries, such as Ghana, bonuses were introduced in addition to pay reforms (Chand and Moene, 1999). For an exploration of the effects of the introduction of *performance-based* wages in the Brazilian tax administration, see Kahn et al. (2000).

[37]See Nashashibi et al. (1992), pp. 40–41.

ruption may be stronger, and wages at which no corruption occurs lower, than predicted by models postulating self-interested behavior (i.e. shirking models), especially when bribe levels are high and the probability of detection of corrupt acts is low. This result has obvious implications for optimal wage policy, whether the government's goal is to maximize social welfare or its cost-effectiveness. If the "fair wage-corruption" hypothesis holds, paying wages that ensure low corruption may not necessarily be very costly (though this would depend on civil servants' standards of fairness), and paying wages that ensure an honest civil service may be cost-effective.

We have presented suggestive evidence of a negative relationship between civil-service pay and corruption. The cross-country or "between" regressions for a sample of 31 developing countries indicate that increasing relative pay from 1 to 2 is associated with an improvement in the corruption index on the order of 0.5 points excluding any indirect effects of wages on the quality of the bureaucracy and the rule of law, and more including indirect effects. Quasi-eradication of corruption is associated with a relative wage of two to eight times the manufacturing wage, not taking into account indirect effects. This is more than one would expect if the fair-wage hypothesis held in pure form, but less than predicted by the shirking hypothesis, suggesting that neither hypothesis holds in pure form.

Some caution is needed in drawing policy implications or carrying out cost-benefit analysis based on our cross-country regression analysis. First, the existence of a relationship cannot be confirmed based on regressions with country-fixed effects (the "within" estimates), which means that the cross-country results could reflect a spurious correlation notwithstanding our attempts to control for other factors. This also means that higher pay does not lead to lower corruption in the *short run*.[38] Second, the cross-country correlation need not reflect a causal link from government wages to corruption. The fact that corrupt countries tend to have poor budgetary performance and face strong budgetary pressures, or may subscribe to the view that civil servants al-

---

[38]As explained in Section 2, the fact that the within estimates are not significant could reflect a lack of power to reject the null and the omission of dynamics. This is because the variance of relative civil-service wages is low in our sample and because corruption may not respond to pay increases, except when pay increases are sustained (in that case, no effect would be detected in country-fixed effects regressions of corruption on *contemporaneous* wages).

ready earn sufficient income from corruption, may lead them to pay less well. In view of the findings from case studies that point to increases in revenues following pay reforms in tax administration, we believe that, these caveats notwithstanding, our results support the presumption that an active wage policy can help in fighting corruption. This is not to say that other instruments are not important. Indeed the results of the paper suggest that strengthening the rule of law, in particular, will also have beneficial effects on corruption.

Appendix A. Econometric Specification

Supposing the dynamic model underlying the relationship between x and y is as follows (where i denotes the country, t denotes time, T_{i0+1} denotes the first period for country i, and T_{i1} the last period):

$$y_{i,t} = \alpha_i + \beta_0 x_{i,t} + \beta_1 x_{i,t-1} + \epsilon_{i,t},$$

$$t = T_{i0+1}, \ldots T_{i1},$$

$$\alpha_i = \alpha + n_i,$$

$$\epsilon \approx iid(0, \epsilon_i^2).$$

Aggregating over country observations, we obtain:

$$\frac{1}{T_i} \sum_{t=i_{0}+1}^{T_{i1}} y_{it} = \alpha + n_i + \beta_0 \frac{1}{T_i} \sum_{t=T_{i0}+1}^{T_{i1}} x_{it}$$

$$+ \beta_1 \frac{1}{T_i} \sum_{t=T_{i0}+1}^{T_{i1}} x_{i,t-1} + \frac{1}{T_i} \sum_{t=T_{i0}+1}^{T_{i1}} \epsilon_{it}.$$

Removing and adding x_{i0} and adding and removing x_{i1}, we find:

$$\text{let } \overline{y_{i,T_i}} = \frac{1}{T_i} \sum_{t=T_{i0}+1}^{T_{i1}} y_{it},$$

$$\overline{y_{i,T_i}} = \alpha + (\beta_0 + \beta_1)\overline{x_{i,T_i}} + \overline{v_{i,T_i}},$$

$$\overline{v_{i,T_i}} = n_i + \beta_1 \frac{(x_{i,T_i 0} - x_{i,T_{i1}})}{T_i} + \overline{\epsilon_{i,T_i}}.$$

From this it follows that: (1) a regression on country averages will yield the long-term coefficient ($\beta_0 + \beta_1$), and (2) that the error term exhibits heteroscedasticity, since (ignoring end effects for simplicity) the variance of the error term is:

$$V(\overline{v_{i,T_i}}) = \sigma_\eta^2 + \frac{\sigma_\epsilon^2}{T_i}.$$

Appendix B. Calibration Exercise for Shirking and Fair-Wage Models

This section calibrates a theoretical model of corruption with shirking and the fair-wage hypotheses as special cases. The section has two purposes. First, it illustrates that corruption is much more responsive to wages under fair wages and shows that civil-service wages would have to be raised to very high levels to eradicate corruption if the shirking hypothesis in fact holds. Second, it makes the case that the empirical estimate for wages at which corruption is eliminated is an upper bound because fair-wages and shirking hypotheses are observationally equivalent for certain parameters. The shirking model—which is a variant of the well-known Becker-Stigler model—is presented mainly to facilitate comparison with the fair wages model.

A.1. The Shirking Hypothesis: Corruption in a Maximizing Framework

The analysis draws heavily on Becker and Stigler (1974), with the exception that corruption is modeled as a continuous variable rather than a binary variable. Government employees are assumed to maximize the present discounted value of a stream of expected income. In so doing, they balance the benefits from corrupt behavior against the penalties when caught and punished. These penalties are assumed to include dismissal (with a cost equal to the wage differential with the private sector plus bribes foregone) and other penalties. In a multi-period model, the present discounted value (PDV), of expected income, in the *last period* of employment, period T, can be expressed as follows:

$$\text{PDV}_T = (1 - pC)(CB + W_g) + pC(W_p - f). \tag{1a}$$

Here PDV is the present discounted value of expected income. The equation expresses expected income as a weighted average of the income when corruption is not detected and when it is detected. When corruption is not detected, income equals income from bribery, CB, where C is the number of corrupt acts and B is the level of the bribe, plus the government wage, W_g. W_g can be thought of as including the government pension. When corruption is detected, the wage, pension, and bribery income is foregone and income equals the private sector wage, W_p, minus penalties or jail terms, f. This formulation assumes for simplicity that the probability of detection equals pC, or the probability of detection for an individual corrupt act, p, times the number of corrupt acts, C.[39] Except for C, all variables are assumed to be exogenous. Furthermore, all variables, except for C and W_g are assumed constant over time.

Taking the first derivative of PDV with respect to C and solving gives the amount of corruption that a civil servant who maximizes expected income would chose to engage in, in the last period of employment:

$$C = \frac{1}{2} \frac{B - p(W_s - W_p + f)}{pB}.$$

In this formulation, government wage policy has an effect on corruption. However, high wages are not necessary for low corruption, if the government can manipulate p and f at will.[40]

The government can ensure that corruption equals zero by providing the wage for which $C = 0$ in the above equation. We label this condition the No Corruption Condition (NCC), in parallel with the No Shirking Condition in the efficiency wage literature:

$$W_g = W_p + B/p - f. \tag{1b}$$

Note from this NCC that very high wages are required in order to eradicate corruption when the probability of detection is low and/or the level of bribes is high. Solutions for earlier periods are obtained by backward induction (see

---

[39]This is a good approximation of the true probability of detection of at least one act (when these probabilities are independent), or $1 - (1 - p)^C$, for low p and C. Note also that the assumption of a fixed probability of detection abstracts from the possibility of multiple equilibria. See Lui (1986) and Andvig and Moene (1990) for models of multiple equilibria and Bardhan (1997) for a review of this literature.

[40]It is interesting to note that in reality p and f tend to be endogenous, rendering the task of controlling corruption through p or f, but without using wage policy, difficult. Thus, cooperation with enforcement agencies is diminished (p is low) when civil servant wages are low. Similarly, high penalties (f) tend not to be enforced by the courts, that is a high f leads to low p. For example, Thailand had the death penalty for corruption at one point, but this penalty was never imposed. See Akerlof and Yellen (1994) for a model where cooperation with the police in controlling gangs (p) depends on penalties (f).

Becker and Stigler, 1974). PDV in the second to last period of employment can be expressed as follows:

$$PDV_{T-1} = (1-pC)(CB + W_g + PDV_T/(1+r)) + pC(W_p - f + W_p/(1+r)),$$

where r represents the discount rate. Assuming the NCC holds in the last period, PDV_{T-1} is obtained by setting PDV_T equal to W_g from Eq. (1b). Maximizing PDV_{T-1} subject to C and then equating C to zero provides the NCC for the second to last period, *conditional on the NCC holding in the last period*:

$$W_g = W_p + (B/p - f)r/(1 + r). \qquad (2)$$

Note that when the NCC is not expected to hold in later periods, higher wages than indicated by Eq. (2) have to be paid in earlier periods. In practice in developing countries, the NCC is not expected to hold in later periods; that is, future wages are likely to be such that corruption "pays" (i.e. future wages are below the PDV that civil servants can obtain when corrupt). Therefore, the results given by Eq. (2) provide a lower bound to the actual wage required to eradicate corruption.

A calibration can illustrate the magnitudes involved. Assuming that the probability of detection and punishment of an individual act of corruption is 0.1%,[41] that penalties consist of dismissal, foregone bribes, and additional penalties of 150, that the private sector wage equals 100, that the bribe level equals 20, and that the discount rate is 10%, one finds that corruption is eradicated when government wages equal 200 times the private sector wage in the last period of employment and 19 times in all earlier periods. If wages fall short of 200 times the private sector wage in the last period of employment, a factor greater than 19 is required in order to eradicate corruption in earlier periods.

A.2. The Fair-Wage Hypothesis: Corruption in a Satisficing Framework

Individual behavior may not be appropriately described by the optimizing framework laid out above. According to the psychological literature on "fair wages," "workers who do not receive a fair wage [. . .] may change actual ef-

---

[41]The choice of $p = 0.1$ reflects anecdotal information for India (see Section 3), which rates about average on p in our sample using our empirical proxies for internal and external controls.

fort. [. . .] or their perceived level of remuneration (by redefining the nonpecuniary terms of the job)" (Akerlof and Yellen, 1990, p. 257).[42]

What we will call the "fair wage-corruption" hypothesis is the hypothesis that workers choose levels of C in an attempt to reach an expected income level EI = W^*.

$$\text{EI} = (1 - pC)(CB + W_g) + pC(W_p - f) = W^*, \tag{3}$$

The solution for C, as we shall see, is a function of government wages, W_g, relative to the fair wage, W^*.[43] The "fair" wage could be determined according to a variety of mechanisms: wages of peers within or without the place of employment, societal expectations, the market clearing wage, subsistence requirements, the status of civil servants, etc.[44] Solving for C and choosing the negative root, one obtains:[45]

$$C = \frac{1}{2} \frac{B - p(W_g - W_p + f) - \sqrt{D}}{pB},$$

where:

$$D = [B - p(W_g - W_p + f)]^2 - 4pB(W^* - W_g).$$

Setting $C = 0$, we find that the NCC is simply:

$$W_g = W^*. \tag{4}$$

This means that a higher W^* implies a higher government wage is necessary to eliminate corruption, as one would expect. Under certain circumstances—high W^*, low W_g, low B, high p or f—D is negative and there is no solution for C (i.e. the solution is imaginary): targeted income cannot be reached whatever the level of corruption. In this situation, one would expect the civil servant to engage in the number of corrupt acts that maximizes expected value,

---

[42]See Akerlof and Yellen (1990) for a review of sociological evidence. Fehr et al. (1993) provide experimental evidence suggesting that wages motivate effort even when there are no penalties for shirking, though the effect is not very large. Fehr and Tyran (1996) interpret this finding in terms of "reciprocity," i.e. they see a desire on the part of workers to reward well-paying employers.

[43]Charap and Harm (2000) see predatory states actually setting up systems with low civil-service wages to force civil servants into corruption, so as to create a system of rents.

[44]See Dumont (1979) for some insights on this for the case of Sub-Saharan Africa.

[45]The positive root involving the same expected income; however, more corruption theoretically constitutes a second solution, but this solution is ignored here.

while also reducing effort, say according to effort = $f(EI/W^*)$.[46] That is, one would expect civil servants to act as maximizers even when they are truly satisficers. Thus, satisficing behavior can be observationally equivalent to maximizing behavior. This observational equivalence (which is more likely to occur at low civil-service wages) implies that it may be impossible to test the fair-wage and shirking hypotheses empirically. Linear extrapolation based on observations in the low-wage range may produce a higher intercept (i.e. wages at which corruption is zero) than the true intercept. Under these circumstances, micro data on corruption incidence in the parts of public administration that offer high bribes or have a low probability of detection would be necessary to distinguish the two efficiency wage theories empirically.

References

Acemoglu, D., Verdier, T., 2000. The choice between market failures and corruption. American Economic Review 90 (1), 194–211.

Adamolekum, L., Jah, O. (Eds.), 1997. Enclave Approach to Tax and Customs Administration in Africa: Three Country Studies. Mimeograph, World Bank, Washington, DC.

Ades, A., Di Tella, R., 1997. National champions and corruption: some unpleasant interventionist arithmetic. Economic Journal 107 (443), 1023–1043.

Ades, A., Di Tella, R., 1999. Rents, competition and corruption. American Economic Review 89 (4), 982–994.

Akerlof, G.A., Yellen, J., 1990. The fair wage effort hypothesis and unemployment. Quarterly Journal of Economics 105 (2), 255–283.

Akerlof, G.A., Yellen, J., 1994. Gang behavior, law enforcement, and community. In: Aaron, H.J., Mann, T.E., Taylor, T. (Eds.), Values in Public Policy. Brookings, Washington.

Alfiler, M.C.P., 1986. The process of bureaucratic corruption in Asia: emerging patterns. In: Cariño, L.V. (Ed.), Bureaucratic Corruption in Asia: Causes, Consequences, and Controls. NMC Press, Quezon City, Philippines, pp. 15–68.

Andvig, J.C., Moene, K.O., 1990. How corruption may corrupt. Journal of Economic Behavior and Organization 13 (1), 63–76.

---

[46]The incorporation of both corruption and effort in one model fits the stylized facts described in the corruption literature, see, Gould (1980, p. 71) who explains that "The civil servant who does not wish—or does not have the opportunity—to steal, or whose corruption is not sufficiently remunerative, may engage in another behavior strategy: taking on a second job, moonlighting."

Bardhan, P., 1997. Corruption and development: A review of issues. Journal of Economic Literature 35 (3), 1320–1346.

Becker, G.S., Stigler, G.J., 1974. Law enforcement, malfeasance, and the compensation of enforcers. Journal of Legal Studies 2, 1–19.

Besley, T., McLaren, J., 1993. Taxes and bribery: the role of wage incentives. Economic Journal 103 (416), 119–141.

Brunetti, A., Kisunko, G., Weder, B., 1998. Credibility of rules and economic growth: evidence from a worldwide survey of the private sector. World Bank Economic Review 12 (3), 353–384.

Cariño, L.V. (Ed.), 1986. Bureaucratic Corruption in Asia: Causes, Consequences, and Controls. NMC Press, Quezon City, Philippines.

Chand, S.K., Moene, K.O., 1999. Controlling fiscal corruption. World Development 27 (7), 1129–1140. [Reproduced as Chapter 4 in this volume—ED.]

Charap, J., Harm, C., 2000. Institutionalized corruption and the kleptocratic state. In: Menard, C. (Ed.), Institutions, Contracts and Organizations: Perspectives from New Institutional Economics. Edward Elgar, Cheltenham, UK, pp. 188–209. [Reproduced as Chapter 6 in this volume—ED.]

Coplin, W.D., O'Leary, M.K., Sealy, T., 1993. A Business Guide to Political Risk for International Decisions. Political Risk Services, Syracuse, NY.

Dumont, R., 1979. Remuneration and corruption levels in French-speaking Africa. In: Ekpo, M. (Ed.), Bureaucratic Corruption in Sub-Saharan Africa: Toward a Search of Causes and Consequences. University Press of America, Washington, DC.

Fehr, E., Tyran, J., 1996. Institutions and reciprocal fairness. Nordic Journal of Political Economy.

Fehr, E., Kirchsteiger, G., Riedl, A., 1993. Does fairness prevent market clearing? An experimental investigation. Quarterly Journal of Economics 108 (2), 437–459.

Flatters, F., McLeod, W.B., 1995. Administrative corruption and taxation. International Tax and Public Finance 2 (3), 397–417.

Freedom House (various issues). Freedom in the World: The Annual Survey of Political Rights and Civil Liberties. Freedom House, New York.

Goel, R., Rich, D., 1989. On the economic incentives for taking bribes. Public Choice 61 (3), 269–275.

Gould, D.J., 1980. Bureaucratic Corruption and Underdevelopment in the Third World: The Case of Zaire. Pergamon, New York.

Haque, N., Sahay, R., 1996. Do Government wage cuts close budget deficit? IMF Staff Papers 43 (4).

Israel, A., 1987. Institutional Development: Incentives to Performance. Johns Hopkins Univ. Press, Baltimore.

Kahn, C.M., Silva, E.C.D., Ziliak, J.P., 2000. Performance-Based Wages in Tax Collection: The Brazilian Tax Collection Reform and its Effects. Mimeograph, Tulane University.

[Kaufmann, D., 1997. Corruption: the facts. Foreign Policy 107 (Summer), 114–31—ED.]

Klitgaard, R., 1989. Controlling Corruption. Univ. California Press, Berkeley.

Klitgaard, R., 1991. Adjusting to Reality, Beyond State Versus Market in Economic Development. ICS Press, San Francisco.

Knack, S., Keefer, P., 1995. Institutions and economic performance: cross-country tests using alternative institutional measures. Economics and Politics 7 (3), 207–227.

Lee, R.P.L., 1986. Bureaucratic corruption in Asia: the problem of incongruence between legal norms and folk norms. In Cariño (Ed.), Bureaucratic Corruption in Asia: Causes, Consequences, and Controls. NMC Press, Quezon City, Philippines, pp. 69–107.

Lindauer, D., Nunberg, B. (Eds.), 1994. Rehabilitating Government: Pay and Employment Reform in Africa. World Bank, Washington.

Lui, F.T., 1986. A dynamic model of corruption deterrence. Journal of Public Economics 231 (2), 1–22.

Mauro, P., 1995. Corruption and growth. Quarterly Journal of Economics 110 (3), 681–712.

Mauro, P., 1998. Corruption and the composition of government expenditure. Journal of Public Economics 69 (2), 263–279. [Reproduced as Chapter 10 in this volume—ED.]

Mookherjee, D., Png, I.P.L., 1995. Corruptible law enforcers: how should they be compensated? Economic Journal 105 (428), 145–159.

Myrdal, G., 1968. Asian Drama: an Inquiry into the Poverty of Nations. Twentieth Century Fund, New York.

Nashashibi, K., Gupta, S., Liuksila, C., Lorie, H., Mahler, W., 1992. The Fiscal Dimension of Adjustment in Low-Income Countries. IMF Occasional Paper No. 95. International Monetary Fund, Washington.

Pesaran, M.H., Smith, R., 1995. Estimating long-run relationships from dynamic heterogeneous panels. Journal of Econometrics 68 (1), 79–113.

Political Risk Services, various issues. International Country Risk Guide. Political Risk Services, New York.

Rahman, A.T.R., 1986. Legal and administrative measures against bureaucratic corruption in Asia. In: Cariño (Ed.), Bureaucratic Corruption in Asia: Causes, Consequences, and Controls. NMC Press, Quezon City, Philippines, pp. 109–162.

Rauch, J.E., Evans, P.B., 2000. Bureaucratic structure and bureaucratic performance in less developed countries. Journal of Public Economics 75 (1), 49–71.

Rose-Ackerman, S., 1999, Corruption and Government: Causes, Consequences, and Reform. Cambridge Univ. Press, Cambridge, UK.

Schiavo-Campo, S., de Tommaso, G., Mukherjee, A., 1997. An International Statistical Survey of Government Employment and Wages. World Bank Policy Research Working Paper No. 1806.

Shapiro, C., Stiglitz, J.E., 1984. Equilibrium uemployment as a worker discipline device. American Economic Review 74 (3), 433–444.

Shleifer, A., Vishny, R., 1993. Corruption. Quarterly Journal of Economics 108 (3), 599–617.

Tanzi, V., 1994. Corruption, Governmental Activities, and Markets, IMF Working Paper No. 94/99.

Tanzi, V., Zee, H.H., 1995. Human Capital Accumulation and Public Sector Growth, IMF Working Paper No. 95/95.

Van Rijckeghem, C., Weder, B., 1997. Corruption and the Rate of Temptation: Do Low Wages in the Civil Service Cause Corruption? IMF Working Paper No. 97/73.

Wei, S., 1997. How taxing is corruption on international investors? Review of Economics and Statistics 82 (1), 1–11.

Wei, S., 2000. Natural Openness and Good Government, NBER Working Paper No. 7765.

4

Controlling Fiscal Corruption

Sheetal K. Chand and Karl O. Moene

1. Introduction

It has been widely observed that insufficient domestic resource mobilization and wasteful public expenditures are at the root of the adjustment and growth problems faced by many countries, including especially those in transition to a market economy. To remedy this situation the basic strategy has relied on reforming the design of taxes and their administration, accompanied by efforts to control expenditure waste and fraud. The often less-than-satisfactory outcome of this strategy has led to a growing perception that corruption and its corrosive effects on fiscal performance should also be addressed.[1]

Reprinted from *World Development*, Vol. 27, Sheetal K. Chand and Karl O. Moene, "Controlling Fiscal Corruption," pp. 1129–1140 (1999), with permission from Elsevier Science.

The authors are indebted to Sveinung Skjesol for assistance in the preparation of this paper. They also wish to thank an anonymous referee for very helpful comments.

[1] See especially Klitgaard (1988) and Rose-Ackerman (1978, 1997). For an example of institutional recognition in a multilateral context see the Governance Guidance Note of the IMF (1997).

It is difficult, however, to obtain adequate information on corruption because the involved parties naturally strive for concealment. Broadly, on the side of revenue, some indication of the extent of corruption can be obtained by comparing the theoretical yield of taxes and actual collections, but the shortfall could also be caused by other factors such as the poor organization and administration of tax departments. It is also difficult to establish how much corruption adds to expenditures as standards for comparison are not readily available, especially for public goods, while with respect to procurement and contract specifications, practices may vary between the private and public sectors. Detailed information on behavioral responses is not readily available and therefore researchers have often had to rely on anecdotal accounts.[2] Such a situation does not facilitate the construction of an analytical framework to explain corruption and to develop ways to control it.

In the literature, three basic factors have been identified as contributing to corruption.[3] The first is the overall level of potential benefits from corrupt behavior. Benefits refer to the payoffs from evasion in the case of taxes or excessive billing of government expenditures. The second relates to the costs of bribery, or the penalties and sanctions applicable to briber and bribee. The third concerns the bargaining power of officials, or the extent of exclusive discretionary powers in the hands of individual bureaucrats. High tax rates imply high potential benefits from evasion. A poor record of applying sanctions lowers the costs of being corrupt. Considerable discretionary powers vested in the hands of officers confer the means for extracting bribes. An environment exhibiting all three features is likely to exhibit high levels of corruption. Suggested traditional remedies follow readily: lower tax rates; apply adequate penalties more rigorously; and reduce the discretionary powers of fiscal officers, with the last two also applicable in the area of government outlays.

These remedies however, may not be adequate. It may also be necessary to address issues concerning the conditions of service and more generally the motivation of fiscal officers. Obviously, if officers are poorly paid, or become so as a consequence of an adjustment strategy, for example, wage control in a context of massive price increases, they might be more inclined to engage in corruption.[4] Should the top eche-

---

[2]Klitgaard (1988) presents some intriguing cases. See also Tanzi (1998).
[3]Thus see Rose-Ackerman (1978).
[4]Van Rijckeghem and Weder (1997). The experience of Sierra Leone is instructive. In the last quarter of 1986, an adjustment program was adopted that froze wages of public servants

lons of government be corrupt, there is likely to be a contagion effect on lower levels.[5] This effect could become more pronounced if it is generally perceived that the administrative structures are being used to promote the self-interest of their managements rather than the mandated objectives. The contagion effect may be further stimulated if, as is often the case in such environments, officers view their own career progression to be dependant on the extent to which they compromise with higher levels. Establishing an organizational structure that is less conducive to compromising behavior, combined with the right incentive structure and the appropriate *esprit de corps*, can help contain contagion effects. It is likely that the payment of a properly designed bonus, especially if emoluments are inadequate, could be a powerful incentive. But, for such a measure to be effective it is essential to reduce corruption at higher levels.

Most of the attempts at formal modeling in the literature have focused on the behavior of the briber, for example, the taxpayer.[6] Less attention has been paid to the behavior of the fiscal officer, their conditions of service, and their motivation, which is the focus of this paper.[7] To address these issues, a two-pronged approach is adopted. First, a framework is set up in Section 2 to analyze how bonus payments to tax officers can promote less corrupt outcomes. Second, a case study of how rampant fiscal corruption was brought under control, and revenue performance markedly improved, is presented in Section 3.

---

so as to contain inflation. At the same time, the exchange rate was floated and restrictions on external transactions removed. The exchange rate depreciated rapidly from about US$1 = Leones 5 to US$1 = Leones 35 by the end of the year. While the former rate was overvalued in comparison to a parallel market rate of US$1 = Leones 18, the new rate had widely overshot. Despite a small reduction in import tariff rates, importers confronted an increase in customs duties of severalfold. Removal of price restrictions resulted in full pass-through of the exchange rate effect and the price of imported staples such as rice rose by a factor of about seven. Given the resulting severe erosion in the real wages of customs officers, the stage was set for mutually self-serving deals with importers, and officially recorded imports plummeted. The fiscal deficit jumped from 2.3% of GDP in 1986 to 14.8% in 1987.

[5]See Andvig and Moene (1990).
[6]The classic reference is Allingham and Sandmo (1972).
[7]See, however, Besley and McLaren (1993), Flatters and MacLeod (1995), and Haque and Sahay (1996), who examine incentive effects but without the explicit treatment of bonuses as is done here. Our approach is closer to that of Mookherjee and Png (1995).

2. Modeling Incentive Effects

There are three categories of players in the model that are set out here: taxpayers, tax collectors, and their managers. Taxpayers try to reduce their tax liability through evasion. Should they be caught evading they try to bribe the tax collector. It is assumed that all tax collectors are not well paid and that they supplement their incomes through bribes. It is further assumed that their ability to extort ever higher bribes is limited by the scope for the taxpayer to appeal to the tax collectors' managers, some of whom may be dishonest. On appeal, the latter uncover the true extent of evasion and either levy a penalty, or, if they are corrupt, they ask for a bribe. The tax collector loses in the process.

To capture these interactions we study a four-stage sequential game. The game involves weighing various risks in the course of optimizing the net benefits to be obtained. Into this framework, a bonus scheme is introduced with a view to promoting less corrupt behavior on the part of the tax collector. In order to abstract from the diverse characteristics of taxpayers, the analysis refers to a "firm" that engages in the quintessential activity of attempting to increase its net profits which may include recourses to tax evasion. *Mutatis mutandis*, the same principle applies to other categories of taxpayers. The sequencing of the game is as follows.

(a) Stage (1)—The Firm's Behavior

The true profit is Π, but the firm may find it advantageous to report lower profits R than the true level. According to the books, the reported profit is $R \leq \Pi$. The main idea below is that the firm chooses how much of its profits to report. To disguise the true profit, however, involves costs. The firm cannot run activities that are easily monitored by tax collectors; it must keep double accounts and so on. The costs of trying to evade taxes is captured by assuming that the true profit Π and the reported level R are related as $\Pi(R)$. It is assumed that $\Pi'(R) \geq 0$ for $R \leq \Pi$ and $\Pi'(R) = 0$ for $R = \Pi$. Moreover, $\Pi''(\cdot) < 0$.

(b) Stage (2)—The Tax Collectors' Behavior

The tax collector checks the books with an intensity μ implying that tax evasion is discovered with a probability μ. The tax collector chooses μ by the choice of how much work effort he is willing to put in. The cost of effort is denoted c and μ is increasing in c at a decreasing rate, hence

$\mu = \mu(c)$ with $\mu'(\cdot) > 0$ and $\mu''(\cdot) < 0$. With a bonus scheme, the tax collector receives a fraction γ of all taxes he collects. We derive the impact of a bonus for the amount of tax collected by modeling the case with a bonus parameter γ, and then comparing the cases $\gamma = 0$ with $\gamma > 0$. The tax rate on profits is t.

(c) Stage (3)—Threat Points and the Bribe

A tax collector who has found evidence of tax evasion may take a bribe b_1 for not reporting the firm. The level of the bribe b_1 is determined by bargaining between the firm and the tax collector. The agreement is constrained by the possibilities of both the firm and the tax collector to appeal the case to higher-level tax authorities.

(d) Stage (4)—Behavior of Higher-Level Bureaucrats

Higher-level tax authorities handle the case if there is a disagreement between the firm and the tax collector who claims to have evidence of tax evasion. By inspecting the books in the light of the evidence provided by the tax collector, higher-level tax authorities can always find out what the true profit is. But not all bureaucrats employed at this level are honest. A fraction θ of the higher-level bureaucrats is corrupt and willing to take a bribe b_2 for reporting a taxable profit equal to R. Honest bureaucrats report what they find. The presence of corrupt officials implies that when a tax case is appealed, it is handled by a corrupt official with probability θ and by a noncorrupt official with a probability $(1 - \theta)$.

We start backward at stage (4), when the case is considered by higher-level tax authorities. If the case is handled by a noncorrupt official, he collects the tax $t\Pi$. If the case is handled by a corrupt bureaucrat, he reports tR and receives a bribe b_2, determined by bargaining between the firm and the bureaucrat. The profit of the firm above the disagreement level $(1 - t)\Pi$, is

$$\Pi - tR - b_2 - (1 - t)\Pi = t(\Pi - R) - b_2. \tag{1}$$

The corresponding surplus to the corrupt bureaucrat is simply the bribe b_2. The equilibrium bribe is just a share of the tax saved

$$b_2 = \alpha t(\Pi - R), \tag{2}$$

where α is the bargaining power of the bureaucrat. Eqn. (2) can be justified by applying the asymmetric Nash bargaining approach, or by exploring the bargaining conflict in an extensive form game such as in Rubinstein (1982). The bargaining power coefficient α captures how harmful a postponement of the deal is to the taxpayer relative to the tax collector and may incorporate both specific institutional factors such as the expected future treatment of the tax authorities and general aspects such as the relative impatience of the two.

At stage (3), if tax evasion is identified, the bribe to a nonreporting tax collector b_1 is determined by bargaining. Both can use an appeal to higher-level tax authorities as a threat against the other. Both sides perceive what will happen in that case: the firm obtains π_1 and the tax collector u_1 (in expected terms), given by

$$\pi_1 = \theta[\Pi - tR - b_2] + (1 - \theta)[(1 - t)\Pi], \tag{3}$$

$$u_1 = \theta\gamma tR + (1 - \theta)\gamma t\Pi, \tag{4}$$

where, in both expressions, the probabilities of being treated by a higher-level corrupt official is θ. Letting the bargaining power of the tax collector be β and that of the firm be $(1 - \beta)$, the equilibrium level of the bribe is the value of b_1 that maximizes

$$[\Pi - tR - b_1 - \pi_1]^{1-\beta} [\gamma tR + b_1 - u_1]^\beta \tag{5}$$

which by inserting for π_1, u_1, and b_2 can be expressed as

$$b_1 = \phi t(\Pi - R), \tag{6}$$

where

$$\phi = \phi(\gamma, \theta) \equiv [(1 - \beta)(1 - \theta)\gamma + \beta(1 - \theta) + \beta\theta\alpha]. \tag{7}$$

Observe that ϕ is less than unity and that ϕ, and, therefore, the bribe b_1 is increasing in the bonus parameter γ. The implication is straightforward. The higher the bonus the more income the tax collector forgoes by not reporting the true level of profits, thus the higher the bribe has to be. It is also clear from Eqns. (6) and (7) that ϕ and the bribe b_1 is decreasing in the incidence of corruption θ among higher-level tax authorities. The reason is that an appeal from the tax collector is a less severe threat to the firm as long as it can bribe its way also at this level, while an appeal by the firm would lead to a lower expected bonus to the tax collector, the more corruption there is at this higher level. Thus a high level of corruption among higher-level bureaucrats makes the tax collector weaker and the firm stronger. Finally, it might also be noted that increases in the tax rate raise the level of the bribe.

At stage (2) the tax collector decides his work intensity μ. Consider the case where all tax collectors are dishonest. Thus the tax collector maximizes

$$U = \mu(c)(\gamma tR + b_1) + (1 - \mu(c))\gamma tR - c \tag{8}$$

which give us the first-order condition

$$\phi t(\Pi - R)\mu'(c) = 1. \tag{9}$$

It is clear from Eqns. (7) and (9) that the μ is positive even without a bonus, that is with ($\gamma = 0$). Without a bonus, ϕ in Eqn. (9) is just $\phi(0, \theta) \equiv \beta(1 - \theta) + \beta\theta\alpha$. Thus the possibility of obtaining bribes provides work incentives for the tax collector. Observe, however, that work incentives become weaker, the more higher-level corruption there is, as ϕ declines when θ goes up. Moreover, since ϕ is increasing in the bonus parameter γ, the chosen work intensity μ goes up with the bonus for each level of tax evasion. But, the impact of an increase in the bonus on work effort becomes smaller when corruption of higher-level bureaucrats goes up. In the limit, the impact of γ on work effort is zero when all higher-level bureaucrats are corrupt and $\theta = 1$. The tax collector then obtains no expected gain in bonus income by appealing the case to higher-level authorities. There is no bonus income forgone by accepting the bribe for not reporting. Accordingly, there are no incentives to the tax collector to work harder with a bonus than without when all higher-level bureaucrats are corrupt. Finally, Eqn. (9) shows that for each level of ϕ, tax collectors work harder the more tax evasion they expect to find, i.e., the lower they expect R to be and the higher is t. How work intensity μ is affected by the other variables is summarized in the table.

At stage (1) the firm determines R in order to maximize expected profits net of taxes and bribes. The maximand is

$$V = \mu[\Pi(R) - tR - b_1] + (1 - \mu)[\Pi(R) - tR]. \tag{10}$$

The first-order condition for maximizing V with respect to R is

$$\Pi'(R) = \frac{t(1 - \mu\phi)}{1 - \mu\phi t}. \qquad (11)$$

First, observe that reported profit R is higher the harder tax collectors are supposed to work. This is so since $\Pi''(\cdot) < 0$ and the RHS of Eqn. (11) is decreasing in the work intensity μ. It is also readily seen that higher taxes make tax evasion more tempting. As shown by Eqn. (11), reported profit R declines as t goes up. Next, since ϕ is decreasing in the incidence of higher-level corruption θ (and the RHS of Eqn. (11) is decreasing in ϕ in which case it would increase when ϕ decreases), reported profits are lower and tax evasion higher, the more higher-level corruption there is. Similarly, since ϕ is increasing in the bonus parameter, the level of reported profits R is higher, the higher the bonus. With a bonus scheme tax collectors have to be paid higher bribes to be willing not to report any acts of tax evasion that they identify. The firm would know this, which is captured by the impact on the RHS of Eqn. (11) via the dependence of ϕ on γ in Eqn. (7). (In addition, firms can infer that with a bonus, tax collectors would work harder in order to identify tax evasion. This is captured by the impact on the RHS of Eqn. (11) of the dependence of μ on γ from Eqn. (9), to be incorporated when we solve for the equilibrium behavior of both taxpayers and collectors.) The impacts on reported profits of increases in the variables of the model are summarized in Table 1.

The equilibrium levels of μ and R are those that solve Eqns. (9) and (11) simultaneously as illustrated in Figure 1. The downward sloping curve shows the tax collector's choice of μ for each level of R (since for each R there is a unique $[\Pi(R) - R]$). The upward sloping curve shows the firm's choice of reported profits R for each level of μ. The (Nash) equilibrium of the model is where the two curves intersect.

As illustrated in the figure, an increase in the bonus parameter shifts both curves to the right, implying that the equilibrium level of reported profits goes up. An increase in corruption among higher-level bureaucrats, however, shifts both curves to the left, implying that the equilibrium level of reported profits R goes down. A decline in the tax rate shifts the curve describing the firm's behavior to the right as the direct incentives for tax evasion decline. Yet, in equilibrium, lower taxes do not necessarily imply less tax evasion since a lower tax rate, in addition,

Table 1. Work Intensity Affected by Other Variables

Increase in:	R	μ	θ	γ	t
Effects on: R		+	−	+	−
μ	−		−	+	+

shifts the curve describing tax collectors' behavior to the left as tax collectors work less hard. Thus the net effect on reported profits depends on which is the strongest of the direct incentive effect on taxpayers' behavior and the indirect effect via a less efficient tax collection.

Returning to the bonus, it may seem as if a higher bonus parameter implies increasing corruption among tax collectors since the bribe b_1, all else being given, goes up with the bonus. All else, however, is not given. Tax collectors work harder and firms have fewer incentives to hide their true profits both because they have to pay higher bribes when detected and because for each level of tax evasion the probability of being detected goes up with the bonus. As a consequence, the gap between $\Pi - R$ narrows and even though tax collectors obtain a higher share of the gap with a bonus than without, the equilibrium bribes may very well decline with the introduction of a bonus.

As demonstrated, the efficiency of the bonus scheme depends on the incidence of higher-level corruption. It is, therefore, important to incorporate how the incidence of higher-level corruption θ may be affected by the bonus to tax collectors. A simple and robust way to make θ endogenous is to assume that the incidence is increasing in the potential gain from acting corruptly captured by b_2. Thus let

$$\theta = F(\alpha t(\Pi(R) - R)), \qquad (12)$$

where $F(\cdot) > 0$. Now we have an even more interesting closed loop of the impact of a bonus to tax collectors on the functioning of the tax system: A bonus implies that tax collectors work harder and that firms voluntarily report higher profits. This implies, once more, that the gap between the true and reported profits $(\Pi - R)$ narrows which again reduces the incidence of corruption among higher-level bureaucrats according to Eqn. (12). As θ goes down, work effort of tax collectors increases and reported profits of firms go up both because μ is higher for each level of tax evasion and because there is less to be gained by an appeal to higher-level authorities. Thus introducing a bonus scheme

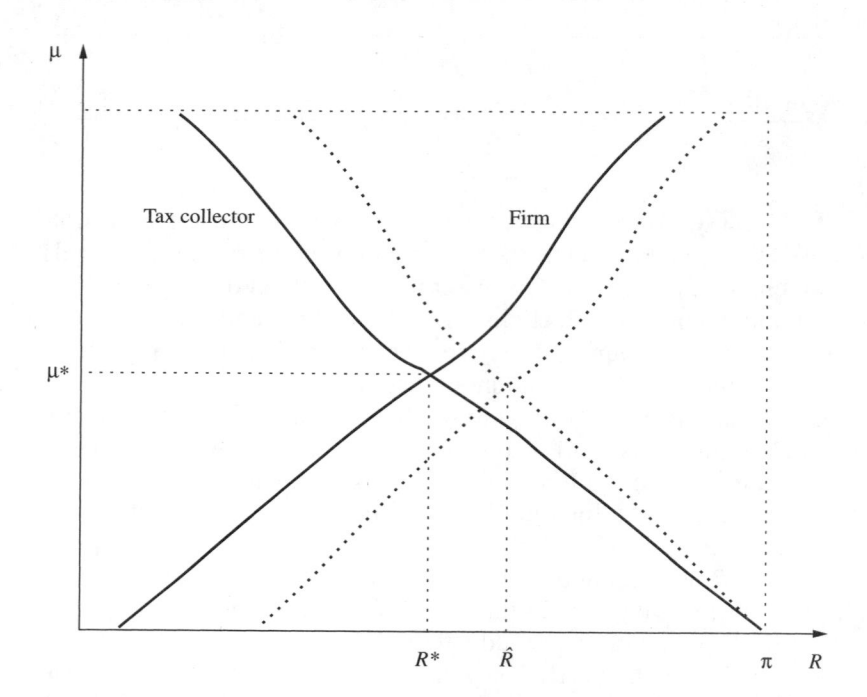

Figure 1. Incentive Policies and Revenue Yield

leads to more honesty in parts of the administration that are not directly affected by the bonus. Moreover, a more honest administration makes the bonus scheme more efficient. Thus, there is an honesty multiplier in the sense that a bonus makes firms act more honestly, which also induces higher-level bureaucrats to act more honestly as there is less to gain from corruption. In turn, this outcome induces firms to engage in less tax evasion and so on.

The honesty multiplier does not require that tax collectors work harder with the bonus than without. As seen from Figure 1, an increase in the bonus may have an ambiguous impact on work effort μ. To see how the multiplier works let us for now assume that μ is given. We then have that Eqn. (11) determines R as a function of $\phi \equiv \phi(\gamma, \theta)$, written $R = R(\phi)$ where $R'(\phi) > 0$, while Eqn. (12) determines the fraction of higher-level authorities who are corrupt as a function of R, expressed as $\theta = \theta(R)$ where $\theta'(R) < 0$. Let us in addition define the following elasticities

$$\sigma \equiv \frac{\theta' R}{\theta}; \quad \rho \equiv \frac{R'\phi}{R}.$$

Using these short-hand expressions, the total effect of an increase in the bonus parameter can be written as

$$\frac{dR}{d\gamma} = mR_\gamma, \qquad (13)$$

where

$$m \equiv \frac{\phi}{\phi - \rho\sigma\theta a} > 1,$$

$a \equiv (1 - \beta)\gamma + (1 - \alpha)$ and

$R_\gamma = (1 - \beta)(1 - \theta)R'.$

As stated before, an increase in the bonus has no effect when $\theta = 1$. When $\theta < 1$ every initial stimulus from a higher bonus $R_\gamma > 0$ is multiplied by $m > 1$ to obtain the overall effect. A higher γ makes tax evasion less profitable simply because the higher bonus implies that tax collectors demand higher bribes in order to report the firm. When firms take that into account, they evade less taxes which again makes it less tempting for higher-level officials to be corrupt. If we assume symmetric bargaining power $\alpha = \beta = \frac{1}{2}$ and that half of the higher-level officials are initially corrupt, $\theta = \frac{1}{2}$ and that $\sigma\rho = \frac{1}{2}$, we get $m = 1.2$. An increase in the response elasticities to $\sigma\rho = 1$ increases the multiplier to $m = 1.5$.

The tax collected is proportional to

$$T = tR \qquad (14)$$

since in equilibrium the same amount is reported whether the tax collector detects tax evasion or not. In both cases, he only reports tR. The value of T is of course a gross tax and one may be concerned that even though R goes up, the net tax income after the bonus to tax collectors is paid, may go down. A bonus scheme, however, does not have to be excessively generous and adjustments can always be made to initial salary levels. The salary could be reduced by an amount not far from that of expected bonus incomes. If a target level of emoluments including bonuses is maintained, then the relevant tax income is rendered proportional to T in Eqn. (14) and tax incomes unambiguously go up with the introduction of the bonus scheme.

3. A Case Study

It is difficult to find well-documented case studies of successful attacks on fiscal corruption, perhaps because there may not be many successful cases. Although it remains to be fully documented, Ghana provides an interesting case of a country that suffered badly from widespread fiscal corruption, but eventually took effective steps to contain it, at least for a while. From the mid-1960s up to the early 1980s, Ghana's economy underwent a sustained decline, owing to adverse terms of trade, and domestic policies that became increasingly more interventionist. During this period there was widespread recourse to price and income controls, comprehensive regulations, and an elaborate licensing system, which had the effect of driving much of the economy underground.[8] This, of course, contributed to a decline in taxable capacity.

(a) Growth in Corruption

Initially, attempts to recoup revenue relied largely on raising tax rates. This stimulated a further erosion of tax bases, however, and the revenue response was inadequate. As indicated in Table 2, by 1983 the tax ratio had progressively collapsed to 4.5% of GDP from around 13% in 1973, and even higher in earlier years. To supplement the dwindling resources of the state, a variety of quasi-fiscal measures, which implicitly tax some in favor of others, were also introduced. In the main, these took the form of multiple exchange rates, foreign exchange rationing, negative real interest rates, and credit rationing, with state controlled agencies and favored individuals being the principal beneficiaries. Political and bureaucratic discretion were relied upon in applying the quasi-fiscal measures. Such conditions stimulated rent seeking which expanded to the point where the productive economy collapsed. Eventually, de-

---

[8]See Chand (1993).

Table 2. Ghana: Fiscal Collapse and Recovery (Ratios to GDP)[a]

	1973[b]	1976[b]	1983	1988	1994
Total revenue and grants	15.0	9.1	5.6	14.6	23.4
Tax revenue	12.8	8.1	4.6	12.3	17.0
Direct taxes	2.8	1.7	1.0	3.9	3.4
Taxes on domestic goods and services	2.8	2.7	0.9	3.7	8.0
Taxes on international trade	7.2	3.5	2.7	4.8	5.6
Total expenditure and net lending	19.1	14.5	8.2	14.3	21.0
Current expenditure	14.6	8.9	7.4	10.6	16.1
Capital expenditure	3.2	2.4	0.6	2.8	4.1
Overall deficit	–4.1	–5.4	–2.7	0.4	2.5

Sources: Statistical Service of Ghana; and Fund staff estimates.
[a] Refers to Central Government.
[b] Refers to fiscal year on a July/June basis. From 1983 onward, the fiscal year was converted to a calendar year basis.

clining state resources forced a curtailment of expenditures, and deep cuts were made in the salaries of civil servants, and in essential infrastructure and social outlays. These moves contributed to a series of major breakdowns that affected critical areas such as telecommunications, energy generation, the transport network, and ports, thereby hampering exports and economic growth. The resulting supply shortages were made worse by droughts and the severe rationing of foreign exchange in the face of export collapse, growing external debt arrears, and exclusion from the international capital markets.[9]

The pronounced and persistent decline in revenue was associated with a tax and customs administration that became increasingly disorganized. This manifested itself in several ways including the haphazard storage of taxpayer files, which were in any case poorly organized; desultory examination of returns; the mixing up of assessment and collection functions in the hands of the same officers; and the virtual cessation of properly conducted audits. Such practices of course made it

---

[9] Even external donor support dwindled. As Roe and Schneider (1992, p. 15) note ". . . the disenchantment of the aid community with Ghana's economic policies in general, its reputation for poor management and corruption, and its extremely poor record in honoring debt commitments . . . ruled out any prospect that external grants and loans could compensate for the collapse of tax revenues."

easier for taxpayers to evade taxes and for corrupt tax officers to collect rents.[10] At the same time, the tax system became riddled with all sorts of devices that were used by fiscal officers to supplement their incomes. A prominent instrument was the use of tax clearance certificates (TCCs). These were required for a wide and growing range of transactions, for example, acquiring trading licenses, a passport, and so forth. The fiscal officer enjoyed considerable discretion in granting TCCs and, according to all accounts, exploited the opportunity to extract bribes.

Both anecdotal accounts and the charges subsequently leveled by the future President Rawlings pointed to widespread corruption at all levels, and most damaging, at higher levels. This is likely to have contributed to widespread demoralization of the tax and customs service, which is no doubt reflected in the poor revenue performance. Civil servants, who had been among the most highly paid in the country, had by 1983 experienced a real erosion in their salaries to one-sixth of what they had been in earlier times. At the same time, because of the loss of job opportunities elsewhere in the economy, employment in the public service increased sharply, further preempting the scope for restoring real wages. Aside from suffering from badly eroded emoluments, what would be the point of applying extra effort to uncover tax evasion if collusion between the taxpayer and higher-level officials would deny the fruits of one's labor?[11]

(b) The Reform

The takeover by the Rawlings regime at end 1981, on an anti-corruption platform, was the start of a far-reaching reform of the economy. At first, in an attempt to contain corruption and to raise revenue, extreme measures were taken. Some officers were charged with corrup-

---

[10] Indeed, anecdotal accounts referred to the tax system as one of more or less voluntary payments of tax, where the amount to be paid bore little relation to the true tax liability but was the outcome of a self-serving bargain between the taxpayer and the tax collector.

[11] According to Roe and Schneider (1992, p. 49) "The respect and influence accorded to the civil service was substantially damaged by the corruption of the later Nkrumah years . . . and chronically impaired by the heightened corruption and mismanagement presided over by the governments of most of the 1970s. . . . extremely tiny differentials of less than 2:1 between the salaries of top civil servants and unskilled workers was guaranteed to make the recruitment and retention of skilled and committed professionals extremely difficult . . . . the failure . . . to match the costs of rising consumption needs inevitably prompted absenteeism, moonlighting, corruption and woefully poor morale."

tion and were executed; untrained revolutionary cadres were assigned to identify potential taxpayers and to collect taxes (in the so-called operation tax harvest); general exhortations to pay taxes were made; and sanctions were threatened in the event of nonpayment. An ominous sounding "National Investigations Committee (NIC)" paralleled by another body called the "Office of Revenue Commissioners (ORC)" were set up to enforce fiscal obligations, if necessary through arrest and seizure. But, these measures appeared to have had only temporary effects. A frightened population or terrified tax officers may turn in more revenue for a time. But, if the incentive structure that concerns taxpayers and tax collectors is not reformed, and reinforced by appropriate organizational and procedural changes, revenue will subside. The likelihood for such an outcome increases when tax collectors are paid well below subsistence levels, and the population remains harassed and subject to very high compliance costs.

What can be done to improve the fiscal situation in a sustainable manner and, in particular, the revenue position? Three essential elements that concern the structure of incentives are involved: first, tax bases need to be coaxed back from the underground; second, taxpayers must be induced to pay taxes; and, third, tax officers must be motivated to collect them. A piecemeal solution involving only one or other of the preceding elements may not work. Thus simply improving the motivation of tax officers, but not reforming a tax system that had become, at least on paper, punitive because of the high rates, could wreak havoc on the private sector. They would now be subject to the full brunt of the higher tax rates, and no doubt would redouble their efforts at evasion. On the other hand, not doing anything to improve the effectiveness of tax administration but merely lowering tax rates may not increase revenue.[12]

The failure of the initial, piecemeal, attempts at reform led the Rawlings Government, late in 1984, to initiate an integrated approach that was pursued over several years involving all of the three requirements mentioned above. Actions had already been taken in the context of the reform program to reduce key distortions such as the overvalued exchange rate, and its concomitant of rationing, which encouraged tax

---

[12]A finding of the model set out earlier is instructive in this regard. Although lower tax rates reduce the costs of complying which would raise revenue, they may also reduce the diligence with which tax officers undertake their work. The supply-side contention that lower tax rates increase revenue needs to be qualified.

bases to emerge from the underground. These were supplemented by the staged lowering in tax rates to more reasonable levels, for example, the top marginal rate of tax on income was reduced in steps from 55% (65% on personal income) to 25%. The large number of excise duties were reduced and merged into a revamped manufacturer's sales tax at substantially lower rates. The tax mix was changed in favor of indirect taxes on domestic production and consumption. In particular, reliance on the harder to evade excise duties on gasoline products was increased sharply. Generally, taxes were simplified and steps taken to document them better so as to render them more transparent. There was more effective enforcement of withholding and the application of presumptive methods, while the use of TCCs was circumscribed.

A central element of the strategy, which was vigorously pursued from 1985 onward, was to reorganize the revenue service and, *inter alia*, restrain the exercise of discretionary powers by tax officers. Considerable emphasis was placed on improving the conditions of service of tax and customs officers. Owing to the legal restrictions imposed by civil service rules, their pay could not be raised without parallel increases for the rest of the civil service. But a general pay increase could not be provided because of the lack of fiscal resources. Part of the solution that could be adopted to break this version of the chicken and egg problem would be to introduce a bonus scheme. But, this could not be granted to each tax officer without providing similar bonuses to other ministry of finance officials. More generally, the required restructuring of the revenue collection function could not be undertaken if the needed recruitment, training, promotion and salary policies differed significantly from those of the civil service. There was also the question of how to ensure that the revenue departments would have sufficient resources to procure the various inputs that would enable them to fulfill their functions. As long as the revenue departments were an integral part of the central government structure, they could not be exempt from any across-the-board cuts that were frequently applied to ensure compliance with overall expenditure targets in the context of adjustment programs.

It was therefore decided to move the two revenue departments—Customs, Excise and Preventive Service (CEPS) and the Internal Revenue Service (IRS)—out of the Ministry of Finance and Economic Planning (MFEP). A new authority, designated the National Revenue Service (NRS), was established to coordinate closely the work of the revenue agencies. The agencies were given considerable operational autonomy, with their own boards, and entrusted with the tasks of assessing and collecting revenue under the overall supervision of the National Revenue Secretariat (NRS). The latter, armed with the clear mandate of ". . . supervising the activities of the revenue institutions and recommending revenue policy directly to the government" (Terkper, 1994a, p. 1394), was headed by a minister of state of known integrity and drive.

An important aspect involved strengthening the surveillance functions of the NRS over the autonomous income tax and customs services, thereby making credible the minister's threat to keep an eye on the tax officers. A key measure was to weed out at the outset those officers who were regarded as irredeemably corrupt, and several officers left. Selective recruitment was initiated to replace incompetent and unmotivated staff. Facilities were also set up to enable the general public to complain about corrupt officers. Significant reforms were undertaken in the organizational structure and work procedures of the IRS and CEPS. These included better separation between different revenue functions such as assessment and collection; offices, whose work was organized more efficiently; examinations that were more assiduously conducted, and more frequent taxpayer audits.[13]

Two innovative schemes were introduced in 1986 for motivating staff and ensuring adequate resources for the revenue departments. The first, involved sizable, across-the-board, annual bonuses to tax and customs officers that would be paid if pre-set revenue targets for the two agencies were exceeded. The bonus rate is 15% of base pay, with a lower floor of 10%. The scheme is nondiscriminatory, applying to all full time employees, which is viewed as contributing to better morale and *esprit de corps*.[14] At the same time, it is compatible with using the regular pay scale and schedule for merit increases to reward superior performance of individual officers.

Second, and parallel with the bonus system, an incentive-based mechanism was employed for some years to provide resources to the

---

[13]More steps however, could have been taken. For example, Ghana still has to introduce a common taxpayers' identification number, which is essential for fully effective control.

[14]A disadvantage of this scheme is that once the revenue target is in sight the incentive to continue working hard may diminish. The disincentive effect can be avoided by setting the bonus as a percentage of the amount by which actual revenues exceed the target. But, the size of the bonus is then less assured. With wage costs of tax officers roughly 2% of total collections, a 15% annual bonus to be paid out of excess revenue would require annual revenue excesses of 10% if 3% of the excess were set aside for this purpose. Clearly, it would be difficult to ensure a 10% revenue excess each year.

revenue agencies to cover their routine operations. The two agencies were allowed to keep a small percentage of the revenue collected, to pay for both the bonus schemes. This procedure conferred the incentive that if they needed more resources they would aim at a higher level of collections. The proceeds could, at the discretion of the heads of the two tax departments, be used for the improvement of facilities.[15] The use of such funds was subjected to *ex post* auditing. This agency bonus system lasted until the end of 1992, by which time it was presumably felt that sufficient improvements in the conditions of service had occurred.[16]

(c) Some Outcomes

Table 2 shows that the results from pursuing the integrated reform strategy were highly favorable. Despite the major reductions in tax rates, the tax ratio rose sharply from 4.5% in 1983 to over 12% of GDP by 1988, reaching 17% by 1994.

It is difficult to disentangle the effects of the three elements mentioned above with respect to the reemergence of tax bases, improved tax compliance, and more effective administration. To some extent, the revenue increases reflect the success of the strategy implemented to reduce the size of the unofficial sector. Some part of the improvement must be attributed however, to the reform of the tax administration and its better motivated officers. This can be established by noting that simply bringing into the open the unofficial sector and subjecting it to taxation need not raise the tax ratio. While revenue will rise, the GDP denominator also increases. Furthermore, with an entrenched behavior of noncompliance, even if the increase in the taxable base is readily observable, for example, goods being brought out into the open for sale, it need not lead to increases in revenue. Ignoring for the moment tax administration, the tax ratio could rise if new taxes are introduced, or the tax system is rendered more progressive. But, the reforms involved reducing the nominal progressivity of the tax system. Furthermore, although there were significant increases in revenue from the introduction of the essentially

---

[15]See Terkper (1994a) for a more detailed description.

[16]Terkper (1994a), mentions additional reasons why this bonus scheme for supplementing departmental resources was discontinued, especially that the practice was never backed by legislation. Retaining part of revenue would violate the constitutional requirement that all revenue collected should be assigned to the consolidated fund.

new tax on petroleum products, losses were sustained from phasing out export duties. It must follow, therefore, that improvements in tax administration made a significant contribution to the observed rise in tax ratios. Doubtless, revamped administrative procedures is a positive factor, but in the end, surely, it is the superior, well-motivated, performance of the fiscal officer that makes the difference.

The revenue improvement enabled the government to increase sharply its outlays. Together with a policy of civil service retrenchment, major wage increases were granted to civil servants. This resulted in big improvements in average real emoluments and was accompanied by an incentive-oriented decompression of the salary scale. Aside from contributing to greater efficiency of the government machine, the revenue increases made possible higher maintenance, infrastructural, and social outlays, which had for long been neglected, and paved the way for the rehabilitation of the economy. On the whole, the expenditure increases were undertaken responsibly as is indicated by the reduction in the overall deficit and its eventual conversion into sizable surpluses.

The success of the Ghanaian experiment has been emulated in several countries both in Africa and elsewhere. For example, Uganda, drawing on technical assistance from the NRS, set up a comparable structure, which helped promote a superior revenue performance, as have Kenya and Malawi.

In 1991, the NRS, whose independence was apparently a source of bureaucratic friction with the Ministry of Finance, was effectively downgraded. It was brought under the direct control of the MFEP, with its head now reporting to one of the deputy ministers in the MFEP, instead of being headed as it had been by a full minister. The downgrading helps explain some of the difficulties that have since been experienced in coordinating and monitoring the work of the two revenue agencies. The autonomy of the two revenue agencies has increased relative to that of the emasculated NRS. There is reason to believe that bribery and corruption, which had abated considerably during the heyday of the NRS has become more pronounced. In particular, the performance of the CEPS has deteriorated.[17] With a view to restoring earlier levels of compliance, the creation of a central revenue board outside the MFEP is now planned. It is intended to confer sufficient powers on this

---

[17]Terkper (1994b, p. 633) notes that "the year (1993) ended with the minister (Dr. Botchwey) himself criticizing the customs administration before Parliament for a series of valuation malpractices . . ."

body so that it can once again effectively monitor and supervise the assessment, collection, and audit activities of the revenue agencies.

(d) Relationship with the Model

For a full empirical evaluation of the model, more information than was generated by the case study is required, for example, the size of the bribes for senior officials, the varying intensity of work effort and the conditions responsible, and so on. Nevertheless, there are some suggestive confirmations. A prediction of the model is that bonuses are more effective in stimulating revenue collection if corruption at the more senior levels is reduced. From its inception, and during its period of autonomy, the NRS exercised firm surveillance over the revenue agencies, and undertook active measures to reduce if not eliminate corruption especially at the higher levels. At the same time, the bonus schemes described above were introduced. It is suggestive that marked increases in the tax ratio should have occurred over this period. After 1991 however, during which the NRS was emasculated, the continued operation of the bonus scheme for emoluments (but not for departmental inputs) was not associated with a pronounced increase in tax ratios. Moreover, it appears that on occasion, the CEPS staff did not achieve the bonus, unlike the IRS. While deficiencies with both agencies were noted by the Minister of Finance, on balance, the CEPS appeared to be worse off.[18] Some confirmation is therefore provided of the model's prediction that a bonus scheme may lose effectiveness if management practices deteriorate.

4. Conclusion

The model set out above provides analytical support to the basic strategy that was pursued in Ghana to restrain corruption and to improve revenue performance. It brings out clearly the importance of attending, in an integrated manner, both to the conditions of service of

---

[18]Tettey (1997, p. 351) provides an interesting account of how computerization of customs operations, including the random selection of customs officers to handle transactions, failed to curb malfeasance, "... the reality is that large-scale corruption continues... An officer can arrange with a colleague, selected by the computer, to 'help' an importer circumvent the system... It is not uncommon to find... importers giving perquisites to officials with whom they may not be dealing in the present in the hope that their good turn will deserve another in the future."

fiscal officers and the organizational setup. Simply providing bonuses is not enough: corruption at higher levels of management has to be contained to allow bonuses to become more effective. The analysis of the model shows that once this process is initiated a virtuous circle can result that involves the progressive shrinkage of the gap between reported and true tax liabilities thereby reducing the incentive for corruption. Obviously, conclusions based on a single case study should be viewed with caution, but if they can be shown to accord with optimization behavior they gain in plausibility.

An extensive bonus scheme can be criticized as leading to an overly zealous tax collection authority. Such criticisms are appropriate when dealing with a country that has a settled, well-run tax system, decently paid tax officers, taxpayers who understand their obligations, proper accounting and reporting systems, and so on. But in a situation where tax officers are not paid a living wage and where the general climate is one of pervasive rent-seeking—unfortunately, a widespread condition in many transition and other developing countries—a less orthodox solution that has been successfully tried in some countries such as Ghana may be much more effective in the interim. Most fiscal officers, if properly trained, have a sense of professional pride and would not condone corruption. They become corrupt partly out of necessity or because of peer group pressure.

References

Allingham, M. and Sandmo, A. (1972) Income tax evasion: A theoretical analysis. *Journal of Public Economics* 1 (November), 323–338.

Andvig, J. C. and Moene, K. O. (1990) How corruption may corrupt. *Journal of Economic Behavior and Organization* 13 (January), 63–76.

Besley, T. and McLaren, J. (1993) Taxes and bribery: The role of wage incentives. *Economic Journal* 103 (January), 119–141.

Chand, S. K. (1993) From controls to sustainable liberalization: Ghanaian lessons. *In Transition to Market*, ed. V. Tanzi. International Monetary Fund, Washington, DC.

Flatters, F. and MacLeod, W. B. (1995) Administrative corruption and taxation. *International Tax and Public Finance* 2 (November), 397–417.

Haque, N. U. and Sahay, R. (1996) Do government wage cuts close budget deficits? Costs of corruption. *IMF Staff Papers* 43 (December), 754–778.

International Monetary Fund (1997) Governance guidance note. *IMF Survey*, August 5, 234–238.

Klitgaard, R. (1988) *Controlling Corruption*. University of California Press, Berkeley.

Mookherjee, D. and Png, I.P.L. (1995) Corruptible law enforcers: How should they be compensated? *Economic Journal* 105 (January), 145–159.

Roe, A. and Schneider, H. and Pyatt, G. (1992) *Adjustment and Equity in Ghana*. OECD Development Centre, Paris.

Rose-Ackerman, S. (1978) *Corruption: A Study in Political Economy*. Academic Press, New York.

Rose-Ackerman, S. (1997) Corruption and development. Paper presented at the *Annual Bank Conference on Development Economics*, Washington, DC, April.

Rubinstein, A. (1982) Perfect equilibrium in a bargaining model. *Econometrica* 50, 97–109.

Tanzi, V. (1998) Corruption around the world: Causes, consequences, scope, and cures. IMF Working Paper/98/63, International Monetary Fund, Washington, DC. [Revised version reproduced as Chapter 2 in this volume—ED.]

Tettey, W. J. (1997) Transforming tax administration in Ghana: The tension between computers and human agency. *Development Policy Review* 15, 339–356.

Terkper, S. E. (1994a) Ghana's tax administration reforms (1985–93). *Tax Notes International* May 23, 1393–1400.

Terkper, S. E. (1994b) Ghana's budget focuses on strengthening fiscal administration. *Tax Notes International* March 7, 633–637.

Van Rijckeghem, C. and Weder, B. S. (1997) Corruption and the rate of temptation: Do low wages in the civil service cause corruption? IMF Working Paper/97/73, International Monetary Fund, Washington, DC. [Revised version reproduced as Chapter 3 in this volume—ED.]

5

A Game Theoretic Analysis of Corruption in Bureaucracies

Era Dabla-Norris

I. Introduction

A fundamental role of the state lies in its provision of a legal order and in its ability to implement and enforce property rights and other formal rules in an economy, thereby enhancing economic activity.[1] However, individuals who make up the state apparatus often abuse this power to appropriate the surplus generated from private economic activity.[2] Governmental corruption can be viewed as one such abuse of authority.

Corruption by government officials encompasses a broad spectrum of abuses. They range from taking bribes while providing public goods such as licenses and permits to malfeasance in tax collection, corruption

---

[1]The formal rules governing the extraction of revenue, enforcement of contracts, and so on.

[2]The view of the state is nested in the neoclassical political economy's approach to the state as a self-interested actor (Bardhan, 1990, and Olson, 1991) that enforces property rights and contracts (North, 1990) but can take advantage of its monopoly power to engage in predatory behavior designed to extract revenue (Levi, 1988) or otherwise acquire rents (Srinivasan, 1985) from the population.

in the enforcement of commercial agreements, tax farming, and even outright expropriation. Examples of such practices abound in many developing countries (see Tanzi, Chapter 2 in this volume). The pervasiveness of governmental corruption in many developing countries today, however, does not imply that this phenomenon is confined to these countries. The sale of public offices and the use of tax farming in ancient Rome and in seventeenth century Europe are important historical instances of corruption in developed countries.

Casual empiricism and country studies suggest that corruption distorts the allocation of resources and discourages investment. Cross-country studies also find that the level of corruption is negatively associated with economic growth (see Mauro, 1995, and Keefer and Knack, 1997). It is easy to see how corruption discourages private sector activity, thereby constraining a state's capacity to tax its constituents. A more difficult question is why any self-interested, revenue-maximizing state, knowing the consequences, would permit widespread corruption among its agents? Casual observation suggests significant variation in the nature and degree of corruption both across countries and across time even for similar activities. For example, the level of corruption in many developed countries is much lower today than was the case historically. What accounts for this variation in the form and levels of corruption? A related question is why does the incidence of corruption vary across otherwise similar countries (e.g., between seventeenth century France and England) or regions within the same country?

Corruption in many developing and transition countries results from a combination of opportunities and incentives. Opportunities for abuse of power are prevalent in discretionary areas of government policy. For instance, complex tax and customs systems, capital controls and financial market regulation, wide-ranging regulations on the private sector, privatization decisions, and discretion over allocation of public expenditure can foster corruption.[3] Lack of transparency and of effective institutional controls are commonly viewed as the main factors contributing to corruption. Incentives to engage in corrupt behavior include lack of meritocratic recruitment and promotion in civil auditing, a general lack of transparency in government operations, and the absence of well-developed "civil society" institutions. Many of these

---

[3] See Tanzi (Chapter 2 in this volume) for a description of areas where opportunity for corruption may arise as a result of excessive government and regulation and discretion in the provision of goods and services in the economy.

factors are, in turn, closely associated with the level of development of an economy. For instance, eradication of corruption may be costlier in countries where the level of institutional development and the general economic environment is weak.[4]

This paper analyzes strategic interactions between opportunistic and self-interested agents at different levels of a government hierarchy in a two-stage game.[5] The general approach is to examine the behavior of these agents and its effect on the underlying level of real economic activity in order to characterize conditions under which governmental corruption can occur as an equilibrium phenomenon. The game we set up is extremely simple: there are three types of agents—a central authority or dictator, deputies, and private agents. The actions of the dictator and deputies influence private sector allocations, in particular, the decisions of private agents to engage in productive or investment activity. Deputies are needed to provide an important service that affects market activity, which provides the tax base for the dictator.[6] The dictator supervises the deputies' activities through monitoring and by providing wage incentives, and has the ability to tax aggregate market activity.

Deputies are assumed to have some discretion in their job that they can misuse for private gain. The type of corruption envisaged here is the abuse of their power over public commerce to solicit bribes from private agents or otherwise expropriate market activity.[7] The dictator can make use of his regulatory powers over deputies (through his choice of monitoring effort and wage rates) and private economic activity (through his choice of tax policy) to independently create rents for himself. The actions of deputies are assumed to be costly to monitor, creating a standard agency problem. Finally, the sequencing of actions is as follows: the dictator first chooses his policy instruments,

---

[4]Dabla-Norris and Freeman (1999) develop a model of the interconnectedness of underdevelopment and corruption, in which pervasive corruption discourages market activity, thereby reducing the incentives to allocate resources for controlling corruption.

[5]The terms government hierarchy and state are used interchangeably in this paper.

[6]For instance, the provision of public goods such as licenses, permits, and import quotas to producers; the collection of duties on legal imports by customs inspectors; the settlement of disputes between private agents, and so on.

[7]This is akin to Shleifer and Vishny's (1993) notion of "public rent-seeking," which they define as a redistribution from the private sector to government bureaucrats who can influence private economic activity.

given which, individual deputies decide on their own actions and the optimal level of private sector activity is determined.

This relatively simple framework provides a rich set of predictions that fit the observed patterns of corruption and anticorruption policy in many countries. First, it shows that the self-interest of a central authority can induce the dictator to provide incentives to eliminate corruption at the lower level of the hierarchy.[8] Hence, corruption arises when the dictator chooses not to deter it. The analysis also provides a number of predictions about the determinants of corruption. In particular, we show that corruption is more likely to arise where supervision is ineffective, monitoring costs are high, wage incentives are costly, and the tax apparatus is weak. Many of these factors are more likely to exist in developing and transition economies. Therefore, as noted by Levi (1988), reductions from historically high levels of corruption in developed countries may reflect improvements over time in monitoring and supervision technologies or reductions in the costs of providing proper incentives.

Low public sector wages are frequently cited as an important cause of bureaucratic corruption in many developing countries.[9] This however begs the question of why the government sets salaries that are so low. Our model explains why the central authority may choose to allow corruption in a wide variety of situations. We show that if monitoring is ineffective and costly, central authorities may economize on the costs of providing efficiency wages by allowing corruption to take place. Further, we show that, under certain conditions, it may even be optimal for the dictator to sell the office of a deputy (tax farming), thereby recouping some of the illicit gains accruing to the deputies.[10]

The underlying idea is that by not rigorously enforcing rules or even encouraging corruption, the central authority offers its deputies "implicit contracts" with provisions that go well beyond the provisions of formal contracts. In particular, if the administrative costs of monitoring or providing wage incentives are substantial, this implicit

---

[8]This result is akin to Olson's (1991) idea that a self-interested ruler with an "encompassing" interest in the domain over which his coercive power is exercised can be led to act in ways that are consistent with those subject to that power.

[9]In a cross-country regression, van Rijckeghem and Weder (see Chapter 3) find that countries with poorly paid public officials tend toward greater corruption.

[10]See Wade (1984) for a description of the sale of offices associated with the right to allocate irrigation water in southern India.

part of the contract—that is, turning a blind eye to corrupt activities can be far more lucrative (in terms of revenue raised for the central authority) than the official part, and may be a part of a larger political spoils scheme.[11]

Finally, we show that in the presence of strategic complementarities, multiple equilibria may arise even if the central authority can set levels of bureaucratic monitoring and wages.[12] In particular, we show that with costly or ineffective monitoring, there can be two subgame perfect equilibrium in the game: one characterized with a high level of corruption and a low level of private sector activity; the other with a low level of governmental corruption and a high level of economic activity, as shown in Dabla-Norris and Freeman (1999) and Shleifer and Vishny (1993). This multiplicity of equilibria suggests that identically endowed economies can end up with very different outcomes.

This paper adds to the growing literature on corruption. Mookherjee and Png (1995), Besley and McLaren (1993), Banerjee (1997), and Acemoglu and Verdier (1998) develop models where corruption arises due to agency problems. Each of these papers, however, ignores the possibility of multiple equilibria in the presence of efficiency wages. More important, our paper differs from most of the literature in its level of generality. While other papers tell stories related to particular situations where corruption may arise, the present paper captures a wide variety of situations in which corruption can occur.

The remainder of the paper proceeds as follows. In Section II, we describe a general game in which each deputy acts independently of the other deputies in the hierarchy and characterize some important properties of its equilibrium set. In Section III, we extend this game to allow for strategic interactions among deputies and describe the general properties of a game in this environment. Section IV concludes.

---

[11]In her study of revenue in production in Republican Rome, Levi (1988) notes that high measurement, monitoring, and delegation costs were responsible for the rise of tax farming as a means of securing revenue for the state.

[12]In this context, strategic complementarity refers to the increasing profitability of engaging in corrupt acts when all others are acting in the same way. For example, an increase in the number of corrupt agents may raise the cost of an effective audit as in Lui (1986), thereby reducing the chance that each corrupt agent will be caught, or the severity of punishment upon detection may decline as more officials become corrupt, thus increasing the payoff from engaging in corruption.

II. Basic Game

Environment and Technology

In the analysis that follows, we assume that the size of the second tier of government hierarchy is fixed and equal to a continuum of measure one. We describe a game in which each deputy acts independently of the other deputies in the hierarchy. The decision variable of each deputy $i \in [0,1]$ is a level of corruption $c_i \in [0,1]$, where $c_i = 0$ denotes perfect honesty. Let $x \in [0,1]$ denote the level of private sector activity in the economy.[13] Let $w \in \mathbb{R}$ denote the wage received by each deputy i in the public sector, where $w < 0$ denotes a transfer from deputy j to the dictator. Finally, let e denote the enforcement effort chosen by the dictator to monitor a deputy, where, e, by assumption, affects all deputies identically. The preferences of deputy i are represented by a utility function V_i that depends on w, e, c_i, and x, where $V_i : \mathbb{R} \times [0,1] \times [0,1] \times [0,1] \to \mathbb{R}$. Let $\overline{V}$ denote the reservation utility of a deputy.

Assumption A1. *$V_i(c_i, x, e, w)$ is continuous in its arguments, increasing in w, x, e. $\forall x$, w there exists an $e^0 > 0$ such that V is increasing for c_i for $e \leq e^0$ and V is decreasing in c_i for $e > e^0$.*

The first part of Assumption A1 states that the utility from being a deputy is increasing in the wage rate received in the public sector and in the level of private economic activity. The latter condition captures the idea that the payoff to a deputy is increasing in the level of economic activity under his control. The assumption that $V(\cdot)$ is decreasing in e implies that a higher level of monitoring effort reduces the utility obtained by a deputy. To see this, suppose that, for all $c_i > 0$, each deputy faced a probability of apprehension that was increasing in the dictator's monitoring effort. Then, this condition would hold if the expected utility to a deputy when apprehended was lower than his expected utility from not being apprehended (say, because he is fired). The last condition implies that there is a positive level of monitoring effort above which a deputy's utility is decreasing in his level of corruption.[14] In terms of our earlier example, this would be the case if, for

---

[13]If we interpret economic activity to denote aggregate investment in the economy, then x can be regarded as the aggregate of investment decision. Alternatively, x can be regarded as the aggregate decision whether or not to engage in productive market activity.

[14]Note that this assumption is satisfied by expected utility maximization.

all $e > 0$, the probability of apprehension faced by a deputy was increasing in his level of corruption; and the greater the dictator's monitoring effort, an increase in c_i caused a greater increase in the probability with which a deputy is apprehended.

Notationally, a deputy's best response is

Definition 1.

$$c_i^*(x, w, e) \in \arg\max_{c_i \in [0,1]} V_i(c_i, x, e, w).$$

Given that $c \in [0,1]$, Assumption A1 implies that, for all x and w, a deputy's best response is to be honest if $e > e^0$ and to be corrupt if $e < e^0$. Formally,

$c_i^* = 1$ for $e \geq e^0$

$c_i^* \in 1$ for $e = e^0$

$c_i^* = 1$ for $e < e^0$.

A deputy's best response correspondence is, therefore, discontinuous at $e = e^0(x, w)$. This discontinuity implies that a deputy is indifferent between corruption and honesty at that level of enforcement. We make the following assumption about $e^0(x,w)$.

Assumption A2. *$e^0(x, w)$ is continuous in its arguments, nondecreasing in x, and nonincreasing in w.*

The assumption that $e^0(w, e)$ is nondecreasing in x captures the idea that a deputy's incentive to be corrupt is increasing in the amount of private sector activity he can appropriate for himself, either in the form of higher bribes or outright expropriation. The level of monitoring effort for which a deputy chooses perfect honesty is therefore (weakly) increasing in the level of economic activity. Similarly, the assumption that e^0 is nonincreasing in w implies that there is a trade-off between the wage rate offered in the public sector and the level of monitoring effort required to ensure honesty at the lower tier. The intuition is that a higher public sector wage also deters corruption by raising the opportunity cost of losing one's job when corruption is detected and punished, thus inducing the deputy to be less corrupt. The level of private sector activity in the economy is represented by a reduced form function $x(c, \tau) \in X = [0,1]$. The function $x : [0,1] \times [0,1] \to [0,1]$ relates the level of economic activity to the average level of corruption c in the economy, where $c = \int_{i=0}^{1} c_i d_i$ and the tax rate, $\tau \in [0,1]$, set by the dictator.[15] Note that the return on economic activity is a function of the average level of corruption in the economy, c, and not the level of corruption of any given deputy, c_i. Given that all deputies are assumed to be identical, however, the average level of corruption in the economy is identical to the level of corruption of any given deputy. Let x_i^* denote the optimal level of private sector economic activity. We make the following assumptions about x_i^*:

Assumption A3. *$x_i^*(c, \tau)$ is continuously differentiable in its arguments and decreasing in c and τ.*

Assumption A3 implies that a higher tax rate and a higher average level of corruption in the economy both result in a lower level of economic activity. The assumption that high tax rates have a disincentive effect on market activity is fairly standard. In our analysis, however, bureaucratic corruption is also assumed to discourage economic activity. The idea is that, as in the case of taxation, economic activity is reduced through a decline in the expected return on investment or productive activity due to a higher threat of expropriation.[16] Finally, the dictator's decision variables are the vector of policy instruments (w, e, τ). Let $U(w, e, \tau, x)$ denote the utility function of the dictator. The function $U : \mathbb{R} \times [0,1] \times [0,1] \times [0,1] \times [0,1] \to \mathbb{R}$ is assumed to satisfy the following properties:

Assumption A4. *$U(w, e, \tau, x)$ is continuously differentiable in its arguments, decreasing in w and e, and increasing in τ and x.*

The assumption that $U(\cdot)$ is decreasing in e and w implies that there are costs to the dictator of providing incentives for the deputies. For instance, if monitoring costs are increasing in effort, increases in e may translate into a lower level of utility for the dictator. Similarly, if the

---

[15]We are assuming that the dictator can precommit to a preannounced tax rate. The failure of a dictator who exercises sovereign power to irrevocably commit himself to a preannounced tax rate has been discussed elsewhere in the literature, See, for example, Grossman and Noh (1994).

[16]As discussed in Banerjee (1997) and Acemoglu and Verdier (1998), corruption can be thought of as deterring ex ante incentives to invest because ex post individuals do not reap the full benefits of such investment. This assumption is consistent with empirical findings on the links between bureaucratic corruption and investment. For instance, both Mauro (1995) and Keefer and Knack (1997) find that bureaucratic corruption is negatively correlated with private investment and growth.

number of deputies in the public sector is large, higher wages may reduce the dictator's utility by raising his total wage bill. In a general sense, therefore, this assumption captures the idea that prevention of corruption is costly. Finally, the assumption that the dictator's utility is increasing in τ and x reflects the idea that his tax revenues are increasing in his tax rate and in the level of economic activity. Note that this specification of the dictator's utility function implicitly assumes that "lower tier" corruption only affects his utility indirectly through its effect on the level of private sector activity.[17]

To complete the specification of this game, we define $\bar{w}$ as the reservation wage offered by the dictator.

Definition 2.

$$\tilde{w}(e, \tau, \bar{V}) \equiv \inf\{w : V(e, w, x^*, c^*) \geq \bar{V}, x^* = x^*(c^*, \tau), c^* = (x^*, e, w)\}.$$

The above definition implies that $\forall e, \tau, \bar{V}$, if $w \geq \tilde{w}(e, \tau, \bar{V})$, all deputies are at least as happy being deputies as pursuing outside options. The wage offered by the dictator, therefore, lies in the interval $[(\tilde{w}, \infty)$. Let $\Gamma(X, U, V_{i \in [0,1]})$ define a game in this environment. The equilibrium notion we use is that of a perfect equilibrium. We therefore assume that at each move, each agent chooses so as to maximize his utility and takes into account that in the subsequent moves everyone will choose so as to maximize his utility. An outcome that emerges from such a sequence of decisions is referred to as a Stackelberg perfect equilibrium. Formally, we define

Definition 3. A *Stackelberg perfect equilibrium* $\Gamma(X,U,V_{i\in[0,1]})$ *is a quintuple* $(e^*, w^*, \tau^*, c^*, w^*)$,

1. $x^* = x^*(c^*, \tau^*)$
2. $c^* = c^*(x^*, e^*, w^*)$
3. $(w^*, e^*, \tau^*) \in \arg\max_{w, e, r} U(w, e, \tau, x^*)$.

Theorem 1. *Under Assumptions A1–A4, $\Gamma(X,U,V_{i\in[0,1]})$ has an equilibrium.*

---

[17]This assumption does not restrict the ability of our model to explain how corruption propagates in the government hierarchy. We capture the recursive property of corruption by assuming that the dictator can extract rents from those below him in the hierarchy by setting $w < 0$.

Proof. Without loss of generality, one may assume that w is in a bounded interval $[\tilde{w}, W]$.[18] The dictator then chooses a vector of actions, $a = (w, e, \tau)$, from the dictator's compact set A $[\tilde{w}, W] \times [0,1] \times [0,1]$. The equilibria of this game correspond to solutions of the following maximization problem:

$$\max_{w,e,T} U(w, e, \tau, x^*)$$

subject to

$$x^* = x^*(c^*, \tau)$$

$$c^* = c^*(x^*, e, w).$$

The constraints define a closed nonempty subset of A. Given that U is continuous, a maximum exists.

Properties of Equilibrium

Let $E(\Gamma)$ denote the set of all equilibria of this game.[19] We now turn to the characterization of some properties of the equilibrium set, $E(\Gamma)$. The first result characterizes conditions on the dictator's optimum choice of policy instruments such that all deputies choose corruption or honesty, respectively. Define the vector of policy actions of the dictator for which each deputy's best response is to either be corrupt or perfectly honest as follows:

Definition 4.

$$B \equiv \{(w, e, \tau) : c^*(e, w, x^*) = 1, x^* = x^*(1, \tau), w \geq \tilde{w}\}$$

$$D \equiv \{(w, e, \tau) : c^*(e, w, x^*) = 0, x^* = x^*(0, \tau), w \geq \tilde{w}\}.$$

B and D define sets whose typical elements are a vector of policy actions such that deputies choose corruption or perfect honesty, respec-

---

[18]Although the dictator can, in principle, select any wage rate above $\tilde{w}$, there are wage rates so high that they cannot, under any circumstances, be optimal. Thus W can be regarded as the largest wage rate that satisfies the dictator's budget constraint.

[19]Note that there are only pure strategy equilibria in this game.

tively, and the participation constraints of deputies are satisfied. The following lemma provides us with conditions that the set of policy instruments chosen by the dictator must satisfy in an equilibrium with perfect honesty or corruption, respectively.

Lemma 1.

(1) There exists $(w, e, \tau) \in E(\Gamma)$ s.t. $c^* = 0$ iff $\sup_{b \in B} U(b) \geq \sup_{d \in D} U(d)$.

(2) There exists $(w, e, \tau) \in E(\Gamma)$ s.t. $c^* = 0$ iff $\sup_{b \in B} U(b) < \sup_{d \in D} U(d)$.

Proof. The proof follows from the definition of equilibrium (Definition 3) and the definition of the sets B and D (Definition 4). Lemma 1 states that the dictator's choice of policy instruments, for which perfect honesty or corruption, respectively, are the best responses, depends on the payoffs attainable to him from that set of policy actions relative to another. Perfect honesty at the lower level of the hierarchy therefore requires that the payoff to the dictator from choosing a policy mix that induces honesty exceed his payoff from any other policy alternative. An important implication of this result is that the self-interest of a dictator can induce him to adopt policies that ensure honesty at the lower levels of the government hierarchy. Moreover, in light of the assumption that economic activity is decreasing in lower level corruption (Assumption A3) and the assumption that the dictator's utility is increasing in the level of economic activity (Assumption A4), Lemma 1 suggests that a self-interested, opportunistic dictator can, in effect, act as if he has an equity stake in economic activity.

In general, however, the existence of this result depends on the responsiveness of economic activity to the level of corruption in the economy, monitoring costs, the effectiveness of monitoring effort in controlling lower level corruption, the administrative costs of providing wage incentives, and the efficiency of the tax apparatus. Intuitively, an equilibrium with perfect honesty is more likely to exist if economic activity is very responsive to corruption, the costs of providing monitoring and wage incentives are low, and economic activity is not very responsive to the dictator's choice of a tax rate.

In what follows, we characterize conditions under which the dictator chooses to monitor deputies. As discussed earlier, the best response of a deputy is to be honest $\forall e \geq e^0(x, w)$. By Assumption A4, $U(\cdot)$ is decreasing in e. From Assumption A1, e^0 can be regarded as the smallest level of monitoring effort of the dictator for which each deputy chooses to be perfectly honest, for all x and w. Note that the sequence of actions in this game implies that the dictator can commit to a level of monitoring before the deputies have an opportunity to act. Therefore, e^0 can be regarded as the minimum level of monitoring to which a dictator must precommit.[20] The following proposition characterizes the equilibrium precommitment of monitoring effort by the dictator.

Proposition 1.

(1) If $c^* = 0$ in equilibrium, then $e^* > 0$

(2) If $c^* = 1$ in equilibrium, then $e^* = 0$.

Proof. The proof follows from Assumption A1, the definition of equilibrium, and Definition 5. Condition (1) states that in an equilibrium with perfect honesty, the dictator commits a positive amount of monitoring effort to deter corruption. Condition (2) implies that an equilibrium with corruption arises if the dictator gives up on monitoring effort. To see this, suppose that the dictator chooses a level of monitoring such that there is a positive level of lower-tier corruption. From Assumption A1 and Definition 1, we know that the level of monitoring effort chosen by the dictator, e^* must be less than e^0. Given that for all $e < e^0$, $c^* = 1$ (from Assumption A1), the dictator is best off reducing monitoring effort to zero, since, by Assumption A4 monitoring is costly.

The intuitive argument behind Proposition 1 is clear: if corruption is not to be deterred, the dictator has no incentive in making a costly commitment. Hence, $e^0 = 0$. If corruption is deterred, the dictator is expending effort to control corruption with the monitoring effort necessary to deter corruption. Hence, the dictator sets $e^* = e^0 > 0$. In general, the existence of this result depends on monitoring costs, the effectiveness of monitoring effort in reducing corruption, and the responsiveness of economic activity to corruption. For example, if the dictator's utility is increasing in private sector activity, as is assumed in Assumption A4, he may precommit to a positive level of monitoring effort if a higher level of corruption in the economy reduces his total payoffs. Intuitively, an equilibrium with lower-level corruption and

---

[20]We can interpret e as the effort by the dictator to install legal infrastructure or auditing procedures in the hierarchy to deter lower-level corruption.

zero monitoring is more likely to exist when monitoring costs increase sharply in effort, the probability of apprehending corrupt deputies is sufficiently inelastic, and economic activity is not very responsive to bureaucratic corruption.

An important implication of Proposition 1 is that if corruption is not deterred, then for any given tax rate, τ, and reservation utility for a deputy, $\bar{V}$, the dictator is best off choosing the lowest wage that satisfies each deputy's participation constraint. Let w^0 define the smallest wage offered by the dictator if he precommits nothing, that is $e = 0$.

Definition 5.

$$w^0(\tau, \bar{V}) \equiv \inf\{w : V(0, w^*, c^*) \geq \bar{V}, x^* = x^*(c^*, \tau), c^* = c^*(x^*, 0, w)\}$$

The above condition implies that for $e = 0$ and $\forall \tau, \bar{V}, w^0 \geq \tilde{w}(0, \tau, \bar{V})$.

Corollary 1. *If $c^* = 1$ in equilibrium then $w^* = w^0$.*

This result follows directly from Lemma 2, Definition 6, and the assumption that the dictator's payoff is decreasing in the public sector wage (Assumption A4). The intuitive reasoning behind this result is clear. In the absence of monitoring, for all x and w, the economic activity is decreasing in the level of lower-tier corruption (Assumption A3), for any given τ, total revenues (τx) for the dictator fall. If the provision of public sector wages is costly, as is assumed in this game, the administrative cost of providing wage incentives may exceed tax revenues. As a result, in the absence of monitoring, the optimal strategy for the dictator will always be to choose the lowest wage rate that satisfies deputies' participation constraints.

One consequence of this result is that if deputies are not liquidity constrained, the dictator may extract some (and perhaps all) of the corrupt rents that accrue to deputies by setting a fixed fee for the office of a deputy (say, by setting $w^* < 0$, where $w^* \geq (0, \tau, \bar{V})$. Moreover, in the absence of effective monitoring, if the specific source of bureaucratic inefficiency is corruption by tax collectors, then selling the office of a tax collector may be a preferred regime from the point of view of tax revenues raised. Tax farming in this context refers to a situation where deputies bid for the rights to collect taxes, paying a specified sum before collection, and buying the right to pocket the surplus collected from taxpayers. The use of tax farming as a means to raise revenues, however, depends on the responsiveness of economic activity to bureaucratic corruption, since a higher level of taxation by rapacious bureaucrats may result in a lower aggregate level of revenues raised for the dictator.[21]

III. Strategic Complementarity Between Deputies

In this section, we analyze a game in which the optimal action of a deputy is an increasing function of the actions of other deputies in the hierarchy.[22] In particular, we make the assumption that the optimal level of corruption chosen by a deputy is an increasing function of the level of corruption chosen by other deputies in the public sector (so that the game exhibits strategic complementarity).[23] Introducing such strategic interactions between deputies allows us to capture a fundamental observation on corruption. The expected profitability of engaging in corrupt acts depends crucially on the behavior of others acting in the same way.

For deputy i, let $\bar{c} = \int_0^1 c_j dj$ denote the average level of corruption of all deputies other than i. The preferences of deputy i are flow represented by a function $V_i(c_i, \bar{c}, x, e, w)$, where the payoff to deputy i is assumed to be a function of the average level of corruption of other deputies in the economy. The literature on corruption emphasizes the external benefits inherent from engaging in corrupt activity. For example, it may become very costly to audit officials when a greater proportion of them become corrupt, or the expected probability of being punished when detected may decline with the general level of corruption in the civil service. We capture this observation using the following assumption.

Assumption A5. V_i *is continuously increasing in $\bar{c}$, for all other variables.*

---

[21]In general, the dictator's proclivity for regulating tax farming is likely to be related to his security of tenure. A government run by a succession of self-interested central authorities, with the short horizons inevitable given their insecurity of tenure, would have a greater propensity to engage in tax farming than a more stable government.

[22]The class of games that satisfy this property is called "supermodular" games. For an analysis of supermodular games, see Topkis (1978).

[23]The term "strategic complements" was introduced by Bulow, Geanakoplos, and Klemperer (1985) to refer to games in which the best-response functions of the players are upward sloping.

Assumption A5 captures the idea that an increase in the strategy of all but one deputy bestows an external benefit, or a positive externality, on the remaining agents.[24]

In Section II, we assumed that a deputy's payoff is decreasing in his level of corruption for a fixed level of monitoring effort, e^0 (Assumption A1). We now modify this assumption by making the enforcement effort targeted toward a given deputy be a function of the level of corruption of other deputies in the economy. Formally,

Assumption A6. *For a given $\hat{c}$, there exists $\tilde{e}(\hat{c})$ such that V_i is decreasing in c_i for $e > \tilde{e}(\hat{c})$ and increasing in c_i for $e < \tilde{e}$; further, $\tilde{e}(\cdot)$ is increasing in $\hat{c}$.*

This first part of Assumption A6 implies that for a given behavior $\hat{c}$ by other deputies, there is a level of monitoring effort $\tilde{e}(\hat{c})$ above which a deputy's utility is decreasing in his level of corruption. As in Section II, let $e = \tilde{e}$ denote the level of monitoring effort sufficient to eliminate corruption at the lower tier. Therefore, if the dictator chooses any level of monitoring e above $\tilde{e}$, the utility of deputy i is decreasing in his level of corruption, regardless of the behavior of other deputies in the economy. The assumption that $\tilde{e}$ is increasing in $\hat{c}$ captures the idea that the level of corruption chosen by deputy i is an increasing function of the behavior of other deputies in the economy.[25] As a result, for all x and w, a higher level of monitoring effort is required to eliminate corruption at the lower tier of the hierarchy.

Let $c_i^*(\hat{c}, x, w, e)$ denote the best response correspondence of each deputy i to given values of x, e, w, and $\hat{c}$. Note that unlike the game in Section II, deputies now take as given the behavior of other deputies in the hierarchy. The following example provides an illustration of Assumptions A5 and A6.

Example. Suppose all deputies are risk neutral and have utility functions that are linear in their wage and corrupt incomes. Assume there is a continuum of identical private agents in the economy. For

---

[24] In different terms, this assumption is equivalent to requiring that utility functions be continuously differentiable, with the partial derivative $\partial V_i / \partial \hat{c} > 0$.

[25] In general, we can characterize this condition in differential terms for the case of smooth utility functions with Euclidean domains by requiring that utility functions be twice continuously differentiable with the cross partial derivative $\partial^2 V / \partial c_i \partial \hat{c} \geq 0$. This condition implies that an increase in the level of corruption of all deputies j increases the marginal return to corruption for deputy i.

simplicity, suppose that each deputy interacts with a single producer (or investor). Let x denote the return from economic activity for each private agent under the control of a deputy. Each corrupt deputy, then, chooses the amount of economic activity under his control to appropriate for himself. Let $c_i x$ denote the corrupt income of each deputy i. Assume that each corrupt deputy i faces a probability of arrest that is a function $(1 - \phi(c_i, \hat{c}, e))$. For simplicity, assume that monitoring effort by the dictator is fixed, so that this variable can be suppressed as an argument in the apprehension function. Let $\phi_1 > 0$, $\phi_{11} > 0$, and $\phi_2 > 0$. Assume that a deputy who is apprehended receives a utility normalized to zero (say, because he is fired). The income of a deputy is therefore $(w + c_i x)$ with probability $1 - \phi(c_i, \hat{c})$ and zero with probability $\phi(c_i, \hat{c})$. These preferences, together with the probability of arrest function, generate deputy i's payoff function:

$$V_i(c_i, \hat{c}; x, w, e) = (1 - \phi(c_i, \hat{c}))[c_i x + w].$$

Since all agents are identical, we can replace $V_i(\cdot)$ with $V(\cdot)$. Note that $V_2(\cdot) = \phi_2[c_i x + w] > 0$ so that the model displays positive spillovers. Differentiating the payoff function with respect to c_i and $\hat{c}$ yields

$$V_{12} = \phi_2 x - \phi_{12}[c_i x + w].$$

A necessary and sufficient condition for strategic complementarity in this environment is that $\phi_{12} < 0$.[26] This example shows that the expected utility to a deputy i from corruption increases as more deputies in the hierarchy become corrupt (positive externality), and a higher level of corruption in the hierarchy increases the profitability of engaging in corrupt acts, so deputy i will increase c_i (strategic complementarity).

In this example, the strategic complementarity arises because the greater the average level of corruption in the economy, a given increase in c_i is assumed to decrease the probability with which a given deputy is apprehended.[27]

---

[26]Note that this is a necessary as well as sufficient condition because the deputy's utility function is assumed to be linear. For more general utility functions, additional restrictions may be required for increases in $\hat{c}$ to induce increases in c_i.

[27]Note that the strategic complementarity in the above example depends on the implicit assumption that corrupt deputies do not crowd out each other by competing for private

Let $\Gamma^* = \Gamma^*(X, U, V_{i\in[0,1]})$ define a game in this environment. The equilibrium notion we use is that of a subgame perfect Nash equilibrium. A subgame perfect Nash equilibrium can be defined as a behavior strategy combination of each agent such that the behavior strategy of each player is a best-response strategy against the behavior strategies of the other agents in every subgame. In this game, the subgame consists of the second-stage interaction between deputies given the policy actions taken by the dictator in the first stage of the game. Let $\Gamma_s(e)$ denote a subgame of this game, where the subgame depends on the level of monitoring chosen by the dictator in the first stage of the game for a given w and τ for a given e, if the vector $(c_i^*, \hat{c})_{i\in[0,1]}$ is to be a Nash equilibrium of $\Gamma_s(e)$, then for each i, if all deputies are choosing an action, it is in the interest of the remaining agent to choose c as well. Under relatively simple assumptions, the game only has symmetric Nash equilibria.

Assumption A7. *$\Gamma_s(e)$ has multiple symmetric Nash equilibria.*

In general, a necessary condition for multiple equilibria is upward-sloping reaction functions for agents, a condition that is satisfied by our assumption of strategic complementarity. In terms of our earlier example, let λ denote the slope of deputy i's reaction function.

$$\lambda = \frac{-V_{12}}{V_{11}} = \frac{-\phi_2 x - \phi_{12}[c_i x + w]}{\phi_{11}[c_i x + w] + 2\phi_1 x} > 0.$$

A necessary condition for multiplicity is that $\lambda > 1$.[28] Rearranging the above expression, we get

$$-(\phi_1 + \phi_2)x - (\phi_{11} + \phi_{12}[c_i x + w]) \geq 0$$

where

$$\phi_1 > 0; \phi_2 < 0; \phi_{11} > 0; \phi_{12} < 0.$$

---

sector activity. In reality, the return from corruption may actually fall if a higher level of corruption in the hierarchy implies a lower return per corrupt deputy. In the example above, we avoid this property of crowding out by assuming that each deputy interacts with a single producer or investor.

[28] A sufficient condition for multiple equilibria in this environment is that $\lambda > 1$.

In terms of the above example, multiple equilibria in corruption are, thus, more likely when the probability of being caught and punished is small, the apprehension function is not very concave with respect to the level of corruption of any given deputy, and when the probability of apprehension faced by a given deputy is sharply decreasing for a higher level of corruption in the economy.

Let $E(\Gamma_s(e))$ denote the symmetric Nash equilibria of the subgame $\Gamma_s(e)$. We now turn to the characterization of the equilibrium set of the whole game. Note that the sequence of actions in this game implies that the dictator can anticipate that there will be multiple Nash equilibria in the subgame. The dictator, therefore, knows the level of lower-tier corruption associated with any given level of monitoring effort. Let $\bar{c} = sup\{c^* : c^* \in E(\Gamma_s(e))\}$ and $\underline{c} = inf\{c^* : c^* \in E(\Gamma_s(e))\}$ denote the largest and smallest Nash equilibria, respectively. We now turn to the characterization of the equilibrium set of the whole game. First, note that the sequence of actions in this game implies that the dictator can anticipate that there will be multiple Nash equilibria in the subgame. The dictator, therefore, knows the level of lower-tier corruption associated with any given level of monitoring effort. Note that by Assumption A6, an increase in monitoring effort does not reduce lower-tier corruption to zero as long as e is less than $\tilde{e}$, the minimum level of monitoring effort for which each deputy chooses to be perfectly honest. Therefore, for any change in e such that $e \in (0, \tilde{e})$, the level of lower-tier corruption is unaffected.

In the low-corruption equilibrium, the level of monitoring effort chosen by the dictator does not have a significant effect on the level of lower-tier corruption. Given that the payoff attainable to a deputy from choosing a level of corruption $\underline{c}$ in the low-corruption equilibrium exceeds the payoff from any other alternative. An increase in monitoring effort decreases a deputy's payoff from corruption, but for any $\underline{c}$ close to zero, has no significant effect on the level of corruption at the lower level of the hierarchy. Given that $U(\cdot)$ is increasing in e, for all w and τ, in a low-corruption equilibrium the dictator, therefore, has an incentive to choose the lowest level of monitoring effort such that $c^* = \underline{c}$.

In the high-corruption equilibrium, the level of monitoring effort chosen by the dictator affects the level of lower-tier corruption. Increasing monitoring effort decreases a deputy's payoff from corruption for any given behavior of other deputies in the hierarchy, and thus decreases the level of corruption in the hierarchy. By Assumption A6, however, all x and w and $c^* = \bar{c}$, a sufficiently high level of monitoring effort is required to eliminate corruption at the lower tier of the hierarchy. If $U(\cdot)$ is sharply increasing in monitoring effort, in a high-corruption equilibrium, the dictator has an incentive to choose a level of monitoring effort such that $c^* = \bar{c}$.

Let $\underline{e}$ and $\bar{e}$ define the smallest and the largest level of monitoring effort of the dictator such that deputies choose a low or high level of corruption, respectively, for all w and τ.

Definition 6.

$$\underline{e} \equiv inf\{e : \forall(w, \tau), c^*(e, w, x^*) = \underline{c}, x^* = x^*(\tau, \underline{c})\}$$

$$\bar{e} \equiv sup\{e : \forall(w, \tau), c^*(e, w, x^*) = \bar{c}, x^* = x^*(\tau, \bar{c})\}.$$

The following lemma characterizes the equilibrium precommitment of monitoring effort by the dictator in the presence of the strategic complementarity between deputies.

Lemma 2.

(1) *If* $c^* = \underline{c}$ *in equilibrium, then* $e^* = \underline{e}$

(2) *If* $c^* = \bar{c}$ *in equilibrium, then* $e^* = \bar{e}$.

Proof. The proof follows from Assumption A6, the definition of a subgame perfect equilibrium and Definition 6.

Condition (1) states that if the economy is in a low-corruption equilibrium, the optimal level of monitoring effort chosen by the dictator must be sufficient to ensure that deputies choose a $\underline{c} \in E(\Gamma_s(e))$. Similarly, condition (2) states that if a high-corruption equilibrium obtains, the dictator must be choosing a level of monitoring effort such that $\bar{c} \in E(\Gamma_s(e))$. Note that in both instances, the dictator has to commit to a positive amount of monitoring effort. An important implication of this lemma is that the level of private sector activity in a low-corruption equilibrium will be higher than that in a high-corruption equilibrium. This implication follows directly from Assumption A3, which states that the level of private sector activity is decreasing in the level of corruption in the government.

In general, the set of equilibria for the entire game depends on the dictator's utility function U and a mapping $M : e \to E(\Gamma_s(e))$. Formally,

Definition 7. *A subgame perfect equilibrium for* $\Gamma^*(X, U, V_{i \in [0,1]})$ *is a quintuple* $(e^*, w^*, \tau^*, c^*, x^*)$ *and a mapping* $M : e \to M(e \in E[\Gamma_s(e)])$ *such that*

1. $x^* = x^*(c^*, \tau^*)$,

2. $c^* = c^*(x^*M(e), w^*)$,

3. $(w^*, e^*, \tau^*) \in \arg\max_{w,e,\tau} U(w, e, \tau, x^*)$.

The following observation states the main result of this section:

Observation 1. *Depending on $M(e)$ and $U(\cdot)$, $\Gamma^*(X, U, V_{i\in[0,1]})$ may have multiple Nash equilibria.*

This observation states that in the presence of the strategic complementarity between deputies, there may be multiple Nash equilibria in the whole game. This multiplicity of equilibria suggests that even with endogenous monitoring, identically endowed economies can end up in very different equilibria. One can have high corruption and a low level of private sector activity, while the other can have a low level of corruption in the government hierarchy and a high level of economic activity. Note, however, that if the dictator chooses a level of monitoring effort $e = \tilde{e}$, the game has a unique equilibrium with perfect honesty at the lower tier of the government hierarchy. Through sufficient monitoring effort, therefore, an economy can move from a high-corruption equilibrium to an equilibrium with no corruption.

The existence of an equilibrium with a perfectly honest lower tier, however, depends on whether the benefits of eradicating corruption exceed the costs. In general, if monitoring costs are sharply increasing in monitoring effort, the monitoring technology is inefficient, and the level of economic activity is not very responsive to lower-level corruption, then the optimal level of corruption in the economy will not be zero.

IV. Conclusion

This paper has attempted to explain the observable variation in the nature and level of corruption both across countries and across time by analyzing the strategic interactions between self-interested agents that compose the state. We have shown that the self-interested behavior of central authorities determines the optimal level of corruption in the hierarchy. Our analysis also highlights factors that could lead authorities to choose policy instruments that allow lower-tier corruption. In particular, we have shown that an equilibrium with corruption arises when a central authority chooses not to make a commitment to monitoring deputies.

This paper also provides an important implication about the relationship between monitoring and the provision of wage incentives. We have shown that in the presence of poor and ineffective monitoring, it may be optimal for a central authority to allow corrupt lower-tier activities as a means of economizing on the costs of providing wage incentives. A noteworthy implication of this result is that in economies with high levels of corruption, we may expect to observe low public sector wages coexisting with weak monitoring. This prediction is borne out by observations for many developing countries. Our analysis also brings out the factors that could lead central authorities to choose the sale of offices or tax farming as a form of agency.

The trade-off between the reduction in corruption and the higher fiscal costs of providing appropriate wage incentives is likely to be higher in developing and transition economies. More generally, large and bloated bureaucracies can substantially increase the cost of providing proper wage incentives. An important policy implication of these results is that to the extent that providing wage incentives is costly, this measure should be considered as part of general civil service reform effort, which involves a combination of civil service restructuring, increasing salaries, as well as measures to strengthen institutional controls. The latter include enforcing standards for ethical behavior, improvements in accounting and auditing practices, and transparent and well-defined rules, laws, and processes.

Finally, we have shown that in the presence of strategic interactions between deputies, even with endogenous monitoring, countries in very similar circumstances can end up with widely different outcomes. We show that only through sufficient monitoring can an economy move from a high-corruption equilibrium to a low-corruption one. From a policy perspective, the existence of two stable equilibria in corruption implies that ad hoc anticorruption campaigns have little effect on the level of corruption in an economy. For anticorruption policy to be effective, it must be sustained.

An added implication of this paper is that providing appropriate incentives to central authorities may ensure the existence of low-corruption equilibrium. For instance, a high-corruption equilibrium is characterized by a low level of private sector activity, thereby signifying low tax revenues for the central authority. If higher levels of economic activity push a self-interested authority to its most profitable equilibrium, it is more likely to adopt monitoring policies and wage incentives that reduce or even eliminate lower-tier corruption.

More important, an environment that promotes political competition and relates the probability of being reelected to the level of corruption in society can serve as important incentives for central authorities to adopt policies that control corruption and promote economic growth. Therefore, measures that eliminate discretionary elements of government policy, strengthen the rule of law, including setting up an independent and impartial judicial system, and enhance the transparency and accountability of government actions can serve as important deterrents to corruption.

References

Acemoglu, D., and T. Verdier, 1998, "Property Rights, Corruption and the Allocation of Talent: A General Equilibrium Approach," *Economic Journal*, Vol. 108 (September), pp. 1381–1403.

Andvig, J., and K. Moene, 1990, "How Corruption May Corrupt," *Journal of Economic Behavior and Organization*, Vol. 13 (January), pp. 63–76.

Banerjee, A.V., 1997, "A Theory of Misgovernance," *Quarterly Journal of Economics*, Vol. 112, pp. 1289–1332.

Bardhan, P., 1990, "Symposium on the State and Economic Development," *Journal of Economic Perspectives*, Vol. 4, No. 3 (Summer), pp. 3–7.

Besley, T., and J. McLaren, 1993, "Taxes and Bribery: The Role of Wage Incentives," *Economic Journal*, Vol. 103 (January), pp. 119–41.

Bulow, J., J. Geanakoplos, and P. Klemperer, 1985, "Multimarket Oligopoly: Strategic Substitutes and Complements," *Journal of Political Economy*, Vol. 93 (June), pp. 488–511.

Cadot, O., 1987, "Corruption as a Gamble," *Journal of Public Economics*, Vol. 33 (July), pp. 223–44.

Carillo, J.D., 1995, "Grafts, Bribes, and the Practice of Corruption" (unpublished; Toulouse: GREMAQ).

Dabla-Norris E., and S. Freeman, 1999, "The Enforcement of Property Rights and Underdevelopment," IMF Working Paper 99/127 (Washington: International Monetary Fund).

Evans, P., 1989, "Predatory, Developmental, and Other Apparatuses: A Comparative Political Economy Perspective on the Third World State," *Sociological Forum*, Vol. 4 (December), pp. 561–87.

Freeman, S., J. Grogger, and J. Sonstelie, 1996, "The Spatial Concentration of Crime," *Journal of Urban Economics*, Vol. 40 (September), pp. 216–31.

Gibbons, R.G., 1992, *Game Theory for Applied Economists* (Princeton: Princeton University Press).

Gould, D. J., 1980, *Bureaucratic Corruption and Underdevelopment in the Third World: The Case of Zaire* (New York: Pergamon Press).

———, and J.A. Amaro-Reyes, 1983, "The Effects of Corruption on Administrative Performance: Illustrations from Developing Countries," World Bank Staff Working Paper 580 (Washington: World Bank).

Grossman, H.I., and S.J. Noh, 1994, "Proprietary Public Finance and Economic Welfare," *Journal of Public Economics*, Vol. 53 (February), pp. 187–204.

Keefer, P., and S. Knack, 1997, "Why Don't Poor Countries Catch Up? A Cross-National Test of an Institutional Explanation," *Economic Inquiry*, Vol. 35 (July), pp. 590–602.

Klitgaard, R., 1988, *Controlling Corruption* (Berkeley: University of California Press).

Krueger, A.O., 1974, "The Political Economy of the Rent-Seeking Society," *American Economic Review*, Vol. 64 (June), pp. 291–303.

Levi, M., 1988, *Of Rule and Revenue* (Berkeley: University of California Press).

Lui, F. 1986, "A Dynamic Model of Corruption Deterrence," *Journal of Public Economics*, Vol. 31 (November), pp. 215–36.

Mauro, P., 1995, "Corruption and Growth," *Quarterly Journal of Economics*, Vol. 110 (August), pp. 681–712.

Mookherjee, D., and I.P.L. Png, 1995, "Corruptible Law Enforcers: How Should They Be Compensated?" *Economic Journal*, Vol. 105 (January), pp. 145–59.

Murphy, K, A. Shleifer, and R. Vishny, 1993, "Why Is Rent-Seeking So Costly to Growth?" *American Economic Review, Papers and Proceedings*, Vol. 83 (May), pp. 409–14.

North, D.C., 1990, *Institutions, Institutional Change and Economic Performance* (Cambridge, England: Cambridge University Press).

Olson, M., 1991, "Autocracy, Democracy, and Prosperity," in *Strategy and Choice,* ed. by Richard J. Zeckhauser (Cambridge, Massachusetts: MIT Press).

Rauch, J.E., 1995, "Choosing a Dictator: Bureaucracy and Welfare in Less Developed Polities," NBER Working Paper No. 5196 (Cambridge, Massachusetts: National Bureau of Economic Research).

Rose-Ackerman, S., 1978, *Corruption: A Study in Political Economy* (New York: Academic Press).

Shleifer, A., and R. Vishny, 1993, "Corruption," *Quarterly Journal of Economics,* Vol. 108 (August), pp. 599–617.

Srinivasan, T.N., 1985, "Neoclassical Political Economy, the State and Economic Development," *Asian Development Review*, Vol. 3 (No. 2), pp. 38–58.

Tirole J., 1993, *A Theory of Collective Reputations with Applications to the Persistence of Corruption and to Firm Quality* (unpublished; Toulouse: Institut d'Economie Industrielle).

Topkis, D., 1978, "Minimizing a Supermodular Function on a Lattice," *Operations Research*, Vol. 26, pp. 305–21.

Wade, R., 1984, "Market for Public Office: Why the Indian State Is Not Better at Development," Institute of Development Studies Discussion Paper No. 194 (Brighton: University of Sussex).

6

Institutionalized Corruption and the Kleptocratic State

Joshua Charap and Christian Harm

Introduction

Corruption and governance are increasingly popular topics for analysis. In contrast to the mainstream discussion of corruption,[1] we propose that patterns of corruption must be analysed in their political context because corruption is endogenous to the political process. Drawing from the literature on the economics of conflict and appropriation, the economics of organized crime, and the political economy of dictatorships, we derive the endogenous genesis of the *"kleptocratic state"*

Reprinted from *Institutions, Contracts and Organizations: Perspectives from New Institutional Economics*, edited by Claude Ménard, published by Edward Elgar Publishing Ltd., pp. 188–208.

The authors would like to thank Adnan Mazarei for helpful comments on a previous version of this chapter. The views expressed are those of the authors and do not necessarily represent those of the institutions with which they are affiliated. All remaining errors are their own.

[1]For example, see Shleifer and Vishny (1993), Bardhan (1997), or Elliott (1997).

from a state of pure anarchy.[2] Warlords and their collaborators emerge as successful adaptations to the game of anarchy and they seek to usurp one another in a quest for hegemonic rule.

In our view, however, the internal organization of predatory teams is inadequately explained in the literature, which affects the understanding of the optimal span of control of dictatorship. As a partial answer to the problem of internal cohesion of predatory teams, we offer the explanation that corrupt offices are created to satisfy a leader's desire to foster loyalty through patronage. The predatory hierarchy, established in order to extract rents from the economy, is based on a system of low civil service wages, which mandate corrupt activity and serve to reinforce the system of rent extraction to the ultimate benefit of the ruler. Thus, we suggest that corruption is endogenous to the political regime and predatory activity on the part of low-level bureaucrats must be judged in its political context since different political regimes generate different patterns of corruption.

Our analysis builds upon the insights summarized by Bardhan (1997) in two important respects. First, Bardhan asserts that theories of the kleptocratic state cannot determine whether the corruption patterns that arise in an economy would be competitive or monopolistic. By contrast, we endogenize corruption patterns within a model of political structures, which allows us to predict under which regimes competitive or monopolistic corruption patterns are likely to be encountered. Second, our analysis can be extended to explain political corruption—which Bardhan omitted from his survey—as rent-seeking behavior of the polity in democratic rather than dictatorial regimes.

In our view, the endogenization of corruption patterns to the political structure marks an important step in the evolution of research on corruption. The early—apologetic—literature on corruption sought to make arguments in favor of corrupt behavior under the premise that it increased economic efficiency.[3] More recent research by a variety of authors has documented the ill effects of corrupt activity on economic growth.[4] Nevertheless, corruption is largely viewed as a decentralized and coincidental phenomenon. Instead, we posit that corruption should

---

[2]Elsewhere in the literature, this has long been claimed by Mancur Olson, for example in Olson (1993).

[3]For example, see Leff (1964) and Huntington (1968).

[4]For example, see Kaufmann (1997) or Mauro (1995, 1997).

be considered as systemic and deliberate: it is the natural result of efficient predatory behavior in a lawless world.

The chapter is organized as follows. The next section reviews the current literature on conflict, appropriation and dictatorship to conclude that the internal organization of predatory teams remains insufficiently discussed. The third section describes how gangs can emerge as superior adaptations to the game of anarchy and establishes conditions that determine optimal gang size and the optimal size of the territory controlled by the gang. The fourth section presents our arguments that predatory hierarchies are an organizational innovation that increases the span of control of warlords and that nations evolve via the quest of warlords for hegemony. The fifth section links our insights with respect to predatory hierarchies to existing research on organized crime and corruption and we posit that corrupt bureaucracies are an application of our concept of predatory hierarchies. The final section concludes and provides views on the applicability of our theories to public sector reform.

Production, Predation and Dictatorship

This section summarizes the economic literature on conflict and appropriation in a variety of settings. With few exceptions, unquestioned acceptance of property rights in the "state of law" has dictated the course of economic inquiry.[5] However, the universal acceptance of the concept of property rights leads much of the analysis to overlook instances of legal failure.

In the economics literature, Becker's (1968) seminal inquiry into the economics of crime and punishment offers an explicit recognition of the incentives for individuals to redistribute rather than produce. Tullock (1974, 1980) was among the first to analyse rent-seeking activities in totalitarian societies within the economic paradigm.

More generally, Hirshleifer (1987, ch. 6) distinguishes a hierarchy of theories: "constitutional economics," which models systems with functional property rights; "constitutional politics," which allows for redistribution by the polity within the confines of democratically legitimized

---

[5]Hirshleifer (1987, ch. 8) quotes Rousseau's *Discourse on the Origin of Inequality*: "The first man who, having enclosed a piece of ground, bethought himself of saying: 'This is mine,' and found people simple enough to believe him, was the real founder of civil society."

constitutions; and "non-constitutional politics," which analyses social interactions guided solely by the laws of nature.[6] Hirshleifer (1996) describes an economy in the absence of law and property rights. In an environment of abundance, where it is not necessary to safeguard territory or supplies, Hirshleifer labels social organization as "amorphy."

Accordingly, if resources are not abundant and investment and stock keeping can increase utility, a lawless environment (Hirshleifer's non-constitutional politics) provides the opportunity for an individual to satisfy consumption demands via *predation* rather than production. This is the premise of the first set of models to be reviewed here.

Combat and Appropriation

We begin by discussing simple models wherein two individuals allocate their time among production, predation and defense, and time acts as a resource constraint. These models specify a production and a combat technology, and agents maximize utility derived from consumption.

First, consider the case where the two individuals have *equal endowments*. In equilibrium, the players commit equal resources to production and military activities. A crucial variable in the models is the decisiveness of combat. Hirshleifer (1996) shows that, as the decisiveness of combat increases,[7] more time is allocated to military activity and social output decreases due to the resource constraint. Skaperdas (1992) shows that in cases of very low combat decisiveness, a cooperative outcome with no combat and maximal production is feasible.

Second, if the players have *unequal endowments*, the decisiveness of combat technology determines the nature of the resulting equilibrium. Under low combat decisiveness, individuals with low resource endowments invest more in combat technology and relative income distribution shifts in favor of the poor.[8] On the other hand, high combat decisiveness under unequal endowments may lead to the poor acquiescing completely, investing only in production. Hirshleifer (1996) calls this "hierarchy," while Skaperdas labels it "an equilibrium of semi-cooperation." We treat it here as an economic description of subjugation.

---

[6] In the absence of a functioning legal framework, Coase is replaced by Machiavelli.
[7] Small changes in relative combat technology have great consequences for the likely outcome.
[8] Hirshleifer (1991b) labels this the "paradox of power."

Lastly, Hirshleifer (1996) examines the impact of increasing the number of players in the simple game of anarchy. Holding combat decisiveness constant, an increase in the number of players increases each player's allocation to combat rather than production, and thus decreases per capita social output. If the population becomes excessively large, it may disintegrate into amorphy if that equilibrium satisfies the individuals' viability constraint. Otherwise, a Hobbesian "each against all" would ensue until the population has shrunk to a sustainable level.

Dictatorship and Kleptocracy

The "kleptocratic state" exists to maximize the welfare of its ruler.[9] In Grossman's (1991) "A general equilibrium model of insurrections," peasants allocate their time among production, soldiering for the elite, or insurrection activities, while the ruler taxes farmers, and hires soldiers against insurrection at a wage rate that is a decision variable. Hence, the ruler's taxation and soldiering decisions have to find equilibrium with the peasant's decisions on how to allocate time between the competing activities. This model focusses on the relative merits of peasants' insurrection technology versus the ruler's defense through soldiering. If the combat technology is favorable to the ruler, he may, in the extreme, lower the tax rate and hire a sufficient number of soldiers to eliminate insurrection activity completely. If the combat technology shifts against the ruler, the discount rate he applies to future consumption increases, leading him to increase the tax rate, albeit at the loss of total taxation revenues and decreased social welfare because greater effort is allocated to combat.

There are important parallels between Grossman's model and the anarchy models introduced above, particularly Hirshleifer's concepts of the "paradox of power" and "hierarchy." Grossman's model is somewhat richer, in that combat outcome is not a "winner-take-all-contest," but the dictator has the discretion to set the tax rate, which allows him to affect peasants' military activity. Nevertheless, Grossman's results

---

[9]Herschel Grossman (1995a, p. 143) quotes Edwin Mills: "Until two or three hundred years ago, it was characteristic almost anywhere—and to this day, it is characteristic in the majority of countries and in countries containing the majority of the world's population—that the primary government activity was and is extraction of surpluses from the predominantly agricultural population and use of such surplus, to benefit tiny groups of people in and near the government." Later, he quotes Robert Claiborne: "The distinction between robber and cop, between extortion and taxation, has been blurred at many times in history."

mirror those of the two-player anarchy game with unequal endowments: a weak dictator finds himself more often threatened by insurrection, output is reduced, but the peasants' share in total output is relatively increased. Due to a combination of military strength and low tax rates, a strong dictator finds no opposition, output is increased, and the resulting equilibrium can be interpreted as a "humane" form of subjugation due to the lower tax rate.[10]

This section has contrasted models of two-player anarchy games with dictatorial equilibria to examine their similarities. Grossman's model could be considered as a refinement of a two-player game between one dictator and one peasant. Models of dictatorship have remained silent on the issue of how the dictator avoids a "palace revolution" in an environment of anarchy since government is considered a monolithic institution concerned with survival and taxation. We assert that existing theories of dictatorship do not model social aggregation adequately.

Predatory Teams

In the economics literature, one of the less understood aspects of social organization is the natural emergence of predatory teams and social contracts.[11] The rudimentary structure provided by mafias has been analysed in the sense that they not only produce output of "criminal goods," but they also define and police the behavior of their members. For example, Skaperdas and Syropoulos (1995) describe the rudimentary constitutional role of predatory teams and liken them to "primitive states."

---

[10]Usher (1989) combines several of the arguments above into a theory of dynastic cycles. In his model, peasants can be either farmers or bandits who steal from farmers. The ruler taxes farmers and tries to hunt down and kill bandits in order to protect his tax base. This dictatorial equilibrium is superior to an anarchic world until population growth motivates the ruler to turn to banditry, since he can no longer expend sufficient resources on policing bandits. This causes a reversal to anarchy when the tax base can no longer satisfy the consumption demand of the ruler. Under anarchy, the population shrinks to sustainable levels, and a new dynasty may develop. The dynasty can achieve a steady state, however, if the population remains sufficiently small and all members of society are better off under despotism rather than anarchy. The shrinking of the population after the dynasty disintegrates into anarchy mirrors Hirshleifer's (1996) result of anarchy being unable to sustain more than a particular number of individuals in the economy. Due to the superior efficiency of the despotic rather than the anarchic regime, the breakup of the dynasty is followed by population reduction.

[11]See Skogh and Stuart (1982) for an early attempt to explain the endogenous genesis of social contracts under anarchy in an economic framework.

One explanation for the emergence of gangs is that they represent an efficiency adaptation to the game of anarchy itself. Usher (1989) speculates that economies of scale in combat technology imply that the group as a whole is stronger than the sum of its individuals, and the individual possessing the most powerful combat technology may assume the position of leader. However, the ambitions of team members to become leaders themselves may upset this fragile equilibrium. Hirshleifer (1996) maintains that powerful groups have (by some yet-to-be-understood mechanism) solved the problem of anarchy within their structure, but anarchy continues between rival groups.[12]

Because of the absence in the literature of models of the internal cohesion of predatory teams in lawless systems, the forces determining the optimal size of predatory teams are not well explained.[13] Our contribution to that literature begins by considering the case where there are economies of scale in combat technology. A gang consisting of a few people is stronger than the same number of individuals and the gang will be more likely to achieve an equilibrium of subjugation with neighboring individuals. But how are the gains from predation shared among gang members? Three questions arise: the determination of gang leadership; the optimal size of the gang; and the optimal span of territorial control.

Gang Leadership and the Palace Revolution

One possible answer to the question of gang leadership[14] is that the individual with the best combat technology will be the leader. This is

---

[12]Skaperdas and Syropoulos (1995) argue that team cohesion can be maintained in an infinitely repeated game where reputation overrides the prisoner's dilemma outcome of the one-period Nash equilibrium.

[13]Polo (1995) addresses the internal organization of gangs as an agency problem between gang leadership and soldiers. The model explains the hegemonic rule of a gang in a geographically concise area, with different gangs controlling different areas. Yet, it lacks an important step in the analysis, as there is an assumed *ex ante* asymmetry between principal and agent: the agent can never usurp the principal. Thus, the model presupposes an existing gang, and analyses its relationship to "the marginal agent." Findlay (1996) also examines "the limits of empire" in a relevant context, but fails to explain the source of diminishing returns to territory.

[14]As Radner (1992) shows, the economics of leadership and management is still insufficiently understood. Thus, we do not claim to capture the full richness of the determinants of leadership, but maintain that the analysis of leadership under anarchy adds an important dimension to the discussion.

an inadequate explanation, however, since leadership is the skill demonstrated in *organizing* combat activity. While the first element is a "supply-side" argument in that the leader establishes his role by force, the second element is a "demand-side" consideration since gang members want the most skilled person in charge. This demand element is an important consideration when analysing the potential for a palace revolution.

One way to envisage group formation is that the winner of a combat situation does not subjugate the loser, but offers integration to fight under his command in the future. The *leader* is the person organizing gang warfare. For simplicity, we assume that in combat situations decisions are made by order of the leader, since consensus weakens the timeliness of the gang's combat skills and autonomous decision making is inconsistent with the assumed economies of scale in combat technology. In determining leadership, we can treat individual combat technology and individual leadership skills in combat situations as exogenous, while the sharing rule of combat proceeds is endogenous.

The leader can be expected to obtain the largest relative share of predation gains because of his individual combat skills and the willingness of gang members to accept a smaller share of the gains in exchange for the presumed skills of the combat leader. In an environment of anarchy, however, each gang member has the incentive to contract out the largest share to the leader *ex ante*, and renegotiate and expropriate the leader *ex post*. This is the problem of the palace revolution.[15]

Accordingly, it is necessary but not sufficient for the leader to have high individual combat skills, since gang members could prefer a weaker leader with better management skills. In any case, the leader would be expected to obtain the largest share from predatory activity for himself, while ensuring that gang members are sufficiently well rewarded to be induced to be part of a gang. In light of the incentive of every gang member to renegotiate *ex post*, the question for the leader is how to avoid a palace revolution by a potential challenger. The probability of a palace revolution is a function of the surplus share extracted by the leader.

If the leader has high combat skills, the probability of success for an individual gang member trying to overthrow the leader is small. Therefore, the challenger must find an ally who is convinced that his future

---

[15] The game is understood as a repeated game where players have incomplete information about other players' combat and management skills.

share from predatory activity under new leadership is larger than his present share and is prepared to face the risks inherent in combat. Because of uncertainty, *ceteris paribus*, gang members will prefer the status quo in leadership. Given the *ex ante* preference for the status quo, however, the approach to another gang member with a plan to topple the incumbent is risky. The potential ally knows that the initiator of the overthrow may seek an alternative collaborator in his place if he declines to participate. Thus, if the potential ally in the overthrow declines to participate, his rational response will be to try to avert the overthrow actively. Since the initiator of the revolt understands these considerations, the likelihood of revolt initiation is reduced.

Optimal Team Size

Consider the case of a gang of three members including the leader. The initiator of a revolt has only one potential ally. If the ally declines to participate, he knows that the initiator only has the choice to acquiesce, or to try to topple the leader by himself. If the former is more likely, the potential ally has no reason to inform the leader in order not to reduce the group size to two and lose economies of scale in combat technology due to downsizing of the group. If the latter is more likely, the group will downsize anyway, and the ally will choose his side depending on who he expects will win the contest, which is likely to be the incumbent.

Now consider a gang of four including the leader. A potential ally has to consider that in the case where he declines, the fourth person will be an ally in the revolt. There is thus an increased chance that a successful revolt will take place without him. This, in turn, will increase the likelihood that he will side with the leader immediately to avert the revolt, since *ceteris paribus* the initial preference favors the status quo. Given the individual combat skills and combat management skills of the leader, and given the leader's optimal sharing rule of proceeds from predatory activity, the addition of a fourth gang member increases the incentives for self-monitoring. This, in turn, reduces the likelihood of a successful palace revolution. Accordingly, when gang size is small, the leader has an incentive to expand gang size in order both to increase economies of scale in combat technology, and to reduce the probability of a successful overthrow.

As the gang becomes ever larger, however, there are more individuals to aspire for the position of leadership. Even a strong leader can be toppled by a dissenting group of only a few people. And, in a very large group, even a potential ally to prevent a coup might join the revolt in order to preempt yet another group from staging the coup first. Thus, in a group that is large enough to host several rival teams aspiring to produce the new leader, the self-monitoring forces are diminished, and the probability of a revolt increases.

From this we conclude that optimal group size is thus a policy variable of the leader to balance an increase in the gang's strength against an increased likelihood of a palace revolution due to reduced self-monitoring activities at the margin. With this, we have a theory of social aggregation at the micro level arising from a condition of pure anarchy. We explain the endogenous genesis of a group with one layer of hierarchy: gang members and their leader.

Optimal Size of Terrain Controlled

In its immediate environment, the gang will attempt to achieve an equilibrium of subjugation with individual peasants, but these peasants have an incentive to create a gang of their own in order to escape the equilibrium of subjugation. The optimal size of territory controlled is a function of the optimal size of an individual gang. By definition, optimal gang size dictates how many individual peasants can be controlled in an equilibrium of subjugation while taking account of the risk of some peasants banding together in a peasant revolution. Ignoring competing gangs elsewhere, and given optimal gang size, the optimal size of the territory is determined by the gang balancing additional income from larger territory against the probability of a peasant revolution at the margin.

From Gang Warfare Towards Hegemony

Competing gangs are likely to vie for control over the peasantry. As Hirshleifer noted, with the problem of anarchy within gangs solved, anarchy between gangs will persist. While the results from the two-player anarchy equilibrium apply, we now add the feature that gangs try to protect "their" peasants from assaults by rival gangs.

Assume that two neighboring gangs enter into a combat situation and one gang wins. One option is that the victors force losing gang members into peasantry and subjugation. The winning gang also "takes over" the peasants previously controlled by the gang that lost in combat. Since optimal gang size is endogenous, however, and because optimal gang size determines the optimal size of the territory controlled, such subjugation of a rival gang increases the probability of a peasant revolution. That is, the territory under control now exceeds the optimum. Therefore, if gangs have established the optimal size of their territory, subjugation after inter-gang warfare is not efficient.

Predatory Hierarchies

A key contribution of this chapter is to argue that there are organizational solutions to expand the span of control of predatory teams beyond the endogenously determined size of the nucleus gang. Borrowing from Findlay (1996), we assert that integration of the rival gang is a meaningful alternative to complete subjugation. Our solution to the problem of integration, however, is different: the creation of multi-layered hierarchies in predatory teams. The gang that emerges as winner from gang warfare integrates the losing gang in an equilibrium of *subordination* rather than subjugation. This is accomplished by reducing the size of the losing gang below its optimum to render it weaker than the winning gang; allowing the losing gang to continue extracting rents from parts of its previous area of control so that losing gang members remain better off than peasants; and demanding that a fraction of the proceeds are passed up to the winning gang.[16]

Once such a two-layered hierarchy is recognized as an organizational solution to the problem of the optimal span of control of a predatory leader, the central gang can manage several such subordinated units in order to exploit forces of self-monitoring analogous to those that were at work in the nucleus gang. At least to some extent, the subordinated gangs monitor one another so that the probability of an uprising is limited,

This devolution of power to the "second in line" may be an appropriate description of the aristocracy under the king in England after Magna Carta. The king needs to relinquish a sufficient share of his in-

---

[16]Such equilibrium is then stabilized by the provision of hostages as described by Williamson (1983). In the absence of legal enforcement, the provision of hostages is the only possible way to ensure that "contractual" obligations are met. One way to implement such an equilibrium would be to have the losing gang pay its dues *ex ante* to make it economically inevitable that the losing gang still enforces an equilibrium of subjugation with the peasants it controls, rather than hiring them as new gang members to regain strength.

come to make self-policing of the aristocracy succeed to the point that no one lord can usurp the king. The surplus of extortion proceeds for the aristocracy over and above the wage rate of peasants determines self-monitoring activity within the aristocracy.

This logic can be extended to multilayered hierarchies. The necessary conditions for a multilayered hierarchy to be sustainable are that each layer must be strictly better off than the next-lower level; the central institution at each layer must be stronger than each individual group at the next-lower level; each layer manages an optimal number of subordinate groups so that the probability of a revolt is minimized due to self-monitoring; and even the lowest-level group within the hierarchy is strictly better off than the peasantry.[17]

In a probabilistic sense, the individuals at each layer of the hierarchy expect to be worse off in combat with a rival structure, thereby strengthening the internal cohesion of the hierarchy. That is, the hierarchy itself is stronger than the sum of the individual gang parts. This rent-extraction hierarchy is therefore an organizational innovation expanding the limits of empire. Once we understand the limits of empire, we assert that nations may have developed as the hegemonic results of gang warfare and represent the optimal span of control of warlords.[18]

The question that remains to be addressed is whether nations so-defined can achieve some stability in the anarchic equilibrium with their neighbors. For this we have to make another assumption: the geographic landscape features spaces that either favor offensive or defensive military technology. An area encircled by a stretch of land favoring defensive military technology will then define the limits of empire. A hegemonic hierarchy arises within the controlled territory as a result of gang warfare, while its borders produce the anarchic equilibrium of cooperation between neighbors due to poor combat technology as defined by Skaperdas (1992). This is synonymous with "peaceful coexistence."

---

[17]The provision of hostages, as discussed below, can help to ensure that the rents extracted from the peasantry are passed upstream.

[18]Baumol (1995, p. 84), speculates that a fruitful approach to research would be to: "Interpret most governments in human history as gangster associations," and he maintains that "Governments concerned with the welfare of the governed and constrained by rule of law from arbitrary and violent measures are the rare exception in human history, perhaps most realistically interpreted as a curious aberration of a very recent period in rather limited portions of our planet."

Toward an Evolution of Political Structures

An important question remains unanswered, however: "How would a dictator in peaceful coexistence with his neighbors maximize income by sponsoring economic growth?."[19] A fundamental problem in the equilibrium of pure subjugation is that the peasantry lacks incentives to invest in entrepreneurial talent, since the dictator cannot commit not to renegotiate the tax rate *ex post*. This is a key feature in the model by Grossman and Noh (1994). The ruler is not able to commit to a tax rate below a certain threshold, which leads peasants to restrict production to a level compatible with the minimum credible tax rate. This minimum credible tax rate, in turn, is a function of the stability of the dictatorship. Secure dictators can commit to a lower tax rate and thus become more benevolent. The model allows for a poverty trap in the case of stronger insurrection technology, but a move toward a state of law in the case of weaker insurrection technology and stronger dictators.[20] Thus, it opens the way for the evolution to more modern societies.

Finally, Grossman (1995b) motivates the endogenous development of the welfare state in an environment of redistributive activities. If wage income in an economy is small versus property income, the property class has an incentive to redistribute wealth to wage earners in a "Robin Hood" equilibrium in order to preempt predatory redistributive efforts of the wage earners. This model does not explicitly mention dictators, but can be interpreted in that vein. It mirrors the dictator's incentive to reduce taxes if his seat is relatively secure.

Rent Seeking in the Kleptocratic State: Monopolization and Corruption

This section seeks to draw parallels between corrupt bureaucracies and the predatory hierarchies discussed above. In our view, corrupt bureaucracies are an extension of the logic of predatory hierarchies,

---

[19]Some analysis of this issue can be found in Usher (1989), who assumes that peasants can be either farmers or bandits (who steal from farmers), while rulers tax farmers and hunt bandits. Thus, even a predatory dictator would install a system of law and order to increase his tax base.

[20]With regard to the equilibrium of a "poverty trap," Colombatto and Macey (1998) argue that the dictator may seek to retard growth in order to prevent an evolution of income distribution that would be unfavorable to his interests.

which in turn are an efficient organizational adaptation for mafias and dictators alike. In particular, we describe how corrupt bureaucracies are an efficient form of rent extraction for the dictator, especially when compared to other forms of tax administration. Low civil service wages underpin loyalty to the dictator and reduce the probability of a palace revolution.

Monopolies and Cartels in the Business Process

First, we consider the problem of revenue mobilization faced by a dictator seeking to maximize the proceeds from rent-seeking activity. The relevant literature typically considers rent extraction via a tax *rate*. To gain further insights, we assume transaction costs to be linked to the method of taxation. Consider an equilibrium in which a secure dictator is concerned with increasing the tax base while keeping taxes sufficiently low to curtail revolutionary activity. Economic theory tells us that to maximize the tax base the dictator should seek to maximize output, which is accomplished in a competitive and entrepreneurial environment with secured property rights. To the extent that tax collection entails fixed costs, however, it may be inefficient to tax a large number of firms and consumers. More importantly, if taxing consumer surplus is burdened by prohibitive transaction costs, and since the loss of consumer surplus is largely external to the dictator's maximization problem, in the limit the rational dictator's interests are interchangeable with those of a monopolist.[21] Accordingly, the monopolization of industries through close associates of the dictator (crony capitalism) is one example of an efficient form of a predatory hierarchy.

In the literature on organized crime, Gambetta and Reuter (1995) have extended this analysis beyond extracting rents from monopolies to argue that mafias have incentives to create cartels rather than monopolies. While the pecuniary proceeds can be identical, the mafia has a more favorable power balance versus smaller cartel members (as opposed to a large monopolist). Since individual cartel members benefit from mafia enforcement of the cartel, they can be regarded as "partners

---

[21]Bigsten and Moene (1996) document a tendency towards rent extraction from monopolies for the case of Kenya. Regarding organized crime, Fiorentini and Peltzman (1995b, p. 9) state: "In competitive markets . . . the high number of agents involved and the logic of competition do not allow for the collection of large rents from regulation net of its cost." Thus, similar to dictatorial regimes, the mafia prefers to extract rents from monopolies.

in crime." Hence, cartel members can be regarded as part of the mafia itself. Accordingly, gang leaders can be viewed as maximizing revenue by delegating the task of extortion to lower levels in the mafia hierarchy, and then collecting a share of the revenue from the decentralized units,[22] while maintaining a monopolistic hold over business processes. Thus, arguments from the organized crime literature support our reasoning, both as regards the method of taxation through vested monopolies as well as with respect to the stability of predatory teams.

Institutionalized Corruption

We have argued that the decentralization of extortionary activity involving partial devolution of power, as well as efficient extortion via cartelization or monopolization of productive activity, belong to the set of efficient strategies of mafias and dictators alike. We can now make the link to corrupt activities.

Corrupt Bureaucracy as a System of Patronage and Loyalty

Corrupt activities should be considered as rent-seeking activities associated with the predatory hierarchies discussed above. Thus, we consider corruption to be a systemic device for the ruler to extract rents from the populace while at the same time securing loyalty, which protects him from revolt. This is in contrast to the mainstream literature on corruption,[23] which defines corruption as an agency problem where lower-level bureaucrats pervert sensible rules.[24]

Corrupt bureaucracy can be viewed as an extension of the principle of efficient rent extraction via monopolies: the bureaucracy can be considered as a monopoly on the granting of licenses that permit private sector activity, rather than direct monopolization of the business

---

[22]Franzini (1995, p. 58) asked: "What is to prevent us from regarding the mafia as an organizational structure that protects mafia firms on the basis of the advantages it offers with respect to individual protection?"

[23]For example, see Shleifer and Vishny (1993), Bardhan (1997), or Elliott (1997).

[24]Support for our theory is provided by a quotation found in Bardhan's (1997, p. 1329) survey article: "As Ronald Wraith and Edgar Simpkins say of English history: 'For two hundred and fifty years before 1688, Englishmen had been killing each other to obtain power . . . The settlements of 1660 and 1688 inaugurated the Age of Reason, and substituted a system of patronage, bribery and corruption for the previous method of bloodletting.'" Centralized power was strengthened by patronage and tendencies towards anarchy were contained.

process. First, rents may be extracted more efficiently through the sale of a limited number of licenses, rather than vesting a monopoly over a particular sphere of economic activity. Second, endowing only a few bureaucrats with the power to grant licenses enables the diversion of the licensing proceeds away from the budget towards private gain. Since the dictator depends on lower levels of the bureaucracy for rent collection and is himself vulnerable to overthrow by insiders, the role of corruption is to implement an effective extraction and reward mechanism.

The corrupt bureaucracy can be seen as an extension of the logic defining the relationship between king and aristocracy. Under the Roman dictum of *divide et impera*, the corrupt bureaucracy represents the organizational form facilitating an increase in the optimal span of control of warlord or king, and thus an increase in the limits of empire. Corrupt bureaucracy *is* the predatory hierarchy defined in the previous section, in that it provides the optimal mechanism for rent extraction by a predatory ruler.

Also, corruption serves as a hostage mechanism to minimize the probability of defection or insurrection by lower-level insiders of the corrupt bureaucracy: they are effectively constrained—due to their own participation—from turning to the public to denounce the system. On the other hand, the dictator can, when necessary, find a reason why an uncooperative bureaucrat is found guilty of corruption. Corruption is both the carrot and the stick that strengthen loyalty.

A mechanism with which to implement a predatory hierarchy of corruption is to provide the public sector bureaucrat with wages below subsistence.[25] By accepting the contract, the bureaucrat has given himself to his superiors as a hostage in the sense of Williamson (1983).[26] The bureaucrat must exploit the corruption potential inherent in public office in order to make good on low official wages.[27] Superiors can ensure that most of the rents are passed upstream by threatening to dilute the relevant signature authority over the licensing monopoly. This is a

---

[25]Ul Haque and Sahay (1996) recognize the linkage between official wages and corruption: at some point, public sector revenues fall with falling public sector wages due to increased corruption.

[26]The arguments in favor of portraying low wages as a hostage mechanism are supported by anecdotal evidence from the developing world that some civil service positions in some countries are sold for the cash equivalent of several years' worth of wages.

[27]De Soto (1989) asserts that corruption-inducing regulation exists solely for the purpose of generating corruption revenues.

particularly effective method of enforcing subservience in that it lacks transparency or accountability.

In the point of view portrayed here, corruption is endogenous to a political system since the regime itself is predatory. Licensing monopolies maximize the dictator's income while allowing a decentralized organization of economic activity where appropriate. Low public sector wages serve as a commitment mechanism to ensure that rents are passed upstream, while the probability of a palace revolution is contained. This is in contrast to other arguments about the causes of corruption, which portray the phenomenon as exogenous to the government that fostered such a system.

Corruption in Different Political Systems

Once corruption is treated as endogenous to the political system of predatory dictatorship, we must address the issue of how corruption changes in changing political conditions.[28] This requires further clarification of the term "corruption." After all, the bandit stealing the farmer's crop would hardly be labeled a corrupt individual. Yet, he performs the same predatory act as the corrupt bureaucrat holding hostage applicants to his services. The only difference is that the applicant to the government service may presume a legality to the regulation in question.

We posit that corruption is a term that was developed to symbolize deviation from "morally right" or "legitimate" behavior, and that government regulation and legislation—for sometimes ill-defined reasons—has come to be considered "legitimate." Our analysis now turns to adaptations of internal organization to rent seeking in different political contexts. Since predatory hierarchies are only stable in a probabilistic sense, Machiavellian politics is still feasible, and the time path of actual regimes oscillates among strong dictatorships, dictators subject to a likely overthrow, and possibly anarchy. In addition, benevolent monarchs and democracies constitute feasible paths of political development. Corruption patterns are determined by the mode of rent extraction associated with the respective political systems.

Under anarchy, predation typically takes place in a decentralized setting. Hence, there are few issues of corruption in its classical meaning. As the number of warlords in the economy decreases, and warlord or-

---

[28]Similarly, Johnston (1997) has provided a classification scheme of analysing corruption in different political regimes.

ganizations evolve to resemble the institutions of organized crime, rent-seeking activities would still be labeled extortionary rather than corrupt. We argued above that despotic systems are less damaging to general economic welfare than anarchic ones—hence it is unsurprising that seemingly more corrupt systems may have better growth performance than seemingly less corrupt but more openly extortionary systems.

Predatory hierarchies associated with weak and contested dictatorship can be expected to be poorly organized precisely because the dictatorship is weak and contested. The weakness stems from a lack of allies due to an insufficiently developed system of patronage. And the system lacks coordination in extortion by low-level bureaucrats due to an insufficiently developed internal organization of predation. There are possible contenders to the ruler's authority, which have varying degrees of autonomy over their own territory, some of whom are able to impose extortionary taxes outside the ruler's control. Shleifer and Vishny (1993) describe this mechanism of weakly coordinated predatory activity as a system of decentralized corruption, which is the most damaging to economic activity since bribe payers are ultimately faced with higher extortion rates. In turn, this reduces economic activity and leads to lower total corruption proceeds. We assert that this pattern is motivated by the political equilibrium of weak and contested dictatorship.

On the other hand, strong predatory rulers have successfully developed a patronage system for their defense, and therefore corruption is correspondingly well developed. The political economy of predatory dictatorships implies that economic performance is better than in anarchic or contested systems. This is a system that Shleifer and Vishny (ibid.) and Bardhan (1997) would classify as monopolistic corruption: users of government services are charged only once at specified rates. The system is sufficiently developed to credibly commit *ex ante* to bribery rates in the sense of Grossman and Noh's (1994) tax rates. Shleifer and Vishny (1993) show that monopolistic corruption is less detrimental to economic performance than decentralized corruption. Against the benchmark of contested dictatorship, bribery rates go down, but total bribery proceeds go up.

The alternative view of corruption that prevails in the literature, namely that corruption represents an agency problem of sensible government rules being abused by corrupt bureaucrats—as defined by Shleifer and Vishny (ibid.)—becomes relevant as the process of political development progresses further down the path toward democracy. At some point, the predatory dictator receives more legitimacy (job security) from benevolence, rather than loyalty through patronage. Over time, an extortionary bureaucracy may outlive its usefulness and become a hindrance to the changing objectives of the increasingly benevolent ruler. With changing government objectives, previously desirable behavior within an extortionary hierarchy becomes "corrupt." In other words, corruption is a term that wrongly legitimizes all government action, and confusion as to efficiency consequences springs from there.

A weak democracy typically features meaningful constitutional protection of the citizenry against government-sponsored rent seeking for private gain, but nonetheless has weak political institutions. In this case, political rent seeking may take on the form of what Bardhan (1997) labels "political corruption": the use of corruption proceeds to maximize re-election chances, rather than the pursuit of rents solely for private consumption.

The culminating point of political development may be found in modern-day democracies, which have actively combated the old structures of patronage in exchange for democratically legitimized systems of law. Predatory behavior of the polity expresses itself through maximizing re-election chances by securing funding from interest groups in society. As compared to the benchmark of political corruption, interest group rent seeking represents a constitutionally legitimized form of predatory political activity. The previous discussion is summarized in Table 1.

This table complements Table 2 in Johnston (1997, p. 71) in that the Johnston allocation of corruption patterns to various regimes is consistent with our theoretical analysis. In addition, we wish to postulate the existence of an evolutionary time line with regard to the regimes identified in Table 1. While we have argued the case for the development from anarchy towards stable dictatorship, Grossman and Noh (1994) have suggested a path towards a benevolent monarchy. Grossman (1995b) develops arguments towards the evolution of the welfare state, but the genesis of democracies is still an unsolved mystery within this paradigm. Our main contribution is to relate various corruption patterns to different politically motivated rent-seeking regimes.[29]

---

[29] One unanswered question in this literature is why contested dictatorships impose higher taxes, while the threat of a contested election leads politicians in democracies to improve the level of public services to their constituents. Our answer would be that the modern state has evolved to the point where rent seeking for private gain under dictatorship is supplanted by the rent seeking of legitimized interest groups through the democratic process.

Table 1. Rent-Seeking Patterns and Political Regimes

Political Regime	Rent-Seeking Pattern
Anarchy	"Each against all"
Warlordism/Weak dictatorship	Competitive corruption
Strong dictatorship	Monopolistic corruption
Benevolent monarchy	"True" corruption
Weak democracy	Political corruption
Functioning democracy	Interest-group rent seeking

Corruption: A Misnomer

The confusion surrounding the term corruption stems from modern societies that have come to take political legitimacy for granted and liberally transposes the term to societies based on wholly different objectives and structures. The above analysis has argued that once corruption is viewed as a predatory activity that symbolizes a precondition to stable dictatorship, the very term "corruption" is misleading, since it has to be examined in the context of a particular political system. Accordingly, published corruption statistics based on subjective perceptions of individuals (for example, business people from developed nations) probably confuse corruption with other, similar, predatory activity, and therefore, empirical studies will continue to suffer from shortcomings surrounding ambiguities of the concept of corruption.[30]

The more apologetic literature on corruption assumes governmental legitimacy as a matter of course. Accordingly, much of that literature describes the ill effects of corruption versus the benchmark of mature economies. But the very means of facilitating economic growth in benevolent dictatorships or stable democracies may not be useful in preventing predatory dictatorship from descending into anarchy.

Discussion and Conclusion

The key contribution of this chapter to the literature is to sketch a process of social aggregation at the micro level in an environment of

---

[30]Mauro (1995, 1997), who established an empirical link between nations' corruption and growth performance, acknowledged a potential endogeneity bias caused by survey respondents commingling traditional corruption activities with other extortionary activities and a country's growth record.

pure anarchy. Warlords (mafias) and dictators emerge endogenously as efficiency adaptations to the game of anarchy. Efficient rent-seeking patterns seek to balance positive income effects against negative outcomes as defined by dictator or warlord. We have argued that predatory hierarchies satisfy such characteristics. Judged against the background of the literature on economic organization,[31] predatory hierarchies offer an additional perspective into the genesis of organizations.

We have argued that dictators favor taxation via monopolies due to the administrative cost of taxing consumer surplus. The creation of monopolistic firms (crony capitalism) is a rational strategy whereby the dictator can maximize expected income. Alternatively, corrupt bureaucracies endowed with licensing privileges constitute an organizationally efficient form of rent extraction.

Thus, we have linked the literature on kleptocratic regimes to the literature on corruption, and we have argued that many activities typically defined as "corruption" are in effect predatory in nature. This chapter has described "corruption" as an organizational solution to the expansionary intent of warlords and dictators alike. When analysed in the light of rent-seeking dictatorship, "corruption" is systemic rather than coincidental.

The effects of corruption are evident.[32] The fundamental question, however, is whether the problem is corruption or politics. That is, what would be the impact on the political structure in a particular country if anti-corruption efforts were to be pursued independently of their environment? Can corruption be rooted out without a change toward a legitimate political process? If the arguments in this chapter are correct, elimination of corruption in some instances could lead to anarchy rather than efficiency since it destabilizes predatory dictatorship and hastens the path towards internal revolt.

Civil service reform or demonopolization of industry are particularly interesting issues because we posit that, in some countries, the true objective of the bureaucracy is the extraction of rents and the channeling of a share of those rents to the top of the hierarchy. If this supposition is correct, failures of efforts at reform might, in some instances, be explained through the logic of predatory kleptocracy. When reforms are consistent with a ruler's evolution toward benevolence,

---

[31]For example, Coase (1937) and Williamson (1985).

[32]For example, see Krueger (1974), Keefer and Knack (1997), Kaufmann (1997), Tanzi and Davoodi (1997), or Tanzi (1998).

they serve to reinforce a virtuous process. For example, comprehensive reform of civil administration comes to fruition when a ruler gains more stability from benevolence rather than patronage. On the other hand, when reforms would threaten the survival of the regime, they may be systematically rejected, or—in the worst case—lead the country on to a path back towards anarchy.

References

Anderson, Anneliese (1995), "Organized crime, mafia and governments," in Fiorentini and Peltzman (eds) (1995a) pp. 33–53.

Bardhan, Pranab (1997), "Corruption and development: a review of the issues," *Journal of Economic Literature*, 35, 1320–46.

Baumol, William J. (1995), "Comment on Skaperdas and Syropoulos," in Fiorentini and Peltzman (eds) (1995a) pp. 83–86.

Becker, G. S. (1968), "Crime and punishment: an economic approach," *Journal of Political Economy*, 76, 217–24.

Bigsten, Arne and Karl Ove Moene (1996), "Growth and rent-dissipation: the case of Kenya," *Journal of African Economies*, 5 (2), 177–98.

Coase, Ronald H. (1937), "The nature of the firm," *Economica*, N.S., 386–405.

Colombatto, Enrico and Jonathan Macey (1998), "Information and transaction costs as the determinants of tolerable growth levels," mimeo.

De Soto, Hernando (1989), *The Other Path*, New York: Harper & Row.

Elliott, Kimberley Ann (ed) (1997), *Corruption and the Global Economy*, Washington, DC: Institute for International Economics, June.

Findlay, Robert (1996), "Towards a model of territorial expansion and the limits of empire," in Garfinkel and Skaperdas (eds), pp. 41–56.

Fiorentini, Gianluca and Sam Peltzman (eds) (1995a) *The Economics of Organized Crime*, Cambridge, UK: Cambridge University Press.

Fiorentini, Gianluca, and Sam Peltzman (1995b), "Introduction," in Fiorentini and Peltzman (eds) (1995a), pp. 1–32.

Franzini, Maurizio (1995), "Comment on Anderson," in Fiorentini and Peltzman (eds) (1995a), pp. 55–60.

Gambetta, Diego and Peter Reuter (1995), "Conspiracy among the many: the mafia in legitimate industries," in Fiorentini and Peltzman (eds) (1995a), pp. 116–135.

Garfinkel, Michelle R. and Stergios Skaperdas (1996), *The Political Economy of Conflict and Appropriation*, Cambridge, UK: Cambridge University Press.

Grossman, Herschel (1991), "A general equilibrium model of insurrections," *American Economic Review*, 81 (4), 912–21.

Grossman, Herschel (1995a), "Rival Kleptocrats: the mafia vs. the state," in Fiorentini and Peltzman (eds) (1995a).

Grossman, Herschel (1995b), "Robin Hood and the redistribution of property income," *European Journal of Political Economy*, 11 (3), 399–410.

Grossman, Herschel and Suk-Jae Noh (1994), "Proprietary public finance and economic welfare," *Journal of Public Economics*, 53 (2), 187–204.

Hirshleifer, Jack (1987), *Economic Behavior in Adversity*, Brighton, UK: Wheatsheaf Books.

Hirshleifer, Jack (1991a), "The technology of conflict as an economic activity," *American Economic Review*, 81 (2), 130–134.

Hirshleifer, Jack (1991b), "The paradox of power," *Economics and Politics*, 3 (3), 177–200.

Hirshleifer, Jack (1996), "Anarchy and its breakdown," in Garfinkel and Skaperdas (eds), pp. 15–40.

Huntington, Samuel P. (1968), *Political Order in Changing Societies*, New Haven, CT: Yale University Press.

Johnston, Michael (1997), "Public officials, private interests, and sustainable democracy: when politics and corruption meet," in Elliott (ed), pp. 61–82.

Kaufmann, Daniel (1997), "Corruption: The facts," *Foreign Policy*, 107, 114–31.

Keefer, Philip and Stephen Knack (1997) "Why don't poor countries catch up?" *Economic Inquiry*, 35, 590–602.

Krueger, Anne O. (1974) "The political economy of the rent-seeking society," *American Economic Review*, 64 (3), 291–303.

Leff, Nathaniel H. (1964), "Economic development through bureaucratic corruption," *American Behavior Scientist*, November 8–14 .

Mauro, Paolo (1995) "Corruption and growth," *Quarterly Journal of Economics*, 110 (3) 681–712.

Mauro, Paolo (1997), "The effect of corruption on growth, investments, and government expenditure: a cross-country analysis," in Elliott (ed.), pp. 83–107. [Revised version reproduced as Chapter 9 in this volume—ED.]

Olson, Mancur (1993), "Dictatorship, democracy, and development," *American Political Science Review*, 87 (3), September, 567–76.

Polo, Michele (1995), "Internal cohesion and competition among criminal organizations," in Fiorentini and Peltzman (eds) (1995a), pp. 87–108.

Radner, Roy (1992), "The economics of management," *Journal of Economic Literature*, 30, 1382–415.

Shleifer, Andrei and Robert W. Vishny (1993), "Corruption," *Quarterly Journal of Economics,* 108, 599–617.

Skaperdas, Stergios (1992), "Cooperation, conflict, and power in the absence of property rights," *American Economic Review*, 82 (4), 720–39.

Skaperdas, Stergios and Constantinos Syropoulos (1995), "Gangs as primitive states," in Fiorentini and Peltzman (eds) (1995a), pp. 61–81.

Skogh, Goran and Charles Stuart (1982), "A contractarian theory of property rights and crime," *Scandinavian Journal of Economics*, 84 (1), 27–40.

Tanzi, Vito (1998), "Corruption around the world," *IMF Staff Papers*, 45 (4), 559–94, Washington DC. [Reproduced as Chapter 2 in this volume—ED.]

Tanzi, Vito and Hamid Davoodi (1997), "Corruption, public investment, and growth," IMF Working Paper 97/139, Washington, DC: International Monetary Fund. [Revised version reproduced as Chapter 11 in this volume—ED.]

Tullock, Gordon (1974), *The Social Dilemma: The Economics of War and Revolution*, Fairfax, VA: Center for the Study of Public Choice.

Tullock, Gordon (1980), "Efficient rent-seeking," in *Toward a Theory of the Rent-Seeking Society*, College Station, TX: Texas A&M University Press, pp. 97–112.

Ul Haque, Nadeem and Ratna Sahay (1996), "Do government wage cuts close budget deficits? Costs of corruption," *IMF Staff Papers*, 43 (4), Washington, DC, 754–78.

Usher, Dan (1989), "The dynastic cycle and the stationary state," *American Economic Review*, 79 (5), 1031–44.

Williamson, Oliver E. (1983) "Credible commitments: using hostages to support exchange," *American Economic Review*, 73 (4), 519–40.

Williamson, Oliver E. (1985): *The Economic Institutions of Capitalism*, New York: Free Press.

7

Does Mother Nature Corrupt? Natural Resources, Corruption, and Economic Growth

Carlos Leite and Jens Weidmann

I. Introduction

The intensification of the public debate on governance, together with the increased emphasis on governance issues in policy deliberations, has stimulated considerable research aimed at examining the effects of institutional quality on economic performance. Many studies, for example, North (1990) and Shleifer and Vishny (1993), have argued that malfunctioning government institutions severely harm economic performance by reducing incentives and opportunities to invest and innovate. Among the different aspects of governance, corruption has received particular attention by both policymakers and researchers as the recent availability of corruption measures has helped to quan-

---

We would like to thank Benedikt Braumann, Peter Isard, Menachem Katz, and Robert Klitgaard for helpful comments and discussions.

tify its extent and allowed international comparisons. In a pioneering study, Mauro (1995) emphasizes that corruption may constitute a significant obstacle to investment. Nevertheless, different economic aspects of the corruption issue remain unexamined. In particular, the determinants of corruption and its effect on growth through channels other than investment have so far received scant attention.

Issues of corruption may be particularly relevant in the context of natural resources, as natural resource exploration is an extremely high-rent activity likely to foster rent-seeking behavior. The associated increase in rent-seeking opportunities may help to explain Sachs and Warner's (1995a) paradoxical finding of a negative relationship between the abundance of natural resources and long-run economic growth. While a casual glance through history may suffice to turn up enough anecdotal examples to informally support Sachs and Warner (1995a), and while bad management of windfall gains bears clear dangers for economic prosperity, theoretical explanations are anything but conclusive. The Dutch disease mechanism does suggest that a resource boom tends to reduce the level of competitiveness of the nonresource sector, but economic policymakers should be able to attenuate this tendency. Furthermore, standard economic theory makes a case, but only for a temporary negative growth effect; in the long run, the wealth effects associated with natural resources should lead to increased investment and higher economic growth. This paper argues that part of the apparent negative correlation between natural resource abundance and growth may be due to an endogeneity issue: corruption is determined within the economic system, and it should therefore be seen as a consequence of the interaction of economic interests and the use of policy instruments.

Thus, the aim of this paper is twofold. First, we investigate the determinants of corruption with a special emphasis on the role of natural resource abundance. Second, we examine the growth effects of corruption. Both issues are studied theoretically within an open economy, general equilibrium framework, as well as empirically within a simultaneous equation model with both economic growth and corruption endogenized. An additional question addressed in the paper centers on the possibility of attributing to specific components of natural resources a negative (or a positive) growth effect. Presumably, the amalgamation of the components of natural resources (fuel, ores and metals, agricultural products, and food) into one measure may obscure differences in their growth impact.

Section II of this paper provides a brief review of the literature on corruption and growth. Within a simple theoretical setting, Section III then discusses the effects of natural resource abundance on corruption, and illustrates how the latter may affect economic growth. Section IV examines the empirically testable implications of the theoretical model and evaluates the relevance of corruption as a transmission channel of natural resource effects on growth. Section V concludes and discusses the policy implications of the results.

II. Corruption and Natural Resources in the Growth Literature

Increasing recognition of the role of corruption in the process of economic development has been fueled in part by U.S. political concerns about uneven rules on the legality of bribery.[1] This, in turn, has prompted a wide-ranging debate on the political-economy considerations of corruption, leading recently to significant anticorruption efforts on the part of some nongovernmental and international organizations.[2] The academic literature does include some studies on the benefits of corruption, but on the whole, theoretical work tends to support the notion that corruption has a negative impact on development. Recently, econometricians have weighed in with evidence suggesting that investment flows are one transmission channel for the deleterious effect of corruption on growth. However, quantitative evidence on the direct impact of corruption on growth and on the determinants of the level of corruption remains scant. In this section, we review the theoretical and empirical evidence on the role of corruption in economic growth,[3] discuss possible determinants of the

---

[1] U.S. concerns center on the perceived disadvantage faced by U.S. firms in the wake of the Foreign Corrupt Practices Act of 1997. This act not only makes bribes ineligible for tax deduction but formally forbids U.S.-based companies from bribing foreign officials. Only very recently have other member countries of the Organization for Economic Cooperation and Development (OECD) started to adopt similar legislation to govern the behavior of their own firms.

[2] See, for example, World Bank (1997), OECD (1998), and the directory of anticorruption programs maintained on the Transparency International web page at http://www.transparency.org.

[3] Our brief survey draws extensively on two excellent reviews of the corruption literature, Bardhan (1997) on analytical issues and Tanzi (Chapter 2 in this volume) on policy issues.

level of corruption, and examine the role of natural resources in economic growth.

The Role of Corruption in Economic Growth

The strand of the theoretical literature arguing that corruption can play a positive role in the development process relies on static efficiency arguments, essentially viewing bribing as a type of Coasean bargaining process. In this context, Leff (1964) and Huntington (1968) suggest that corruption may allow entrepreneurs to work around extensive bureaucratic procedures, circumventing some of the negative effects of red tape; Lui (1985) uses an equilibrium-queuing model to suggest that corruption allows the queue to be rearranged in a way that brings about an efficient allocation of time, giving those for whom time is most valuable the opportunity to move to the front of the line; and Beck and Maher (1986) and Lien (1986) suggest that corruption may serve to ensure that projects are awarded to the most efficient firms, who stand to gain the most from payment of bribes.

On the first argument, Tanzi (Chapter 2 in this volume) counters that bureaucratic procedures should be seen as the consequence, and not strictly as the initiators, of rent-seeking activities; and Myrdal (1968) suggests that, aside from the possible changes in the order in the queue, bribes may actually induce public servants to reduce the speed with which they process the queue. On the second and third arguments, Boycko, Shleifer, and Vishny (1995) emphasize the added uncertainty resulting from the enforceability problems associated with corruption contracts. Notwithstanding the possible discipline imposed on the bribee by concerns about reputation, enforcement costs are liable to be larger than with regular contracts, and moral hazard about the reliability of the transaction may be an important consideration. Lui's (1985) conclusions may not be robust to such considerations. Furthermore, Baumol (1990), Murphy, Shleifer, and Vishny (1991), and Lui (1996) contend that existing practices in more corrupt societies tend to encourage the most able to engage in rent-seeking activities. It follows that the beneficiaries of corrupt practices are the most successful at rent seeking, and not necessarily the most economically efficient. The reallocation of talent from productive to rent-seeking activities is posited to have a negative impact on economic growth. The important corollary from each of the counterarguments is that it may not be entirely appropriate to look at bribes as a simple Coasean bargaining process.

Efficiency assessments of corruption may also be significantly affected by two additional considerations: the nature of the corrupt system and the extent of corruption. Shleifer and Vishny (1993) note that, in a centralized system of corruption, the bribetaker internalizes some of the distortionary effects, thereby reducing the inefficiency consequences of corruption. Rose-Ackerman (1978) emphasizes that, once entrenched, bribery is difficult to limit to areas in which it might be economically desirable.

A second strand of the theoretical literature suggests that corruption reduces both investment and growth. On investment, Murphy, Shleifer, and Vishny (1993) comment that the prevalence of increasing returns to rent seeking may crowd out productive investment; Romer (1994) notes that corruption, by imposing a tax on ex post profits, may in general reduce the flow of new goods and technology, particularly if an initial fixed cost investment is required; and the argument in Boycko, Shleifer, and Vishny (1995) mentioned above suggests that the added uncertainty may also serve to reduce investment flows.

On the direct effects of corruption on growth, Shleifer and Vishny (1993, p. 612) note that the illegality associated with corruption necessitates efforts to avoid detection and punishment, causing "corruption to be more distortionary than taxation." Indeed, the same study suggests that a detection-avoiding strategy may explain the preference of some officials toward the financing of projects on which the collection of bribes is easier, leading to the choice of infrastructure and defense projects over health and education expenditures, and reducing the quality of public services. Furthermore, Krueger (1993) contends that "vicious circles" of rent seeking and stifling regulations, for example in the context of an import substitution policy, might become entrenched, and even misdirected, and might only be resolved with the advent of an economic crisis. Finally, the labor misallocation emphasized by Baumol (1990), Murphy, Shleifer, and Vishny (1991), and Lui (1996) would be expected to have a direct negative impact on economic growth.

Econometricians have recently weighed into the debate as Mauro's (1995) pioneering study, together with the surveys now widely disseminated by Transparency International (TI),[4] brought to the attention of researchers the availability of corruption indices, and prompted a

---

[4]See TI's home page at http://www.transparency.org or its joint initiative with Goettingen University, the Internet Center for Corruption Research, at http://www.gwdg.de/~uwvw/icr.htm.

number of empirical investigations into the effects of corruption on various aspects of economic performance. Tanzi (Chapter 2 in this volume) lists the significant econometric findings to date, namely the effects of corruption on (1) the level of investment, (2) the productivity of public investment and the level of maintenance expenditures, (3) the level of foreign direct investment, (4) the level of education and health expenditures, and (5) the level of tax revenue. Given our interest in estimating a growth model, we restrict our review to empirical studies assessing either the role of investment as a transmission channel, namely Mauro (1995), Wei (1997), and Tanzi and Davoodi (Chapter 11 in this volume), or the direct impact of corruption on growth, namely Poirson (1998) and Rama (1993).

Mauro (1995) uses subjective indices on institutional efficiency to analyze the relationship between institutional efficiency and economic growth, both directly and through the investment channel. The results provide some evidence that corruption affects investment although the probability value does fall to 12 percent when corruption is instrumented using an index for ethnic diversity.[5] On the direct relationship between corruption and growth, Mauro (1995, p. 704) provides only "weak support," with corruption becoming insignificant in the growth equation once investment is held constant.

The other two studies on the role of investment focus on particular components, Wei (1997) on foreign direct investment and Tanzi and Davoodi (Chapter 11 in this volume) on public investment. Wei (1997) uses individual survey responses to construct a measure of corruption-induced uncertainty. The results are consistent with an explanation that the uncertainty associated with corruption reduces foreign direct investment as suggested by Boycko, Shleifer, and Vishny (1995). Tanzi and Davoodi (Chapter 11 in this volume) provide cross-sectional evidence that higher corruption is associated with a lower quality of public infrastructure, consistent with the conjecture by Shleifer and Vishny (1993) on the choice of projects by corrupt officials. Neither Wei (1997) nor Tanzi and Davoodi (Chapter 11 in this volume) estimate the subsequent impact on growth.

The only econometric evidence of a statistically significant direct effect of corruption on growth is provided by Poirson (1998) and Rama (1993). Poirson (1998) analyzes the effect of economic security for 53

---

[5]Replacing corruption with an index on bureaucratic efficiency yields a probability value of 8 percent.

countries over the period 1984–95. In the context of a growth equation typical of the recent empirical growth literature, she includes measures on investment, openness, and corruption as exogenous explanatory variables and finds that corruption significantly reduces economic growth rates. Within a reduced form (AK) endogenous growth model, Rama (1993) endogenizes lobbying costs incurred by the firm. Using data for Uruguay over the period 1947–98, and regressing long-run growth rates on sectoral and aggregate investment rates, this study finds that lagged values of restrictive regulations decrease growth at the aggregate level.

The Determinants of Corruption

Corruption can take many forms, and it can even be embedded in cultural traditions, but its analysis generally focuses on the variant associated with government activity. Early studies followed Krueger (1974) in investigating the effects of regulations on foreign trade and in pointing out that government restrictions on economic activity tend to generate both rents and rent-seeking behavior. We briefly discuss below some of the factors suggested as contributors to the incidence of corruption.

Viewing corruption as an illegal activity, we can follow Becker's (1968) suggestion that the probability of committing a crime depends primarily on the penalty imposed and on the probability of being caught. In addition, the deterrent value of the penalties depends crucially on the ability and willingness of the authorities to enforce the relevant regulations, as well as on the level of acceptance, by the citizenry, of the judgments rendered by the country's institutions. Two corollaries are that political stability and transparency of rules are likely to be necessary conditions for an effective anticorruption strategy. That is, countries beset by political instability are unlikely to generate the political muscle necessary to adequately empower judicial institutions, and situations of confusing rules and perplexing procedures are unlikely to generate the required widespread understanding and support.

The trade literature suggests that trade restrictions lead to a significant amount of rents and rent-seeking activities, noted by Bhagwati (1982) to include not only attempts to evade tariffs but also efforts at premium seeking when agents compete for premium-fetching licenses, revenue seeking when agents try to appropriate a share of the revenue resulting from import restrictions, and tariff seeking when agents lobby for the imposition of protectionist tariffs. Krueger (1974) estimates that rents generated by government regulations in import licenses exceeded 5 percent of national income for India in 1964 and about 15 percent of GNP for Turkey in 1968, suggesting that rents accruing from the imposition of trade regulations are both theoretically and quantitatively significant. It follows that the degree of openness to foreign trade should be an important factor in determining the level of rent-seeking activities, or the extent of corruption.

The paucity of empirical work on the determinants of corruption is reflected in the existence of only two empirical studies, Van Rijckeghem and Weder (Chapter 3 in this volume), and Rauch and Evans (1999). The first study uses the idea of efficiency wages to argue that, under certain circumstances, higher wages in the public sector can deter corruption by increasing the potential loss in case of detection. Using data on some 25 developing countries, this study finds a significant impact of the public-private sector wage differential on the level of corruption.[6] In a similar vein, Rauch and Evans (1999), in a study covering 35 developing countries, present quantitative evidence suggesting that the extent of corruption is higher in countries in which civil service recruitment and promotion procedures rely less on merit-based considerations.

The Role of Natural Resources in Economic Growth

Similar to the case of corruption, the role of natural resources in economic development has been an area of ardent debate in economics. From earlier findings of a secularly declining price to later evidence on higher price volatility, policymakers have been encouraged not to rely extensively on resource-based growth, and theorists have debated widely on the optimal stance of public policy in the face of abundant natural resources. For purposes of our discussion, it is useful to distinguish between direct and indirect effects of natural resources. Direct effects have been labeled as the Dutch disease since the 1960s, when large discoveries of natural gas led to a recession in the Netherlands.[7]

---

[6]More specifically, Van Rijckeghem and Weder (Chapter 3 in this volume) find that, in a cross-country regression, the differential between wages in the civil service and in manufacturing is a significant determinant of the corruption index assembled by the IRIS Center of the University of Maryland. The same independent variable, however, turns out to be insignificant in a panel setup.

[7]More recent examples of recessions induced by resource booms include the United Kingdom in the late 1970s, following the discovery and exploitation of the North Sea oil

Indirect effects we ascribe to the impact of natural resources on rent-seeking activities and institution building.

The direct effects of a resource boom (either in the form of new discoveries or price improvements) mainly affect the nonresource traded goods sector. First, increased disposable income will be partly spent on nontraded goods, for example, construction and services, causing prices in these sectors to rise. To restore equilibrium in the labor and nontraded goods market, the real exchange rate has to rise and real wages in the nontraded goods sector have to fall. This, in turn, reduces the competitiveness of the traded nonresource goods sector, partially crowding it out (spending effect). Second, factor remuneration will increase in the booming natural resource sector and lure workers and capital away from the other sectors (resource pull effect). The size of both effects is thus, to a large extent, determined by the sector's labor intensity and ownership: the higher the labor intensity and the greater the level of domestic ownership, the more severe are the two effects.[8]

The contraction in the traded goods sector following an increase in natural resource revenues is frequently referred to as the Dutch disease. In reality, the adjustment process can be thought of as a rational response of the economy, although overall welfare losses through a reduction in long-term growth can occur if linkages between the sectors, or more precisely the lack of positive externalities of the resource sector, are considered.[9]

Sachs and Warner (1995a), using data for some 70 countries, find a negative relationship between the ratio of natural resource exports and the rate of economic growth, even after controlling for variables such as initial per capita income, trade policy, and investment rates.[10] Quantitatively, the Sachs and Warner (1995a) estimates imply that an in-

---

fields, and other oil-exporting economies in the late 1970s and early 1980s, following the reversion of the price of oil to its longer-term trend (after the large increases of 1974/75 and 1978/79). In contrast, some countries, for example, Malaysia and Botswana, have managed to harness the power of natural resources and maintain both economic stability and above-average growth rates.

[8]The second effect tends to be less relevant in the case of oil, since the production process is not very labor intensive and the domestic financing effects are generally limited.

[9]For an overview, see Sachs and Warner (1995a).

[10]As a robustness check, Sachs and Warner (1995a) reestimate the main equations in Barro (1991), King and Levine (1993), Mankiw, Romer, and Weil (1992), and DeLong and Summers (1991) while adding natural resource intensity and the openness variable. In all cases, the negative effect of natural resource intensity on long-run growth remains statistically significant.

crease of one standard deviation in natural resource intensity (on average, 16 percent of GNP) leads to a reduction of about 1 percent a year in economic growth.

Indirect effects describe potential negative growth effects linked to the impact of resource abundance on the institutional quality of a country. The problem arises from the possible impact of windfall gains on rent-seeking behavior, as discussed in the previous section. Khan (1994), for example, attributes the pervasiveness of corruption in Nigeria to the oil boom. Lane and Tornell (1997) point out that windfall gains may cause a "feeding frenzy" in which competing groups fight for the natural resource rents, thereby inefficiently exhausting the public good. This effect is exacerbated by the direct accrual to the government of a significant portion of the rents, possibly impeding the implementation of needed structural reforms and sometimes distracting public officials from investing in growth-supporting public goods. Sachs and Warner (1995a) empirically show that resource-abundant economies choose a more protective trade policy, liberalizing later than resource-poor economies.

III. A Simple Analytical Model

In this section, we model the influence of natural resources on, and the growth effects of, corruption within a neoclassical general equilibrium framework. In an open economy infinite horizon growth model, we assume that investment projects need administrative approval, which is granted after the firm pays a bribe to the government employee. Hence, corruption acts like an investment tax borne by firms,[11] and ultimately by all shareholders, to the benefit of government employees who constitute a fixed share $0 < s < 1$ of the total population. $1 - s$ will subsequently also be interpreted, and referred to, as an indicator for the concentration of bureaucratic power in the economy or, put differently, s can be viewed as the extent to which the utility of the nongovernment sector enters the utility function of bureaucrats.[12]

---

[11] Strictly speaking, bribes, compared with taxes, are associated with higher uncertainty and require costly efforts to avoid detection (see Section II). Adding uncertainty to the model, however, would only strengthen the main results.

[12] Aside from analyzing corruption, this model can be easily modified to apply to the more general case where a fraction of the population has the revocable power to impose a burden on the entire population.

Households

Households earn wages and receive interest income. They purchase goods for consumption and save by accumulating additional assets. The current household head maximizes "family utility" by taking into account the well-being of all his descendants; we thus face an infinite horizon maximization problem. In the setting considered here, there are two types of households: government employees and private sector employees, the difference between the two types being that the former have the power to impose bribe payments on investment. In other words, government employees have an additional income: bribe receipts.

Labeling the population growth rate n and normalizing the number of adults at time 0 to unity, the total adult population at time t is $L(t) = e^{nt}$, of which $L_g(t) \equiv se^{nt}$ agents are government employees. The subscripts g and p denote variables referring to the government and private sector employees, respectively, and are omitted whenever no ambiguity arises. Lowercase symbols represent variables per adult person; for example, $C(t)$ is total consumption at time t, while $c(t) \equiv C(t)/L(t)$.

Households maximize overall utility, U, which can be represented as a weighted sum of all future discounted utility flows, $u(c)$:

$$U = \int_0^\infty u[c(t)] e^{nt} e^{-\rho t}\, dt, \tag{1}$$

where $\rho > 0$ is the rate of time preference. We assume that $\rho > n$ to ensure that U is bounded for constant c and that $u(c)$ has the usual properties and satisfies the Inada conditions.[13]

Government employees dispose of three sources of income: labor income, interest income, and bribes.[14] Agents are competitive, that is, they take the wage rate, w, and the interest rate, r, as given and supply inelastically 1 unit of labor services per time unit. The bribe is a fraction γ of gross investment $I = \dot{K} + \delta K$, where δ is the rate of depreciation. The corrupt bureaucrat is detected and punished with probability $\bar{p}$, increasing with the extent of corruption, γ, and the monitoring technology of the society, M, so that $\bar{p} = \bar{p}(\gamma, M)$, with $\partial \bar{p}/\partial \gamma > 0$, and $\partial \bar{p}/\partial M > 0$. Conversely, let $p \equiv 1 - \bar{p}$ denote the likelihood of not being

---

[13] Thus, $u'(c) > 0$, $u''(c) < 0$, $\lim_{c \to \infty} u'(c) \to \infty$, and $\lim_{c \to 0} u'(c) \to 0$.

[14] It proves convenient to start with the government employees' utility maximization problem, as the private sector agents' problem turns out to be a special case thereof.

detected. Upon being caught, the corrupt bureaucrat forgoes his bribe payment and is forced to pay a penalty, z.[15] The expected flow budget constraint faced by the government employee household can thus be written:

$$\dot{a} = w + ra + \frac{\gamma p(\gamma, M)}{s}(\dot{k} + [n+\delta]k) - [1 - p(\gamma, M)]z - c - na, \quad (2)$$

where a denotes the household's total, that is, domestic and foreign assets, and a dot over a variable marks a time derivative. Thus, the increase in assets per capita equals the sum of the three income types less per capita consumption and an adjustment term for population growth. The expected bribe receipt, the third component in equation (2), amounts to γ times gross investment weighted by the probability of not being caught divided by the number of government employees.[16]

To rule out Ponzi schemes, we impose a constraint on the amount of borrowing by households, the so-called transversality condition, ensuring that the present value of their assets remains nonnegative:

$$\lim_{t \to \infty} \left\{ a(t) \exp\left[-\int_0^t (r(v) - n) dv \right] \right\} \geq 0. \quad (3)$$

Maximization of U in equation (1) subject to the budget constraint in equation (2), the stock of initial assets, $a(0)$, and the credit constraint in equation (3) yields the following present-value Hamiltonian:

$$H = u(c)e^{-(\rho-n)t} + v[w + ra + \gamma p(\dot{k} + [n+\delta]k)/s - (1-p)z - c - na]. \quad (4)$$

The first-order conditions for a maximum are

$$\frac{\partial H}{\partial c} = 0 \Rightarrow v = u'(c)e^{-(\rho-n)t}, \quad (5)$$

$$\frac{\partial H}{\partial a} = -\dot{v} = -(r-n)v, \quad (6)$$

---

[15] If we imposed a penalty as a function of the wage rate, for example, through a loss in retirement benefits, our model would show that, ceteris paribus, higher wages deter corruption.

[16] Note that $\dot{K}/L = \dot{k} + nk$ and therefore $(\dot{K} + \delta K)/L_g = (\dot{k} + [n + \delta]k)/s$.

$$\frac{\partial H}{\partial \gamma} = 0 \Rightarrow \gamma^* = \frac{1}{2\bar{p}(1, M)} - \frac{zs}{\dot{k} + [n + \delta]k}. \tag{7}$$

While equations (5) and (6) describe the optimal consumption pattern, equation (7) derives the optimal extent of corruption, γ^*, for the atomistic bureaucrat under the simplifying assumption that $\bar{p}$ is a linear function of γ so that $\bar{p} = \bar{p}(1,M)\gamma$ and $\partial \bar{p}/\partial \gamma = \bar{p}(1,M)$ is independent of γ. As $\partial \bar{p}/\partial M > 0$, an increase in the penalty, z, or the monitoring effort, M, or a reduction in the concentration of power to impose bribes, s,[17] decreases the revenue-maximizing extent of corruption for the bureaucrat. On the other hand, a more capital-intensive mode of production—for example, through a larger share of relatively capital-intensive natural resource extraction activities in the economy—has the opposite effect, leading to a rise in corruption.

Following common practice in the literature, we assume that $u(c)$ takes the form of a constant intertemporal elasticity of substitution (CIES) function,[18] in which case the optimal consumption path, derived by differentiating equation (5) with respect to time and using equation (6), becomes

$$\dot{c}/c = (1/\theta)(r - \rho). \tag{8}$$

This standard Euler equation implies that an interest rate greater than the rate of time preference leads to an increasing consumption pattern over time, with the opposite true for interest rates smaller than the rate of time preference. On the contrary, agents prefer a constant consumption stream if the interest rate happens to equal the rate of

---

[17]Intuitively, the more bureaucrats have to share the revenue from bribes, the higher the relative risk of corruption as the "best case" payoff decreases while at the same time the risk of being detected remains unaffected. Note, however, that this result crucially hinges on the assumption that the likelihood of being detected is independent of s. In a closed economy setting, where public servants and private sector employees differ only in their capacity to impose bribes, and where both groups are shareholders, a rising s increases the costs of corruption borne by government employees (they are more and more "taxing themselves") and induces them to internalize the distortionary effects caused by corruption. This argument is similar to the one put forward by Shleifer and Vishny (1993), and it should not be taken to mean that a reduction in corruption can be brought about by a larger government sector, but only that the inefficiency consequences of corruption diminish as s increases.

[18]That is, $u(c) = (c^{1-\theta} - 1)/(1 - \theta)$, and therefore the elasticity of marginal utility equals the constant $-\theta$ and the elasticity of substitution is $\sigma = 1/\theta$ with $\theta > 0$.

time preference. Note that, as equation (8) is independent of γ or s, it applies to both government and civil sector employees, and it stands for the consumption pattern of the aggregated economy.[19]

Firms

Firms produce the economy's single good, Y, employing a production technology with neoclassical properties, that is, constant returns to scale in K and L and positive and decreasing marginal products. For ease of presentation, the level of technology is assumed to be independent of time. The production technology can be written as

$$Y = F(K,L). \tag{9}$$

The firms' net cash flow is defined as sale proceeds net of wage payments and investment costs, CI:

$$\Pi = F(K,L) - wL - CI, \tag{10}$$

where CI equals the physical cost of investment plus the "unavoidable" bribe payment, that is,

$$CI = I[1 + \gamma].$$

The firm's objective is to maximize the present value of net cash flows between time 0 and infinity by an appropriate choice of L and I, subject to $\dot{K} = I - \delta K$ and an initial value $K(0)$. Let $\bar{r}(t)$ be the average interest rate between times 0 and t, that is, $\bar{r}(t) \equiv (1/t)\int_0^t r(v)dv$, in which case the firm's optimization problem can be represented by the following Hamiltonian:

$$J = e^{-\bar{r}(t)t}\{F(K,L) - wL - I(1 + \gamma)\} + v(I - \delta K). \tag{11}$$

In equation (11), v is the shadow price associated with installed capital in units of time 0 output, that is, the present-value shadow price of installed capital. The current-value shadow price of installed capital, q,

---

[19]Given their extra sources of income, government employees still enjoy a level of consumption higher than private sector employees.

is then $q = v/e^{-\bar{r}(t)t}$. Firms are competitive, taking w and γ as given, and hence the first-order conditions are[20]

$$\frac{\partial J}{\partial L} = 0 \Rightarrow F_L(K,L) = f(k) - kf'(k) = w, \qquad (12)$$

$$\frac{\partial J}{\partial I} = 0 \Rightarrow q = 1 + \gamma, \text{ and} \qquad (13)$$

$$\dot{v} = -\frac{\partial J}{\partial K} \Rightarrow \dot{q} = (r + \delta)q - f'(k), \qquad (14)$$

where $f(k)$ is the intensive form of the production function. Equation (12) represents the usual result that the marginal product of labor equals the wage rate, and equation (13) shows that the shadow price of installed capital exceeds unity by the extent of corruption. Equation (14) can be rewritten to yield $r = f'(k)/q - \delta - \dot{q}/q$, which differs from the conventional results, $r = f'(k) - \delta$ by the terms in q. This equation for r indicates that—with a given world interest rate—the steady-state capital stock will be lower in the presence of corruption as $q > 1$ for $\gamma > 0$. Using equations (7) and (13), as well as $\dot{k} = i - (n + \delta)k$, the motion equation for $\dot{k}$ can be derived as a function of the model's parameters and the shadow price, q:

$$\dot{k} = \frac{zs\,\bar{p}(1, M)}{2\bar{p}(1,M)(1 - q) + 1} - (n + \delta)k. \qquad (15)$$

Equations (14) and (15) constitute a two-dimensional system of differential equations in k and q. Note that in the small open economy setting, the path of $r(t)$ is independent of savings or the capital stock, and thus, the consumers' optimization problem. The condition $\dot{k} = 0$ can be used to derive

$$q = 1 + \frac{1}{2\bar{p}(1,M)} - \frac{zs}{2(n + \delta)k}. \qquad (16)$$

---

[20]The transversality condition is $\lim_{t \to \infty}(vK) = 0$.

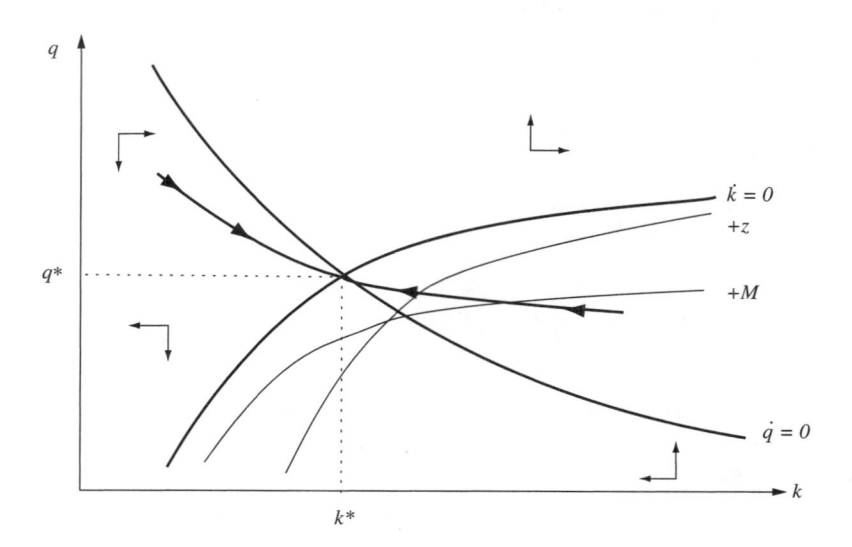

Figure 1. A Small Open Economy with Corruption

Thus, the value of q exceeds 1 for $k > zs\ \bar{p}(1,M)/(n + \delta)$. As indicated above, a higher q^* is tantamount to a lower steady-state capital stock k^*. The phase diagram in Figure 1 illustrates the steady-state and the transitional dynamics of the system. It is straightforward to show that the system exhibits saddle-path stability, the stable arm being depicted by the thick solid line with arrows.

Figure 1 also demonstrates the economic ramifications of fighting corruption, be it through improved monitoring (the line labeled as "+M") or enhanced incentive schemes (the line labeled as "+z"). Both policies lead to a reduction in the steady-state shadow price of capital and, ipso facto, an increase in the steady-state capital stock and also steady-state output. Likewise, fighting corruption implies a higher speed of convergence and thus a higher growth rate of per capita output during convergence to the steady state, as the convergence coefficient can be shown to depend positively on z and M. Conversely, economies with weaker institutional control, or with incentive schemes that do not effectively discourage bribery, tend to grow slower.

Another noteworthy feature of the model is the implication that the impact of the two anticorruption policies depends on the state of economic development or, more precisely, on the capital intensity of the

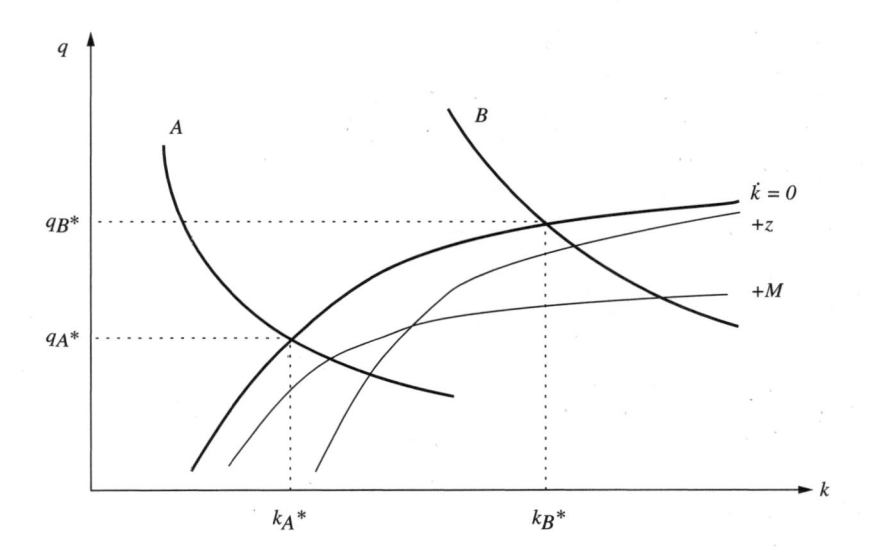

Figure 2. The Effects of Anticorruption Policies

[Figure: Graph with axes q (vertical) and k (horizontal), showing curves A and B, with the $\dot{k}=0$ locus and shifts labeled $+z$ and $+M$. Dashed lines mark steady-state values q_B^*, q_A^* on the q-axis and k_A^*, k_B^* on the k-axis.]

economy. Figure 2 depicts two economies: A is characterized by low values of steady-state q and k, whereas B corresponds to high values of steady-state q and k, so that, generally speaking, they could be thought of as a developing and developed economy, respectively. Now, if each government wants to engage in combating corruption, it can either strengthen the monitoring technology, that is, increase M, or punish the detected bribee more severely, that is, raise z. As Figure 2 shows, the increased penalty generates a larger increase in the steady-state capital stock, and thus output, in the developing economy than the improved monitoring technology, whereas the opposite is true for the developed economy.[21] Thus, the battle against corruption should be fought with different weapons depending on the development of the economy. The different impact of the two policies stems from the fact that an increase in M, in raising the likelihood of being caught, leads to two separate effects: a reduction in the expected bribe payment and an increase in the expected penalty. As the bribe payment relative to k increases with k,

---

[21]As the output increase caused by a rise in z depends positively on s, the effectiveness of the anticorruption policy based on increasing the penalty increases with rising s, that is, reducing the concentration of power.

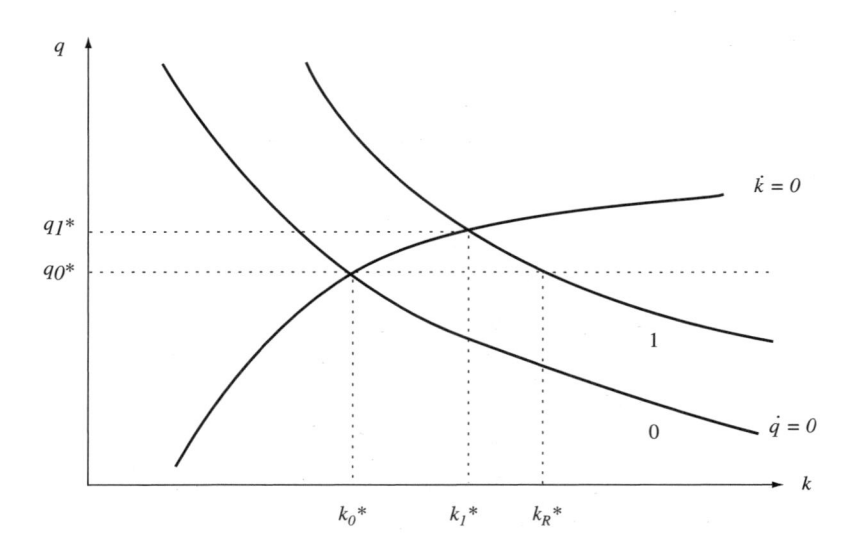

Figure 3. The Effect of an Increase in Natural Resources

the potential loss for the corrupt government employee through enhanced monitoring is relatively higher for large k.

The model also yields insights into the economic effects of a natural resource discovery, viewed as a technology shock shifting the $\dot{q} = 0$ curve outward; in Figure 3, the movement is from 0 to 1. Two observations stand out. First, the technology-induced increase in the steady-state level of both capital stock and output is reduced as a consequence of corruption. Without corruption, the $\dot{k} = 0$ curve would be a horizontal line through q_0^* and the outward shift of the $\dot{q} = 0$ curve would leave q^* unaffected while increasing k^* to k_R^*, instead of k_1^*. It is straightforward to show that this result carries over to the output growth rates during the transition to the new steady state. Second, due to the curvature of the $\dot{k} = 0$ curve, the negative impact of corruption differs depending on the initial steady state of the economy with the effect being more pronounced in less capitalized, that is, less developed, countries. The reason for this nonlinearity follows from equation (7), where it can be seen that a given change in the capital stock has a higher effect on the extent of corruption at low levels of k than at higher levels of k.

This property of the model also suggests that the opportunity costs of corruption, in terms of relative output (growth) forgone, are related to the degree of capital intensity in the resource-extracting industries. More specifically, the shortfall of output (growth) from its potential due to the existence of corruption is more pronounced after an increase in (labor-intensive) food production than after an increase in (capital-intensive) oil extraction. In the empirical section, we investigate dissimilarities in the growth effects of the different resource-extracting industries by disaggregating the natural resource variable into its components.

The implications of our model for the subsequent empirical investigation can be summarized in three points. First, the endogeneity of corruption has to be accounted for, otherwise the empirical estimates of the growth effects of natural resource abundance might be biased downward. Second, the various subcategories of natural resources potentially differ in their effect on corruption and growth, and some insights might be gained by disaggregating the natural resource variable into its components. Finally, the growth effects of natural resources also depend on institutional factors such as the concentration of bureaucratic power, the monitoring technology, and the penalty system.

IV. Empirical Results

Data

The working definition of corruption usually invokes some notion of illegality, and despite the fact that bribery can obviously take place in the private sector, typically focuses on the use of public office for private gain. Notwithstanding the obvious difficulties in measuring illegal activities, several indices that attempt to measure some facet of corruption are available from various investment advisory services, such as the Economist Intelligence Unit (EIU), Political Risk Services Group (which publishes the *International Country Risk Guide* (*ICRG*)), and Business and Environmental Risk Intelligence (BERI). The typical clients for these surveys are reportedly banks, multinational companies, and other international investors, and the definitions of corruption used by the rating agencies tend to focus on measuring the degree to which business transactions involve corruption or "questionable" payments. Mauro (1995) used data from an agency now incorporated into the EIU, while Knack and Keefer (1995) and Easterly and Levine (1996) used data from both *ICRG* and BERI. More recently, the nongovernmental organization Transparency International has made widely available its collection of surveys on levels of corruption in various countries. Fortunately, the data for the various indices, including measures of various aspects of bureaucratic efficiency, are highly correlated, as detailed in Mauro (1995).

As a measure of corruption, we use the *ICRG* corruption index originally introduced into the academic literature by Knack and Keefer (1995). The index is scored on a scale of zero to six with lower scores indicating that "high government officials are likely to demand special payments" and "illegal payments are generally expected throughout lower levels of government" in the form of "bribes connected with import and export licenses, exchange controls, tax assessment, policy protection, or loans" (Knack and Keefer, 1995, p. 225).

The variables on the quality of legal and political institutions and on political instability are taken from Barro and Lee (1994), and are originally from *ICRG* and Banks (1979). As a measure of the quality of legal and political institutions, we use an index on the "rule of law," which subjectively measures the degree to which the citizens of a country are willing to grant to the established institutions the authority to make and implement laws and adjudicate disputes. Higher scores on the scale of zero to six indicate "sound political institutions, a strong court system, and provisions for an orderly succession of power" (Knack and Keefer, 1995, p. 225). The political instability variable, revolutions and coups, is the period average of revolutions per year and political assassinations per million inhabitants per year.

The data on natural resource exports as a share of GNP are originally from Sachs and Warner (1995a), with the definition of natural resources following convention in including SITC categories 0 (live animals and all unprocessed and processed food products), 1 (beverages and tobacco), 2 (inedible crude materials except fuels), 3 (mineral fuels, lubricants, and related materials), 4 (animal and vegetable oil and fats), and 68 (nonferrous metals). The disaggregated data on exports of fuel, minerals, and agricultural and food products were gathered from the World Bank's World Development Indicators (WDI).

We measure trade policy stance by the Sachs and Warner (1995a) trade openness variable, defined as the fraction of years (over the period 1970–90) that a particular economy is classified as open. In any one year, an economy is considered open if none of the following five characteristics are present: tariffs exceeding 40 percent; nontariff barriers covering more than 40 percent of trade; a black market premium more than 20 percent relative to the official exchange rate, on average; a centrally planned economic system; or a state monopoly on major exports.

The dummy variable on public participation in fuels and ores is defined to equal 1 for countries with public sector involvement in the particular industry, 0 otherwise, and was constructed from information on industry coverage of public enterprises found in Table 3 of Short (1984). The measure of country-specific commodity price variability was calculated as the standard deviation, over the period 1970–90, of WDI price indices for fuel, ores, and agricultural and food products weighted by each country's share of exports of the specific commodity. The remainder of the data is taken from Sachs and Warner (1995a).

Regression Results

This section considers the empirical determinants of corruption and its effect on growth. Two key propositions from the theoretical model presented above are that corruption (1) takes the form of rent-seeking activities, with the level of corruption positively related to the incidence of high-rent activities and negatively related to monitoring efforts, and (2) lowers the steady-state income level, thereby reducing the economy's growth rate. Consistent with our interest in the role of natural resources, we endogenize corruption within the growth-regression framework of Sachs and Warner (1995a). The two-equation econometric specification is then

$$Corruption_i = Z\theta + \delta_1 Natural\ Resources_i + \delta_2 Trade\ Openness_i + \delta_3 Rule\ of\ Law_i + \delta_4 Political\ Instability_i + e_{1,i}$$

$$\frac{\ln(Y_i^{1990}/Y_i^{1970})}{20} = X\beta + a_1 \ln Y_i^{1970} + a_2 Corruption_i + a_3 Natural\ Resources_i + e_{2,i},$$

where Y_i^t stands for country i's GDP per economically active person at time t. In the corruption equation, the availability of rent-seeking opportunities is measured by the structure of the economy (particularly endowments of natural resources) and the degree of openness to trade, while monitoring efforts by the government are measured by the strength of the institutions charged with the implementation of laws (rule of law) and the level of political instability (the incidence of revolutions and coups). The set of additional conditioning variables, Z, includes the rate of economic growth over the period 1970–90; a measure of ethnic diversity, the ethnolinguistic fractionalization index introduced by Mauro (1995); and a dummy variable for sub-Saharan African countries. We also test for robustness, in the sense of Levine and Renelt (1992), by the addition of a wider set of variables, as detailed in the footnotes to the relevant tables.

Economic growth, particularly rapid economic growth, entails substantial changes in production methods and social relationships, including changes in the importance of different industries, skills, and business practices. At the same time, there is no guarantee that the evolution of the new institutions (be they government agencies, social or professional organizations, or even social norms) required to either manage or support these changes will take place in concert with the changes themselves. Consider, for example, the following set of stylized facts. On its path through economic development, a low-income country begins to invest in larger capital-intensive natural resource projects. With government revenues increasing and institutional development lagging behind the pace of change in the economic structure, conditions become auspiciously favorable for engagement in revenue-raising activities of the directly unproductive type of Bhagwati (1982).

In the specific case of rapid economic growth brought on by oil and mineral discoveries, the accrual of a majority of the revenue directly to the government is liable to exacerbate the incidence of rent-seeking behavior, as claimed by Khan (1994) for the case of Nigeria. In contrast, economic growth driven by the acquisition of human capital would likely generate fewer easily appropriable rents, and would in any case, tend to simultaneously lead to an improvement in the quality of the institutions (to the extent that basic skills and leadership would be enhanced by the higher level of human capital). As a corollary, we would also posit that more labor-intensive natural resources, such as food and agricultural products, would tend to generate fewer rents and be associated with less corruption. Given the expected differences in behavior for the different components of natural resources, we split the natural resources variable of Sachs and Warner (1995a) into its four components (fuel, ores, agriculture, and food), originally adding each component as a separate variable. We also add the rate of economic growth, along with the different components of natural resources, in order to control for the effects of non-resource-based rapid growth.

The rent-seeking literature suggests that the incidence of bribery is also likely to be associated with the extent of trade regulations, the quality of legal and political institutions, and the level of political instability. Ceteris paribus, we would expect that an economy more open to trade (a higher value for trade openness), with stronger institutions (a higher score for rule of law), and with a higher degree of political stability (a lower value for political instability) would tend to have less corruption.

The inclusion of the ethnic diversity variable is an attempt to assess whether societal divisions along ethnic and linguistic lines contribute to rent-seeking behavior. It may be, for example, that the prevalence of strong family ties, together with a lack of national identity and the absence of accountability of government officials, leads people in positions of power to favor friends and relatives, at the expense of the greater public good. The impact of ethnic diversity may also be related to the theoretical prediction of our model on the effect of bureaucratic power concentration. It may be, for example, that an ethnic group in power will find it easier to pass on the costs of bribe payments to other ethnic groups, reducing the incentive for the former to internalize the costs of corruption.[22] Under both explanations, a more ethnically diverse society (a higher value on the ethnic fractionalization measure) would be expected to have more corruption.[23]

Finally, the rationale for the inclusion of the Africa variable is straightforward: corruption is widely regarded as endemic, and inherently different, in certain parts of the world, particularly in Africa (Shleifer and Vishny, 1993, p. 611). These types of explanations are not well grounded in economic theory, and presumably, if the set of conditioning variables adequately captures the incidence of corruption, dummy variables for any regional grouping should be statistically insignificant (enhancing the applicability of policy prescriptions).

For the growth equation, we follow Sachs and Warner (1995a) in testing our propositions in the context of the trade policy regime. Our main variables of interest are corruption and natural resources. Our

---

[22]The effect of bureaucratic concentration (and, more specifically, the degree of internalization of the costs of corruption) may otherwise be proxied by the share of government employment in total employment or by the share of government current expenditures in GDP.

[23]It may also be that leadership, which Tanzi (Chapter 2 in this volume) suggests is associated with less corruption, is more likely to flourish in more ethnically homogeneous societies.

theoretical model predicts that more corruption is, ceteris paribus, associated with lower rates of growth, while the original Sachs and Warner (1995a) results suggest that an abundance of natural resources tends to reduce economic growth. In endogenizing corruption, we impose an exclusion restriction on the original Sachs and Warner (1995a) growth specification: rule of law, which they originally include as an explanatory variable, is posited to work only through corruption.

The set of additional conditioning variables, X, includes as in Sachs and Warner (1995a), the period average for the ratio of investment to GDP, the level of trade openness over the period, and the change in the terms of trade over the period. For our specification, we also include a measure of the country-specific variability in commodity prices. The rationale for the first three variables is straightforward and clearly articulated in Sachs and Warner (1995a). The addition of price variability is intended to control for the potentially negative impact of commodity price fluctuations, the rationale for which is clearly articulated in the literature on the Dutch disease, as reviewed above. Ceteris paribus, we would expect that an economy with a higher investment ratio, a more open trade policy, with more favorable changes in the terms of trade (higher value for terms of trade), and facing less commodity-based export price variability (lower value for commodity price variability) would tend to have a higher rate of growth.

In the context of the neoclassical growth model, the incidence of natural resources is interpreted as an exogenous technology shock affecting growth through the aggregate production function. By raising the steady-state level of income and leaving the economy farther from its long-run target, natural resources should, ceteris paribus, stimulate economic growth (intuitively, the economy can always stay with the original technology). However, as highlighted in our discussion on the direct (Dutch disease) and indirect (institutional impact) effects, some of the characteristics of resource-led growth can induce a net negative effect on growth, even as average income increases. That is, the initial increase in production (and growth) may be accompanied by policy and institutional changes that, after some time, leave the steady-state level of income closer to the current level of income, thereby reducing the rate of economic growth over the medium term. Given the specification for the corruption regression, we can now assess the strength of corruption as a transmission mechanism from natural resource abundance to economic growth.

The next two sections present the results for the corruption and the growth regression, while the third section provides further evidence on the role of natural resources in the growth process.

Corruption Regression

Table 1 presents the results using the corruption index as the dependent variable, with a high score—on a scale of zero to six—indicating less corruption. The first regression suggests that natural resources should be decomposed into just two variables, "fuel and ores" and "agriculture and food," rather than the usual four components. Not only are the signs on fuel and ores (agriculture and food) consistently negative (positive) for a variety of specifications, but F-tests on the equality of coefficients uniformly fail to reject two null hypotheses:

H_0: $\delta_{Fuel} = \delta_{Ores}$; and

H_0: $\delta_{Agriculture} = \delta_{Food}$.

The suggested groupings are in line with the general characterization of fuel and ores as relatively capital intensive, and agricultural and food industries as relatively labor intensive, and the obtained results are in line with earlier theoretical predictions: capital- (labor-)intensive natural resource industries tend to induce a higher (lower) level of corruption, ceteris paribus.

The coefficient on "trade openness" identifies corruption as a channel through which trade restrictions affect growth, consistent with the rent-seeking literature. The obtained results suggest that countries more open to external trade (i.e., with fewer trade restrictions), indicated as a high score on the openness measure, tend to have less corruption, consistent with the explanation from the rent-seeking literature that regulations on foreign trade tend to generate both substantial rents and rent-seeking behavior.

The results also support the hypothesis that monitoring efforts tend to dampen corruption. Sounder institutions, indicated as a high score on rule of law, tend to be associated with lower corruption, while more political instability, indicated as a high score on revolutions and coups, tends to foster a higher level of corruption.

The conclusions on the role of both rent-seeking opportunities and monitoring are robust, both in the sense of Levine and Renelt (1992) and with respect to estimation technique. As detailed in the note to

Table 1. Corruption Regression

	Corr1	Corr2	Corr3	Corr4	Corr5
GDP growth 1970–90	−0.21*	−0.22*	−0.22**	−0.03	
Initial income				0.62*	0.75***
Fuel_1970	−2.85*				
Ores_1970	−5.47***				
Fuel and ores_1970		−4.19***	−4.16***	−4.02***	−2.73***
Agriculture_1970	4.79				
Food_1970	4.55*				
Agriculture and food_1970		4.81***	4.12**	4.54***	4.36***
Rule of law	0.68***	0.69***	0.61***	0.43***	0.33***
Revolutions and coups			−1.09**	−1.20**	−1.38***
Trade openness	1.19**	1.11**	1.23***	0.93**	1.18***
Fraction	−0.002	−0.003	−0.002	0.002	0.001
Africa	0.26	0.21	0.09	0.51	0.60
Constant	0.98**	1.00***	1.43***	−3.63	−4.53**
Adjusted *R*-squared	0.74	0.74	0.75	0.79	0.79
Number of observations	72	72	72	72	72

Note: Specifications, including GDP growth rate, are estimated using 2SLS with GDP growth rate endogenized. Coefficients significant at the 1 percent, 5 percent, and 10 percent level of significance are indicated with ***, **, and *, respectively. Qualitative results are robust to the presence or absence of a wide set of additional variables, including bureaucratic quality, arms imports as a percentage of GDP, regional dummies, indicators on the incidence of civil conflicts, indicators on the state of property rights, foreign aid flows, share of government current expenditure in GDP, and cross variables between rule of law and regional dummies and between natural resources and regional dummies. Qualitative results are robust to estimation by a tobit procedure to account for both the upper and lower limits in the dependent variable.

Table 1, we tested for robustness by the inclusion of a series of variables commonplace in the economic growth literature, and the qualitative conclusions remained intact. We also estimated the regressions shown in Table 1 by a tobit procedure, to account for both the upper and the lower limits in the dependent variable, and again the results remain qualitatively unchanged.

Three other results are worth noting. First, it appears that the level of corruption is not inherently affected by ethnic diversity, contrary to the suggestions in Mauro (1995) and Tanzi (Chapter 2 in this volume). On a related level, we find no evidence for the predicted effect of bureaucratic power concentration: the results in Table 1 are robust to the addition of a variable on government current expenditures as a share of GDP. Second, it appears that corruption in Africa takes the same form as elsewhere: once account is taken of the key determinants of the level of corruption, the coefficient on the Africa dummy variable is insignificantly different from zero. Third, the coefficient on the GDP growth rate suggests that rapid growth leads to more corruption, a result robust to instrumenting long-run growth with initial income. From our previous discussion, the inference is not that a lower growth rate is somehow to be preferred but simply that rapid economic progress, if its beneficial effect is to be fully felt, requires special attention to be paid to the social and institutional fabric.

Growth Regression

The results for the growth regression are presented in Table 2. The first regression reproduces equation (4) of Sachs and Warner (1995a), while the others endogenize corruption. The third and fourth regressions specifically account for the possible effects of commodity price volatility, measured by the standard deviation of the WDI commodity price indices (fuel, ores, agriculture, and food) weighted by the country's export share of the specific commodity. The rationale for including this variable is that commodity prices are renowned for their volatility that tends to, inter alia, increase ex ante uncertainty and cause substantial variation in government revenues.

Consistent with the growth literature, the conditional convergence hypothesis is confirmed by the negative coefficient on initial income; the positive impact of trade (or the absence of trade restrictions) is confirmed by the positive coefficient on trade openness; and positive terms of trade shocks are associated with higher growth. In the context of the neoclassical model, these results confirm that countries converge faster the farther they are from their own steady state. Consistent with predictions from the Dutch disease literature, our results suggest that natural resource abundance tends to reduce long-run growth rate. Unlike other studies, however, we find no evidence that, ceteris paribus, the growth process in Africa is different from other parts of the world. In fact, the fourth regression, LW3, suggests that the addition of the Africa dummy leads simply to some multicollinearity with the price variability measure, reducing each variable to insignificance.

In accordance with our theoretical model, long-term growth is negatively affected by the level of corruption: the average annual GDP

Table 2. Growth Regression

	SW4	LW1	LW2	LW3
Corruption	...	0.43**	0.71***	0.72***
Initial income	−1.47***	−1.50***	−1.90***	−1.90***
Natural resources	−7.19***	−7.51***	−6.29***	−6.41***
Trade openness	1.69***	1.55***	0.88*	0.90*
Investment/GDP[1]	0.94***	0.73*	0.31	0.31
Terms of trade	0.16***	0.19***	0.30***	0.29***
Rule of law	0.30***	...	...	...
Africa	...	...	...	−0.04
Commodity price variability in Africa	...	...	−0.05**	−0.05
Commodity price variability in non-Africa	...	...	−0.01	...
Constant	10.29***	10.78***	14.86***	14.80***
Adjusted R-squared	0.65	0.66	0.65	0.65
Number of observations	78	72	72	72

Note: SW4 refers to regression (4) in Sachs and Warner (1995a). LW1–3 refer to our regressions estimated using 2SLS with corruption endogenized. A lower score on the corruption index indicates less corruption. Coefficients significant at the 1 percent, 5 percent, and 10 percent level of significance are indicated with ***, **, and *, respectively. Qualitative results are robust to the presence or exclusion of additional variables including political indicators on the incidence of civil conflicts and revolutions, institutional indicators on the state of property rights, and public sector participation in the petroleum and mineral extraction industries.

[1]Qualitative results are robust to instrumenting the investment ratio with the relative price of investment goods in 1970 (log of the ratio of the investment deflator to the overall GDP deflator in 1970).

growth rate is raised by some 1.4 percentage points with a one standard deviation improvement in the corruption ranking (equivalent to Venezuela reducing its corruption to the level of Chile, Chile to the United States, or Kenya to Taiwan Province of China). From the results for the corruption regression, we can identify three mechanisms for such an improvement in corruption rankings: trade policy, quality of institutions, and political stability. We present below suggestive calculations for the impact on both corruption and growth of a change in the first two mechanisms. Table 3 considers the impact of a more open trade policy, while Table 4 estimates the impact of a combined policy effort: a more open trade policy and an improvement in the quality of institutions.

Table 3. Improvements in Trade Regime

From	To	Effect on Corruption[1]	Effect on Growth[2]
Venezuela	Chile	0.66	0.95
Chile	United States	0.52	0.74
Kenya	Taiwan Province of China	1.09	1.55
Cameroon	Taiwan Province of China	1.23	1.75
Cameroon	Chile	0.71	1.01
Nigeria	Chile	0.52	0.74

[1]One standard deviation is equal to 1.93 in the corruption ranking.
[2]One standard deviation is equal to 1.95 in the annual average (1970–90) GDP growth rate.

The implication from Table 3 is the following: had Venezuela's trade policies been as liberal as Chile's over the period 1970–90, Venezuela would have experienced a significant improvement in the corruption ranking (equivalent to 35 percent of one standard deviation), and an increase of close to 1 percentage point in the average annual GDP growth rate; and if Cameroon had similarly emulated Chile, Cameroon's corruption ranking and growth rate would have improved by similar magnitudes.

In this case, if Venezuela had opened its economy and strengthened its legal institutions to the same degree as Chile, Venezuela's corruption ranking would have improved by close to one standard deviation and its average annual GDP growth rate would have risen by some 1.8 percentage points; similar policy actions for Cameroon would have had broadly the same impact.

It is also instructive to evaluate the effects of these policy improvements on the level of income. Table 5 compares the actual and the projected level of income in 1990 for the countries implementing the policy changes detailed in Tables 3 and 4. That is, if Cameroon had emulated Taiwan Province of China in terms of trade policy and institutions over the period 1970–90, Cameroon's level of income per economically active person would have been, by 1990, more than US$2,000 higher than the observed outcome, an increase of some 84 percent in the purchasing power of the average Cameroonian!

Operationally, the normative implication is that to attenuate the extent of corruption and to foster significant improvements in the standards of living, policymakers should focus on liberalizing the external

Table 4. Improvements in Trade Regime and Rule of Law

From	To	Effect on Corruption[1]	Effect on Growth[2]
Venezuela	Chile	1.88	1.81
Chile	United States	1.13	1.17
Kenya	Taiwan Province of China	3.53	3.28
Cameroon	Taiwan Province of China	3.06	3.05
Cameroon	Chile	1.93	1.88
Nigeria	Chile	2.96	2.03

[1] One standard deviation is equal to 1.93 in the corruption ranking.
[2] One standard deviation is equal to 1.95 in the annual average (1970–90) GDP growth rate.

trade regime and enhancing the quality of legal and political institutions. Given our finding that neither the corruption nor the growth process has specific regional dimensions, this recommendation remains as valid in Africa as in any other region of the world.

Natural Resource Components

Although Table 1 confirms that natural resources affect economic growth partly through their effect on corruption, the regressions in Table 2 reveal that the Sachs and Warner (1995a) proposition on the negative effect of natural resources on growth remains intact, even after accounting for the endogeneity of corruption and the effects of commodity price variability and trade liberalization. To further investigate the impact of natural resources on growth, we reestimate the previous growth equation by disaggregating natural resources into its constituent components, accounting for the possible effects of the (nonrandom) regional distribution of natural resource endowments, and also controlling for the effects of government consumption.

There are substantial differences in the characteristics of the four components of commodities originally grouped by Sachs and Warner (1995a) under natural resources. Consider not just the aforementioned differences with respect to factor intensity, but also differences in ownership (with fuel production most often dominated by foreign capital but with public enterprises playing a significant role in mining), the longer extraction time required for capital recovery in both fuel and ores, and the higher export share for fuel and ores, whereas food and

Table 5. Improvements in Policy Stance 1970–90: Projected Impact on 1990 GDP per Economically Active Person (EAP)

| | | 1990 GDP per EAP[1] | | |
| | | | Including improvement in[2] | |
From	To	Actual	Trade regime	Trade regime and rule of law
Venezuela	Chile	10,411	12,577	14,956
Chile	United States	6,806	7,895	8,609
Kenya	Taiwan Province of China	1,918	2,616	3,700
Cameroon	Taiwan Province of China	2,434	3,456	4,482
Cameroon	Chile	2,434	2,980	3,543
Nigeria	Chile	1,963	2,277	2,948

[1] GDP per EAP for the country implementing the policy change; in current U.S. dollars.
[2] Policy regime improvements from Table 3 (trade) and Table 4 (trade and rule of law).

agricultural raw material production is primarily oriented to the domestic market (although this pattern may change with increases in income).[24] Furthermore, the low productivity sectors of agriculture and food tend to tie a large share of the labor force to rural areas, hampering labor migration to more urban areas with potentially more productive occupations and thereby limiting a country's growth potential. To allow the effects of each category to be different, we again disaggregate the natural resource variable into the four components, fuel, ores, agriculture, and food.

On a similar note, a glance at external trade statistics should suffice to convince anyone of the tendency for the distribution of natural resources to be geographically concentrated. Radetzki (1990) points out that while total commodities are almost equally distributed between in-

---

[24] The difference between home consumption and export may have a significant impact on the empirical results. Whereas it is customary to proxy production with export figures, since the latter are often incomplete and unreliable, the differences between commodity groups may imply that the production of food and agricultural raw material is generally underestimated in a manner not unrelated to the stage of economic development. Assuming that a higher proportion of food production in lower-income countries is for domestic consumption, relying on export statistics instead of production data would tend to overestimate the potentially negative impact of food on growth. Unfortunately, we are unable to avoid this potential bias as we have not been able to locate food production statistics.

dustrial and developing countries, ores are produced predominantly in industrial countries, whereas the opposite holds for fuels. To account for these structural differences, we substitute the natural resource variables by the residuals of a regression of the original commodity data on a set of regional dummy variables (Africa, Latin America, Middle East, other nonindustrial, and industrial).

A resource boom has often triggered an (unsustainable) increase in government spending, an effect particularly important in developing countries and in cases of fuel or ore discoveries, where the additional revenue mostly accrues directly to the government. To the extent that such spending spurts reflect current consumption instead of investment in economically justifiable projects, long-run economic growth should be negatively affected, partly in the likely event of a downturn in commodity markets. To account for this effect, we include, as an explanatory variable, the beginning of period ratio of government consumption to GDP, where government consumption is defined as government expenditure net of spending on defense and on education, and is originally taken from Sachs and Warner (1995a).

The results, as reported in Table 6, reveal that the negative effect of natural resources on growth is now confined to the food industry with the conclusion robust to the inclusion of the variable on government consumption and to the aggregation of fuel, ores, and agriculture into one variable. In NatRes6, the stability of the coefficients when food is omitted suggests that the negative effect of food is not an artifact of a high correlation with the remaining explanatory variables. Whether this result could be reversed by the use of data on food production instead of food exports, as discussed in footnote 24, remains an issue for further research.

In the end, what do these results suggest about the effect of natural resources on growth? Table 7 calculates the total effect from previously estimated regressions. While the Sachs and Warner (1995a) results indicate that, on average, a one standard deviation increase in the ratio of natural resource exports to GNP is associated with a decrease of just over 1 percent in the growth rate, the results for our preferred specification, the equations previously labeled as Corr3 and NatRes3, indicate that the negative effect for fuel and ores is approximately half of that, at some 0.6 percent, and due entirely to the indirect effect through corruption. Meanwhile, the effect for agriculture, owing to the latter's beneficial impact on corruption, is actually positive, whereas the effect for food, as emphasized above, remains negative.

Table 6. The Growth Effects of Natural Resources[1]

	NatRes1	NatRes2	NatRes3	NatRes4	NatRes5	NatRes6
Corruption	0.79	0.94***	0.92***	0.92***	0.98***	0.69***
Initial income	−2.15***	−2.02***	−2.22***	−2.09***	−2.30***	−1.94***
Fuel_1970; Res_fuel 1970[2]	3.50	−1.39	−1.22	−1.54	...	...
Ores_1970; Res_ores 1970	−3.58*	−2.80	−2.62	−3.13	...	...
Agriculture_1970; Res_agriculture 1970	3.34	2.36	0.85	2.48	...	...
Food_1970; Res_food 1970	−11.32***	−11.02***	−8.90**	−9.18**	−8.69**	...
Fuel, ores, and agriculture	...	...	...	...	−1.30	−1.51
Trade openness	1.01	1.04*	1.04*	1.08**	0.98*	1.53***
Investment/GDP[3]	0.21	0.80	0.99*	1.15**	1.13**	0.97**
Terms of trade	0.24***	0.34***	0.32***	0.31***	0.34***	0.31***
Commodity price variability in Africa	−0.09***	−0.09***	−0.07***	−0.07**	−0.08***	−0.06***
Commodity price variability in non-Africa	−0.03	−0.03	−0.03	−0.02	−0.03	−0.02
Government consumption	...	...	−10.04***	−10.06***	−10.82***	−12.89***
Public participation in fuels	...	...	...	−0.29	...	...
Public participation in ores	...	...	...	0.56	...	...
Constant	17.81***	15.34***	17.82***	16.31***	18.35***	16.17***
Adjusted R-squared	0.66	0.58	0.64	0.64	0.63	0.67
Number of observations	72	72	72	72	72	72

[1] All regressions are estimated using 2SLS with "corruption" endogenized. Coefficients significant at the 1 percent, 5 percent, and 10 percent level of significance are indicated with ***, **, and *, respectively. A lower score on the corruption index indicates more corruption.

[2] NatRes1 includes the components of the original "Natural resources" (e.g., Fuel_1970) as independent variables. NatRes2–4 include the residuals from regressing each of the components of "Natural resources" (e.g., Res_fuel 1970) on a set of geographical dummy variables (Africa, Middle East, Latin America, other nonindustrial, and industrial). "Fuel, ores, and agriculture" in NatRes5–6 is the sum of Res_fuel 1970, Res_ores 1970, and Res_agriculture 1970.

[3] The investment ratio is instrumented with the relative price of investment goods in 1970 (log of the ratio of the investment deflator to the overall GDP deflator in 1970).

Table 7. One Standard Deviation Increase in Natural Resource Exports[1]

	Effect on Long-Run GDP Growth Rate[2]			
	SW4	LW2	NatRes1	NatRes3
Fuel	−1.15	−1.48	−0.53	−0.61
Ores	−1.15	−1.48	−1.10	−0.61
Agriculture	−1.15	−0.54	0.52	0.61
Food	−1.15	−0.54	−1.29	−0.82

[1]For SW4 and LW2, one standard deviation (of the aggregate measure "Natural resources") equals 16 percent of GNP. For NatRes1 and NatRes2, one standard deviation is 17 percent for fuel, 9 percent for ores, 3 percent for agriculture, and 7 percent for food.

[2]LW2, NatRes1, and NatRes3 include the indirect effects of corruption as estimated by Corr3. Coefficients statistically insignificant at the 10 percent level were set to zero.

V. Conclusions

The present paper theoretically and empirically investigated a, thus far ignored, channel through which natural resources might affect a country's economic growth, that is, through an increase in rent-seeking activities. More generally, the paper analyzed two inextricably intertwined broader issues. First, what factors determine the incidence of corruption, and in particular, what role does the abundance of natural resources play? Second, what factors affect economic growth, and how can one explain the stylized fact that resource-rich economies tend to grow slower?

Given the scope of the paper, our analytical model focused on four major determinants of the extent of corruption in an economy. It demonstrated the corruption-dampening effects of improvements in monitoring technology and increases in penalties, and the corruption-fostering effects of capital-intensive production and concentration of bureaucratic power. In the framework of our model, natural resource discoveries were interpreted as technology shocks, with their extent depending on the specific type of commodity considered. Empirically, one of the main results was to confirm that capital-intensive natural resources are a major determinant of corruption.

Other interesting features of the analytical model concerned the growth effects of natural resource–induced corruption and anticorruption policies. Whereas the existence of corruption always reduced growth compared with the noncorruption case, the negative effects exhibited some nonlinearities and were more pronounced in less-developed economies (characterized by a lower initial steady-state capital stock). Correspondingly, the effectiveness of the two anticorruption policies considered also depended on the state of development of the economy. Institution building, that is, improvements in monitoring technology, tends to be more effective in less-developed countries, while stricter enforcement, that is, increases in penalties, are predicted to be more effective in more-developed countries. Empirically, the growth regressions unambiguously corroborate the negative growth effect of corruption and support our initial hypothesis of the corruption channel being an important explanation for the slow growth of resource-rich economies.

Both our theoretical and empirical results stress the importance of strong (or at least strengthened) institutions in the wake of natural resource discoveries as a means to curb the associated negative growth effects of corruption. This is especially true in less-developed countries where natural resource discoveries have a much higher relative impact on the economy's capital stock and on the extent of corruption, and are confronted with generally weaker and less adaptable institutions. Other interesting empirical results are the findings that, ceteris paribus, neither the corruption nor the growth process are different in Africa than elsewhere, and that rapid growth induces an increase in corruption.

This study constitutes a first step toward an investigation of the effect of natural resources on corruption and growth. In this context, it would be useful to model the government's anticorruption policies as the response of an optimizing agent, which would allow, inter alia, a formal derivation of the need for, and the extent of, institutional and administrative adjustments in response to resource discoveries. Empirically, production, instead of export, data for natural resources may help to explain the persistently negative coefficient of food items in the growth equation, and the addition of a time dimension to our empirical analysis would allow some understanding of the economic dynamics of natural resource discoveries.

References

Banks, A.S., 1979, *Cross-National Time-Series Data Archive* (Binghampton: Center for Social Analysis, State University of New York).

Bardhan, P., 1997, "Corruption and Development: A Review of Issues," *Journal of Economic Literature,* Vol. 35 (September), pp. 1320–46.

Barro, R.J., 1991, "Economic Growth in a Cross Section of Countries," *Quarterly Journal of Economics*, Vol. 106 (May), pp. 407–43.

———, and J. Lee, 1994, "Data Set for a Panel of 138 Countries" (unpublished and data diskette).

Baumol, W.J., "Entrepreneurship: Productive, Unproductive, and Destructive," *Journal of Political Economy*, Vol. 98 (October), pp. 893–921.

Beck, Paul J., and Michael W. Maher, 1986, "A Comparison of Bribery and Bidding in Thin Markets," *Economics Letters*, Vol. 20, No. 1, pp. 1–5.

Becker, G., 1968, "Crime and Punishment: An Economic Approach," *Journal of Political Economy*, Vol. 76 (March/April), pp. 169–217.

Bhagwati, J.N., 1982, "Directly Unproductive, Profit-Seeking (DUP) Activities," *Journal of Political Economy*, Vol. 90 (October), pp. 988–1002.

Boycko, M., A. Shleifer, and R. Vishny, 1995, *Privatizing Russia* (Cambridge, Massachusetts: MIT Press).

DeLong, J.B., and L. Summers, 1991, "Equipment Investment and Economic Growth," *Quarterly Journal of Economics*, Vol. 106 (May), pp. 455–502.

Easterly, W., 1993, "How Much Do Distortions Affect Growth?" *Journal of Monetary Economics,* Vol. 32, pp. 187–212.

———, and R. Levine, 1996, "Africa's Growth Tragedy" (unpublished; Washington: World Bank).

Huntington, S. P., 1968, *Political Order in Changing Societies* (New Haven: Yale University Press).

Khan, S.A., 1994, *Nigeria: The Political Economy of Oil* (Oxford: Oxford University Press).

King, R.G., and R. Levine, 1993, "Finance and Growth: Schumpeter Might Be Right," *Quarterly Journal of Economics*, Vol. 108 (August), pp. 717–37.

Knack, S., and P. Keefer, 1995, "Institutions and Economic Performance: Cross-Country Tests Using Alternative Institutional Measures," *Economics and Politics*, Vol. 7 (November), pp. 207–27.

Krueger, A.O., 1974, "The Political Economy of the Rent-Seeking Society," *American Economic Review*, Vol. 64 (June), pp. 291–303.

———, 1993, "Virtuous and Vicious Circles in Economic Development," *American Economic Review, Papers and Proceedings*, Vol. 83 (May), pp. 351–55.

Lane, P., and A. Tornell, 1997, "Voracity and Growth," Harvard Institute for Economic Research Discussion Paper No. 1807 (Cambridge, Massachusetts).

Leff, N., 1964, "Economic Development through Bureaucratic Corruption," *American Behavioral Scientist*, pp. 8–14.

Levine, R., and D. Renelt, 1992, "A Sensitivity Analysis of Cross-Country Growth Regressions," *American Economic Review*, Vol. 82 (September), pp. 942–64.

Lien, D.H.D., 1986, "A Note on Competitive Bribery Games," *Economics Letters*, Vol. 22, No. 4, pp. 337–41.

Lui, F. T., 1985, "An Equilibrium Queuing Model of Bribery," *Journal of Political Economy*, Vol. 93 (August), pp. 760–81.

———, 1996, "Three Aspects of Corruption," *Contemporary Economic Policy*, Vol. 14 (July), pp. 26–29.

Mankiw, N., D. Romer, and D. Weil, 1992, "A Contribution to the Empirics of Economic Growth," *Quarterly Journal of Economics*, Vol. 107, pp. 407–37.

Mauro, P., 1995, "Corruption and Growth," *Quarterly Journal of Economics*, Vol. 110 (August), pp. 681–712.

Murphy, K., A. Shleifer, and R. Vishny, 1991, "The Allocation of Talent: Implications for Growth," *Quarterly Journal of Economics*, Vol. 106 (May), pp. 503–30.

———, 1993, "Why Is Rent-Seeking So Costly to Growth?" *American Economic Review, Papers and Proceedings*, Vol. 83 (May), pp. 409–14.

Myrdal, G., 1968, *Asian Drama: An Inquiry into the Poverty of Nations* (New York: Twentieth Century Fund).

North, D.C., 1990, *Institutions, Institutional Change, and Economic Performance* (New York: Cambridge University Press).

Organization for Economic Cooperation and Development (OECD), 1998, *Convention On Combating Bribery of Foreign Public Officials in International Business Transactions* (Paris).

Poirson, H., 1998, "Economic Security, Private Investment, and Growth in Developing Countries," IMF Working Paper No. 98/4 (Washington: International Monetary Fund).

Radetzki, M., 1990, *A Guide to Primary Commodities in the World Economy* (Oxford: Basil Blackwell).

Rama, M., 1993, "Rent Seeking and Economic Growth: A Theoretical Model and Some Empirical Evidence," *Journal of Development Economics*, Vol. 42 (October), pp. 35–50.

Rauch, J., and P. Evans, 1999, "Bureaucratic Structure and Bureaucratic Performance in Less Developed Countries," University of California at San Diego Working Paper 99-06 (San Diego: University of California).

Rebelo, S., 1991, "Long-Run Policy Analysis and Long-Run Growth," *Journal of Political Economy*, Vol. 99 (June), pp. 500–21.

Romer, P., 1994, "New Goods, Old Theory, and the Welfare Costs of Trade Restrictions," *Journal of Development Economics*, Vol. 43 (February), pp. 5–38.

Rose-Ackerman, S., 1978, *Corruption: A Study in Political Economy* (New York: Academic Press).

Sachs, J., and A. Warner, 1995a, "Natural Resource Abundance and Economic Growth," NBER Working Paper No. 5398 (Cambridge, Massachusetts: National Bureau of Economic Research).

———, 1995b, "Economic Reform and the Process of Global Integration," *Brookings Papers on Economic Activity: 1*, pp. 1–118.

Shleifer A., and R. Vishny, 1993, "Corruption," *Quarterly Journal of Economics,* Vol. 108 (August), pp. 599–617.

Short, R., 1984, "The Role of Public Enterprises: An International Statistical Comparison," in *Public Enterprise in Mixed Economies: Some Macroeconomic Aspects*, ed. by R. Floyd, C. Gray, and R. Short (Washington: International Monetary Fund).

Wei, S., 1997, "Why Is Corruption So Much More Taxing Than Tax? Arbitrariness Kills," NBER Working Paper No. 6255 (Cambridge, Massachusetts: National Bureau of Economic Research).

World Bank, 1997, *Helping Countries Combat Corruption: The Role of the World Bank* (Washington).

8

Corruption, Growth, and Public Finances

Vito Tanzi and Hamid R. Davoodi

Introduction

In the last decade corruption has received a great deal of attention from a broad spectrum of the public. The study of corruption is no longer regarded as a subject of inquiry exclusively by students of politics and sociology. It now occupies the attention of many other fields such as political economy, public administration and law. Many international and regional organizations now regard corruption and poor governance as major obstacles to good policy-making. The current interest in corruption probably reflects an increase in the scope of corruption over the years, and is in part fueled by a better understanding of the economic costs of corruption. Thus it does not just reflect a greater awareness of an age-old problem.

Until recently segments of the economic literature had presented a romantic view of corruption. This view made corruption seem an almost

---

Reprinted from *Political Economy of Corruption*, edited by Arvind K. Jain (London, Routledge, 2001), pp. 89–110.

virtuous activity and possibly good for growth in a world stifled by bad governments. For example, in various theoretical studies it was argued that corruption removes or relaxes government-imposed rigidities; greases the wheels of commerce; allocates investment and time to the most efficient users; keeps wages low; and may even act as a political glue that holds a country together.[1] The romantic view of corruption has been replaced, in more recent years, by a more realistic and much less favorable view. According to this new view, the payment of bribes is not a panacea for overcoming red tape and cumbersome government regulations; the highest bribes are paid by rent-seekers and not by the most efficient individuals; a comprehensive civil service reform is better at reducing corruption than simply raising wages; corruption is subject to increasing returns which perpetuate it; and corruption creates an environment that, in time, can lead to the collapse of political regimes.

This chapter elaborates on these contrasting views of corruption and, from this perspective, analyzes the conceptual and empirical links between corruption, economic growth, and public finances. There are many indirect channels through which corruption lowers growth, and recently some formal models have been developed that link corruption directly to growth. By contrast, there are papers in the public finance literature, and particularly on the tax side, which systematically investigate corruption, tax evasion and the incentive structure of tax inspectors and the public. This chapter discusses some related issues.

Corruption and Growth

As a point of departure, it is important to describe two associations that have appeared prominently in the recent empirical literature on corruption. First, there is a negative association between corruption perception indexes and levels of economic development measured by real per capita GDP.[2] Figure 1 shows, for a sample of ninety-seven countries in 1997, that countries with higher perceived corruption tend to have

---

[1]For a concise survey of this literature, see Tanzi (1998a).

[2]The corruption perception index is the extended Transparency International index and is taken from Lambsdorff (1998) and real per capita GDP is in purchasing power parity US dollars and is taken from International Monetary Fund's World Economic Outlook database. The original index which ranges from 0 (highly corrupt) to 10 (highly clean) has been rescaled (i.e., adjusted index = 10 − original index) so that higher values of the adjusted index represent higher perceptions of corruption.

lower real per capita GDP. Or, putting it differently, countries with low per capita income tend to have higher corruption. The correlation coefficient is −0.80, which is statistically significant with a t-ratio of −13.2.[3] Second, there is a negative association between corruption perception indexes and economic growth as measured by growth in real per capita GDP.

The relation shown in Figure 2 for the same countries as in Figure 1 indicates that countries with higher corruption tend to have a lower growth rate. The correlation coefficient is −0.32 which is statistically significant with a t-ratio of −3.2. Although, this association is consistent with causation running in both directions, some studies have used econometric techniques, such as instrumental variable techniques (Mauro 1995), to argue that the causality is from corruption to economic growth. Nevertheless, regardless of the position taken on the direction of causality, the simple negative association between corruption and growth is supported by the data. This chapter presents some arguments to explain why this relation exists. It analyzes some direct and indirect channels through which corruption may affect economic growth. No attempt is made to formalize these channels in an explicit framework. The channels analyzed are: (a) the impact of corruption on enterprises with particular attention on small enterprises and its differentiated effect between large and small enterprises; (b) the impact of corruption on investment; and (c) the impact of corruption on the allocation of talent. In the last section, we will investigate some relationships between corruption and the composition of taxes and spending.

Corruption and Enterprise Growth

The increase in development of enterprises as a building block of growth (at industry and national level) is an old and respected topic in economics, dating back to Adam Smith's notion of scale economies, Alfred Marshall's description of industrial evolution of small firms, and Schumpeterian forces of creative destruction and entrepreneurship. Historically, large enterprises had been viewed as the most important source of jobs, innovation and growth. However, in recent

---

[3]Similar results are obtained using other corruption indexes. Recent studies of causes of corruption interpret this correlation as causation running from per capita GDP to corruption; see Treisman (2000).

Figure 1. Corruption and Development in Ninety-Seven Countries

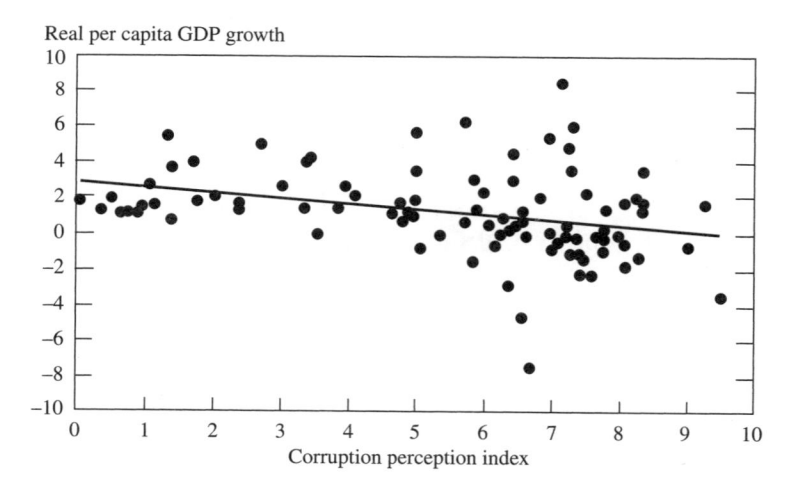

Real per capita GDP (in 1,000US$)

Figure 2. Corruption and Growth in Ninety-Seven Countries

Real per capita GDP growth

years, public policy has increasingly focused on the contributions of small and medium-size enterprises (SMEs) to these objectives. Considerable empirical research conducted on OECD countries over the last decade has established a number of interesting facts which lie behind the changing perception of the role of SMEs in the economy. These are:[4]

- SMEs may comprise a smaller share of value added in the economy than large enterprises, but they employ the bulk of the labor force and create most of the new jobs.
- SMEs tend to be less capital intensive, consistent with their importance in the employment share.
- SMEs tend to be product-innovative whereas large firms tend to be process-innovative.[5]
- SMEs are more financially constrained than large enterprises which have easier access to the capital market; in the United States, for example, SMEs make up half of the value added in the economy, but represent only 6 percent of total business finance.
- SMEs contribute to growth in normal as well as recession times in ways that large firms do not. In a study of twelve European countries during the first half of 1990s, a greater increase in the smaller firm sales, compared to large firm sales, led to more growth in the national GNP in the following year.[6] During the deep recession of 1990–3 in Sweden, the SMEs' share of job gains was larger than the SMEs' share of job losses and as a result SMEs performed better than large firms.
- The survival of SMEs depends on access to finance, but also on competent entrepreneurship and talented management. It also depends on the environment that they face.

The above description of the role of SMEs is not limited to OECD countries but it covers also transition economies and developing countries. Thus, if corruption were to be more damaging to small and new enterprises than to large enterprises, it would imply that corruption would be putting brakes on the forces that promote growth. We will argue that, in fact, the effect of corruption is differentiated among the enterprises and is particularly pronounced on the small enterprises.

---

[4]See Acs, Carlsson, and Karlsson (1999) and Acs and Yeung (1999).
[5]Large enterprises tend to dominate in process innovations because they have the capacity to appropriate the returns to research and development.
[6]See Acs and Yeung (1999).

In a survey of 3,000 enterprises across twenty transition economies, conducted jointly for the European Bank for Reconstruction and Development (EBRD) and the World Bank—referred to as the Business Environment and Enterprise Performance Survey (BEEPS)—enterprises were asked to assess the major impediments in their business environment in terms of the extent of competition, corruption, taxes and regulations, inflation, financing and infrastructure. The results of the survey show the differential impact of corruption on firm size. Across all regions, corruption and anti-competitive practices were perceived as the most difficult obstacles by start-up firms with both barriers being ranked on average as 13 percent greater by start-ups, which tend to be largely SMEs, than by state-owned enterprises (SOEs) which tend to be older and large enterprises.[7]

A detailed breakdown of other impediments have shown that it is the access to essential business services, rather than the cost of finance per se, that is the greatest problem for start-ups. These findings seem to be consistent with other survey-based studies. For example, in a study of eighty-four wholesale trade enterprises in the city of Moscow in 1993, a dummy variable representing connection of the head of the enterprise to the relevant city government officials was a good predictor of which enterprises got soft credit. This dummy was a better predictor than the profit of the enterprise or other economic factors (Treisman 1995).

The role of connections in the allocation of credit is, of course, not unique to transition economies. In a study of Japanese firms of varying size, investment in physical capital by firms with close ties to banks was found to be much less sensitive to their liquidity than for firms raising their capital through arms' length transactions (Hoshi, Kashyap, and Scharfstein 1991). Although this finding is consistent with the role of financial intermediaries as monitoring agents that are in the business of reducing incentive problems and solving asymmetric information problems, it is also consistent with the observation that the allocation of credit based on arms' length relationships is perhaps good for growth in the long run, given the subsequent state of financial and enterprise restructuring in Japan in the 1990s and the long recession.

These findings from the experience of OECD countries and transition economies have important public policy implications. In general, the lessons are that factors that impede the growth of SMEs and stifle the entry of new firms, which tend to be small and important to a dy-

---

[7]See EBRD (1999).

namic economy, will also tend to slow down the growth rate of the economy.

The conceptual link between corruption, size of enterprises and growth runs along the following lines. Large enterprises are known to find it easier to protect themselves from corrupt officials; they have specialized departments; they can use "facilitators"—individuals with skills to bypass the regulations and tax laws; their size protects them from petty bureaucrats; and they can use political power to further their rent-seeking corruption to their advantage. For large enterprises corruption is often of a cost-reducing kind as it allows them to enjoy monopoly rents and scale economies; whereas for SMEs it is often of a cost-increasing kind because they have to make payments which do not contribute to the productivity or profitability of the firm but that are necessary for their survivability. SMEs are normally preyed upon by petty bureaucrats and corrupt tax inspectors and are forced into making substantial payments and abiding by cumbersome regulations. Bribes may be required to obtain various authorizations or freedom from bureaucratic harassment. Bribe payments may amount to a substantial portion of SMEs' operating costs which can drive them out of business since they tend to operate in more competitive environments than large enterprises. In a study in Indonesia it was reported that these payments may have been as high as 20 percent of the sales of shops or small enterprises.

A growing number of surveys provides empirical support for the conceptual link:

- In a sample of 176 Ugandan firms in 1997, the median firm paid bribes equivalent to 28 percent of its investment in machinery and equipment; and there was no evidence that firms that paid higher bribes on average received more beneficial government favors (Svensson 2000). In Uganda, SMEs represent 50 percent of total employment and 96 percent of business establishments.

- Ugandan firms that are involved in exports and receive tax exemptions have a higher probability of facing corrupt bureaucrats and having to pay bribes (Svensson 2000). The implications of this finding are that (a) corruption does not grease the wheels of commerce; (b) those who can afford to pay more will be asked to pay more; and (c) trade liberalization and tax reform can reduce the opportunities for corruption. However, trade liberalization, though good for the economy as a whole, is more likely to benefit larger

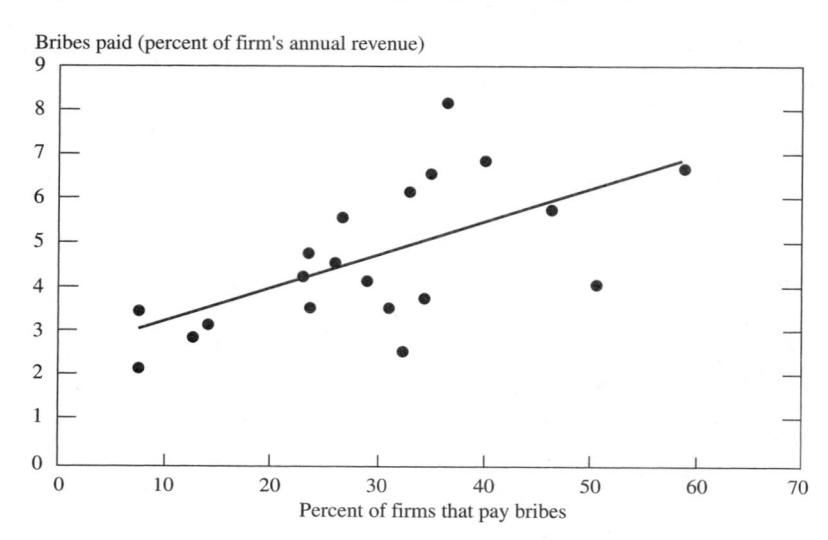

Figure 3. Bribes Paid and Their Frequency in Twenty Transition Economies

Bribes paid (percent of firm's annual revenue)

Percent of firms that pay bribes

firms than smaller firms since traditionally the tradable sector has been dominated by large firms.

- In a survey of some 3,000 enterprises in twenty transition economies, conducted by the EBRD and the World Bank, bribes are found to act like a regressive tax (EBRD 1999); the bribes paid by smaller firms amount to about 5 percent of their annual revenue compared with 4 percent for medium-size firms, and slightly less than 3 percent for large firms.[8]

- Smaller firms pay bribes more frequently than medium size and large firms; so do the new entrants and newly privatized state enterprises (ibid.). In addition, enterprises that pay bribes more frequently also tend to pay a higher bribe per unit of revenues, in other words, a higher tax in addition to other taxes. Figure 3 demonstrates the relationship between frequency of bribes and their total costs to the firms.

---

[8]EBRD defines smaller firms as having less than forty-nine employees; medium-size firms as having between fifty and 499 employees and large firms as having more than 500 employees.

- The evidence on the length of time spent by senior management of firms of different sizes with government bureaucrats seems to be mixed at best. This is a widely used indicator in the literature on corruption which may represent various costs of doing business with a government bureaucracy. The cost may involve forgone valuable time of a manager and may represent the time spent complying with regulations, lobbying for benefits, negotiating tax payments or bribes. The evidence based on Global Competitive Report data indicates that large firms waste less time with government bureaucrats. See Kaufmann and Wei (1999, Table 5). However, the BEEPS survey for the EBRD and the World Bank shows that senior management of state enterprises, which tend to be large, spend more time with government bureaucrats (about 12 percent of their time) than senior management of privatized and new entrants (10 percent each) which tend to be small firms.[9] The evidence from Ukraine is consistent with that of Kaufmann and Wei (1999, Table 5); management of new private entrants spend about 37 percent of their time with government bureaucracy, followed by 29 percent by privatized firms and 21 percent by state enterprises (Kaufmann 1997).

- Corruption can reduce the rates of return on capital of small firms by more than those of large firms. It has been estimated that public sector bureaucratic corruption in Argentina reduces the expected rates of return on invested capital by 1 to 2.5 percentage points for large firms, 2 to 2.5 percentage points for medium-sized firms and 3 to 3.6 percentage points for small enterprises (Buscaglia and Ratliff 2000). The effect is attributed by the authors to high regulatory fees and taxes. Corruption may not be expected to explain the entire difference. For example, in a different, but related study of rate of return on 1,163 World Bank–funded investment projects in sixty-one developing countries, it was found that poor quality of economic policy can reduce the rate of return by some 10 percentage points (Isham and Kaufmann 1999). However, corruption may also reduce the quality of economic policy.

In conclusion, although the evidence is often indirect and not as clear as one would wish, it is consistent with the hypothesis that corruption increases the costs of enterprises and reduces their rates of re-

---

[9] See Hellman, Jones, Kaufmann, and Schankerman (2000).

turn. Furthermore, it tends to have more damaging effects on small enterprises than on large enterprises.

Corruption and Investment

Most economists and much economic theory assume a positive relationship between investment and growth.[10] Therefore, if corruption affects investment, it must also affect growth.

Corruption may affect investment in different ways. It may affect (a) total investment, (b) the size and composition of foreign direct investment, (c) the size of public investment, and (d) the quality of the investment decisions and of investment projects.

In several papers, Paolo Mauro (1995, 1996) has shown that corruption can have a significant negative impact on *the ratio of investment to GDP*. Regressing the investment ratio on a constant, the corruption index, GDP per capita in an earlier period (1960), secondary education in 1960, and population growth, he has shown that an improvement in the corruption index (i.e. a reduction in corruption) can significantly increase the investment-GDP ratio. The fall in investment-GDP ratio caused by corruption is shown to have an important effect on growth. Mauro estimates that a reduction in corruption equivalent to two points in the corruption index, through its positive effect on the investment-GDP ratio, could raise the growth rate by about 0.5 percent. In this relationship, the impact of corruption on the quality of investment is ignored. If the reduction in investment improved the quality of investment, the positive impact on growth could be higher.

In a recent study of transition economies, Abed and Davoodi (2000) show that the impact of corruption on growth is reduced once one controls for structural reforms. These authors argue and provide evidence that structural reforms are perhaps the driving force behind the impact of corruption on growth. This interpretation and the findings have not been tested for other countries besides the transition economies and they depend on specific assessments of structural changes.

In a paper focusing on *Foreign Direct Investment* (FDI), Shang Jin Wei (1997a) has shown that while a 1 percentage point increase in the

---

[10]This by no means represents a unanimous view as argued in Tanzi and Davoodi (1997). See also Devarajan, Easterly, and Pack (1999), Easterly (1999), and Easterly and Levine (2000) for new international evidence in the case of Africa, and a large sample of developed and developing countries.

marginal tax rate on foreign direct investment (FDI) reduces incoming FDI by about 3.3 percent, an increase in the corruption index by 1 point reduces the flow of FDI into a country by about 11 percent. This would be equivalent to a 3.6 percentage points increase in the marginal tax rate. He has calculated that an increase in the corruption index, from the Singapore level to the Mexican level, would have an impact similar to that of 21–4 percentage points increase in the marginal tax rate. There is evidence in the literature that higher FDI leads to higher growth through several channels: transfer of technology, improving productivity of domestic investment and providing the necessary capital to work with complementary skilled labor (Borensztein, De Gregorio, and Lee 1998). Hence, by increasing FDI, lower corruption will lead to higher growth.

New evidence indicates that corruption also affects the composition of FDI. Using firm-level data, Smarzynska and Wei (2000), show that higher corruption in a host country shifts the composition of inward FDI towards joint ventures and away from wholly owned subsidiaries of foreign enterprises. Although the authors do not investigate the growth implications of this shift, growth is likely to be higher if such a shift re-enforces the channels identified by Borensztein, De Gregorio, and Lee (1998).

In a related work, using data from the Global Competitiveness Report, Wei (1997b) has shown that the *predictability of corruption* is also important. The less predictable the level of corruption (the higher the dispersion of individual ratings of corruption level of host countries), the greater is the impact of corruption on FDI. A higher level of dispersion makes corruption behave like an unpredictable and random tax.

> The effect of uncertainty on FDI is negative, statistically significant and . . . large. An increase in uncertainty from the level of Singapore to that of Mexico . . . is equivalent to raising the tax rate on multinational firms by 32 percentage points.
>
> (Wei 1997b)

The evidence presented by Wei (1997b) has also been corroborated using the private sector survey carried out for the World Bank's 1997 *World Development Report* (Campos, Lien, and Pradhan 1999).

Tanzi and Davoodi (1997) have argued that corruption is likely to *increase public investment but to reduce its productivity*. They have argued that public investment is easily manipulated by powerful political or bureaucratic personalities. They have tested the hypothesis that, other things being equal, higher corruption is associated with higher public investment.

Regressing public investment (as a share of GDP) against a constant, the corruption index, real per capita GDP, and the share of government revenue in GDP, Tanzi and Davoodi show that the corruption index is highly significant (at the 1 percent level) and that the more corruption there is, the more *public* investment.

Subject to the caveat expressed earlier, the reduction in the investment-GDP ratio and in the FDI-GDP ratios can be assumed to have a clear, negative impact on growth. However, the increase in the share of public investment in GDP has a more questionable impact on growth. Some related evidence is provided by Tanzi and Davoodi (1997), Reinikka and Svensson (1999), and Ades and Di Tella (1997).

Although the difficulties in getting good data are great, Tanzi and Davoodi have presented evidence that other things being equal, (a) *high corruption is associated with low operation and maintenance expenditure*; and (b) *high corruption is associated with poor quality of infrastructure*. Thus, while corruption is likely to increase public investment by distorting the composition of that investment and by causing a deterioration of a country's infrastructure, it is likely to reduce a country's growth prospects. Poor public infrastructure reduces private productivity or forces private investment to compensate for the poor infrastructure. In terms of statistical significance, the impact of corruption on the quality of infrastructure is strongest on the quality of roads (paved roads in good condition), on power outages, and on railway diesels in use. Most of these relationships survive when real per capita GDP is added to the equation as an independent variable. Thus: "the costs of corruption should also be measured in terms of the deterioration in the quality of the existing infrastructure. These costs can be very high in terms of their impact on growth" (Tanzi and Davoodi 1997). Studies at the micro, country level also confirm the above evidence. In a study of 243 Ugandan firms observed during the period 1995–7, Reinikka and Svensson (1999) show that poor public capital, proxied by unreliable and inadequate power supply, significantly reduced productive private investment. This evidence is consistent with responses from managers of the Ugandan firms who had cited poor utility services as well as corruption as major constraints to investment; the evidence is also consistent with inefficiency in investments observed across a large cross-section of countries in Africa (Devarajan, Easterly, and Pack 1999).

Ades and Di Tella (1997) have tried to estimate the impact of industrial policies (identified with procurement preferences to "national champions" and unequal fiscal treatment to enterprises). They find that corruption is higher in countries pursuing active industrial policy. In the presence of corruption, the total effect of industrial policy on investment ranges between 84 and 56 percent of the direct effect.

In conclusion, the above evidence supports a strong presumption that the net impact of corruption on investment is to reduce its size and its quality. As a consequence, growth must also be reduced.

Corruption and the Allocation of Talent

Corruption and rent-seeking may have a negative impact on growth if they create incentives for highly talented individuals to go toward rent-seeking and other unproductive activities rather than toward productive activities. This connection was also seen as important in the discussion of SMEs and their growth potential. In these enterprises, managers spent a significant amount of time dealing with rent-seeking or trying to defend their enterprises from corrupt bureaucrats. This was surely an unproductive use of their time.

The hypothesis of a connection between rent-seeking and the allocation of talent was first suggested by Baumol (1990), and by Murphy, Shleifer, and Vishny (1991). Recently it has been given a more rigorous treatment by Ehrlich and Lui (1999). Unfortunately, data on use of talent and growth by firm size are not available. Therefore, only data at the aggregate level are used to investigate the issue. These data are only suggestive of a possible relationship.

We follow the approach of Murphy, Shleifer, and Vishny (1991) that one way in which rent-seeking and corruption may influence growth is by pushing able individuals toward law rather than toward more directly productive activities such as engineering. Using data from UNESCO for fifty-three countries on enrollment in law and in engineering, we found the following result:

$$\text{Corr} = 18.50 + 0.60 \text{ Laweng} - 1.64 \text{ GDP}$$
$$(5.79) \quad (3.07) \quad\quad (-4.47)$$

$R^2 = 0.50$, number of countries = 53 (numbers in parenthesis denote t-ratios).

Here Laweng is the ratio of college enrollment in law to college enrollment in engineering in 1980; corr refers to the corruption perception index (averaged over the period 1989–97); and GDP refers to real per capita GDP in early 1960s. The latter has been found to be a robust determinant of corruption (Treisman 2000). The regression shows that countries with high corruption tend to have a low per capita GDP and a high ratio of lawyers to engineers. *Ceteris paribus*, it would seem that a more corrupt society needs more lawyers.

Separating lawyers from engineers gives:

$$\text{Corr} = 18.00 + 0.18 \text{ Law} + 0.02 \text{ Eng} - 1.70 \text{ GDP}$$
$$(5.89) \quad (3.59) \quad\quad (0.82) \quad\quad (-5.00)$$

$R^2 = 0.56$, number of countries = 53.

Thus, the correlation is between corruption and the number of lawyers. The higher the index of corruption, the more individuals are attracted to degrees in law.

Furthermore, the higher the ratio of lawyers to engineers, the lower the rate of growth.

$$\text{Growth} = 21.10 - 0.36 \text{ Corr} - 0.22 \text{ Laweng} - 2.04 \text{ GDP} + 1.39 \text{ Schooling}$$
$$(4.47)(-3.00) \quad\quad (-1.86) \quad\quad\quad (-4.06) \quad\quad\quad (3.04)$$

Adjusted $R^2 = 0.39$, number of countries = 50.

Where,

Growth = Average real per capita GDP over the 1980–97 period (source: *World Economic Outlook*).
Corr = Index of corruption, the same as used in previous regressions.
Laweng = as defined previously.
GDP = Real per capita GDP in 1980 (source: *World Economic Outlook*).
Schooling = Mean years of secondary schooling in 1980 (source: Barro and Lee 1996).

The above regression suggests a negative impact on growth of a higher allocation of talent to law as opposed to engineering. Along with the previous regression, it shows that the allocation of talent has an indirect impact on growth and that corruption allocates talent in a growth reducing fashion. The equation suggests that growth will be lower by 0.4 percentage points as a result of the combined direct and indirect impact of allocation of talent to law.

Corruption and Public Finances

In the above section, corruption and some aspects of public finance such as public investment were discussed. In the remainder of this section, additional public finance considerations which might have growth effects are taken into account, but the discussion is less directly linked to growth.

Corruption and the Composition of Public Spending

Corruption may have additional effects beyond those identified earlier. Some of these have been identified in recent papers; and some may have an impact on growth.

Mauro (1998) has shown that corruption may have no impact on total government spending.[11] He has also shown that *corrupt countries spend less for education and health*. This result has been confirmed by Gupta, Davoodi, and Alonso-Terme (1998). Because social spending is assumed to promote growth, it must be concluded that this might be another channel through which corruption may affect growth negatively.

Gupta, de Mello, and Sharan (2000) have shown that corruption also leads to higher military spending, expressed either as a share of GDP or of total government expenditure, given other determinants of military spending. There is also some evidence that cuts in military spending can lead to higher growth (Knight, Loayza, and Villanueva 1996). Therefore, higher corruption can reduce growth through higher military spending.

Corruption and the Tax Structure

The impact of corruption, and of tax evasion on tax collection is not new in the public finance literature. See Tanzi (1998b). A recent theoretical paper (Hindriks, Keen, and Muthoo 1999) has shown that in addition to loss in tax collection, the more bribes are collected, the more a tax inspector can resort to extortion in order to collect even more.[12] The existing tax system may be regressive if tax inspectors tend to go after poorer taxpayers rather than rich ones. An implication of this

---

[11]However by reducing government tax revenue, it may reduce spending or increase the fiscal deficit.

[12]See also Shleifer and Vishny (1993).

chapter is that collecting progressive taxes without inducing evasion or corruption may require commissions to be paid to tax inspectors when they report high revenue; and there will be a tradeoff between enhancing equity and efficiency in pursuing a progressive tax system.

Hindriks, Keen, and Muthoo (1999) do not investigate the growth implications of the tradeoff between equity and efficiency. However, the presence of such a tradeoff implies that lowering corruption through the payment of commissions to tax inspectors has an ambiguous impact on growth since enhancing equity is good for growth, as demonstrated by Persson and Tabellini (1994) and Alesina and Rodrik (1994), but efficiency losses from a progressive tax system are bad for growth. It is not clear, however, whether such a tradeoff is quantitatively important for growth.

In a series of papers, Tanzi and Davoodi (1997), Johnson, Kaufmann, and Zoido-Lobatón (1999) and Friedman, Johnson, Kaufmann, and Zoido-Lobatón (2000) have provided evidence that countries with high levels of corruption tend to have lower collection of tax revenues in relation to GDP, given other factors. This finding implies that some of the taxes paid by taxpayers are diverted toward the pockets of the tax administrators. Thus, the true burden of taxation on the taxpayers may not fall as much as the fall in the tax receipts of the government; and as a result, the tax system in practice may become less progressive.[13] Also some taxes are not collected from some taxpayers leading to less neutrality of the tax system. These arguments demonstrate that a distinction needs to be made between taxes collected by the administrators and taxes received by the treasury. Low level of taxation may lead to a sub-optimal level of public spending, which may reduce its productivity and lead to higher fiscal deficits. Higher deficits may in turn lower the growth rate (Fischer 1993). Therefore, corruption may also affect growth through its effect on fiscal deficits.

Previous studies of corruption and tax collection have addressed the effect of corruption on the level of taxation and not on its composition. One may expect that different types of taxes respond differently to corruption since payment of some taxes, but not of others, may be negotiated; some taxes are self-assessed in some countries (for example, income taxes); some are assessed by tax inspectors; hence, they are

---

[13]Gupta, Davoodi, and Alonso-Terme (1998) provide evidence that corruption increases income inequality by reducing the progressivity of the tax system.

subject to opportunistic behavior and extortion on the part of tax inspectors; and some are easier to administer than others (such as international trade taxes). Recent surveys eliciting respondents' views on the prevalence of corruption in different occupations often cite customs as an area rampant with corruption and kickbacks. Does corruption reduce taxes received from customs more than other types of taxes? Are weaknesses in the administration of certain taxes systematically related to corruption? Should one expect corruption to affect value added taxes (VAT) less than other taxes because VATs, in principle, require better book-keeping and tax records and because an overwhelming share of VAT revenue is collected from a few large enterprises? An understanding of the basic facts of the tax structure is needed to understand the impact of corruption on the tax structure. The analysis that follows should be seen as only suggestive.

Table 1 presents the average value of each tax revenue (expressed as a fraction of GDP) and the determinants of the tax structure for a sample of up to ninety countries, and two sub-samples of developing and developed countries. Developing countries tend to rely more on indirect taxes (trade taxes and taxes on domestic goods and services); they tend to have a high share of agriculture in GDP, a low tax-GDP ratio, and a high non-tax-GDP ratio. Can corruption explain any of these differences?

Relying on the empirical models of tax structure *à la* Tanzi (1987), each type of tax revenue, expressed as a fraction of GDP, is regressed on the same set of regressors. These are: a constant, share of agriculture in GDP, real per capita GDP, share of international trade in GDP; and the corruption perception index.[14] The results are shown in Table 2 and can be summarized as follows.[15]

- *Level and composition effects*: A 1 point increase in the corruption index is associated with 1.5 percentage point decline in total revenue-GDP ratio, 2.7 percent decline in tax-GDP ratio, and 1.3 percentage point increase in non-tax revenue-GDP ratio.

---

[14]The corruption perception index is based on Business International data and International Country Risk Guide data, used previously by Tanzi and Davoodi (1997). A higher value of the index represents a higher perception of corruption.

[15]The table represents the estimated coefficient on the corruption index only. Results for other variables included in the regression are identical to what are found in the literature. Tax revenues increase with per capita GDP, and openness, but fall with agriculture share of GDP.

Table 1. Average of Measures of Tax Structure and Their Determinants, 1980–97

Variable	World	Developed countries	Developing countries
Total revenue	26.00	33.30	24.40
Tax revenue	20.60	29.70	18.70
Income, profit, capital gains taxes	6.80	9.70	6.10
Individual	3.12	7.57	2.13
Corporate	3.38	2.36	3.61
Social security tax	3.74	7.97	2.55
Payroll tax	0.31	0.32	0.30
Property tax	0.42	0.65	0.37
Domestic taxes on goods and services	6.65	9.68	6.01
Sales, VAT, turnover	3.97	5.77	3.57
Excise	2.07	2.97	1.86
Trade taxes	3.65	0.83	4.28
Import	3.18	0.80	3.73
Export	0.44	0.01	0.53
Non-tax revenue	5.33	3.47	5.72
Determinants of tax structure:			
Real capita GDP (PPP$)	5,120	14,100	3,780
Agriculture share of GDP	20.90	4.51	22.90
Trade share of GDP	81.20	66.10	83.50
Corruption index	4.26	1.21	4.95

Note

All variables are measured as fractions of GDP except for the corruption index. The measure of corruption is based on ICRG and BI indexes; see Tanzi and Davoodi (1997) for details. It ranges from 0 to 10 where higher values of the corruption index refer to higher values of corruption. Averages are unweighted.

- Higher corruption is associated with lower revenues of all types, except for non-tax revenues. The latter finding is consistent with the fact that non-tax revenues are dominated by revenues from natural resources (at least for developing countries). Some studies have shown that natural resource abundance is an important determinant of corruption (Leite and Weidmann 1999).

- Corruption has a statistically significant correlation with individual income taxes, a finding that is consistent with individuals negotiating their tax liability with corrupt tax inspectors. It is in the mutual interests of the individual taxpayer as well as the tax inspector who would conduct business as usual by living with underreporting and

Table 2. Determinants of Tax Structure

Dependent variable	Corruption	Adjusted R-squared	Number of countries
Total revenue	−1.47***	0.41	90
	(−1.90)		
Tax revenue	−2.73***	0.42	89
	(−4.05)		
Income, profit, capital gains taxes	−0.79**	0.24	89
	(−2.25)		
Individual	−0.63**	0.46	86
	(−2.29)		
Corporate	−0.16	0.08	86
	(−0.71)		
Social security tax	−0.92***	0.39	74
	(−3.25)		
Payroll tax	−0.04	−0.02	75
	(−1.16)		
Property tax	−0.05**	0.37	85
	(−1.84)		
Domestic taxes on goods and services	−1.08***	0.29	90
	(−4.47)		
Sales, VAT, turnover	−0.79***	0.24	86
	(−4.40)		
Excise	−0.23**	0.11	88
	(−1.98)		
Trade taxes	−0.06	0.41	90
	(−0.52)		
Import	0.03	0.33	90
	(0.23)		
Export	−0.07*	0.12	89
	(−1.43)		
Non-tax revenue	1.27	0.16	89
	(1.21)		

Notes

Regression includes an intercept, real per capita GDP, agriculture share of GDP, and trade share of GDP. It is estimated on a cross-section of countries over the period 1980–97. The corruption perception index is taken from Tanzi and Davoodi (1997) who based it on data from International Country Risk Guide and Business International. The index has been rescaled so that higher values of the index represent higher perception of corruption. Only the coefficient on the corruption perception index is shown. Numbers in parenthesis denote t-ratios based on heteroskedastic-consistent standard errors.

*** Significant at 1 percent level; ** significant at 5 percent level; and * significant at 10 percent level.

collecting bribes on a sustained basis. The point estimate shows that a 1 point increase in corruption is associated with a 0.63 percent of GDP decline in individual income taxes received.

- A 1 point increase in corruption reduces the ratio of direct taxes to GDP by more than the drop in the ratio of indirect taxes to GDP (1.8 percentage point vs. 1.2 percentage point, respectively).[16] Given the higher level of corruption in developing countries, corruption has therefore a larger impact on direct taxes in developing countries than in developed countries. This finding helps explain the predominance of indirect taxes in developing countries compared to developed countries. It is also consistent with the prevalence of tax evasion from income taxes in developing countries. By reducing corruption, developing countries could help correct the imbalance between direct and indirect taxes. A 4 point reduction in corruption, which is the average difference in corruption between developed and developing countries, can increase direct taxes for the developing country as a group by 7.2 percent of GDP, bringing their ratio of direct taxes to GDP within 2 percent of GDP of developed countries.

- The larger impact of corruption on direct taxes compared to indirect taxes also implies that the progressivity of the income tax system is reduced.

- Surprisingly corruption has no statistically significant correlation with trade taxes even though surveys of the public indicate the significant presence of corruption in the customs.

- Higher corruption is also associated with lower revenues collected from VAT, sales tax, and turnover tax.[17]

Many countries have adopted value added taxes to simplify their tax system and increase their revenue performance. Are corruption and VAT performance related? More specifically, is higher corruption associated with lower VAT productivity? One measure of VAT produc-

---

[16]Direct taxes are assumed to consist of four taxes in Table 2 (income, profit, and capital gains taxes), social security tax, payroll tax, and property tax.

[17]Two caveats should be mentioned regarding the impact of corruption on VAT. First, the regression does not control for the nominal rate of the VAT; a higher rate can create greater incentives for corruption and tax evasion. Second, the available data do not allow a distinction of the revenues from VAT from those of turnover and sales taxes.

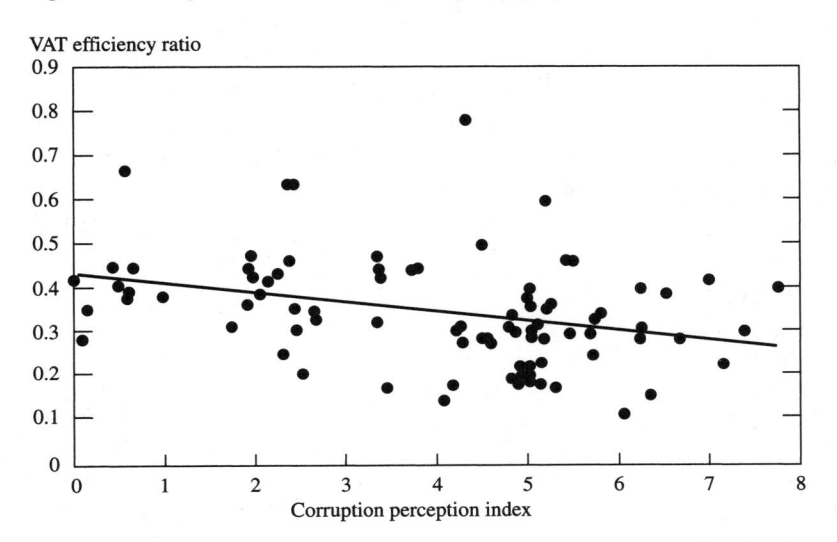

Figure 4. Corruption and VAT Productivity in Eighty-Three Countries

tivity is the so-called VAT efficiency ratio: the ratio of VAT revenues received to GDP divided by the standard VAT rate. This measure is bounded between 1 and 0. The higher the ratio, the more productive the VAT system. The lower the ratio, the more widespread the extent of exemptions, zero rating, tax evasion, or weak tax administration. The simple association between corruption and the VAT efficiency ratio for a sample of eighty-three countries shows that countries with high perception of corruption tend to have low VAT efficiency ratios (Figure 4). The correlation coefficient is –0.34 which is statistically significant at the 1 percent level. This correlation does not imply that every exemption in the VAT system is necessarily the outcome of rent-seeking activities or corruption. For example, basic food stuffs are routinely exempt from VAT in many countries; but then there are also many instances where VAT exemptions tend to grow when vested interests attempt to regain the exemptions that they used to enjoy under the previous sales taxes replaced by the VAT.

There is also some evidence to show that countries which introduced value added taxes earlier tend to have lower levels of corruption and higher VAT efficiency ratios. Specifically, the correlation coefficient for the same group of eighty-three countries, as shown in Figure 4, between the date of adoption of the VAT and the subsequent level of corruption is 0.23 which is statistically significant at the 5 percent level. The correlation between the date of adoption of VAT and VAT efficiency ratio is –0.2 which is statistically significantly at the 10 percent level. It should be pointed out that these correlations might be suggestive of the role that the VAT system can play in improving book-keeping records, and tax compliance, thus reducing corruption and increasing revenues.

Conclusions

This chapter has analyzed some conceptual as well as empirical direct and indirect links between corruption, growth, and public finance. Apart from reviewing the channels discussed in the literature such as the impact of corruption on investment (public and private), and its composition, the chapter has also discussed the role of small and medium-size enterprises in OECD countries and has shown that this role is not unique to OECD countries; SMEs in many developing and transition economies are also important contributors to growth. This chapter has discussed the constraints facing SMEs and the regressive nature of bribery they encounter. It has argued that such constraints affect the allocation of time on the part of talented entrepreneurs, restrict the availability of finance to SMEs and, given their importance as engines of growth, ultimately reduce the national growth rate of the economy.

The chapter provides some evidence that there is a positive and significant association between the allocation of talent to unproductive activities and corruption. Given that corruption has a negative impact on growth, this misallocation has negative direct and indirect effects on growth of about 0.4 percentage points.

It also provides new evidence that corruption affects the structure of taxes. The evidence shows that the presence of higher corruption in developing countries may in part explain the predominant share of indirect taxes in total tax revenues. Given the spread of VATs worldwide, the chapter has also analyzed whether its adoption bears any relationship to the prevalence and awareness of corruption. Some evidence is provided that countries which adopted the VAT earlier tend to have a lower level of corruption *and* higher VAT productivity *subsequently*. However, these conclusions must be considered as highly tentative. Also the direction of the causation is not obvious.

The last decade has seen a proliferation of surveys of firms and the public about costs of corruption and other obstacles of doing business worldwide. These surveys are qualitative in nature and do not replace more objective ways of measuring such costs, but they have nevertheless provided a wealth of information consistent with objective and hard evidence provided by earlier studies conducted by researchers such as De Soto and others. In conclusion, although much of the evidence available is only suggestive, it points to a probable negative relationship between corruption and the growth rate of countries.

References

Abed, G. and Davoodi, H.R. (2000) "Corruption, Structural Reforms and Economic Performance in the Transition Economies," IMF Working Paper Series no. 132, Washington DC: International Monetary Fund. [Revised version reproduced as Chapter 18 in this volume—ED.]

Acs, Z.J., Carlsson, B., and Karlsson, C. (eds) (1999) *Entrepreneurship, Small and Medium-Sized Enterprises and the Macroeconomy*, New York: Cambridge University Press.

Acs, Z. J. and Yeung, B. (eds) (1999) *Small and Medium-Sized Enterprises in the Global Economy*, Ann Arbor, Mich.: University of Michigan Press.

Ades, A. and Di Tella, R. (1997) "National Champions and Corruption: Some Unpleasant Interventionist Arithmetic," *Economic Journal* 107 (July): 1023–42.

Alesina, A. and Rodrik, D. (1994) "Distributive Policies and Economic Growth," *Quarterly Journal of Economics* 108: 465–90.

Barro, R.J. and Lee, J.W. (1996) "International Measures of Schooling Years and Schooling Quality," *American Economic Review* 86 (2): pp. 218–33.

Baumol, W.J. (1990) "Entrepreneurship: Productive, Unproductive, and Destructive," *Journal of Political Economy* 98: 893–921.

Borensztein, E., De Gregorio, J., and Lee, J.W. (1998) "How Does Foreign Direct Investment Affect Economic Growth," *Journal of International Economics* 45 (June):115–35.

Buscaglia, E. and Ratliff, W. (2000) *Law and Economics in Developing Countries*, Stanford: Hoover Institution.

Campos, E. E., Lien D., and Pradhan, P. (1999) "The Impact of Corruption on Investment: Predictability Matters," *World Development* 27 (June): 1059–67.

De Soto, H. (1989) *The Other Path: The Invisible Revolution in the Third World*, New York: Harper and Row.

Devarajan, S., Easterly, W.R., and Pack, H. (1999) "Is Investment in Africa Too High or Too Low? Macro and Micro Evidence," manuscript, Washington, DC: World Bank.

Easterly, W. (1999) "The Ghost of Financing Gap: Testing the Growth Model Used in the International Financial Institutions," *Journal of Development Economics* 60: 423–38.

Easterly, W. R. and Levine, R. (2000) "It is not Factor Accumulation: Stylized Facts and Growth Models," manuscript, Washington DC: World Bank.

Ehrlich, I. and Lui, F.T. (1999) "Bureaucratic Corruption and Endogenous Growth," *Journal of Political Economy*, 107: S270–93.

European Bank for Reconstruction and Development (1999) *Ten Years of Transition*, London: European Bank for Reconstruction and Development.

Fischer, S. (1993) "Role of Macroeconomic Factors in Growth," *Journal of Monetary Economics:* 32, 485–512.

Friedman, E., Johnson, S., Kaufmann, D., and Zoido-Lobatón, P. (2000) "Dodging the Grabbing Hand: The Determinants of Unofficial Activity in 69 Countries," *Journal of Public Economics*, 76: 459–93.

Gupta, S., Davoodi, H.R., and Alonso-Terme, R. (1998) "Does Corruption Affect Income Inequality and Poverty?" IMF Working Paper Series WP/98/76, Washington DC: International Monetary Fund. [Revised version reproduced as Chapter 17 in this volume—ED.]

Gupta, S., de Mello, L., and Sharan, R. (2000) "Corruption and Military Spending," IMF Working Paper Series WP/00/23, Washington DC: International Monetary Fund. [Revised version reproduced as Chapter 12 in this volume—ED.]

Hellman, J. S., Jones, G., Kaufmann, D., and Schankerman, M. (2000) "Measuring Governance, Corruption, and State Capture: How Firms and Bureaucrats Shape the Business Environment in Transition Economies," World Bank Discussion Paper Series no. 2312, Washington DC: World Bank.

Hindriks, J., Keen, M., and Muthoo, A. (1999) "Corruption, Extortion and Evasion," *Journal of Public Economics*, 74: 395–430. [Reproduced as Chapter 15 in this volume—ED.]

Hoshi, T., Kashyap, A., and Scharfstein, D. (1991) "Corporate Structure, Liquidity, and Investment: Evidence from Japanese Industrial Groups," *Quarterly Journal of Economics* 106(1): 33–60.

Isham, J. and Kaufmann, D. (1999) "The Forgotten Rationale for Policy Reform: The Productivity of Investment Projects," *Quarterly Journal of Economics:* 149–84.

Johnson, S., Kaufmann, D., and Zoido-Lobatón, P. (1999) "Corruption, Public Finances, and the Unofficial Economy," World Bank Discussion Paper Series no. 2169, Washington DC: World Bank.

Kaufmann, D. (1997) "The Missing Pillar of a Growth Strategy for Ukraine: Institutional and Policy Reforms for Private Sector Development," Harvard Institute for International Development Discussion Paper Series no. 603, Cambridge, Mass.: Harvard University.

Kaufmann, D. and Wei, S. (1999) "Does 'Grease Money' Speed up the Wheel of Commerce?" World Bank Discussion Paper Series no. 2254, Washington DC: World Bank.

Knight, M., Loayza, N., and Villanueva, D. (1996) "The Peace Dividend: Military Spending Cuts and Economic Growth," *IMF Staff Papers*, March: 1–37.

Lambsdorff, J.G. (1998) "Corruption in Comparative Perception," in A.K. Jain (ed.), *Economics of Corruption*, Boston: Kluwer Academic.

Leite, C., and Weidmann, J. (1999) "Does Mother Nature Corrupt? Natural Resources, Corruption and Economic Growth," International Monetary Fund Working Paper WP/99/85, Washington, DC: International Monetary Fund. [Reproduced as Chapter 7 in this volume—ED.]

Mauro, P. (1995) "Corruption and Growth," *Quarterly Journal of Economics*: 110 (August): 681–712.

—— (1996) "The Effects of Corruption on Growth, Investment, and Government Expenditure," IMF Working Paper WP/96/98, Washington, DC: International Monetary Fund. [Revised version reproduced as Chapter 9 in this volume—ED.]

—— (1998) "Corruption and the Composition of Government Expenditure," *Journal of Public Economics* 69: 263–79. [Reproduced as Chapter 9 in this volume—ED.]

Murphy, K., Shleifer, A., and Vishny, R. (1991) "The Allocation of Talent: Implications for Growth," *Quarterly Journal of Economics* (May): 503–30.

Persson, T. and Tabellini, G. (1994) "Is Inequality Harmful for Growth?" *American Economic Review* 84: 600–22.

Reinikka, R. and Svensson, J. (1999) "How Inadequate Provision of Public Infrastructure and Services Affects Private Investment," World Bank Discussion Paper Series no. 2262, Washington, DC: World Bank.

Shleifer, A. and Vishny, R.W. (1993) "Corruption," *Quarterly Journal of Economics* 108: 599–617.

Smarzynska, B. K. and Wei, S. (2000) "Corruption and the Composition of Foreign Direct Investment: Firm-Level Evidence," World Bank Discussion Paper no. 2360, Washington, DC: World Bank.

Svensson. J. (2000) "Who Must Pay Bribes and How Much? Evidence from a Cross-Section of Firms," unpublished manuscript, Washington DC: World Bank.

Tanzi, V. (1987) "Quantitative Characteristics of the Tax Systems of Developing Countries," in D.M.G. Newbery and N. Stern (eds), *The Theory of Taxation for Developing Countries*, New York: Oxford University Press.

—— (1998a) "Corruption Around the World: Causes, Consequences, Scope, and Cures," *IMF Staff Papers*, December, 559–94, Washington, DC: International Monetary Fund. [Reproduced as Chapter 2 in this volume—ED.]

—— (1998b) "Corruption and the Budget: Problems and Solutions," in A.K. Jain (ed.), *Economics of Corruption*, Boston: Kluwer Academic.

Tanzi, V. and Davoodi, H.R. (1997) "Corruption, Public Investment and Growth," IMF Working Paper Series WP/97/139, Washington, DC: International Monetary Fund. [Revised version reproduced as Chapter 11 in this volume—ED.]

Treisman, D. (1995) "The Politics of Soft Credit in Post-Soviet Russia," *Europe-Asia Studies* 47(6): 949–76.

—— (2000) "The Causes of Corruption: A Cross-National Study," *Journal of Public Economics* 76 (June): 399–458.

Wei, S. (1997a) "How Taxing is Corruption on International Investors?" NBER Working Paper no. 6030, Cambridge, Mass.: National Bureau of Economic Research.

—— (1997b) "Why is Corruption So Much More Taxing than Tax?" NBER Working Paper no. 2048, Cambridge, Mass.: National Bureau of Economic Research.

Part II

Corruption and Government Expenditures

9

Corruption and the Composition of Government Expenditure

Paolo Mauro

1. Introduction

In a world in which governments do not always act in their citizens' best interest, corrupt politicians may be expected to spend more public resources on those items on which it is easier to levy large bribes and maintain them secret. This paper provides the first cross-country evidence that corruption does indeed affect the composition of government expenditure. In particular, education spending is found to be adversely affected by corruption.

Both economic theory and common sense suggest the types of government expenditure that provide more lucrative opportunities. First,

---

Reprinted from *Journal of Public Economics*, Vol. 69, Paolo Mauro, "Corruption and the Composition of Government Expenditure," pp. 263–279 (1998), with permission from Elsevier Science.

Helpful conversations with Andrei Shleifer and Vito Tanzi and sugggestions by Roberto Perotti, Phillip Swagel and two referees are gratefully acknowledged. The views expressed are strictly personal and do not necessarily represent those of the International Monetary Fund. The author does not necessarily agree with the subjective indices relating to any given country.

the seminal contributions of Krueger (1974) and others stressed that it is the existence of rents that motivate rent-seeking behavior. As a consequence, large bribes will be available on items produced by firms operating in markets where the degree of competition is low. Second, the illegal nature of corruption and the ensuing need for secrecy imply that corrupt officials will choose goods whose exact value is difficult to monitor. Therefore, specialized, high-technology goods will be particularly sought after (Shleifer and Vishny, 1993). Hines (1995) argues that, for example, international trade in military aircraft—high-technology goods produced by a limited number of oligopolistic firms—is particularly susceptible to corruption. By contrast, basic education only requires mature technology that can be provided by a relatively large number of suppliers. On the basis of these considerations, one might therefore expect that it will be easier to collect substantial bribes on large infrastructure projects or highly sophisticated defense equipment than on textbooks or teachers' salaries.

In other areas, such as health or transfers and welfare payments, the picture is less clear-cut. In the case of health, opportunities to collect bribes may be abundant on state-of-the-art medical equipment or advanced hospital facilities designed to boost national prestige, but may be more limited in the case of doctors' and nurses' salaries. In the case of transfers and welfare payments, many of which constitute rents, bureaucrats sometimes enjoy considerable discretion in how to allocate them, even though the rents per individual transaction may be relatively limited. For example, bureaucrats may have little room for maneuver on old-age pensions, but anecdotal evidence suggests that, in some countries, fraud is widespread on disability pensions or unemployment benefits. Education is not free from the scope for patronage, but it seems easier to hand out a disability pension to a healthy person than to give a teaching job to an unqualified person. In the case of the former, a pure rent is transferred with no further visible consequences, while in the case of the latter, it would be difficult—in egregious cases—for the unqualified teacher to face a class of students on a daily basis. Therefore, on a priori grounds, it is not always possible to make a precise guess on how corruption affects a particular spending item, but education seems to stand out as an area where it is relatively difficult to levy bribes.

The question whether corruption affects the composition of government expenditure may have important implications. First, while the empirical literature has so far yielded mixed results on the effects of government expenditure and, in particular, its composition, on economic growth,[1] most economists seem to think that the level and type of spending undertaken by governments do matter for economic performance. For example, even though cross-country regression work has not conclusively shown the existence of a relationship between government spending on education and economic growth, it has gathered robust evidence that school enrollment rates (Levine and Renelt, 1992) and educational attainment (Barro, 1992) play a considerable role in determining economic growth. Second, measuring the effects of corruption on the composition of government expenditure may help quantify the severity of the principal-agent problem that exists in this respect between citizens and politicians or, following the literature on the fungibility of aid resources, aid donors and recipient governments.

In order to study empirically the relatively unexplored relationship between corruption and the composition of government expenditure, this paper uses corruption indices produced by a private firm for a cross-section of countries.[2] It finds that corruption alters the composition of government expenditure, specifically by reducing government spending on education. Therefore, it confirms that more corrupt countries choose to spend less on education, since it does not provide as many lucrative opportunities for government officials as other components of spending do.[3] There is also some evidence that corruption reduces spending on health.

---

[1]Concerning the overall level of government expenditure, Levine and Renelt (1992) show that it does not seem to be robustly associated with economic growth. Previous work on the composition of government expenditure has been relatively limited. Devarajan et al. (1996) find that, with the exception of current expenditure, no component of government expenditure bears a significant relationship with economic growth. Easterly and Rebelo (1993) also find few significant relationships: public investment on transport and communications is positively associated with economic growth, though not with private investment; public investment in agriculture is negatively associated with private investment; general government investment is positively correlated with both growth and private investment; and public enterprise investment is negatively correlated with private investment.

[2]The only previous related empirical work that I am aware of is that of Rauch (1995), who uses a data set on U.S. cities to show that the wave of municipal reform that took place during the Progressive Era increased the share of total municipal expenditure allocated to road and sewer investment, thereby raising the growth in city manufacturing employment.

[3]Mauro (1996) derives a simple generalization of the Barro (1990) model that shows that if corruption acted simply as though it were a tax on income, then the amount and composition of government expenditure would be independent of corruption. As a consequence, it seems reasonable to interpret any empirical relationships between corruption indices and particular components of government spending as evidence that bribes can be collected more efficiently on some government expenditure components than on others.

2. Description of the Data

This paper uses the indices of corruption and other institutional variables drawn from *Political Risk Services, Inc.*, a private firm which publishes the *International Country Risk Guide*, used and described in detail by Keefer and Knack (1993).[4] The indices were compiled by the IRIS Center (University of Maryland) and are available for over 100 countries. I use the 1982–1995 average of the "corruption" index. Low scores on the ICRG corruption index indicate "high government officials are likely to demand special payments" and "illegal payments are generally expected throughout lower levels of government" in the form of "bribes connected with import and export licenses, exchange controls, tax assessment, police protection, or loans." All indices are on a scale from 0 (worst, most corrupt) to 6 (best, least corrupt). There are 106 observations in the Barro (1991) sample for which the corruption index is available. The sample statistics are as follows: mean = 3.37, standard deviation = 1.45, minimum = 0.10, maximum = 6.00.

In estimating the relationship between corruption indices and the components of government expenditure, the fact that the indices are subjective is unlikely to constitute a source of endogeneity bias. In fact, it does not seem plausible that the consultants that produce the indices be influenced in their judgement by the composition of government expenditure. However, the issue of causality is relevant when one wonders whether the composition of government expenditure causes corruption (by creating opportunities for it) or corruption alters the composition of government expenditure. Therefore, in some estimates in this paper, a number of instrumental variables are used to address potential endogeneity bias. The first three have been used and described in further detail in Mauro (1995).

The first instrument is an index of ethnolinguistic fractionalization drawn from Taylor and Hudson (1972), which measures the probability that two randomly selected persons from a given country will not belong to the same ethnolinguistic group. This variable is a good in-

---

[4]Mauro (1996) obtains broadly similar results using also data from another firm, *Business International*.

strument because, in accordance with Shleifer and Vishny (1993) arguments, more fractionalized countries tend to have more dishonest bureaucracies. The index of ethnolinguistic fractionalization has a correlation coefficient of 0.36 (significant at the conventional levels) with the corruption index. The second and third are two dummy variables (compiled by consulting the Encyclopaedia Britannica) related to whether (following Taylor and Hudson, 1972) the country ever was a colony (after 1776), and whether the country achieved independence after 1945. The colonial dummies are highly correlated with a country's corruption index, perhaps because countries that have been colonized have found it difficult to develop efficient institutions. The simple correlation coefficients are 0.58 and 0.41 respectively, both significant at the conventional levels.

As additional instruments, I use the black market premium from Levine and Renelt (1992), the ratio of the sum of imports plus exports to GDP from the World Bank's STARS database and the "oil" dummy from Barro (1991). The first two variables are proxies for the extent to which a country is protected by restrictions to trade with the rest of the world, which the original rent-seeking literature emphasized as a potential source of rents. Ades and Di Tella (1994) show that the second variable is a significant determinant of corruption. In this paper's sample of countries, the simple correlation coefficients with the corruption index are 0.31 and 0.21 respectively. The "oil" dummy, which indicates whether oil production represents a large fraction of a country's GDP, is used following the arguments by Sachs and Warner (1995) that natural resources constitute an important source of rents. The simple correlation coefficient is 0.23 in this case. All correlation coefficients are significant at the conventional levels. All these variables are likely to be valid instruments, since a priori they should be unrelated to the composition of government expenditure, other than through their effects on corruption.

This paper uses two standard sources of data on the composition of government expenditure:[5]

(1) The Barro (1991) data set, which provided the basis for much recent empirical work on the determinants of economic growth. It contains the 1970–85 averages of government spending on defense, education, transfers, social security and welfare, and total government consumption expenditure for over 100 countries. The primary sources

---

[5]Mauro (1996) also reports estimates obtained using the Easterly and Rebelo (1993) data set on the composition of public investment. The results are mostly insignificant.

are Unesco and the International Monetary Fund's *Government Finance Statistics* (GFS). The basic sample of countries in this study is also the same as Barro (1991), subject to data availability.

(2) The Devarajan et al. (1996) data set of developing countries, to which I added the industrial countries, so as to obtain data for around 90 countries. The data are drawn from the GFS and refer to the 1985 observation. The sub-components of education (school, university and other education) and health (hospitals, clinics and other health) expenditure are available for thirty to sixty countries.

The data on population by age group refer to 1985 and are drawn from United Nations (1990). I use the share of population aged 5–20 in total population.

3. Empirical Results

This section analyzes empirically the relationship between corruption and various components of government expenditure. It finds that corruption lowers expenditure on education, and perhaps on health.

Table 1 analyzes the relationship between each component of public expenditure (as a ratio to GDP) reported in the Barro (1991) data set, and the corruption index.[6] Government spending on education as a ratio to GDP is negatively and significantly correlated with corruption. The magnitude of the coefficient is considerable: a one-standard-deviation improvement in the corruption index is associated with an increase in government spending on education by 0.6% of GDP. Taken at face value, this result implies that if a given country were to improve its "grade" on corruption from, say, a "4 out of 6" to a "5½ out of 6," on average its government would increase its spending on education by about 0.6% of GDP. The coefficient is broadly unchanged and the relationship remains significant when estimated through widely-used robust regression techniques (see notes to the tables). Fig. 1 provides direct visual evidence that this result is not driven by a small group of countries.

Other components of government expenditure are also significantly associated with the corruption index at the conventional levels, most

---

[6]The reason why the various components of government spending are analyzed *as a share of* GDP is that the simple generalization of the Barro (1991) that is derived in Mauro (1996) implies that if bribes could be levied just as easily on all income (rather than more easily on some government expenditure components than others), then each component of government expenditure *as a share of* GDP should be unrelated to corruption.

notably in the case of transfer payments, and social insurance and welfare payments. However, it is important to take into account the well-known empirical observation that government expenditure as a ratio to GDP tends to rise as a country becomes richer—a relationship known as Wagner's law.[7] When the level of per capita income in 1980 is used as an additional explanatory variable, education turns out to be the only component of public spending whose association with the corruption index remains significant at the 1% level. The magnitude of the coefficient remains broadly the same as in the univariate regression.

Table 2 reports the results obtained by using the *Government Finance Statistics*, which include more finely disaggregated data, though at the cost of a reduction in the number of countries for which data are available and possibly of lower cross-country comparability at the level of the more detailed items. Total government expenditure is again unrelated to corruption, and the results obtained when public expenditure is split by function are in line with those obtained using the Barro data set. In particular, controlling for per capita GDP, government expenditure on education is negatively and significantly associated with corruption, the magnitude of the coefficient being larger by about a third in this sample. In addition, government expenditure on health is found to be negatively and significantly associated with corruption in univariate regressions (see Fig. 2) and when controlling for GDP per capita. In the latter case, the link between corruption and health expenditure is significant at the conventional levels in the estimates presented in Table 2, but it was only significant at the 10% level in a previous version of this paper, which used a slightly different proxy for corruption (which included corruption indices from another private firm, *Business International*).[8] Therefore, the results on the relationship between corruption and health expenditure should only be considered tentative. Finally, neither defense, nor transportation display any significant relationship with corruption. Of course, this does not necessarily mean that corruption is unrelated to spending on these items. On the contrary, it is highly likely that the relationship between corruption and defense spending in particular is being blurred by the presence of a large number of other factors that cannot easily be controlled for.

---

[7]Easterly and Rebelo (1993) provide a literature review on Wagner's law and show that, in a panel of countries, several components of public spending rise (as a ratio to GDP) as income per capita rises.

[8]By contrast, the relationship between corruption and government spending on education has proved robust to changes in the source of the proxies for corruption.

Table 1. Corruption and the Composition of Government Expenditure, Barro (1991) Data

Dependent variable (average 1970–85, in percent of GDP)	N	R^2	Constant	Per capita GDP (1980)	Corruption index OLS	Corruption index ROBUST	Corruption index MEDIAN
Government expenditure on education	103	0.14	0.029 (7.95)		0.0039 (4.00)	0.0039 (3.75)	0.0040 (2.93)
Government consumption expenditure	106	0.03	0.212 (12.47)		−0.0080 (−1.75)	−0.0083 (−1.79)	−0.0077 (−1.23)
Government consumption expenditure excluding education and defense	93	0.10	0.144 (10.99)		−0.0114 (−3.29)	−0.0114 (−3.04)	−0.0126 (−1.97)
Government expenditure on defense	93	0.00	0.033 (4.18)		0.0004 (0.19)	0.0003 (0.31)	0.0003 (0.18)
Government transfer payments	73	0.45	−0.036 (−2.01)		0.0348 (7.41)	0.0347 (7.20)	0.0371 (5.12)
Social insurance and welfare payments	75	0.47	−0.041 (−4.04)		0.0258 (7.83)	0.0248 (7.41)	0.0205 (6.22)
Government expenditure on education	103	0.14	0.030 (7.56)	0.0003 (0.50)	0.0034 (2.41)	0.0036 (2.54)	0.0039 (2.02)
Government consumption expenditure	106	0.15	0.194 (11.56)	−0.0089 (−0.57)	0.0069 (1.28)	0.0070 (1.24)	0.0085 (1.03)

	N	R^2						
Government consumption expenditure excluding education and defense	93	0.25	0.117 (8.30)	−0.011 (−4.73)	0.0080 (1.43)	0.0089 (1.53)	0.0107 (1.16)	
Government expenditure on defense	93	0.00	0.032 (2.91)	0.0002 (−0.07)	0.0007 (0.14)	0.0023 (1.19)	0.0032 (1.03)	
Government transfer payments	73	0.64	0.013 (0.84)	0.0185 (5.62)	0.0004 (0.06)	−0.0038 (−0.57)	−0.0052 (−0.80)	
Social insurance and welfare payments	75	0.58	−0.011 (−1.25)	0.0110 (4.56)	0.0052 (1.22)	0.0027 (0.54)	0.0018 (0.45)	

Data sources: Barro (1991) and Political Risk Services/IRIS.

The corruption index is the simple average of the corruption indices produced by Political Risk Services (compiled by IRIS) for 1982–95. One standard deviation of the corruption index equals 1.45. A high value of the corruption index means that the country has good institutions in that respect. The number of observations, N, the R^2, the constant, and the coefficients on per capita GDP in 1980 and the corruption index (OLS) refer to the OLS estimates, with White-corrected t-statistics in parentheses. The ROBUST coefficients on the corruption index refer to robust regressions (with an identical specification to the OLS regression in the same row) that perform an initial OLS regression, calculate Cook's distance, eliminate the gross outliers for which Cook's distance exceeds 1, and then perform iterations based on Huber weights followed by iterations based on a biweight function. The MEDIAN coefficients refer to quantile (median) regressions that minimize the sum of the absolute residuals. Both routines are programmed in the STATA econometric software. The remainder of these regressions is omitted for the sake of brevity.

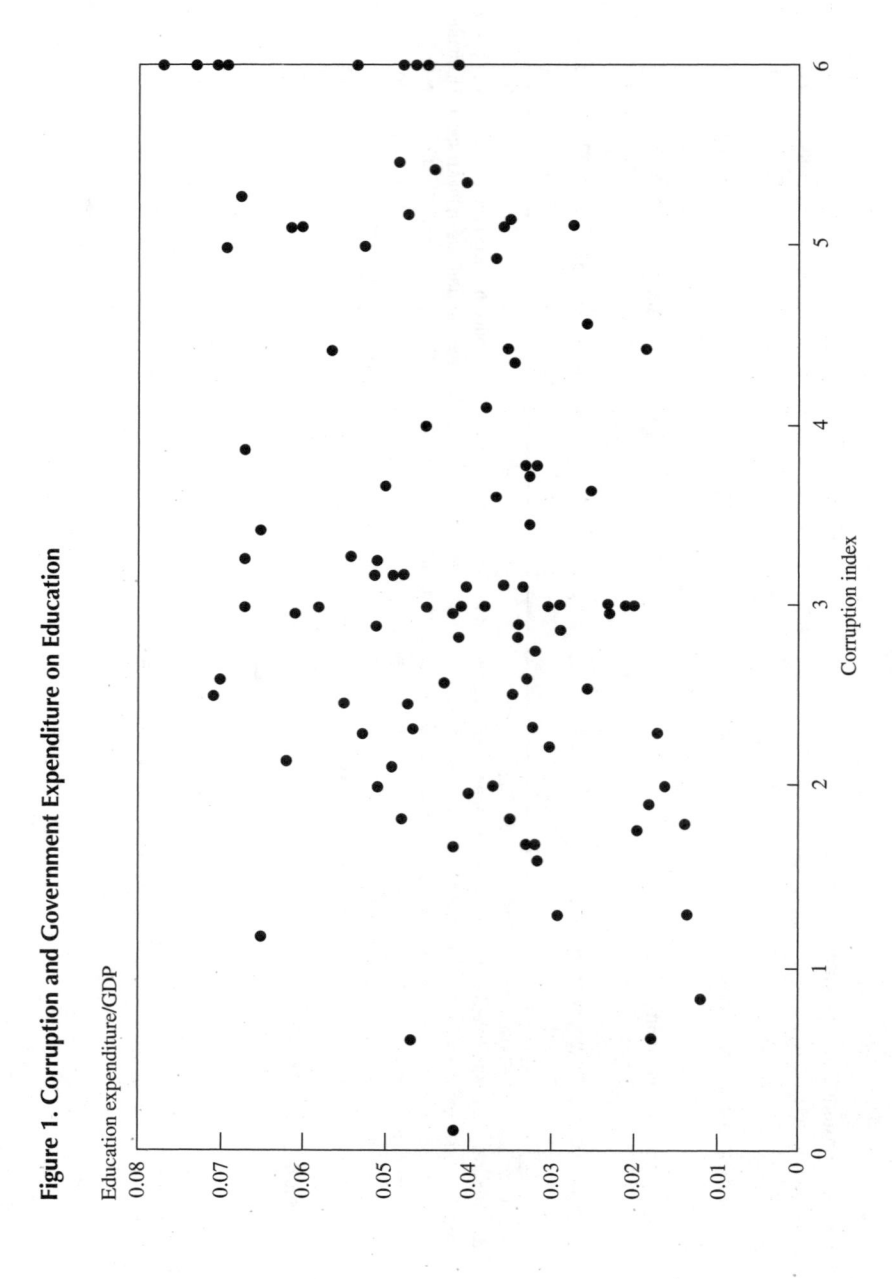

Figure 1. Corruption and Government Expenditure on Education

While the relationship between corruption and government expenditure on education is strongly significant, the link between corruption and the sub-components of education expenditure (schools, universities, and other) is less clear, and it is significant (though just at the 10% level) only for spending on universities.

Table 2 also shows the results of the test of a hypothesis that is often heard in popular debate, namely that corruption is likely to lead to high capital expenditure by the government, perhaps on "white elephant" projects (prestigious projects that do not serve useful economic or social objectives). The data are somewhat in line with this hypothesis, with improvements in the corruption index coinciding with declines in capital expenditure and increases in current expenditure, but neither relationship is significant at the conventional levels. Therefore, these results are interesting, but not too much should be made of them.

Table 3 analyzes the relationship between corruption and government expenditure on education in further detail. It shows that the relationship is robust to controlling for additional determinants of education expenditure. Most notably, the inclusion of the share of population aged between 5 and 20 over total population (an obvious determinant of the need for expenditure on schooling) raises the magnitude of the coefficient on corruption by around one third, and the relationship retains its strong significance. The association between corruption and government expenditure on education remains strongly significant when total government consumption expenditure as a ratio to GDP is included among the explanatory variables. The association is also largely unaffected by controlling for the degree of political stability, which turns out to be insignificant in this multivariate regression. In all of these cases, the coefficient on the corruption index remains broadly unchanged when using robust regression techniques. It is also interesting to note that the coefficient does not change much when dropping one observation at a time—a more rudimentary approach to robustness: in the case of the regression reported in row 6, the largest value for the corruption coefficient amounts to 0.0060 (when dropping Nicaragua, t-statistic 3.89) and the smallest amounts to 0.0043 (obtained by dropping Kuwait, t-statistic 2.73). The same coefficient amounts to 0.0058 (t-statistic 3.07) when dropping the 15 poorest countries, 0.0044 (t-statistic 2.51) when dropping the 15 richest countries, 0.0063 (t-statistic 3.66) when dropping the (5) countries with corruption indices more than 1½ standard deviations worse than the mean, and 0.0047 (t-statistic 2.69) when dropping the (ten) countries with

Table 2. Corruption and the Composition of Government Expenditure, Government Finance Statistics Data

Dependent variable 1985, observation, as ratio of GDP	N	R^2	Constant	Per capita GDP (1980)	Corruption index OLS	Corruption index ROBUST	Corruption index MEDIAN
Total government expenditure	88	0.12	0.229 (4.56)	0.0105 (1.55)	0.0094 (0.51)	0.0215 (1.53)	0.0215 (1.04)
Current government expenditure	85	0.24	0.140 (3.55)	0.0086 (1.56)	0.0227 (1.54)	0.0296 (2.41)	0.0357 (2.26)
Capital government expenditure	86	0.12	0.082 (4.80)	0.0014 (0.56)	−0.0114 (−1.78)	0.0023 (0.70)	−0.0019 (−0.64)
Government expenditure on education	85	0.06	0.023 (4.60)	−0.0018 (−1.86)	0.0046 (2.23)	0.0048 (2.27)	0.0054 (3.09)
Government expenditure on schools	57	0.05	0.016 (2.80)	−0.0017 (−1.50)	0.0035 (1.37)	0.0022 (0.95)	−0.0003 (−0.09)
Government expenditure on universities	56	0.06	0.005 (2.84)	−0.0006 (−2.17)	0.0012 (1.85)	0.0012 (1.90)	0.0022 (3.09)
Other government expenditure on education	54	0.01	0.008 (2.17)	−0.0001 (−0.11)	−0.0003 (−0.19)	0.0004 (0.83)	0.0001 (0.17)
Government expenditure on health	86	0.29	0.002 (0.45)	0.0013 (1.38)	0.0040 (2.05)	0.0039 (2.55)	0.0036 (2.37)
Government expenditure on hospitals	54	0.06	0.009 (2.13)	0.0010 (1.41)	−0.0003 (−0.16)	−0.0003 (−0.23)	−0.0002 (−0.08)

Government expenditure on clinics	28	0.14	−0.006 (−1.15)	−0.0005 (−0.52)	0.0039 (1.74)	0.0007 (0.70)	0.0010 (0.68)
Other government expenditure on health	44	0.03	0.002 (0.71)	−0.0008 (−1.17)	0.0014 (0.78)	0.0003 (0.92)	0.0002 (0.63)
Government expenditure on defense	82	0.01	0.037 (3.01)	0.0015 (0.65)	−0.0027 (−0.51)	0.0023 (1.31)	0.0014 (0.48)
Government expenditure on transportation	85	0.01	0.014 (4.52)	−0.0000 (−0.03)	0.0008 (0.49)	0.0016 (1.33)	0.0011 (0.62)

Data sources: *Government Finance Statistics*, International Monetary Fund; and Political Risk Services/IRIS.

The corruption index is the simple average of the corruption indices produced by Political Risk Services (compiled by IRIS) for 1982–95. One standard deviation of the corruption index equals 1.45. A *high* value of the corruption index means that the country has good institutions in that respect. The number of observations, N, the R^2, the constant, and the coefficients on per capita GDP in 1980 and the corruption index (OLS) refer to the OLS estimates, with White-corrected t-statistics in parentheses. The ROBUST coefficients on the corruption index refer to robust regressions (with an identical specification to the OLS regression in the same row) that perform an initial OLS regression, calculate Cook's distance, eliminate the gross outliers for which Cook's distance exceeds 1, and then perform iterations based on Huber weights followed by iterations based on a biweight function. The MEDIAN coefficients refer to quantile (median) regressions that minimize the sum of the absolute residuals. Both routines are programmed in the STATA econometric software. The remainder of these regressions is omitted for the sake of brevity.

Figure 2. Corruption and Government Expenditure on Health

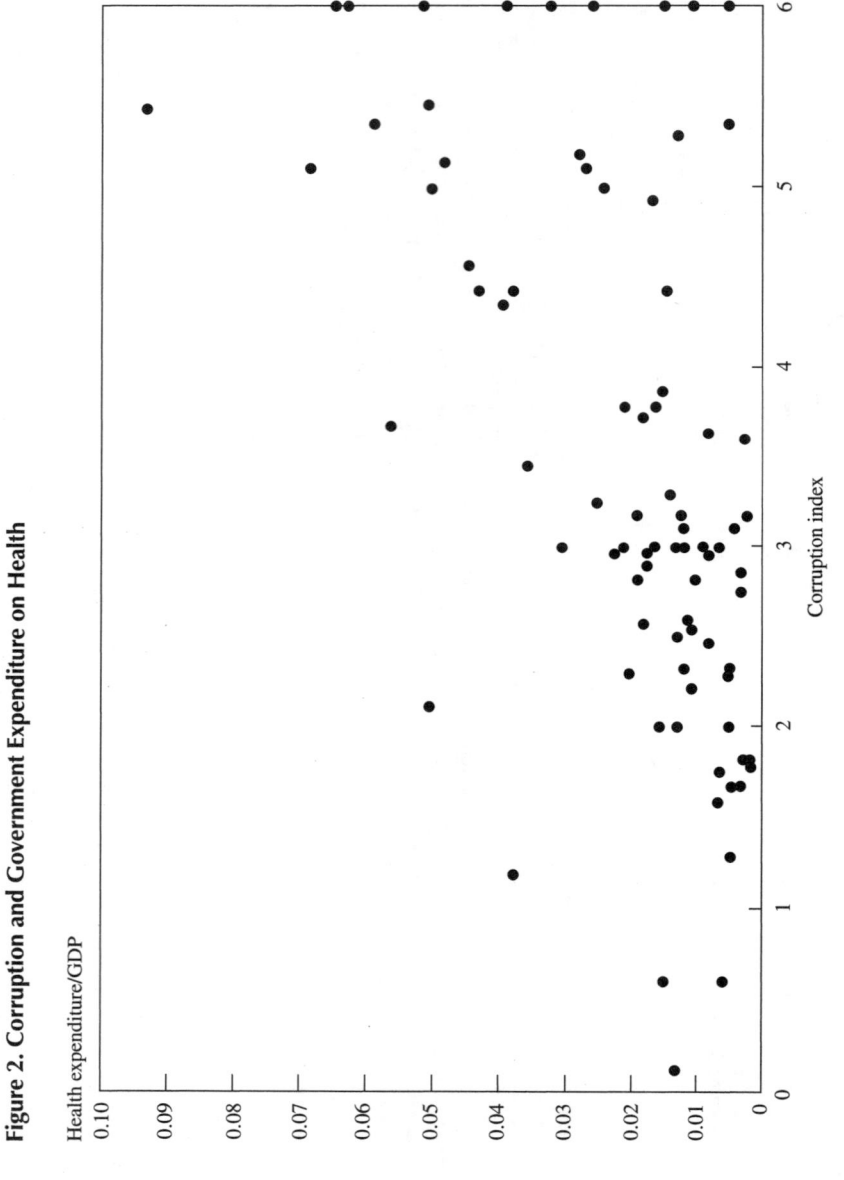

corruption indices more than 1½ standard deviations better than the mean. Finally, it is worth noting that the association between corruption and expenditure on education is broadly the same when estimated in sub-samples of developed or developing countries. For example, the following text table reports the results obtained by splitting the sample into countries with above-average and below-average per capita GDP in 1980. A log-likelihood ratio test is far from rejecting the null of equality of the coefficients in the regressions for the high-income and low-income countries (Table 4).

Table 3 also conducts a number of simple robustness tests of the relationship between corruption and government expenditure on education by, first, relaxing some of the assumptions on functional form that have been made in the previous estimates and, second, controlling for possible endogeneity problems by using instrumental variables. To explore the effects of changing the functional form of the relationship, government expenditure on education as a share of total government consumption expenditure is used as the dependent variable, and turns out also to be significantly associated with the corruption index. The magnitude of the coefficient is considerable: a one standard-deviation improvement in the corruption index leads education expenditure to rise by over six percentage points of total government consumption expenditure. The relationship expressed in this form becomes weaker only when using robust estimation techniques and controlling for GDP per capita and the share of schooling age population. Overall, the relationship between corruption and government expenditure on education seems to be robust to a number of changes in specification.[9]

To address issues of endogeneity and ensure that the direction of causality being captured is that from corruption to government spending on education, it is interesting to use instrumental variable estimation (Table 3). I use two sets of instrumental variables. The first is the same as in Mauro (1995) and includes the index of ethnolinguistic fractionalization and the two colonial history dummies. In this first case, the use of instrumental variables lowers the coefficient on corruption by about a third in the regression of government expenditure on education as a ratio to GDP (row 10 compared to row 1), but raises it slightly in the regression of government expenditure as a share of total government

---

[9]I also experimented with adding various combinations of per capita GDP squared, the log of GDP, and the square of the log of GDP to the list of explanatory variables, and did not find notable changes in the main relationship of interest, which remained significant.

Table 3. Corruption and Government Expenditure on Education, Health, Robustness Tests

Dependent variable (average 1970–85)	N	R^2	P-value	Constant	Per capita GDP (1980)	Cons. ex./GDP	Pop. 5–20/tot. pop.	Polit. stabil.	Corruption index OLS	Corruption index ROBUST	Corruption index MEDIAN
Exp. on educ./GDP	103	0.14		0.029 (7.95)					0.0039 (4.00)	0.0039 (3.75)	0.0040 (2.93)
Exp. on educ./GDP	103	0.14		0.030 (7.56)	0.0003 (0.49)				0.0034 (2.41)	0.0036 (2.54)	0.0039 (2.02)
Exp. on educ./GDP	103	0.29		0.011 (2.34)		0.0871 (4.72)			0.0046 (5.54)	0.0046 (4.87)	0.0045 (4.05)
Exp. on educ./GDP	102	0.16		0.005 (0.31)			0.0553 (1.75)		0.0058 (3.71)	0.0062 (3.82)	0.0067 (3.48)
Exp. on educ./GDP	102	0.35		−0.015 (−0.98)	0.0017 (1.96)	0.0988 (4.49)	0.0600 (1.65)		0.0039 (2.60)	0.0039 (2.83)	0.0040 (1.90)
Exp. on educ./GDP	102	0.18		−0.008 (−0.49)	0.0010 (1.30)		0.0884 (2.30)		0.0052 (3.16)	0.0055 (3.35)	0.0064 (3.52)
Exp. on educ./GDP	67	0.24		−0.020 (−0.74)	0.0010 (1.14)		0.0958 (1.85)	0.0012 (0.75)	0.0053 (2.50)	0.0055 (2.75)	0.0067 (2.69)
Exp. on educ./Cons. exp.	103	0.27		0.109 (4.43)					0.0428 (5.33)	0.0371 (5.34)	0.0344 (4.56)
Exp. on educ./Cons. exp.	102	0.44		0.042 (0.41)	0.0198 (4.46)		0.2366 (0.97)		0.0178 (1.93)	0.0154 (1.57)	0.0045 (0.33)
Exp. on educ./GDP instr: fraction., col. hist.	100	*	0.75	0.033 (5.79)					0.0025 (1.55)		

Exp. on ed./cons. ex. instr: fraction., col. hist.	100	*	0.01	0.082 (1.89)		0.0509 (3.86)
Exp. on ed./GDP instruments: all	88	*	0.90	0.029 (5.82)		0.0038 (2.81)
Exp. on ed./cons. ex. instruments: all	88	*	0.95	0.098 (2.38)		0.0472 (3.92)
Exp. on health/GDP	86	0.28		-0.001 (-0.32)	0.0047 (5.35)	0.0064 (4.57)
Exp. on health/GDP instr: fraction., col. hist.	84	*	0.25	-0.014 (-1.82)		0.0099 (4.26)
Exp. on health/GDP instruments: all	77	*	0.25	-0.009 (-1.64)	0.0057 (7.67)	0.0085 (4.56)

Data sources: Barro (1991), Business International, Political Risk Services/IRIS, United Nations (1990).

The corruption index is the simple average of the 1982–95 indices produced by Political Risk Services (compiled by IRIS). One standard deviation of the corruption index equals 1.45. A *high* value of the corruption index means that the country has good institutions in that respect. The number of observations, N, the R^2, the constant, and the coefficients on per capita GDP in 1980, government consumption expenditure as a share of GDP, the share of population aged between 5 and 20 (from United Nations, 1990), the Business International "political stability" index for 1980–83 (see Mauro, 1995), and the corruption index (OLS) refer to the OLS estimates, with White-corrected *t*-statistics in parentheses. The ROBUST coefficients on the corruption index refer to robust regressions (with an identical specification to the OLS regression in the same row) that perform an initial OLS regression, calculate Cook's distance, eliminate the gross outliers for which Cook's distance exceeds 1, and then perform iterations based on Huber weights followed by iterations based on a biweight function. The MEDIAN coefficients refer to quantile (median) regressions that minimize the sum of the absolute residuals. Both routines are programmed in the STATA econometric software. The remainder of these regressions is omitted for the sake of brevity. "Fractionalization" is the index of ethnolinguistic fractionalization in 1960, from Taylor and Hudson (1972). "Colonial history" indicates dummies for whether the country was ever a colony (after 1776) and for whether the country was still a colony in 1945. "All" adds to this instrument list the ratio of imports plus exports to GDP from the World Bank STARS database, the "oil" dummy from Barro (1991) and the black market premium from Levine and Renelt (1992).

(*) The R^2 is not an appropriate measure of goodness of fit with instrumental variables (Two-Stage Least Squares). The *P*-value refers to the test of the overidentifying restrictions.

Table 4. Corruption and Government Expenditure on Education, Developed and Developing Countries

Sample	Constant	Corruption index	Per capita GDP in 1980	Share of the population aged 5–20	N	R^2
Above-average GDP per capita	0.027 (2.84)	0.0041 (2.08)			40	0.11
Below-average GDP per capita	0.028 (5.10)	0.0044 (2.30)			63	0.09
Above-average GDP per capita	−0.016 (−0.69)	0.0064 (2.49)	0.0011 (1.15)	0.0933 (1.68)	40	0.20
Below-average GDP per capita	−0.016 (−0.67)	0.0044 (2.03)	0.0013 (0.67)	0.1157 (1.91)	62	0.12

Data sources: Barro (1991) and Political Risk Services/IRIS.

The *corruption* index is the simple average of the *corruption* indices produced by Political Risk Services (compiled by IRIS) for 1982–95. One standard deviation of the *corruption* index equals 1.45. A *high* value of the *corruption* index means that the country has *good* institutions in that respect. White-corrected *t*-statistics in parentheses.

consumption expenditure (row 11 compared to row 8). The second set of instruments adds the black market premium, imports plus exports as a ratio of GDP, and the oil dummy to the previous set. In this second case, the use of instrumental variables yields a coefficient on corruption almost identical to that in the ordinary least squares regression both in the regression of government expenditure on education as a ratio to GDP (row 12 compared to row 1) and in the regression of government expenditure as a share of total government consumption expenditure (row 13 compared to row 8). The null of appropriate specification of the system is not rejected by tests of the overidentifying instruments when using the first set of instruments and is rejected when using the second set of instruments. Overall, there is tentative support for the hypothesis that corruption causes a decline in government expenditure on education. The last rows in Table 3 report some evidence that corruption may also cause a decline in government spending on health.

To sum up, there is significant evidence that corruption is negatively associated with government expenditure on education, and the relationship is robust to a number of changes in the specification. There is also some evidence of an association between corruption and government expenditure on health. The fact that significant relationships have been found is even more interesting when one recalls that the quality of the available data on spending may be relatively low, both because not all countries may apply the same criteria in allocating projects among the various categories of government expenditure and because each public expenditure component presumably contains both productive and unproductive projects.[10] The results are consistent with the hypothesis that education provides more limited opportunities for rent-seeking than other items do, largely because for the most part it requires widely available, mature technology. There is also tentative evidence that the direction of the causal link is at least in part from corruption to the composition of spending. That is, it seems that the existence of corruption causes a less-than-optimal composition of government expenditure, rather than merely high government expenditure on unmonitorable items causing corruption.

4. Concluding Remarks

This paper has presented evidence of a negative, significant, and robust relationship between corruption and government expenditure on education, which is a reason for concern, since previous literature has shown that educational attainment is an important determinant of economic growth. A possible interpretation of the observed correlation between corruption and government expenditure composition is that corrupt governments find it easier to collect bribes on some expenditure items than on others. Education stands out as a particularly unattractive target for rent-seekers, presumably in large part because its provision typically does not require high-technology inputs to be provided by oligopolistic suppliers. A potential policy implication might be that it would be desirable to encourage governments to improve the composition of their expenditure by increasing the share of those spending categories that are less susceptible to corruption. However, an important issue remains whether, as a practical matter, that composition could be specified in such a way that corrupt officials would not be able to substitute publicly unproductive but privately lucrative projects for publicly productive but privately non-lucrative ones *within* the various expenditure categories.

---

[10]The noisy quality of the data might explain why in previous literature it has proved difficult to find significant and robust effects of the composition of government expenditure on economic growth (see footnote 1).

References

Ades, A., Di Tella, R., 1994. Competition and Corruption. Institute of Economics and Statistics Discussion Papers 169, University of Oxford.

Barro, R., 1992. Human capital and economic growth. In: Federal Reserve Bank of Kansas City, Policies for Long-Run Economic Growth, pp. 199–216.

Barro, R., 1991. Economic growth in a cross-section of countries. Quarterly Journal of Economics CVI, 407–43.

Barro, R., 1990. Government spending in a simple model of endogenous growth. Journal of Political Economy 98 (5), S103–125.

Devarajan, S., Swaroop, V., Zou, H., 1996. What do governments buy? The composition of public spending and economic performance. Journal of Monetary Economics 37, 313–344.

Easterly, W., Rebelo, S., 1993. Fiscal policy and economic growth: an empirical investigation. Journal of Monetary Economics 32 (2), 417–458.

Hines, J., 1995. Forbidden Payment: Foreign Bribery and American Business. NBER Working Paper 5266.

Keefer, P., Knack, S., 1993. Why Don't Poor Countries Catch Up? A Cross-National Test of an Institutional Explanation. Center for Institutional Reform and the Informal Sector Working Paper 60.

Krueger, A., 1974. The Political Economy of the Rent-Seeking Society. American Economic Review 64 (3), 291–303.

Levine, R., Renelt, D., 1992. A sensitivity analysis of cross-country growth regressions. American Economic Review 82 (4), 942–963.

Mauro, P., 1996. The effects of corruption on investment, growth, and government expenditure. International Monetary Fund Working paper 96/98. [Revised version reproduced as Chapter 9 in this volume—ED.]

Mauro, P., 1995. Corruption and growth. Quarterly Journal of Economics CX (3), 681–712.

Rauch, J., 1995. Bureaucracy, infrastructure and economic growth: evidence from U.S. cities during the progressive era. American Economic Review 85 (4), 968–979.

Sachs, J., Warner, A., 1995. Natural Resource Abundance and Economic Growth. NBER Working Paper 5398.

Shleifer, A., Vishny, R., 1993. Corruption. Quarterly Journal of Economics CVIII, 599–617.

Taylor, C. L., Hudson, M.C., 1972. World Handbook of Political and Social Indicators. ICPSR, Ann Arbor, MI.

United Nations, 1990. Sex and Age. Computer disk. United Nations, New York.

10

Corruption and the Provision of Health Care and Education Services

Sanjeev Gupta, Hamid R. Davoodi, and Erwin R. Tiongson

Introduction

Social sectors in an economy are often characterized by market failures. To correct such failures, governments intervene through the public provision, financing, and regulation of services. There is recognition that corruption emerges as a by-product of government intervention (Acemoglu and Verdier 2000); what is not well understood, however, is that corruption can adversely affect the provision of publicly provided social services. The theoretical literature identifies three channels through which this can happen. First, corruption can drive up the price and lower the level of government output and

---

Reprinted from *The Political Economy of Corruption*, edited by Arvind K. Jain (London: Routledge, 2001), pp. 111–141.

The views expressed in this chapter are those of the authors and do not necessarily represent those of the IMF or IMF policy. The authors wish to thank Emanuele Baldacci, Luiz de Mello, Gabriela Inchauste, Arvind K. Jain, and Luc Leruth for their comments. The usual disclaimer applies.

services (Shleifer and Vishny 1993), including the provision and financing of health care and education services in many countries.[1] Second, corruption can reduce investment in human capital (Ehrlich and Lui 1999). Finally, corruption can reduce government revenue (Shleifer and Vishny 1993; Hindriks, Keen, and Muthoo 1999), which in turn can lower the quality of publicly provided services (Bearse, Glomm, and Janeba 2000).[2] The latter discourages some individuals from using these services and reduces their willingness to pay for them (through tax evasion), which shrinks the tax base and diminishes the government's ability to provide quality public services.[3] The lower quality also creates incentives for individuals to opt for privately provided services. However, in countries where private markets for health care and education services are limited, this can lead to congestion, increased delays in obtaining public services, rising opportunities for rent-seeking, and frequent use of discretionary power by government officials. Even in cases where private markets are well developed and extensive, the poor may lack the ability to pay for private services and outputs.

These predictions are consistent with a growing empirical literature on the economic consequences of corruption as well as results from surveys of users of public services. The existing empirical evidence, for example, shows that corruption reduces spending on operations and maintenance, such as medicine and textbooks (Tanzi and Davoodi 1997). Higher corruption is associated with rising military spending (Gupta, de Mello, and Sharan 2000), and lower spending on health care and education services (Mauro 1998; Gupta, Davoodi, and Alonso-Terme 1998). Corruption has also been found to lower tax revenues (Ul Haque and Sahay 1996, Tanzi and Davoodi 1997, Johnson, Kaufmann, and Zoido-Lobatón 1999a). The newly instituted surveys of users of public services further confirm the adverse impact of corruption on social services. The surveys rely on users who come in contact with officials in charge of providing social services.

---

[1] Governments provide a wide range of services in social sectors, as measured by intermediate health care and education indicators (e.g. immunization and school enrollment) and outcomes (e.g. literacy and mortality).

[2] Government revenues are lower according to these two models because different government agencies act as independent rent-seeking, monopolist providers of complementary goods and services or because of corrupt and extortionist tax inspectors.

[3] Alesina (1999) discusses this "vicious cycle" in developing countries and contrasts it with a "virtuous cycle" in developed countries.

Sanjeev Gupta, Hamid R. Davoodi, and Erwin R. Tiongson

Although corruption shifts the composition of public spending away from social sectors, its impact on health care and education indicators through spending may not be significant. In the empirical literature, the link between public spending and indicators of service provision, such as enrollment rate and infant mortality rates, is weak (Hanushek 1995, Jack 1999, Gupta, Verhoeven, and Tiongson 1999). The impact of corruption on indicators of provision of health care and education services can then be either direct or indirect, working through some of the channels discussed above. This paper shows that corruption, measured by corruption perception indices, adversely affects the indicators of provision of health care and education services. Despite the overwhelming evidence from surveys of users of public services and the theoretical literature on the adverse consequences of corruption for provision of health care and education services, no systematic investigation has yet been made of the relationship between corruption and provision of health care and education services.[4]

The rest of this paper is organized as follows. The first section below illustrates how corruption can impact on the provision of social services using a theoretical model introduced by Shleifer and Vishny (1993). The subsequant section summarizes findings from national service delivery surveys to bolster the predictions from theoretical models. The data and econometric results are described in the section that follows. The last section contains the conclusions and policy implications.

Theoretical Framework

Among models of corruption, the one by Shleifer and Vishny (1993) provides the simplest framework for analyzing the causes and consequences of corruption as affecting the public provision of social services. In their framework, bribes are paid by consumers to obtain government services or output. Government officials are assumed to exercise monopoly power by determining the quantity of services or output provided, either by delaying or by simply withholding them. Two cases of corruption are considered, both of which have adverse consequences for the provision of services, and are relevant in many settings.

---

[4]Kaufmann, Kraay, and Zoido-Lobatón (1999a) test a simple association between two social indicators and various measures of governance.

In the first case, an official overprices by providing a service or an output at a government-established charge plus a bribe. Marginal cost to the government agent is the official price and the agent determines the quantity supplied by equating marginal revenue and marginal cost as with a typical monopolist. The bribe constitutes a tax. The official retains the bribe and transfers the official charge to the treasury. Figure 1a illustrates this case as "corruption without theft." The result is that the bribe drives up the price and lowers the output. Under these circumstances, some consumers will inevitably be crowded out of the market.[5] Moreover, when services affected by corruption are critical for the population, such as basic health care and education services, the full impact of government spending will not be realized. Furthermore, if teachers accept bribes for providing government-funded books or for admitting students, it will be more difficult to achieve the objective of a literate population through universal school enrollment. In fact, it has been suggested that large irregular payments required for school entrance or for passing examinations help explain low enrollment rates (Cockroft 1998). Similarly, the payment of bribes for gaining access to medical services could impact on health care indicators over time.

That government officials have the ability to limit the supply of public services has been highlighted by recent research (Kaufmann 1997, Bardhan 1997, Kaufmann and Wei 1999)—a view that was also propounded by Myrdal (1968) some thirty years ago.

In the second case, the official does not turn over to the treasury the government-imposed charge for the service or an output. This case has been referred to as "corruption with theft" (Figure 1b), as the government service or output is, in a way, stolen by the government official in charge of delivering it, and a bribe is collected for providing the service and output to a consumer. In this case, the official still equates marginal revenue with marginal cost, but marginal cost to the official is now zero. Thus, the bribe a consumer pays may be lower than the official price. In a sense the official "under-invoices" the cost of providing the service and output. Such a situation is attractive to the con-

---

[5]This is similar to Alam's (1989, 1990) model, where managers increase their illicit revenues by reducing output. The result is also consistent with studies of benefit incidence of public social spending, which point to significant leakages. Benefits from public spending disproportionately accrue to the rich; the poor simply do not utilize public services as intensively as the rich, despite the fact that the poor tend to have lower levels of health care and education achievements (Castro-Leal et al. 1999; Davoodi and Sachjapinan 2001). Corruption, of course, is not the only reason for this leakage.

Figure 1a. Corruption Without Theft

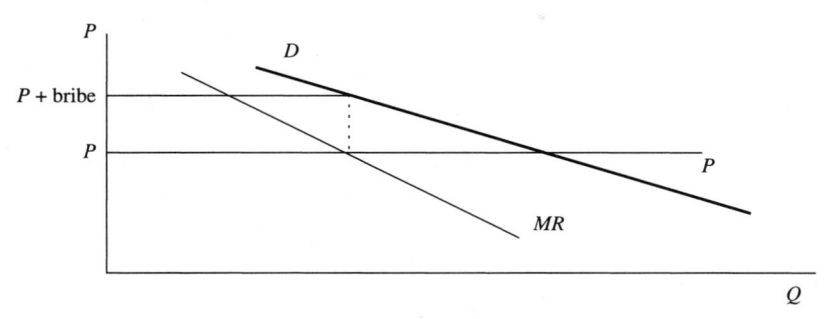

Source: Shleifer and Vishny (1993).

Figure 1b. Corruption With Theft

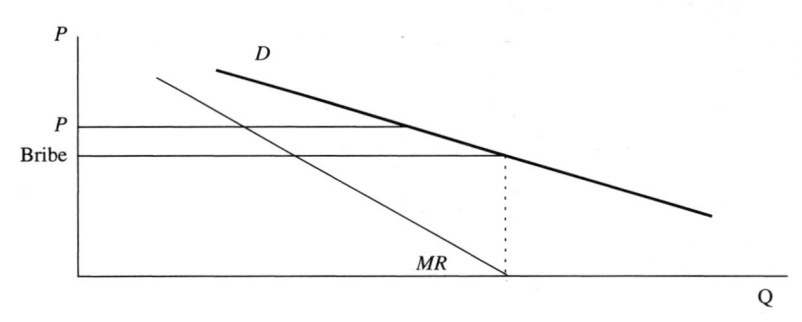

Source: Shleifer and Vishny (1993).

sumer and aligns his interest with that of the official, which makes corruption more difficult to detect. This creates a revenue loss for the treasury and the government official is able to exercise more discretion than in "corruption without theft." The corrupt official can choose to lower bribe level, thereby increasing the demand for a service or an output and raising revenue loss to the treasury. A smaller bribe also has the advantage of lowering the risk of detection.

The difference between the two cases is that revenue loss under the second case can be significantly higher. Although a lower bribe increases demand in the short run, it would restrict supply in the long run because of larger revenue losses.

Shleifer and Vishny's model offers policy prescriptions for anti-corruption strategies. In corruption without theft, competition in the provision of government service or output could reduce possibilities for corruption. In corruption with theft, competition complemented with enhanced monitoring of government officials and better procurement policies would help curb corruption.

Although the above model has important policy implications, it overlooks the fact that the government does not provide a single service or output. In an extension of their original model, Shleifer and Vishny (1993) present another model in which the government is still a monopolist but provides complementary services and output. The extended model recognizes that publicly provided health care and education services are complementary inputs to households' "production function" of health care and education services.[6] The government official can act as a joint monopolist and lower the bribe on a service or an output to expand demand for the complementary services and output. However, when different government agencies act as independent monopolists and do not consider the complementarity of services and outputs, the adverse impact of corruption is significant. In comparison with the joint monopolist model, a higher bribe is charged to the consumer, a lower output is supplied, and government revenue is even lower. A first-best anti-corruption solution is to allow for many producers of complementary goods and services. In comparison with joint and independent monopolist cases, this results in the lowest price, highest output, and zero bribe.

In contrast, there exists a class of models that predict exactly the opposite result. According to these models, bribes provide a mechanism for overcoming an overly centralized and overly extended government bureaucracy, red tape, and delays (Leff 1964, Lui 1985). This interpretation of bribery and corruption, sometimes referred to as the "efficient-grease" hypothesis (Kaufmann and Wei 1999), views the size of a bribe as a reflection of an individual's opportunity cost. Hence, the payment of a bribe is an efficient solution to the acquisition of a public service or output, with no adverse consequences. The next section shows that the efficient-grease hypothesis runs counter to findings of national service delivery surveys. In general, these surveys point toward the negative impact of corruption on the provision of services.[7]

---

[6] See, for example, Hanushek (1995) and Filmer, Hammer, and Pritchett (1998).

[7] Kaufmann and Wei (1999) also report that the efficient-grease hypothesis is not supported by data.

Sanjeev Gupta, Hamid R. Davoodi, and Erwin R. Tiongson

National Service Delivery Surveys

In recent years, an increasing number of public service delivery surveys have been conducted in developing and transition economies by international organizations, such as the World Bank and CIET (Community Information, Empowerment, Transparency) International, as well as by local agencies, such as the Public Affairs Center (PAC) in Bangalore, India.[8] These surveys are designed to elicit responses from users of social services, including their views on the impact of corruption on service delivery. Although most reports based on these surveys are still preliminary, they nevertheless confirm the pervasiveness of corruption and bribery in the public provision of health care and education services.

One major survey conducted worldwide by the World Bank for the 1997 *World Development Report* (WDR) examined perceptions of institutional uncertainty as viewed by the private sector.[9] This survey provides an internationally comparable dataset of indicators of perceived uncertainty about laws, policies, and regulations, the level and unpredictability of corruption, as well as the perceived quality and efficiency of government services and the quality of health care provision. This aspect of the WDR survey provides interesting insights for this study. Figure 2 illustrates the relationship between an index of corruption and its unpredictability, on one hand, and government service provision, on the other, for a group of seventy-one countries.[10]

The scatterplots suggest a strong correlation between corruption and service provision; that is, countries with less corruption and higher predictability of corruption tend to have better quality of health care and more efficient provision of public services.[11] The correlation coefficients range from –0.59 to –0.66 and are significant at the 1 percent

---

[8]The CIET social audits are available via the Internet: www.ciet.org.
[9]Available via the Internet: www.unibas.ch/wwz/wifor/staff/bw/survey/index.html.
[10]In the survey, corruption was defined as irregular payments made to officials, and corruption uncertainty as firms asked to pay more, in addition to irregular payments. Respondents were required to rate their responses from 1 (worst) to 6 (best). Respondents were also asked to rate the quality of health care services and efficiency of government services provided in their country, following the same scale. For ease of interpretation, this paper rescales the corruption and uncertainty indices from 1 (best) to 6 (worst), with higher values of each index representing higher corruption and higher uncertainty.
[11]See Campos, Lien, and Pradhan (1999) and Wei (1997) for the concepts of corruption unpredictability and corruption uncertainty, both of which are found to have adverse impact on development.

Figure 2. Corruption and the Provision of Government Services in Seventy-One Countries

Panel A. Corruption and Health Care

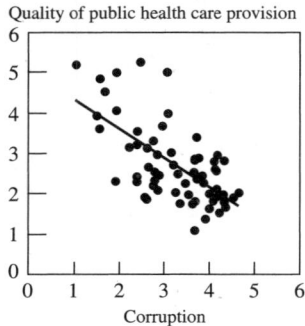

Panel B. Corruption Uncertainty and Health Care

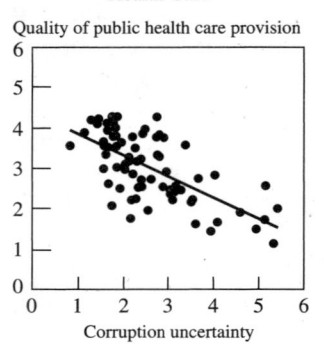

Panel C. Corruption and Government Services

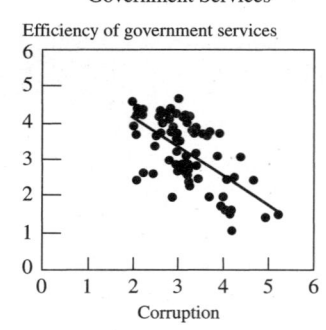

Panel D. Corruption Uncertainty and Government Services

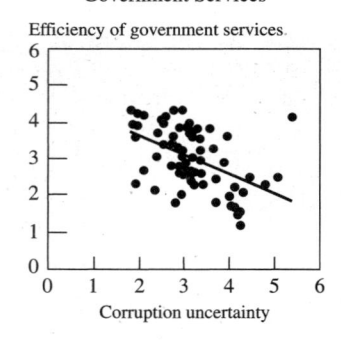

Source: World Bank (1997).
Note: The indices used in the charts correspond to the following survey questions: For corruption: Are irregular payments commonly made to officials? For corruption uncertainty: Are firms asked to pay more—in addition to irregular payments—by other officials? For quality of government services: How efficient are government sevices? And for quality of public health care: How is the quality of public health care provision? In the survey, these are questions 14, 16, 25, and 22d, respectively. Respondents were required to rate their responses from 1 (worst) to 6 (best). For this paper, the corruption and uncertainty indices have been rescaled from 1 (best) to 6 (worst).

level. This high correlation further suggests that corruption and the efficient-grease hypothesis are at odds with each other.

The above results are reinforced by a simple regression of child mortality rate on a constant, the index of corruption, and the indicator of quality of health care provision for a group of sixty-two countries.[12] The results confirm the association between corruption and health outcomes: countries with higher corruption tend to have higher child mortality.

These results can be used to quantify the interaction between corruption and quality of health care provision and child mortality rate. Using the estimated coefficients on the explanatory variables and the mean and standard deviation of each variable in the regression, four cells are constructed, each representing a different scenario for corruption and quality of health care and the associated value for child mortality.[13] The results are shown in Figure 3a. The difference between the two polar cases is considerable; countries with low corruption and high quality of health care provision tend to have fifty-nine fewer child mortality per 1,000 live births than countries with high corruption and low quality of health care provision. The results are subjected to further scrutiny in the next section.

Similarly, the student dropout rate is regressed on a constant, the corruption index and the indicator of efficiency of government services for a group of fifty-three countries.[14] The results shown in Figure 3b are consistent with theoretical predictions. Countries with higher levels of corruption tend to have higher student dropout rates. The difference

---

[12]The regression produces an adjusted R-squared of 0.13, with variations explained mostly by corruption and not by the quality of health care provision:

$$\text{Child mortality} = 178.8 + 22.9^* \text{ (Corruption)} - 9.1^* \text{(Quality)},$$
$$(5.50) \quad (1.75) \quad\quad\quad (-0.78)$$

where t-statistics are in parentheses. The regression does not control for other determinants of child mortality, hence the low R-squared, and does not address the endogeneity of corruption or reverse causality. These issues are discussed in section four of this chapter.

[13]Each cell is calculated as one standard deviation around the mean; the results are the same when two standard deviations are used. Child mortality rates refer to under-age-five mortality rates.

[14]The survey does not provide data on the quality of education service provision; the indicator of the efficiency of government services is used instead. The regression produces an adjusted R-squared of 0.29:

$$\text{Dropout rate} = 78.5 + 12.3^* \text{ (Corruption)} - 2.32^* \text{ (Efficiency)},$$
$$(8.39) \; (3.90) \quad\quad\quad (-0.52)$$

where t-statistics are in parentheses. Like the previous regression, the variation in the dependent variable is accounted for by variation in corruption rather than efficiency of government services, with the latter being statistically insignificant. Statistical inadequacy of this regression, as in the previous one, is addressed in section four of this chapter.

Figure 3a. Corruption, Quality of Health Care, and Child Mortality in Sixty-Two Countries
(Circa 1997)

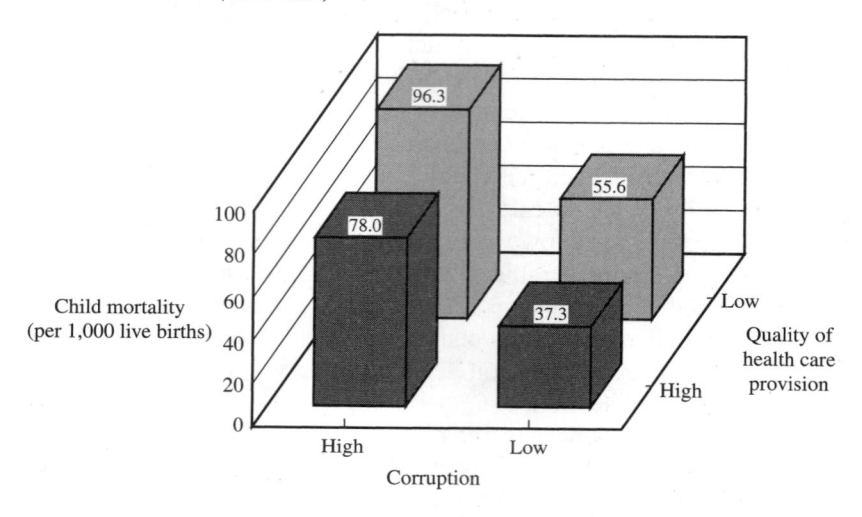

Figure 3b. Corruption, Efficiency, and Dropout Rates in Fifty-Three Countries
(Circa 1997)

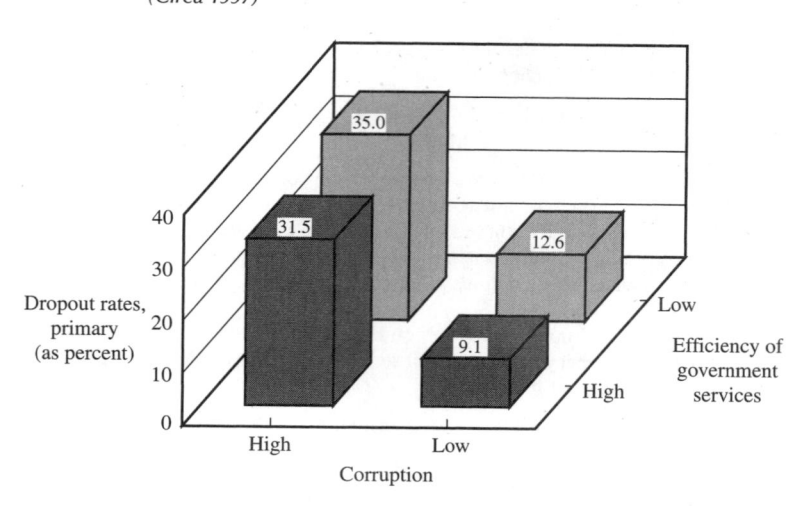

between the two polar cases is revealing: countries with low corruption and high efficiency of government services tend to have about 26 percentage points fewer student dropouts than countries with high corruption and low efficiency of government services.

Other surveys of national service delivery have solicited answers to a range of questions that were not covered in the WDR survey. The findings from these surveys can be summarized as follows.

First, *corruption can increase the cost of health care and education services.* Although primary health care and primary education are often provided by the government free of charge or at very low cost in the countries surveyed, service users often find themselves paying unofficial fees or illegal charges. The CIET social audits suggest that the percentage of students paying extra charges for education range from 10 percent to 86 percent.[15] A World Bank country study likewise finds that parents are asked to pay illegal stipends for enrolling their children in school (Langseth and Stapenhurst 1997). A PAC survey reveals that as much as 38 percent of total hospital expenses borne by households are in the form of bribes, and some 17 percent of households claim to have made unofficial payments to public hospitals (Paul 1998). One study reveals that even staff of a maternity hospital were bribed to obtain medical services (Gopakumar 1998). Another survey confirms that perception of corruption in the health sector is strongly correlated with input overpricing and unofficial payments (Gray-Molina, Perez de Rada, and Yanez 1999).

Higher user costs also create a disincentive for using government facilities. Surveys suggest that that illegal payments for school entrance and other hidden costs help explain dropout rates and low school enrollment rates in developing countries (CIET 1999, Cockroft 1998).

Second, *corruption may decrease the volume of publicly provided services.* Service delivery surveys show that theft of medicines and textbooks is a common form of leakage.[16] In one country, health staff reportedly expropriated and sold drugs and medicine, depriving the poor of basic health services (Reinikka 1999). In another country, despite significant public expenditures on textbooks, only 16 percent of children have actually received them. Similarly, education supplies have been lost to payoffs, under-deliveries, and overpricing (Chua 1999).

---

[15]Not all informal charges are necessarily bribe payments.
[16]*The Economist* (1994) reports on the theft of medical supplies.

Finally, *corruption may lower the quality of health care and education services*. In one country, bribes and payoffs in teacher recruitment and promotion have lowered the quality of public school teachers (Chua 1999); in another, inadequate treatment and lack of drugs have been attributed to corruption (CIET 1996). Officials may also create delays or bottlenecks in order to extract bribes. One survey confirms that bribes are indeed associated with slower service (Villegas, Morales, and Andersson 1998).

The next section ascertains whether these service delivery surveys are consistent with data across a range of countries.

Data and Estimation

The preceding sections suggest a framework for evaluating the relationship between corruption and social indicators:

$$Y_i = \alpha + \beta X_i + \gamma Z_i + \epsilon_i \tag{1}$$

where Y_i is a measure of aggregate education outcome or health status; X_i is an index of corruption perception in country i; and Z_i are control variables such as per capita income, public spending on health care and education services, average years of education, and other known determinants of health care and education indicators.

Although this framework addresses the adverse impact of corruption on health care and education indicators, the available data do not allow one to distinguish between the two cases of corruption discussed in the section on theoretical framework. This regression should then be seen as a reduced-form specification.

The use of aggregate data to estimate this equation has other limitations. The factors that affect health care and education indicators are often poorly captured by aggregate indicators, such as average years of education. However, there is evidence that cross-country analyses based on aggregate data are not inconsistent with findings of micro-level studies (Schultz 1993 and 1998).

The technique of Ordinary Least Squares (OLS) is used to estimate equation (1) for both cross-section and panel data covering 128 advanced and developing countries.[17] Panel data results may be less reli-

---

[17]Cross-sectional data are averages of each variable by country over the 1985–97 period. The actual number of observations varies depending on specifications. Descriptive statistics are provided in the appendix.

able because of the persistence of corruption over time in the sample countries, the limited annual data on social indicators, and the quality of reported social indicators that are often based on interpolations or estimates from demographic models. For these reasons, this chapter relies largely on cross-sectional regressions.

Semilog regressions are used to estimate various specifications of equation (1). Except for corruption, all other variables are specified in logarithmic form. This is consistent with other studies suggesting a nonlinear relationship between social indicators and their standard explanatory variables.[18]

The corruption indices were drawn from various sources. The main index is from the Political Risk Services/International Country Risk Guide (PRS/ICRG) database. This corruption index has been rescaled and ranges from 0 (least corrupt) to 10 (most corrupt).[19] Recent research by Kaufmann, Kraay, and Zoido-Lobatón (1999b) suggests the inadequacy of existing individual indices of corruption, due to high variance among the surveys that underlie these indices. These authors combine related measures of governance into aggregate indicators for what they consider to be six fundamental concepts of governance, including graft or corruption.[20] Their index of graft, with estimates ranging from about –2.5 (most corrupt) to 2.5 (least corrupt), is also used as an alternative measure of corruption. This was rescaled and ranges from –2.5 (least corrupt) to 2.5 (most corrupt). This chapter uses the PRS/ICRG index more extensively than the graft index because the graft index covers only the 1997–8 period, whereas the PRS/ICRG index covers the 1985–97 period—the same period as the health care and education indicators and the control variables.[21]

Indices of corruption constructed by Transparency International (TI), which are based on at least three surveys, are also used for testing the sensitivity of results.

At the outset, it needs to be recognized that the above indices of perception of corruption do not necessarily capture corruption in the

---

[18]See, for example, Pritchett and Summers (1996) on the nonlinear relationship between income and health.

[19]This procedure has been used by Tanzi and Davoodi (1997), and Gupta, Davoodi, and Alonso-Terme (1998).

[20]The methodology is described in detail in Kaufmann, Kraay, and Zoido-Lobatón (1999b).

[21]As noted later in the robustness tests, however, using the graft index in place of the PRS/ICRG index yields the same overall results.

health care and education sectors. For example, the PRS/ICRG index reflects the assessment of foreign investors about the degree of corruption in an economy. Investors are asked whether high government officials are likely to demand special payments (high-level corruption) and whether illegal payments are generally expected throughout lower levels of government especially those connected with import and export licenses, exchange controls, tax assessment, police protection, or loans (low-level corruption). However, these indices are likely to capture corruption at the service provision level to the extent they refer to corruption in the public sector as a whole.

This study uses health care and education indicators that are common to four sets of indicators endorsed at different international fora.[22] These include rates for immunization, births attended by health staff, child and infant mortality, enrollment and persistence to Grade 5, repeater, dropout, and illiteracy. Data on social indicators and the control variables are primarily drawn from the 1999 World Development Indicators, UNESCO, and Barro and Lee (1996).[23] A detailed list is provided in Tables 8 and 9 in the appendix.

OLS Regressions

Table 1 presents baseline regressions of indicators of health care and education services on a constant and the PRS/ICRG corruption index. The results show that better health care and education indicators are positively and significantly correlated with lower corruption. When per capita GDP, considered as a major determinant of corruption (Treisman 2000), is added to the baseline regressions,[24] the corruption index remains significantly correlated with all measures of health outcomes, except for immunization rates (Table 2).[25] The coefficient estimates, how-

---

[22]The indicators have been endorsed by the OECD, the World Bank, and the UN; the Common Country Assessment (CCA) of the UN Development Assistance Framework; the UN/CCA Task Force on Basic Social Services; and by the UN Statistical Commission under the Minimum National Social Data Set (MNSDS).

[23]Other data are taken from Davoodi and Sachjapinan (2001), and International Monetary Fund, *World Economic Outlook* (1999).

[24]The link between income and social indicators is well documented. See, for example, Jack (1999) for a brief survey of the relevant health literature.

[25]In general, the estimated coefficient of per capita income in the mortality regressions is consistent with previous cross-country estimates. Wang *et al.* (1999), for example, suggest that income elasticity for child mortality in 1990 was –0.71 in low-income and middle-income countries, which is close to the estimate of –0.73 obtained in this chapter.

Table 1. Baseline Regressions, 1985–97: Cross-Sectional Analysis[1]

Dependent variable	N	R^2	F statistic	Constant	Corruption
Health outcomes					
Child mortality (per 1,000 live births)	116	0.44	92.26***	5.75*** (28.01)	0.37*** (12.26)
Infant mortality (per 1,000 live births)	117	0.48	107.77***	5.37*** (30.22)	0.35*** (12.72)
Births attended by health staff (percent of total)	110	0.25	38.18***	3.42*** (22.05)	−0.13*** (−6.06)
Immunization, DPT (percent of children under 12 months)	117	0.15	21.68***	3.92*** (49.73)	−0.06*** (−5.61)
Low-birthweight babies (percent of births)	113	0.33	55.38***	3.02*** (23.34)	0.14*** (7.20)
Education outcomes					
School enrollment, primary (percent net)	111	0.05	6.24***	4.34*** (57.02)	−0.03*** (−3.30)
Repeater rates, primary (percent)	87	0.13	14.09***	3.17*** (9.51)	0.24*** (3.47)
Dropout rates, primary (percent)	88	0.32	41.30***	4.70*** (16.32)	0.36*** (7.02)
Persistence to grade 5, total (percent of cohort)	81	0.12	11.47***	4.13*** (67.58)	−0.04*** (−4.30)
Illiteracy rates (percent of population age 15 and older)	86	0.08	8.53***	4.01*** (9.09)	0.23*** (2.71)

Sources: World Bank (1999), Barro and Lee (1996), and Political Risk Services.
Note
[1] Variables are means covering the period 1985–97. N denotes the number of countries. Except for corruption, all the variables are in logs. A low value of the corruption index means that a country is perceived to be less corrupt. White's heteroskedastic-consistent t-statistics are in parentheses. (***), (**), and (*) denote significance at the 1 percent, 5 percent, and 10 percent levels, respectively.

ever, are generally lower. Corruption ceases to be significantly correlated with indicators of education services when per capita income is added as a control variable, except for repeater rates and dropout rates at the primary level.

The overall results continue to hold when four other control variables are added. First, average years of education in the female population—a measure of maternal education—could have a positive impact on health outcomes (Schultz 1993, 1998) and on student

Table 2. Corruption, Health Care and Education Services, 1985–97: Cross-Sectional Analysis[1]

Dependent variable	N	R²	F statistic	Constant	Income	Corruption
Health outcomes						
Child mortality (per 1,000 live births)	116	0.82	254.42***	10.45*** (18.07)	−0.73*** (−9.11)	0.13*** (4.30)
Infant mortality (per 1,000 live births)	117	0.81	255.43***	9.35*** (19.22)	−0.62*** (−9.17)	0.14*** (5.14)
Births attended by health staff (percent of total)	110	0.48	50.52***	1.79*** (4.88)	0.25*** (5.12)	−0.05** (−2.01)
Immunization, DPT (percent of children under 12 months)	117	0.31	27.06***	3.07*** (12.31)	0.13*** (4.10)	−0.02 (−1.40)
Low-birthweight babies (percent of births)	113	0.55	68.13***	4.55*** (17.93)	−0.24*** (−7.63)	0.06*** (2.87)
Education outcomes						
School enrollment, primary (percent net)	111	0.24	18.01***	3.52*** (12.75)	0.13*** (3.51)	0.01 (0.82)
Repeater rates, primary (percent)	87	0.22	12.98***	5.63*** (6.87)	−0.36*** (−3.49)	0.15** (2.16)
Dropout rates, primary (percent)	88	0.44	35.78***	7.89*** (11.88)	−0.50*** (−5.15)	0.20*** (3.39)
Persistence to grade 5, total (percent of cohort)	81	0.43	31.71***	3.14*** (14.97)	0.15*** (4.78)	−0.00 (−0.30)
Illiteracy rates (percent of population age 15 and older)	86	0.26	16.14***	7.46*** (8.46)	−0.50*** (−4.27)	0.11 (1.34)

Sources: World Bank (1999), Barro and Lee (1996), and Political Risk Services.

Note

[1]Variables are means covering the period 1985–97. N denotes the number of countries. Except for corruption, all the variables are in logs. A low value of the corruption index means that a country is perceived to be less corrupt. White's heteroskedastic-consistent t-statistics are in parentheses. (***), (**), and (*) denote significance at the 1 percent, 5 percent, and 10 percent levels, respectively.

performance (Barro and Lee 1997). Second, public expenditures on health care and education services are added, although evidence on their impact on social indicators is mixed.[26] Third, age-dependency

---

[26]See, for example, Filmer and Pritchett (1999), Gupta, Verhoeven, and Tiongson (1999) and Jack (1999) for health care, and Anand and Ravallion (1993), Noss (1991), Mingat and Tan (1998) for education.

ratio is meant to capture the constraints on public resources.[27] Finally, health status and education outcomes are expected to improve with increased urbanization.[28] For brevity, Table 3 reports the results of this exercise for child mortality alone, but this holds for infant mortality and percent of low-birthweight babies as well.[29]

Some additional controls were also tried, which did not affect the statistical significance of corruption. These were access to safe water and access to sanitation, which were both found to be statistically significant.[30] Physicians per 1,000 people, another measure of available health resources, is also significant, while adding benefit incidence as a control variable shows that corruption remains significant at the 5 percent level.[31]

As regards regressions for education indicators, corruption is consistently correlated with dropout rates at conventional levels of significance when various controls are added (Table 4).[32] However, this is not the case for the remaining education indicators. It is noteworthy that the presence of multicollinearity—in particular, the correlation between corruption and public spending—requires some caution in the interpretation of these results.[33]

Instrumental Variable Regressions

Corruption could be an endogenous variable, which would render the OLS technique inappropriate. First, both corruption and health or

---

[27]Dependency ratios have been used in regressions of education outcomes. See, for example, Tan and Mingat (1992). Behrman, Duryea, and Szekely (1999) suggest that dependency ratios change the relative share of public resources available for school-age children. This effect may hold for health as well.

[28]According to Schultz's (1993) survey of the literature, studies suggest that mortality is higher for rural, low-income households. Plank (1987) finds that access to education is typically better in urban areas.

[29]For lack of annual data from 1985–97, 1990 data on average years of education of adult females are used. The regressions also hold when 1990 data on average years of education of all adults are used.

[30]Shi (2000) finds that access to potable water and sewerage connection has a significant impact on child mortality.

[31]This follows Davoodi and Sachjapinan (2001). To keep the sample size as large as possible, this chapter restricts the controls to the strongest and consistent determinants of health outcomes, limiting the sample to thirty-one countries.

[32]These results also hold when pupil-teacher ratio is added as well.

[33]Corruption, for example, is correlated with public spending on education and health. The health regression results generally hold even when per capita health expenditures, including private spending, is used in place of public health spending.

Table 3. Child Mortality and Corruption, 1985–97: Cross-Sectional Analysis[1]

	OLS							2SLS
	(1)	(2)	(3)	(4)	(5)	(6)	(7)	(8)
Constant	5.75***	10.45***	10.42***	10.21***	9.37***	9.31***	8.65***	8.97***
	(28.01)	(18.07)	(17.90)	(21.55)	(24.46)	(22.71)	(16.69)	(21.00)
Corruption (PRS/ICRG)	0.37***	0.13***	0.12***	0.08***	0.07***	0.07***		0.10**
	(12.26)	(4.30)	(4.28)	(3.44)	(2.70)	(2.59)		(2.03)
Corruption (graft)							−0.20***	
							(3.95)	
Per capita income		−0.73***	−0.73***	−0.67***	−0.55***	−0.58***	−0.53***	−0.49***
		(−9.11)	(−8.98)	(−9.22)	(−9.75)	(−8.08)	(−6.24)	(−5.04)
Public health spending			−0.01	0.04	0.04	0.04	0.03	0.05
			(−0.30)	(0.87)	(0.90)	(0.86)	(0.80)	(0.95)
Average years of education, females, age 15 and older				−0.36***	−0.22***	−0.23***	−0.26***	−0.31**
				(−3.96)	(−2.84)	(−2.76)	(3.18)	(−1.96)
Dependency ratio					1.16***	1.13***	1.00***	0.98***
					(5.58)	(5.48)	(4.73)	(3.52)
Urbanization						0.07	0.04	0.04
						(0.15)	(0.30)	(0.28)
F statistic	92.26***	254.42***	168.27***	184.43***	195.54***	161.76***	169.36***	
Adjusted R-squared	0.44	0.82	0.81	0.89	0.91	0.91	0.92	
N	116	116	116	89	89	89	89	73
First-stage R-squared								0.69
Sargan's p-value								0.77

Sources: World Bank (1999), Barro and Lee (1996), Political Risk Services, Kaufmann et al. (1999b), and Treisman (2000).

Note

[1] Variables are means covering the period 1985–97. N denotes the number of countries. Except for corruption, all the variables are in logs. A low value of the corruption index means that a country is perceived to be less corrupt. White's heteroskedastic-consistent t-statistics are in parentheses. (***), (**), and (*) denote significance at the 1 percent, 5 percent, and 10 percent levels, respectively. The instruments used were (log of) 1985 per capita income, democracy index, and percent Protestants. See text.

Table 4. Dropout Rates and Corruption, 1985–97: Cross-Sectional Analysis[1]

	OLS							2SLS
	(1)	(2)	(3)	(4)	(5)	(6)	(7)	(8)
Constant	4.70***	7.89***	8.06***	6.64***	5.16***	4.73***	3.25**	3.83**
	(16.32)	(11.88)	(11.32)	(4.97)	(3.98)	(3.44)	(1.99)	(2.52)
Corruption (PRS/ICRG)	0.36***	0.20***	0.18***	0.20***	0.14**	0.13**		0.36**
	(7.02)	(3.39)	(3.08)	(2.74)	(2.12)	(2.00)		(2.51)
Corruption (graft)							0.50***	
							(2.72)	
Per capita income		−0.50***	−0.52***	−0.29***	−0.08***	−0.28	−0.15	−0.00
		(−5.15)	(−5.16)	(−1.42)	(−0.46)	(−1.28)	(−0.65)	(−0.02)
Public education spending			−0.07	−0.13	−0.23	−0.24	−0.31**	−0.08
			(−0.36)	(−0.66)	(−1.20)	(−1.20)	(1.65)	(−0.34)
Average years of education, females, age 15 and older				−0.17	0.17	0.05	0.00	0.17
				(−0.65)	(0.66)	(0.17)	(0.00)	(0.35)
Dependency ratio					2.50***	2.29***	1.95**	1.76*
					(3.49)	(3.07)	(2.53)	(1.92)
Urbanization						0.55	0.47	0.37
						(1.39)	(1.30)	(0.89)
F statistic	41.30***	35.78***	22.69***	10.95***	12.63***	11.16***	12.76***	
Adjusted R-squared	0.32	0.44	0.43	0.35	0.45	0.46	0.49	
N	88	88	86	72	72	72	72	59
First-stage R-squared								0.69
Sargan's P-value								0.17

Sources: World Bank (1999), Barro and Lee (1996), Political Risk Services, Kaufmann et al. (1999b), and Treisman (2000).

Note

[1]Variables are means covering the period 1985–97. N denotes the number of countries. Except for corruption, all the variables are in logs. A low value of the corruption index means that a country is perceived to be less corrupt. White's heteroskedastic-consistent t-statistics are in parentheses. (***), (**), and (*) denote significance at the 1 percent, 5 percent, and 10 percent levels, respectively. The instruments used were (log of) 1985 per capita income, democracy index, and percent Protestants. See text.

education indicators could be correlated with an unobserved, country-specific variable. The statistical relationship between corruption and health care or education may then be simply incidental. Second, the possibility of reverse causality cannot be ruled out as people with poor health status may be more willing to pay bribes to obtain services that otherwise would not be available; or poor levels of education could create an environment conducive to corruption. The instrumental variable technique addresses both possibilities. The difficulty lies in finding appropriate instruments for corruption.

For this study, the variables identified by Treisman (2000) are used as instruments. He finds that countries with lower corruption tend to be largely Protestant, former British colonies, have high per capita income, a high ratio of imports to GDP, long exposure to democracy, and a unitary form of government.[34] These variables can be taken as potential instruments for the corruption index. In the current sample, corruption is found to be highly correlated with the share of Protestants in the population, per capita income, and exposure to democracy.[35]

The results of 2SLS regressions are presented in Tables 3 and 4 (columns 8). The instruments used are the (log of) the initial value of per capita income, the share of Protestants in the population, and exposure to democracy.[36] The specification test indicates that the instruments are correctly specified and the first-stage adjusted R-squared is generally high—about 0.69 for both regressions.

In general, the results in Tables 3 and 4 indicate a statistically significant relationship between corruption and both child mortality rates and dropout rates. The 2SLS regressions of infant mortality rates and percent of low-birthweight babies are not shown but the results hold for these regressions as well. Sargan's specification test also indicates that the instruments are correctly specified for all 2SLS regressions. A

---

[34]La Porta, Lopez-de-Silanes, Shleifer, and Vishny (1999) also find that countries that are less developed have higher Catholic and Muslim populations, and countries with French or socialist laws tend to have inferior measures of government performance, including higher corruption.

[35]Further difficulties arise if per capita income is regarded as endogenous to health care and education indicators. Good health or better education could raise living standards, thus implying reverse causality. To address this concern, the initial value of per capita income (1985) is used as an instrument for per capita income averaged over the 1985–97 period.

[36]The other control variables are assumed to act as their own instruments.

Figure 4. Corruption and Child Mortality

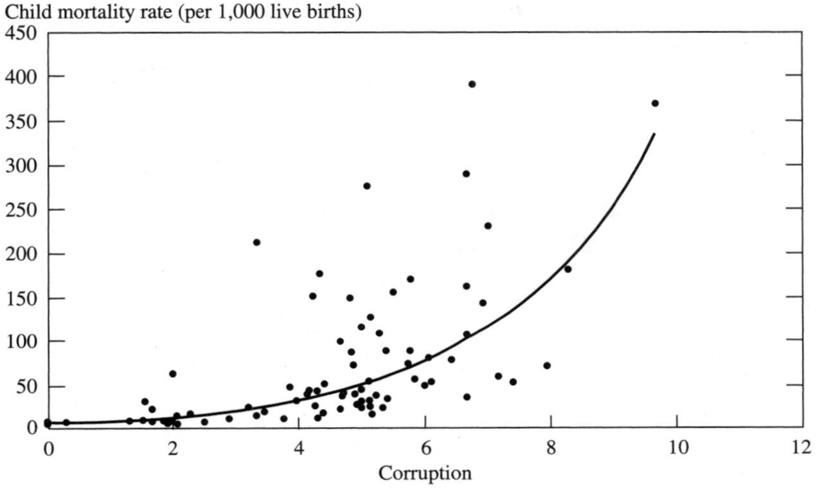

Child mortality rate (per 1,000 live births)

Source: See Table 3.

partial scatterplot of the 2SLS regression in Table 3, column 8, is displayed in Figure 4.[37]

The results suggest that when corruption is reduced, the social gains, as measured by improvement in health care and education indicators, are immense. Figure 5 illustrates these gains, using the estimated coefficients and the mean of each variable in the 2SLS regressions.[38] The polar cases of corruption are based on its standard deviation. Although the gains are not quite as dramatic as those suggested by the simple regression in the previous section, they remain considerable. Infant mortality rates in countries with high corruption, for example, could be almost twice as high as in countries with low corruption, holding other factors constant; dropout rates could be five times as high.

---

[37]Removal of apparent outliers in Figure 4, for example, those associated with child mortality rates well above 200, in fact strengthens the relationship.

[38]The relative rankings based on the OLS regression (columns 6 in Tables 3 and 4) are the same as the 2SLS regression.

Figure 5. Corruption and Social Indicators

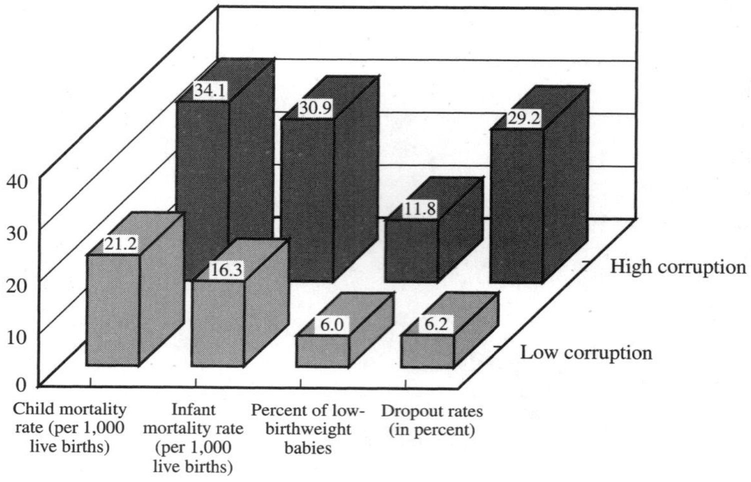

[Bar chart showing:
- Child mortality rate (per 1,000 live births): High corruption 34.1, Low corruption 21.2
- Infant mortality rate (per 1,000 live births): High corruption 30.9, Low corruption 16.3
- Percent of low-birthweight babies: High corruption 11.8, Low corruption 6.0
- Dropout rates (in percent): High corruption 29.2, Low corruption 6.2]

Source: See Tables 3 and 4.

Further Robustness Test

Estimating OLS regressions using the aggregate governance indicator for graft produced by Kaufmann, Kraay, and Zoido-Lobatón (1999b) yields similar results (Tables 3 and 4, columns 7).[39] The adjusted R-squared is somewhat higher at 0.79 but the basic results hold.

In addition, two other indices of corruption, the 1995–98 TI index and the expanded 1997 corruption perception index constructed by Lambsdorff (1998) are also significantly correlated with child and infant mortality rates, percent of low-birthweight babies, and dropout rates.[40] These results hold when income per capita, public spending on health or education, average years of education in the female population, dependency ratio, and urbanization are employed as control variables.[41] The

---

[39]This is not surprising, considering the high degree of correlation between the PRS/ICRG index and the graft indicator.

[40]These indices are both scaled from 0 (most corrupt) to 10 (least corrupt).

[41]The TI corruption index is also significantly correlated with immunization and persistence rates, controlling for all these variables. These results are available from authors upon request.

coefficient estimates are broadly similar to those in regressions based on the PRS/ICRG index.

Previous regressions treated corruption as a continuous variable. Kaufmann, Kraay, and Zoido-Lobatón (1999b) note the imprecision of existing continuous measures of corruption. Given this uncertainty, the findings of these authors imply that corruption indices should be used to classify countries into three groups: the most corrupt, the least corrupt, and those in-between.

Table 5 reports the results of regressions with a two-way (high and low) and a three-way (high, medium, and low) classification of corruption scores. Dummy variables are used to define each classification.[42] For brevity, the table omits the coefficient estimates of the control variables in the regression model. In general, the results suggest that relative to countries with low corruption, countries with high and medium corruption have worse health care and education outcomes. The difference between high and medium corruption, however, is generally not significant, suggesting that a two-way classification may better characterize the data.[43]

Alternatively, the importance of corruption could also be ascertained by splitting the countries into categories of high and low corruption. Table 6 reports the results that use the graft index to group countries into these categories.[44] In general, the impact of health or education spending on social indicators remains insignificant. There is some evidence that corruption reduces the effectiveness of public education spending, as such spending is significant in reducing dropout rates in countries with low corruption but not in countries with high corruption. Meanwhile, the income elasticity of child mortality, infant mortality, and percent of low-birthweight babies in countries with low corruption is about twice the elasticity in high-corruption countries,

---

[42]In the two-way classification case, the high corruption dummy takes a value of 1 when corruption scores are above the mean (or median) and 0 otherwise. In the three-way classification case, a high corruption dummy takes a value of 1 when corruption scores are greater than one standard deviation above the mean and 0 otherwise. The medium corruption is defined as 1 when corruption scores lie within one standard deviation around the mean and 0 otherwise. The low corruption dummy takes a value of 1 when corruption scores are less than one standard deviation below the mean.

[43]When high corruption is used as benchmark, the dummy for low corruption is significant but medium corruption is not.

[44]A country is classified under high corruption if its corruption score is higher than the median graft score; otherwise, it is classified under low corruption. The results hold when the mean is used in place of the median.

Table 5. Cross-Sectional Analysis with Dummy Variables, 1985–97[1]

Corruption classification	Dependent variable					Dependent variable			
	Child mortality	Infant mortality	Low birthweight	Dropout		Child mortality	Infant mortality	Low birthweight	Dropout
	PRS/ICRG corruption index					Graft index			
	(Coefficient estimates)								
Two-way									
High (mean)	0.25**	0.29***	0.25***	0.08		0.42***	0.48***	0.26***	0.93***
	(2.54)	(2.99)	(3.57)	(0.33)		(3.19)	(3.71)	(2.82)	(2.83)
High (median)	0.30***	0.30***	0.29***	0.49**		0.24**	0.25**	0.08	0.56*
	(3.31)	(3.37)	(4.16)	(2.13)		(2.12)	(2.30)	(1.03)	(1.90)
Three-way									
High	0.34*	0.43***	0.35**	0.81*		0.33**	0.46***	0.33**	1.04*
	(1.96)	(2.62)	(2.34)	(1.81)		(2.39)	(3.31)	(2.59)	(1.81)
Medium	0.33***	0.41***	0.29***	0.52		0.38***	0.49***	0.30***	1.02**
	(3.17)	(3.75)	(3.31)	(1.37)		(3.81)	(4.63)	(3.25)	(2.26)
N	89	89	87	72		89	89	87	72

Sources: Political Risk Services and Kaufmann et al. (1999b).

Note

[1]These regressions, following previous regressions, control for log of income, sectoral spending, average years of female schooling, dependency ratio, urbanization. White's heteroskedastic-consistent t-statistics are in parentheses. (***), (**), and (*) denote significance at the 1 percent, 5 percent, and 10 percent levels, respectively. See text for classification of corruption dummies.

suggesting that income is more effective in improving social indicators in countries with low corruption. Dependency ratios, however, pose a greater resource constraint in countries with low corruption, whereas female education is a bigger factor in reducing child and infant mortality in countries with high corruption. The finding on dependency ratios implies that as more resources are allocated toward old-age rather than younger populations, social indicators for the latter worsen. The finding on female education is equally important because it shows that social gains from increasing females' access to education can be significant, particularly in countries with high corruption.

To further address the problem of imprecision in existing corruption indices, it has been argued that weighting an index by the inverse of its standard deviation could give more accurate results (Treisman 2000). This gives more weight to corruption rankings in which there is less uncertainty or more agreement among the different surveys on which they are based. Table 7 presents the results of regressions of social indicators on the graft index divided by its standard deviation, along with the same control variables as in Tables 5 and 6. The results indicate that variance-weighted corruption is significantly related to child mortality, infant mortality, percent of low-birthweight babies, and dropout rates.

Panel Data Regressions

Panel data regressions generally yield weaker results. Controlling for per capita income, public spending on health, dependency ratio, and urbanization rate, corruption remains significantly correlated with child mortality rates in both fixed effects and random effects regressions, and with percent of low-birthweight babies in the random effects regression.[45]

Data limitations preclude the application of panel data techniques to education outcomes. For instance, there are relatively few observations for dropout rates for the 1985–97 period. In addition, the baseline regressions are not significant for either fixed effects or random effects.

---

[45]Average years of education in the female population was dropped as a control variable, due to lack of annual data. These results are in Appendix Table 8. These results hold when the regressions also control for physicians per 1,000 and, for a much smaller sample, safe water and sanitation.

Table 6. Social Indicators and Low and High Graft, 1985–97: Cross-Sectional Analysis[1]

	Child mortality		Infant mortality		Low birthweight		Dropout	
	Low graft	High graft	Low graft	High graft	Low graft	High graft	Low graft	High graft
Constant	9.98***	8.23***	9.98***	6.95***	5.96***	3.65***	2.91	4.74**
	(8.91)	(16.69)	(8.91)	(16.35)	(9.42)	(5.35)	(1.56)	(2.40)
Per capita income	−0.70***	−0.41***	−0.70***	−0.29***	−0.35***	0.14	−0.19	−0.13
	(−4.38)	(−4.36)	(−4.38)	(−3.62)	(−3.87)	(1.22)	(−0.53)	(−0.40)
Public health or education spending	0.04	−0.01	0.04	−0.02	0.02	0.03	−0.40*	−0.31
	(0.73)	(−0.09)	(0.73)	(−0.39)	(0.42)	(0.47)	(−1.79)	(−1.10)
Average years of education, females, age 15 and older	−0.28	−0.25**	−0.28	−0.21**	0.09	−0.08	−0.68	0.42
	(−1.62)	(−2.56)	(−1.62)	(−2.67)	(0.73)	(−0.90)	(−1.42)	(1.14)
Dependency ratio	1.15***	0.91***	1.15***	0.66**	−0.13	0.37	2.29**	1.96**
	(3.01)	(3.35)	(3.01)	(2.61)	(−0.39)	(1.10)	(2.06)	(2.46)
Urbanization	0.07	−0.06	0.07	−0.09	−0.24	−0.57***	0.89	−0.03
	(0.22)	(−0.51)	(0.22)	(−0.84)	(−1.31)	(−2.81)	(0.98)	(−0.08)
Adjusted R-squared	0.87	0.84	0.87	0.81	0.61	0.35	0.37	0.14
F statistic	60.65***	46.48***	60.65***	37.34***	14.64***	5.57***	4.54***	2.32*
N	45	44	45	44	44	43	31	41

Sources: World Bank (1999), Barro and Lee (1996), Political Risk Services, and Kaufmann et al. (1999b).
Note
[1]Variables are means covering the period 1985–97. N denotes the number of countries. Except for corruption, all the variables are in logs. A low value of the corruption index means that a country is perceived to be less corrupt. White's heteroskedastic-consistent t-statistics are in parentheses. (***), (**), and (*) denote significance at the 1 percent, 5 percent, and 10 percent levels, respectively.

Table 7. Social Indicators and Variance-Weighted Corruption, 1985–97: Cross-Sectional Analysis[1]

	Child mortality	Infant mortality	Low birthweight	Dropout
Constant	8.56***	7.46***	4.23***	2.94*
	(16.47)	(15.28)	(7.94)	(1.85)
Graft/standard deviation of graft	0.05***	0.06***	0.03***	0.12***
	(4.28)	(5.67)	(2.72)	(3.30)
Per capita income	−0.52***	−0.43***	−0.03	−0.09
	(−6.16)	(−5.35)	(−0.37)	(−0.41)
Public health or education spending	0.04	0.04	0.03	−0.35**
	(0.80)	(0.92)	(0.70)	(−2.06)
Average years of education, females, age 15 and older	−0.30***	−0.26***	−0.06	−0.08
	(−3.51)	(−3.14)	(−0.85)	(−0.25)
Dependency ratio	0.96***	0.74***	0.12	1.92**
	(4.37)	(3.58)	(0.50)	(2.51)
Urbanization	0.05	0.04	−0.41***	0.47
	(0.37)	(0.35)	(−2.90)	(1.34)
Adjusted R-squared	0.93	0.92	0.62	0.56
F statistic	176.49***	157.06***	21.79***	13.86***
N	89	89	87	72

Sources: World Bank (1999), Barro and Lee (1996), Political Risk Services, and Kaufmann et al. (1999b).

Note

[1] Variables are means covering the period 1985–97. N denotes the number of countries. Except for corruption, all the variables are in logs. A low value of the graft index means that a country is perceived to be less corrupt. White's heteroskedastic-consistent t-statistics are in parentheses. (***), (**), and (*) denote significance at the 1 percent, 5 percent, and 10 percent levels, respectively.

Conclusions and Policy Implications

This chapter provides a cross-country analysis of the relationship between corruption perception indices and indicators of provision of health care and education services. The empirical analysis shows that a high level of corruption has adverse consequences for a country's child and infant mortality rates, percent of low-birthweight babies in total births, and dropout rates in primary schools. In particular, child mortality rates in countries with high corruption are about one-third higher than in countries with low corruption; infant mortality rates and percent of low-birthweight babies are almost twice as high, and dropout rates are five times as high. The results are consistent with predictions stemming from theoretical models and service delivery surveys.

The results have four important policy implications in light of the dominant role played by governments in the provision of health care and education services. First, improvements in indicators of health care and education services do not necessarily require higher public spending. It is equally, if not more, important to institute transparent procurement procedures and to enhance financial accountability of public spending. Second, it is likely that a reduced level of corruption in the provision of services would help improve their quality. This, in turn, would induce individuals to use these services more intensely and pay official charges for their provision.[46] Third, conditions that facilitate private sector entry into the provision of public services would help curb the monopoly power of government service providers and limit their ability to charge bribes. Finally, participation of the poor in the decisions that influence the allocation of public resources would mitigate corruption possibilities.[47] Empowerment of the poor would thus limit the monopoly power exercised by the government officials responsible for the provision of public services and outputs.

---

[46]It is, however, possible that the supply of basic public services is constrained in some countries, and would need to be expanded.

[47]This participatory principle underlies the preparation of recently introduced poverty reduction strategy papers for the Heavily Indebted Poor Countries (HIPCs). It is envisioned that all stakeholders in the economy will participate in the process leading to the preparation of anti-poverty programs, including for health and education, that are consistent with the overall macroeconomic framework.

Appendix Table 8. Descriptive Statistics: Country Averages, 1985–97[1]

Variable	Data source	Mean	Std. Dev.	Minimum	Maximum	Observations
PRS/ICRG corruption index[1]	PRS/ICRG database	5.7	2.0	0.3	10.0	128
Graft governance indicators[1]	Kaufmann, Kraay, Lobatón, 1999	0.1	0.9	−1.6	2.1	128
Mortality rate, under 5 (per 1,000 live births)	WDI database, 1999	66.5	70.1	5.5	320.0	116
Mortality rate, infant (per 1,000 live births)	WDI database, 1999	46.0	40.6	4.5	183.5	117
Births attended by health staff (percent of total)	WDI database, 1999	72.2	27.6	7.7	100.0	110
Immunization, DPT (percent of children under 12 months)	WDI database, 1999	74.4	18.6	18.3	99.5	117
Low-birthweight babies (percent of births)	WDI database, 1999	10.6	6.2	3.2	46.0	113
School enrollment, primary (percent gross)	WDI database, 1999	95.6	20.4	27.8	133.8	111
Repeater rate, primary (percent)	UNESCO database, 1998	9.6	9.6	0.0	41.4	97
Dropout rate, primary (percent)	Barro and Lee, 1996	22.4	23.7	0.0	92.0	105
Persistence to grade 5, total (percent of cohort)	WDI database, 1999	82.0	17.3	32.9	100.0	81
Illiteracy rate, total (15 yrs old+)	WDI database, 1999	26.7	22.5	0.4	87.8	86
Per capita income (PPP)	WEO database, 1999	7,212.6	6,804.5	141.4	28,212.5	118
Public spending on health (percent of GDP)	National authorities; IMF staff estimates	2.3	1.8	0.1	8.4	117

Appendix Table 8 (concluded)

Variable	Data source	Mean	Std. Dev.	Minimum	Maximum	Observations
Public spending on education (percent of GDP)	National authorities; IMF staff estimates	3.5	1.7	0.2	8.7	116
Average years of education, female (15 yrs old+)	Barro and Lee, 1996	5.3	2.8	0.5	11.5	91
Average years of education, all (15 yrs old+)	Barro and Lee, 1996	5.8	2.7	0.7	11.7	91
Health expenditure per capita, PPP (current international $)	WDI database, 1999	583.8	671.0	11.3	3,462.9	93
Age dependency ratio (dependents to working-age population)	WDI database, 1999	0.7	0.2	0.4	1.1	117
Urban population (percent of total)	WDI database, 1999	55.0	24.1	11.5	100.0	117
Democracy dummy	Treisman, 2000	0.2	0.4	0.0	1.0	89
Protestants (percent of population)	Treisman, 2000	15.4	24.2	0.0	97.8	89
Benefit incidence (ratio of q1 to q5)	Davoodi and Sachjapinan, 2001	1.5	1.9	0.1	9.6	31
Pupil-teacher ratio, primary	WDI database, 1999	28.4	12.5	6.1	66.0	110
Physicians per 1,000 people	WDI database, 1999	1.2	1.1	0.0	3.9	115

Note:

[1]The corruption indices retain their original scaling from worst to best.

Appendix Table 9. Health Indicators and Corruption, 1985–97: Panel Data Analysis[1]

	Child mortality		Infant mortality		Low-birthweight babies	
Dependent variable	Fixed effects	Random effects	Fixed effects	Random effects	Fixed effects	Random effects
Corruption (PRS/ICRG)	0.02**	0.04***	−0.00	0.00	0.03	0.07***
	(2.08)	(4.63)	(−1.10)	(0.70)	(0.94)	(4.91)
Per capita income	−0.58***	−0.56***	−0.70***	−0.64***	−0.14	−0.02
	(−7.14)	(−12.13)	(−14.47)	(−20.57)	(−0.95)	(−0.43)
Public health spending	−0.26	−0.03	−0.02	−0.03*	−0.06	−0.02
	(−0.79)	(−1.46)	(−0.98)	(−1.80)	(−0.47)	(0.76)
Dependency ratio	0.16	0.95***	0.05	0.67***	0.67	0.22
	(0.59)	(6.35)	(0.34)	(5.58)	(0.64)	(1.47)
Urbanization	0.04	−0.10	0.31*	0.06	−0.01	−0.41
	(0.18)	(−1.01)	(1.83)	(0.84)	(−0.04)	(−4.54)
Adjusted R-squared	0.99	0.68	0.99	0.78	0.65	0.13
N	204	204	468	468	229	229

Sources: World Bank (1999), Barro and Lee (1996), and Political Risk Services.

Note

[1]Except for corruption, all the variables are in logs. A low value of the corruption index means that a country is perceived to be less corrupt. White's heteroskedastic-consistent t-statistics are in parentheses. (***), (**), and (*) denote significance at the 1 percent, 5 percent, and 10 percent levels, respectively.

Bibliography

Acemoglu, D. and Verdier, T. (2000) "The Choice Between Market Failures and Corruption," *American Economic Review* 90 (March): 194–211.

Alam, M. S. (1989) "Anatomy of Corruption: An Approach to the Political Economy of Underdevelopment," *American Journal of Economics and Sociology* 48 (October): 441–56.

—— (1990) "Some Economic Costs of Corruption in LDCs," *Journal of Development Studies* 27 (October): 89–97.

Alesina, A. (1999) "Too Small and Too Large Governments," in V. Tanzi, K. Chu, and S. Gupta (eds), *Equity and Economic Policy,* Washington, DC: International Monetary Fund.

Anand, S. and Ravallion, M. (1993) "Human Development in Poor Countries: On the Role of Private Incomes and Public Services," *Journal of Economic Perspectives* 7 (Winter): 133–50.

Anderson, J. (1998) "Corruption in Latvia: Survey Evidence," Washington, DC: World Bank Institute.

Bardhan, P. (1997) "Corruption and Development: A Review of Issues," *Journal of Economic Literature* 35 (September): 1320–46.

Barro, R. and Lee, J. (1996) "International Measures of Schooling Years and Schooling Quality," *American Economic Review* 86 (May): 218–23.

—— (1997) "Schooling Quality in a Cross Section of Countries," NBER Working Paper no. 6198, Cambridge, Mass.: National Bureau of Economic Research.

Bearse, P., Glomm, G., and Janeba, E. (2000) "Why Poor Countries Rely Mostly On Redistribution In-Kind," *Journal of Public Economics* 75 (March): 463–81.

Behrman, J. R., Duryea, S., and Szekely, M. (1999) "Aging and Economic Opportunities: Major World Regions Around the Turn of the Century," Office of the Chief Economist Working Paper no. 405, Washington, DC: Inter-American Development Bank.

Campos, J. E., Lien, D., and Pradhan, S. (1999) "The Impact of Corruption on Investment: Predictability Matters," *World Development* 27 (June): 1059–67.

Castro-Leal, F., Dayton, J., Demery, L., and Mehra K. (1999) "Public Social Spending in Africa: Do the Poor Benefit?" *The World Bank Research Observer* 14 (February): 49–72.

Chua, Y. T. (1999) *Robbed: An Investigation of Corruption in Philippine Education,* Quezon City: Philippine Center for Investigative Journalism.

CIET (1996) "Final report: Baseline Service Delivery Survey in Support of Results Oriented Management in the Uganda Institutional Capacity Building Project," New York: CIET International.

—— (1999) "Corruption: The Invisible Price Tag on Education," CIET media release, October 12, New York: CIET International.

Cockroft, L. (1998) "Corruption and Human Rights: A Crucial Link," TI Working Paper, Berlin: Transparency International.

Davoodi, H., and Sachjapinan, S. (2001) "How Useful are Benefit Incidence Studies?" Unpublished, Washington, DC: International Monetary Fund.

Economist (1994) "Sick Ukrainians," October 8: 56.

Ehrlich, I. and Lui, F. T. (1999) "Bureaucratic Corruption and Endogenous Growth," *Journal of Political Economy* 107 (December): S270–93.

Filmer, D., Hammer, J., and Pritchett, L. (1998) "Health Policy in Poor Countries: Weak Links in the Chain," World Bank Policy Research Working Paper no. 1874, Washington, DC: World Bank.

Filmer, D. and Pritchett, L. (1999) "The Impact of Public Spending on Health: Does Money Matter?" *Social Science & Medicine* 49: 1309–23.

Gopakumar, K. (1998) "Citizen Feedback Surveys to Highlight Corruption in Public Services: The Experience of Public Affairs Center, Bangalore," TI Working Paper, Berlin: Transparency International.

Gray-Molina, G., Perez de Rada, E. P., and Yanez, E. (1999) "Transparency and Accountability in Bolivia: Does Voice Matter?" OCE Working Paper no. R-381, Washington, DC: Inter-American Development Bank.

Gupta, S., Davoodi, H., and Alonso-Terme, R. (1998) "Does Corruption Affect Income Inequality and Poverty?" IMF Working Paper 98/76, Washington, DC: International Monetary Fund. [Revised version reproduced as Chapter 17 in this volume—ED.]

Gupta, S., de Mello, L., and Sharan, R. (2000) "Corruption and Military Spending," IMF Working Paper 00/23, Washington, DC: International Monetary Fund. [Revised version reproduced as Chapter 12 in this volume—ED.]

Gupta, S., Verhoeven, M., and Tiongson, E. (1999) "Does Higher Government Spending Buy Better Results in Education and Health Care?" IMF Working Paper 99/21, Washington, DC: International Monetary Fund.

Hanushek, E. E. (1995) "Interpreting Recent Research on Schooling in Developing Countries," *World Bank Research Observer* 10 (August): 227–46.

Hindriks, J., Keen, M., and Muthoo, A. (1999) "Corruption, Extortion, and Evasion," *Journal of Public Economics* 74 (December): 395–430. [Reproduced as Chapter 15 in this volume—ED.]

International Monetary Fund (1999) *World Economic Outlook*, available via Internet: www.imf.org/external/pubs/ft/weo/1999/01/data/index.htm, Washington, DC: International Monetary Fund.

Jack, W. (1999) *Principles of Health Economics for Developing Countries*, Washington, DC: World Bank Institute.

Johnson, S., Kaufmann, D., and Zoido-Lobatón, P. (1999) "Corruption, Public Finances and the Unofficial Economy," World Bank Policy Research Paper no. 2169, Washington, DC: World Bank.

Kaufmann, D. (1997) "Corruption: The Facts," *Foreign Policy* 107 (Summer): 114–31.

Kaufmann, D., Kraay, A., and Zoido-Lobatón, P. (1999a) "Governance Matters," World Bank Policy Research Paper no. 2196, Washington, DC: World Bank.

——— (1999b) "Aggregating Governance Indicators," World Bank Policy Research Paper no. 2195, Washington, DC: World Bank.

Kaufmann, D., Pradhan, S., and Ryterman, R. (1998) "New Frontiers in Diagnosing and Combating Corruption," *PREM Notes* 7 (October): 1–6.

Kaufmann, D. and Wei, S. (1999) "Does Grease Money Speed Up the Wheels of Commerce?" NBER Working Paper no. 7093, Cambridge, Mass.: National Bureau of Economic Research.

La Porta, R., Lopez-de-Silanes, F., Shleifer, A., and Vishny, R. (1999) "The Quality of Government," *Journal of Law, Economics, and Organization* 15 (April): 222–79.

Lambsdorff, J. (1998) "Corruption in Comparative Perception," in A. K. Jain (ed.), *The Economics of Corruption*, Boston: Kluwer Academic.

Langseth, P. and Stapenhurst, R. (1997) "National Integrity System Country Studies," EDI Working Paper, Washington, DC: World Bank Economic Development Institute.

Leff, N. H. (1964) "Economic Development Through Bureaucratic Corruption," *American Behavioral Scientist* 8(2): 8–14.

Lui, F. (1985) "An Equilibrium Queuing Model of Bribery," *Journal of Political Economy* 93(4) (August): 760–81.

Mauro, P. (1998) "Corruption and the Composition of Government Expenditure," *Journal of Public Economics* 69 (August): 263–79. [Reproduced as Chapter 9 in this volume—ED.]

Mingat, A. and Tan, J. (1998) "The Mechanics of Progress in Education: Evidence from Cross-Country Data," Policy Research Working Paper no. 2015, Washington, DC: World Bank.

Myrdal, G. (1968) *Asian Drama: An Inquiry into the Poverty of Nations*, New York: Twentieth Century Fund.

Narayan, D. (2000) *Voices of the Poor: Can Anyone Hear Us?* Washington, DC: World Bank.

Noss, A. (1991) "Education and Adjustment: A Review of the Literature," PRE Working Paper WPS 701, Washington, DC: World Bank.

Paul, S. (1998) "Making Voice Work: The Report Card on Bangalore's Public Services," World Bank Policy Research Paper no. 1921, Washington, DC: World Bank.

Plank, D. N. (1987) "The Expansion of Education: A Brazilian Case Study," *Comparative Education Review* 31 (August): 361–76.

Political Risk Services, International Country Risk Guide (CD-ROM version).

Pritchett, L. and Summers, L. H. (1996) "Wealthier is Healthier," *Journal of Human Resources* 31 (Fall): 841–68.

Reinikka, R. (1999) "Using Surveys for Public Sector Reform," *PREM Notes* 23 (May): 1–4.

Schultz, T. P. (1993) "Mortality Decline in the Low Income World: Causes and Consequence," Economic Growth Center Discussion Paper no. 681, New Haven: Yale University.

——— (1998) "The Formation of Human Capital and the Economic Development of Africa: Returns to Health and Schooling Investments," Economic Research Paper no. 37, Ivory Coast, African Development Bank.

Shi, A. (2000) "How Access to Urban Potable Water and Sewerage Connections Affects Child Mortality," World Bank Policy Research Paper no. 2274, Washington, DC: World Bank.

Shleifer, A. and Vishny, R. W. (1993) "Corruption," *Quarterly Journal of Economics* 108 (August): 599–617.

Tan, J. and Mingat, A. (1992) *Education in Asia: A Comparative Study of Cost and Financing,* Washington, DC: World Bank.

Tanzi, V. and Davoodi, H. (1997) "Corruption, Public Investment, and Growth," IMF Working Paper 97/139, Washington, DC: International Monetary Fund. [Revised version reproduced as Chapter 11 in this volume—ED.]

Treisman, D. (2000) "The Causes of Corruption: A Cross-National Study," *Journal of Public Economics* 76 (June): 399–457.

Ul Haque, N., and Sahay, R. (1996) "Do Government Wage Cuts Close Budget Deficits? Costs of Corruption," *IMF Staff Papers,* vol. 43 (December): 754–78, Washington, DC: International Monetary Fund.

United Nations Educational, Scientific, and Cultural Organization, *UNESCO Statistical Yearbook,* Paris: UNESCO.

Villegas, A., Morales, A., and Andersson, N. (1998) "Popular Perceptions of Corruption in Public Services: Key Findings of the First National Integrity Survey in Bolivia, 1998," unpublished manuscript, New York: CIET International.

Wang, J., Jamison, D. T., Bos, E., Preker, A., and Peabody, J. (1999) *Measuring Country Performance on Health: Selected Indicators for 115 Countries,* Washington, DC: World Bank.

Wei, S. (1997) "Why Is Corruption So Much More Taxing Than Tax? Arbitrariness Kills," NBER Working Paper no. 6255, Cambridge, Mass.: National Bureau of Economic Research.

World Bank (1997) *World Development Report 1997: The State in a Changing World,* New York: Oxford University Press for the World Bank.

——— (1999) *World Development Indicators,* Washington, DC: World Bank.

11

Corruption, Public Investment, and Growth

Vito Tanzi and Hamid R. Davoodi

Introduction

Up to the time when a huge corruption scandal, popularly labeled "tangentopoli" (bribe city), brought down the political establishment that had ruled Italy for several decades, that country had reported one of the largest shares of capital spending in GDP among the OECD countries. After the scandal broke out and several prominent individuals were sent to jail, or even committed suicide, capital spending fell sharply. The fall seems to have been caused by a reduction in the number of capital projects being undertaken and, perhaps more importantly, by a sharp fall in the costs of the projects still undertaken. Information released by *Transparency International* (*TI*)[1] reports that, within the space of two or three years, in the city of Milan, the city

---

Reprinted from *The Welfare State, Public Investment and Growth*, edited by Hirofumi Shibata and Toshihiro Ihori (Springer-Verlag Tokyo, 1998), pp. 41–60.

[1] *TI* is a nongovernmental organization with headquarters in Berlin which traces corruption trends around the world and which has as its goal the elimination of corruption.

where the scandal broke out in the first place, the cost of city rail links fell by 52 percent, the cost of one kilometer of subway fell by 57 percent, and the budget for the new airport terminal was reduced by 59 percent to reflect the lower construction costs. Although one must be aware of the logical fallacy of *post hoc, ergo propter hoc,* the connection between the two events is too strong to be attributed to a coincidence. In fact, this paper takes the view that it could not have been a coincidence.

The basic hypothesis of this paper is that corruption, and especially political or "grand" corruption,[2] is often tied to capital projects. Corruption is likely to increase the number of projects undertaken in a country, and to change the design of these projects by enlarging their sizes and their complexity. The net result is: (a) an increase in the share of public investment in GDP; (b) a fall in the average productivity of that investment; and, because of budgetary constraints and other considerations, (c) a possible reduction in some other categories of public spending, such as "operation and maintenance," education, and health. As a consequence of these and other effects of corruption on the economy, the rate of growth of a country where corruption is significant is negatively affected.

In the next section we discuss reasons why we assume that public investment is particularly sensitive to the existence of (political) corruption. We then present empirical evidence on the basic hypotheses. Finally, we draw conclusions.

Corruption and Government Spending

At least from the time, after World War II, when influential economists such as Harrod, Domar, Rostow, and others argued that countries need capital to grow and, more importantly, that there is an almost mechanical relation (the capital-output ratio) between increased capital spending and increased growth, there has been a strong intellectual bias in the economic profession in favor of capital spending. For example, when economists evaluate the allocation of public money between current and capital spending in government budgets, they tend to be critical of countries that allow the share of current spending to grow.

---

[2]The literature distinguishes between petty or bureaucratic corruption and "grand" or political corruption.

On the other hand, they generally praise countries where the share of capital spending in total government expenditure goes up.

The above bias is enshrined in the "golden rule" that many economists advocate for countries. That rule essentially states that it is all right to borrow as long as the borrowing is for investment projects.[3] Thus, it is all right to borrow to finance the building of new roads but not to finance the repairs of existing roads; or to borrow for the building of a new hospital, but not for the hiring of doctors or nurses or for buying medicines. This rule continues to be invoked as a good guide to policy even in the face of much evidence that some current spending—such as "operation and maintenance" that keeps the existing infrastructure in good condition or spending that contributes to the accumulation of human capital—can promote growth more than capital spending.

Politicians have internalized this bias and to some extent have exploited it. For example, ribbon-cutting ceremonies, when new investment projects related to roads, dams, irrigation canals, power plants, ports, airports, schools, and hospitals are completed and inaugurated, are very popular with politicians. They like to be pictured in newspaper articles in the act of cutting the ribbons and, thus, presumably, contributing to the future growth of the country. In a particular Latin American country, capital projects completed under the current administration have been painted orange to send a clear signal to the population that the present government is promoting growth. This pro-investment bias increases the investment budget. We will argue that another factor that also increases the size of the investment budget is corruption.

There is nothing routine about the investment budget and its composition. While much current government spending reflects, to a large extent, explicit or implicit entitlements or previous commitments,[4] thus allowing limited discretion, in the short run, to politicians and, especially, to specific politicians, capital spending is highly discretionary.[5] For the latter, high political figures—members of parliament, general secretaries, ministers, or even heads of state—must make some of the basic decisions. These decisions relate to: (a) the size of the total pub-

---

[3]The rule simply states that only current expenditure needs to be balanced by ordinary revenue: a country can have a fiscal deficit equal to the net capital spending of the government.

[4]Pensions, interest payments on the debt, salaries, subsidies, and so on.

[5]Specific politicians generally do not have the power to change the pensions, salaries, or subsidies of specific individuals.

lic investment budget; (b) the general composition of that budget, i.e., the broad allocation among different categories of capital spending; (c) the choice of the specific projects and their locations; and (d) even the size and the design of each project. In these decisions, and especially those in (c) and (d), some high-level individuals will have considerable control or influence. This will happen especially when some of the essential controlling or auditing institutions are not well developed and, therefore, institutional controls are weak.

Public investment projects tend to be large and in some cases they are very large. Their execution is often contracted out to domestic or foreign private enterprises. There is thus a need to choose the enterprise that will be responsible for undertaking the project. For a private enterprise, getting a contract to execute a project, and especially a large one, can be very profitable. Therefore, the managers of these enterprises may be willing to pay a "commission" to the government officials that help them win the contract.[6] In some countries, commissions paid by their enterprises to foreign politicians are both legal and tax deductible. Such "commissions" are often calculated as percentages of the total cost of the projects.

A commission of even a few percentage points on a project that costs millions or even hundreds of millions of dollars can be a large sum, one large enough to exceed the temptation price for many individuals.[7] When commissions are calculated as a percentage of projects' costs, the public officials who receive the payments for helping the enterprises win the bid will have a vested interest in increasing the scope or the size of the projects so that they can get larger commissions.[8]

The process of approval of an investment project involves several phases. For example, a civil construction project (roads, buildings, ports) requires decisions related to: (a) specification and design issues; (b) issue of tender (limited or open?); (c) tender scrutiny; (d) tender negotiations; and (e) tender approval and contracting process. The completion of the project will require verification that the work has been done according to the stipulated contract. It will also require some ar-

---

[6]Commission is often a euphemism for what is essentially a bribe.

[7]Actually, in many cases the act of bribery may not start with the enterprises but with the officials who control the decisions. Foreign enterprises report that in some countries it is impossible to get a government contract without paying a bribe.

[8]For a useful discussion of corruption in public investment, see Patrick Meagher (1997).

bitration about points of disagreement. The writing of contracts for complex projects is very difficult and inevitably there will be many areas of uncertainty and eventual disagreement.

In some of these phases, it will be possible for a strategically-placed high-level official to influence the process in ways that lead to the selection of a particular enterprise. For example, the specifications of the design can be tailor-made for a given enterprise. The issuance of tenders can be accompanied by the provision of insider information to favored enterprises, and so on.

The enterprise that pays the commission will not suffer from the payment of the bribe if it is able to recover that cost in several ways: (a) through up-front cost recovery if it can win the bidding competition with an offer that includes the cost of the commission; (b) it can have an understanding with the influential official that the initial low bid can be adjusted upward along the way, presumably, to reflect modifications to the basic design;[9] or (c) reduce its project costs by skimping on the quality of the work done and on the materials used, thus delivering, at completion, an inferior product.[10] In cases when the contract is stipulated in a cost-plus fashion, the enterprise can recover the cost of the commission by overpricing.

In all these alternatives which require the collaboration of the corrupt official, the country will end up with either a higher cost for the specified project than would have been the case in the absence of corruption; with a bigger or more complex project than would have been necessary; or with a project of inferior quality that will not perform up to the anticipated standards and will require costly upkeeping and repairs. The experience with public sector projects, especially in developing countries, is full of stories about roads that needed to be repaired a short time after completion, power plants that worked at much lower capacity than anticipated, and so on.

The above discussion has highlighted cases where corrupt high-level officials or political personalities steer the approval of investment

---

[9]This second option may be less attractive to the enterprise if it fears that the official may require additional payments when the cost-increasing modifications are made or if it fears that the official may no longer have the power to influence the process. In countries where the same individuals remain in power for a long time, the strategy of the low initial bid followed by adjustments over the period when the project is executed is a common strategy.

[10]This has been a frequent occurrence in road building where the thickness of the base of the road may be much reduced. It has also been an occurrence in the building of bridges and buildings which, at times, have collapsed causing loss of lives and economic costs.

projects towards particular domestic or foreign enterprises in exchange for bribes. This is an important part of the way in which corruption, defined in the broader sense of rent seeking, affects public investment. However, it is not the full story. Important cases of corruption exist also when political personalities steer public investments towards their home districts or their own land. In a recent case reported in the *Financial Times* of July 29, 1997, the President of a country was accused of having built an airport with public funds in his small home town even though there seemed to be little economic justification for it. This is far from an isolated case. At other times, projects are steered toward particular areas in order to increase the value of assets (such as lands owned by political personalities) in those areas.

In all of these cases, the productivity of the capital spending is reduced, thus reducing the growth rate of the country. Therefore, corruption can significantly distort the relationship between the capital input and the output generated by that capital, thus increasing the capital-output ratio.

When the approval of investment projects comes to be much influenced by corrupt, high-level officials, the rate of return of projects as calculated by cost-benefit analysis ceases to be the criterion for project selection.[11] Capital spending becomes much less productive and much less of a contributor to growth than generally believed. Unfortunately, situations of this type are far from rare. In these situations, those who carry out the projects (the executing enterprises) come to care mostly about the profits that they make. And the political figures that authorize the projects and choose the enterprises care mostly about the bribes, or the other advantages that they get. Thus, corruption distorts the whole decision-making process connected with the investment budget. In the extreme case of a totally corrupt country, projects are chosen exclusively for their bribe-generating capacity and not for their productivity. The productivity of the projects becomes almost irrelevant.[12]

When corruption plays a large role in the selection of projects and contractors, the result of this process is a capital budget that is highly distorted. "White elephants" and "cathedrals in the desert" are produced. Some projects are completed but never used. Some are much

---

[11]In Italy, before tangentopoli, those hired to evaluate projects often found that they were totally ignored.

[12]This may be part of the reason why we observe extremely high capital-output ratios in some countries.

larger and complex than necessary. Some are of such low quality that they will need continuous repairs and their output capacity will be much below initial expectations. In these circumstances, it is not surprising that capital spending does not generate the results in terms of growth that economists expect.

Widespread corruption in the investment budget will not only reduce the rate of return to *new* public investment, but will also affect the rate of return that a country gets from its existing infrastructure. The reasons are several.

First, to the extent that corruption is not a new phenomenon but one that has been around for some time, the existing infrastructure has also been contaminated because *past* investments were also misdirected or distorted by corruption.

Second, higher spending on capital projects will reduce the resources available for other spending. Of the other spending one that is not protected by the existence of entitlements or implicit commitments is "operation and maintenance," that is the kind of current public spending that is required to keep the existing physical infrastructure of a country in good working conditions. Therefore, a frequently observed phenomenon is the poor conditions of the existing infrastructure (roads with potholes, buildings badly in need of repairs, etc.). One often observes situations where new projects are undertaken while the existing structure is left to deteriorate.

Third, and more speculatively, in cases of extreme corruption, operation and maintenance on the physical infrastructure of a country may be intentionally reduced so that some infrastructures, such as roads, will deteriorate quickly to the point where they will need to be rebuilt, thus allowing some high-level officials the opportunity to extract another commission from the enterprise that will undertake the project. Some World Bank Reports have hinted that this may have happened in some countries.

A country can squeeze more output out of the existing infrastructure by keeping it in good working condition so that it can be used at close to 100 percent capacity.[13] It is easy to think of situations where the deterioration of this infrastructure retards growth more than the new capital projects add to growth. Additionally when generalized corruption

---

[13]World Bank studies indicate that in many countries public infrastructure including roads, power plants, irrigation canals, often can be used only at a fraction of their full capacity.

in a country reduces resources because of the negative impact on tax revenue that is caused by corrupt tax administrators, operation and maintenance will be reduced far more than public investment because of the intellectual bias listed above that supports borrowing for capital projects but not for current expenditure.

Empirical Analysis

Data Description

In our empirical analysis we use indices of corruption data from two sources: *Business International (BI)* and *Political Risk Services, Inc.* The *BI* index has been used by Mauro (1995), among others, and is available for 68 countries over the 1980–83 period (one observation per country). The second source publishes a closely related index in the *International Country Risk Guide (ICRG)*. Unlike the *BI* index, the *ICRG* index is annual; it covers the 1982–95 period and, depending on the year, is available for 42 to 128 countries. This index has been used by Knack and Keefer (1995) and many others.

Both indices are assessments of the degree of corruption in a country by informed observers, the *BI*'s network of correspondents, in the case of the *BI* index, and foreign investors, in the case of the *ICRG* index. The *BI* index has been discontinued, while the *ICRG* index is updated annually and is sold as part of a package to potential investors worldwide. Corruption in the *BI* indicates "The degree to which business transactions involve corruption or questionable payments." The index ranges from 0 (most corrupt) to 10 (least corrupt). In the *ICRG* index higher corruption indicates that "high government officials are likely to demand special payments" and "illegal payments are generally expected throughout lower levels of government" in the forms of "bribes connected with import and export licenses, exchange controls, tax assessment, police protection, or loans." The *ICRG* index ranges from 0 (most corrupt) to 6 (least corrupt).

We have re-scaled the *ICRG* index by multiplying it by 10/6 so that both indexes range from 0 to 10 and have spliced them to form a single corruption index from 1980 to 1995.[14] For ease of interpretation of

---

[14]The two indices are highly correlated with a correlation coefficient of 0.81. Other indices are also available including one issued by *Transparency International*. These indices are also highly correlated.

the regression results, we have multiplied the resulting index by minus one so that higher values of the index imply higher corruption.

The discussion in the previous section underscored the interaction between corruption, public investment, operations and maintenance (O&M) expenditures, and other aspects of the government's budgetary position. For public investment, capital expenditure data from the International Monetary Fund's *Government Finance Statistics* (*GFS*) are used. Unfortunately, cross-country data on O&M expenditures are not available. We have, thus, chosen two proxies called "expenditure on other goods and services" which includes O&M expenditures, and "wages and salaries as a fraction of current expenditures." The rationale behind these proxies will be explained below.

To investigate the impact of corruption on the *quality* of public investment, we use the following indicators of quality of infrastructure:

- Paved roads in good condition as a percentage of total paved roads
- Electric power system losses as a percentage of total power output
- Telecommunication faults per 100 mainlines per year
- Water losses as a percentage of total water provision
- Railway diesels in use as a percentage of total diesel inventory

The above data are often referred to as performance indicators of infrastructure and seem adequate for our purpose; they are measured from the perspective of both infrastructure providers and the users; they cover a large number of countries and most importantly, they have many characteristics that make them the responsibility of governments. These data are taken from International Telecommunications Union and the World Bank's *World Development Indicators* data base. Paved roads in good condition are roads substantially free of major problems and requiring only routine maintenance. Electric power system losses consist of technical losses such as resistance losses in transmission and distribution and non-technical losses such as illegal connection to the electricity and other sources of theft. System losses are then expressed as a fraction of total output. Telecommunication faults per 100 mainlines per year refer to the number of reported faults per 100 main lines for each year. Water losses include physical losses (pipe breaks and overflows) and commercial losses (meter under-registration, illegal use including fraudulent or unregistered connections, and legal, but not usually metered, uses such as firefighting). Railway diesels in use as a percentage of total diesel inventory measures technical and managerial performance.

Finally, government revenue data, taken from the *GFS*, are expressed as fractions of GDP. Data on GDP and real per capita GDP (the latter is a control variable in regression) come from the World Bank's *World Development Indicators* data base.

Regression Results

The previous discussions suggest testable hypotheses about the relationship between corruption on one hand and public investment, government revenue, O&M expenditures and quality of infrastructure on the other. We use regression analysis to test these hypotheses using cross-country data. It is of course difficult to draw causality statements from regression equations, and one must guard against spurious regression results. We do so by controlling for other variables, such as real per capita GDP, government revenue-GDP ratio, and public investment-GDP ratio.

(1) Corruption and Public Investment

Hypothesis 1: Other things being equal, high corruption is associated with high public investment.

To test this hypothesis, we regress the public investment-GDP ratio on a constant and the corruption index. We subsequently add real per capita GDP and government revenue-GDP ratio to see if the corruption-investment relationship is robust to the inclusion of these two variables. We add real per capita GDP since it is typically a proxy for the stage of economic development and different levels of development may require different needs for public investment. Government revenue-GDP ratio is added because the higher are these revenues the easier it is to finance public investment. The results are three regressions shown in Table 1. In all the regressions, we cannot reject hypothesis 1 at the 1 percent significance level.[15] Government revenue-GDP variable has a statistically significant positive coefficient indicating that such revenues are important sources of financing public investment. The results shown in Table 1 are for the world sample, but they also hold up for the sub-samples of developing countries and members of the Organization for Economic Cooperation and Development (OECD).

---

[15]Note that corruption reduces aggregate investment (Mauro, 1995) which is the sum of public and private capital investment. Thus, corruption must reduce private capital investment by more than it increases public capital investment.

Table 1. The Effects of Corruption on Public Investment, 1980–95
(As a ratio of GDP; annual data)

Independent Variables	(1)	(2)	(3)
Constant	6.75	6.47	4.71
	(23.4)	(19.5)	(13.9)
Corruption index	0.38	0.27	0.48
	(8.97)	(4.15)	(7.48)
Real per capita GDP*		−0.71	−1.21
		(−2.94)	(−5.18)
Government revenue-GDP ratio			0.13
			(12.6)
Adjusted R^2	0.069	0.082	0.207
Number of observations	1,081	1,011	1,000

Sources: IMF, *Government Finance Statistics; World Tables; Business International;* and *Political Risk Services.* The corruption index is taken from Mauro (1995) and *International Country Risk Guide* compiled by Political Risk Services. A high value of the index means a country has high corruption; t-statistics are in parentheses. Estimation technique is OLS.

*Indicates that the coefficient is multiplied by 10,000.

(2) Corruption and Government Revenues

Regressions in Table 1 show the direct impact of corruption on public investment and do not rule out the possibility of an indirect impact, say, through government revenues. Corruption can reduce government revenues if it contributes to tax evasion, improper tax exemptions or weak tax administration. This leads to the second hypothesis:

Hypothesis 2: Other things being equal, high corruption is associated with low government revenue.

To test this assertion we regress government revenue-GDP ratio on a constant and corruption. We then add real per capita GDP to control for stage-of-economic development effects. The results given in Table 2 for the world sample show that we cannot reject hypothesis 2 at the 1 percent significance level. Similar results also hold up for sub-samples of developing and OECD countries.

(3) Corruption and O&M Expenditures

An observation made previously, and one closely related to Hypotheses 1 and 2, is the underfunding of O&M expenditure. Since corruption

Table 2. The Effects of Corruption on Government Revenue, 1980–95
(As a ratio of GDP; annual data)

Independent Variables	(1)	(2)
Constant	9.99	12.9
	(12.1)	(13.7)
Corruption index	–2.51	–1.71
	(–20.4)	(–9.28)
Real per capita GDP*		3.73
		(5.34)
Adjusted R^2	0.272	0.28
Number of observations	1,114	1,042

Sources: IMF, *Government Finance Statistics; World Tables; Business International;* and *Political Risk Services*. The corruption index is taken from Mauro (1995) and *International Country Risk Guide* compiled by Political Risk Services. A high value of the index means a country has high corruption; t-statistics are in parentheses. Estimation technique is OLS.

*Indicates that the coefficient is multiplied by 10,000.

and bribery are more effectively related to new investments, corruption may result in lower O&M expenditure. These observations lead to the third hypothesis:

Hypothesis 3: Other things being equal, high corruption is associated with low O&M expenditures.

As stated earlier, direct cross-country data on O&M expenditures are not available.[16] We therefore use two proxies: (1) "expenditures on other goods and services," a component of current expenditure, expressed as a fraction of wages and salaries; and (2) wages and salaries expressed as a fraction of current expenditure. These data are taken from the IMF's *GFS* data base. The rationale behind the first proxy is obvious since, according to the *Government Finance Statistics Manual*, expenditures on other goods and services include O&M expenditures. We have expressed this expenditure relative to wages and salaries in order to highlight potential trade-offs between O&M expenditure and expenditure on wages and salaries. The ratio of wages and salaries to current expenditure is a reasonable proxy for O&M expenditures be-

---

[16]Ideally, we want shortfalls in O&M expenditures. This requires knowledge of the so-called "r" coefficients and actual O&M expenditures. The r coefficient is the ratio of net recurrent expenditure requirements to the total investment cost of a project; see Heller (1991).

cause governments often tend to award wage increases but cut O&M expenditures. Hence, increases in wages and salaries can be interpreted as cuts in O&M expenditures.

To test hypothesis 3, we regress each of the above proxies on a constant and a corruption index and, as usual for sensitivity analysis, we add real per capita GDP to each regression. The results are shown in Table 3. Unlike the previous regressions, we present the results for three samples (world, OECD and developing) as there are differences across these samples. With respect to the first proxy, results in Table 3 indicate that high corruption is indeed associated with low O&M expenditures. However, one can reject hypothesis 3 at the 1 percent significance level only for the developing country sample. Once we control for real per capita GDP, hypothesis 3 is rejected at the 1 percent significance level for all three samples. One interpretation of this finding is that the first proxy is a noisy indicator of O&M expenditure.

As regards the second proxy for O&M expenditures, we cannot reject hypothesis 3 for all three samples at the 1 percent significance level whether or not we control for real per capita GDP (Table 3, panel b). Countries with high corruption do tend to have high ratio of wages and salaries to current expenditure.[17] The evidence is much stronger statistically and economically for the developing country sample than the OECD sample.

(4) Corruption and Quality of Public Investment

Infrastructure investments are often lumpy and require substantial up-front financial capital. It has been known for some time that corruption is most prevalent in the infrastructure sector (Wade, 1982; Rose-Ackerman, 1996). Regressions in Table 1 in this paper have provided evidence that high corruption is indeed associated with high public investment. See also Mauro (1997). However, this evidence links corruption to *quantity* of investment, and not the *quality*. We argued previously that countries take on new infrastructure investment without maintaining the existing infrastructure capital stock. Therefore, we expect the quality of the infrastructure to deteriorate and

---

[17]This does not mean that the level of salaries in corrupt countries is higher. In fact a recent study has found a negative relationship between salary levels in the public sector and corruption. See Van Rijckeghem and Weder (1997).

Table 3. The Effects of Corruption on O&M Expenditure

a. Expenditures on Other Goods and Services, 1980–95
(As a ratio of wages and salaries, 1980–95)

	World		OECD		Developing	
Independent Variable	(1)	(2)	(1)	(2)	(1)	(2)
Constant	72.9	97.2	–20.2	43.4	84.2	82.3
	(8.15)	(9.29)	(–0.558)	(1.19)	(7.08)	(6.65)
Corruption index	–3.54	4.44	–14	5.96	–1.24	1.43
	(–2.69)	(2.20)	(–3.53)	(1.23)	(–0.57)	(0.60)
Real per capita GDP*		0.42		0.81		0.63
		(5.55)		(6.99)		(3.93)
Adjusted R^2	0.006	0.038	0.037	0.182	–0.01	0.021
Number of observations	999	927	300	273	699	654

b. Wages and Salaries, 1980–95
(As a ratio of current expenditure; annual data)

	World		OECD		Developing	
Independent Variable	(1)	(2)	(1)	(2)	(1)	(2)
Constant	47.3	42.2	34.2	30.8	39.7	39.7
	(41.7)	(33.2)	(12.2)	(11.3)	(26.1)	(25.2)
Corruption index	3.1	1.48	2.17	0.75	1.22	1.16
	(18.5)	(6.03)	(7.02)	(2.07)	(4.43)	(3.83)
Real per capita GDP**		–0.84		–0.65		–0.067
		(–9.13)		(–7.54)		(–0.327)
Adjusted R^2	0.255	0.319	0.139	0.31	0.026	0.023
Number of observations	1,000	925	300	273	700	652

Sources: IMF, *Government Finance Statistics; World Tables; Business International;* and *Political Risk Services*. The corruption index is taken from Mauro (1995) and *International Country Risk Guide* compiled by Political Risk Services. A high value of the index means a country has high corruption; t-statistics are in parentheses. Estimation technique is OLS.

* and ** indicate that the coefficients are multiplied by 100 and 1,000, respectively.

more so if corruption leads to O&M expenditure cutbacks. These observations lead to the fourth hypothesis:

Hypothesis 4: Other things being equal, high corruption is associated with poor quality of infrastructure.

To test this hypothesis we regress indicators of quality of infrastructure on a constant, the corruption index and real per capita GDP. The results are given in Table 4 for five indicators of quality of infrastructure. Hypothesis 4 cannot be rejected at the usual significance levels: Countries with high corruption do tend to have poor quality of infrastructure. In terms of statistical significance, the impact of corruption is strongest on the quality of roads (paved roads in good condition), power outages, and railway diesels in use. When we control for real per capita GDP, corruption changes its sign in only one regression (telecommunication faults) and loses its statistical significance at the usual levels in three regressions (telecommunication faults, water losses, and railway diesels in use). The fit of every regression improves, as judged by the adjusted R-squared, when we add real per capita GDP. Moreover, real per capita GDP in every regression has the right sign: countries with higher real per capita GDP tend to have better quality of infrastructure. An important implication of the results in Table 4 is that the costs of corruption should also be measured in terms of the deterioration in the quality of the existing infrastructure. These costs can be very high in terms of their impact on growth.

Does corruption reduce the quality of infrastructure through public investment?

To answer the above question, we conduct a more rigorous test of hypothesis 4 for the quality of roads.[18] We regress paved roads in good condition on a constant, real per capita GDP, the corruption index (i.e., the same regression as in Table 4) and two additional variables: public investment-GDP ratio and its interaction with the corruption index. Results are shown in Table 5. Columns (1) and (2) show that even when we control for public investment, we still cannot reject hypothesis 4 at the 1 percent significance level. The regression in column (3) shows that corruption is still significant in the presence of the interaction variable. If corruption reduces the quality of roads through public investment, we should find that corruption loses its significance when the interaction variable is added to the regression, given the presence of public investment-GDP ratio and real per capita GDP. Comparison of columns (4) and (2)—with and without the interaction term respectively—shows this to be the case. In addition, the statistically significant interaction term in column (4) shows that the impact of corruption on the quality of roads depends on public investment. The negative sign on the interaction term suggests that the higher is the public investment, the higher is

---

[18]Results with other measures of quality of infrastructure are similar.

Table 4. Corruption and Quality of Infrastructure, 1980–95
(Annual data)

Dependent Variable	Constant	Corruption Index	Real Per Capita GDP*	Adjusted R^2	N
Paved roads in good condition	19.2 (4.97)	–3.84 (–5.40)		0.052	513
Paved roads in good condition	15.5 (3.87)	–2.22 (–2.89)	5.4 (9.85)	0.268	373
Power outages	18.7 (27.7)	1.1 (8.69)		0.07	997
Power outages	18.8 (32.5)	0.95 (8.17)	–0.56 (–7.07)	0.162	922
Telecommunication faults	97.6 (6.93)	4.17 (1.63)		0.007	241
Telecommunication faults	94.5 (6.31)	–0.54 (–0.18)	–9.33 (–5.01)	0.127	201
Water losses#	43.8 (6.89)	2.25 (1.86)		0.089	26
Water losses#	43.6 (7.19)	1.52 (1.14)	–2.92 (–1.63)	0.186	25
Railway diesels in use##	47.1 (7.45)	–3.66 (–3.80)		0.17	67
Railway diesels in use##	59.4 (8.62)	–0.58 (–0.46)	1.37 (3.39)	0.285	67

Sources: IMF, *Government Finance Statistics; World Tables; Business International;* and *Political Risk Services*. The corruption index is taken from Mauro (1995) and *International Country Risk Guide* compiled by Political Risk Services. A high value of the index means a country has high corruption; t-statistics are in parentheses. Estimation technique is OLS.

and ## denote averages of data over 1980–89 and 1990–95 periods, respectively.

* Indicates that the coefficient is multiplied by 10,000.

the negative impact of corruption on the quality of roads. This additional evidence is consistent with the finding in Table 1 that higher corruption is indeed associated with higher public investment.

Does higher corruption reduce the productivity of public investment?

Suppose that we measure productivity of public investment by improvements in the quality of roads per dollar of public investment. The regression in column (4) of Table 5 shows that the impact of investment

Table 5. The Effects of Corruption on Quality of Roads, 1980–95

Dependent variable: Paved roads in good condition
as a percentage of total paved roads
(Annual data)

Independent Variables	(1)	(2)	(3)	(4)
Constant	−1.03	7.55	1.83	19.6
	(−0.150)	(1.01)	(0.193)	(1.82)
Corruption index	−7	−2.56	−6.51	−0.32
	(−8.68)	(−2.20)	(−4.74)	(−0.17)
Public investment-GDP ratio	2.03	3.09	1.15	−0.2
	(2.65)	(4.00)	(0.53)	(0.10)
Public investment-GDP ratio × corruption index			−0.16	−0.58
			(−0.44)	(−1.56)
Real per capita GDP*		0.24		0.25
		(6.38)		(6.57)
Adjusted R²	0.186	0.326	0.184	0.329
Number of observations	322	269	322	269

Sources: IMF, *Government Finance Statistics; World Tables; Business International;* and *Political Risk Services.* The corruption index is taken from Mauro (1995) and *International Country Risk Guide* compiled by Political Risk Services. A high value of the index means a country has high corruption; t-statistics are in parentheses. Estimation technique is OLS.

*Indicates that the coefficient is multiplied by 100.

on the quality of roads depends on the existence of corruption. Specifically, the negative sign on the interaction term shows that higher corruption can reduce the productivity of public investment.

Concluding Remarks

There are many channels through which higher corruption reduces economic growth. Mauro (1995, 1997) provides evidence and summarizes some of these arguments. The new evidence presented in this paper supports four additional arguments.

First, corruption can reduce growth by increasing public investment *while reducing its productivity.*[19] This finding is consistent with

---

[19] Please note that because corruption reduces tax revenue, the relative increase in public investment (i.e., its share of the total government budget) is likely to be higher than the absolute increase in public investment.

typical reduced-form cross-country growth regressions. For example, Devarajan, Swaroop and Zou (1996) have found that higher public investment is associated with lower growth, given other determinants of growth and Tanzi (1994) found that the relation between growth and investment is highly sensitive to the inclusion of a couple of countries.

Second, corruption can reduce growth by increasing public investment *that* is not accompanied by its recurrent current expenditure, i.e., adequate non-wage O&M expenditures. Our evidence shows that higher corruption is associated with higher total expenditure on wages and salaries. Wages and salaries are a large component of government consumption and higher government consumption has been shown to be unambiguously associated with lower growth (Commander et al., 1997; Barro, 1996; Barro and Sala-i-Martin, 1995).

Third, corruption can reduce growth by reducing the quality of the existing infrastructure. A deteriorating infrastructure increases the cost of doing business for both government and private sector (e.g., congestion, delays, break-downs of machineries, etc.) and thus leads to lower output and growth. The importance of infrastructure in growth has been shown in many cross-country growth regressions (Canning and Fay, 1993; Easterly and Levine, 1996; Hulten, 1996).

Finally, corruption can reduce growth by lowering government revenue needed to finance productive spending.

The implication of this paper is that economists should be more restrained in their praise of high public sector investment spending and of rules such as the golden rule, especially in countries where corruption, and especially high level corruption, is a problem.

This paper has focused on the problem of corruption and not on solutions. As far as corruption relates to the activities of foreign enterprises, the OECD is currently attempting to induce industrial countries: (a) to make the payments of bribes to foreign officials not tax deductible; and (b) to criminalize the payment of bribes. So far the ministers representing the OECD countries have accepted these recommendations, but the legislative bodies of those countries must still act. The OECD proposal, however, would not affect public investment projects in non-OECD countries carried out by domestic contractors or by contractors from non-OECD countries.[20]

---

[20] For a discussion of steps to reduce corruption, see Tanzi (1997).

References

Barro, Robert J. (1996), "Determinants of Economic Growth: A Cross-Country Empirical Study," *NBER Working Paper*, No. 5698.

Barro, Robert J. and X. Sala-i-Martin (1995), *Economic Growth*, McGraw Hill, New York.

Canning, David and Marianne Fay (1993), "The Effect of Transportation Networks on Economic Growth," *mimeo*, Columbia University.

Commander, Simon, Hamid R. Davoodi, Une J. Lee (1997), "The Causes of Government and the Consequences for Growth and Well-Being," *World Bank Policy Research Paper* No. 1785.

Devarajan, Shantayanan, Vinaya Swaroop and Heng-fu Zou (1996), "The Composition of Public Expenditure and Economic Growth," *Journal of Monetary Economics*, 37, pp. 313–344.

Easterly, William and R. Levine (1996), "Africa's Growth Tragedy," *mimeo*, The World Bank.

Heller, Peter S. (1991), "Operations and Maintenance," *Public Expenditure Handbook*, edited by Ke-young Chu and Richard Hemming, IMF.

Hulten, Charles R. (1996), "Infrastructure and Economic Development: One More Unto the Beach," *mimeo*, World Bank and University of Maryland, College Park.

Knack, Stephen and Philip Keefer (1995), "Institutions and Economic Performance: Cross-Country Tests Using Alternative Institutional Measures," *Economics and Politics*, Vol. 7, No. 3, pp. 207–227.

Klitgaard, Robert (1988), *Controlling Corruption*, Berkeley, University of California.

Mauro, Paolo (1997), "The Effects of Corruption on Growth, Investment, and Government Expenditure: A Cross Country Analysis" in *Corruption and the Global Economy*, edited by Kimberly Ann Elliott, Washington: Institute for International Economics. [Revised version reproduced as Chapter 9 in this volume—ED.]

Mauro, Paolo (1995). "Corruption and Growth," *Quarterly Journal of Economics*, CX, No. 3 (August), pp. 681–712.

Meagher, Patrick (1997), "Combating Corruption in Africa; Institutional Challenges and Response," paper presented at the IMF Seminar on Combating Corruption in Economic and Financial Management, Lisbon, May 19–21.

Olson, Mancur (1996), "Big Bills Left on the Sidewalk: Why Some Nations are Rich and Others Poor," *Journal of Economic Perspectives*, 10, 2, pp. 3–24.

Pritchett, Lant (1996), "Mind Your P's and Q's: The Cost of Public Investment is not the Value of Public Capital Stock," Policy Research Working Paper, No. 1660, The World Bank, Washington D.C.

Rose-Ackerman, Susan (1996), "When is Corruption Harmful?" Background paper for the *1997 World Development Report*.

Svensson, Jacob (1996), "Foreign Aid and Rent-Seeking," World Bank, Macroeconomics and Growth Division, *mimeo*.

Tanzi, Vito (1991), *Public Finance in Developing Countries*, Aldershot: Edward Elgar.

Tanzi, Vito (1994), "The IMF and Tax Reform," in *Tax Policy and Planning in Developing Countries*, edited by Amaresh Bagchi and Nicholas Stern, Delhi: Oxford University Press.

Tanzi, Vito (1995), "Corruption, Government Activities, and Markets" in *The Economics of Organized Crime*, edited by Gianluca Fiorentini and Sam Peltzman, Cambridge: Cambridge University Press.

Tanzi, Vito (1997), "Corruption, Governmental Activities and Policy Instruments: A Brief Review of the Main Issues," (*mimeo*: May 1997).

Van Rijckeghem, Caroline and Beatrice Weder (1997), "Corruption and the Rate of Temptation: Do Low Wages in the Civil Service Cause Corruption?" IMF *Working Paper*. [Revised version reproduced as Chapter 3 in this volume—ED.]

Wade, Robert (1982), "The System of Administrative and Political Corruption: Canal Irrigation in South India," *Journal of Development Studies*, 18, pp. 287–328.

Wei, Shang-Jin, "How Taxing is Corruption on International Investors," NBER Working Paper Series, *Working Paper* 6030.

12

Corruption and Military Spending

Sanjeev Gupta, Luiz de Mello, and Raju Sharan

1. Introduction

In recent years, increasing attention has been devoted to understanding the reasons for, and economic consequences of, corruption. The existing literature can be divided into two broad strands. The first focuses on the determinants of corruption. Various studies have shown that the main factors affecting the scope and breadth of corruption are the quality of the civil service (Rauch and Evans, 2000); the level of public sector wages (van Rijckeghem and Weder, 1997); rule of law, particularly anticorruption legislation and the availability of natural resources (Leite and Weidmann, 1999); the economy's degree of competition and

---

Reprinted from *European Journal of Political Economy*, Vol. 17, Sanjeev Gupta, Luiz de Mello, and Raju Sharan, "Corruption and Military Spending," pp. 749–777 (2001), with permission from Elsevier Science.

The authors wish to thank two anonymous referees, Arye Hillman, Hamid Davoodi, Robert Gillingham, Gabriela Inchauste, Luc Leruth, Ali Mansoor, Randa Sab, Erwin Tiongson, and Marijn Verhoeven for helpful comments. The usual disclaimer applies.

trade openness; and the country's industrial policy (Bhagwati, 1982; Krueger, 1993).[1, 2]

The second strand of literature shifts attention from the determinants to the consequences of corruption. Recent studies have analyzed the impact of corruption on, among other things, output growth (Shleifer and Vishny, 1993; Murphy, et al., 1993; Mauro, 1995), the quality of public infrastructure and public investment (Tanzi and Davoodi, 1997), foreign direct investment (Wei, 1997), and income inequality and poverty (Gupta et al., 1998). These studies have shown that corruption is likely to have a detrimental impact on economic efficiency, growth, equity, and the overall welfare of a society. In the early literature, however, ethical considerations aside, corruption was seen as a means to achieve a higher degree of economic efficiency by "greasing the wheels" of government and overcoming cumbersome government regulation. By corollary, the absence of corruption would prevent the smooth functioning of markets, government, and economic institutions (Leff, 1964; Huntington, 1968; Lui, 1985; Beck and Maher, 1986; Lien, 1986). More recently, the negative aspects of corruption have been found to outweigh its efficiency-enhancing properties (Kaufmann and Wei, 1999).

A comprehensive definition of corruption is lacking in the literature. Different aspects of the problem are often highlighted in different definitions depending on the object of investigation. Nevertheless, corruption can be generally described as the abuse of government authority for private benefit (Bardhan, 1999; Tanzi, 1998). Corruption also involves some notion of illegality, and has been defined as "be-

---

[1] Economies experiencing exchange rate controls are likely to have other distortions that provide opportunities for rent seeking and hence corruption (Wei, 1999). Indicators of regulatory discretion (Johnson et al., 1998) and competition (Ades and di Tella, 1999) are also used to measure the extent of distortion in the economy.

[2] In cross-section studies, a number of time-invariant explanatory variables are often used in corruption models. These are the index of ethnolinguistic fractionalization, measuring the probability that two randomly selected persons from a given country do not belong to the same ethnolinguistic group (Taylor and Hudson, 1972; and Mauro, 1995); the distance from the Equator, measured as the distance in latitudes of a given country's capital from the Equator; and the share of a country's population that speaks English at home (Hall and Jones, 1999). These variables are expected to capture cultural factors including the strength of a culture of arms-length relationships and societal acceptance of corruption, and the possibility that ethnolinguistic divisions in society create opportunities for rent seeking. La Porta et al. (1998) also use religion and legal systems as controls in corruption equations.

havior which deviates from the formal duties of a public role because of private-regarding (personal, close family, private clique) pecuniary or status gain; or violates rules against the exercise of certain types of private-regarding behavior" (Nye, 1967, p. 419; Klitgaard, 1988, p. 23). Corruption is defined by Shleifer and Vishny (1993), whose focus is on privatization, as "the sale by government officials of government property for personal gain" (p. 599).

This paper empirically investigates the relationship between corruption and military spending. Various aspects of military spending lend themselves to acts of corruption. The basic hypothesis proposed in this paper is that corruption is correlated with (1) the share of defense outlays in both GDP and total government spending, and (2) military procurement in relation to both GDP and total government spending.

To our knowledge, our investigation is the first systematic cross-country empirical analysis relating military spending with corruption.[3] Our study supplements anecdotal evidence for a wide variety of countries that details instances of payment of commissions and bribes associated with public spending on the military, in particular on arms procurement.[4] It has been estimated that bribes account for as much as 15% of the total spending on weapons acquisition (Tanzi, 1998).[5] Hines (1995) observes that trade in military aircraft is particularly susceptible to corruption.

---

[3]In analyzing the relationship between corruption and government spending, Mauro (1997) provides some evidence that military spending is associated with corruption.

[4]While addressing a press conference in Manila on October 1, 1999, Mark Pieth, Chairman of the OECD Working Group on bribery said "If you look at the figures, far more [bribes] are actually paid in industrialized countries, for example, in the arms trade." Corruption can also be found in the form of campaign financing in return for favorable legislation for continued spending on military R&D and for lifting bans on exports of arms, sometimes even seeking involvement of government officials to actively promote such trade. See Lambsdorff (1998) and Naylor (1998) for more information and anecdotal evidence of corruption in arms trade and procurement.

[5]In fact, the internet has become an important vehicle for the dissemination of corruption indicators, case studies, anecdotal evidence, reports, and surveys. See the Transparency International website (www.transparency.de) for a wealth of information on this subject. In the case of corruption and military spending, see the World Policy Institute website (www.worldpolicy.org) for some anecdotal evidence of corruption in military procurement. Also, the website of the Stockholm International Peace Research Institute, SIPRI (www.sipri.se), contains information on arms production, arms transfers, military expenditures and military technology, as well as links to many sites with information on this subject.

The paper is organized as follows. Section 2 delineates the channels that link corruption to military spending. Section 3 sets out the model of military spending and corruption and the data set is described. The empirical results are reported in Section 4. Section 5 concludes.

2. Corruption and Military Spending

Corruption is a multifaceted phenomenon that can affect military spending through a variety of channels. Corruption may be affected by supply-side considerations, in the sense that arms producers may resort to bribes (or inappropriate commissions) to win contracts, and/or demand-side considerations, insofar as the military may engage in activities which are prone to corruption.

Supply-side considerations are as follows:

- Foreign suppliers may bribe the officials of countries importing arms and military equipment. This can be facilitated by the tax code of arms-exporting countries, according to which bribery may be deducted as a cost. Payment of bribes to foreign officials is typically not considered as a criminal act in these countries. To address this issue, the OECD called for greater transparency in the legal treatment of bribery to foreign counterparts among member countries (OECD, 1997).[6]

- Since the mid-1980s, a persistent fall in military spending throughout the world has increased competition among arms producers.[7] The end of the Cold War and the breakup of the former Soviet Union changed countries' perceived threats and national security priorities. In some countries, the defense industry was saddled with idle capacities and huge fixed sunk costs. Large R&D costs have often compelled arms producers to scout aggressively

---

[6]The OECD Convention on Combating Bribery of Foreign Public Officials in International Business Transactions, in effect since February 15, 1999, makes it a "crime to offer, promise, or give a bribe to a foreign public official in order to obtain or retain institutional business deals. [It also] puts an end to the practice according tax deductibility to bribe payments made to foreign officials." See www.oecd.org/daf/nocorruption/index.htm for more details. The United States' Foreign Corrupt Practice Act of 1977 also makes it a crime for American firms to bribe foreign government officials.

[7]See Gupta et al. (1996) and IMF (2000) for further details.

for markets abroad (see www.worldpolicy.org/arms/papi2rep.txt for more information) by, for instance, resorting to bribery.[8, 9]

Demand-side considerations are listed below:

- Governments are typically the sole providers of defense services. Certain aspects of defense provision are particularly susceptible to corruption. Regulations typically confer power on the officials in charge of authorizing contracts. Limited competition among suppliers encourages rent seeking and provides incentives for officials to engage in malfeasant behavior (Ades and Di Tella, 1999; Kimenyi and Mbaku, 1996; Mbaku, 2000).

- The secrecy surrounding defense outlays gives rise to corruption. In general, there is less transparency in government operations in the defense sector, particularly with respect to procurement of military equipment, than in other sectors.[10] Defense contracts are often excluded from freedom of information legislation, where available; and are also often drawn in secrecy and under considerable discretionary power by the authorities. Administrative procedures in military spending may not be closely monitored by tax and customs administration authorities and defense contracts may

---

[8]This argument does not apply in the case of countries where the bulk of military procurement is not carried out through the standard commercial channels. In these countries, the supply of military equipment may have involved donations of surplus military equipment from former colonizers, and from other suppliers during the Cold War (Levine, 1975; Gould, 1980). Non-commercial access to military equipment has also been important in "embargoed" countries. Nevertheless, corruption may still occur in these non-commercial transactions, but it takes a different form from the types described above. It may involve, for instance, bribes paid to the employees of parastatal companies that trade and/or produce military equipment. These companies have often been set up to circumvent the sanctions imposed on formal bilateral trade in "embargoed" countries (Ellis, 1998).

[9]The combination of cost negligence on the part of arms importers and the monopsonistic nature of the military procurement process creates opportunity for overinvoicing in procurement contracts. As a result, the companies paying bribes and commissions can subsequently recover these costs, at least in part, by (i) overpricing arms and ammunition; (ii) overcharging for spare parts and minor add-ons which are specific to the system and of which they are the lone producer; and (iii) obtaining lucrative contracts to train the officers of the armed forces in the use of the weapons purchased.

[10]See www.transparency.de for further details. Military procurement is defined in this paper principally as nonwage outlays, such as the purchase of services, arms, and military equipment.

not be liable to standard budget oversight (such as auditing and legislative approval).[11]

The stock of defense assets—such as military-controlled land, hardware, testing grounds, transport vehicles, and facilities such as housing and training centers—tends to be large and provide further opportunities for corruption. By controlling land, for instance, the military often controls the use and exploitation of natural resources.[12] The military is also known to engage in business operations in a number of countries, ranging from producing arms, military equipment, and steel, to managing airports and duty-free shops. Commercial activities by the military may limit entry of private firms and encourage smuggling and commodity stockpiling.

There are additional features that make military spending particularly open to corruption. Defense projects tend to be relatively capital-intensive, which increases willingness of firms to bribe government officials to help them win a contract or tender.[13] Access to information on the design and/or specifications of a tender can also be acquired by bribing government officials in the tender process.[14]

---

[11]Defense-related operations may not always be consolidated in the budget. For instance, the revenues of state-owned enterprises in the defense sector may be transferred to off-budgetary funds that in turn finance spending on defense. Again, the existence of off-budgetary funds and operations is not confined to the defense sector but is likely to be pervasive in this sector, particularly in developing countries, where the coverage of the public sector may not be comprehensive and budgetary oversight inadequate.

[12]In a number of countries, natural resource tax revenues are earmarked to finance military spending or extrabudgetary funds for military use. The military are also responsible for issuing licenses and concessions for logging and mining and for transportation of natural resources, particularly crude oil and fuel.

[13]Indeed, corruption has also been shown to alter the composition of government spending in favor of capital-intensive projects (Rose-Ackerman, 1996; Tanzi and Davoodi, 1997; UNDP, 1997). It also increases public investment, particularly in unproductive projects, thereby squeezing public resources away from current expenditures such as operations and maintenance (Mauro, 1997).

[14]It can also be argued that bureaucrats in poor countries may opt for imports of complex technology, rather than more standardized—and possibly more appropriate—technology, because it is hard to detect improper valuation and/or overinvoicing in the former case (Bardhan, 1997). Corruption may in this case induce excessive capital intensity in government procurement. In many developing countries, advanced weapons are purchased even in the absence of adequately trained soldiers who can use them. Again, the importation of inadequate technology is not unique to the military but is more likely to occur in certain types of public procurement, of which defense is a key example.

3. The Theoretical Model and Empirical Evidence

3.1 The Theoretical Model

There is no unique theoretical model of military spending. The model developed by Hewitt (1992, 1993) adopts a public-choice framework for analyzing the relationship between military spending and overall government expenditures. This model and subsequent applications do not deal with the connection between corruption and military outlays, or indeed any other type of government spending.

In line with this strand of literature, we have modeled the relationship between corruption and military spending as follows. Government spending (G) is a composite of military (M) and nonmilitary (N) outlays, such that $G = M + N$, and is financed through taxation such that $G = T$, where $T = \tau Y$, T is taxation, Y is national income, and $0 \leq \tau \leq 1$. To complete the model, we specify a utility function U that is twice-continuously differentiable on private consumption (C) and government spending (G), with $U_i > 0$ and $U_{ii} < 0$, for $i = C, G$. For simplicity, we adopt the form $U(C, M, N) = C^\beta M^\gamma M^\delta$, where $\delta = 1 - \beta - \gamma$. Finally, for tractability, we assume no private investment.

We omit time indices for notational simplicity. The utility maximization problem is then:

$$\max U(C, M, N), \tag{1}$$

subject to:

$$Y = C + G, \tag{2}$$

$$G = M + N. \tag{3}$$

In this corruption-free model, utility maximization requires:

$$\frac{M}{Y} = \frac{\gamma}{\beta}(1-\tau) \text{ and } \frac{M}{G} = \frac{\gamma}{\beta}(1-\tau)\frac{Y}{G}.^{15} \tag{4}$$

---

[15]Note that, similarly, $\frac{N}{Y} = \frac{\delta}{\beta}(1-\tau)$ and $\frac{N}{G} = \frac{\delta}{\beta}(1-\tau)\frac{Y}{G}$.

By Eq. (4), for a given level of taxation τ, the share of military (and nonmilitary) spending in income (and total government spending) depends on the parameters of the utility function (γ and β). A higher γ, relative to β, leads to an increase in military spending relative to private consumption. Against this background, the association between corruption and military spending can be described as follows. Let the parameters of the utility function (β, γ, and δ) be affected by corruption R such that Eq. (4) becomes:

$$\frac{M}{Y} = \frac{\gamma(R)}{\beta(R)}(1-\tau) \text{ and } \frac{M}{G} = \frac{\gamma(R)}{\beta(R)}(1-\tau)\frac{Y}{G}.^{16} \qquad (5)$$

By Eq. (5),

$$\frac{\partial(M/Y)}{\partial R} = (1-\tau)\left[\frac{\gamma_R\beta - \beta_R\gamma}{\beta^2}\right] \text{ and } \frac{\partial(M/G)}{\partial R} = (1-\tau)\frac{Y}{G}\left[\frac{\gamma_R\beta - \beta_R\gamma}{\beta^2}\right],$$

where

$$\gamma_R = \frac{d\gamma}{dR} \text{ and } \beta_R = \frac{d\beta}{dR}.$$

In this case,

$$\frac{\partial(M/Y)}{\partial R} > 0 \text{ and } \frac{\partial(M/G)}{\partial R} > 0 \text{ if } \frac{\gamma_R}{\gamma} > \frac{\beta_R}{\beta}.$$

Corruption therefore affects the parameters of the utility function, but is not introduced in the model as an argument of the utility function. That is, corruption is associated with higher military spending as long as the utility maximiser perceives an increase in military outlays as an opportunity to use public spending for private benefit to achieve a higher personal utility.

---

[16]Note that, similarly, $\frac{N}{Y} = \frac{\delta(R)}{\beta(R)}(1-\tau)$ and $\frac{N}{G} = \frac{\delta(R)}{\beta(R)}(1-\tau)\frac{Y}{G}$.

3.2. Empirical Evidence

By Eq. (5),

$$\frac{M}{Y} = f(\gamma, \beta, \tau, R) \text{ and } \frac{M}{G} = h\left(\gamma, \beta, \tau, R, \frac{Y}{G}\right).$$

Because γ, β, τ and R are not directly observable, the impact of corruption on military spending can be estimated as follows:

$$\left(\frac{M}{Y}\right)_i(t) = \theta_0 + \theta_1 R_i(t) + \theta_2 C_i(t) + \epsilon_i(t), \tag{6a}$$

and

$$\left(\frac{M}{G}\right)_i(t) = \zeta_0 + \zeta_1 R_i(t) + \zeta_2\left(\frac{G}{Y}\right)_i(t) + \zeta_3 C_i(t) + \epsilon_i(t), \tag{6b}$$

where t is a time index and i indexes the countries in the panel, $M/Y_i(t)$ is the ratio of military spending to GDP, $M/G_i(t)$ is the ratio of military spending to total government spending, $G/Y_i(t)$ is the ratio of government spending to GDP, $R_i(t)$ is a corruption indicator, $C_i(t)$ is a vector of controls, and ϵ_{it} is an error term.

The corruption indicators used here are the Transparency International (TI) index, compiled by Goettingen University;[17] and the International Country Risk Guide (ICRG) index.[18,19] The control variables are as follows. Real GDP per capita is used as a scale variable. Sec-

---

[17] Available via the Internet: http://www.transparency.de.

[18] The ICRG index measures corruption in a country as perceived by foreign investors. It varies from 0 (most corrupt) to 6 (least corrupt). Corruption is defined as the likelihood of a government official "to demand special payments," whether "illegal payments are expected throughout lower levels of government" in the form of "bribes connected with import and export licenses, exchange controls, tax assessment, police protection, or loans." See Knack and Keefer (1995), for further details.

[19] The ICRG index spans 1985 through 1998 while the TI index covers the period 1995 onward. To create a single continuous index from 1985 to 1998, the ICRG index was rescaled by multiplying it by 10/6 and then splicing the two indices, as in Tanzi and Davoodi (1997). Mauro (1995) presents a detailed analysis of different corruption indices, including the ones used in this paper, and shows that these indices are highly correlated. A sensitivity analysis of the econometric results using different corruption indices tends to yield robust parameter estimates (Gupta et al., 1998).

ondary school enrolment measures the country's level of social development. The urbanization rate and the age dependency ratio measure the demand for public goods and services.[20] The size of the armed forces, measured as the number of military personnel per thousand population, proxies for pressures on the government's wage bill. Large armies increase the operating costs of government, and hence military spending. Military spending in neighboring countries, defined as the unweighted average of neighboring countries' ratio of military spending to GDP, is an indicator of regional tension and a country's perceived threats that may lead to an increase in military spending (Davoodi et al., 1999). The ratio of government spending to GDP is also routinely used as an explanatory variable in structural models of military spending (see for example, Hewitt, 1992).

We proceed with an empirical analysis of the relationship between corruption and military spending using annual data for up to 120 countries in the period 1985–1998. Country selection was based primarily on the availability of internationally comparable data on military spending and arms imports for a sufficiently long time span. The list of countries is set out in Appendix A. The relevant variables are defined in Appendix B. Descriptive statistics are reported in Appendix C.

3.3. Military Spending Trends and Corruption

Data show that there has been a downward trend in worldwide military expenditures during the 1990s.[21] The reduction in military spending has been described as a peace dividend (Knight et al., 1996). According to the World Economic Outlook database of the IMF, the share of military expenditures in GDP fell gradually from 5.1% in 1985 to 3.4% in 1990 and to 2.1% in 1999. As a share of total government spending, military outlays fell from 14.2% in 1990 to 10.0% in 1999.

This downward trend in worldwide military spending is confirmed by other sources of data on military expenditures: the Stockholm International Peace Research Institute (SIPRI), the International Institute for Strategic Studies (IISS), and the US Arms Control and Disarmament Agency (ACDA). In a sample of 96 countries, SIPRI reports a fall

---

[20]Real GDP per capita, the urbanization rate, and the age dependency ratio have also been used in military spending equations (Hewitt, 1992, 1993; and Davoodi et al., 1999).

[21]For further details, see Hewitt (1993), Bayoumi et al. (1995), and Knight et al. (1996).

in worldwide military expenditures to 2.1% of GDP in 1998 from 3.3% of GDP in 1990. For a sample of 89 countries, IISS data show that worldwide military expenditures fell by 0.7% of GDP since 1990 to 2.5% of GDP in 1998. The data produced by ACDA, available only up to 1997, show a decline in military spending for 107 countries of 1.1% of GDP since 1990 to 2.7% of GDP in 1997.[22]

The association between corruption and military spending is illustrated in Fig. 1. Panels A and B plot the corruption index against the ratios of military spending to GDP and total government expenditures, respectively, for all countries in the sample. The downward-sloping trend lines suggest that more corrupt countries tend to have higher military spending as a share of GDP and total government expenditures.[23] The bivariate correlation between the military spending-to-GDP ratio and corruption is –0.15 (Appendix D).

Procurement is an important channel through which corruption affects military expenditures, as we have suggested above. Panels C and D of Fig. 1 plot the corruption index against military procurement (arms imports) as a share of GDP and total government expenditures, respectively, for all countries that we examine. Arms imports are taken as a proxy for procurement because most countries in the sample do not produce arms domestically. The trend lines are also downward sloping. The correlation coefficient between arms imports as a share of GDP and corruption is –0.29 (Appendix D).

Some caution is required in this type of empirical analysis. Lack of suitable, good-quality data has been the main deterrent to empirical research on corruption and its association with military and other types of spending. The notable constraints are: (1) data on all the possible channels through which corruption affects military spending are simply not available; (2) information on military assets and military engagements in commercial activities is hard to come by and often unreliable; (3) in most countries, budgetary data do not specify in full all military outlays, reflecting the confidential nature of military activities;

---

[22]In line with the fall in military spending in the 1990s, ACDA data show a reduction in the size of the armed forces per thousand population between 1990 and 1995. According to data for 134 countries, the size of the armed forces has fallen since 1990 for all regions in the world from 6.7 per thousand population to 5.7 per thousand population, except in the newly industrialized Asian countries. Countries in Africa and the Western Hemisphere have the smallest armed forces as a share of population (IMF, 1999 and 2000, *World Economic Outlook, October 1999:* Box No. 6.1, pp. 138–140).

[23]A high score in the corruption index indicates a low level of corruption.

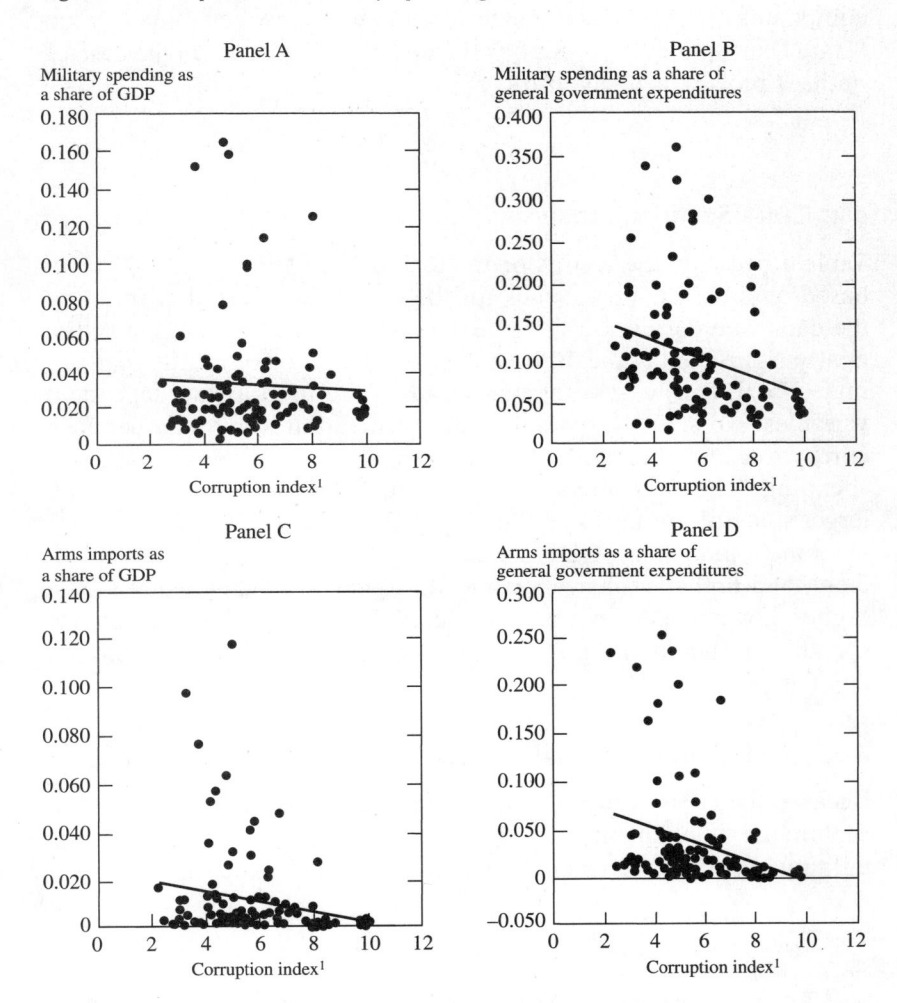

Figure 1. Corruption and Military Spending

Panel A
Military spending as a share of GDP

Panel B
Military spending as a share of general government expenditures

Panel C
Arms imports as a share of GDP

Panel D
Arms imports as a share of general government expenditures

Source: IMF staff calculations.
[1]A high score in the corruption index indicates a low level of corruption.

and (4) a focus on arms trade flows is an imperfect proxy for military procurement and neglects purchases of domestically produced military equipment. Corruption indices tend to focus on subjective assessments of business risk and efficiency and financial corruption, and do not necessarily take into account issues related to procurement of military equipment. These indices do not distinguish between "small" and "large" corruption; the latter type is more likely to occur in the case of military procurement activities.

4. Results

4.1. Cross-Sectional Analysis

Table 1 presents the results of the estimation of Eqs. (6a) and (6b), based on cross-country means for the entire time period covered by the data. The corruption variable has the expected sign and is statistically significant at the 10% level when the ratios of military spending to GDP and to government spending are used as the dependent variables. No statistically significant association was found between corruption and the ratio of arms imports to GDP or government spending. The coefficients of the control variables suggest that a larger share of military spending in GDP is associated with lower development indicators (GDP per capita, gross secondary school enrolment, and higher urbanization rates), higher age dependency ratios, higher government spending in relation to GDP, higher defense spending in neighboring countries, and larger armies (per thousand population).[24,25]

4.2. Panel Regression Analysis

Because the cross-sectional estimation of Eqs. (6a) and (6b) does not capture the time dimension of the relationship between corruption and military spending, the models were re-estimated as a panel.[26] Three

---

[24]A political regime variable has also been included in the set of control variables in cross-sectional military spending regressions.

[25]To deal with the possibility of reverse causality, we re-estimated the equations using the two-stage least squares estimator. Corruption was instrumented by the ethnolinguistic fractionalization index, the share of people speaking English at home, and distance from the Equator, as discussed above. As reported in the literature, all explanatory factors are correctly signed and statistically significant at classical levels. In the second-stage regressions, in general, the coefficient of corruption in the government spending equations loses significance. In the arms procurement equations, the corruption coefficients are significant, albeit only at the 10% level, but no longer correctly signed. The coefficients are also smaller in magnitude when the equations are estimated by two-stage least squares.

[26]Other cross-sectional studies (Mauro, 1997) have shown a relatively weak association between military spending and corruption.

Table 1. Corruption and Military Spending: Cross-Sectional Analysis, 1985–1998

	Dependent variable			
	Military spending as a share of GDP	Military spending as a share of government spending	Arms imports as a share of GDP	Arms imports as a share of government spending
Corruption	−0.48***	−0.44**	−0.76	−0.62
	(−1.880)	(−1.673)	(−1.495)	(−1.172)
Real GDP per capita	−0.005	−0.05	−0.45***	−0.18
	(−0.039)	(−0.355)	(−1.717)	(−0.654)
Gross secondary school enrollment	−0.23	−0.19	−0.47	−0.05
	(−1.431)	(−1.142)	(−1.499)	(−0.149)
Age dependency ratio	0.50	0.51	0.91	0.67
	(1.324)	(1.346)	(1.237)	(0.881)
Urbanization rate	−0.09	−0.08	−0.48	−0.43
	(−0.473)	(−0.404)	(−1.151)	(−1.066)
Government spending as share of GDP	0.66**	−0.34	1.28**	0.32
	(3.201)	(−1.623)	(2.993)	(0.767)
Average of military spending of neighbors	0.29**	0.26*	0.47*	0.28
	(2.868)	(2.468)	(2.404)	(1.344)
Soldiers per thousand population	0.53**	0.53**	0.87**	0.22
	(6.554)	(6.514)	(5.279)	(1.350)
Constant	−0.39	−0.48	5.30**	3.62*
	(−0.452)	(−0.540)	(3.006)	(2.032)
No. of observations	79	79	79	77
Adjusted R squared	0.60	0.55	0.58	0.26
F-test	15.54	12.89	14.70	4.27

(*), (**), and (***) denote, respectively, significance at the 5%, 1%, and 10% levels. All models are estimated by OLS. The numbers in parentheses are heteroscedasticity-consistent t-statistics. All variables are defined in logarithms. In all models, a high score on the corruption index indicates a low level of corruption.

basic different panel data estimators are considered: pooled OLS; one-way (country dummy) fixed effects, estimated by OLS; and random effects, estimated by GLS. Model selection is based on log-likelihood and the adjusted R^2 for the pooled OLS and fixed-effects estimator

(FEM). To deal with possible reverse causality biases, the models have also been estimated by two-stage least squares (2SLS) and generalized method of moments (GMM).

4.3. Military Spending Equations

Table 2 reports the results of the estimation of Eqs. (6a) in which the ratio of military spending to GDP is used as the dependent variable. The explanatory variables account for 52% to 55% of the variation in military spending across countries and over time, depending on model specification. The F-test is significant at classical confidence levels for all models. In the baseline model, the corruption indicator has a negative, although statistically insignificant, impact on military spending.[27] In Model 1, the control variables are included in the estimating equation.[28] The corruption indicator has the expected sign: the societies that are perceived as being more corrupt have a higher share of military spending in GDP. The point estimate suggests that a 1% increase in the corruption index is associated with an increase in military spending as a share of GDP of 0.32%.

It can be proposed that the true relationship between military spending and corruption involves a distributed lag. To deal with this possibility, Model 2 was estimated with the corruption indicator lagged 3 years. It can be argued that the inclusion of the lagged, rather than contemporaneous, values of the corruption indicator reduces the risk of bias in parameter estimates due to reverse causality.[29] The results are consistent with the previous findings. The point estimate is nevertheless lower than in Model 1, which is not surprising given the lagged response.

We also used the ratio of military spending to total government spending as the dependent variable, as in Eq. (6b). Table 3 reports the results. The F-test is significant at classical confidence levels for all models. As in the case of Table 2, different model specifications are used to test for the robustness of the parameter estimates reported in

---

[27]The LM and Hausmann tests recommend rejection of the OLS model and the GLS coefficients are reported instead. In what follows, the FEM/GLS coefficients are reported, together with the LM and Hausmann tests, whenever the OLS model is rejected.

[28]The age dependency ratio and the urbanization rate may be proxying demand for government provision. Estimating the models without these control variables when the ratio of government spending to GDP is included in the estimating equation produced similar results.

[29]We also experimented with different lag structures (1, 5, 7, and 10 years) yielding consistent results.

Table 2. Corruption and Military Spending: Panel Regression Analysis, 1985–1998
(Dependent variable: military spending as a share of GDP)

	Baseline	(1)	(2)	(3)	(4)	(5)
			Models			
Corruption	−0.03	−0.32**	−0.21*	−0.08	−0.41*	−0.38*
	(−0.627)	(−3.420)	(−2.061)	(−1.035)	(−2.064)	(−2.050)
Real GDP per capita		−0.02	−0.0001	−0.52**	0.07	0.10
		(−0.342)	(−0.001)	(−3.066)	(0.570)	(0.873)
Gross secondary school enrollment		−0.22**	−0.19*	−0.05	−0.19	−0.21
		(−3.151)	(−2.458)	(−0.297)	(−1.313)	(−1.575)
Age dependency ratio		0.44**	0.56**	−0.05	0.50	0.51***
		(2.711)	(3.161)	(−0.008)	(1.605)	(1.714)
Urbanization rate		−0.03	−0.06	0.46	−0.08	−0.07
		(−0.393)	(−0.596)	(1.178)	(−0.433)	(−0.421)
Government spending a share of GDP		0.56**	0.56**	0.43**	0.49**	0.49**
		(7.098)	(6.302)	(5.124)	(3.638)	(3.592)
Average of military spending of neighbors		0.26**	0.27**	0.21**	0.27**	0.27**
		(5.890)	(5.402)	(2.341)	(3.061)	(3.074)
Soldiers per thousand population		0.48**	0.46**	0.15	0.45**	0.43**
		(13.916)	(11.774)	(1.243)	(7.403)	(8.028)
IMF-supported program dummy				−0.14**	−0.03	−0.76
				(−3.097)	(−0.294)	(−0.084)
Conflict-country dummy						0.36**
						(2.740)
Constant	−3.72**	−1.03**	−1.28**	−0.91**	−1.51***	−1.81*
	(−35.899)	(−2.843)	(−3.184)	(−1.930)	(−1.963)	(−2.383)
Estimator	GLS	OLS	OLS	FEM	GMM	GMM
No. of observations	1,249	430	374	430	332	332
Adjusted R squared		0.55	0.52	0.56		
F-test		66.51	51.15	33.59		
LM test	462.72			593.52		
	[0.000]			[0.000]		
Hausmann test	0.03					
	[0.866]					
P-test (overidentification of instruments)					0.918	0.833

(*), (**), and (***) denote, respectively, significance at the 5%, 1%, and 10% levels. All variables are defined in logarithms, except for the IMF dummy. The numbers in parentheses are heteroscedasticity-consistent t-statistics. The corruption indicator is lagged 3 years in Model 2. Significant values of the Lagrange Multiplier (LM) test reject the pooled regression model (OLS). Significant values of the Hausmann test reject the random effects model (GLS). P-value in brackets. FEM denotes the fixed effects estimator. GMM denotes the generalized method of moments estimator. In all models, a high score on the corruption index indicates a low level of corruption.

Table 3. All models suggest that the countries perceived as being more corrupt tend to have a higher share of military spending in total government spending.[30]

4.4. Military Procurement Equations

The findings reported above confirm the hypothesis that corruption is associated with higher military spending, and that countries with worse corruption indicators tend to spend more on defense outlays, as a share of both GDP and total government spending. As noted above, procurement is likely to be an important channel through which corruption affects military expenditures. To test this hypothesis, we re-estimated equations (6a) and (6b) using military procurement (arms imports) as a share of both GDP and total government spending. The regressions reported in Tables 4 and 5 use the same set of right-hand side variables as in Tables 2 and 3. The results suggest that corruption is associated with higher procurement spending, as illustrated in Fig. 1.[31]

To deal with reverse causality, the equations were also re-estimated using the two-stage least squares (2SLS) estimator, as the government spending equations. Overall, in the panel regressions reported in

---

[30]To deal with the possibility of reverse causality, we also used the instrumental variables estimator to re-estimate the regressions in Tables 2 and 3 treating the contemporaneous values of corruption as endogenous. The selection of instruments is not trivial in this type of regression and we opted for the most conservative choice: the lagged values of the corruption index were used as instruments and different lag structures were experimented with (1, 5, 7, and 10 years). The set of instruments used in the cross-sectional regressions are time-invariant and therefore cannot be used in the panel regressions. Lagged corruption is correctly signed and statistically significant in the first-stage regressions. In the second-stage regressions, corruption remains negatively signed. The coefficients are smaller in magnitude than those estimated by OLS for the uninstrumented lagged values of corruption. The t-statistics are also typically lower but still in general significant at classical levels. When the fixed-effects estimator was used, the models were estimated in first differences, given the bias due to the correlation between the fixed effects and the lagged dependent variable. The results, omitted to economize on space, are in line with those reported in the tables. Lagged corruption remains correctly signed and statistically significant in the first-stage regressions. In the second-stage regressions, corruption remains negatively signed, although smaller in magnitude. Significance is nevertheless only obtained at the 10% level.

[31]As in the case of the military spending equations, estimation of Eq. (6b) assumes that the right-hand side variables are exogenous. To address concerns about the possible endogeneity of corruption, we also experimented with the instrumental variables estimator. Lagged values of the corruption index were used as the instruments. The results, available upon request, are in line with those reported in Tables 4 and 5.

Table 3. Corruption and Military Spending: Panel Regression Analysis, 1985–1998
(Dependent variable: military spending as a share of government spending)

	Baseline	(1)	(2)	(3)	(4)	(5)
			Models			
Corruption	−0.54**	−0.37**	−0.20*	−0.10	−0.42*	−0.39*
	(−11.147)	(−4.261)	(−2.049)	(−1.425)	(−2.136)	(−2.114)
Real GDP per capita		0.04	−0.05	−0.53**	0.09	0.12
		(0.746)	(−0.355)	(−3.187)	(0.761)	(1.056)
Gross secondary school enrollment		−0.24**	−0.20**	−0.08	−0.19	−0.21
		(−3.574)	(−2.763)	(−0.449)	(−1.290)	(−1.567)
Age dependency ratio		0.51**	0.68**	−0.15	0.60**	0.60*
		(3.406)	(4.135)	(−0.254)	(2.007)	(2.100)
Urbanization rate		0.008	0.01	0.50	−0.09	−0.08
		(0.094)	(0.109)	(1.299)	(−0.510)	(−0.501)
Government spending as share of GDP		−0.48**	−0.52**	−0.54**	−0.51**	−0.50**
		(−6.506)	(−6.303)	(−6.436)	(−3.716)	(−3.632)
Average of military spending of neighbors		0.27**	0.29**	0.22**	0.24**	0.25**
		(6.553)	(6.155)	(2.867)	(2.911)	(2.969)
Soldiers per thousand population		0.44**	0.41**	0.13	0.45**	0.44**
		(13.248)	(11.006)	(1.189)	(7.515)	(8.147)
IMF-supported program dummy				−0.14**	−0.05	−0.26
				(−3.357)	(−0.549)	(−0.298)
Conflict-country dummy						0.37**
						(2.843)
Constant	−1.63**	−1.41**	−1.88**	−0.85	−1.69*	−1.98*
	(−19.151)	(−4.164)	(−4.972)	(−1.882)	(−2.230)	(−2.66)
Estimator	OLS	OLS	OLS	FEM	GMM	GMM
No. of observations	1,221	430	371	430	334	334
Adjusted R squared	0.09	0.57	0.55	0.90		
F-test	124.25	71.27	56.94	47.12		
LM Test				529.55 [0.000]		
P-test (overidentification of instruments)					0.480	0.748

(*), (**), and (***) denote, respectively, significance at the 5%, 1%, and 10% levels. All variables are defined in logarithms, except for the IMF dummy. The numbers in parentheses are heteroscedasticity-consistent t-statistics. The corruption indicator is lagged 3 years in Model 2. Significant values of the LM test reject the pooled regression model (OLS). P-value in brackets. FEM denotes the fixed effects estimator. GMM denotes the generalized method of moments estimator. In all models, a high score on the corruption index indicates a low level of corruption.

Table 4. Corruption and Military Spending: Panel Regression Analysis, 1985–1998

(Dependent variable: arms imports as a share of GDP)

	Baseline	(1)	(2)	(3)	(4)	(5)
Corruption	−1.07**	−0.85**	−0.82**	−0.85**	−1.10*	−1.05*
	(−8.486)	(−3.776)	(−3.487)	(−3.812)	(−2.320)	(−2.216)
Real GDP per capita		−0.29*	−0.19	−0.42**	−1.06*	−0.37
		(−2.063)	(−1.298)	(−2.877)	(−2.216)	(−1.288)
Average of military spending of neighbors		0.67**	0.69**	0.57**	0.50*	0.50*
		(6.301)	(6.502)	(5.280)	(2.224)	(2.269)
Gross secondary school enrollment		−0.12	−0.18	−0.17	−0.06	−0.07
		(−0.705)	(−1.087)	(−0.989)	(−0.257)	(−3.031)
Age dependency ratio		0.86*	0.90*	0.80*	0.92	0.91
		(2.254)	(2.332)	(2.107)	(1.548)	(1.548)
Urbanization rate		−0.41***	−0.46*	−0.32	−0.44	−0.42
		(−1.856)	(−2.035)	(−1.450)	(−1.552)	(−1.490)
Soldiers per thousand population		0.78**	0.73**	0.79**	0.73**	0.73**
		(9.214)	(8.393)	(9.430)	(6.277)	(6.386)
Government spending as share of GDP		0.61**	0.59**	0.63**	0.59*	0.59*
		(3.320)	(3.082)	(3.500)	(2.041)	(2.023)
IMF-supported program dummy				−0.46**	−0.51*	−0.49**
				(−2.992)	(−2.633)	(−2.568)
Conflict-country dummy						0.29
						(1.042)
Constant	−3.87**	2.23*	1.95*	2.95**	3.02***	2.77
	(−17.139)	(2.490)	(2.209)	(3.216)	(1.867)	(1.587)
Estimator	OLS	OLS	OLS	OLS	GMM	GMM
No. of observations	888	340	333	340	291	291
Adjusted R squared	0.07	0.50	0.51	0.51		
F-test	72.02	43.12	44.17	40.25		
P-test (overidentification of instruments)					0.296	0.238

(*), (**), and (***) denote, respectively, significance at the 5%, 1%, and 10% levels. All variables are defined in logarithms, except for the IMF dummy. The numbers in parentheses are heteroscedasticity-consistent t-statistics. The corruption indicator is lagged 3 years in Model 2. GMM denotes the generalized method of moments estimator. In all models, a high score on the corruption index indicates a low level of corruption.

Table 5. Corruption and Military Spending: Panel Regression Analysis, 1985–1998
(Dependent variable: arms imports as a share of government spending)

	Baseline	(1)	(2)	(3)	(4)	(5)
Corruption	−0.87**	−0.85**	−0.82**	−0.85**	−1.10*	−1.09*
	(−8.766)	(−3.778)	(−3.488)	(−3.814)	(−2.318)	(−2.214)
Real GDP per capita		−0.29*	−0.19	−0.42**	−1.06*	−0.37
		(−2.068)	(−1.303)	(−2.881)	(−2.214)	(−1.290)
Average of military spending of neighbors		0.67**	0.69**	0.57**	0.50*	0.506*
		(6.303)	(6.504)	(5.282)	(2.224)	(2.268)
Gross secondary school enrollment		−0.12	−0.18	−0.17	−0.06	−0.074
		(−0.704)	(−1.086)	(−0.988)	(−0.256)	(−0.301)
Age dependency ratio		0.86*	0.90*	0.80*	0.92	0.91
		(2.255)	(2.334)	(2.108)	(1.549)	(1.549)
Urbanization rate		−0.41***	−0.46*	−0.32	−0.44	−0.42
		(−1.857)	(−2.035)	(−1.450)	(−1.553)	(−1.492)
Soldiers per thousand population		0.78**	0.73**	0.79**	0.73**	0.73**
		(9.223)	(8.402)	(9.438)	(6.282)	(6.391)
Government spending as share of GDP		−0.39*	−0.41*	−0.37*	−0.41	−0.40
		(−2.161)	(−2.145)	(−2.041)	(−1.422)	(−1.381)
IMF-supported program dummy				−0.46**	−0.51**	−0.49**
				(−2.991)	(−2.624)	(−2.569)
Conflict-country dummy						0.29
						(1.040)
Constant	−0.65**	2.23*	1.95*	2.95**	3.02***	2.77
	(−3.665)	(2.494)	(2.213)	(3.219)	(1.868)	(1.588)
Estimator	OLS	OLS	OLS	OLS	GMM	GMM
No. of observations	795	340	333	340	291	291
Adjusted R squared	0.09	0.54	0.55	0.55		
F-test	76.84	49.87	51.50	46.39		
P-test (overidentification of instruments)					0.296	0.238

(*), (**), and (***) denote, respectively, significance at the 5%, 1%, and 10% levels. All variables are defined in logarithms, except for the IMF dummy. The numbers in parentheses are heteroscedasticity-consistent t-statistics. The corruption indicator is lagged 3 years in Model 2. GMM denotes the generalized method of moments estimator. In all models, a high score on the corruption index indicates a low level of corruption.

Tables 2–5, both OLS and 2SLS estimators yield similar parameter estimates. Given the adequacy of the instruments in the first-stage regressions, it is fair to say that taking account of the information provided in the time dimension of the panel reduces the risk of bias in the parameter estimates due to reverse causality. This is particularly true when lagged, rather than contemporaneous, values of the corruption indicator are included in the estimating equations. In the cross-sectional equations, however, for which the literature offers more guidance on the choice of instruments, the results are weaker for the 2SLS regressions.

4.5. Does Conditionality in Adjustment Programs Play a Role?

Policy advice from international financial institutions, in particular the IMF, has focused, among others, on improving the composition of government expenditures in favor of programs with higher productivity, including those in support of human development.[32] To ascertain whether this is the case, a dummy variable was introduced to identify the countries in the sample that have, or have had, IMF-supported programs.[33] This dummy variable takes the value of one if there is a program in a given year and zero, otherwise.

The results reported in Model 3 (Tables 2–5) suggest that IMF program countries tend to have lower military spending as a share of GDP and total government spending. Unlike Davoodi et al. (1999), who consider a different time period and sample of countries in their analysis, we found the IMF dummy to be strongly significant when military procure-

---

[32]To support poverty reduction efforts in poor countries, a number of donors have banned export credits for the purpose of buying arms and military equipment. Others, in the context of debt relief for Heavily Indebted Poor Countries (HIPCs), have restricted credit guarantees to imports that support productive investment and social development.

[33]Davoodi et al. (1999) also include an IMF program country dummy in the military spending regressions because IMF-supported adjustment programs are likely to affect both the level and the composition of government spending. Gupta et al. (1996) show that countries with stand-by arrangements and systemic transformation facility programs have a substantially larger decline in military spending as a share of GDP than countries with SAF/ESAF programs in the period 1990–1995. The authors also show that program countries have relied more heavily than nonprogram countries on cuts in military spending to implement fiscal adjustment. See also Harris and Kusi (1992) for evidence of lower military spending in African countries with IMF-supported programs.

ment was used as the dependent variable.[34] In this case, military procurement tends to be lower in countries with IMF-supported programs.

Evidence of serial correlation in the residuals was found for most models. Serial correlation is expected because military spending levels in one given year affect spending levels in subsequent years. To address this issue and the possibility of heterogeneity and endogeneity of the regressors, the models were re-estimated by GMM.[35] In general, the results reported in Tables 2–5 are in line with the previous findings, but the IMF dummy loses significance in the military spending equations.

4.6. Military Spending and Involvement in Armed Conflict

A conflict-country dummy was introduced in the equations reported in Tables 2–5. We used SIPRI's definition of major armed conflict, defined "as a prolonged combat between the military forces of two or more governments, or of one government and at least one organized armed group, and incurring the battle-related deaths of at least 1000 people during the entire conflict. A conflict location is the territory of a state." SIPRI covers the post-1992 period. As in Davoodi et al. (1999), for years prior to 1992, we use the list of conflict countries in Sivard (1993). The variable takes value one in conflict years for each country, and zero otherwise. In the military spending equations (Model 5, Tables 2 and 3), the conflict-country dummy was found to affect military spending positively, as expected, and to be statistically significant at classical confidence levels. In the military procurement equations (Model 5, Tables 4 and 5), the coefficient of the conflict-country dummy was found to be positively signed but not statistically different from zero.[36]

---

[34] When the military procurement variables are used as the dependent variable, the corruption indicator fails to be statistically significant at classical confidence levels. This may be attributed to the high correlation between corruption and the IMF-program dummy, and between the corruption index and the fixed effects (Tables 2 and 3).

[35] The instruments used are the explanatory variables included in the OLS models and the corruption index lagged one and two periods. We also experimented with different lag structures (3, 5, and 7 years).

[36] The inclusion of the conflict-country dummy in the equations results in the loss of significance of the corruption indicator when the models are estimated by FEM and GLS, but not when the models are estimated by OLS.

4.7. Further Robustness Checks

To further evaluate the robustness of the results reported above, we also introduced a dummy variable to identify the OECD member countries in the sample. OECD membership was found to be associated with higher military spending as a share of GDP (Table 6). A dummy variable was also introduced to identify the arms-exporting countries in the sample. In these countries, it can be argued that the relationship between military spending and corruption differs from that in arms-importing countries. The dummy was found to be positively associated with military spending, but not statistically significant at classical levels of significance. Moreover, we experimented with time dummies to capture the downward trend in military spending over time (Section 3.3). The time dummy was not found to be statistically significant.[37] A regional dummy was also included in the estimation of equations to identify the African countries in the sample. The African dummy was found to be positively signed and statistically significant in most models when ACDA data are used in the construction of the dependent variables. This is not surprising because Africa had the vast majority of conflict countries in recent years.[38]

4.8. Different Data Sources

The findings reported above are robust to the use of the different sources of military spending data referred to in Section 3.3. These data sources differ primarily in country coverage and the definition of expenditures. The WEO data set contains defense budget outturns reported by IMF country desk officers and has the widest coverage of countries. SIPRI uses the NATO definition of defense spending and includes military pensions, military interest payments, and paramili-

---

[37]The results of the sensitivity analysis for the arms procurement equations (omitted to economize on space) are in line with the coefficients reported in Table 6.

[38]Military outlays remain relatively high in Africa, at 2.3% of GDP in 1999, compared to 1.4% of GDP in Asia, and 1.2% of GDP in the Western Hemisphere. Military spending has been higher in Africa than in these two regions as a share of GDP throughout the 1990s, even if conflict countries are excluded from the analysis. Among developing and transition economies, Africa spends more as a share of GDP on the military than all other regions except the Middle East (IMF, 2000, *World Economic Outlook, October 1999:* Box No. 6.1, pp. 138–140). See also Sollenberg et al. (1999), for more details.

Table 6. Corruption and Military Spending: Panel Regression Analysis, 1985–1998
(Dependent variable: military spending as a share of GDP)

	(1)	(2)	(3)	(4)
Corruption	−0.38*	−0.34*	−0.41*	−0.38*
	(−2.050)	(−2.089)	(−2.109)	(−2.033)
Real GDP per capita	0.10	0.24*	0.11	0.10
	(0.873)	(2.320)	(0.949)	(0.944)
Gross secondary school enrollment	−0.21	−0.30*	−0.20	−0.21
	(−1.575)	(−2.402)	(−1.508)	(−1.542)
Age dependency ratio	0.51***	0.33	0.60	0.52***
	(1.714)	(1.176)	(1.876)	(1.738)
Urbanization rate	−0.07	−0.14	−0.07	−0.07
	(−0.421)	(−0.918)	(−0.459)	(−0.448)
Government spending as share of GDP	0.49**	0.59**	0.48**	0.49**
	(3.592)	(4.335)	(3.505)	(3.601)
Average of military spending of neighbors	0.27**	0.25**	0.27**	0.27**
	(3.074)	(3.221)	(3.193)	(3.086)
Soldiers per thousand population	0.43**	0.412**	0.43**	0.438**
	(8.028)	(8.489)	(7.984)	(7.872)
Conflict-country dummy	0.36**	0.37**	0.36**	0.35**
	(2.740)	(2.970)	(2.714)	(2.640)
OECD dummy		0.37**		
		(2.970)		
Arms exporters dummy			0.13	
			(1.124)	
Time trend				−0.26
				(−0.129)
Constant	−1.8*	−2.29**	−1.80*	−2.29*
	(−2.383)	(−3.28)	(−2.461)	(−3.283)
P-test (overidentification of instruments)	0.833	0.715	0.756	0.831

(*), (**), and (***) denote, respectively, significance at the 5%, 1%, and 10% levels. All variables are defined in logarithms. The numbers in parentheses are heteroscedasticity-consistent *t*-statistics. The number of observations is 332 in all models. All models are estimated by GMM. In all models, a high score on the corruption index indicates a low level of corruption.

tary expenditures in total outlays, but excludes police expenditures. IISS uses the NATO definition only for NATO countries, and defense budget outturns for non-NATO countries. These sources also differ in the treatment of calendar and fiscal year data. For instance, WEO and

Table 7. Corruption and Military Spending: Panel Regression Analysis, 1985–1998

(Dependent variable: military spending as a share of GDP)

	Data Sources			
	WEO	SIPRI	ACDA	IISS
Corruption	−0.32**	−0.27*	−0.30*	−0.35*
	(−2.816)	(−2.442)	(−2.276)	(−2.253)
GDP per capita	0.004	0.11***	−0.42**	−0.13
	(0.065)	(1.847)	(−5.682)	(−1.462)
Gross secondary school enrollment	−0.40**	−0.55**	−0.35**	−0.27*
	(−4.228)	(−6.038)	(−3.221)	(−2.111)
Age dependency ratio	0.30	0.30	−1.03**	0.29
	(1.500)	(1.585)	(−4.453)	(1.082)
Urbanization rate	0.11	−0.07	0.43**	0.007
	(1.070)	(−0.707)	(3.630)	(0.047)
Government spending as share of GDP	0.54**	0.68**	0.40**	0.57**
	(5.803)	(7.618)	(3.663)	(4.537)
Average of military spending of neighbors	0.44**	0.50**	0.59**	0.43**
	(8.145)	(9.766)	(9.411)	(5.978)
Soldiers per thousand population	0.40**	0.42**	0.49**	0.44**
	(8.931)	(9.967)	(9.359)	(7.242)
Constant	−0.30	0.29	1.79**	0.79
	(−0.650)	(0.653)	(3.291)	(1.263)
Adjusted R squared	0.59	0.67	0.56	0.45
F-test	51.20	70.06	43.96	28.80

(*), (**), and (***) denote, respectively, significance at the 5%, 1%, and 10% levels. All variables are defined in logarithms. The numbers in parentheses are heteroscedasticity-consistent t-statistics. The corruption indicator is lagged 3 years in Model 2. All models are estimated by OLS. The number of observations is 275. In all models, a high score on the corruption index indicates a low level of corruption.

SIPRI data are calculated on a calendar year basis, while IISS uses a mix of fiscal and calendar year data. The timeliness with which data are reported also varies among these data sources.

Table 7 reports the estimations of Eq. (6a) using military spending data from WEO, ACDA, SIPRI, and IISS. The same sample of countries is used in these regressions. The association between corruption and military spending was found to have the correct sign and to be strongly significant, regardless of the data set used. The coefficients vary between –0.27 when SIPRI data are used and –0.35 when IISS data are used.[39]

5. Conclusions

This paper has shown that corruption is associated with higher military spending as a share of GDP and total government expenditures, and with larger procurement outlays in relation to both GDP and government spending. Although some caution is needed, owing to the data limitations, the evidence reported in this paper is suggestive—but by no means conclusive—that countries perceived as being more corrupt tend to spend more on the military. The results are fairly robust to different model specifications, estimation techniques, and data sources. The paper contributes to the ongoing debate in international fora on the choice of appropriate governance indicators, and supports the possible use of military spending in relation to GDP and total government spending as such indicators.

The principal policy conclusion of this paper is that, other things being equal, we can expect policies aimed at reducing corruption to change the composition of government spending toward more productive, nonmilitary outlays. Corruption in military spending/procurement can of course be reduced through greater transparency and reduced patronage at the level of officials receiving bribes. Defense contracts could also be included in freedom of information legislation, when available. Arms procurement contracts could be liable to standard budgetary oversight (such as auditing procedures and legislative approval), in the same way as other expenditure programs in the budget.

Deficiencies in budget oversight and associated corruption are not unique to the defense sector. Transparent budget preparation, execution, and reporting, as well as subjecting fiscal information to independent assurances of integrity would however weaken the channels through which corruption affects public procurement, including in the military sector.

---

[39]Note that while the sources of military spending data vary in different equations, only one source of data (WEO) is used for the government spending variable.

Appendixes

Appendix A. Country Annual Data Used

1. Albania	41. Guatemala	81. Pakistan
2. Algeria	42. Guinea	82. Papua New Guinea
3. Angola	43. Guinea-Bissau	83. Paraguay
4. Argentina	44. Guyana	84. Peru
5. Australia	45. Haiti	85. Philippines
6. Austria	46. Honduras	86. Poland
7. Bahrain	47. Hungary	87. Portugal
8. Bangladesh	48. India	88. Romania
9. Belgium	49. Indonesia	89. Russia
10. Bolivia	50. Iran, Islamic Republic of	90. Saudi Arabia
11. Botswana		91. Senegal
12. Brazil	51. Ireland	92. Sierra Leone
13. Bulgaria	52. Israel	93. Singapore
14. Burkina Faso	53. Italy	94. Slovak Republic
15. Cameroon	54. Jamaica	95. South Africa
16. Canada	55. Japan	96. Spain
17. Central African Republic	56. Jordan	97. Sri Lanka
	57. Kenya	98. Sudan
18. Chile	58. Korea, Dem. People's Rep. of	99. Suriname
19. China		100. Sweden
20. Colombia	59. Korea, Republic of	101. Switzerland
21. Congo, Dem. Republic of	60. Kuwait	102. Syrian Arab Republic
	61. Lebanon	103. Taiwan Province of China
22. Costa Rica	62. Libya	104. Tanzania
23. Côte d'Ivoire	63. Luxembourg	105. Thailand
24. Cuba	64. Madagascar	106. Togo
25. Cyprus	65. Malawi	107. Trinidad and Tobago
26. Czech Republic	66. Malaysia	108. Tunisia
27. Denmark	67. Mali	109. Turkey
28. Dominican Republic	68. Malta	110. Uganda
29. Ecuador	69. Mexico	111. United Arab Emirates
30. Egypt	70. Mongolia	112. United Kingdom
31. El Salvador	71. Morocco	113. United States
32. Ethiopia	72. Mozambique	114. Uruguay
33. Fiji	73. Myanmar	115. República Bolivariana de Venezuela
34. Finland	74. Namibia	
35. France	75. Netherlands	116. Vietnam
36. Gabon	76. New Zealand	117. Yemen, Republic of
37. Gambia, The	77. Niger	118. Yugoslavia, Federal Republic of
38. Germany	78. Nigeria	
39. Ghana	79. Norway	119. Zambia
40. Greece	80. Oman	120. Zimbabwe

Appendix B. Variable Definitions and Sources

Variable	Description	Source
CORIN	Corruption index.	ICRG, TI
GDPPC	Real per capita GDP in PPP terms.	World Bank: 1999 WDI
GESGDP	Ratio of government expenditure to GDP.	WEO, World Bank
AFTHP	Armed Forces per thousand population.	ACDA
DSGDP	Ratio of military spending to GDP.	WEO, SIPRI, ACDA, IISS
DEFSGE	Ratio of military spending to government expenditures.	WEO
AIMPSGDP	Ratio of arms imports to GDP.	ACDA, World Bank
AISDEF	Ratio of arms imports to military spending.	ACDA, WEO
AISGE	Ratio of arms imports to government expenditures.	ACDA, WEO
AVNEB	Unweighted average of military spending as a share of GDP of neighboring countries.	WEO
SENROL	Gross secondary school enrollment.	World Bank: 1999 WDI
URBAN	Urbanization rate.	World Bank: 1999 WDI
AGEDEP	Age dependency ratio.	World Bank: 1999 WDI
IMF program	Dummy variable taking value 1 for countries with IMF-supported program, and 0 otherwise.	IMF

Appendix C. Descriptive Statistics
(Unweighted averages)

Variable	Mean	Standard deviation	Minimum	Maximum	Number of observations
DSGDP (ACDA)	4.4	6.4	0.2	95.6	833
DSGDP (IISS)	3.7	4.6	0.2	68.3	907
DSGDP (WEO)	3.3	4.2	0.2	86.2	1,355
DSGDP (SIPRI)	3.2	3.5	0.2	48.5	964
AVNEB	3.7	3.4	0.5	19.2	1,260
CORIN	5.7	2.2	0.8	10.0	1,556
GDPPC	6,712	6,609	290	30,140	1,383
AFTHP	7.55	8.51	0.41	62.17	1,236
AIMPSGDP	1.1	2.7	0.0	36.5	997
DEFSGE	10.3	8.4	1.2	88.1	1,326
AISGE	3.4	7.5	0.0	81.4	980
AISDEF	19.4	19.8	0.0	99.1	822
GESGDP	33.1	13.4	6.6	78.1	1,605
SENROL	58.4	32.9	3.3	148.3	1,140
AGEDEP	0.7	0.2	0.4	1.2	1,074
URBAN	53.2	23.6	9.9	100.0	1,547

The sample covers 1985–1998. All values are defined in percent form, except for CORIN, GDPPC, and AGEDEP.

Appendix D. Raw Correlations

	DSGDP (WEO)	DEFSGE	AIMPSGDP	AISDEF	AVNEB	CORIN	GDPPC	AFTHP	GESGDP	SENROL	AGEDEP	URBAN
DSGDP (WEO)	1.00											
DEFSGE	0.89	1.00										
AIMPSGDP	0.57	0.57	1.00									
AISDEF	0.15	0.21	0.68	1.00								
AVNEB	0.68	0.60	0.62	0.28	1.00							
CORIN	−0.15	−0.38	−0.29	−0.32	−0.12	1.00						
GDPPC	0.02	−0.22	−0.08	−0.29	0.02	0.72	1.00					
AFTHP	0.41	0.31	0.37	0.20	0.40	0.16	0.22	1.00				
GESGDP	0.21	−0.16	0.12	−0.10	0.18	0.65	0.70	0.36	1.00			
SENROL	−0.10	−0.37	−0.16	−0.25	−0.08	0.75	0.83	0.23	0.74	1.00		
AGEDEP	0.18	0.38	0.23	0.27	0.24	−0.60	−0.68	−0.09	−0.50	−0.82	1.00	
URBAN	0.18	−0.08	0.07	−0.18	0.14	0.46	0.74	0.35	0.61	0.72	−0.56	1.00

References

Ades, A., Di Tella, R., 1999. Rents, competition, and corruption. American Economic Review 89, 982–993.

Bardhan, P., 1997. Corruption and development: a review of issues. Journal of Economic Literature 35, 1320–1346.

Bayoumi, T., Hewitt, D., Schiff, J., 1995. Economic consequences of lower military spending: some simulation results. In: Klein, L., Lo, F., McKibbin, W. (Eds.), Arms Reduction: Economic Implications in the Post-Cold War Era. United Nations Univ. Press, New York.

Beck, P., Maher, M., 1986. A comparison of bribery and bidding in thin markets. Economics Letters 20, 1–5.

Bhagwati, J.N., 1982. Directly unproductive, profit-seeking (DUP) activities. Journal of Political Economy 90, 988–1002.

Davoodi, H. et al., 1999. Military spending, the peace dividend, and fiscal adjustment. Working paper no. 99/87, International Monetary Fund, Washington, DC.

Ellis, S., 1998. Africa and international corruption: the strange case of South Africa and Seychelles. In: Mbaku, J.M. (Ed.), Corruption and the Crisis of Institutional Reforms in Africa. Edwin Mellen Press, Lewinston, NY, pp. 198–236.

Gould, D.J., 1980. Bureaucratic Corruption and Underdevelopment in the Third World: The Case of Zaire. Pergamon, New York.

Gupta, S., Schiff, J., Clements, B., 1996. Worldwide military spending, 1990–95. Working paper no. 96/64, International Monetary Fund, Washington, DC.

Gupta, S., Davoodi, H., Alonso-Terme, R., 1998. Does corruption affect income inequality and poverty? Working paper no. 98/76, International Monetary Fund, Washington, DC. [Revised version reproduced as Chapter 17 in this volume—ED.]

Hall, R., Jones, C., 1999. Why do some countries produce so much more output per worker than others?. Quarterly Journal of Economics 114, 83–116.

Harris, G., Kusi, N., 1992. Impact of the IMF on government expenditures: a study of African LDCs. Journal of International Development 4, 73–85.

Hewitt, D., 1992. Military expenditures worldwide: determinants and trends, 1972–88. Journal of Public Policy 12 (12), 105–152.

Hewitt, D., 1993. Military expenditures 1972–1990: the reason behind the post-1985 fall in world military spending. Working paper no. 93/18, International Monetary Fund, Washington, DC.

Hines, J.R. Jr., 1995. Forbidden payment: foreign bribery and American business after 1977. Working paper no. 5266, National Bureau of Economic Research, Cambridge, Massachusetts.

Huntington, S., 1968. Political Order in Changing Societies. Yale Univ. Press, New Haven, CT.

IMF, 1999. World Economic Outlook, October 1999: A Survey by the Staff of the International Monetary Fund. World Economic and Financial Surveys. International Monetary Fund, Washington, DC.

IMF, 2000. Military expenditures stabilize during 1999; variations persist in different regions. IMF Survey, 175–76. International Monetary Fund, Washington, DC.

Johnson, S., Kaufmann, D., Zoido-Lobatón, P., 1998. Regulatory discretion and the unofficial economy, American Economic Review 88, 387–392.

Kaufmann, D., Wei, S., 1999. Does "grease money" speed up the wheels of commerce? Policy research paper no. 2254, The World Bank, Washington, DC.

Kimenyi, M.S., Mbaku J.M., 1996. Rents, military elites, and political democracy. European Journal of Political Economy 11, 699–708.

Klitgaard, R., 1988. Controlling Corruption. University of California Press, Berkeley, CA.

Knack, S., Keefer, P., 1995. Institutions and economic performance: cross-country tests using alternative institutional measures. Economics and Politics 7, 207–227.

Knight, M., Loayza, N., Villanueva, D., 1996. The peace dividend: military spending cuts and economic growth. Staff papers 43, 1–37, International Monetary Fund, Washington, DC.

Krueger, A., 1993. Virtuous and vicious circles in economic development. American Economic Review 83, 351–355.

Lambsdorff, J., 1998. An empirical investigation of bribery in international trade. European Journal of Development Research 10, 40–59.

La Porta, R. et al., 1998. The quality of government. Working paper no. 6727, National Bureau of Economic Research, Cambridge, Massachusetts.

Leff, N., 1964. Economic development through bureaucratic corruption. The American Behavioral Scientist 8, 8–14.

Leite, C., Weidmann, J., 1999. Does mother nature corrupt?: natural resources, corruption, and economic growth. Working paper no. 99/85, International Monetary Fund, Washington, DC. [Reproduced as Chapter 7 in this volume—ED.]

LeVine, V.T., 1975. Political Corruption: The Ghanian Case. Hoover Institution, Stanford, CA.

Lien, D., 1986. Note on competitive bribery games. Economics Letters 22, 337–341.

Lui, F., 1985. Equilibrium queuing model of bribery. Journal of Political Economy 93 (4), 760–781.

Mauro, P., 1995. Corruption and growth. Quarterly Journal of Economics 110, 681–712.

Mauro, P., 1997. The effects of corruption on growth, investment, and government expenditure: a cross-country analysis. In: Elliott, K. (Ed.), Corruption and the Global Economy. Institute for International Economics, Washington, DC. [Revised version reproduced as Chapter 9 in this volume—ED.]

Mbaku, J.M., 2000. Bureaucratic and Political Corruption in Africa: The Public Choice Perspective. Krieger, Malabar, FL.

Murphy, K., Shleifer, A., Vishny, R., 1993. Why is rent-seeking so costly to growth? American Economic Review 83, 409–414.

Naylor, R.T., 1998. Corruption in the modern arms business: terms from the pentagon scandals. In: Jain, A. (Ed.), Economics of Corruption. Kluwer Academic Publishing, Boston.

Nye, J.S., 1967. Corruption and political development: a cost-benefit analysis. American Political Science Review 51, 417–429.

OECD, 1997. Convention on Combating Bribery of Foreign Public Officials in International Business Transactions. Organisation for Economic Co-operation and Development, Paris.

Rauch, J.E., Evans, P.B., 2000. Bureaucratic structure and bureaucratic performance in less developed countries. Journal of Public Economics 75, 49–71.

Rose-Ackerman, S., 1996. When is corruption harmful? Working paper, The World Bank, Washington, DC.

Shleifer, A., Vishny, R., 1993. Corruption. Quarterly Journal of Economics 59, 599–617.

Sivard, R., 1993. World Military and Social Expenditures. WMSE Publications, Leesburg, VA.

Sollenberg, M., Wallensteen, P., Jato, A., 1999. Major Armed Conflicts. SIPRI Yearbook.

Tanzi, V., 1998. Corruption around the world: causes, consequences, scope, and cures. Staff papers 45, 559–594, International Monetary Fund, Washington, DC. [Reproduced as Chapter 2 in this volume—ED.]

Tanzi, V., Davoodi, H., 1997. Corruption, public investment, and growth. Working paper no. 97/139, International Monetary Fund, Washington, DC. [Revised version reproduced as Chapter 11 in this volume—ED.]

Taylor, C., Hudson, M., 1972. World Handbook of Political and Social Indicators. Yale Univ. Press, New Haven, CT.

UNDP, 1997. Human Development Report. United Nations Development Programme, New York.

van Rijckeghem, C., Weder, B., 1997. Corruption and the rate of temptation: do low wages in the civil service cause corruption? Working paper no. 97/73, International Monetary Fund, Washington, DC. [Revised version reproduced as Chapter 3 in this volume—ED.]

Wei, S., 1997. Why is corruption so much more taxing than tax? Arbitrariness kills. Working paper no. 6255, National Bureau of Economic Research, Cambridge, Massachusetts.

Wei, S., 1999. Does corruption relieve foreign investors of the burden of taxes and capital controls? Policy research working paper no. 2209, The World Bank, Washington, DC.

13

Fiscal Decentralization and Governance: A Cross-Country Analysis

Luiz de Mello and Matias Barenstein

I. Introduction

Strengthening governance—the institutions by which a country exercises authority and manages its public resources—has been a key objective of most economic reform programs implemented in recent years. Countries that have already achieved macroeconomic stability through first-generation reforms have designed and implemented second-generation reforms to upgrade the social and legal institutions that encourage and support better governance.

Some countries, in preparing their Poverty Reduction Strategy Papers (PRSPs), have identified decentralization as an explicit policy

---

The authors are grateful to Juan Pablo Cordoba for his active participation in this research project and would like to thank Pranab Bardhan, Ke-young Chu, Ki Fukasaku, Sanjeev Gupta, Philippe Le Houerou, Calvin McDonald, Gerd Schwartz, Teresa Ter-Minassian, and Daniel Treisman for comments and helpful discussions. The authors remain solely responsible for any remaining errors and omissions.

instrument to improve governance.[1] In these documents, emphasis is placed on judicial reform, fighting against corruption, and strengthening the rule of law. Decentralization is also pursued to (1) improve service delivery; (2) coordinate, implement, and monitor donor-financed poverty-alleviation programs; (3) strengthen budget preparation and execution; (4) bring the administration closer to the people and encourage their participation in the management of public affairs; and (5) enable local governments and grassroots communities to take responsibility for their own development.

Fiscal decentralization—the assignment of expenditure functions and revenue sources to subnational levels of governments—has a recognized bearing on governance and on the quality of government (Humplick and Estache, 1995; Huther and Shah, 1998; Fisman and Gatti, 2000; and Treisman, 2000). Related literature shows that macroeconomic governance is affected not only by fiscal decentralization but also by how subnational expenditures are financed. Decentralization programs that encourage revenue mobilization, rather than reliance on grants and transfers from higher levels of government to finance local expenditures, are known to have smaller governments (measured as the share of government spending to GDP) and lower budget deficits (Ter-Minassian, 1997; Stein, 1998; Fukasaku and de Mello, 1998 and 1999; and de Mello, 1999 and 2000a). This paper aims to test the hypotheses that (1) fiscal decentralization improves governance and (2) the association between decentralization and governance is stronger when decentralization promotes subnational revenue mobilization.

Lack of data has limited this type of empirical analysis. The data needed to construct decentralization indicators have been widely available for many countries over a considerable time span. However, because governance is a multidimensional concept, quantitative indicators are much harder to construct and require data not readily available, particularly for developing countries. In recent years, considerable effort has been made to construct governance indicators for a cross-section of developing and developed countries.

---

[1]In late 1999, the Executive Boards of the IMF and the World Bank approved a new approach to reducing poverty in low-income countries, based on country-owned poverty reduction strategies. These strategies were expected to be results-oriented, comprehensive, and long term in perspective and were to be embodied within a PRSP that would serve as a framework for development assistance from the IMF, the World Bank, and other donors.

The data set available from Kaufmann, Kraay, and Zoido-Lobatón (1999a) focuses on different aspects of governance such as corruption, rule of law, voice and accountability, political instability, and quality of the bureaucracy. This is the main source of governance data to be used in this paper. Other governance indicators that have been widely used in the empirical literature are the Heritage Foundation's index of property rights, the Freedom House's indices of equality of citizens before the law and economic freedom (Messick, 1996), and the indices of perceived corruption available from Transparency International, the Political Risk Services Group, which produces the *International Country Risk Guide (ICRG)*, and Gallup, among others.[2]

The rest of this paper is organized as follows. Section II surveys the literature on decentralization and governance. Section III describes the data used in the empirical sections and provides preliminary evidence of an association between decentralization and governance. Section IV reports the econometric results. Section V focuses on revenue mobilization capacity and the association between governance and decentralization. Conclusions and policy implications are provided in Section VI.

II. Review of the Literature

A growing body of literature has emerged in recent years hypothesizing a positive association between decentralization and governance. Based on the public finance principle of subsidiarity, a better match can be achieved between the supply of goods and services provided by the public sector and the demands of the population, as long as the costs associated with revenue mobilization are borne by the same jurisdiction that can internalize the benefits of public sector provision. This closer association between expenditures and revenue mobilization at the subnational level may lead to better accountability of government actions (Inter-American Development Bank, 1997; Bahl, 1999; and Oates, 1999). Corruption may also be reduced in decentralized governments as long as autonomous jurisdictions compete with each other for bribes and kickbacks (Weingast, 1995; Breton, 1996; and Treisman, 2000). Fiscal decentralization may lead to allocative ineffi-

---

[2]For more information on these indices, see www.heritage.org/index/methodology.html and www.freedomhouse.org/survey99/method. See also Messick (1996) and de Mello and Sab (2000) for more information.

ciencies, as well as poor accountability and governance, if expenditures and revenue mobilization functions are not clearly assigned across the different levels of government (Hommes, 1995; Inter-American Development Bank, 1997; World Bank, 1999; and Fukasaku and de Mello, 1999). Fiscal decentralization has also been shown to strengthen social capital and encourage political participation (Inman and Rubinfeld, 1997; and de Mello, 2000b).[3] Electoral rules and other mechanisms are nevertheless needed to encourage voter participation and improve accountability through more general and continuous participation of civil society in the political process (World Bank, 1999).

Related literature focuses on the relationship between fiscal and political decentralization.[4] Bardhan and Mookherjee (1998) argue that an agency problem arises when local bureaucrats are appointed by the central government, rather than elected locally, because the central government may have limited ability to monitor their performance.[5] In the same vein, Seabright (1996) notes that decentralization can strengthen accountability because it increases the proximity between representatives and the electorate. Central government representatives do not necessarily need to be elected in all subnational jurisdictions, whereas each local representative has to win the election in his or her own jurisdiction. Subnational governments may therefore be more accountable to their electorate than the central government.

The literature also recommends caution in assessing the benefits of fiscal and political decentralization as catalysts for improved governance. Blanchard and Shleifer (2000) discuss the risks of local capture of political power by vested interests in transition economies and argue that some degree of political centralization may be warranted. Bardhan and Mookherjee (1998) also argue that if local accountability is limited, decentralization will lead to local capture. Political decentralization

---

[3]It has also been argued that "when a country finds itself deeply divided, especially along geographic or ethnic lines, decentralization provides an institutional mechanism for bringing opposition groups into a formal, rules-bound bargaining process" (World Bank, 1999, p. 107).

[4]Some authors have distinguished devolution of fiscal functions in decentralized systems from deconcentration within a centralized system (Parker, 1995).

[5]This may be attributed "to costs of communication and supervision, better information held at the local level regarding delivery costs and needs, and the conflict of interest between corrupt bureaucrats and elected politicians" (Bardhan and Mookherjee, 1998, p. 6). Local capture of the democratic process by special interest groups may depend on various factors, such as income inequality, which reflects the ability of the wealthy to use the political process to their advantage.

may therefore simply transfer power from national to local elites. In this respect, it has often been stated that the institutional foundations for fiscal decentralization, such as revenue-sharing arrangements and expenditure rules, should be in place before political liberalization begins. Fiscal decentralization may lead to allocative inefficiencies, as well as poor accountability and governance, if expenditures and revenue mobilization functions are not clearly assigned across the different levels of government (Hommes, 1995; Inter-American Development Bank, 1997; World Bank, 1999; and Fukasaku and de Mello, 1999).

The potential for increased efficiency in the provision of local public goods may not be fulfilled if institutional capacity is weak at the subnational level. It can also be argued that corruption may increase in decentralized governments, rather than decline, because of the proximity between local government officials and private individuals (Prud'homme, 1995; and Tanzi, 1995). When subnational governments, in addition to the central government, are granted autonomy to regulate economic activity, decentralization may increase corruption through the "overgrazing" of the bribe base (Shleifer and Vishny, 1993). These are issues of particular concern for developing countries. Other problems include limited exploitation of economies of scale in the decentralized provision of goods and services and lack of coordination and equity across jurisdictions (Bardhan and Mookherjee, 1998).[6]

Despite its comprehensiveness, the main weakness of the literature, which this paper does not aim to overcome, is the absence of formal theoretical models dealing with the different aspects of the relationship between decentralization and governance (Bardhan and Mookherjee, 1998). This is due, at least in part, to the multidimensional nature of governance, which makes it hard for the analyst to model its different aspects in a single theoretical framework.

The empirical literature has not tested all of the theoretical hypotheses mentioned earlier. Using cross-country data, Humplick and Estache (1995) estimate the impact of decentralization on the performance of several infrastructure projects, including roads, electricity, and water. Using different measures of decentralization in each sector, the authors find that at least one performance indicator improved in each sector under examination as a result of decentralization. Nev-

---

[6]A case in point is the provision of regional public goods, which may suffer as a result of decentralization, unless coordination is strengthened among subnational jurisdictions to avoid underprovision and disruption in service delivery.

ertheless, the correlation between decentralization and performance was not strong in general. Also in a cross-section of countries, Huther and Shah (1998) report positive correlations between decentralization and various governance indicators. By not controlling for any other determinants of governance, however, their findings are potentially subject to omitted variable biases. In a similar manner, Fisman and Gatti (2000) focus primarily on corruption as their governance indicator. They find that decentralization is strongly and significantly associated with less corruption, even after including various control variables in the estimating equation, such as GDP per capita and population, and dealing with the potential problem of endogeneity. More recently, in a paper dealing with the causes of corruption, Treisman (2000) reports cross-country evidence that corruption is perceived as more widespread in federal governments. Although Treisman uses similar corruption data, he measures decentralization by political autonomy rather than by the revenue and expenditure share indicators used by Huther and Shah (1998) and Fisman and Gatti (2000).[7]

Case studies are less numerous in the empirical literature. For instance, Galasso and Ravallion (2000) use data on the implementation of a partially decentralized food-for-schooling program in Bangladesh. In this program, the central government decides on the intercommunity allocation of funds, while local governments focus on intracommunity assignments.[8] They find that targeting is somewhat propoor, and local capture does not seem to be sizable. Isham, Kaufmann, and Pritchett (1997) and Pritchett and Kaufmann (1998) also assess the determinants of governance in public investment projects.

III. Data and Preliminary Findings

Decentralization Indicators

Decentralization indicators can be constructed using the data available in the IMF's *Government Finance Statistics (GFS) Yearbook*. GFS data

---

[7]The classification of federal states used in the paper is that of Elazar (1995). This classification focuses on the constitutional division of powers between central and regional governments, rather than the relative size of each level of government in expenditure and revenue mobilization.

[8]See also Barenstein (1994 and 2000).

are available for many developing and industrial countries since the early 1970s.

The main decentralization indicator used in the empirical analysis is the share of subnational spending in total government expenditures.[9] Subnational governments may comprise local and middle-tier jurisdictions.[10] Out of the more than 90 countries for which *GFS* data are reported for at least two levels of government, just over 20 countries provide information on spending at both the local and the middle-tier levels and about half of these countries are defined as federal.[11] For the remaining 70 or so countries, 5 countries provide information only at the middle-tier level, and the remaining 65 countries report subnational spending data at the local level only, including those countries, such as Belgium and Italy, where data are reported for middle-tier and local governments together.

The coverage of the expenditure data needed for the construction of decentralization indicators varies across countries. In the case of central government spending, for instance, in 14 countries out of the potential sample of 90 countries, data are available for the budgetary central government only, rather than for the consolidated central government, thereby excluding, among others, social security funds and public enterprises. In this case, the narrower the coverage of the public sector, the lower the spending share of the central government

---

[9]Other decentralization indicators have also been widely used in the literature. For example, a commonly used indicator measuring vertical imbalances in intergovernmental fiscal relations is the share of transfers and grants from higher levels of government in total subnational government revenues. To measure the extent of fiscal decentralization from the revenue perspective, a standard indicator is the ratio of subnational governments' own revenues to their total revenues. These indicators will be discussed and used later. For more information, see de Mello (1999 and 2000b).

[10]Most countries for which *GFS* data are available only report data for one subnational level, typically local governments. There can be several reasons for this. One possibility is that the country does not have formally defined middle-tier governments: this is typically the case in smaller countries. Another possible reason is that, whereas a particular level of government may exist as a separate entity, it is not really independent from higher levels of government. The 1986 *GFS Manual* states: "A central issue in the separate reporting of statistics for both regional and local governments, therefore, is whether they may be judged to have a separate existence, that is, whether they have sufficient discretion in the management of their own affairs to distinguish them as separate from the administrative structure of another government. A government may be considered to have substantial autonomy when it has the power to raise a substantial portion of its revenue from sources it controls and its officers are independent of external administrative control in the actual operation of the unit's activities" (p. 14).

[11]For the whole sample, only about 20 percent of the countries are defined as federal.

relative to subnational governments and the higher the implied degree of decentralization.

Governance Indicators

Indicators of governance should, in principle, provide information not only on the way governments are elected, monitored, and replaced, as well as their capacity to formulate and implement sound policies effectively, but also on the attitude of the citizenry or the electorate, as well as of their representatives, toward the institutions that govern economic, political, and social interactions. A number of such indicators are now available. Their main limitations are the small number of countries and the short time span for which internationally comparable information is available. Typically, there is a trade-off between the cross-country and the time-series dimensions of the data. For instance, the widely used corruption indicator constructed by the *International Country Risk Guide (ICRG)* is available for the post-1982 period only. The governance indicators constructed by Kaufmann, Kraay, and Zoido-Lobatón (1999a and 1999b) are available for 1997–98 only.

Another important shortcoming is that, unlike the decentralization indicators, which are based on standard public finance aggregates, the governance indicators are subjective. These indicators use the information collected through market and business confidence surveys, polls of experts, and commercial and political risk assessment reports; they reflect the subjective perception of the citizenry and/or the business community of different aspects of governance in a given country. Data are typically available from a variety of sources, ranging from political and business risk rating agencies and think tanks to international financial institutions and nongovernmental organizations.

The governance indices used in the empirical section are as follows:[12]

- The *ICRG corruption index* measures the degree to which special or illegal payments are expected and demanded at various levels of

---

[12]More detailed definitions of these indicators are provided in the Appendix. Kaufmann, Kraay, and Zoido-Lobatón (1999a) explain how they construct these aggregate governance indicators, using an unobserved components model. Their data are available via the Internet at www.worldbank.org/wbi/governance/datasets.htm. For a discussion of why such inherently subjective data are useful in measuring governance, see Kaufmann, Kraay, and Zoido-Lobatón (1999b, pp. 2–5). The authors also comment on the advantages and disadvantages of polls as opposed to surveys in obtaining such data.

government within each country.[13] We use annual data for the period 1984–98 (unlike Fisman and Gatti (2000), who only use data for 1982–90), from which we construct a single average for each country.

- Additional governance indices are available from Kaufmann, Kraay, and Zoido-Lobatón (1999a and 1999b). The authors organize governance data from different sources into six clusters corresponding to basic aspects of governance. Two of these, *graft* and *rule of law*, summarize the respect of citizens and the state for the institutions that govern their interactions. *Government effectiveness* and *regulatory burden*, on the other hand, include various indicators of the government's ability to formulate and implement sound policies. The final two indicators, *voice and accountability* and *political instability and violence*, measure the process by which those in authority are elected and replaced. Data are available for these indicators for 1997–98, from which a single average is constructed for each country.

Preliminary Findings

Preliminary statistical interpretations of the data are reported in Table 1. Simple correlations between the decentralization indicator (the share of subnational spending in total government expenditures) and selected governance indicators are presented in Figure 1. The two top panels show the correlation between the *ICRG* corruption index (in its original scale and after rescaling) and the decentralization indicator. Note that a higher score in the original *ICRG* index denotes less, not more, perceived corruption. The remaining panels show the correlations between the decentralization indicator and four of the governance indicators available from Kaufmann, Kraay and Zoido-Lobatón (1999a and 1999b): graft, voice and accountability, government effectiveness, and rule of law. These bivariate correlations provide prima facie evidence of a statistical association between governance and decentralization, as hypothesized above. More rigorous multivariate tests are presented in the following section.

---

[13]The *ICRG* index is available via the Internet at www.prsgroup.com. This is the main governance indicator used by Fisman and Gatti (2000), who rescale the index to take on values between zero (least corrupt) and one (most corrupt). In order to make our results comparable to theirs, we have performed the same rescaling.

Table 1. Descriptive Statistics

	Number of Observations	Mean	Standard Deviation	Minimum	Maximum
Governance indicators					
ICRG corruption index	76	0.36	0.21	0.00	0.79
Graft	79	0.31	0.95	−1.00	2.13
Government effectiveness	79	0.34	0.85	−1.13	2.03
Voice and accountability	79	0.48	0.86	−1.30	1.69
Rule of law	79	0.35	0.86	−1.22	2.00
Political instability and violence	79	0.28	0.82	−1.69	1.69
Regulatory burden	79	0.42	0.55	−1.47	1.21
Decentralization indicators					
Expenditure share	81	0.21	0.17	0.00	0.77
Vertical imbalances	78	0.35	0.23	0.02	0.96
Tax autonomy	78	0.45	0.21	0.02	0.85
Nontax autonomy	78	0.20	0.13	0.03	0.61
Other variables					
GDP per capita	79	7,492	6,171	438	21,573
Population (in millions)	80	48.54	156.27	0.19	1,114.24
Land area (in squared kilometers)	80	1,189,190	2,834,523	690	17,075,400
Gastil civil liberties index	77	3.21	1.60	1.00	6.45

Note: Sample averages using 1980 data until most recent (except for expshare, which uses earliest available expshare figure from 1970 onward).

IV. Main Findings

Testable Hypothesis

The association between fiscal decentralization and governance can be estimated by regressing the cross-section of the above-described governance indicators on a set of regressors of two types: a measure of fiscal decentralization and control variables. The basic equation to be estimated is as follows:

$$I_{ij} = \beta_{0j} + \beta_{1j}D_{ij} + \beta_{2j}C_{ij} + \epsilon_{ij}, \tag{1}$$

where I_{ij} denotes the *j*-th governance index, with $j = (1, \ldots, M)$, for the *i*-th country in the sample; D_{ij} denotes the fiscal decentralization indi-

Figure 1. Governance and Decentralization: Period Averages, 1980–98

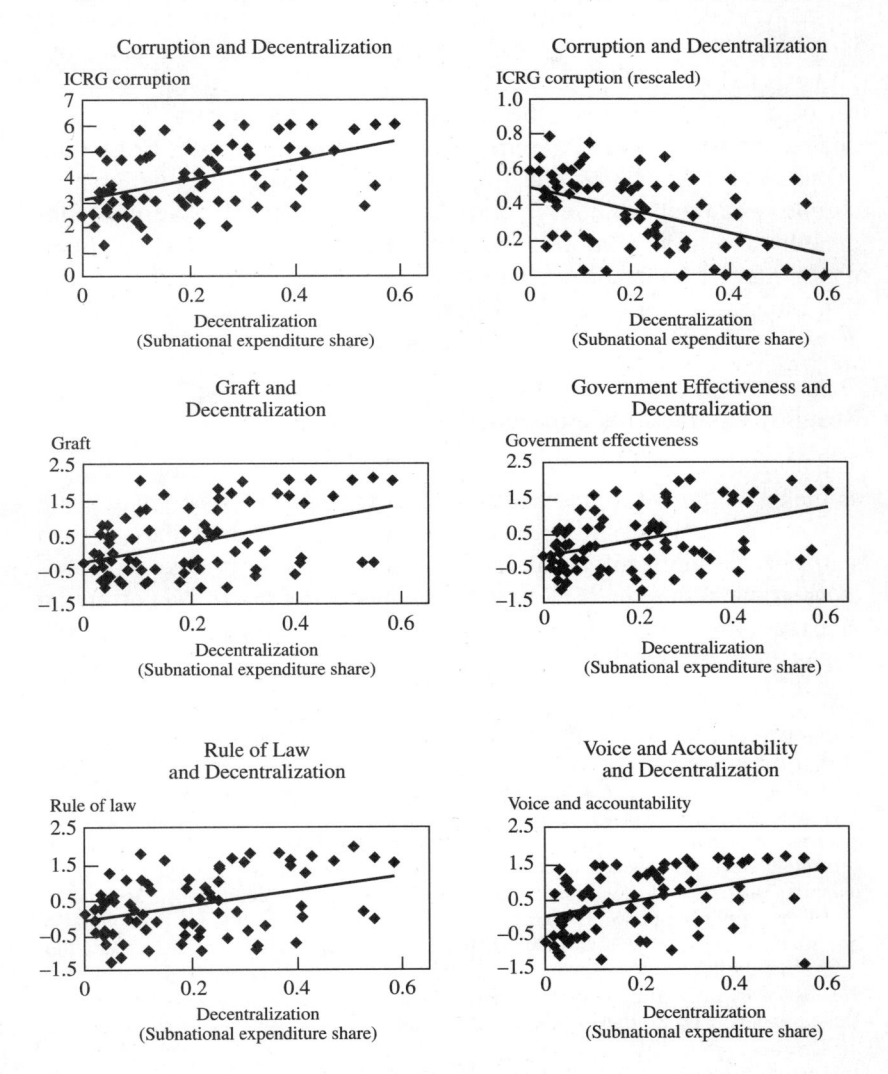

Corruption and Decentralization
ICRG corruption vs Decentralization (Subnational expenditure share)

Corruption and Decentralization
ICRG corruption (rescaled) vs Decentralization (Subnational expenditure share)

Graft and Decentralization
Graft vs Decentralization (Subnational expenditure share)

Government Effectiveness and Decentralization
Government effectiveness vs Decentralization (Subnational expenditure share)

Rule of Law and Decentralization
Rule of law vs Decentralization (Subnational expenditure share)

Voice and Accountability and Decentralization
Voice and accountability vs Decentralization (Subnational expenditure share)

Sources: IMF, *Government Finance Statistics Yearbook*; Political Risk Services Group, *International Country Risk Guide*; Kaufmann, Kraay, and Zoido-Lobatón (1999a and 1999b); and IMF staff calculations.

cator in country i when indicator j is used as the governance indicator; C_{ij} is a vector of control variables; and ϵ_{ij} is an error term. Equation (1) is estimated separately for each governance indicator. The basic hypothesis to be tested is whether $\beta_{1j} \neq 0$, for each j, in equation (1). The set of controls comprises the (logarithm of) GDP per capita in purchasing power parity (PPP) terms (period averages), and the (logarithm of) population.[14] The rationale for the use of these control variables is simple: wealthier societies tend to have better scores in governance indicators and to have more solid and mature institutions. Also, governance may be more difficult in more populous countries for reasons that range from regional disparities in income, climate, and ethnicity, as well as needs and preferences, among others.

Baseline Regressions and Sensitivity Analysis

The baseline regressions are reported in Table 2. Cross-sectional data for as many as 78 countries are used in the estimations.[15] The relationship between governance and decentralization is signed as hypothesized and statistically significant at classical levels for a number of governance indicators, including the *ICRG* corruption index. For the *ICRG* corruption index, a tobit estimation procedure was used due to the presence of limit

---

[14]Unlike Fisman and Gatti (2000), we exclude the civil liberties indicator from the baseline regressions because it is highly correlated with the decentralization indicator: countries that have better civil liberty scores also tend to be more decentralized. This correlation is likely to produce an upward bias in the parameter estimate of the decentralization indicator. Also, measures of civil liberties are included, by construction, in several governance indicators, such as voice and accountability. Likewise, indices of perceived corruption are used in the construction of the civil liberties indicator. It would therefore be inappropriate to include civil liberties as a right-hand-side variable in the regressions.

[15]Our sample comprises 22 member countries of the Organization for Economic Cooperation and Development (OECD) (Australia, Austria, Belgium, Canada, Denmark, Finland, France, Germany, Greece, Iceland, Ireland, Italy, Luxemburg, the Netherlands, New Zealand, Norway, Portugal, Spain, Sweden, Switzerland, the United Kingdom, and the United States); 13 transition economies (Albania, Azerbaijan, Belarus, Bulgaria, Croatia, the Czech Republic, Estonia, Hungary, Latvia, Lithuania, Poland, Romania, and Russia); 16 Latin American countries (Argentina, Bolivia, Brazil, Chile, Colombia, Costa Rica, the Dominican Republic, Ecuador, Guatemala, Mexico, Nicaragua, Panama, Paraguay, Peru, Trinidad and Tobago, and Uruguay); 12 African countries (Botswana, Burkina Faso, Ethiopia, The Gambia, Kenya, Malawi, Mauritius, South Africa, Swaziland, Uganda, Zambia, and Zimbabwe); 3 Middle Eastern and North African countries (Bahrain, Egypt, and Tunisia); 11 Asian countries (China, Fiji, India, Indonesia, the Islamic Republic of Iran, Malaysia, Papua New Guinea, the Philippines, Sri Lanka, Mongolia, and Thailand); as well as Israel.

observations for about 10 percent of the sample. This was not the case for the other governance indices, which were constructed so as to avoid observations at the limit of the scale. For these indices, the weighted OLS estimator was used. The weights were the relevant index's standard deviation for each country (as various sources were used in each country to construct the aggregate index). The weights place greater emphasis on the cases where different governance indices produce similar predictions. Our findings, however, are robust to other estimation techniques, including straight OLS, which produced very similar results. Note that when the (rescaled) *ICRG* index is used as the dependent variable, a negatively signed expenditure share indicator shows that more decentralization is associated with less, not more, perceived corruption. The finding that fiscal decentralization reduces corruption is in line with the evidence reported by Fisman and Gatti (2000), although our parameter estimates are slightly lower.[16]

When the other governance indicators are used as the dependent variables, the parameter estimates are also statistically significant, except for the indicators of regulatory burden and voice and accountability. The coefficients are nevertheless smaller in magnitude than in the case of the *ICRG* corruption index: a one-standard deviation increase in the decentralization indicator improves governance by 20 percent of a standard deviation, instead of approximately 40 percent in the case of the *ICRG* corruption indicator.

The baseline regressions include the (logarithm of) GDP per capita in PPP terms and the (logarithm of) population to control for income and size, as discussed earlier. Both variables are signed as expected. Income (population) is associated with better (worse) governance indicators. The results are robust to the inclusion of the Gastil index of civil liberties in the regressions, as in Fisman and Gatti (2000), in the case of both the *ICRG* corruption index and the graft indicator. The results

---

[16]Our sample is larger (even if we restrict attention to the 1980s and to the countries that report *GFS* data for the consolidated central government). Also, Fisman and Gatti (2000) use GDP and population data from the Summers-Heston Penn World dataset, which does not cover the late 1990s, thus excluding information on most transition countries. Instead, we use more updated data available from the World Bank's World Development Indicators (WDI). Incidentally, we experimented with including a dummy variable to identify the transition economies in the sample. The transition economy dummy tends to be significant, suggesting that these countries, controlling for all else, have worse governance outcomes. Nevertheless, the interaction of the transition country dummy and the decentralization indicator is not in general statistically significant.

Table 2. Expenditure Decentralization and Governance: Cross-Sectional Analysis, 1980–98

	Corruption	Graft	Government Effectiveness	Voice and Accountability	Rule of Law	Political Instability and Violence	Regulatory Burden
Expenditure share	−0.51***	1.14**	0.83*	0.94	0.74*	1.14**	−0.21
	(−3.60)	(2.24)	(2.02)	(1.54)	(1.70)	(2.46)	(−0.41)
Log of GDP per capita	−0.11***	0.58***	0.56***	0.55***	0.51***	0.43***	0.31***
	(−5.45)	(6.89)	(7.26)	(5.81)	(6.22)	(4.97)	(6.11)
Log of population	0.03***	−0.10**	−0.05	−0.06	−0.06	−0.06	0.00
	(2.73)	(−2.23)	(−1.32)	(−1.23)	(−1.34)	(−1.11)	(−0.10)
Fraction positive	0.92						
Log-likelihood	28.34						
Number of observations	75	78	78	78	78	78	78
Adjusted R^2		0.56	0.55	0.52	0.50	0.39	0.26
F-statistic		33.06	32.25	29.18	26.21	17.45	10.08
Estimator	Tobit	Weighted OLS	Weighted OLS	Weighted OLS	Weighted OLS	Weighted OLS	Weighted OLS

Sensitivity Analysis

Expshare w/ Gastil	−0.48***	0.86*	0.62	0.57	0.50	0.89*	−0.42
	(−3.46)	(2.00)	(1.41)	(1.02)	(1.18)	(1.68)	(−0.87)
Expshare w/ OECD dummy	−0.49***	0.91**	0.65*	0.87	0.53	1.02**	−0.31
	(−3.97)	(2.07)	(1.78)	(1.48)	(1.36)	(2.19)	(−0.62)
Expshare w/ democracy	−0.40***	0.61	0.31	1.22	0.15	0.58	−0.27
	(−2.88)	(1.13)	(0.66)	(0.26)	(0.29)	(0.92)	(−0.43)

Expshare w/ Protestant	−0.29**	0.40	0.48	0.91	0.41	0.97*	−0.37
	(−2.05)	(0.72)	(0.95)	(0.96)	(0.73)	(1.63)	(0.59)
Expshare w/ autonomy	−0.47***	0.48	−0.05	0.55	0.30	0.58	−0.76
	(−2.59)	(0.51)	(−0.07)	(0.73)	(0.31)	(0.83)	(−0.80)
Expshare w/ state constitution	−0.66***	1.37**	1.14*	1.67*	1.07	1.27	−0.39
	(−4.20)	(2.29)	(1.76)	(1.90)	(1.61)	(1.62)	(−0.70)
Expshare w/ state or local election	−0.52***	1.04*	0.83	1.00	0.74	0.86	−0.09
	(−3.40)	(1.85)	(1.64)	(1.36)	(1.36)	(1.41)	(−0.16)

Note: White's heteroscedastic-consistent t-statistics are in parentheses. ***, **, and * denote significance at the 1 percent, 5 percent, and 10 percent levels, respectively.

also hold, in general, when the equations are reestimated including the OECD country dummy to identify the countries in the sample that are most likely to have a better governance track record (Huther and Shah, 1998). Moreover, the parameter estimates, slightly lower in these regressions, are in general robust to the inclusion of variables capturing religious tradition and democracy.[17] These variables have been identified as important determinants of corruption.

Political decentralization may affect governance, particularly corruption, as discussed previously. The baseline parameter estimates are also robust to the inclusion of three indicators of political decentralization: (1) an indicator of whether state or local governments are locally elected;[18] (2) a dummy variable identifying the countries in the sample where subnational governments have significant authority over taxing, spending, and legislating; and (3) a dummy variable identifying the countries where the senate is appointed or elected through middle-tier constituencies (i.e., states and provinces), rather than on a national basis. It can be argued that subnational interests are reinforced when the constituencies of national legislators match those of subnational jurisdictions. These indicators are obtained from the political institutions data set constructed by Beck and others (2000). Moreover, the sensitivity analysis shows that the state or local election indicator is positively associated with political instability and violence, the subnational authority dummy is positively associated with graft and government effectiveness, and the senate election dummy is positively associated with corruption at classical levels.

Dealing with Reverse Causality

Parameter estimates may be biased due to reverse causality, as well as omitted variables. It can be argued that reverse causality is unlikely in

---

[17]The proportion of Protestants in a country's population is used to identify for religious traditions. Democracy is proxied by a dummy variable identifying the countries in the sample that have had democratic governments continuously since 1950. Both variables are available from Treisman (2000). Protestantism and democracy are both expected to be associated with less perceived corruption. Although not reported in Table 2, the coefficient of Protestantism and democracy are indeed associated with better governance in the relevant equations.

[18]The variable takes a value of zero, if neither the local executive nor the local legislature are locally elected; one, if the local executive is appointed, but the local legislature is elected; and two, if both the executive and the legislature are elected. Separate scores for local and middle-tier jurisdictions are averaged.

the estimation of equation (1) because decentralization and governance indicators have been constructed using data for different time periods. Earlier data were used to construct the decentralization averages, starting in the early 1980s, whereas the governance indicators have been constructed using data for 1997–98, with the exception of the *ICRG* corruption index.

Notwithstanding these considerations, we examined the possibility of reverse causality more thoroughly by reestimating the baseline regressions by two-stage least squares. The choice of adequate instruments for the decentralization indicator is far from settled in the literature. For instance, Fisman and Gatti (2000) use dummies identifying the countries' legal origins (British, French, Socialist, Germanic, or Scandinavian) as instruments for decentralization. This choice of instruments was motivated by La Porta and others (1999). The argument is that a country's political and social institutions determine governance outcomes and that these institutions can be inherited from colonial powers (Acemoglu, Johnson, and Robinson, 2000; and Treisman, 2000). In line with the literature, we also used these legal origin dummies as the instruments for decentralization and obtained consistent results.[19]

The results reported in Table 3 show that, in several cases, the coefficient of the decentralization indicator is still statistically significant and signed as expected, and greater in magnitude when instrumented by the legal origin dummies. Statistical significance of the decentralization indicators is nevertheless lost when equation (1) is estimated for the indicators of graft, government effectiveness, voice and accountability, and rule of law. We also experimented with other possible instruments, including the initial expenditure share for each country.

---

[19]Based on a later paper on corporate governance by Rajan and Zingales (1998), Fisman and Gatti (2000) argue that legal origin affects corruption primarily through its association with fiscal decentralization. The legal origin dummies performed well in the first-stage equations, which also included an intercept. The explanatory power of the first-stage regression is large, with an *R*-squared statistic of 0.25. Unlike the French origin dummy, most of the dummies were significant relative to the omitted British origin dummy. However, most countries in the sample have either French or British legal origin. When we tested for a direct impact of these instruments on corruption, in a regression that also included the expenditure share indicator as an explanatory variable, we found, as expected, that most dummies were not statistically significant, except for the Scandinavian legal origin dummy. See Treisman (2000) for a detailed discussion on the association between legal origin, colonial heritage, and corruption.

Table 3. Instrumental Expenditure Decentralization and Governance: Cross-Sectional Analysis, 1980–98

	Corruption		Graft		Government Effectiveness		Voice and Accountability		Rule of Law		Political Instability and Violence		Regulatory Burden	
	Legal origin	Initial expenditure share	Legal origin	Initial expenditure share	Legal origin	Initial expenditure share	Legal origin	Initial expenditure share	Legal origin	Initial expenditure share	Legal origin	Initial expenditure share	Legal origin	Initial expenditure share
Expenditure share	−0.57*** (−2.77)	−0.51*** (−4.81)	1.04 (1.15)	1.56*** (2.97)	0.20 (0.24)	1.08** (2.46)	0.56 (0.68)	0.84 (1.34)	1.08 (1.38)	0.97** (2.10)	1.49* (2.02)	1.36*** (2.85)	−1.28* (−1.69)	−0.07 (−0.14)
Log of GDP per capita	−0.10*** (−4.25)	−0.10*** (−5.54)	0.59*** (5.99)	0.55*** (6.53)	0.61*** (6.58)	0.54*** (7.16)	0.58*** (5.78)	0.56*** (6.00)	0.48*** (5.12)	0.49*** (6.18)	0.40*** (4.06)	0.41*** (4.89)	0.39*** (5.79)	0.30*** (6.22)
Log of population	0.03*** (3.09)	0.03*** (3.46)	−0.09* (−1.86)	−0.11** (−2.60)	−0.03 (−0.61)	−0.06 (−1.57)	−0.05 (−0.90)	−0.06 (−1.16)	−0.07 (−1.53)	−0.07 (−1.58)	−0.08 (−1.34)	−0.07 (−1.32)	0.04 (0.72)	−0.01 (−0.22)
Number of observations	75	75	78	78	78	78	78	78	78	78	78	78	78	78
Adjusted R^2	0.53	0.53	0.56	0.55	0.54	0.55	0.52	0.52	0.49	0.49	0.39	0.39	0.21	0.26
First-stage R^2 without controls	0.22	0.78	0.22	0.78	0.22	0.78	0.22	0.78	0.22	0.78	0.22	0.78	0.22	0.78
First-stage R^2 with controls	0.57	0.89	0.57	0.89	0.57	0.89	0.57	0.89	0.57	0.89	0.57	0.89	0.57	0.89
Sargan's P	0.17	0.00	9.14	0.00	4.52	0.00	1.16	0.00	4.51	0.00	1.61	0.00	1.17	0.00
E'PZ*E														

Note: White's heteroscedastic-consistent t-statistics are in parentheses. ***, **, and * denote significance at the 1 percent, 5 percent, and 10 percent levels, respectively. For corruption, the first-stage regressions have four additional observations.

The results are reported in Table 3.[20] Moreover, we experimented with the country's land area as an alternative instrument for decentralization, in the belief that it would be positively associated with decentralization, for geographical reasons that might affect communications and logistics. The results compare poorly with those obtained when the legal origin dummies are used as instruments for decentralization, and were therefore omitted.[21]

V. Decentralization and Subnational Revenue Mobilization

Revenue Mobilization Capacity

It has often been argued that governance is affected not only by fiscal decentralization but also by how subnational expenditures are financed. The key argument is that, as discussed earlier, a closer match between local expenditures and revenue mobilization is likely to improve accountability (Ter-Minassian, 1997; and de Mello, 1999 and 2000a). To test the hypothesis that subnational revenue mobilization affects the association between decentralization and governance, we created three separate expenditure share indicators depending on their financing sources: tax revenues, nontax revenues, and grants and transfers from higher levels of government.

Equation (1) was redefined as:

$$I_{ij} = \beta_{0j} + \Sigma_k \beta_{1jk}(D_{ij} * R_{ijk}) + \beta_{2j}C_{ij} + \epsilon_{ij}, \tag{2}$$

---

[20]It may be argued that the initial expenditure share is not a good instrument for current decentralization because decentralization indicators tend to exhibit little variation over time. In this case, the difference between current and initial values of decentralization may be too small. Because of the limited within-country variation in the data, we did not proceed to estimate the equations as a panel.

[21]In the first-stage regression, the association between land area and expenditure share is statistically significant and correctly signed, and the R-squared statistic is about 0.15. The explanatory power of land area remains significant even after we control for GDP per capita and population. However, in the second-stage regression, the instrumented expenditure share loses significance. Panizza (1999) finds that a country's land area is significantly correlated with decentralization, even after controlling for other determinants of decentralization, such as ethnic fractionalization and indices of democracy. The association between decentralization and democracy and ethnic fractionalization is nevertheless not robust to different sample sizes.

Table 4. Financing Source Decentralization and Governance: Cross-Sectional Analysis, 1980–98

	Corruption		Graft		Government Effectiveness		Voice and Accountability		Rule of Law		Political Instability and Violence		Regulatory Burden	
Expshare * vertical imbalance	−0.69** (−2.17)	−0.54* (−1.90)	0.32 (0.27)	1.75 (1.30)	1.00 (0.95)	1.77 (1.52)	1.36 (1.33)	0.99 (0.67)	0.29 (0.25)	1.03 (0.68)	0.54 (0.40)	0.08 (0.06)	−0.24 (−0.20)
Expshare * tax autonomy	−0.19 (−0.76)	−0.37 (−1.58)	0.10 (0.12)	−0.60 (−0.44)	0.15 (0.15)	−0.84 (−0.68)	−0.39 (−0.34)	−0.49 (−0.39)	0.15 (0.19)	0.79 (0.65)	1.24 (1.26)	−1.81 (−1.40)	−1.54 (−1.27)
Expshare * nontax autonomy	−1.54* (−1.92)	−0.77 (−1.04)	10.86** (2.05)	5.97* (1.80)	6.03 (0.94)	1.76 (0.36)	5.80 (1.07)	3.44 (0.72)	7.02 (1.61)	2.93 (1.20)	4.19 (0.98)	1.53 (0.48)	6.66 (1.20)	4.97 (0.96)
Log of GDP per capita	−0.11*** (−5.16)	−0.03 (−1.16)	0.56*** (5.62)	0.15* (1.76)	0.55*** (5.37)	0.18* (1.83)	0.56*** (5.11)	0.33** (2.63)	0.48*** (4.75)	0.11 (0.84)	0.42*** (4.11)	0.17 (1.18)	0.27*** (3.69)	0.14 (1.62)
Log of population	0.04*** (3.37)	0.04*** (3.44)	−0.13*** (−3.03)	−0.12*** (−3.30)	−0.08* (−1.77)	−0.06* (−1.71)	−0.08* (−1.74)	−0.08 (−1.66)	−0.08 (−1.64)	−0.07* (−1.87)	−0.08 (−1.34)	−0.08 (−1.31)	−0.01 (−0.19)	−0.01 (−0.13)
OECD dummy		−0.24*** (−4.16)		1.32*** (6.01)		1.16*** (5.00)		0.68*** (3.06)		1.23*** (4.54)		0.78** (2.51)		0.44** (2.30)
Fraction positive	0.91	0.91												
Log-likelihood	25.97	33.80												
Number of observations	66	66	69	69	69	69	69	69	69	69	69	69	69	69
Adjusted R^2			0.63	0.77	0.58	0.71	0.60	0.64	0.50	0.65	0.38	0.43	0.28	0.31
F-statistic	23.93	38.00	19.90	28.34	21.15	21.33	14.84	22.30	9.26	9.59	6.34	6.20

Note: White's heteroscedastic-consistent t-statistics are in parentheses. ***, **, and * denote significance at the 1 percent, 5 percent, and 10 percent levels, respectively.

where I_{ij} denotes the j-th governance indicator for the i-th country in the sample; D_{ij} is the fiscal decentralization indicator; R_{ijk} denotes the k-th revenue mobilization indicator, for $k = (1, \ldots, N)$; C_{ij} is a vector of control variables; and ϵ_{ij} is an error term. The basic hypothesis to be tested is $\beta_{1jk} \neq 0$, for each j and at least one k.

The revenue mobilization indicators are (1) the tax autonomy indicator, defined as the share of local governments' own tax revenues in total subnational revenues; (2) the vertical imbalance indicator, defined as the share of grants and transfers from the central government in total subnational revenues; and (3) the nontax autonomy indicator, defined as the share of nontax revenues in total subnational revenues. The results of the estimation of equation (2) for each separate governance indicator are reported in Table 4.[22] In general, some parameter estimates tend to be statistically significant when the *ICRG* corruption and graft indices are used as the dependent variables, even after controlling for OECD membership.

When the *ICRG* corruption index is used as the dependent variable, we find that governance is improved by increasing the share of subnational expenditures financed through grants and transfers from higher levels of government and nontaxes. For the indicator of graft, subnational expenditures financed through nontax revenues have a statistically significant association with governance, even after controlling for OECD membership. These results are consistent with the literature in that the mobilization of nontax revenues at the subnational level—primarily via user charges—is associated with better governance (Humplick and Estache, 1995).

Does the Level of Decentralization Matter?

Expenditure decentralization financed through subnational tax revenues does not seem to affect governance strongly. This is surprising

---

[22]We started by including the revenue mobilization indicators in the estimating equation one by one, without controlling for the level of subnational expenditures, and found that these indicators do not seem to have an impact on governance. The findings are robust, however, to the inclusion of the expenditure share indicator in the regressions, together with the tax revenue mobilization indicator (except when the indices of graft and voice and accountability are used as the dependent variables), and the nontax revenue mobilization indicator. These results suggest that subnational nontax revenue is positively associated with better governance, as expected. The empirical results, not reported to economize on space, are available on request.

because taxes are the main source of subnational revenues in the sample, with a mean share in total subnational revenues of 45 percent, relative to 20 percent for nontax revenues. Moreover, we argue that the impact of subnational revenue mobilization on governance depends on the country's level of decentralization.[23] To this end, we experimented with including the revenue mobilization and decentralization indicators as interaction terms in the estimating equation. In this case, for instance, the interaction of the expenditure share indicator with the local financing ratio, defined as the share of tax and nontax revenues in total subnational revenues, is included together with the local financing ratio and the expenditure share indicator as separate regressors.[24] The results are reported in equation (3):

$$I_i = -4.32 + 5.77 D_i - 6.67(D_i * R_i) + 1.27 R_i$$
$$(-3.43) \quad (2.97) \quad (-2.20) \quad\quad (2.10)$$

$$+ 0.61 \ln(GDP/pop)_i - 0.10 \ln(pop)_i \quad\quad (3)$$
$$(6.98) \quad\quad (-2.34)$$

where I_i is the graft index for country i, D_i is the subnational expenditure share in country i, and R_i is the local financing ratio (taxes and nontaxes combined) in country i. The numbers in parentheses are t-statistics. All coefficients are significant at the 5 percent level or higher.[25] Equation (3) shows that the interaction term is statistically significant, as well as the direct effect of local financing and the coefficient of the

---

[23]Stein (1998), in a different context, also makes the argument that the coefficient on the revenue source should not be of the same magnitude and significance at different levels of local expenditure.

[24]In this case, equation (1) was reestimated as follows: $I_{ij} = \beta_{0j} + \beta_{1j}D_{ij} + \beta_{2j}(D_{ij} * R_{ij}) + \beta_{3j}R_{ij} + \beta_{4j}C_{ij} + \epsilon_{ij}$, where I_{ij} denotes the governance indicator, as before; D_{ij} is the fiscal decentralization indicator; R_{ij} is the revenue mobilization indicator; C_{ij} is a vector of control variables; and ϵ_{ij} is an error term. The basic hypotheses to be tested are $\beta_{1j} \neq 0$, $\beta_{2j} \neq 0$, and $\beta_{3j} \neq 0$, for each j. The results of the estimation of this equation are available upon request.

[25]Seventy-three observations were used in this regression, and the F-statistic for zero slopes is 20.31. The results using the government effectiveness index as the dependent variable are similar in magnitude and statistical significance. For the *ICRG* corruption index, the expenditure share and the interaction term are still significant, but the coefficient of the separate local financing ratio is not. For the other governance indices, the results are also not significant for this variable, or even its interaction with the expenditure share.

expenditure share indicator.[26] Nevertheless, the interaction term is negatively signed, suggesting that governance deteriorates through decentralization when subnational revenue mobilization is high.[27] The turning point for the decentralization indicator is 19 percent (1.27 divided by 6.67), which is close to the sample mean of 21 percent. In other words, governance deteriorates when further subnational revenue mobilization is pursued in the course of decentralization in countries where subnational governments already account for more than 19 percent of total government spending. This may be primarily due to lack of accountability, or weak capacity at the local level, or both. By corollary, subnational revenue mobilization is associated with improved governance for those countries with smaller subnational governments, which comprise most of the developing countries in the sample.[28] The results also show that expenditure decentralization remains positively associated with governance, unless local revenue mobilization is extremely high, at 87 percent (5.77 divided by 6.67) or higher. These levels of decentralization are not common in a sample of countries where the mean local financing ratio is 65 percent and the standard deviation 22 percent.

More on the Level of Decentralization

To further examine the relationship between governance and decentralization, we broke down the expenditure share indicator into quartiles and tested for possible nonlinearities in the relationship between decentralization and governance. To this end, dummy variables were constructed to identify each separate quartile in the cross-country distribution of expenditure shares.

Equation (1) was redefined as:

$$I_{ij} = \beta_{0j} + \Sigma_q \beta_{1jq}(D_{ij} * Q_{ijq}) + \beta_{2j}C_{ij} + \epsilon_{ij}, \tag{4}$$

---

[26]Tax and nontax revenues were combined in a single local financing variable. When these terms, as well as their interactions with the expenditure share, were included separately in the estimating equation, the results were found to be less promising, especially for the nontax autonomy indicator.

[27]We also performed an F-test of joint significance for the expenditure share and the interaction term, and could not accept the hypothesis that they are jointly equal to zero.

[28]Some of these findings are not robust to the inclusion of the OECD country dummy.

where, as above, I_{ij} denotes the governance indicator, D_{ij} is the fiscal decentralization indicator, Q_{ijq} denotes the q-th quartile dummy with $q = (1, \ldots, Z - 1)$, C_{ij} is a vector of control variables, and ϵ_{ij} is an error term.[29]

The hypothesis to be tested is that a minimum level of decentralization is needed for governance to improve. In other words, the basic hypothesis to be tested is $\beta_{1jq} \neq 0$, for each j and at least one q included in the regression.

The results reported in Table 5 show that only the highest quartile is statistically significant, even when the OECD country dummy is included in the estimating equation. This is suggestive that decentralization is associated with improved governance only at relatively high levels of expenditure decentralization. For the *ICRG* corruption index, we find that the coefficient of the highest quartile is statistically significant, whereas, for the remaining governance indicators, none of the coefficients on the expenditure quartiles is statistically significant.[30]

Discussion

To summarize these ideas, the empirical findings reported above show that governance is improved when subnational spending is financed by mobilizing nontax revenues. This is not controversial. However, the weak correlation between governance and the mobilization of tax revenues to finance subnational spending is surprising, given that the share of tax revenues in total subnational revenues is more than double that of nontax revenues. We also find that governance is improved if subnational spending levels are very high.

These findings imply that expenditures should not be decentralized regardless of subnational revenue mobilization capacity and effort. This is in line with the literature, which recommends avoiding a mismatch between subnational revenues and expenditures in the course of decentralization (Tanzi, 1995; Prud'homme, 1995; Ter-Minassian, 1997; Bahl, 1999; and de Mello, 2000a). We show that governance deteriorates when subnational revenue mobilization is pursued in countries where subnational governments already account for more

---

[29]The dummy omitted in the estimation of equation (4) was that identifying the lowest quartile in the distribution of expenditure shares in the sample.

[30]These coefficients are significant, however, for a subsample that excluded the 15 countries for which only budgetary central government expenditures were available.

Table 5. Nonlinear Decentralization Effect and Governance: Cross-Sectional Analysis, 1980-98

	Corruption		Graft		Government Effectiveness		Voice and Accountability		Rule of Law		Political Instability and Violence		Regulatory Burden	
Second-quartile expenditure share	0.01	(0.17)	−0.08	(−0.39)	−0.03	(−0.17)	0.05	(0.30)	0.13	(0.60)	0.21	(0.93)	−0.02	(−0.08)	0.07	(0.29)	0.12	(0.48)	0.06	(0.33)	0.08	(0.46)
Third-quartile expenditure share	−0.05	(−0.81)	−0.08	(−1.64)	0.03	(0.14)	0.06	(0.28)	0.14	(0.71)	0.16	(0.64)	0.24	(0.96)	−0.03	(−0.16)	0.17	(0.69)	0.22	(0.86)	−0.03	(−0.13)	−0.01	(−0.05)
Fourth-quartile expenditure share	−0.14**	(−2.19)	−0.15***	(−2.78)	0.21	(0.81)	0.26	(1.19)	0.17	(0.69)	0.22	(1.09)	0.30	(0.97)	0.36	(1.29)	0.08	(0.31)	0.13	(0.64)	0.27	(0.96)	0.30	(1.15)	−0.13	(−0.45)	−0.13	(−0.49)
Log of GDP per capita	−0.12***	(−5.69)	−0.03	(−1.04)	0.64***	(7.33)	0.21**	(2.40)	0.60***	(7.38)	0.21**	(2.18)	0.57***	(5.67)	0.31**	(2.50)	0.57***	(6.84)	0.18*	(1.68)	0.46***	(5.24)	0.21	(1.64)	0.32***	(4.85)	0.18*	(1.79)
Log of population	0.02*	(1.82)	0.02**	(2.16)	−0.07*	(−1.67)	−0.08**	(−2.33)	−0.04	(−0.87)	−0.04	(−1.31)	−0.05	(−0.97)	−0.06	(−1.22)	−0.04	(−0.78)	−0.05	(−1.48)	−0.04	(−0.76)	−0.05	(−0.99)	0.00	(−0.00)	0.00	(−0.09)
OECD dummy			−0.25***	(−4.86)			1.22***	(5.43)			1.05***	(5.29)			0.68**	(2.99)			1.09***	(5.04)			0.69**	(2.68)			0.41**	(2.22)
Fraction positive	0.93		0.93																					
Log-likelihood	27.53		37.88																					
Number of observations	74		74		78		78		78		78		78		78		78		78		78		78		78		78
Adjusted R^2	0.54		0.69		0.53		0.66		0.50		0.55		0.48		0.63		0.35		0.41		0.25		0.29
F-statistic	19.12		29.69		18.15		26.02		16.42		16.84		15.10		22.80		9.40		9.82		6.16		6.28

Note: White's heteroscedastic-consistent t-statistics are in parentheses. ***, **, and * denote significance at the 1 percent, 5 percent, and 10 percent levels, respectively.

than 19 percent of total government spending. The estimated ratio is close to the sample mean of 21 percent. The finding implies that, if a country is already beyond this critical level, further expenditure decentralization should be financed through nontax revenue mobilization and/or greater reliance on grants and transfers from higher levels of government, rather than increased decentralization of tax bases.

We venture three explanations for the estimated association between subnational revenue mobilization and governance.

- These findings may suggest that the countries in the sample have already reached the optimal level of tax base decentralization. To explore this line of argument fully, information would be needed on measures of optimality in the allocation of tax bases to subnational governments and tax compliance at the subnational level. Unfortunately, the former is not measurable and the latter is not readily available. In any case, the argument is as follows. Mobile tax bases are best managed by higher levels of government due to the possibility of tax exportation, factor mobility, and economies of scale, among others. In principle, these tax bases should not be assigned to subnational governments.[31] If the tax bases that are best managed by subnational governments have already been assigned to them—as in the likely case of countries where subnational tax autonomy ratios are already high—further decentralization of tax bases to finance subnational expenditures may lead to allocative inefficiencies, which may in turn worsen governance scores.[32]

- Alternatively, subnational governments may face soft budget constraints. In this case, governance may deteriorate because of the mismatch between subnational governments' expenditure functions and revenue-raising capacity. Because of this mismatch, subnational spending may rise regardless of the tax autonomy facing subnational jurisdictions. Consequently, further decentralization of tax bases may weaken governance, not because of the extent of

---

[31]See de Mello (2000a), for further information.

[32]Unfortunately, it is not possible to ascertain whether subnational tax autonomy is low because tax bases are not assigned to subnational governments or, alternatively, whether subnational governments do not fully exploit the tax bases that are assigned to them. Tax autonomy may be low at the subnational level due to noncompliance, for example, rather than lack of tax bases.

expenditure decentralization per se, but due to the lack of hard budget constraints at the subnational level.[33]

- Another possible explanation for the weak correlation between governance and decentralization financed through subnational tax revenue mobilization is the political capture of local government by interest groups. A possible argument is that local elites may not fully exploit local tax bases to reduce their own tax burden, particularly when subnational governments face soft budget constraints, as discussed above. Alternatively, as suggested by Bardhan and Mookherjee (1998), local elites may increase the local tax burden on the middle class to finance the projects that benefit them (the local elites) more. The possibility of local capture supports the introduction of user charges, and nontax revenue mobilization in general, rather than general local taxation, to finance subnational government spending.

Against this background, we tested the hypothesis that governance can be improved not only as a result of fiscal decentralization but also due to political decentralization, to the extent that local officials are elected, rather than centrally appointed. The argument is that political decentralization, proxied by local elections, may provide the checks and balances needed to avoid, or at least reduce, local capture in the context of fiscal decentralization. We used the local or municipal elections variable obtained from Beck and others (2000) interacted with the expenditure share indicator. The results were not found to be robust to the different governance indicators. However, we did find a positive association between local elections and governance for the sample of developing countries. The weak results may be due to the difficulty in assessing the degree of decision-making autonomy enjoyed by local governments, which is not captured by the local or municipal elections variable.

VI. Conclusions and Policy Implications

This paper sought to shed more light on the relationship between fiscal decentralization and governance. The empirical evidence provided for a sample of both developing and developed economies suggests

---

[33]Testing this hypothesis empirically is not an easy task because the data sets used in this paper do not allow for a qualitative assessment of the budget constraints facing subnational governments.

that, despite data inadequacies and methodological limitations, governance can be enhanced through the decentralization of expenditure functions to subnational governments. Moreover, the higher the share of subnational spending in total government expenditures, the stronger the positive association between decentralization and governance. The results are in general robust to the inclusion of standard controls and a number of widely used governance indicators.

We have shown that governance is affected not only by fiscal decentralization but also by how subnational expenditures are financed. This is a considerable improvement on the previous studies in the literature, which focus almost exclusively on political and/or expenditure-based indicators of decentralization. The empirical results show that

- For any level of fiscal decentralization, the higher the share of nontax revenues and grants and transfers from higher levels of government in total subnational revenue, the stronger the association between decentralization and governance.

- For a broader measure of subnational revenue mobilization that includes tax and nontax revenues, the level of expenditure decentralization affects the association between governance and revenue mobilization. In countries where subnational governments are large, governance may worsen when local tax revenue mobilization is pursued in the course of decentralization. Further decentralization of tax bases may therefore lead to allocative inefficiencies and hence poorer governance. This may be due to, among other things, soft budget constraints at the subnational level.

With regard to policy recommendations, the empirical evidence reported in this paper underscores the need for caution in the use of decentralization as a tool for improving governance. For decentralization to be a catalyst for improved governance and accountability in government, appropriate economic and political institutions are needed to insulate the decentralization process from excessive capture of the benefits of government provision by local, rather than national, elites, and to ensure that subnational governments operate under hard budget constraints. The possibility of local capture supports greater reliance on nontaxes and grants and transfer from higher levels of government to finance subnational spending, rather than local tax revenue mobilization. Moreover, limited capacity at the subnational level may impose constraints on the ability of the government to extract information on local preferences and needs and, therefore, to provide local goods and services efficiently and adequately. Furthermore, allocative inefficiencies may result from the suboptimal allocation of tax bases to subnational governments to finance decentralized provision.

Cognizant of the need for caution in implementing decentralization programs, several PRSPs have highlighted preconditions for successful decentralization in terms of (1) strengthening managerial, administrative, and supervisory capacity at the local level; (2) establishing sustained partnership within the government and with decentralized administrations; (3) encouraging pragmatism and gradualism to allow the communities to organize themselves and to respond to local expectations; and (4) fostering citizen participation through civil society organizations in local development, not only in the formulation of objectives and choice of means but also in execution and supervision of actions undertaken.

The empirical results reported above also warrant, albeit indirectly, a word of caution on the appropriate sequencing of reform in countries where fiscal decentralization is to be used as a policy instrument for improving governance. Because improvements in governance take time to mature, fiscal decentralization should not be used as a catalyst for improving governance in the short term. Moreover, fiscal decentralization affects governance through different revenue mobilization instruments. In this case, institutional capacity should be built in subnational jurisdictions to allow them to fully exploit the tax bases and nontax instruments that they are best equipped to manage and administer. Capacity should also be built in the areas of tax administration, as well as budget preparation, execution, and supervision, so that local government officials can handle the increased volume of resources assigned and/or devolved to them through decentralization and are faced with hard budget constraints. In the course of political, rather than fiscal, decentralization, citizen participation should be encouraged through civil society organizations, not only in formulating objectives and choosing means but also in executing and supervising government actions.

Appendix

Governance Indices: Additional Information

The ICRG corruption index measures corruption within the political system. It is argued that this type of corruption distorts the economic and financial environment, reduces the efficiency of government and business by enabling people to assume positions of power through patronage rather than ability, and introduces inherent instability in the political system. The most common form of corruption met directly by business is financial corruption in the form of demands for bribes connected with import and export licenses, exchange controls, tax assessments, and police protection. This measure is also concerned with actual or potential corruption in the form of patronage, nepotism, job reservation, "favor-for-favor," secret party funding, and suspiciously close ties between politics and business.

With regard to the other governance indicators used in the empirical section, the following definitions are taken from Kaufmann, Kraay, and Zoido-Lobatón (1999b, pp. 7–8):

- "Graft" measures the perception of corruption, generally defined as the exercise of public power for private gain. The particular aspect of corruption measured by the various data sources included in the construction of the index ranges from the frequency of additional payments to "get things done" to the effects of corruption on the business environment.

- "Rule of law" includes several indicators measuring the extent to which agents have confidence in, and abide by, the rules of society. The index is constructed using information on the perceived incidence of both violent and nonviolent crime, the effectiveness and predictability of the judiciary, and the enforceability of contracts.

- "Government effectiveness" combines perception of the quality of public service provision, the quality of the bureaucracy, the competence of civil servants, the independence of the civil service from political pressures, and the credibility of the government's commitment to policies.

- "Regulatory burden" includes measures of the incidence of market-unfriendly policies, such as price controls or inadequate bank supervision, as well as perception of the burdens imposed by excessive regulation in several areas, such as foreign trade and business development, among others.

- "Voice and accountability" is composed of several measures relating to the political process, civil liberties, and political rights. The index is constructed using information on the extent to which citizens of a country are able to participate in the selection of governments, and various measures of the independence of the media.

- "Political instability and violence" combines several indicators measuring perception of the likelihood that the government in power will be destabilized or overthrown by possibly unconstitutional or violent means.

References

Acemoglu, Daron, Simon Johnson, and James A. Robinson, 2000, "The Colonial Origins of Comparative Development: An Empirical Investigation," NBER Working Paper No. 7771 (Cambridge, Massachusetts: National Bureau of Economic Research).

Bahl, Roy, 1999, "Fiscal Decentralization as Development Policy," *Public Budgeting and Finance*, Vol. 19 (Summer), pp. 59–75.

Bardhan, Pranab, and Dilip Mookherjee, 1998, "Expenditure Decentralization and the Delivery of Public Services in Developing Countries," CIDER Working Paper No. C98-104 (Berkeley: Center for International and Development Economics Research, University of California).

Barenstein, Jorge, 1994, "The Fiscal Misery of Local Government in Bangladesh: Some Reflections and a Book Review," *Journal of Social Studies,* Vol. 66 (October), pp. 97–105.

———, 2000, "Local Governance and Civil Society in the 1990s: A Rapid Empirical Probe in Bangladesh," *Bangladesh National Institutional Review* (BNIR) (Washington: World Bank).

Beck, Thorsten, and others, 2000, "New Tools and New Tests in Comparative Political Economy: The Database of Political Institutions," World Bank Policy Research Working Paper No. 2283 (Washington: World Bank).

Blanchard, Olivier, and Andrei Shleifer, 2000, "Federalism With and Without Political Centralization: China Versus Russia," NBER Working Paper No. 7616 (Cambridge, Massachusetts: National Bureau of Economic Research).

Breton, Albert, 1996, *Competitive Governments: An Economic Theory of Politics and Public Finance* (Cambridge, England; New York: Cambridge University Press).

de Mello, Jr., Luiz R., 1999, "Intergovernmental Fiscal Relations Coordination Failures and Fiscal Outcomes," *Public Budgeting and Finance*, Vol. 19 (Spring), pp. 3–25.

———, 2000a, "Fiscal Decentralization and Intergovernmental Fiscal Relations: A Cross-Country Analysis," *World Development,* Vol. 28 (February), pp. 365–80.

———, 2000b, "Can Fiscal Decentralization Strengthen Social Capital?" IMF Working Paper No. 00/129 (Washington: International Monetary Fund).

———, 2001, "Fiscal Federalism and Government Size in the Transition Economies: The Case of Moldova," *Journal of International Development*, Vol. 13 (March), pp. 255–68.

———, and Randa Sab, 2000, "Government Spending, Rights, and Civil Liberties," IMF Working Paper No. 00/205 (Washington: International Monetary Fund).

Elazar, Daniel J., 1995, "From Statism to Federalism: A Paradigm Shift," *Publius*, Vol. 25 (Spring), pp. 5–18.

Fisman, Raymond, and Roberta Gatti, 2000, "Decentralization and Corruption: Evidence Across Countries." World Bank Policy Research Working Paper No. 2290 (Washington: World Bank).

Fukasaku, Kiichiro, and Luiz R. de Mello, 1998, "Fiscal Decentralisation and Macroeconomic Stability: The Experience of Large Developing and Transition Economies," in *Democracy, Decentralisation and Deficits in Latin America*, ed. by Kiichiro Fukasaku and Ricardo Hausmann (Paris: Inter-American Development Bank and Development Center of the Organization for Economic Cooperation and Development).

———, eds., 1999, *Fiscal Decentralisation in Emerging Economies: Governance Issues* (Paris: Inter-American Development Bank and Development Center of the Organization for Economic Cooperation and Development).

Galasso, Emanuela, and Martin Ravallion, 2000, "Distributional Outcomes of a Decentralized Welfare Program," World Bank Policy Research Working Paper No. 2316 (Washington: World Bank).

Hommes, Rudolf, 1995, "Conflicts and Dilemmas of Decentralization," paper prepared for the World Bank's Annual Bank Conference on Development Economics, Washington, May.

Humplick, Frannie, and Antonio Estache, 1995, "Does Decentralization Improve Infrastructure Performance?" in *Decentralizing Infrastructure: Advantages and Limitations*, World Bank Discussion Paper Series, No. 290, ed. by Antonio Estache (Washington: World Bank).

Huther, Jeff, and Anwar Shah, 1998, "Applying a Simple Measure of Good Governance to the Debate on Fiscal Decentralization," World Bank Policy Research Working Paper No. 1894 (Washington: World Bank).

Inman, Robert P., and Daniel L. Rubinfeld, 1997, "Rethinking Federalism," *Journal of Economic Perspectives*, Vol. 11, No. 4 (Fall), pp. 43–64.

Inter-American Development Bank, 1997, "Estabilidad Fiscal con Democracia y Descentralización?" in *Informe Progreso Económico y Social 1997: América Latina tras una Década de Reformas* (Washington).

International Monetary Fund, *Government Finance Statistics Yearbook* (Washington, various issues).

———, 1986, *A Manual on Government Finance Statistics* (Washington).

Isham, Jonathan, Daniel Kaufmann, and Lant H. Pritchett, 1997, "Civil Liberties, Democracy, and the Performance of Government Projects," *World Bank Economic Review*, Vol. 11 (May), pp. 219–42.

Kaufmann, Daniel, Aart Kraay, and Pablo Zoido-Lobatón, 1999a, "Aggregating Governance Indicators," World Bank Policy Research Working Paper No. 2195 (Washington: World Bank).

———, 1999b, "Governance Matters," World Bank Policy Research Working Paper No. 2196 (Washington: World Bank).

La Porta, Rafael, and others, 1999, "The Quality of Government," *Journal of Law, Economics, and Organization*, Vol. 15 (April), pp. 222–79.

Messick, Richard E., ed., 1996, *World Survey of Economic Freedom, 1995–1996: A Freedom House Study* (New Brunswick, New Jersey: Transaction Publishers).

Oates, Wallace, 1999, "An Essay on Fiscal Federalism," *Journal of Economic Literature*, Vol. 37 (September), pp. 1120–49.

Panizza, Ugo, 1999, "On the Determinants of Fiscal Centralization: Theory and Evidence," *Journal of Public Economics*, Vol. 74 (October), pp. 97–139.

Parker, Andrew N., 1995, "Decentralization: The Way Forward for Rural Development?" World Bank Policy Research Working Paper No. 1475 (Washington: World Bank).

Pritchett, Lant, and Daniel Kaufmann, 1998, "Civil Liberties, Democracy, and the Performance of Government Projects," *Finance & Development* (March), pp. 26–29.

Prud'homme, Rémy, 1995, "Dangers of Decentralization," *World Bank Research Observer*, Vol. 10 (August), pp. 201–10.

Rajan, Raghuram G., and Luigi Zingales, 1998, "Financial Dependence and Growth," *American Economic Review*, Vol. 88 (June), pp. 559–86.

Seabright, Paul, 1996, "Accountability and Decentralisation in Government: An Incomplete Contracts Model," *European Economic Review*, Vol. 40 (January), pp. 61–89.

Shleifer, Andrei, and Robert W. Vishny, 1993, "Corruption," *Quarterly Journal of Economics*, Vol. 108 (August), pp. 599–617.

Stein, Ernesto, 1998, "Fiscal Decentralization and Government Size in Latin America," Inter-American Development Bank Working Paper No. 368 (Washington: Inter-American Development Bank).

Tanzi, Vito, 1995, "Fiscal Federalism and Decentralization: A Review of Some Efficiency and Macroeconomic Aspects," paper prepared for the World Bank's Annual Bank Conference on Development Economics, Washington, May.

Ter-Minassian, Teresa, ed., 1997, *Fiscal Federalism in Theory and Practice* (Washington: International Monetary Fund).

Treisman, Daniel, 2000, "The Causes of Corruption: A Cross-National Study," *Journal of Public Economics*, Vol. 76 (June), pp. 399–457.

Weingast, Barry R., 1995, "The Economic Role of Political Institutions: Market-Preserving Federalism and Economic Development," *Journal of Law, Economics, and Organization*, Vol. 11 (April), pp. 1–31.

World Bank, 1999, *World Development Report* (New York: Oxford University Press).

Part III

Corruption and Taxes

14

Tax Revenue in Sub-Saharan Africa: Effects of Economic Policies and Corruption

Dhaneshwar Ghura

I. Introduction

Large fiscal deficits have been a daunting problem for a number of countries in sub-Saharan Africa over the past several years. Rapid expansions in expenditure and declining or low revenue levels have been the main cause of fiscal imbalances.[1] Recent endogenous growth models have demonstrated that growth can be enhanced by, inter alia, reducing fiscal imbalances, which, in turn, can be achieved by either

---

I would like to thank Marcel Fafchamps, Menachem Katz, Carlos Leite, Ian Lienert, Joseph Ntamatungiro, Dominique Simard, and Janet Stotsky for useful comments. Yasuyuki Todo contributed to an earlier version of this paper as a summer intern in the IMF's African Department in 1997.

[1]Nashashibi and Bazzoni (1994) provide an analysis of the trends in revenue and expenditure, as well as economic performance, in the region during 1980–91.

lowering expenditure or raising revenue.[2] However, many countries in the region have reduced expenditure to minimum sustainable levels, especially in health, education, and infrastructure. Thus, raising tax revenue to achieve fiscal sustainability would be a feasible alternative. Also, in order to improve the environment for private sector development and sustained economic growth, governments need to play a supportive role by investing in physical and human capital, and institutional infrastructure. Tax revenue is needed for such expenditure if inflationary financing and the crowding out of the private sector are to be avoided (Hamada, 1994).

The mobilization of tax revenue is an important policy objective. While governments can do little in the short run to change the structural determinants of the tax revenue (such as the composition of value added), they can alter other factors that influence tax revenue, such as the economic policies, the level of corruption, and the quality of tax administration. As documented by Nashashibi and Bazzoni (1994), the wide divergences between the effective and statutory tax rates in many countries in the region indicate that there is scope for raising tax revenue without increasing tax rates by reinforcing tax and customs administrations, reducing tax exemptions, and fighting fraud and corruption. Nevertheless, Heller (1997, p. 41) cautions that "one must be realistic in terms of improvement in revenue ratios that can be reasonably expected to be achieved in many African countries, given the low level of development and the heavily agricultural and informal sector character of their economies." In addition, Tanzi (Chapter 2 in this volume) cautions that the fight against corruption takes time, needs to be undertaken on several fronts, and can be costly. Furthermore, tax mobilization and reform can be achieved only when there is strong political will and leadership to adopt the necessary measures (Hamada, 1994).

A number of empirical studies have investigated the determinants of tax revenue in developing countries.[3] Few of them, however, have focused on the effects of economic policies and corruption on tax revenue, even though these variables have been shown to influence other

---

[2] See Tanzi and Zee (1997) for a survey of the literature on the effects of fiscal policies on growth.

[3] See, for example, Heller (1975), Tanzi (1981, 1987, and 1992), Farhadian-Lorie and Katz (1989), Leuthold (1991), Nashashibi and Bazzoni (1994), and Stotsky and Wolde-Mariam (1997). Stotsky and WoldeMariam (1997) provide a survey of previous empirical work.

aspects of economic performance.[4] Tanzi (1989) argues that the wide fluctuations in tax ratios observed in several countries over short time periods cannot be satisfactorily explained by variations in the traditional determinant of tax revenue—the tax base; rather, changes in the macroeconomic policy environment have played an important role. Also, Chand and Moene (Chapter 4 in this volume) note that fiscal corruption has been a key factor behind the poor revenue performance in a number of developing countries.

This paper contributes to the empirical literature by focusing on the impact of economic policies and corruption on tax revenue, using data for 39 sub-Saharan African countries during 1985–96. Among the economic policy–related variables considered in this study are the rate of inflation, the percentage change in the real effective exchange rate, the implementation of structural reforms, and the provision of public services by the government. The effect of corruption, which is typically defined as the abuse of public power for private benefit, is captured by an index that measures the extent to which bribes are generally expected by government officials in relation to, inter alia, tax assessments, trade licenses, and exchange controls.

The tax performance of sub-Saharan African countries varied widely during 1985–96. For example, while the average total tax revenue–GDP ratio for these countries was about 17 percent during this period, 9 countries had ratios below 10 percent and 10 countries had ratios above 20 percent (Table 1). The majority of countries had average tax revenue–GDP ratios below 15 percent during 1985–96. On average, the total tax revenue–GDP ratio declined over time from 18.4 percent in 1985 to 16.3 percent in 1996. The largest decline was experienced by the oil producers—Cameroon, the Republic of Congo, Gabon, and Nigeria—whose average tax ratio fell from 25½ percent in 1985 to 18½ percent in 1996, largely reflecting the decline in oil prices.[5] For the non-oil producers, the ratio declined from 17.3 percent to 16 percent.

---

[4]Bardhan (1997) reviews the literature on corruption and development. Mauro (Chapter 9 in this volume) finds evidence of adverse effects of corruption on economic growth. Ghura and Hadjimichael (1996) find evidence to support the positive effects of macroeconomic stability on economic growth in sub-Saharan Africa.

[5]For the oil producers in the sample, tax revenue includes oil revenue from all sources—that is, from oil production shared between private oil companies and the government and oil company profits or income taxes.

Table 1. Sub-Saharan Africa: Tax Revenue in Selected Countries[1]
(In percent of GDP)

	Average 1985–90	Average 1991–96	Average 1985–96
Benin[2]	9.6	10.9	10.2
Botswana	40.9	34.1	37.5
Burkina Faso[2]	9.4	10.1	9.7
Burundi	13.6	14.6	14.2
Cameroon[2,3]	16.2	12.5	14.3
Central African Republic[2]	9.7	7.6	8.6
Chad[2]	7.1	7.5	7.3
Comoros[2]	10.9	11.8	11.4
Congo, Republic of[2]	25.2	24.2	24.7
Côte d'Ivoire[2]	18.7	16.9	17.5
Equatorial Guinea[2]	14.7	11.7	13.2
Ethiopia	12.2	8.5	10.4
Gabon[2,3]	24.9	23.7	24.3
Gambia, The	19.1	19.4	19.2
Ghana	11.6	14.2	12.9
Guinea	13.7	10.9	11.6
Guinea-Bissau	6.5	6.0	6.2
Kenya	19.9	22.7	21.3
Lesotho	34.4	40.0	37.2
Madagascar	9.8	8.0	8.9
Malawi	18.6	17.0	17.8
Mali[2]	9.6	11.2	10.4
Mauritius	20.4	19.0	19.7
Mozambique	16.2	17.4	16.8
Namibia	25.6	33.3	29.4
Niger[2]	8.5	6.5	7.5
Nigeria[3]	13.7	12.5	13.1
Rwanda	9.9	7.6	8.8
São Tomé and Príncipe	11.8	10.9	11.3
Senegal[2]	14.3	13.7	14.0
Seychelles	34.7	32.4	33.5
Sierra Leone	5.4	9.7	8.6
South Africa	24.4	25.0	24.7
Swaziland	26.3	30.3	28.3
Tanzania	14.3	12.0	13.2
Togo[2]	20.1	12.6	16.3
Uganda	5.8	7.8	6.8
Zambia	18.1	16.2	17.0
Zimbabwe	32.4	30.9	31.6

Table 1 *(concluded)*

	Average		
	1985–90	1991–96	1985–96
Unweighted averages			
Sub-Saharan Africa	17.3	16.4	16.9
Oil-producing countries	20.0	18.2	19.1
Non-oil-producing countries	16.9	16.2	16.6
CFA franc countries	14.1	12.9	13.5
Oil-producing countries	22.1	20.1	21.1
Non-oil-producing countries	11.8	10.9	11.3
Non-CFA franc countries	19.1	18.4	18.8
Oil-producing countries[4]	13.7	12.5	13.1
Non-oil-producing countries	19.4	18.7	19.0

[1] See the Appendix for the sources and definitions of the variables.
[2] CFA franc countries.
[3] Oil-producing countries.
[4] Nigeria.

While controlling for the elements of the tax base, this paper investigates whether economic policies and corruption can account for part of the variation observed in tax revenue performance in sub-Saharan African countries. The results indicate that, in addition to variables related to income and the structure of the tax base, a number of other factors influence tax revenue, including macroeconomic and structural policies, the provision of public services by the government, and the level of corruption. The rest of the paper is organized as follows. The next section presents the theoretical model and discusses the hypotheses. Section III presents the empirical results, and the last section draws conclusions and suggests possible policy implications.

II. Theoretical Considerations

In order to account for the effects of economic policies and corruption, along with the impact of the elements of the tax base, this paper extends the tax model developed by Heller (1975).

The public decision maker's utility function is given by

$$U = U(Y - T, G, D; F + L), \tag{1}$$

U_{Y-T} and $U_G > 0,$

U_D and $U_{F+L} < 0$ if D and $F + L > 0$, and

U_D and $U_{F+L} > 0$ if D and $F + L < 0$,

where $Y - T$ (equal to GDP, Y, minus tax revenue, T) is the private sector's disposable income; D is net domestic government borrowing,[6] G is total government expenditure, and $F + L$ is net foreign financing, consisting of grants (F) and loans (L), including external arrears accumulation or decumulation (net of amortization). The variables D and ($F + L$) can be either positive or negative, and thus the first derivatives of U with respect to D and ($F + L$) are either negative (D and $F + L > 0$) or positive (D and $F + L < 0$). All variables in the model are in real per capita terms. The budget constraint faced by the decision maker is given by

$$T + F + L + D = G. \tag{2}$$

Expanding on Leuthold's (1991) applied tax model, it is assumed that the actual tax revenue–GDP ratio (T/Y) is a function of the desired tax revenue–GDP ratio (T/Y)* and the availability of certain tax bases (B), as well as the status of economic policies (E) and the level of corruption (C). That is,

$$T/Y = f\{(T/Y)^*, B, E, C\}. \tag{3}$$

Desired tax revenue is determined by maximizing (1) subject to (2). Following Heller (1975), it is assumed that the utility function takes a quadratic form as follows:

$$U = \alpha_1(Y-T-Y_S) - \frac{\alpha_2}{2}(Y-T-Y_S)^2 + \alpha_3(G-G_S) - \frac{\alpha_4}{2}(G-G_S)^2$$

$$- \alpha_5 D - \frac{\alpha_6}{2}D^2 - \alpha_7(F+L) - \alpha_8(F+L)^2, \tag{4}$$

where the α's are positive constants, and Y_S and G_S are subsistence levels of income and government expenditure, respectively. Empirically, a

---
[6]The variable D includes net bank and nonbank financing, net domestic arrears, and, for simplicity, nontax revenue.

quadratic utility function is preferable to a log-linear one because the terms D and $F + L$ can be either positive or negative. Since Y_S and G_S are not observable, following Leuthold (1991), it is assumed that they are simple linear functions of income, as follows:

$$G_S = g_0 + g_1 Y, \tag{5a}$$

and

$$Y_S = y_0 + y_1 Y. \tag{5b}$$

Maximizing equation (1) with respect to T, G, and D, subject to constraint equation (2), yields the following reduced form for the desired equation for the tax revenue–GDP ratio:

$$\left(\frac{T}{Y}\right)^* = \left(\frac{\alpha + \alpha_4 g_0 - \beta y_0}{\beta + \alpha_4}\right)\left(\frac{1}{Y}\right) - \left(\frac{\alpha_4}{\beta + \alpha_4}\right)\left(\frac{F+L}{Y}\right)$$

$$+ \left(\frac{\alpha_4 g_1 - \beta y_1}{\beta + \alpha_4}\right), \tag{6}$$

where $\alpha = (-\alpha_1 + \alpha_3 - \alpha_1\alpha_4/\alpha_6 + \alpha_4\alpha_5/\alpha_6)$ and $\beta = \alpha_2(\alpha_4 + \alpha_6)/\alpha_6$. Combining equations (3) and (6) yields

$$T/Y = f(1/Y, (F+L)/Y, B, E, C). \tag{7}$$

Since β is positive and α could be either positive or negative, $(T/Y)^*$ is a negative function of $(F + L)/Y$ and an ambiguous function of the inverse of per capita income $(1/Y)$.

The literature on the determinants of tax revenue provides a set of testable hypotheses. This paper focuses on those hypotheses—on income, the tax base, economic policies, corruption, and the external environment—that can be tested using available data for sub-Saharan African countries. The rest of this section briefly discusses the hypotheses relating to the actual variables used; detailed discussions are provided by Tanzi (1989), Farhadian-Lorie and Katz (1989), and Nashashibi and Bazzoni (1994). The Appendix gives the definitions and sources of the variables used in this study.

The theoretical model predicts an ambiguous effect of increases in per capita income on tax revenue. This effect stems from the differential impact of an increase in income on different categories of tax revenues. While a higher level of economic development would be expected to raise the ratio of indirect tax revenue to GDP, it would be expected to lower the trade tax revenue–GDP ratio; thus, the effect on aggregate tax revenue is ambiguous. Farhadian-Lorie and Katz (1989) have noted that trade taxes have historically been a major source of government revenue during the early stages of economic development because they are easier to collect than domestic income or consumption taxes, owing to the rudimentary status of tax administration, as well as the limited availability of "tax handles." During the later stages of development, however, collection costs are expected to fall, dependence on trade taxes to decline, and dependence on indirect taxes to rise.

Elements of a country's tax base—better known as tax handles—considered in this study are the share of agriculture in GDP (*AGS*), the share of oil and non-oil mining activities in GDP (*OIL* and *MINE*), and the ratio of the sum of exports and imports to GDP (*OPEN*).[7] The sectoral composition of value added constitutes a key element of the tax base. In many sub-Saharan African economies, a large share of GDP results from agricultural activities.[8] However, the agricultural sector is difficult to tax owing to the prevalence of subsistence activities, which are largely informal. The administrative costs for the tax department of organizing and monitoring subsistence activities can be prohibitively high in relation to potential revenue yield. In general, therefore, a negative relationship would be expected between the tax revenue–GDP ratio and the share of agriculture in GDP. Mining activities, on the other hand, are organized, and thus easy to monitor and tax.[9] A positive correlation would be expected between the variable *OPEN* and the tax revenue–GDP ratio: as the international trade sector is a well-

---

[7]The concept of tax handles is explained by Musgrave (1987, p. 244). Leuthold (1991, p. 175) summarizes tax handles as "tax bases that lend themselves to taxation."

[8]See, for example, Aguirre, Griffith, and Yücelik (1981).

[9]Data on mining shares are incomplete for the set of countries included in this study. To circumvent this problem, two dummy variables are used to represent oil-producing countries (*OIL*), and non-oil producers whose average share of mining value added in GDP during 1985–96 was greater than or equal to 5 percent of GDP (*MINE*). The oil producers are Cameroon, the Republic of Congo, Gabon, and Nigeria. The other mining countries are Botswana, Equatorial Guinea, Guinea, Namibia, Niger, Sierra Leone, Togo, Zambia, and Zimbabwe.

organized and monetized sector, administrative costs of the tax system related to this sector should be lower than others.

Tanzi (1989) argues that one has to look beyond the traditional determinants of tax revenue—elements of the tax base—to obtain a satisfactory explanation of the wide fluctuations in tax ratios observed in several countries over short time periods; macroeconomic policy plays an important role. The effect of macroeconomic policy is captured by the inflation rate (*INF*) and the percentage change in the real effective exchange rate (*RERG*).[10] The effect of inflation on tax revenue can be registered through three main channels. First, according to the Tanzi-Olivera effect, in an inflationary environment, when actual tax payments lag the transactions to be taxed, tax obligations are lower in real terms at the time of tax payments (Tanzi, 1977). Second, excise duties on a number of products (e.g., tobacco, alcohol, and gasoline) may be levied at specific rates that may not necessarily be adjusted in line with inflation (Tanzi, 1989). Finally, high inflation rates reduce the tax base because in order to protect the real value of their wealth, economic agents make portfolio adjustments in favor of assets that typically escape the domestic tax net (such as land, livestock, jewels, and foreign capital). An appreciation of the real effective exchange rate is expected to raise imports and lower exports. The overall effect of a real effective exchange rate appreciation on tax revenue could be positive, given the greater dependence of tax receipts on import rather than export taxes. Nevertheless, an overvaluation of the real effective exchange rate—typically brought about by expansionary financial policies—would be expected to adversely affect overall economic activity, and thus to lower tax revenue.

Tax revenue can also be influenced by the implementation of structural reforms (*STRUC*). Such reforms can raise tax revenue by improving economic efficiency and resource allocation, enhancing external competitiveness, expanding the productive capacity of the economy, and broadening the tax base.[11] In recent years, a number of sub-Saharan African countries have made progress in the implementation of struc-

---

[10]In the empirical literature, the impact of macroeconomic policies on tax revenue has received little attention; the papers by Farhadian-Lorie and Katz (1989) and Nashashibi and Bazzoni (1994) are among the few exceptions.

[11]See Khan (1987) for a general analysis of structural reforms. The effects of these reforms are captured by the use of a dummy variable for countries classified as sustained adjusters, which are considered to have made relatively good progress in implementing structural reforms (see the Appendix).

tural reforms. These have included (1) public enterprise restructuring and privatization; (2) retail and producer price decontrol; (3) exchange and trade liberalization; (4) financial sector reform; (5) tax reform; (6) civil service reform; and (7) legal reform. A number of countries that have made progress in structural reforms have benefited from technical assistance aimed at increasing voluntary compliance and self-assessment, expanding the use of final withholding, improving collection procedures, developing audit plans and procedures, and reorganizing tax administration along functional lines (Abed and others, 1998).

Finally, in the area of economic policies, it is hypothesized that, when taxpayers see the benefit of their tax payments in terms of government's provision of public services, proxied by improvements in an index of human capital development (*HCI*), their willingness to pay taxes would be expected to increase.[12] In a number of developing economies, owing especially to weaknesses in the expenditure management process and the existence of corruption, part of the budgeted outlays do not reach their intended final destinations. Indeed, for the set of countries used in this study, there is a large positive correlation between declining corruption and rising human capital (a correlation coefficient of 0.48; see Appendix Table A1).[13] The index of human capital is intended to measure the visible impact of government expenditure on actual priority outlays.

It is hypothesized that corruption (*CORRUPT*) lowers the tax revenue–GDP ratio. Klitgaard (1998) notes that acts of corruption include (but are not limited to) bribery, extortion, influence peddling, nepotism, fraud, and embezzlement. Tanzi (Chapter 2 in this volume) provides a set of factors that encourage fiscal corruption, including complicated tax laws, excessive discretionary power vested in tax administrators, the necessity for frequent contacts between taxpayers and tax officials, weak legal and judicial systems, lack of accountability and transparency in the tax administration, and low salaries in the public sector. Corrupt tax and custom officials allocate a proportion of their working hours to (1) collecting bribes in exchange for alleviating

---

[12]Four social indicators are used to construct this variable—secondary school enrollment ratio, literacy rate, life expectancy at birth, and the infant survival rate. See the Appendix for a description of the procedure used for the aggregation.

[13]Tanzi (Chapter 2 in this volume) discusses how spending decisions are affected by corruption.

tax burdens of taxpayers offering these bribes; and (2) complicating procedures for taxpayers who refuse to participate in the bribery scheme, thus forcing them out of business or into the informal sector. These activities lower tax revenue for the public treasury.[14] Pervasive corruption in an economy is expected to lower investment and economic growth, and thus weaken the tax base.[15] The index of corruption used in this study is taken from the *International Country Risk Guide*, published by the Political Risk Services Group in Syracuse, New York. This index, which takes integer values ranging from 0 (high corruption) to 6 (low corruption), measures the extent to which bribes are generally expected by government officials in relation to, inter alia, tax assessments, trade licenses, and exchange controls.[16]

With respect to the external environment, the theoretical model predicts a negative effect of increases in external financing on the domestic tax revenue–GDP ratio. Two variables are used to capture this effect—the ratio of external grants to GDP (*GRANTY*) and the change in the debt stock–GDP ratio (*CHDETY*).[17] The effects of changes in the terms of trade on the tax revenue–GDP ratio are ambiguous. If a large proportion of a country's imports is price inelastic, a deterioration in the terms of trade owing to an increase in import prices could improve the tax base. However, if the deterioration in the terms of trade is due to a decline in export prices and the country depends on revenue from export taxes, the tax base would be expected to shrink. In addition, the decline in income associated with a decline in the terms of trade would be expected to lower the tax base.

III. Empirical Framework and Results

Empirical Framework

An empirical counterpart of equation (7) for the ith sub-Saharan African country at time t is written as follows:

---

[14]See Chand and Moene (Chapter 4 in this volume) for an analysis of this phenomenon.

[15]Empirical evidence provided by Mauro (Chapter 9 in this volume) suggests that large economic payoffs can be achieved by reducing corruption.

[16]Data on the level of corruption are available for only 27 of the 39 countries included in the study. See the next section for the methodology used to estimate the data for the countries for which data are missing.

[17]A large stock of external public debt can lower the tax base; see Tanzi (Chapter 2 in this volume).

$$TRY_{it} = \alpha_0 + t_1\log_e(1/PCI_{it}) + t_2AGS_{it} + t_3OPEN_{it} + t_4OIL_i$$
$$+ t_5MINE_i + n_1INF_{it} + n_2RERG_{it} + n_3STRUC_i + n_4HCI_{is}$$
$$+ n_5CORRUPT_{it} + n_6GRANTY_{it} + n_7CHDETY_{it}$$
$$+ n_8TTG_{it} + u_i + v_t + e_{it}, \qquad (8)$$

where TRY is the tax revenue–GDP ratio; PCI is per capita income;[18] AGS is the share of agriculture in GDP; $OPEN$ is the ratio to GDP of the sum of exports and imports; INF is the rate of inflation; OIL is a dummy variable that takes a value of 1 if the ith country is an oil producer; $MINE$ is a dummy variable that takes a value of 1 if the ith country is not an oil producer but whose mining share is at least 5 percent of GDP; $RERG$ is the percentage change in the real effective exchange rate; $STRUC$ is a dummy variable capturing the implementation of structural reforms by the ith country; HCI is an index of human capital; $CORRUPT$ is an index of corruption that varies from 0 (high corruption) to 6 (low corruption); $GRANTY$ is the external grants–GDP ratio; $CHDETY$ is the change in the stock of external debt–GDP ratio; and TTG is the percentage change in the terms of trade. The subscript s for HCI denotes that this variable is time-invariant over two subperiods (1985–90 and 1991–96). The coefficients $t_1 - t_5$ broadly capture the effects of variables related to income and the tax base that are typically used in the literature. The coefficients $n_1 - n_8$ are intended to capture the effects of variables related to economic policies and corruption, typically ignored in the empirical literature. The Appendix provides the definitions and sources of the variables; Appendix Table A1 provides the matrix of correlation coefficients for these variables; and Appendix Table A2 provides the period averages of the data.

A regression framework is used to estimate the tax equation, with an unbalanced panel data set for 39 countries covering the period 1985–96.[19] As the data are in panel form, the error term for equation (8) accordingly has three components: u_i and v_t, which capture country- and

---

[18]The best equation fit was obtained when the natural logarithm of (1/PCI) was used in the estimation of equation (8).

[19]With a one-period lag used for instruments, one observation is lost per country. Thirty-one countries have data for the full period (1986–96); out of the eight remaining countries, four have data for the period 1987–96, two have data for 1988–96, and two have data for 1989–96. A total of 415 observations are available for the regression estimation.

time-specific effects, respectively, and e_{it}, which is an error term common to all observations. To deal with time effects, the data are processed to remove the time means from the series, and the resulting model is estimated without an intercept. Country heterogeneity is captured by the inclusion of country-specific information in the indicators for the level of human capital development, the stance of economic policies, changes in the terms of trade, the levels of external indebtedness and grants, and the level of corruption. In addition, dummy variables for subgroups of countries (*CFA*, *STRUC*, *OIL*, *MINE*) are used to account for the possibility of fixed effects stemming from a priori information regarding country characteristics and institutional arrangements.

In order to correct for possible simultaneity bias stemming from the variables *PCI*, *OPEN*, *INF*, *STRUC*, and *CORRUPT*, an instrumental variables technique is used.[20] Since the variable *STRUC* is binary (0,1), a logistic model of the following type is used obtain its predicted values: $\log_e(p/(1-p)) = a + bX$, where $p = Pr(Y = 1 \mid X)$ is the response probability to be modeled, Y is the binary (0,1) response, X is the vector of instruments, and b is the vector of coefficients. To deal with the problem of heteroscedasticity, a feasible instrumental variables generalized least squares (IV-GLS) procedure is used.[21]

As noted above, data on the level of corruption are available for only 27 of the 39 countries. To avoid losing observations in the regression analysis, the instrumental variables mentioned above are used to estimate the missing data for this variable. As shown in Appendix Table A2, this set of instruments reproduces the available data fairly accurately, thereby providing a reasonable degree of confidence in the data that are generated for the countries with no available data. The correlation coefficient between the generated corruption (*CORRUPTP*) and actual corruption (*CORRUPT*) variables is 0.74 (Appendix Table A1).

---

[20]The instruments used are the contemporaneous, squared, and lagged values of population, population growth, urbanization rate, growth in the terms of trade, agriculture share, the external grants–GDP ratio, the change in external debt–GDP ratio, the external debt–GDP ratio, and growth in the real effective exchange rate. In addition, an index of human capital (*HCI*), *HCI* squared, the lagged broad money–GDP ratio, *CFA*, *OIL*, and *MINE* are used.

[21]This procedure is implemented in two steps. First, an instrumental variables technique is used to estimate the regression equation with pooled data. Second, the residuals from this step are used to calculate the standard deviation for each country; the inverse of the country-specific standard deviations are then used to weigh all the included variables (including predicted ones), and the equation is reestimated with the pooled transformed data.

Econometrics Results

The regression results are given in Table 2. Following the traditional empirical literature, regression (1) includes only variables related to income and the tax base; this is taken to be the base regression. Regressions (2)–(4) also use variables related to macroeconomic and structural policies, the extent of public services provided by the government, corruption, and the external environment. The last column of Table 2 provides an indication of the relative importance of the explanatory variables in explaining the tax revenue–GDP ratio, as captured by the beta coefficients using the results of regression (4). The following observations can be made based on the results.

- The results of the base regression are broadly consistent with those available in the empirical literature. They indicate that the tax revenue–GDP ratio grows with an increase in income, a decline in the share of agriculture in GDP, greater openness of the economy, and the existence of oil and non-oil mining sectors.[22] As indicated by the beta coefficients, among the variables capturing the effects of income and the tax base, the degree of openness (*OPEN*) exerts the largest impact on the tax ratio, followed by the income variable (1/*PCI*), the existence of an oil sector (*OIL*), the agricultural share (*AGS*), and the existence of a non-oil mining sector (*MINE*).

- When the base regression is augmented to include other variables, the main results relating to income and the elements of the tax base do not change by much. Nevertheless, owing to the high degrees of correlations between human capital (*HCI*), on the one hand, and the inverse of per capita income (*PCI*) and the agriculture share (*AGS*), on the other—correlation coefficients of –0.72 and –0.66, respectively (see Appendix Table A1)—the magnitude and statistical significance of the impact of $\log_e(1/PCI)$ and *AGS* on the tax ratio fall.

- The results support the theoretical view provided by Tanzi (1989) and some existing empirical evidence that the macroeconomic policy environment matters for tax revenue performance.[23] An increase in inflation (a proxy for expansionary financial policies) lowers the

---

[22]See, for example, Tanzi (1981, 1987, and 1992); Leuthold (1991); and Stotsky and WoldeMariam (1997). See also Farhadian-Lorie and Katz (1989) for an analysis with respect to trade taxes.

[23]Empirical evidence is provided by Farhadian-Lorie and Katz (1989) and Nashashibi and Bazzoni (1994).

tax ratio. An appreciation of the real effective exchange rate has a positive although statistically insignificant effect on the tax ratio.

- Structural reforms (*STRUC*) have positive and significant effects on the tax revenue–GDP ratio. This result indicates that, on average, countries that made progress in the implementation of structural reforms were able to raise their average tax revenue–GDP ratios higher than countries that did not.

- The effect of human capital development (*HCI*), another economic policy–related variable used as a proxy for the provision of public services by the government, is positive and significant. It could be inferred from this result that, when taxpayers see the benefits of their tax contributions, their willingness to voluntarily comply with their tax obligations increases. It should be noted that *HCI* is measured in such a way as to avoid the problem of causality and simultaneity bias (see the Appendix).

- As shown by the beta coefficients, of the economic policy–related variables, inflation exerts the largest impact on the tax revenue–GDP ratio, followed by the implementation of structural reforms. Thus, economic policies that emphasize a prudent financial stance and the implementation of structural reforms can be expected to raise tax revenue. The relative impact of the provision of public services by the government is small.

- There is strong evidence that an increase in the level of corruption (as captured by a decline in *CORRUPTP*) lowers the tax revenue–GDP ratio. The important role played by corruption in influencing tax revenue is confirmed by its relatively high beta coefficient. Thus, efforts to lower corruption would be expected to increase tax revenue significantly.

- As the levels of corruption and human capital development are highly correlated (see Appendix Table A1), when these two variables are included in the same regression the magnitude and statistical significance of their impact fall.

- Increases in external grants lower tax revenue. While this result could be indicative of substitution between domestic tax revenue mobilization and the availability of external grants, it could also reflect a reverse causality problem, whereby countries with lower tax revenue–GDP ratios have been recipients of larger amounts of grants. Several factors guide the flow of grants, including the

Table 2. Estimates of the Tax Equation and Beta Coefficients[1]

Explanatory Variables[2]	(1)	(2)	(3)	(4)	Beta Coefficients[3]
Income $\log_e(1/PCI)$	−3.223*** (8.83)	−1.248** (2.51)	−2.407*** (6.72)	−1.696*** (3.38)	−0.190
Tax base					
Share of agriculture in GDP ratio (AGS)	−0.078*** (4.41)	−0.105*** (5.59)	−0.045** (2.22)	−0.065*** (2.89)	−0.121
Openness (OPEN)	0.127*** (17.51)	0.106*** (12.59)	0.122*** (13.10)	0.118*** (12.57)	0.412
Dummy variable for oil-producing countries (OIL)	2.384*** (3.96)	3.031*** (4.76)	4.456*** (6.79)	4.044*** (5.91)	0.144
Dummy variable for non-oil mining countries (MINE)	1.643*** (5.38)	2.184*** (5.31)	1.501*** (3.58)	1.722*** (4.01)	0.088
Economic policies					
Inflation (INF)		−0.096*** (7.24)	−0.082*** (5.69)	−0.084*** (5.87)	−0.284
Percentage change in real effective exchange rate (RERG)		0.010 (0.92)	0.015 (1.42)	0.015 (1.35)	0.025
Structural reforms (STRUC)		1.292*** (3.36)	1.443*** (3.84)	1.132*** (2.83)	0.066
Provision of public services, proxied by human capital index (HCI)		0.149*** (4.44)		0.080** (2.08)	0.005

Corruption (*CORRUPTP*)			1.686*** (5.24)	1.242*** (3.28)	0.143
External environment					
External grants–GDP ratio (*GRANTY*)		−0.092** (2.51)	−0.080** (2.44)	−0.030** (2.54)	−0.002
Change in external debt–GDP ratio (*CHDETY*)		0.020 (1.07)	0.021 (1.09)	0.019 (0.99)	0.027
Percentage change in terms of trade (*TTG*)		0.001 (0.14)	0.007 (0.76)	0.005 (0.58)	0.009
Dummy variable for CFA franc countries *CFA*	−3.706*** (16.13)	−5.149*** (10.69)	−4.815*** (9.16)	−4.659*** (8.78)	−0.263
Mean square error	0.947	0.947	0.975	0.964	
F-value[4]	486.84***	212.79***	228.96***	216.33***	
Number of observations	415	415	415	415	

[1] An instrumental variables generalized least squares (IV-GLS) procedure is used for estimation. The numbers in parentheses below the estimated coefficients are the absolute values of the *t*-ratios. ***, **, and * denote statistical significance at the 0.1, 0.05, and 0.10 levels, respectively.
[2] See the Appendix for definitions and sources of variables used.
[3] Beta coefficients using the estimated coefficients reported in regression (4). The beta coefficient of an explanatory variable *X*, for example, is the ratio of the product of its estimated coefficient and its standard error to the standard error of the dependent variable.
[4] Test statistic for the test of the null hypothesis that the joint effect of all variables included on the right-hand side of the estimated equations is zero.

level of development, the status of implementation of macroeconomic and structural policies, and the level of corruption. The regression analysis controls for these factors and still finds a significant independent effect of external grants on tax revenue, indicating that, on average, grants tend to substitute for domestic tax revenue mobilization.

IV. Conclusions and Policy Implications

This paper analyzes tax revenue performance in sub-Saharan Africa, using panel data for 39 countries in the region during 1985–96. A relatively large set of factors that can potentially influence tax revenue performance—income, the structure of the economy, macroeconomic and structural policies, the extent of provision of public goods by the government, the level of corruption, and the external environment—is considered in the econometrics analysis. The effect of corruption, which is typically defined as the abuse of public power for private benefit, is captured by an index that measures the extent to which bribes are generally expected by government officials in relation to, inter alia, tax assessments, trade licenses, and exchange controls.

The analysis confirms the important role played by income and the elements of the tax base in influencing the tax revenue–GDP ratio. The latter rises with income and the level of openness of the economy, as well as with reductions in the share of agriculture in GDP. The results also indicate that a number of other factors typically not considered in the empirical literature significantly influence the tax ratio. In particular, the economic policy environment and the level of corruption matter for the tax revenue–GDP ratio: the latter declines with rising inflation—a proxy for expansionary financial policies—and corruption. Also, there is evidence that countries that have implemented structural reforms on a sustained basis have raised their tax revenue higher than countries that have not. Furthermore, an increase in the level of human capital—a proxy for the extent of public service provided by the government—is associated with an increase in tax revenue. In addition, increases in the level of external grants are associated with lower tax ratios.

An analysis of beta coefficients indicates that, among the economic policy–related variables, inflation has the largest impact on the tax revenue–GDP ratio, followed by the implementation of structural policies. Thus, for a given tax regime and rate, economic policies that promote a noninflationary environment (through a prudent financial stance) and the implementation of structural reforms can be expected to raise tax revenue. Also, the evidence strongly suggests that measures taken to reduce corruption would be expected to enhance tax revenue significantly. Among the variables capturing the effects of income and the tax base, the degree of openness of the economy exerts the largest impact on the tax ratio, followed by income and the agricultural share.

Although measures taken to promote economic reforms and reduce corruption would be expected to enhance tax revenue, a number of caveats are in order. The fight against corruption takes time, needs to be undertaken on several fronts, and can be costly (Tanzi, Chapter 2 in this volume). In addition, the implementation of policies to lower inflation and promote structural reforms may encounter resistance both from the government (which stands to lose seigniorage revenue) and special interest groups (which stand to lose certain privileged positions, such as monopoly power). Thus, projections of large tax revenue gains over a short time period through economic policy reforms and measures to reduce corruption (including through the reform of tax administration) may not be realistic. Finally, in view of the generally low levels of development of sub-Saharan African economies, as well as of the agricultural and informal character of these economies, caution must be exercised in projecting revenue improvements that can reasonably be expected in many of these countries (Heller, 1997).

Appendix

Definitions and Sources of Variables[24]

Tax revenue

TRY   Total tax revenue–GDP ratio (in percent, in real terms).

Income

PCI   Per capita income, calculated as per capita real GDP, converted into U.S. dollars using 1990 nominal exchange rate.

---

[24]Unless otherwise indicated, data are from the IMF, World Economic Outlook database. The data on tax revenue were obtained from the IMF's African Department database. See Table 1 for a list of countries included in this study. Angola, Cape Verde, the Democratic Republic of Congo (formerly Zaïre), Eritrea, and Liberia are excluded from the study owing to data limitations.

Tax base

AGS Share of agriculture in GDP (in percent). Source: World Bank, World Development Indicators database.

OPEN The ratio to GDP of the sum of exports and imports (in percent).

OIL A dummy variable that takes a value of one for oil-producing countries—Cameroon, the Republic of Congo, Gabon, and Nigeria—and zero otherwise.

MINE A dummy variable that takes a value of one for non-oil mining countries—Botswana, Equatorial Guinea, Guinea, Namibia, Niger, Sierra Leone, Togo, Zambia, and Zimbabwe—and zero otherwise.

Macroeconomic and structural policies

INF Rate of change of the consumer price index (in percent).

RERG Percentage change in the real effective exchange rate (*RER*). A positive value for *RERG* denotes an appreciation of the *RER*. Owing to data limitations for Comoros and São Tomé and Príncipe, the following proxy is used: $CPI/(ERI*WPIUS)$, where *CPI* is the domestic consumer price index, *ERI* is an exchange rate index, and *WPIUS* is the U.S. wholesale price index. Source for *RER*: IMF, Information Notice System.

STRUC A dummy variable for capturing the effects of structural reforms. It takes a value of one for sustained adjusters and zero otherwise. Two sets of countries are included. First, there are 5 countries with small macroeconomic imbalances during 1985–96—Botswana, Mauritius, Namibia, Seychelles, and Swaziland— that implemented structural reforms without IMF-supported programs. Second, there are 19 countries that successfully implemented Structural Adjustment Facility (SAF) or Enhanced Structural Adjustment Facility (ESAF)–supported programs on a sustained basis. This country group includes countries that have completed three years of SAF/ESAF-supported programs and excludes countries with large undrawn balances at the expiration or cancellation of the programs. The dummy variable takes a value of one starting in the first year of the IMF-supported program to the end of the period. The sustained adjusters and their first program years are as follows: Benin (1989), Burundi (1987), Burkina Faso (1993), Côte d'Ivoire (1994), Ethiopia (1993), The Gambia (1987), Ghana

(1988), Guinea (1992), Kenya (1988), Lesotho (1988), Malawi (1988), Mali (1989), Mozambique (1987), Niger (1987), Senegal (1987), Tanzania (1988), Togo (1987), Uganda (1987), and Zimbabwe (1993). Burundi and The Gambia are taken to be sustained adjusters only through 1993, owing to political difficulties during 1994–96. Other countries that had SAF- or ESAF-supported programs during the period 1985–97 but which are not classified as sustained adjusters are Cameroon, the Central African Republic, Comoros, Equatorial Guinea, Madagascar, and Sierra Leone.

Provision of public services by government

HCI   Index of human capital development. Four variables are used to construct this index (secondary school enrollment ratio; literacy rate; life expectancy at birth; and 1,000 minus the infant mortality rate).[25] These variables are available only at irregular intervals for most countries and fluctuate substantially over time. For each variable, averages are computed over two subperiods: 1985–90 and 1991–96. These averages are transformed such that their mean values are equal to 100 and their standard deviations are equal to ten. The average of these four transformed variables is used for *HCI*.[26] Source: World Bank, World Development Indicators database, 1997.

Corruption

CORRUPT   An index of corruption, which takes integer values ranging from zero (high corruption) to six (low corruption). Source: *International Country Risk Guide*, published by Political Risk Services Group in Syracuse, New York.

CORRUPTP Data on the level of corruption are available for only 27 of the 39 countries included in the study. In order to avoid the loss of valuable data in the regression analysis, a methodology is used to estimate the data for the countries for which data are missing (see text).

---

[25]Infant mortality rate is the number of infants per thousand live births who die before reaching one year of age.

[26]For Namibia and São Tomé and Príncipe, only three out of the four human capital indicators were available. The average of the three transformed indicators is defined as *HCI* for these two countries. For a few countries, no data were available for one of the two subperiods. In such a case, the value of *HCI* for the subperiod for which the data were available is used for the other subperiod.

External environment

GRANTY External grants–GDP ratio (in percent, in real terms).

CHDETY Net external indebtedness (including arrears accumulation or decumulation), as measured by the change in the external debt-to-GDP ratio (in percent). In order to exclude the impact of revaluation stemming from changes in exchange rates, dollar values are used in the estimation of this variable. Source: World Bank, World Development Indicators database.

TTG Percentage change in the terms of trade.

Dummy variable

CFA A dummy variable that takes a value of one for the CFA franc countries—Benin, Burkina Faso, Cameroon, the Central African Republic, Chad, Comoros, the Republic of Congo, Côte d'Ivoire, Equatorial Guinea, Gabon, Mali, Niger, Senegal, and Togo—and zero otherwise.

Table A1. Matrix of Correlation Coefficients

	ATRY	$\log_e(1/PCI)$	AGS	OPEN	INF	RERG	GRANTY	CHDETY	TTG	HCI	CORRUPT	CORRUPTP
$\log_e(1/PCI)$	−0.63***	1.00										
AGS	−0.74***	−0.81***	1.00									
OPEN	0.67***	−0.36***	−0.52***	1.00								
INF	−0.16***	0.29***	0.16***	−0.05	1.00							
RERG	0.08	−0.12**	−0.13**	0.04	−0.10**	1.00						
GRANTY	−0.26***	0.36***	0.22***	−0.06	0.19***	−0.08	1.00					
CHDETY	−0.10**	0.14**	0.08	0.03	0.21***	−0.16***	0.37***	1.00				
TTG	0.15**	−0.14**	−0.15**	0.08	−0.04	0.10**	−0.03	0.00	1.00			
HCI	0.64***	−0.72***	−0.66***	0.39***	−0.14***	0.08	−0.21***	−0.03	0.14**	1.00		
CORRUPT	0.27***	−0.11	−0.24***	0.16**	−0.11	0.05	0.06	−0.12**	0.02	0.37***	1.00	
CORRUPTP	0.43***	−0.28***	−0.44***	0.20***	−0.05	0.05	−0.07	−0.19***	−0.01	0.48***	0.74***	1.00
CFA	−0.27***	−0.10**	0.10**	−0.17***	−0.37***	0.03	−0.01	−0.06	−0.03	−0.26***	−0.25***	−0.39***
STRUC	0.27***	−0.05	−0.09	0.30***	−0.09	0.00	−0.07	−0.21***	0.03	0.18***	0.20***	0.37***
OIL	0.09	−0.31***	−0.23***	−0.01	−0.07	0.01	−0.25***	0.01	0.00	0.08	−0.33***	−0.25***
MINE	0.22***	−0.19***	−0.23***	0.14**	0.10**	0.04	−0.20***	−0.10**	0.03	0.02	0.18**	0.08

[1]See Appendix text for definitions and sources of variables. ***, **, and * denote statistical significance at the 0.01, 0.05, and 0.10 levels, respectively.

Table A2. Period Average of Data by Variable and Country, 1986–96[1]

Country	TRY	PCI	AGS	OPEN	INF	RERG	GRANTY	CHDETY	TTG	HCI	CORRUPT	CORRUPTP	SUS[2]	CFA	OIL	MINE
Benin	10.2	408	35.8	45.1	6.4	−1.3	4.6	4.9	−1.8	95	...	2.6	0.7	1	0	0
Botswana	37.4	2,844	5.4	89.5	11.3	0.3	1.3	1.1	6.0	110	3.7	3.8	1.0	0	0	1
Burkina Faso	9.9	300	34.6	29.1	3.4	−4.0	5.7	2.9	3.3	91	3.6	3.8	0.4	1	0	0
Burundi	14.2	200	54.7	26.0	9.2	−4.5	5.2	5.8	0.4	94	...	3.3	0.6	0	0	0
Cameroon	14.0	959	28.3	27.0	5.4	−1.3	0.2	7.5	−5.7	105	2.5	2.0	0.0	1	1	0
Central African Republic	8.5	473	45.7	26.4	3.1	−2.9	6.1	4.2	−3.1	97	...	2.5	0.0	1	0	0
Chad	7.5	214	40.9	39.5	4.6	−5.0	12.4	6.3	5.0	93	...	2.6	0.0	1	0	0
Comoros	11.4	525	38.8	28.3	5.2	2.0	14.0	2.9	−3.1	101	...	2.8	0.0	1	0	0
Congo, Republic of	23.9	1,243	11.8	72.0	6.7	−0.8	0.3	11.9	5.3	104	3.0	3.1	0.0	1	1	0
Côte d'Ivoire	17.5	899	31.4	55.3	6.5	0.5	0.3	8.8	−3.7	101	3.5	3.0	0.3	1	0	0
Equatorial Guinea	13.0	430	56.1	87.1	3.6	−5.0	1.9	12.6	−0.6	95	...	2.1	0.0	1	0	1
Ethiopia	10.3	167	55.7	17.7	7.5	−8.1	2.9	3.6	−3.8	93	2.6	2.9	0.4	0	0	0
Gabon	23.0	4,990	8.9	59.5	4.7	−3.0	0.3	6.8	−1.1	101	1.6	1.9	0.0	1	1	0
Gambia, The	19.4	308	29.3	87.4	14.0	−2.5	5.4	6.2	−4.6	92	3.1	3.0	0.6	0	0	0
Ghana	13.2	421	48.1	40.2	31.1	−8.5	2.9	5.7	−3.1	106	3.0	3.2	0.8	0	0	0
Guinea	11.6	489	23.8	47.9	17.0	0.3	3.5	6.6	2.8	89	3.6	2.8	0.5	0	0	1
Guinea-Bissau	6.2	225	45.1	34.4	55.2	−7.5	17.7	19.5	−4.9	90	2.0	2.1	0.0	0	0	0
Kenya	21.5	324	30.3	40.8	16.3	−2.0	1.5	3.5	3.5	107	3.0	3.8	0.8	0	0	0
Lesotho	37.0	358	15.8	133.0	13.0	−0.6	6.7	7.5	1.5	106	...	3.7	0.8	0	0	0
Madagascar	8.8	253	34.5	27.2	19.8	−3.8	2.8	5.8	−2.0	103	4.0	3.4	0.0	0	0	0

Malawi	17.7	213	43.0	41.7	27.9	−1.1	0.3	7.8	−2.9	93	3.6	3.2	0.8	0	0
Mali	10.5	288	46.0	42.3	3.0	−4.6	1.7	7.4	−1.6	92	1.9	2.1	0.7	1	0
Mauritius	19.7	2,302	11.4	93.3	7.2	−1.6	0.4	4.1	4.2	119	⋯	3.9	1.0	0	0
Mozambique	17.2	101	39.3	60.1	57.4	−9.4	16.6	19.7	1.0	92	4.0	3.6	0.9	0	0
Namibia	30.0	1,816	12.3	93.2	12.1	−1.0	3.4	0.2	−3.1	110	4.4	4.3	1.0	0	1
Niger	7.4	312	36.8	29.9	3.2	−6.0	4.8	1.8	−1.6	90	3.5	2.9	0.9	1	1
Nigeria	13.1	369	33.4	46.4	34.5	−5.5	0	4.1	−3.8	101	2.0	2.2	0.0	0	0
Rwanda	8.7	337	38.0	19.9	13.4	−2.8	4.1	3.2	−1.1	93	⋯	3.4	0.0	0	0
São Tomé and Príncipe	11.1	509	27.1	57.0	38.9	−3.6	15.2	46.1	−6.0	113	⋯	4.0	0.0	0	0
Senegal	13.8	747	21.0	38.1	3.8	−3.7	1.8	2.9	−2.1	98	2.9	3.0	0.9	1	0
Seychelles	33.8	5,178	4.3	50.9	1.6	−1.6	1.5	2.6	3.4	126	⋯	6.0	1.0	0	0
Sierra Leone	8.6	196	44.6	30.8	65.7	−5.6	0	6.6	3.5	84	1.6	2.0	0.0	0	1
South Africa	24.7	2,758	5.2	40.6	12.8	−0.6	0	0.1	−0.8	116	5.2	4.7	0.0	0	1
Swaziland	28.4	1,080	12.9	140.4	11.4	−0.9	0.8	0.5	0.6	109	⋯	3.9	1.0	0	0
Tanzania	12.8	156	56.8	44.3	29.8	−9.9	3.1	6.1	−3.6	100	3.6	2.9	0.8	0	0
Togo	15.8	423	36.4	56.3	6.0	−2.1	1.8	4.4	−0.7	100	2.0	2.7	0.9	1	1
Uganda	6.7	207	53.5	21.7	62.0	−3.2	2.9	4.8	−6.3	96	2.8	3.2	0.9	0	0
Zambia	17.0	442	19.6	61.0	88.5	1.8	4.2	13.8	0.9	100	2.7	3.0	0.0	0	1
Zimbabwe	31.8	671	14.2	59.2	20.4	−4.4	1.7	3.5	2.2	111	3.5	3.8	0.4	0	1

[1] See Appendix text for definitions and sources of variables.
[2] Proportion of time during the 11-year sample period characterized by sustained adjustment.

References

Abed, George, and others, 1998, *Fiscal Reforms in Low-Income Countries: Experience Under IMF-Supported Programs*, IMF Occasional Paper No. 160 (Washington: International Monetary Fund).

Aguirre, Carlos A., Peter S. Griffith, and M. Zühtu Yücelik, 1981, "Tax Policy and Administration in Sub-Saharan Africa," Part I, in *Taxation in Sub-Saharan Africa*, IMF Occasional Paper No. 8, by the Fiscal Affairs Department (Washington: International Monetary Fund).

Bardhan, Pranab, 1997, "Corruption and Development: A Review of Issues," *Journal of Economic Literature*, Vol. 35 (September), pp. 1320–46.

Farhadian-Lorie, Ziba, and Menachem Katz, 1989, "Fiscal Dimensions of Trade Policy," in *Fiscal Policy, Stabilization, and Growth in Developing Countries*, ed. by Mario I. Blejer and Ke-young Chu (Washington: International Monetary Fund).

Ghura, Dhaneshwar, and Michael T. Hadjimichael, 1996, "Growth in Sub-Saharan Africa," *Staff Papers*, International Monetary Fund, Vol. 43 (September), pp. 605–34.

Hamada, Koichi, 1994, "Broadening the Tax Base: The Economics Behind It," *Asian Development Review*, Vol. 12 (No. 2), pp. 51–84.

Heller, Peter S., 1975, "A Model of Public Fiscal Behavior in Developing Countries: Aid, Investment, and Taxation," *American Economic Review*, Vol. 65 (June), pp. 429–45.

———, 1997, "Strengthening Revenue Mobilization Efforts in Sub-Saharan Africa," in *Deepening Structural Reform in Africa: Lessons from East Asia*, ed. by Laura Wallace (Washington: International Monetary Fund).

Khan, Mohsin S., 1987, "Macroeconomic Adjustment in Developing Countries: A Policy Perspective," *World Bank Research Observer*, Vol. 2 (January), pp. 23–42.

Klitgaard, Robert, 1998, "International Cooperation Against Corruption," *Finance & Development* (March), pp. 3–6.

Leuthold, Jane H., 1991, "Tax Shares in Developing Economies: A Panel Study," *Journal of Development Economics*, Vol. 35 (January), pp. 173–85.

Musgrave, Richard, 1987, "Tax Reform in Developing Countries," in *The Theory of Taxation for Developing Countries*, ed. by David Newbery and Nicholas Stern (New York: Oxford University Press).

Nashahibi, Karim, and Stefania Bazzoni, 1994, "Exchange Rate Strategies and Fiscal Performance in Sub-Saharan Africa," *Staff Papers*, International Monetary Fund, Vol. 41 (March), pp. 76–122.

Stotsky, Janet G., and Asegedech WoldeMariam, 1997, "Tax Effort in Sub-Saharan Africa," IMF Working Paper 97/107 (Washington: International Monetary Fund).

Tanzi, Vito, 1977, "Inflation, Lags in Collection, and the Real Value of Tax Revenue," *Staff Papers*, International Monetary Fund, Vol. 24 (March), pp. 154–67.

———, 1981, "A Statistical Evaluation of Taxation in Sub-Saharan Africa," Part II in *Taxation in Sub-Saharan Africa,* IMF Occasional Paper No. 8, by the Fiscal Affairs Department (Washington: International Monetary Fund).

———, 1987, "Quantitative Characteristics of the Tax Systems of Developing Countries," in *The Theory of Taxation for Developing Countries*, ed. by David Newbery and Nicholas Stern (New York: Oxford University Press).

———, 1989, "The Impact of Macroeconomic Policies on the Level of Taxation and the Fiscal Balance in Developing Countries," *Staff Papers*, International Monetary Fund, Vol. 36 (September), pp. 633–56.

———, 1992, "Structural Factors and Tax Revenue in Developing Countries: A Decade of Evidence," in *Open Economies: Structural Adjustment and Agriculture*, ed. by Ian Goldin and L. Alan Winters (Cambridge, England; New York: Cambridge University Press).

———, and Howell H. Zee, 1997, "Fiscal Policy and Long-Run Growth," *Staff Papers*, International Monetary Fund, Vol. 44 (June), pp. 179–209.

15

Corruption, Extortion and Evasion

Jean Hindriks, Michael Keen, and Abhinay Muthoo

1. Introduction

Tax revenue does not collect itself. Instead its collection invites several forms of dishonesty and malpractice: taxpayers may try to evade their legal liabilities, while tax inspectors may solicit bribes in order to connive at such evasion or, more generally, may abuse the authority with which they are entrusted. Firm evidence on the extent of such practices is naturally hard to come by. But anecdotal evidence abounds, and can be stunning.[1] Moreover, any illusion that such practices are limited to

---

Reprinted from *Journal of Public Economics,* Vol. 74, Jean Hindriks, Michael Keen, and Abhinay Muthoo, "Corruption, Extortion and Evasion," pp. 395–430 (1999), with permission from Elsevier Science.

Financial support from the European Commission, both under contract ERBFM-BICT971968 and for the research network on Fiscal Implications of European Integration, is acknowledged with thanks. We also greatly appreciate helpful comments from participants in seminars at Bristol, Istanbul, Kyoto, Leicester, the LSE, Maastricht, Memorial and Warwick, and from Tim Besley, Nicolas Marceau, Steve Coate and the referees. Errors and views are ours alone, not necessarily those of any institution with which we are affiliated.

[1]Surveys in Taiwan Province of China, for example, report 94% of interviewees as having been "led to" bribe corrupt tax administrators and 80% of certified public accountants as admitting to bribing tax officials (Chu, 1990). For India, Mookherjee and Png (1995)—

developing countries has been dispelled by recent high profile cases in, for example, Italy and the UK. Not least, the Senate Hearings on the Internal Revenue Service (IRS) in autumn 1997 have raised in stark form the potential for abuse that lies in the considerable powers vested in tax collection agencies.

Dishonesty and corruption can make the real effects of the tax system very different from those that the formal tax system would have if honestly implemented. Even when such behaviour does not occur in equilibrium, moreover, the possibility of its occurring must be a central consideration in designing fair and effective tax collection mechanisms. A host of issues arise. How do dishonesty and corruption affect the distributional impact of the tax system? How should potentially corruptible tax inspectors be remunerated? Is it possible to eliminate evasion and corruption without compromising either the revenue raised by the tax system or its distributional effects?

The aim of this paper is to address these and other issues by developing and exploring a model of the encounter between a taxpayer and a tax inspector, both potentially corruptible, within the setting of a very general form of tax collection mechanism; a mechanism that is ultimately a matter for choice by the government. There are three key aspects of the generality that we seek.

The first is that we allow for the possibility of *extortio*n: the tax inspector can report, or threaten to the taxpayer that he will report, a taxable income higher than the true. For tax inspectors commonly possess many devices by which they may over-state taxable income: they might disallow or challenge legitimate deductions; they might charge tax on non-taxable incomes; they might simply lie about the taxpayer's characteristics (the floor space of her shop under a presumptive tax system, for example, or the number and age of her dependents). Appeals procedures provide some safeguard against over-assessment, but it is implausible to suppose them sufficiently perfect to preclude it altogether, and indeed the corrupt inspector has an incentive to use intimidatory methods to impede their effectiveness. Practitioners have little doubt as to the prevalence and importance of extortion by tax

---

citing Goswami et al. (1990)—report a confidential survey as finding that 76% of all government tax auditors took bribes, and that 68% of taxpayers had paid bribes. Ul Haque and Sahay (1996) report estimates that 20–30% of Nepalese tax revenue has been lost through bribery, and cite a former prime minister of Thailand as reckoning that the elimination of corruption would raise tax revenues by nearly 50%.

inspectors. The classic discussion of corruption by Klitgaard (1988) reports the response of Justice Plana, a senior official credited with a successful anti-corruption campaign in the Internal Revenue Service of the Philippines, when asked what he felt to be the most serious form of corruption: "It was extortion. When you resort to intimidation, when you threaten the taxpayer with a fantastic assessment—that to me is the most serious form of corruption. This practice was fairly extensive and very pernicious." (Klitgaard, 1988, p. 49).[2]

The second aspect of generality is the remuneration of tax inspectors. We allow a very general reward scheme, comprising a fixed wage and—in particular—a possibly non-linear commission payment on revenues collected.[3] Paying tax inspectors a commission gives them an incentive to resist the evasion of taxes. By the same token, however, it also gives them an incentive to over-state taxes: paying inspectors a commission may thus enhance their ability to extort by rendering credible the threat to over-report the taxpayer's income. Thus this second aspect of generality is closely linked to the first.[4]

The third aspect of generality is that—in order to address distributional issues—we allow for non-linear tax schedules. Such distributional complexities prove to be closely related to the possibility of non-linear commission schedules.

This generality is not pursued for its own sake. It generates what proves a rich framework, with each element generating distinctive and powerful conclusions. Two of these are especially striking:

---

[2]The IRS hearings in the US alleged abusive practices that have a similar taste: see, for example, the evidence of Jennifer Long (Finance Committee Press Release, 24th September 1997; http://www.senate.gov/finance/long.htm).

[3]Increased concern with the extent of evasion and corruption amongst tax collectors has indeed led to suggestions for some form of commission payment: see, for instance, Bagchi et al. (1995).

[4]Some countries, such as Belarus and Senegal, have indeed adopted explicit commission systems for tax inspectors. Reward systems within tax collection agencies may also have implicit commission-like features. As a less structured form of commission, Bird (1992) notes that banks used to collect taxes benefit from the use of these funds over some period; and a firm required to withhold taxes on the wages and salaries it pays will typically find that reporting rather than concealing a given gross wage payment reduces its profit tax liability, akin to a receipt of commission. Not least, it is worth remembering that a central method of tax collection throughout most of recorded history has been tax farming: the extreme form of commission system in which the collector pays the government a fixed fee in return for the right to retain all revenues legitimately collected. There has recently been a revival of interest in the possibilities for this ultimate form of privatisation: see, for example, Stella (1993).

- for tax schemes of broadly the kind usually observed, the impact of evasion and corruption in tax collection is unambiguously regressive: the richest have most to gain from evading taxes and are least vulnerable to extortion (because it is harder to credibly over-report their incomes); the poor, on the other hand, have few taxes to evade and their incomes can more plausibly be over-reported;

- the honest implementation of progressive taxation requires that the inspector be paid a commission on high income reports (but not on low). Financing that commission, however, requires that the average level of taxation be higher than would otherwise be the case. Costs of implementation—quite distinct from standard incentive effects in the generation of taxable income—thus create a trade-off between equity and efficiency objectives that seems previously to have been unnoticed.

There have of course been many previous studies of dishonesty in taxation. Almost all, however, deal only with evasion by dishonest taxpayers, under the assumption that tax collectors themselves are intrinsically honest.[5] In emphasising collusion between taxpayer and inspector we follow Basu et al. (1992), Besley and McLaren (1993), Chander and Wilde (1992), Carillo (1995a), Flatters and MacLeod (1995) and—with environmental regulation rather than tax collection in mind—Mookherjee and Png (1995). But none of these contains any of the distinctive features just described (except that Mookherjee and Png allow for linear (only) commissions).[6] Closest to the analysis here is Mookherjee (1998),[7] which extends the Mookherjee-Png framework (retaining the linearity restrictions) to raise some of the extortion-related issues addressed here.

There is also of course a large literature on corruption more generally (a recent review being Bardhan (1997)) with key contributions including those of Tirole (1986, 1992) and, on the empirical side, Mauro (1995) and Tanzi and Davoodi (1997). The present analysis has appli-

---

[5] See for example Border and Sobel (1987), Chander and Wilde (1998), Cowell (1990) and Reinganum and Wilde (1985).

[6] By the same token, we wish to abstract from the issues that these authors focus on: those that arise when the corrupt have corrupt supervisors (Basu et al., 1992; Carillo, 1995a), for example, or the inspector plays the same game over several periods, and so may be discouraged from taking bribes by payment of an efficiency wage and the threat of dismissal (Besley and McLaren, 1993; Flatters and MacLeod, 1995).

[7] We became aware of this paper after circulating earlier versions of the present one.

cations in these wider contexts. Recent treatments of collusion within institutions by Kofman and Lawarree (1993), Carillo (1995a,b), and Strausz (1995), for example, preclude extortion of the kind addressed here by arbitrarily assuming that the inspector cannot send a report to the principal that is less favourable to the agent than the truth.[8] Certainly the analytical framework here is open to many other interpretations;[9] the general structure of the problem with which we deal—a principal seeking to extract some payment from an agent and hiring an inspector to uncover and report private information upon which that payment can be based—fits a very wide variety of circumstances in which the possibility of corruption is a key concern.

The rest of the paper is organised as follows. Section 2 sets out the framework of analysis, and Section 3 then addresses a series of positive issues concerning the bargaining equilibrium. Section 4 considers the joint design of optimal tax, remuneration and penalty schedules. Section 5 summarises, and discusses some of our key modelling assumptions.

2. The Model

As described in Section 1, the aspect of tax collection on which we focus is the encounter between taxpayer and tax inspector. To this end we abstract from some features of the tax collection process that are important in some contexts. In particular, the model we use is most naturally interpreted as one in which all taxpayers will meet an inspector.[10] In practice, such encounters happen only to taxpayers selected for audit. In some cases—as with the US income tax—that audit selection

---

[8]Extortion has been examined in the contexts—very different from the present—of organised crime (by Konrad and Skaperdas (1995, 1997)) and public procurement (by Mogiliansky (1994) and Auriol (1996)).

[9]One might for example conceive of the principal as the owner of a firm run by the agent, with the former hiring an auditor (the supervisor) to uncover the firm's true profitability, upon which dividend payments can be based, in the knowledge that the manager retains use of funds not distributed and that manager and auditor may collude to misreport profitability. Or the principal might be a landlord, seeking to extract rents from her tenants but unsure of the profitability of their various holdings and to discover this employing a land agent.

[10]There are alternatives. One could read the model, for example, as having only one taxpayer encounter an inspector with all non-audited paying some fixed amount of tax (possibly zero).

process reflects the application of systematic rules, and there then arise further strategic considerations in the tax collection and design process that we do not address. In many cases, however, audit selection is de facto unsystematic, and one might with little loss think of the taxpayer population we examine as a random draw from a wider universe.[11] Moreover, there are contexts in which all taxpayers are audited: VAT administrations, for example, generally aim to audit all taxpayers within a cycle of a few years; and in some developing countries assessment (for land tax, for instance) is by local figures of authority, taken to have knowledge of each taxpayer's circumstances. The model developed here is not intended as a realistic representation of any actual tax system. Indeed part of the ultimate purpose is to explain why observed systems are not closer to that described here: why it is, for example, that the UK Inland Revenue does not routinely include revenue targets in its performance evaluations. Whilst the model used here is not a full representation of any real tax system, it addresses a feature—an encounter between taxpayer and inspector—that is common to all.

It may be helpful, before turning to its detail, to outline the essence of that model. Discussion of some of the key assumptions is deferred until the final section.

2.1 Outline

The government, G, wishes to raise some revenue, and may (or may not) also have distinct concerns with the levels of tax evasion and/or corruption, and also with the distribution of tax payments across taxpayers of differing incomes. Tax collection is delegated by G to an inspector I, who operates within the framework of a set of policy instruments and incentive schemes specified by G. It is common knowledge that I is corruptible, in the sense that he pursues his own interest and not necessarily that of G: in particular, I is open to bribery. The inspector encounters one of many citizens, C. The taxable income θ of each citizen is her own private information, but its distribution in the population is common knowledge. All citizens are open to the payment (or, conceivably, receipt) of bribes. The encounter between I and C may thus lead to the former receiving a bribe of B from the latter and reporting to G that C's income is r, which may differ from her true in-

---

[11]Though of course the question then remains as to the determination of the tax payments of those not audited.

come θ. This mis-reporting may be in either direction: income may be under-reported, with C and I colluding in the evasion of taxes, or it may be over-reported, corresponding to extortion. The citizen may (at some cost) appeal against the assessment by I. If she does not, then the income reported by I is subject to random audit by an honest collector. Both C and I are risk-neutral.

2.2 Details

The structure just outlined is modelled as a three-stage game.

2.2.1. Stage 1: G Announces the Tax Scheme

The government G announces (and commits itself to) a set of policy instruments $M \equiv \langle T, f_C, f_I, \lambda, \omega \rangle$ comprising: (i) a tax schedule $T: \Gamma \to \Gamma$, where Γ denotes the interval $[0, \infty)$ (thus $T(\theta)$ denotes the legal tax liability on income θ), (ii) a penalty schedule $f_i: \Gamma^2 \to \Re$, where $f_i(r, \theta)$ is the monetary fine imposed by G on player i ($i = C, I$) if income is reported as r but subsequently discovered to be θ, and (iii) a reward scheme for I comprising a fixed wage $\omega \in \Re$ and a commission schedule $\lambda : \Gamma \to [0, 1]$. The payment to I for a report r is $\omega + \lambda(r)T(r)$. We refer to any such set of instruments M as a *tax scheme*, and assume that G's choice is restricted to tax schemes that satisfy:

Assumption 1. The government can choose only tax schemes such that: (i) $T(\theta) \in [0, \theta]$, $\forall \theta \in \Gamma$, (ii) $f_i(\theta, \theta) = 0$, $i = C, I$, and (iii) $f_i(r, \theta) \geq 0$, $\forall (r, \theta) \in \Gamma^2$.

Assumption A1(i) merely ensures that average tax rates are non-negative and do not exceed 100% (which implies that $T(0) = 0$). A1(ii) means that those discovered to have reported truthfully are neither punished nor rewarded, and A1(iii) that rewards are never paid. Rewarding truthtelling is indeed never optimal in any of the problems with which we shall be concerned.[12] Knowing the tax scheme and the distribution of citizens' incomes, I decides whether or not to participate. If he does not, I obtains his reservation payoff, which we normalise to zero. The participation constraint is then that I's expected payoff be non-negative. We restrict attention in the positive part of the analysis to schemes

---

[12]This reflects our later assumption that the probability with which the income reported by I is audited by an honest inspector is exogenous and fixed.

that satisfy this condition, and in the normative part impose the stronger requirement that the ex post payoff to I be non-negative.

2.2.2. Stage 2: Income Reporting and Appeal

The inspector meets a citizen C drawn at random from the population. Before they talk, the citizen's true income $\theta \in \Gamma$ becomes common knowledge between them.[13] They then bargain (talk) according to a *game form* ϕ, which has two types of outcome: (i) the players reach an agreement $(m, B) \in \Gamma \times \Re$, with the interpretation that I certifies to the government that the true income of C is m, and C pays I a bribe of B, and (ii) the players fail to reach an agreement and the inspector unilaterally chooses an income report $n \in \Gamma$—since no agreement has been reached between I and C, no bribe is paid. With either type of outcome, I reports to G some income $r \in \Gamma$.[14]

For most of our results we shall need no further restrictions on ϕ. By way of illustration, one possible form for ϕ would be that in which: with probability 0.5, player i ($i = C, I$) makes an offer (m, B), which player j ($j \neq i$) can either accept or reject; if she rejects then the tax inspector I chooses n unilaterally.

The citizen is now given an opportunity to appeal against the income r reported by I. Appeals are always successful, in the sense that C's true income is certain to be revealed and—appeal judges being assumed incorruptible[15]—her liability restored to its correct level. But appealing incurs a fixed cost for C of $\alpha \geq 0$. For the most part we shall assume α to be strictly positive, as seems evidently realistic in many tax settings (and as may indeed be optimal, if appeals involve real resource cost, as a means of discouraging frivolous appeals).[16]

---

[13]This is clearly restrictive, but we focus here on other aspects of a problem that is already rather rich. The role of this assumption—and others—is discussed in the concluding section.

[14]It should be noted that G cannot control and choose the game form ϕ through which I and C bargain over the collusive agreement (side-contract). An implication of this observation is that the results from the standard mechanism design/implementation literature with complete information are inapplicable to our problem.

[15]Banerjee (1994) examines what happens when this assumption is violated.

[16]That appealing is costly, and that tax enforcers may exploit this, is again illustrated by the IRS hearings, with one irate taxpayer alleging that in his dealings with them: "... the government extorted $50,000 ... The government attorneys knew that it was going to cost an additional $50,000 to litigate the case and used it to leverage the IRS' position." (Evidence of Tom Savage) (Finance Committee Press Release, 24th September 1997; http://www.senate.gov/finance/savage.htm).

We do not allow either C or I to renege on any agreement (m, B) that is struck, though they may have an incentive to do so. The inspector, for example, having perhaps pocketed a bribe in return for condoning understatement of income, would now benefit, if λT is increasing, from raising the income report and so receiving a higher commission. One can also conceive of circumstances in which C would wish to appeal against an income report m to which she had agreed. We preclude such reneging by assuming any agreement struck to be enforceable by some means.[17]

2.2.3. Stage 3: Audit by an Honest Inspector

With probability $\pi \in (0, 1)$ (and unless it was the subject of appeal at Stage 2, in which case the truth is already known) I's report at Stage 2 is audited by an honest tax collector,[18] and C's true income discovered for sure. We assume π to be both exogenous and independent of the income report.

2.2.3.1. Payoffs

The payoffs to I and C depend on the circumstances that materialise. Consider in turn the two kinds of outcomes that the game form ϕ admits. The first is that an agreement is reached, in which case there are again two possibilities. Either there is an audit by an honest superior, in which case payoffs (that of player i being denoted by P_i) are

$$P_I = \omega + \lambda(\theta)T(\theta) - f_I(r, \theta) + B \tag{1}$$

$$P_C = \theta - T(\theta) - f_C(r, \theta) - B \tag{2}$$

or there is not such an audit, in which case

$$P_I = \omega + \lambda(r)T(r) + B \tag{3}$$

$$P_C = \theta - T(r) - B. \tag{4}$$

---

[17]The issue is a familiar one in analyses of collusion, as is our response to it: enforceability might be achieved through reputation effects whose modelling would considerably complicate the analysis. Tirole (1992) suggests that many of the qualitative insights obtained in models which assume that such side-contracts are enforceable might be robust to a relaxation of this assumption.

[18]Corruptible hierarchies are examined by Basu et al. (1992) and Carillo (1995a).

The second type of outcome is that in which no agreement is reached (in which case of course $B = 0$). If C chose to appeal at Stage 2, payoffs are[19]

$$P_I = \omega + \lambda(\theta)T(\theta) - f_I(r, \theta) \tag{5}$$

$$P_C = \theta - T(\theta) - \alpha. \tag{6}$$

If C chose not to appeal, then the outcome depends whether or not there turns out to be a random audit of the report made unilaterally by I; payoffs are thus as in (1)–(4) above, but with $B = 0$. Weighting the outcomes in (1)–(4) by the probability of audit π, note for later use that expected payoffs conditional on there being no appeal are:

$$P_I^e(r, B; \theta) \equiv \omega + \pi\lambda(\theta)T(\theta) + (1-\pi)\lambda(r)T(r) - \pi f_I(r, \theta) + B \tag{7}$$

$$P_C^e(r, B; \theta) \equiv \theta - \pi T(\theta) - (1-\pi)T(r) - \pi f_C(r, \theta) - B. \tag{8}$$

2.3. Bargaining Equilibrium

Stage 3 of the game being mechanical, we start to solve the game by considering C's decision in Stage 2 as to whether or not to appeal (given that no agreement is reached at Stage 2). Clearly she will not appeal if and only if

$$\theta - T(\theta) - \alpha \leq P_C^e(n, 0; \theta) \tag{9}$$

(our assumption being that when indifferent C does not appeal). At Stage 2, I will bear in mind this possibility of appeal when choosing the unilateral report to make if no agreement is reached. Intuition suggests that it can never be in the interest of the inspector to over-report to such an extent that C will choose to appeal. It is indeed easily verified that: *the citizen does not appeal in any subgame perfect equilibrium (SPE) of the sequential "disagreement" game that follows if C and I fail to agree at Stage 2.*[20]

---

[19]Any compensation paid to C is akin to a reduction of α. It should be noted, however, that C cannot be overcompensated.

[20]Proof is available on request.

Thus, the report that I makes if agreement is not reached at Stage 2 will be such as to maximise his expected payoff in the event of there being no appeal, $P_I^e(r, 0; \theta)$, subject to the condition ((9) above) that there will indeed be no appeal. It is assumed throughout that the set of such maximising reports is not empty. Denoting the generic element of the set by $n^*(\theta)$, equilibrium payoffs in the event that C and I do not reach agreement at Stage 2, which we refer to as *disagreement payoffs*, are:

$$d_I = P_I^e(n^*(\theta), 0; \theta) \tag{10}$$

$$d_C = P_C^e(n^*(\theta), 0; \theta). \tag{11}$$

The other possible outcome at Stage 2 is that C and I reach agreement. It is straightforward to show that an agreement (m, B) is Pareto efficient if and only if m maximises the *surplus*

$$S(\theta, m) \equiv P_I^e(m, B; \theta) + P_C^e(m, B; \theta) \tag{12}$$

$$= \theta + \omega - \pi[[1 - \lambda(\theta)]T(\theta) + f(m, \theta)] - (1 - \pi)[1 - \lambda(m)]T(m) \tag{13}$$

where $f \equiv f_C + f_I$ denotes the collective fine. Note that surplus is independent of the bribe, which simply determines its distribution between C and I. We take it that the set of surplus-maximising income reports—with generic element $m^*(\theta)$—is non-empty.

Assuming that the equilibrium outcome at Stage 2 is Pareto efficient and individually rational, it follows that C and I will indeed reach agreement at Stage 2: for (10)–(12) imply $d_I + d_C = S(\theta, n^*(\theta)) \leq S(\theta, m^*(\theta))$, and hence it is always possible to find a bribe such that $P_i^e(m^*(\theta), \theta, B) \geq d_i$ for $i = I, C$. Both players, that is, can fare better than in the disagreement game. Thus, for any $\theta \in \Gamma$, the inspector and the citizen reach agreement at Stage 2 on a surplus-maximising income report $m^*(\theta)$. Moreover, $B^*(\theta)$ is such that $P_i^e(m^*(\theta), B^*(\theta); \theta) \geq d_i$ ($i = C, I$). Although the disagreement payoffs and the possibility of appeal thus have no impact on the income report, they do of course potentially affect the negotiated bribe $B^*(\theta)$.

3. Positive Issues

Continuing the backward induction, the next step would be to characterise G's choice of tax scheme at Stage 1. We postpone this, however, until the next section. Instead we now explore key positive aspects of the bargaining equilibria associated with tax schemes broadly resembling those observed in practice, the wider purpose being to develop some sense of the way in which the structure of the tax scheme affects the outcome of the encounter between C and I.

3.1. Corruption and Tax Evasion

The present framework immediately points to a sharp distinction between two kinds of dishonesty: tax evasion (by which we mean under-reporting of income, $m^*(\theta) < \theta$) and corruption (meaning the payment of bribes, $B^*(\theta) \neq 0$). In previous analyses, which have precluded the threat of over-reporting, these are two sides of a single coin: a bribe is paid to the inspector only in order that he might benefit from, and therefore collude in, under-payment of taxes. Here, in contrast, evasion and corruption are quite different things; and a first task is to establish the precise relationship between them.

Note first that nothing in the specification of the model precludes the possibilities, however unfamiliar, that in equilibrium income will be over-stated and/or bribes paid by the inspector to the citizen. Indeed, one can conceive of circumstances in which the commission payment increases so rapidly with the income report that it becomes worth the inspector's while to bribe the citizen to agree on an over-statement of income. The following establishes, inter alia, seemingly natural restrictions on the tax scheme which suffice to rule out bargaining equilibria with such properties:

Proposition 1. *If both $\lambda(\cdot)T(\cdot)$ and $[1 - \lambda(\cdot)]T(\cdot)$ are strictly increasing, then for each $\theta \in \Gamma$: (i) $m^*(\theta) \leq \theta$, (ii) $B^*(\theta) \geq 0$, (iii) $n^*(\theta) \geq \theta$, and (iv) $m^*(\theta) < \theta \Rightarrow B^*(\theta) > 0$.*

Proof. See Appendix A.

The intuition is straightforward. The collective payment that C and I make, if not audited, is $[1 - \lambda(m)]T(m)$; if this increases with the income they report then—since detection of any misreport can only increase their collective payment—over-reporting can never maximise their surplus (which is part (i) of the proposition). And if the inspector's commission λT is increasing with the income reported, he will have to receive some bribe in order to be willing to submit an under-report (part (ii)); nor will his threat in the disagreement game involve under-reporting, since with an increasing commission the inspector can do better by reporting truthfully (part (iii)). And to tolerate any evasion of taxes, involving both a loss of commission and potential penalties, the inspector will need to be paid off (part (iv)).

Part (iv) of Proposition 1 indicates that, under the conditions given—and using the terms in the senses defined above—evasion implies corruption.[21] The converse, however, is not true: there exist schemes[22] for which (for some θ) $B^*(\theta) > 0$ even though $m^*(\theta) = \theta$. The reason is clear: a citizen confronted by an inspector willing and able to over-report their liability will be willing to pay a bribe simply to prevent their doing so. Bribes thus emerge not only as a means to share the gains from evasion but also as the manifestation of extortion. This is not merely a theoretical possibility. Jain (1997), for example, speaks of the prevalence in India of a "No harassment tax," paid to tax officials simply to be assessed expeditiously and correctly.

3.2. Evaders as Victims

A related implication of the present model is that tax evaders—naturally thought of as villains—may in fact be victims, injured by the power invested in corruptible tax collectors. For it is perfectly possible that the equilibrium payoff to the citizen lies below that she would receive if her true income were reported. That is, it may be that for some θ:

$$P_C^e(m^*(\theta), B^*(\theta); \theta) < P_C^e(\theta, 0; \theta). \qquad (14)$$

In this case we call the type θ citizen a *victim* of extortion, while if the reverse inequality applies she is an *accomplice* in evasion and corruption.[23] This distinction between victims and accomplices is exactly

---

[21]Mookherjee and Png (1995) do not obtain the result that evasion implies corruption. This is because, in their model, to reduce evasion the inspector must be motivated to *work* by the prospect of a bribe payment; corruption is needed as an incentive device to combat evasion when the incentive scheme is linear. In our model, on the other hand, a non-linear incentive scheme replicates the incentive effect of bribery.

[22]See footnote 34 below.

[23]Interestingly, the argument that citizens may be more sinned against than sinning has indeed emerged as a line of defence in recent high-profile anti-corruption cases in Italy. Giorgio Armani, for example, ". . . has admitted handing an envelope stuffed with cash to his tax advisor to keep the inspectors at bay. But he said ". . . It is up to the judicial investigators to determine whether I was guilty of corruption or whether I was the subject of extortion." *(The Independent,* June 8th 1995.)

equivalent to one cast in terms of an *effective surcharge*, Σ, paid by the taxpayer, defined as the excess of her expected payment of taxes, bribes and fines over her true tax liability: from (8),

$$\Sigma(\theta) \equiv (1-\pi)[T(m^*(\theta)) - T(\theta)] + \pi f_C(m^*(\theta), \theta)$$

$$+ (1-\pi)B^*(\theta) \qquad (15)$$

with type θ being a victim (accomplice) iff $\Sigma(\theta) > 0 (< 0)$. We make further use of this notion of an effective surcharge below.

To identify the precise source of this possibility of the victimised evader, note that a citizen with income θ cannot be a victim if $n^*(\theta) = \theta$: for her disagreement payoff d_C is then $P_C^e(\theta, 0; \theta)$, and since (see Section 2.3 above) $P_C^e(m^*(\theta), B^*(\theta); \theta) \geq d_C$ the inequality in (14) cannot hold. From the definition of $n^*(\theta)$, it is clear that either of two conditions is sufficient for $n^*(\theta) = \theta$. The first is that $\lambda(\theta) = 0$; the second that $\alpha = 0$. Thus victims can emerge in equilibrium only if the inspector is paid, at least in part, on commission: without this, the inspector has no incentive to over-report in the disagreement game. And they can also emerge only if appeals are costly to the taxpayer, who can otherwise neutralise any threat of over-reporting. Extortion thus ultimately arises from the combination of two factors: the incentive that performance-related payment gives the inspector to over-report, and imperfections in the appeal process.

It is possible too to derive some sense of the groups most vulnerable to extortion. Note first that in many contexts there is clearly some upper bound on the level of income that a tax inspector may credibly report. A collector visiting a poor rural village or assessing a presumptive tax on small traders, for example, is likely to beware of inviting suspicion and investigation by reporting implausibly high incomes. Suppose then—just for the present—that there exists some maximal possible level of income (normalised at unity), so that $\Gamma = [0, 1]$. Then:

Proposition 2. *Under the conditions of Proposition 1, and with $\Gamma = [0, 1]$:* (i) *the richest citizen ($\theta = 1$) can never be a victim, and* (ii) *the poorest citizen ($\theta = 0$) can never be an accomplice.*

Proof. Part (i) follows from the discussion after (14) on noting that the constraint $n \leq 1$ imposed on the disagreement game combined with (iii) of Proposition 1 together imply $n^*(1) = 1$. For part (ii), note that the constraint $m \geq 0$ on reported incomes combined with part (i) of

Proposition 1 implies that $m^*(0) = 0$. Using this and A1(ii) in (15), the type 0 citizen is an accomplice only if $B^*(0) < 0$, which is precluded by Proposition 1(ii). □

The rich thus enjoy a natural protection against extortion whilst the poor suffer from a natural vulnerability. The richest are protected because their true incomes are so high that they cannot credibly be overstated by the inspector. The poorest, on the other hand, are vulnerable because their true liabilities are so low that the bribe which the inspector is able to extort by threatening to over-report exceeds any conceivable gain from condoning evasion.

3.3. The Regressive Effects of Dishonesty

In practice, fines for tax evasion are almost invariably specified as increasing and convex functions $g_i(u)$ of the amount of tax under-reported,[24] $u \equiv T(\theta) - T(m)$. Such restrictions on the penalty functions f_i may not be optimal, but their pervasiveness in practice makes this an important special case. Consider then:

Example A. Any tax scheme satisfying A1 and such that:

(i) $f_C(m, \theta) = g_C(u)$, with g_C increasing and strictly convex for $u \geq 0$ and zero otherwise.

(ii) $f_I(m, \theta) = g_I(u)$, with g_I strictly convex, strictly increasing for $u > 0$ and strictly decreasing for $u < 0$.

(iii) T strictly increasing and strictly convex.

(iv) T, g_C and g_I twice continuously differentiable on the interior of their domains.

(v) $\lambda(\theta) = \beta$, $\forall \theta \in \Gamma$.

The further and not implausible assumptions have thus been made that: the tax schedule is progressive in the sense of implying an increasing marginal tax rate; the taxpayer pays no fine in the event of over-reporting; fines on the inspector also depend only on the amount of taxes mis-reported; and the commission rate is constant (perhaps zero).

---

[24]In the UK, for example, the maximum fine is specified in the Taxes Management Act as 100% of the tax lost, but the Inland Revenue may accept a lesser amount depending, inter alia, on the "size and gravity" of the offence (*Tolley's Tax Guide, 1992–93*, pp. 121–122).

Suppose too, specialising the example further, that the equilibrium bribe is determined by the familiar "split-the-difference" outcome, with C and I each receiving their disagreement payoff d_i plus one-half the excess of the maximised $S(m^*(\theta), \theta)$ over the sum of those disagreement payoffs.[25] We assume the split-the-difference form for the remainder of this section, though not, it should be emphasised, anywhere else in the analysis. This leads, when embedded in the general framework of the preceding section, to an equilibrium bribe of

$$B^*(\theta) = \frac{1}{2}(1-\pi)[[1 + \lambda(n^*(\theta))]T(n^*(\theta)) \\ - [1 + \lambda(m^*(\theta))]T(m^*(\theta))] \\ + \frac{\pi}{2}[f_I(m^*(\theta), \theta) - f_C(m^*(\theta), \theta) \\ + f_C(n^*(\theta), \theta) - f_I(n^*(\theta), \theta)]. \qquad (16)$$

Combining the plausible form of tax scheme in Example A with the split-the-difference rule gives a very striking pattern of bribery and effective surcharging:

Theorem 1. *For any tax scheme of the form in Example A and with $\Gamma = [0, 1]$, if the bribe is given by the split-the-difference rule then there exist θ_1 and θ_2 such that*:

(i) $B^*(\theta)$ *is strictly increasing in θ on $(0, \theta_1]$, constant on $[\theta_1, \theta_2]$ and strictly decreasing on $[\theta_2, 1]$.*
(ii) $\Sigma(\theta)$ *is strictly decreasing on $[0, \theta_1]$ and $[\theta_2, 1]$ and constant on $[\theta_1, \theta_2]$, with $\theta_2 = 1$ if $\beta\alpha = 0$.*

Proof. See Appendix B.

Part (i) shows the pattern of bribery that emerges in equilibrium to have the general form in Fig. 1, the most notable feature being that the bribe is greater in the middle of the income distribution than at either extreme. Though by no means apparent a priori, this finding that it is the middle classes who pay the biggest bribes has a ready explanation.

---

[25]The split-the-difference rule can be rationalised in several ways. In the symmetric ultimatum bargaining game described above, (16) will be the unique subgame perfect equilibrium bribe. Other game forms ϕ will also generate (as a unique equilibrium) the split-the-difference rule (see, for example, Muthoo (1999)).

Figure 1. The Equilibrium Bribe Under Conditions of Theorem 1

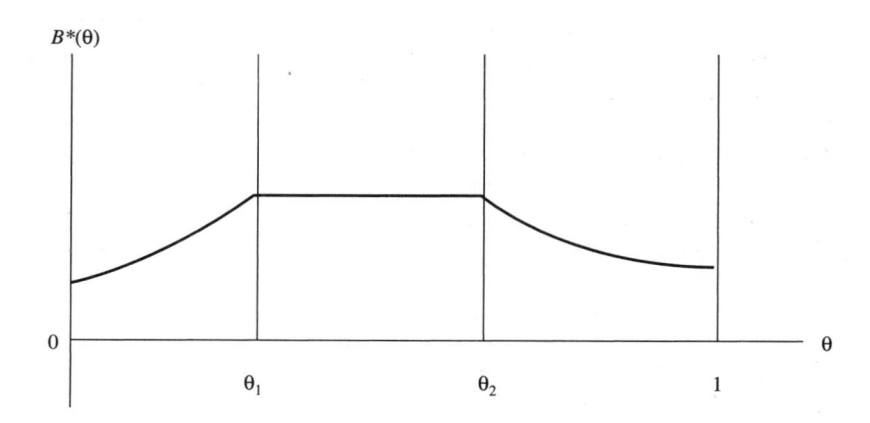

Figure 2. The Effective Surcharge Under Conditions of Theorem 1

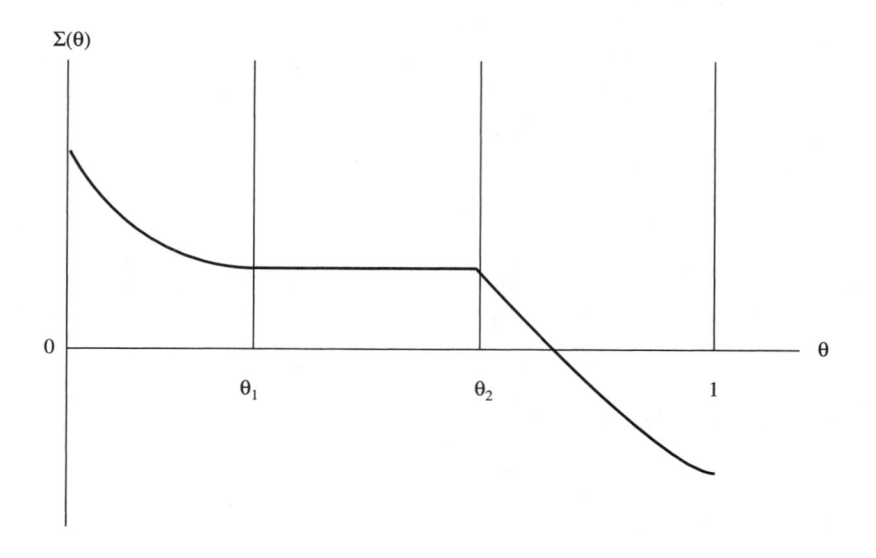

For the poor, their low incomes and hence low tax liabilities offer little scope for collusive gain from evasion and at the same time limit the extent to which bribes can be extracted from them by the threat of over-reporting (both effects being accentuated by progressivity of the tax schedule). The high incomes of the rich protect them from extortion (as discussed after Proposition 2), and so limit the extent to which they must share with the inspector the gains from evasion. The incomes of the middle classes, however, are both high enough to create sizeable gains from evasion and low enough to leave them wide open to extortion.

Part (ii) of the Proposition shows the effective surcharge Σ to have the general shape shown in Fig. 2: strictly decreasing at the extremes and constant in between.[26] This is perhaps as one would expect at the top, given the decreasing bribe displayed in part (i): the rich are less vulnerable to extortion and also have more to gain by evading tax. That the effective surcharge also falls at low levels of income despite an increasing bribe reflects a growing opportunity to evade as income reaches deeper into the range of a progressive system: increased gains from evasion more than offset the larger bribes that must be paid.

The implications for the distributional consequences of equilibrium evasion and corruption are very powerful: part (ii) shows that their effect is equivalent, so far as the taxpayer is concerned, to adding to the statutory tax schedule an effective surcharge that decreases with income in the manner illustrated. Such a surcharge is inherently regressive, implying[27] that the distribution of expected net incomes—net, that is, of taxes, bribes and fines—is unambiguously less equal (in the Lorenz sense) than the distribution of income net only of legal tax liabilities. Tax schemes similar to those often observed thus have the feature that the impact of evasion and corruption are unambiguously regressive.[28]

3.4. Fighting Corruption and Evasion

A central concern in discussions of corruption and evasion is how best to combat them. To this end, and as a source of intuition for the subse-

---

[26] As drawn, Σ becomes negative above θ_2; it might, however, become negative below θ_1.

[27] By for example, Proposition 3 of Jakobsson (1976).

[28] Note that this is true, moreover, even if—because either the commission rate or the cost of appeal is zero—there is no prospect of extortion: this would simply imply $\theta_2 = 1$, eliminating the upper range in the figures. The regressivity result, in particular, would remain entirely clear-cut.

quent analysis of optimal policy, we briefly consider some comparative statics.[29] Consider first the penalty structure. Mookherjee and Png (1995) find that increasing the penalties on corrupt inspectors actually increases the bribe: inspectors demand a higher payment to collude in misleading the government. Focusing on the other side of the encounter, Chander and Wilde (1992) show—in a rather different setting involving asymmetries of information between I and C—that increasing penalties on C can also lead to an increase in the equilibrium bribe: the citizen needs to offer a higher bribe in order to ensure that the inspector colludes in evasion. Here, however, an important distinction emerges between penalties levied in the event of over- and under-reporting. For brevity, we focus on the significance of this for the impact of penalties on the inspector:[30]

Proposition 3. *Consider any tax scheme M satisfying the conditions of Proposition 1, for which T, λ and f_i are differentiable and for which fines are strictly increasing in the extent of misreporting (so that $\nabla_m f_i(m, \theta) < 0 \; (> 0)$ as $m < (>)\theta$). Suppose too that the bribe is given by the split-the-difference rule. Then:*

(i) *a multiplicative increase in the fine on I in the event of under-reporting at all $\theta \in \Gamma$ has an ambiguous effect on $B^*(\theta)$, $\forall \theta \in \Gamma$;*

(ii) *a multiplicative increase in the fine on I in the event of over-reporting at all $\theta \in \Gamma$ reduces $B^*(\theta)$ for all θ.*

Proof. See Appendix C.

The ambiguity in part (i) reflects counter-acting effects. First, an increase in the penalty on I for under-reporting makes the inspector more reluctant to under-report income, which favors an increase in the bribe; this gives the Mookherjee-Png result. But at the same time $m^*(\theta)$ increases, tending to decrease the bribe and so making the overall effect ambiguous. Part (ii) shows that increasing the penalty on I for over-reporting, on the other hand, unambiguously reduces the bribe. Thus it is over-reporting by I that needs to be penalised heavily to discourage corruption, since it is this that reduces I's disagreement payoff. The instinct of Justice Plana cited in Section 1—that the control of corruption requires that extortion be especially heavily punished—is thus borne out.

---

[29] For the rest of the paper, we revert to our assumption that $\Gamma = [0, \infty)$.
[30] Converse remarks apply to penalties on the taxpayer.

Turning to the effects of paying higher commissions, one finds:

Proposition 4. *Under the conditions of Proposition 3, a multiplicative increase in the commission schedule:*

(i) *strictly increases $m^*(\theta)$ for all θ such that $m^*(\theta) > 0$,*

(ii) *strictly reduces the government's net revenue, and*

(iii) *has an ambiguous effect on equilibrium bribes.*

Proof. See Appendix D.

This confirms the intuition of Section 1: giving the inspector an interest in a high income report tends to reduce the extent of evasion (since by Proposition 1 $m^*(\theta) \leq \theta$). Part (ii) indicates, however, that the consequent increase in the government's revenue is more than offset by the increased cost of the commission itself. This is best thought of as an envelope result: a small increase in m has no effect on surplus, and hence also no effect on net revenues (the increased payment of taxes being exactly offset by reduced receipts from fines); thus only the direct cost of the higher commission remains.

What of the impact of commission payments on corruption? In a different context, Mookherjee and Png (1995) show that increasing the commission rate (which they assume to be constant) leads to a higher bribe (at all θ); the intuition being that a higher commission rate increases the disagreement payoff to the inspector. In the present setting, however, the impact is ambiguous. This is at first sight surprising, since the possibility of over-reporting that is allowed here means that an increase in the commission rate increases still further the inspector's disagreement payoff, and to that extent reinforces the tendency for the bribe to increase. But there is also another effect at work: the increase in reported income m^*. The result of Mookherjee and Png (1995) relates to circumstances in which the report remains unchanged at a corner solution implied by linear penalties; thus the only way that the inspector can realise any benefit from his improved disagreement payoff is by an increased bribe. Here, however, he may also benefit from the increased commission payment associated with the higher income report.

4. Optimal Tax Schemes

Continuing the backward induction begun in Section 2 we arrive now at Stage 1 of the game: the government's choice of tax scheme. Thus

G selects the tax schedule T, reward system $\langle \omega, \lambda \rangle$ and penalty functions f_i ($i = C, I$). The government's choice will depend, of course, on its objectives. Four likely concerns come to mind: the revenue raised, the extent of evasion, the degree of corruption and the overall distributional impact of the tax scheme. To bring out the distinctive implications of each, we consider first the case in which G cares only about revenue and then, in turn, add in each of the other concerns. Before doing so, we introduce one further restriction. The design problem in this model is trivial if penalties are unbounded. We therefore now restrict attention to schemes that satisfy the limited liability constraints in:

Assumption 2. For any $\theta \in \Gamma$ and any $r \in \Gamma$: (i) $f_I(r, \theta) \leq \omega + \lambda(\theta) T(\theta)$, and (ii) $f_C(r, \theta) \leq \theta - T(\theta)$.

A2(i) requires that I receive at least his reservation utility (normalised, recall, at zero) even if audited, irrespective of which citizen he encounters and the income he reports. A2(ii) requires that C not need to draw on any other resources to meet her liabilities if audited, again irrespective of the income reported. A tax scheme is henceforth called *admissible* iff it satisfies A1 and A2, and the set of such schemes is denoted by Ω. Note that A1 and A2 imply that $E_\theta[P_I^e(m^*(\theta), B^*(\theta); \theta)] \geq 0$ so that I's participation constraint is satisfied. Moreover, since $T(0) = 0$ and $f_I \geq 0$, A2(i) implies that $\omega \geq 0$. Pure tax farming is thus precluded.

4.1. Maximising Revenue and Minimising Evasion

Suppose first that the government's sole concern is to maximise (any increasing function of) its expected revenue, which is

$$P_G^*(M) \equiv E_\theta[(1 - \pi)[1 - \lambda(m^*(\theta))]T(m^*(\theta))$$

$$+ \pi[[1 - \lambda(\theta)]T(\theta) + f_C(m^*(\theta), \theta)$$

$$+ f_I(m^*(\theta), \theta]] - \omega. \tag{17}$$

Such behaviour can be rationalised in several ways: G might be a leviathan; or G may be benevolently providing a public good that citizens value more highly, at the margin, than their private incomes; or, as we shall prove later, G may ultimately be pursuing a Rawlsian maximin objective. In any event, revenue maximisation proves a useful benchmark, which we shall very soon be tempering by other concerns.

For there are, in general, many revenue-maximising tax schemes. Suppose then that G is also averse to tax evasion; we do not model the reason for this, though it seems clear that evasion is widely seen as costly not only in terms of its direct impact on tax revenues but also, and perhaps more fundamentally, in jeopardising the perceived integrity and legitimacy of the tax system. The question then immediately arises as to whether it is possible for G to eliminate evasion without compromising its revenue objective. This in turn is essentially the question of whether the revelation principle applies in our framework, despite the restrictions imposed on in A1–A2, so that attention can be confined to schemes that induce truthful reporting. Denoting by $\Omega^{ep} \subseteq \Omega$ the set of admissible schemes that are *evasion-proof* in the sense that

$$S(\theta, \theta) \geq S(m, \theta), \forall \theta \in \Gamma, \forall m \neq \theta (m \in \Gamma) \tag{18}$$

the following shows that it does indeed apply:[31]

Lemma 1. *For any tax scheme $M \in \Omega$ there exists $M' \in \Omega^{ep}$ such that $P_G^*(M) = P_G^*(M')$.*

Any tax scheme that maximises revenue over the evasion-proof set Ω^{ep} thus also maximises revenue over the wider set Ω: G can eliminate evasion without foregoing any revenue. The class of schemes that are both revenue-maximising and evasion-proof is of obvious importance. The following provides a complete characterisation:

Theorem 2. *An admissible tax scheme is revenue-maximising and evasion-proof if and only if it has the features*: (a) $\pi\theta = [1 - \lambda(\theta)]T(\theta)$, *for all* $\theta \in \Gamma$, (b) $\omega = 0$, *and* (c) $f(r, \theta) \geq (1 - \pi)(\theta - r)$, $\forall r, \theta \in \Gamma$ *such that* $r < \theta$. *The expected revenue raised by any such scheme is* $\pi\theta^e$, *where θ^e denotes the expected value of θ.*

Proof. See Appendix E.

The proof is somewhat involved, but the underlying reasoning is quite straightforward. Take the necessity part. Suppose first that G has decided to set the maximal penalties allowed by the limited liability condition A2. If C and I are discovered on audit to have misreported they then pay

---

[31]The proof of Lemma 1 is available on request.

to G a total amount (net of remuneration to I) of $T + f_I + f_C - \omega - \lambda T$; which is equal, given maximal penalties, to θ. Their collective payment on a truthful report, $[1 - \lambda(\theta)]T(\theta)$, can thus be raised only to equality with their expected loss if they were to mis-report, which is $\pi\theta$: at any higher level they would make a lesser expected payment by reporting some $m < \theta$. This establishes the necessity of the condition in (a). And G's net receipts from a truthful report, $[1 - \lambda(\theta)]T(\theta) - \omega$, are then maximised by setting $\omega = 0$ (which is condition (b)), in which case the maximised value of expected revenue (from (a)) is $\pi\theta^e$. Finally, it is readily checked that when (a) is satisfied truthful reporting requires that penalties satisfy (c). Verifying sufficiency is routine.

Several conclusions follow from Theorem 2. Part (a) implies that the two requirements of revenue maximisation and evasion-proofness place very few additional restrictions on either tax or commission schedules when each is considered in isolation.[32] Using A1, for example, part (a) of the Theorem implies that the average tax rate $T(\theta)/\theta$ be no less than the probability of audit π, and the commission rate no greater than $1 - \pi$. What Theorem 2 does very substantially restrict, however, is the relationship between T and λ. In particular, part (a) implies that it is perfectly possible for G to raise the maximum feasible revenue by implementing a tax schedule that is progressive (in the sense that the average tax rate rises with income); but only if it also

---

[32]Proposition 4(ii) might suggest that the revenue-maximising commission rate is zero. For it might lead one to suspect that given any mechanism with a positive commission rate, expected revenue could be increased—albeit at the cost of inducing some evasion—by a small reduction in the commission rate. This would appear to contradict Theorem 2. Notice, however, that condition (c) of Theorem 2 (combined with A1(ii)) implies that in any admissible tax scheme that is revenue-maximising and evasion-proof, the collective fine $f(m, \theta)$ is not differentiable in m at $m = \theta$. Hence, such a tax scheme does not satisfy the hypotheses of Proposition 4, which require, in particular, that the collective fine be differentiable in m at $m = \theta$—which, in turn, implies (combined with the monotonicity assumptions) that the derivative of f with respect to m at θ is zero. It should be noted that the proof of Proposition 4(ii) is based on the envelope argument, which requires, in particular, that S be differentiable in m at $m = \theta$—and this would not be true if f is not differentiable in m at $m = \theta$. Hence, any tax scheme considered in Proposition 4 is not an admissible, revenue-maximising and evasion-proof tax scheme—and no admissible, revenue-maximising and evasion-proof tax scheme satisfies the conditions of Proposition 4. In fact, it can be shown (proofs available on request) that if G has to choose a tax scheme from the class of tax schemes that satisfy the conditions of Proposition 4, then: (i) the evasion-proofness requirement implies that the commission rate equals one, and the maximal revenue raised is zero, and (ii) revenue is maximised through a *non* evasion-proof tax scheme, in which the commission rate is zero.

sets a reward structure such that the commission rate λ also increases with the income reported. By the same token, a constant commission rate is optimal only if tax liabilities are proportional to income. Intuitively, a progressive tax schedule means that the tax saved by any under-statement of income is greater at higher incomes; and an increasing commission rate is then needed to counter the consequently greater temptation to evade taxes, which it does by raising the cost to the inspector, in foregone commission, of conniving in an understatement of income.

Part (a) also reveals the key role played in the model by the parameter π: it is the strength of the constraint on dishonesty inherent in the wider economic environment that ultimately determines how much revenue the government can raise.

Part (b) of the theorem indicates that the fixed wage component of remuneration is set at its lowest possible level: any excess of I's expected payment over his reservation utility must come entirely from commission payments.

Part (c) has two useful implications. One is that it is only the collective fine—not its allocation between C and I—that matters for evasion-proofness and revenue-maximisation. The other, more striking, is that the achievement of these objectives does not require that penalties be set at their maximum feasible levels. Indeed these penalties can take a very simple form: it is enough that they be proportional to the extent of understatement, with the factor of proportionality being greater the less effective is the audit check.

Combining these observations, Theorem 2 points to two sets of circumstances in which commission payments may have a role and—consequently, given part (b)—the inspector optimally paid more than his reservation utility level. One (from part (a)) is that in which, for some reason, the preferred tax schedule has a non-constant marginal rate (because, for example, the preferred schedule is progressive). The other is that in which, for some reason, fines on the citizen cannot be set at levels that satisfy part (c): for then, given A2(i) and part (b), (c) can be satisfied only if commissions are non-zero. In both of these cases, the payment to I of an "efficiency wage"—though here, since $\omega = 0$, the surplus comes not from the fixed wage but from the commission—serves to provide scope for punishment that counteracts incentives to dishonesty, whether created by non-linearities in the tax schedule (which we consider in some detail below) or restrictions on the penalties that can be imposed on C.

4.2. Corruption-Aversion

Suppose now that the government's concerns extend beyond the revenue it raises and the extent of tax evasion to include also—again for reasons that we do not model, but seem evident enough in practice[33]—the degree of corruption in tax collection. As emphasised earlier, the possibility of extortion means that corruption is conceptually quite distinct from evasion: the threat of over-reporting may enable I to extract a bribe merely to report the truth. Thus there certainly exist schemes which belong to the revenue-maximising, evasion-proof class Ω^{ep} characterised in Theorem 2 but are not corruption-proof (in the sense that it is not the case that $B^*(\theta) = 0$, $\forall \theta \in \Gamma$).[34]

Are there then any evasion-proof and revenue-maximising schemes that are also corruption-proof? The further requirement imposed by corruption-proofness, it can be shown,[35] is that $n^*(\theta) = \theta \forall \theta \in \Gamma$. This is as intuition would suggest: if there is no prospect of evasion then bribes can arise only in connection with extortion, to prevent which it is necessary to remove any incentive for I to over-report. If appeals are costless (so that $\alpha = 0$), corruption-proofness follows immediately. The more interesting and relevant case, we have argued, is surely that in which $\alpha > 0$. Eliminating extortion is then a matter of ensuring that the gains to I from a disagreement outcome in which C's income is over-reported—which depend on the commission received on the associated tax payments—are outweighed by the penalties I incurs if the over-report is discovered. More precisely, denote by $N^*(\theta)$ the set of income reports that would not be appealed by a citizen with income θ; that is, recalling (9),

$$N^*(\theta) \equiv \{n \in \Gamma | (1-\pi)T(n) + \pi f_C(n, \theta) \le (1-\pi)T(\theta) + \alpha\}. \quad (19)$$

Then it will never be in I's interest to over-report if and only if $P_I^e(\theta, 0; \theta) \ge P_I^e(n, 0; \theta)$ for all $n \in N^*(\theta)$; which, using (7), is the condition

$$(1-\pi)[\lambda(n)T(n) - \lambda(\theta)T(\theta)] \le \pi f_I(n, \theta), \quad (20)$$

---

[33]Nalebuff (1998), for example, argues powerfully for such an aversion to corruption per se.

[34]Consider, for example, the tax scheme with $T(\theta) = t\theta$ for some $t \in (\pi, 1]$, $\lambda(\theta) = 1 - \pi/t$ and satisfying (b) and (c) of Theorem 2. By Theorem 2, this is revenue-maximising and evasion-proof. But it can also be shown to imply $B^*(\theta) > 0$, $\forall \theta \in [0, \hat{\theta})$ where $\hat{\theta} \equiv \min\{\alpha/\pi, 1-\pi\}$. (Proof available on request).

[35]The proof is available on request.

so that the expected gain in commission is less than the increase in the expected penalty paid by I. Clearly then:

Lemma 2. *An admissible tax scheme is evasion-proof, corruption-proof and revenue-maximising if and only if the conditions of Theorem 2 hold and (d) for any $\theta \in \Gamma$, condition (20) holds $\forall n \in N^*(\theta)$.*

There is one obvious way of satisfying these conditions. For the incentive to over-report can be removed by simply paying no commission. Using this in Theorem 2 leads one to:

Corollary 1. *The following tax scheme is evasion-proof, corruption-proof and revenue-maximising*:

(i) $T(\theta) = \pi\theta$, $\forall \theta \in \Gamma$,

(ii) $\lambda(\theta) = 0$, $\forall \theta \in \Gamma$,

(iii) $\omega = 0$, *and*

(iv) $f_I(r, \theta) = 0$ *and* $f_C(r, \theta) = (1 - \pi)(\theta - r) \forall r, \theta \in \Gamma$ *such that* $r < \theta$.

This is a very simple scheme, involving a proportional tax schedule (with average and marginal rate equal to the probability of random audit) and a fixed wage system for inspectors. A government that likes revenue and dislikes evasion and corruption can thus do no better than set a proportional tax and pay its collectors a fixed wage. The tax scheme in Corollary 1 looks very much like the kind of straightforward tax arrangements often recommended by tax policy analysts, especially for developing countries. The rationale, however, is typically in terms of such considerations as administrative ease and the avoidance of creating arbitrage opportunities. The rationale provided here is entirely different: it is that one can preclude extortion by paying no commission to inspectors, but then any progressivity in the tax structure invites evasion and corruption.[36]

There may though be tax schemes other than that in Corollary 1 which maximise revenue without inducing evasion or corruption. The following establishes a striking necessary condition: any such scheme must possess the features of that in Corollary 1 in the lower part of the income distribution:

Proposition 5. *It is necessary for an admissible scheme to be evasion-proof, revenue-maximising and corruption-proof that:*

---

[36]As a referee notes, we should emphasise that the result in Corollary 1 hinges on the assumption that the tax inspector learns the citizen's true income costlessly.

$$T(\theta) = \pi\theta, \forall \theta < \alpha/(1 - \pi) \tag{21}$$

$$\lambda(\theta) = 0, \forall \theta < \alpha/(1 - \pi). \tag{22}$$

Proof. See Appendix F.

At least in the lower reaches of the income distribution, the tax must thus be a simple proportional one and the commission rate must be zero. This result derives from the implication of A2(i) that $f_I(n, 0) = 0$. For the inspector then has nothing to lose in attempting to extort from the poorest individual, who can then be protected from "small" over-reports—her ability to appeal protecting her from "large" over-reports—only by removing any incentive for I to misreport in this range; which requires paying no commission. That the tax must be a proportional one then follows from the linkage between the shape of T and λ discussed after Theorem 2. The sharpness of Proposition 5 clearly reflects the strength of the limited liability condition A2. More broadly, however, the result points again to the potential vulnerability of the poor to extortion: those with low taxable income have little to offer the corrupt inspector in terms of sharing gains from tax evasion, since they have little tax to avoid; paying inspectors a commission at low income reports then does little to combat evasion but does create the possibility of extortion. The lesson, it seems, is that the payment of commission on low income reports can be especially dangerous.

While corruption-proofness thus rules out progressive taxation in the lower part of the income distribution, the preceding results leave open the possibility that it may be possible to achieve progressivity over some upper range of the income distribution, without damaging revenues or creating evasion or corruption, so long as an appropriate commission is paid on these higher income reports. The following verifies that this is indeed the case so long only as the collective fine on I and C exceeds a lower bound:

Proposition 6. *It is sufficient for an admissible scheme to be revenue-maximising, evasion-proof and corruption-proof that the conditions of Theorem 2 hold and*[37]

---

[37] Note that the sufficient condition in (e) differs from the necessary condition of Proposition 5 in requiring zero commission over a wider interval. If attention is restricted to continuous T, however, condition (e) also becomes necessary. The proof of this is available on request.

(e) *The tax and commission schedules satisfy*:

$$T(\theta) = \pi\theta, \forall \theta < \alpha/\pi(1 - \pi) \tag{23}$$

$$\lambda(\theta) = 0, \forall \theta < \alpha/\pi(1 - \pi), \text{ and} \tag{24}$$

(f) *for any* $\theta \in \Gamma$ *and* $r \neq \theta$ *such that* $r \geq \alpha/\pi(1 - \pi)$,

$$f(r, \theta) > \alpha/\pi - (1 - \pi)(r - \theta). \tag{25}$$

Proof. See Appendix G.

Interestingly, the lower bound on the collective fine in (f) not only admits less than maximal penalties but actually decreases with the extent of any over-report. To see why this is, and more generally how it is that this lower bound suffices, note first that the condition can also be written as

$$\pi f(r, \theta) + (1 - \pi)\pi(r - \theta) > \alpha. \tag{26}$$

The left of (26) reflects two kinds of punishment that arise from any over-report: the explicit penalty $f(r, \theta)$ and—recalling condition (a) of Theorem 2—the implicit penalty in the form of an increase in the collective payment $(1 - \lambda)T$ made to the government. The condition in (f) is that this expected punishment exceeds the cost of appealing: intuitively, it must then be the case that either the punishment is so great that the inspector will choose never to over-report or/and the cost of appealing so low that C will indeed choose to appeal. And this condition may hold even if the fine $f(r, \theta)$ decreases with the extent of over-reporting because the implicit component of the punishment automatically increases with r.

Proposition 6 points the way to the construction of many tax schemes that are evasion-proof, corruption-proof, revenue-maximising and—in contrast to the simple proportional tax of Corollary 1 above—progressive in the upper reaches. Consider, for example, the class of tax schemes described in:

Example B. A tax scheme with $\omega = 0$, satisfying (f) of Proposition 6 and:

$$\text{(i)} \ T(\theta) = \begin{cases} \theta - \alpha/\pi & \theta \geq \hat{\theta} \\ \pi\theta & \theta < \hat{\theta} \end{cases} \tag{27}$$

(ii) $\lambda(\theta) = \begin{cases} [(1-\pi)\pi\theta - \alpha]/(\pi\theta - \alpha) & \theta \geq \hat{\theta} \\ 0 & \theta < \hat{\theta} \end{cases}$ (28)

where $\hat{\theta} \equiv \alpha/\pi(1-\pi)$.

This, it is easily checked, satisfies all the conditions of Proposition 6. And it involves a progressive tax schedule, with the average rate strictly increasing at incomes above $\hat{\theta}$, honestly implemented by a scheme involving less than maximal penalties and positive commissions in the progressive range.

There are thus many evasion-proof, corruption-proof revenue-maximising schemes for G to choose from. Since these schemes differ in the progressivity of the tax schedule T, distributional concerns in tax design come to the fore again, and it is to these that we now turn.

4.3. Distributional Considerations

Consider then the comparison, from the perspective of a government with some distributional concerns, between the schemes in Corollary 1 and Example B. They raise the same revenue, and both are evasion-proof and corruption-proof. But the distribution of net incomes implied by the tax scheme in Corollary 1 is unambiguously less equal (in the Lorenz sense) than that implied by the tax scheme in Example B.[38] It might therefore seem that any government with distributional concerns will prefer the latter. But not so. For notice that since expected commission payments are strictly positive under the scheme in Example B but zero under that in Corollary 1, the fact that the two schemes raise the same revenue for the government implies that the average tax burden is actually higher under the scheme in Example B. Honest implementation of the progressive scheme requires a costly commission system that taxpayers themselves must ultimately pay for. Indeed comparing tax payments under the two schemes it can be seen that no taxpayer strictly prefers the progressive tax in Example B to the proportional tax in Corollary 1: the only people who gain from progressivity are the inspectors, who must be paid more than their reservation value in order to implement it. Any distributionally concerned government then needs to trade off the attractions of a progressive tax

---

[38] Assuming, that is, that $\hat{\theta} < 1$: otherwise the two schemes are identical.

system—an equity gain in having a more equal distribution of net incomes—against the higher average level of taxation—and hence lower average net income—that it involves. Though the scheme in Example B is no more than an illustration, the implication may be of some importance: potential evasion and corruption in the tax collection process mean that there are costs involved in the honest implementation of progressive taxation of a kind quite different from the incentive effects on taxpayers usually emphasised.

The discussion so far has taken it that the primary purpose of taxation is to raise revenue, and indeed by restricting taxes $T(\theta)$ to be nonnegative we have precluded purely redistributive taxation. Consider now the opposite extreme, in which taxes are levied *only* in order to redistribute. More precisely, consider the set of redistributive tax schemes defined by a net tax schedule of the form $\tau(\theta) = T(\theta) - b(\theta)$, where $b(\theta) \geq 0 \ \forall \theta \in \Gamma$, $E_\theta[\tau(\theta)] = 0$ and T forms part of an admissible tax scheme as defined after A2 above (but with A2(ii) now amended to reflect the possible receipt of benefit).[39] Suppose too that the government pursues the extreme Rawlsian maximin objective of maximising the net income of the worst-off individual. Our final result shows that such a government, if it confines itself to evasion-proof and corruption-proof schemes[40] can be thought of as optimally proceeding in two steps: first it implements a revenue-maximising tax scheme of exactly the sort considered above, and then it distributes the proceeds as a poll subsidy:[41]

Proposition 7. *An admissible evasion-proof and corruption-proof redistributive tax scheme maximises the net income of the poorest citizen if the net tax schedule is of the form* $\tau^*(\theta) = T^*(\theta) - b$, *where* T^* *forms part of an admissible corruption-proof and revenue-maximising tax scheme and* $b = E_\theta[T^*(\theta)] = \pi \theta^e$.

The bulk of the analysis above thus applies not only to the revenue-maximising government but also, at an opposite extreme, the Rawlsian one.

---

[39]More precisely, in the remainder of this section we replace A2(ii) of the text by the condition A2(ii)*: $f_C(r, \theta) \leq \theta - T(\theta) + b(\theta) - b(0)$, $\forall r, \theta \in \Gamma$. Admissibility is now to be interpreted in terms of A2(ii)*.

[40]These features are assumed rather than proved because of such possibilities as that G might wish to arrange matters so that I finds it optimal to pay a bribe to a citizen with $\theta = 0$.

[41]The proof of Proposition 7 is available on request.

5. Summary and Concluding Remarks

The two most fundamental results are those emphasized in Section 1:

- The impact of evasion and corruption is unambiguously regressive under tax schemes of broadly the kind often observed. For the poor have little to gain from evading taxes and are at the same time vulnerable to over-reporting of their incomes; for the rich, the converse is true.

- Inducing honesty in the collection of progressive taxes can be costly, implying an additional source of inefficiency associated with the pursuit of equity goals. Intuitively, the government can levy progressive taxes without reducing its own payoff by creating countervailing incentives in the form of commissions: the parties are tempted to understate income to evade progressive taxes, and tempted to overstate income to raise the commission payments. Arranging an appropriate balance between the two, however, incurs a real resource cost.

Other points also deserve some emphasis:

- Since the poor are the most vulnerable to extortion, paying tax inspectors commission on low income reports—lending strength to their threat to over-report—runs an especially large risk of inducing abuse and corruption.

- While heavy penalties on inspectors caught conniving in the evasion of taxes may simply lead them to ask for and receive larger bribes, heavy penalties for extortion reduce bribe-taking and may have a key role to play in combating corruption. Corruption and evasion can be eliminated, however, and at no revenue cost, without setting penalties at their maximum feasible levels.

- A government that is concerned only to maximise revenue—or which has a Rawlsian maximin objective—and is averse to both evasion and corruption can do no better than set a proportional tax schedule and pay inspectors a fixed wage (with penalties proportional to extent of mis-reporting); can do no better, that is, than set something resembling a simple flat tax. The reason is nothing to do with incentive effects on taxpayers' effort or administrative simplicity: it is as a means of ensuring honesty in collection.

- It is the threat of extortion which leads to low-powered incentives. There are two opposing forces at work here. On one hand, since collusion defeats the effectiveness of tax instruments in raising revenue and impairs the deterrent effect of penalties, it is desirable to provide high-powered incentives to the inspector (in the form of a commission payment to resist the temptation to collude with the taxpayer). On the other hand, to deter the inspector from abusing his discretionary power through the threat of extortion, it is desirable to have low-powered incentives. In the present context, the latter effect dominates, in the sense that there is never any strict gain from paying positive commissions.[42]

Evasion and corruption are complex matters, and the analysis has abstracted from many aspects that may be important in practice. Some of these simplifying assumptions (such as the absence of any systematic audit selection process) were discussed in the text. We conclude by considering some of the others.

One such is the assumption that the probability of corruption being detected (the parameter π) is exogenous, and independent of the income report. We think of π as describing the degree of intrinsic honesty in the system. It plays a key role in the analysis; it is this, for instance, which determines the maximum amount of revenue that the government can raise. As Klitgaard (1988) emphasizes, it is this degree of intrinsic honesty that ultimately determines the likelihood that corruption will be detected. In the short-run it is hard for the government to affect this variable very significantly: hence the approach taken here. Doubtless there are ways in which governments can have some effect on the probability of an illicit deal between taxpayer and inspector being discovered: it could increase the number of audits double-checked, or seek over time to develop an elite core of incorruptible inspectors. Formally, one can certainly extend the analysis to allow π to be varied by the government, at some cost. But this adds little of real interest. A more substantive question is whether efforts to detect dishonesty—the work of the incorruptible elite team, for instance—should be concentrated on low income reports (as the work of Chander and Wilde (1998), for example, would seem to suggest): the appropriate policy is not clear, since although such a focus of effort would re-

---

[42]It should be noted that although in much of the principal-agent theory (as, for example, surveyed in Hart and Holmstrom (1987)) it is optimal to provide the agent with high-powered, complex, incentive schemes, in some principal-agent contexts—such as in the context of multi-task environments (see Holmstrom and Milgrom, 1991)—it is optimal to provide low-powered, simple, incentive schemes.

duce the incentive to underreport income—the effect emphasised in the previous literature on optimal auditing—it would also exacerbate the risk of extortion.

Second, in assuming that the taxpayer's true taxable income becomes known to the inspector without effort on the part of the latter we preclude an obvious incentive argument for commission payments. The analysis shows that even without this moral hazard dimension some commission payment is needed to implement progressive taxes honestly. The need to motivate inspectors in discovering underlying income will only reinforce this effect. Now, however, commission payments may have an even stronger effect in promoting extortion: not only do they lend credibility to the inspector's threat to over-report (as here), they also provide the inspector with an incentive to acquire information that strengthens his position in bargaining with the taxpayer.

Third, there may in practice be restrictions on acceptable penalties that constrain the government more tightly than we have allowed here; and it may then be optimal for the government to tolerate some degree of evasion and corruption. Suppose, for example—here we take an extreme case, for clarity—that small misreports cannot be penalised. Then the only way to preclude evasion altogether is by paying the inspector entirely on commission. But since one can also show—along the lines of Theorem 2—that ω must be set to zero, the government would then raise no revenue. To collect any revenue, it must tolerate evasion, which in turn opens the way to the payment of bribes.[43]

Appendixes

Appendix A. Proof of Proposition 1

To show that $m^*(\theta) \leq \theta$, note from (12) that, using A.1,

$$S(\theta, \theta) - S(m, \theta) = (1-\pi)[[1-\lambda(m)]T(m) - [1-\lambda(\theta)]T(\theta)] + \pi f(m, \theta) \quad \text{(A.1)}$$

Combining (A.1) with the hypothesis that $[1-\lambda(\cdot)]T(\cdot)$ is strictly increasing implies that no $m > \theta$ can maximise $S(m, \theta)$. To show that $n^*(\theta) \geq \theta$, note from (7), using (A.1),

$$P_I^e(n, 0; \theta) - P_I^e(\theta, 0; \theta) = (1-\pi)[\lambda(n)T(n) - \lambda(\theta)T(\theta)] - \pi f_I(n, \theta). \quad \text{(A.2)}$$

---

[43]Details of these results are available on request.

Combining (A.1) with the hypothesis that $\lambda(\cdot)T(\cdot)$ is strictly increasing then implies that $\forall n < \theta$, $P_I^e(n, 0; \theta) < P_I^e(\theta, 0; \theta)$. Since $n = \theta$ satisfies (9), we have the desired conclusion. We now show that $B^*(\theta) \geq 0$. Since $P_I^e(m^*(\theta), B^*(\theta); \theta) \geq d_I$, and since $n = \theta$ satisfies (9) (which implies $d_I \geq P_I^e(\theta, 0; \theta)$), we have $P_I^e(m^*(\theta), B^*(\theta); \theta) \geq P_I^e(\theta, 0; \theta)$. Consequently,

$$B^*(\theta) \geq (1-\pi)[\lambda(\theta)T(\theta) - \lambda(m^*(\theta))T(m^*(\theta))] + \pi f_I(m^*(\theta), \theta). \quad (A.3)$$

Combining (A.1) with the hypothesis that $\lambda(\cdot)T(\cdot)$ is strictly increasing thus implies (since we have already shown that $m^*(\theta) \leq \theta$) that $B^*(\theta) \geq 0$. Part (iv) of the proposition follows immediately from (A.3), since $\lambda(\cdot)T(\cdot)$ is strictly increasing. □

Appendix B. Proof of Theorem 1

We first establish:

Lemma A. *For any tax scheme of the form in Example A:*

$$m^*(\theta) = \begin{cases} 0 & \forall \theta \in [0, \theta_1] \\ T^{-1}[T(\theta) - u^*] & \forall \theta \in [\theta_1, 1] \end{cases} \quad (B.1)$$

$$n^*(\theta) = \begin{cases} T^{-1}[T(\theta) - \upsilon^*] & \forall \theta \in [0, \theta_2] \\ 1 & \forall \theta \in [\theta_2, 1] \end{cases} \quad (B.2)$$

where $\theta_1 \equiv T^{-1}(u^*)$, $\theta_2 \equiv T^{-1}(\upsilon^* + T(1))$, $\theta_1 < \theta_2$ *and* $u^* > 0$ *and* $\upsilon^* \leq 0$ *are both independent of* θ. *Moreover,* $\upsilon^* = 0$ *if* $\beta\alpha = 0$.

Proof. Consider first the optimal report $m^*(\theta)$. Unconstrained maximisation of the surplus S in (13) gives the necessary condition

$$-\pi g'[T(\theta) - T(m)] + (1 - \pi)(1 - \beta) = 0, \quad (B.3)$$

the prime indicating differentiation and $g \equiv g_C + g_I$. This implies an amount of under-reporting $T(\theta) - T(m^*(\theta)) \equiv u^* > 0$ that is independent of true income θ. Recognising that the report m is constrained to be non-negative, it is then clear that there will exist some critical income level θ_1 such that those above under-report by u^* whilst those below report $m = 0$ and thus under-report by the full amount of their true liability. Hence (B.1).

Consider next the disagreement report $n^*(\theta)$. From (9) and $P_I^e(n, 0; \theta)$ and leaving aside the constraint that $n \in \Gamma$, the outcome of the disagreement game is readily seen to solve

$$\min_v [\pi g_I(v) + (1 - \pi) \beta v] \text{ s.t. } \pi g_C(v) - (1 - \pi)v \le \alpha \qquad (B.4)$$

where $v \equiv T(\theta) - T(n)$. The solution v^* being independent of θ and non-positive (by feasibility of the choice $v = 0$), the result follows. □

To establish the theorem itself, define $z(\theta) \equiv 2B^*(\theta)$ and consider three subintervals of Γ:

(a) For $\theta \in [0, \theta_1]$, using Lemma A in (15) and (16) gives:

$$z(\theta) = (1 - \pi)(1 + \beta)[-v^* + T(\theta)]$$

$$+ \pi[g_I(T(\theta)) - g_C(T(\theta)) + g_C(v^*) - g_I(v^*)] \qquad (B.5)$$

$$\Sigma(\theta) = -(1 - \pi)T(\theta) + \pi g_C(T(\theta)) + (1 - \pi)B^*(\theta). \qquad (B.6)$$

Differentiating (B.5):

$$z'(\theta) = T'(\theta)[(1 - \pi)(1 + \beta) + \pi\{g_I'(T(\theta)) - g_C'(T(\theta))\}]. \qquad (B.7)$$

Since $m^*(\theta) = 0$ for any $\theta \in [0, \theta_1]$, it follows that $\nabla_m S(0, \theta) \le 0$. That is,

$$(1 - \pi)(1 - \beta) > \pi g'(T(\theta)). \qquad (B.8)$$

Using (B.8) in (B.7), the assumption that (for $i = C, I$) $g_i'(u) > 0$ for $u > 0$ implies $z' > 0$. Turning to Σ, differentiating (B.6) and using (B.7) gives

$$\Sigma' = T'(\theta)\left[-(1 - \pi) + \frac{1}{2}[(1 - \pi)(1 + \beta) + \pi g'(T(\theta))]\right] \qquad (B.9)$$

Substituting for $g'(T(\theta))$ from (B.8) gives $\Sigma' < 0$.

(b) For $\theta \in [\theta_1, \theta_2]$, it is immediate from Lemma A that both B^* and Σ are independent of θ.

(c) For $\theta \in [\theta_2, 1]$, Lemma A implies (recalling that $g_C(u) = 0$ for $u \le 0$)

$$z(\theta) = (1 - \pi)(1 + \beta)[u^* + T(1) - T(\theta)]$$

$$+ \pi[g_I(u^*) - g_C(u^*) - g_I(T(\theta) - T(1))] \qquad (B.10)$$

$$\Sigma(\theta) = -(1 - \pi)u^* + \pi g_C(u^*) + (1 - \pi)B^*(\theta). \qquad (B.11)$$

Establishing that $z(\theta)$ is strictly decreasing over this range will thus also establish that Σ is decreasing. Differentiating in (B.10) gives

$$z'(\theta) = T'(\theta)[-(1-\pi)(1+\beta) - \pi g_I'(\upsilon)] \tag{B.12}$$

where $\upsilon = T(\theta) - T(1)$. Note next that it is necessary for the minimisation problem in (B.4) augmented by the binding constraint $\upsilon = T(\theta) - T(1)$ that

$$\pi g_I'(\upsilon) + (1-\pi)\beta - \mu_1(1-\pi) - \mu_2 = 0, \tag{B.13}$$

where $\mu_1 \geq 0$ is the multiplier on the no-appeal constraint in (B.4) and $\mu_2 > 0$ that for the constraint directly on υ. Using (B.13) in (B.12) gives $z'/T' = -(1-\pi)(1+\mu_1) - \mu_2 < 0$. □

Appendix C. Proof of Proposition 3

For part (i), introduce a parameter ζ such that the fines on the inspector are now

$$f_I(m, \theta, \zeta) = \begin{cases} \zeta f_I(m, \theta), & \forall m < \theta \\ f_I(m, \theta), & \forall m \leq \theta \end{cases} \tag{C.1}$$

By a similar argument to that given in the proof to Proposition 4 below, one finds that $\nabla_\zeta m^*(\theta, \zeta) > 0$. Since Proposition 1 applies, so that $n^*(\theta) \geq \theta$, it is easily seen from $P_I^e(n, 0; \theta)$ and (9) that $n^*(\theta)$ is independent of ζ. The ambiguity of the effect of an increase in ζ is straightforward to establish by differentiating in (16) and evaluating at $\zeta = 1$, and then considering the following two cases. If π is sufficiently small, then an increase in ζ decreases $B^*(\theta)$. But if π is sufficiently large, f_I sufficiently small and f_I is relatively flatter than f_C, in the sense that for any $m < \theta$ $\nabla_m f_C(m, \theta) < \nabla_m f_I(m, \theta) (< 0)$, then an increase in ζ increases the equilibrium bribe.

For part (ii), suppose now that the parameter ζ applies to f_I in the event $m \geq \theta$. In this case m^* is easily seen to be independent of ζ, and it then follows from (7)–(8) (using the split-the-difference rule) that it is enough to show that increasing ζ reduces $d_I - d_C$. Given, from Proposition 1, that $n^* \geq \theta$ it is clear from (10) that d_I is strictly decreasing in ζ. From (11) and (A.1), d_C is non-increasing in n^*; and that $\nabla_\zeta n^* \leq 0$ follows on considering the only two possibilities: either the no-appeal constraint (9) bites, in which case n^* cannot strictly increase with ζ (the critical value of n at which C appeals being unaffected by ζ); or n^* is characterised by an interior solution, in which case routine comparative statics give $\nabla_\zeta n^* < 0$. □

Appendix D. Proof of Proposition 4

Define $\lambda(\theta) = \gamma h(\theta)$, where $\gamma \in (0, 1)$ and $h(\theta) \in (0, 1)$. If $m^*(\theta) > 0$, then it must be the case that $\nabla_m S(m^*(\theta), \theta) = 0$ and $\nabla_{mm} S(m^*(\theta), \theta) < 0$. Hence the sign of $\nabla_\gamma m^*(\theta; \gamma)$ is the same as the sign of $\nabla_{m\gamma} S(m^*(\theta), \theta; \gamma)$. $\lambda(\cdot)T(\cdot)$ strictly increasing implies that the latter sign is strictly positive, and hence Proposition 4(i) follows. If $m^*(\theta) = 0$, then it is trivial to show that $\nabla_\gamma m^*(\theta; \gamma) \geq 0$.

We now establish part (ii). Notice that the payoff to the government from type θ is, in fact, $\theta - S(m^*(\theta, \gamma); \gamma)$. Differentiating this w.r.t γ, it follows—since $\nabla_\gamma S(m^*(\theta); \gamma) > 0$ and $\nabla_m S(m^*(\theta, \gamma); \gamma) \nabla_\gamma m^*(\theta, \gamma) = 0$—that if $m^*(\theta, \gamma) > 0$, then that derivative is strictly negative. If, on the other hand, $m^*(\theta) = 0$, then either $\nabla_m S(m^*(\theta); \gamma) = 0$ or < 0. In the latter case $\nabla_\gamma m^*(\theta; \gamma) = 0$, since $\nabla_m S(0, \theta; \gamma)$ is continuous in γ. In either case, therefore, the desired derivative is strictly negative (since $\nabla_\gamma S(m^*(\theta); \gamma) > 0$). Hence, part (ii) follows.

We now show that the effect on the bribe $B^*(\theta)$ is ambiguous. Note first that (in obvious notation) $n^*(\theta; \gamma)$ is non-decreasing in γ, for n^* is either at a corner solution for the constrained maximisation of $P_I^e(n, 0; \theta)$, in which case it is independent of γ, or it is characterised by an interior solution to the maximisation of $P_I^e(n, 0; \theta)$, in which case it is easily seen to be strictly increasing in γ. The ambiguity of the effect of an increase in γ is straightforward to establish by differentiating in (16) and then considering the following two cases, in both of which one assumes π to take a sufficiently high value. If f_C is relatively flatter than f_I, in the sense that (i) for any $m < \theta$ $\nabla_m f_I(m, \theta) < \nabla_m f_C(m, \theta)$ (< 0), and (ii) for any $m > \theta$ $\nabla_m f_I(m, \theta) > \nabla_m f_C(m, \theta)$ (> 0), then an increase in γ strictly decreases the equilibrium bribe. While if f_I is relatively flatter than f_C, then the reverse is the case.

Appendix E. Proof of Theorem 2

Necessity. Using conditions (i) and (ii) in (13), the evasion-proofness requirement (18) (that $S(m, \theta) \geq S(\theta, \theta)$, $\forall m \neq \theta$) reduces to condition (iii). Conditions (i) and (ii), together with evasion-proofness, also imply that G's expected revenue is $\pi \theta^e$.

It thus suffices to show that any evasion-proof, revenue-maximising admissible tax scheme satisfies (i) and (ii). And for this, we now argue, it is enough to show that (i) and (ii) are satisfied by any such scheme that also involves penalties that are maximal in the sense of being the largest consistent with the limited liability restriction in (A.2): that is, for any θ, $r \in \Gamma$ such that $r \neq \theta$, $f_I(r, \theta) = \omega + \lambda(\theta)T(\theta)$ and $f_C(r, \theta) = \theta - T(\theta)$. For consider some evasion-proof revenue-maximising scheme M that does not involve maximal penalties. Let M' be the scheme identical to M in every aspect except that in M' penalties are maximal. It is trivial to verify that M' is evasion-proof (because M is).[44] This implies that M' generates the same, maximal, expected revenue as M. Thus M' is evasion-proof, revenue-maximising, and has maximal penalties. If then M' satisfies conditions (i) and (ii), so too—being identical in every respect except the penalties f_i—does the original scheme M.

Suppose then that penalties are maximal. The evasion-proofness conditions (18) then become the requirement that for any θ, $m \in \Gamma$ such that $m \neq \theta$,

$$(1 - \pi)[1 - \lambda(m)]T(m) \geq [1 - \lambda(\theta)]T(\theta) - \pi(\omega + \theta). \tag{E.1}$$

Since, by (A.1), $T(m)[1 - \lambda(m)] \geq 0 \; \forall m \in \Gamma$ and $T(0)[1 - \lambda(0)] = 0$, this implies (and is implied by)

$$\pi(\omega + \theta) \geq [1 - \lambda(\theta)]T(\theta).$$

Maximising the state's expected revenue then requires setting the right of this latter inequality to its maximum level, i.e.:

$$\pi(\omega + \theta) = [1 - \lambda(\theta)]T(\theta). \tag{E.2}$$

The state's expected revenue then becomes $E_\theta[\pi\theta - (1-\pi)\omega]$ which, since $\omega \geq 0$, is maximised by setting $\omega = 0$; which is condition (ii). Condition (i) then follows from (E.2).

Sufficiency. Conditions (i) and (ii) are readily seen to imply that the evasion-proofness conditions (18) are satisfied; and, with (ii), to generate expected revenue equal to the maximal value of $\pi\theta^e$. □

Appendix F. Proof of Proposition 5

Note first that since $T(0) = 0$ and (from A2(i)) $f_f(r, 0) = 0$ for all $r \in \Gamma$, for $\theta = 0$ condition (20) reduces to $\lambda(n)T(n) \leq 0$ for all $n \in N^*(0)$. Suppose then that there exists $\hat{n} \in (0, \alpha/(1 - \pi))$ such that $\lambda(\hat{n}) > 0$. Since $T(0) = 0$, $T(\hat{n}) \leq \hat{n}$ and (from A2(i)) $f_C(\hat{n}, 0) = 0$, one finds from (19) that $\hat{n} \in N^*(0)$. But since (from Theorem 2) $T(r) > 0$ for all $r > 0$, it then also follows that $\lambda(\hat{n})T(\hat{n}) > 0$, and thus (20) is violated. □

---

[44]Let $S(m, \theta; M)$ and $S(m, \theta; M')$ denote the surplus function associated respectively with tax schemes M and M'. Since M is evasion proof, $S(\theta, \theta; M) \geq S(m, \theta; M)$ for all $m \neq \theta$. Furthermore, since the commission and tax schedules in M and M' are identical, $S(\theta, \theta; M) = S(\theta, \theta; M')$. Hence, $S(\theta, \theta; M') \geq S(m, \theta; M)$ for all $m \neq \theta$. Since the penalties in M' are maximal, and otherwise M and M' are identical, it follows that $S(m, \theta; M) \geq S(m, \theta; M')$ for all $m \neq \theta$. Hence, M' satisfies (18).

Appendix G. Proof of Proposition 6

Given Theorem 2, we need to show that such a tax scheme is corruption-proof. Fix an arbitrary $\theta \in \Gamma$. First note that (24) implies that for any $n \in N^*(\theta)$— where $N^*(\theta)$ is defined in (19)—such that $n < \alpha/\pi(1 - \pi)$, inequality (20) is satisfied—which means that the inspector prefers to report the truth than n. Now fix any $n \geq \alpha/\pi(1 - \pi)$. Inequality (25) implies (using condition (i) of Theorem 2) that $A + B > 0$, where

$$A = (1 - \pi)[T(n) - T(\theta)] + \pi f_C(n, \theta) - \alpha$$

$$B = (1 - \pi)[\lambda(\theta)T(\theta) - \lambda(n)T(n)] + \pi f_I(n, \theta).$$

Thus, either $A > 0$ or $B > 0$. We now note that the citizen appeals against the report n if and only if $A > 0$, and the inspector prefers to report the truth than n if and only if $B \geq 0$. Hence, since if $A > 0$ then $n \notin N^*(\theta)$, it follows that $n^*(\theta) = \theta$. The desired conclusion follows immediately, because, as noted above, any evasion-proof tax scheme is corruption-proof if and only if $n^*(\theta) = \theta$ for all $\theta \in \Gamma$. □

References

Auriol, E., 1996. Delegation under the threat of corruption in procurement and public purchase. University of Toulouse, mimeo.

Bagchi, A., Bird, R., das-Gupta, A., 1995. An economic approach to tax administration reform. Discussion Paper No. 3, International Centre for Tax Studies, University of Toronto.

Banerjee, A., 1994. Eliminating corruption. In: Quibria, M.G. (Ed.), Proceedings of the Third Annual Conference On Development Economics, Asian Development Bank, Manila.

Bardhan, P., 1997. Corruption and development. Journal of Economic Literature 35, 1320–1346.

Basu, K., Bhattacharya, S., Mishra, A., 1992. Notes on bribery and the control of corruption. Journal of Public Economics 48, 349–359.

Besley, T., McLaren, J., 1993. Taxes and bribery: the role of wage incentives. Economic Journal 103, 119–141.

Bird, R.M., 1992. Tax Policy and Economic Development, Johns Hopkins Press, Baltimore.

Border, K., Sobel, J., 1987. Samurai accountant: a theory of auditing and plunder. Review of Economic Studies 54, 525–540.

Carillo, J., 1995a. Corruption in hierarchies. GREMAQ, mimeo.

Carillo, J., 1995b. Grafts, bribes and the practice of corruption. GREMAQ, mimeo.

Chander, P., Wilde, L., 1992. Corruption in tax administration. Journal of Public Economics 49, 333–349.

Chander, P., Wilde, L., 1998. A general characterisation of optimal income taxation and enforcement. Review of Economic Studies 65, 165–183.

Chu, C., 1990. Income tax evasion with venal tax officials — the case of developing countries. Public Finance, 392–408.

Cowell, F., 1990. Cheating the Government, MIT Press, Cambridge, MA.

Flatters, F., MacLeod, W.B., 1995. Administrative corruption and taxation. International Tax and Public Finance 2, 397–417.

Goswami O., Sanyal, A., Gang, I., 1990. Corrupt auditors: How they affect tax collection. Indian Statistical Institute, New Delhi, mimeo.

Hart, O., Holmstrom, B., 1987. The theory of contracts. In: Bewley, T.F. (Ed.), Advances in Economic Theory, Cambridge University Press.

Holmstrom, B., Milgrom, P., 1991. Multitask principal-agent analyses: incentive contracts, asset ownership and job design. Journal of Law, Economics and Organisation 7, 24–51.

Jakobsson, U., 1976. On the measurement of the degree of progression. Journal of Public Economics 5, 161–168.

Jain, A.K., 1997. Tax evasion, economic reforms and corruption in India. Intertax 25, 18–22.

Klitgaard, R., 1988. Controlling Corruption, University of California Press, Berkeley.

Kofman, F., Lawarree, J., 1993. Collusion in hierarchical agency. Econometrica 61, 629–656.

Konrad, K., Skaperdas, S., 1995. Credible threats in extortion. Free University of Berlin, mimeo.

Konrad, K., Skaperdas, S., 1997. Extortion. University of California, mimeo.

Mauro, P., 1995. Corruption and growth. Quarterly Journal of Economics 110, 681–712.

Mogiliansky, A., 1994. Corruption in procurement: the economics of regulatory blackmail. University of Stockholm, mimeo.

Mookherjee, D., 1998. Incentive reforms in developing country bureaucracies: lessons from tax administration. In: Proceedings of the Annual World Bank Conference On Development Economics, World Bank.

Mookherjee, D., Png, I., 1995. Corruptible law enforcers: how should they be compensated? Economic Journal 105, 145–159.

Muthoo, A., 1999. Bargaining Theory with Applications. Cambridge University Press, Forthcoming.

Nalebuff, B., 1998. Comment on "Incentive reforms in developing country bureaucracies: lessons from tax administration" by D. Mookherjee. In: Proceedings of the Annual World Bank Conference On Development Economics, World Bank.

Reinganum, J.F., Wilde, L., 1985. Income tax compliance in a principal-agent framework. Journal of Public Economics 26, 1–18.

Stella, P., 1993. Tax farming: a radical solution for developing country tax problems? IMF Staff Papers 40, 217–225.

Strausz, R., 1995. Delegation of monitoring in principal-agent relationship. Review of Economic Studies 64, 337–357.

Tanzi, V., Davoodi, H., 1997. Corruption, public investment and growth. International Monetary Fund, mimeo. [Revised version reproduced as Chapter 11 in this volume—ED.]

Tirole, J., 1986. Hierarchies and bureaucracies: on the role of collusion in organisations. Journal of Law, Economics and Organization 2, 181–214.

Tirole, J., 1992. Collusion and the theory of organizations. In: Laffont, J.J. (Ed.), Advances in Economic Theory, Vol. 2, Cambridge University Press.

Ul Haque, N., Sahay, R., 1996. Do government wage cuts close budget deficits? Costs of corruption. IMF Staff Papers 43, 754–778.

Part IV

Corruption, Income Distribution, and Poverty

16

Production, Rent Seeking, and Wealth Distribution

Era Dabla-Norris and Paul Wade

I. Introduction

In this paper, we examine the relationship between initial wealth and occupational choice between rent seeking and productive activities. Rent seeking refers to all largely unproductive, expropriative activities that bring positive return to the individual but not to society (Krueger, 1974). The allocation of resources to rent seeking affects aggregate economic activity in several ways. First, to the extent that rent seeking activities, such as corruption and tax farming, lower incentives and opportunities for production and investment, aggregate economic activity is reduced.[1] Second, rent seeking can compete with productive sectors for scarce economic resources, resulting in a misallocation of labor, capital, and talent in the economy.

---

[1]For historical discussions on the role of rent seeking in explaining the differential economic performance of eighteenth century France and England, see North and Thomas (1973) and North (1981). Empirical studies by Magee, Brock, and Young (1989) and Murphy, Shleifer, and Vishny (1991) also provide some evidence to suggest that countries with more rent seeking tend to grow more slowly.

In many countries today as well as historically, people choose the government bureaucracy, army, and other rent seeking activities over productive and entrepreneurial activities. Historical evidence and casual observation from developing countries, however, suggest that often it is the wealthy who are the rent seekers—exactly those who might otherwise become the first capitalists. Baumol (1990), for instance, notes that in China under the Mandarins and in medieval Europe, government service with its attendant ability to solicit bribes and dispose of tax revenue for one's private benefit was the principal career choice for many wealthy individuals in society. In a historical study of seventeenth century France, Braudel (1982) notes that the purchase of government offices and tax farming was commonplace among wealthy landowners and members of the bourgeoisie. Levi (1988) states that an important prerequisite for engaging in tax farming in Republican Rome was the availability of sufficient capital that enabled wealthy Roman citizens to advance funds to rulers and to collect taxes.

More recently, Wade (1984) finds that individuals pay thousands of dollars for positions with the power to allocate supposedly free water to farmers in India, since these jobs give them monopoly rights to charge for water. In some developing countries, it is common for government officials to own businesses run either by themselves or by their relatives, and to protect such businesses from bribes and other forms of appropriation by virtue of their government positions. One example is the establishment of state trading monopolies by government officials in which one has a stake either directly or through relatives.

Why is it that the rich choose to engage in rent seeking rather than productive activities? This paper provides a theoretical explanation for the relationship between the distribution of agents' initial wealth and their occupational choice between rent seeking and production. It determines endogenously the allocation of agents between the two occupations, the subsequent distribution of income and wealth, and the overall income of the economy. We show that persons with initial wealth above a certain threshold become rent seekers and the rest become producers, and examine the role of bequests in determining initial wealth in society.

The general framework we adopt is a modification of Diamond's (1965) overlapping generation model with the absence of labor and credit markets. Agents in this model have identical preferences and abilities and differ only with respect to their initial wealth. We assume that agents can operate in one of two sectors in the economy: rent seeking and production. Entry into rent seeking, however, requires the payment of a lump sum cost. Payment of this cost enables rent seekers to appropriate some portion of the surplus generated by productive economic activity, while allowing them to protect their wealth from expropriation by others. This latter activity can be regarded as hoarding. In the model, rent seeking and production are assumed to be mutually exclusive activities, with the return to hoarding being lower than the return to production.

The mechanism whereby initial inequality in wealth influences individuals' choice of occupation is as follows: by virtue of being a rent seeker an individual can protect himself against expropriation from other rent seekers. This incentive is relatively stronger for the wealthy who have more to lose from expropriation than individuals with lower wealth. In the absence of credit markets and with a lump sum entry fee for rent seeking, only the wealthy will have enough capital to pay for this right. The payment of the lump sum fee can be viewed as analogous to the purchase of weapons used both for protection and for offense. In this interpretation, arms enable agents to protect their wealth from appropriation by others but also to extract rents from other agents.[2] Hence, when property rights protection is poor or ineffective, wealthy agents have an incentive to buy arms (i.e., paying the entrance fee to rent seeking). The purchase of these arms, however, also enables them to prey on the wealth of other agents in the economy.

The model also has implications for the distribution of wealth in society. An extension of the model to allow for altruistic dynastic bequests demonstrates how differences in bequests determine the initial wealth of agents in society. Income and occupational differences are perpetuated in equilibrium from parent to child as in Galor and Zeira (1993), Banerjee and Newman (1993), Aghion and Bolton (1994), and Greenwood and Jovanovic (1990). These papers rely on the assumptions of imperfect credit markets and indivisible inputs to show that occupational choice and the resulting level of aggregate economic activity depend on initial conditions (particularly, initial wealth or income). Our paper illustrates this imperfection with the special case of no credit

---

[2]This is in contrast to Grossman and Kim's (1997) analysis of the relationship between weapons used either for predation or for defensive fortifications. An important distinction between our paper and theirs is that, here, predation and the deterrence of predation are viewed as complementary activities.

markets at all. We model the indivisibility as a lump sum cost, as in Greenwood and Jovanovic (1990).

The link between the relative rewards to rent seeking and productive activities is examined by Baumol (1990), Murphy, Shleifer, and Vishny (1991), Acemoglu (1995), Acemoglu and Verdier (1998), Mehlum, Moene, and Torvik (2000), and Baland and François (2000). These papers focus on the relative returns to engaging in production and rent seeking as a determinant of the allocation of agents between the two activities. They do not, however, examine the relationship between occupational choice and the level of initial wealth in society.

The paper proceeds as follows. Section II specifies the basic model and examines the properties of equilibrium. Section III examines the role of bequests in determining initial wealth in society. Section IV considers extensions to the basic model, and Section V concludes.

II. The Model

Environment and Technology

Consider an economy consisting of a continuum of agents living in two periods distributed over the interval [0, 1]. Agents are assumed to have identical preferences and abilities and differ only in their initial wealth. The preferences of each agent are described by a twice-continuously differentiable quasi-concave utility function $U(c_1, c_2)$, where c_1 and c_2 denote consumption of the economy's single good in each period of life. The arguments of the utility function are gross substitutes with $\lim_{c_i \to 0}[u_i(c_1, c_2)] = \infty$, and u_i represents marginal utility in period i, $i = 1$, 2.[3] Each agent is endowed with $w > 0$ units of the consumption good when young. The initial distribution of goods endowment in the economy is represented by the cumulative distribution function $\Gamma: R_{++} \to [0, 1]$.

There are two sectors in the economy: production and rent seeking. Each agent operates in one of these two sectors in his lifetime. Each producer has access to a standard concave production technology that yields $f(i)$ units of the consumption good in period two of his life to an investment of i units when young (period 1), where $f(0) = 0$ and $f'(0) = \infty$. Producers, however, face appropriation of some share of their market production by rent seekers. Let $0 < \gamma < 1$ denote the proportion

---
[3] A sufficient condition for gross substitutability is a separable utility function and a coefficient of relative risk aversion less than one.

of market production that can be extracted from each producer in the form of bribes, taxes, or outright expropriation.[4] We assume that the probability of dealing with a rent seeker is equal to the proportion of rent seekers in the economy, n. Therefore, the expected second period return to a producer is given by $(1 - n\gamma)f(i)$.

Entry into rent seeking requires payment of a lump sum fee of θ units of the consumption good when young. Payment of this cost allows rent seekers to tax market production in the second period of their lives. Agents are assumed to be unable to borrow to finance entry into rent seeking. The payoff to rent seeking depends on the likelihood of obtaining rents from producers. We assume that the amount collected by each rent seeker is given by a function $R(n, \gamma)$, with $R_n < 0$, $R_\gamma > 0$, $R_{\gamma\gamma} \leq 0$, $R_{nn} \leq 0$ and $R_{n\gamma} \geq 0$. The expected rent to a rent seeker is given by $(1 - n)R(n, \gamma)$. The assumption that the return to rent seeking is decreasing in n captures the idea that rent seekers crowd each other out. We also assume that the first rent seeker can appropriate the maximum potential rent, which is given by $\gamma f(i)$. This assumption implies that $\lim_{n \to 0} R_n(n, \gamma)dn = \gamma f(i)$ (which implies that $R_n(0, \gamma) = \infty$).[5]

Rent seekers are assumed to save only through a simple technology that returns x goods in period 2 of their lives to an input of s when young (period 1). The inputs of rent seekers are assumed to be unobservable, which implies that rent seekers cannot coordinate their saving decisions. Unobservability of a rent seeker's inputs also implies that a rent seeker cannot expropriate the goods controlled by another rent seeker. Therefore, one may think of x as the return on hoarding that allows rent seekers protection from theft by others. We assume that $x < (1-n\gamma)f'(i)\ \forall i$ and n. Thus, the marginal productivity of the production technology is higher than the return on hoarding.[6]

Equilibrium

In this section we describe individual decisions. First, consider the optimization problem faced by an agent who chooses to become a rent

---

[4]Here γ can be regarded as a tax on the proceeds of market production, or, alternatively, the cost of engaging in production in a rent seeking society. In reality, this fraction may depend on the effectiveness of the rent seeking technology or the level of development of an economy.

[5]This assumption gives us a unique equilibrium in production and rent seeking.

[6]Note that the same results follow if x were equal to $(1 - n\gamma)f'(i)$ for any $\theta > 0$. If x is assumed to be greater than $(1 - n\gamma)f'(i)$, this leads to the uninteresting case of rent seeking always being profitable for individuals.

seeker. The budget constraints faced by a rent seeker in each period of his life, are

$$w - \theta - s = c_1 \tag{1}$$

$$(1 - n)R(n, \gamma) + xs = c_2, \tag{2}$$

where s represents the savings of the rent seeker. The first order condition for utility maximization for a rent seeker is given by the Kuhn-Tucker condition:

$$-u_1^R + xu_2^R \leq 0 \text{ for } s \geq 0. \tag{3}$$

If the agent's initial endowment w is sufficient to provide all desired consumption when young, equation (3) is always satisfied with equality. Suppose this is the case. Define as $V^R(w)$ the maximum utility attained by an agent if he chooses to engage in rent seeking given an initial endowment w. When instead the agent chooses to become a producer, he solves

$$V^P(w) = \max_{c1, c2} U(c_1, c_2) \tag{4}$$

s.t.

$$w - i = c_1$$

$$(1 - n\gamma)f(i) = c_2, \tag{5}$$

where $V^P(w)$ denotes the maximum utility attained by a producer taking w as given. The first order condition for utility maximization for a producer is

$$-u_1^P + (1 - n\gamma)f'(i)u_2^P = 0. \tag{6}$$

An equilibrium in this environment is given by an allocation of the population between rent seeking and production and values of s and i such that each agent maximizes his lifetime utility taking as given w, x, θ, and γ. To study the allocation of agents between rent seeking and production, we examine the relationship between $V^R(w)$ and $V^P(w)$ as a function of n, the proportion of rent seekers in the economy. The derivatives of $V^R(w)$ and $V^P(w)$ with respect to n are given by

$$\frac{\partial V^P}{\partial n} = -\gamma f(i)u_2^R < 0 \tag{7}$$

$$\frac{\partial V^R}{\partial n} = u_2^R [-R(n, \gamma) + (1-n)R_n] < 0. \tag{8}$$

Therefore, both curves are downward sloping. The following lemma shows that a corner solution with only rent seeking does not exist.

Lemma 1. *There does not exist an equilibrium in which all agents engage in rent seeking (that is, $n \neq 1$).*

Proof. At $n = 1$, for a given w, the expected rent accruing to each rent seeker, $(1-n)R(n, \gamma)$ is zero. Because the return to hoarding is less than the return to production, the maximum utility attained by a producer exceeds the maximum utility attained by a rent seeker. That is, $V^R(w) < V^P(w)$ at $n = 1$. Therefore, there cannot be an equilibrium in which all agents choose to engage in rent seeking. Q.E.D.

Consider now an equilibrium in which there is no rent seeking. For such an equilibrium, it is necessary that $V^R(w) < V^P(w)$ at $n = 0$.[7] That is, the maximum utility from production is greater than the utility from being the only producer. In what follows, we assume that γ is sufficiently high and/or θ is sufficiently low such that at $n = 0$, the maximum return to rent seeking exceeds the return to production.

Assumption 1. $V^R(w) > V^P(w)$ at $n = 0$.

Lemma 1 and Assumption 1, along with the continuity of the utility functions, yield Proposition 1 (Figure 1).

Proposition 1. *In equilibrium, there is a positive measure of agents engaging in rent seeking and of agents engaging in production.*

Note that if Assumption 1 does not hold, and if both V^P and V^R are downward-sloping curves, they can have more than one intersection, giving rise to the possibility of multiple equilibria. If, for instance, $V^P > V^R$ at $n = 0$, and there exists some $0 < n < 1$ for which $V^R > V^P$, the relative position of the two curves is illustrated by Figure 2. These conditions imply that if there is no rent seeking, the return to rent seeking is lower than the return from production, and that there exists some range over which the return to rent seeking exceeds the return to production. In this case, there can be multiple equilibria in rent seeking and production and our model then delivers qualitative outcomes comparable to

---

[7]A sufficiently high θ or a sufficiently low γ makes this equilibrium more likely.

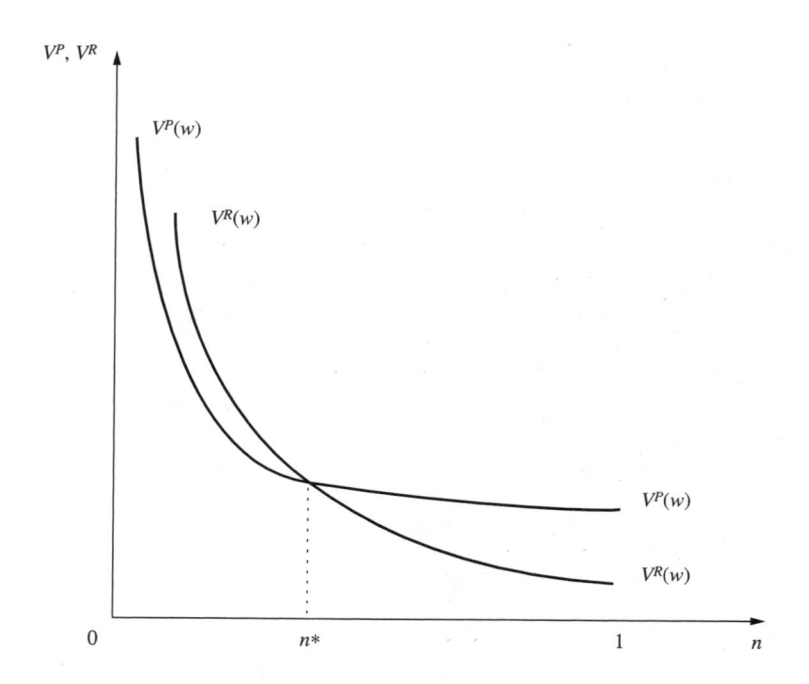

Figure 1. Unique Equilibrium in Production and Rent Seeking

Murphy, Shleifer, and Vishny (1993), Acemoglu (1995), and Baland and François (2000). In this paper, we deliberately abstract from multiple equilibria in order to focus on the relationship between agents' initial wealth and their choice between rent seeking and production.

Properties of Equilibrium

In this section, we examine the relationship between agents' wealth and their choice between rent seeking and production. In the presence of the lump sum cost in the rent seeking sector and in the absence of credit markets, it can be shown that only wealthy agents will choose to engage in rent seeking. The following lemma states that the earned income (second period) of a rent seeker is higher than the earned income of a producer.

Lemma 2. *Each agent enjoys a greater earned income if he engages in rent seeking than in production.*

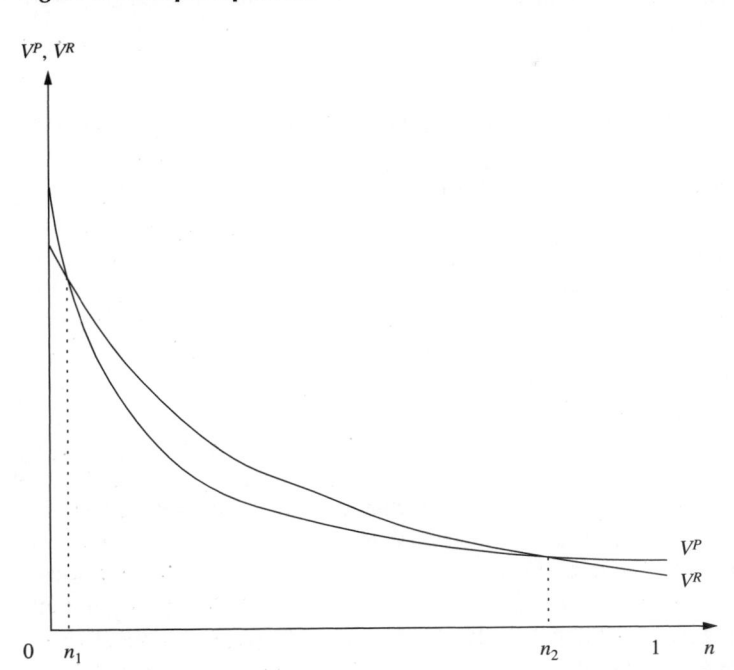

Figure 2. Multiple Equilibria

[Figure: Graph showing V^P and V^R curves as functions of n, both decreasing, intersecting at n_1 and n_2, with axes labeled V^P, V^R vertically and n horizontally from 0 to 1.]

Proof. Because producing has a higher marginal product than hoarding ($x < (1 - n\gamma)f'(i)$), if an agent with a given endowment w chooses to become a rent seeker, it must be the case that $u_2^R < u_2^P$. Q.E.D.

Lemma 3. *For a given endowment w, if an agent is just indifferent between rent seeking and production, it must be true that $u_1^R > u_1^P$.*

Proof. At the point where agents are just indifferent between rent seeking and production, $V^R(w) = V^P(w)$, for any given endowment w. It follows from Lemma 3 that the earned income of a rent seeker is higher than the earned income of a producer, for any given w. Therefore, $u_2^R < u_2^P$ implies that $u_1^R > u_1^P$.

Lemma 3 states for a given w, at the point where agents are indifferent between rent seeking and production, the consumption of a rent seeker when young is lower than the consumption (period 1) of a producer. This result occurs due to the presence of the lump sum cost required to enter into rent seeking. Let $\Omega(w)$ denote the difference between the utility of an agent with endowment w if he chooses to engage in rent seeking and his utility if he chooses to become a producer.

$$\Omega(w) \equiv U(w-\theta-s^*, (1-n)R(n, \gamma)+xs^*) - U(w-i^*,(1-n\gamma)f(i)), \quad (9)$$

where s^* denotes the value of saving that satisfies with equality the first order condition for a rent seeker (equation 3) and i^* represents the value of a producer's saving that satisfies his first order condition (equation 6). Therefore, $\Omega(w)$ represents the difference between the maximum utility obtained from rent seeking, $V^R(w)$, and the maximum utility obtained from production, $V^P(w)$.

The derivative of $\Omega(w)$ with respect to w is given by

$$\Omega'(w) = u_1^R - u_1^P, \quad (10)$$

where u_1^R and u_1^P represent the marginal utility from engaging in rent seeking and in production, respectively. From Lemma 3 we know that at the point where agents are indifferent between the two occupations, the marginal utility of consumption when young is higher for a rent seeker than for a producer, so that $u_1^R > u_1^P$ and $\Omega'(w) > 0$. Because in equilibrium some agents must follow each career path (from Proposition 1), there must exist some borderline endowment $\bar{w}$ defined by $\Omega(\bar{w}) = 0$. The above analysis indicates that $\Omega(\cdot)$ has a positive slope at $w = \bar{w}$; that is, when rent seeking and production offer nearly the same utility, the relative attractiveness of rent seeking to production is increasing with a higher initial wealth. Therefore, Lemma 3, along with the continuity of the utility functions, ensures that $V^P(w)$ and $V^R(w)$ have a single crossing.

We can now characterize the allocation of agents between rent seeking and production. There exists a unique level of endowment $\bar{w} > 0$ such that for $w \geq \bar{w}$ agents will choose to engage in rent seeking, and for all $w < \bar{w}$ will choose production. This result is summarized in Proposition 2.

Proposition 2. In equilibrium, the greater the initial income of an agent, the more attractive is a career in rent seeking relative to producing.

Proposition 2 states that the rich become rent seekers. Rent seeking is limited to agents with high enough initial income due to the presence of the lump sum cost required to enter this sector. Note that it is not the higher wealth itself that creates incentives for wealthy agents to enter into rent seeking but the ability to protect the return from their own wealth that a career in rent seeking affords them. Payment of the fixed cost enables rent seekers not only to extract some portion of the proceeds from market production but also ensures protection of their wealth from appropriation by others. The rich, by virtue of their higher initial income, therefore, have a greater incentive to engage in rent seeking.

Thus, despite the fact that agents are ex ante identical in terms of preferences and abilities, two classes of agents emerge in equilibrium. It is the initial income (w) of an agent that determines his decisions whether to engage in rent seeking or production, and how much to consume and save. Hence, the initial distribution of endowments determines aggregate output in the economy and the measure of agents engaged in rent seeking

$$\int_{\underline{w}}^{\infty} d\Gamma(w) = n \tag{11}$$

and in production

$$\int_{0}^{\overline{w}} d\Gamma(w) = (1 - n). \tag{12}$$

Given that hoarding has a lower marginal product than production, the greater the proportion of rent seekers in the economy, the smaller is aggregate output. Hence, the total level of output in the economy is negatively related to the size of the rent seeking sector.

III. Bequests and Income Classes

The analysis in the previous sections assumed that the distribution of wealth in society was exogenous. But where does this initial distribution come from? In this section, we show that the initial distribution of wealth may represent bequests received from an agent's parents when young. The important question then is which sort of parent will leave larger bequests to induce their children to choose a career in rent seeking versus production? We, therefore, examine equilibrium behavior in the face of a bequest motive on the part of parents.

As in Barro (1974), we assume that parents value the utility of their children, such that an individual born at time t has the utility function:

$$V_t \equiv u(c_{1,t}) + u(c_{2,t+1}) + \beta V_{t+1}, \tag{12}$$

where $0 < \beta < 1$. The budget constraints for producers can be written as:

$$w_t - i_t = c_{1,t} \tag{13}$$

$$(1 - n\gamma)f(i_t) = c_{2,t+1} + w_{t+1} \tag{14}$$

and, for rent seekers as:

$$w_t - \theta - s_t = c_{1,t} \tag{15}$$

$$(1 - n)R(n, \gamma) + xs_t = c_{2,t+1} + w_{t+1}. \tag{16}$$

Assume that bequests are nonnegative (parents cannot extract goods from their children). For both agents, the first order maximization condition with respect to the choice of bequest, w_{t+1}, is given by

$$-u_{2,t} + \beta u_{1,t+1} \leq 0 \text{ for } w_{t+1} \geq 0 \tag{17}$$

with the other conditions remaining the same as in Section II.

Lemma 4. *Agents will leave larger bequests if they are rent seekers than producers.*

Proof. If no bequests are received (i.e., $w_{t+1} = 0$), we know from Lemma 2 that $u_2^R < u_2^P$. From equation (17), this implies that, for any given value of $u_{1,t+1}$, a rent seeker having a lower marginal utility of consumption when old will choose to leave a larger bequest. Q.E.D.

Proposition 3. *In a stationary equilibrium where both agents leave bequests, rent seekers will only engage in hoarding if the amount expropriated from producers is sufficiently low.*

Proof. In a stationary equilibrium with positive bequests, equation (17) implies that $u_1/u_2 = 1/\beta$.[8] Since both rent seekers and producers must leave positive bequests to finance their children's consumption when young, the assumption that $x < (1 - n\gamma)f'(i)$ implies that either

---

[8]Notice that saving from youth to old age requires that $u_1/u_2 = (1 - n\gamma)f'(i)$ for a producer and $u_1/u_2 = x$ for a rent seeker.

(i) $u_1/u_2 = (1 - n\gamma)f'(i) = 1/\beta$ and $x < 1/\beta$ or

(ii) $u_1/u_2 = (1 - n\gamma)f'(i) > 1/\beta$ and $x = 1/\beta$.

From Lemma 3 we know that agents will leave larger bequests if they are rent seekers than producers. Therefore in a stationary equilibrium, (i) suggests that for $\theta > 0$, the expected rent expropriated from producers, $(1 - n\gamma)R(n, \gamma)$, is sufficient to provide all desired consumption when old and to leave larger bequests than producers. As a result, the rent seeker does not need to engage in hoarding ($s = 0$). However, if the rent expropriated from producers is low, due to a low proportion extracted (γ) relative to the degree of crowding out among rent seekers, (ii) implies that a rent seeker must hoard to consume when old and leave a bequest. Q.E.D.

Note that for a given $\theta > 0$, a rent seeker who does not save (engage in hoarding) enjoys higher consumption when young but has a lower second-period income than the case in which he allocates a positive amount of his initial wealth to saving. In the absence of credit markets, a higher initial income is of greater value to rent seekers than producers because it allows them to devote a positive amount of their endowment to hoarding while allowing them to finance a higher consumption when young. As a result, in an equilibrium with more pervasive rent seeking or a sufficiently low γ, which implies lower rents, a rent seeker will choose to save when young. However, if the rent expropriated from producers is sufficiently high or crowding out among rent seekers is not severe, by choosing not to engage in hoarding, he will enjoy a higher consumption when young.

We also know from Proposition 2 that those receiving a larger bequest are more likely to be rent seekers. Since the children of rent seekers are the ones to receive larger bequests, they will therefore become rent seekers themselves as they will be able to meet the lump sum cost required to enter into rent seeking. Similarly, the children of producers will choose to be producers themselves as the bequests they receive may not be sufficient to meet the lump sum cost to rent seeking. Therefore, the children of rent seekers will become rent seekers and the children of producers will become producers. We can, therefore, have a class structure of wealth and occupational choice between rent seeking and production that, in equilibrium, is self-generating and self-perpetuating.

IV. Extensions

Endogenous θ

The equilibrium allocations between production and rent seeking in our analysis so far relied on the assumption of a fixed cost θ of entering into rent seeking. However, the model could easily be extended to endogenize θ. In all cases considered below, it is assumed that there is a maximum potential number of rent seeking cases (P^*), which is ultimately a function of the existing set of rules and regulations and the degree of discretionary power of public officials. P^* is assumed to be at least as large as the maximum number of rent seeking cases in the economy, given the rent seeking technology and the number of rent seekers.

Consider a two-stage game in which a self-interested higher authority in the first stage decides on the size of the rent seeking sector n. In the second stage, there is free competitive bidding for the rent seeking positions, such that all successful bidders pay the same price and agents choose their profession. Assume that there is no taxation in the economy. The central authority then acts as a revenue maximizing Stackelberg leader, choosing the optimum n to maximize its revenues, $n\vartheta(n)$.[9]

Suppose instead, in the absence of a strong centralized authority a (relatively large) number of decentralized government units effectively have power to charge agents an entrance fee into rent seeking, each one in its own area, and the number of potential entrants into rent seeking P^* is the same as in the previous case. Each unit can grant one agent the right to engage in rent seeking and it acts independently of the other units. Hence it does not take into account the effect on the entrance fee θ of increasing the number of rent seekers. Intuitively, the number of rent seekers will be larger, and the equilibrium entrance fee and the threshold initial wealth level ($\bar{w}$) lower than in the previous case. In other words, the revenue-maximizing central authority will choose a smaller, more exclusive, and wealthier club of rent seekers.

This feature of a small "elite" of wealthy individuals engaging in rent seeking is observed in a number of developing countries as well as in medieval Europe. Examples of uncoordinated solicitation of bribes

---

[9] In the absence of effective monitoring and weak law enforcement, the central authority would essentially be extracting some of the rents that accrue to rent seekers. If, for instance, the specific source of bureaucratic inefficiency in the economy is corruption by tax collectors, then tax farming may be a preferred regime from the point of view of tax revenues raised.

and other forms of rent seeking by a large number of government units are seen in many African countries.[10] The large number of units with this power reflects their own low entrance costs into rent seeking. As noted by Shleifer and Vishny (1993), the resulting effect can be an even heavier burden on private producers of rent seeking, which is detrimental to private investment and economic growth.

In the above discussion, it is implicitly assumed that the free competitive bidding in the second stage raises the entrance fee θ to the level where the marginal bidder's excess utility from rent seeking relative to production is reduced to zero. Hence, if all agents had the same initial wealth (say, the same $\bar{w}$), there would be no rent seekers. This would be the case regardless of the higher authority's decision in stage 1 about the size of the rent seeking sector. Only individuals with initial wealth higher than $\bar{w}$ would have positive excess utility from rent seeking relative to production at that level of θ. In other words, an important implication of our model is that there must be initial inequality in wealth for any rent seeking to take place.

Differences in Ability

The model can easily be extended to assume differences in abilities across individuals leading to differing returns in each sector. The link between rent seeking and misallocation of resources in the economy is then reinforced by the finding that the most able persons become rent seekers.

Differences in ability can be incorporated in a number of ways in our model. Suppose that more able individuals have lower costs of entering into rent seeking (lower θ). Assume that an individual's ability a is drawn from a continuous density function $q(a)$, where agents with high a have a comparative advantage for rent seeking relative to production. In this case, it can be shown that the return to rent seeking becomes more attractive for individuals above some average ability a^* and less attractive for those below average ability.[11]

Suppose there exist productivity differences among individuals in both rent seeking and production such that persons with higher ability have higher productivity in both rent seeking and in production than

---

[10]See Fjeldstad (1999).

[11]This is similar to Acemoglu and Verdier (1998) but they assume that the decreasing cost of human capital investment applies to production.

less able individuals. We can formalize this by considering an amended production function, $af(i)$, and rent seeking function, $aR(n)$ as in Murphy, Shleifer, and Vishny (1991). Both rent seeking and production show increasing net returns to ability. This reflects the existence of a cost element in both sectors that is fixed with regard to variations in the level of ability (the entrance fee θ), whereas rents appropriated through rent seeking and output in production both vary with ability. If the elasticity of the net return to ability is higher in rent seeking than in production, rent seeking will be relatively more attractive for the more able individuals in society.

Therefore, the most able individuals will be attracted to rent seeking, resulting in a misallocation of talent in the economy. Aggregate production is decreased because the number of individuals, the amount of capital invested, and the average ability and productivity of persons engaged in production are lower.

V. Conclusion

This paper analyzes the role of initial wealth in determining the choice between engaging in rent seeking and productive activities. We show that in the absence of credit markets, only wealthy agents can overcome the nonconvexity in income-earning possibilities. The wealthy are, therefore, "born into rent seeking." We analyze a model in which rent seeking enables agents not only to extract some portion of the proceeds from market production but also ensures protection of their wealth from appropriation by others. Therefore, wealthy agents avoid the tax from rent seekers by becoming rent seekers themselves, a result that accords well with both historical evidence and casual observation from developing countries today.

The results of the model are robust to alternative specifications of the rent seeking technology. Allowing rent seekers to expropriate a proportion of producers' output simplifies our analysis, but does not affect any of the major results.[12] In the model, agents are assumed to be unable to finance their entry into rent seeking through borrowing. Credit markets in many developing countries are typically character-

---

[12]For instance, even if rent seekers extract a fixed fee instead of expropriating a proportion of market production, the model's implications concerning the relationship between initial income and occupational choice are unchanged.

ized by high collateral requirements. An agent seeking to obtain a loan to finance the entrance fee into rent seeking would need to have substantial capital to meet the collateral requirements. This suggests that even in the presence of capital markets, it is the relatively wealthy who will be able to obtain such loans.

The model abstracts from law enforcement as the rent seekers' probability of being caught and punished is implicitly set equal to zero. Clearly, effective law enforcement would reduce the attractiveness of engaging in rent seeking. Law enforcement can easily be captured in the model by making γ a decreasing function of the economy-wide resources devoted to enforcement. If, for instance, such enforcement is financed through a lump sum tax on producers, the larger the size of the rent seeking sector, the larger would be the tax required to finance a given level of enforcement. As a result, even with positive law enforcement, the implied trade-off for producers between lower expropriation and higher taxes suggests that rent seeking will not be eliminated in equilibrium.

The results of this model require two crucial assumptions, namely that there are nonconvexities in rent seeking and that rent seekers have access to a "protection" technology. These assumptions together ensure that the initial distribution of wealth determines the choice between rent seeking and production. The model also provides implications for this initial distribution of wealth. It is shown that if agents have an altruistic bequest motive, differences in bequests determine the distribution of wealth in society and can explain the perpetuation of rent seeking in society.

The model presented in this paper is essentially static in nature in that it describes the short-run equilibrium where income distribution affects occupational choice, output, and investment. An important extension would be to consider the dynamics of the relationship between wealth distribution and rent seeking as an economy develops. Such an extension would allow us to examine the relationship among income distribution, occupational structure, and economic growth.

References

Acemoglu, D., 1995, "Reward Structures and the Allocation of Talent," *European Economic Review,* Vol. 39 (January), pp. 17–33.

———, and T. Verdier, 1998, " Property Rights, Corruption and the Allocation of Talent: A General Equilibrium Approach," *Economic Journal,* Vol. 108 (September), pp. 1381–1403.

Aghion, P., and P. Bolton, 1994, "A Theory of Trickle-Down Growth with Debt Overhang," London School of Economics Financial Markets Group Discussion Paper No. 170 (London: London School of Economics).

Alfiler, M., 1986, "The Process of Bureaucratic Corruption in Asia: Emerging Patterns," in *Bureaucratic Corruption in Asia: Causes, Consequences and Controls*, ed. by L. Carino (Manila: College of Public Administration, University of Philippines).

Azabou, M., and J. Nugent, 1988, "Contractual Choice in Tax Collection Activities: Some Implications of the Experience with Tax Farming," *Journal of Institutional and Theoretical Economics*, Vol. 144 (September), pp. 684–705.

Baland, J., and P. François, 2000, "Rent Seeking and Resource Booms," *Journal of Development Economics*, Vol. 61, No. 2, pp. 527–42.

Banerjee, A. V., and A. F. Newman, 1991, "Risk-Bearing and the Theory of Income Distribution," *Review of Economic Studies*, Vol. 58 (April), pp. 211–35.

———, 1993, "Occupational Choice and the Process of Development," *Journal of Political Economy*, Vol. 101 (April), pp. 274–98.

Barro, R., 1974, "Are Government Bonds Net Wealth?" *Journal of Public Economy*, Vol. 82, pp. 1095–1117.

Baumol, W. J., 1990, "Entrepreneurship: Productive, Unproductive, and Destructive," *Journal of Political Economy*, Vol. 98 (October), pp. 893–921.

Braudel, F., 1982, *Civilization and Capitalism, 15th–18th Century* (New York: Harper & Row).

Chiu, W. H., and P. Madden, 1998, "Burglary and Income Inequality," *Journal of Public Economics*, Vol. 69 (July), pp. 123–41.

Diamond, P., 1965, "National Debt in a Neoclassical Growth Model," *American Economic Review*, Vol. 55 (December), pp. 1126–50.

Fjelstad, O., 1999, "Korrupsjon," in *Fordeling og vekst i fattige land*, ed. by Rune Jansenagen and Karl R. Pedersen (Norway: Fagbokforlaget).

Galor, O., and J. Zeira, 1993, "Income Distribution and Macroeconomics," *Review of Economic Studies*, Vol. 60 (January), pp. 35–52.

Greenwood, J., and B. Jovanovic, 1990, "Financial Development, Growth, and the Distribution of Income," *Journal of Political Economy*, Vol. 98 (October), pp. 1076–1107.

Grossman, H., and M. Kim, 1997, "Predation, Efficiency and Inequality," NBER Working Paper No. 6301 (Cambridge, Massachusetts: National Bureau of Economic Research).

Krueger, A. O., 1974, "The Political Economy of the Rent-Seeking Society," *American Economic Review*, Vol. 64 (June), pp. 291–303.

Levi, M., 1988, *Of Rule and Revenue* (Berkeley: University of California Press).

Magee, S. P., W. A. Brock, and L. Young, 1989, *Black Hole Tariffs and the Endogenous Policy Theory* (Cambridge, England: Cambridge University Press).

Mehlum, H., K. Moene, and R. Torvik, 2000, "Predator or Prey? Parasitic Enterprises in Economic Development" (unpublished; Oslo: University of Oslo).

Murphy, K., A. Shleifer, and R. Vishny, 1991, "The Allocation of Talent: Implications for Growth," *Quarterly Journal of Economics*, Vol. 106, pp. 503–50.

———, 1993, "Why Is Rent-Seeking So Costly to Growth? *American Economic Review, Papers and Proceedings*, Vol. 83 (May), pp. 409–14.

North, D., 1981, *Structure and Change in Economic History* (New York: Norton).

———, and R. P. Thomas, 1973, *The Rise of the Western World: A New Economic History* (Cambridge, England: Cambridge University Press).

Shleifer, A., and R. Vishny, 1993, "Corruption," *Quarterly Journal of Economics*, Vol. 108 (August), pp. 599–617.

Wade, R., 1984, "Market for Public Office: Why the Indian State Is Not Better at Development," Institute of Development Studies Discussion Paper No. 194 (Brighton: University of Sussex).

17

Does Corruption Affect Income Inequality and Poverty?

Sanjeev Gupta, Hamid R. Davoodi, and Rosa Alonso-Terme

1. Introduction

Government officials may use their authority for private gain in designing and implementing public policies. This phenomenon—defined broadly as corruption (Tanzi, 1997a)—may result in enriching these officials as well as private individuals who obtain a larger share of public benefits or bear a lower share of public costs. In this way, corruption distorts the government's role in resource allocation. It has been argued (Tanzi, 1995) that the benefits from corruption are likely to accrue to the better-connected individuals in society, who belong mostly to high-income groups. Thus, corruption would affect not only broad macroeconomic variables, such as investment and growth, as has been

---

Reprinted from *Economics of Governance*, "Does Corruption Affect Income Inequality and Poverty?" Sanjeev Gupta, Hamid Davoodi, and Rosa Alonso-Terme, Vol. 3, Issue 1, pp. 23–45 (2002), with permission from Springer-Verlag GmbH & Co. KG.

The authors would like to thank Vito Tanzi, Zeljko Bogetic, Benedict Clements, Calvin McDonald, Erwin Tiongson, Edgardo Ruggiero, and two anonymous referees for their comments.

shown previously, but also income distribution. It has been further contended that corruption increases poverty by reducing the level of social services available to the poor, creating incentives for higher investment in capital-intensive projects and lower investment in labor-intensive projects (Rose-Ackerman, 1997a, 1999). Such a bias in investment strategy deprives the poor of income-generating opportunities.

To date, no empirical evidence has been presented to corroborate the relationship between either corruption and income distribution or corruption and poverty. This paper seeks to ascertain if such relationships are supported by cross-country data.

Empirical studies of the impact of corruption have explored the efficiency implications of corruption through its impact on growth and investment (Mauro, 1995, 1998; Knack and Keefer, 1996), composition of government expenditure (Tanzi and Davoodi, 1997; Mauro, 1998), and allocation of foreign direct investment (Wei, 1997).[1] This literature generally finds that corruption reduces growth, and investment; skews expenditure towards public investment and away from operations and maintenance; and redirects foreign direct investment towards countries with lower corruption.

While underscoring the efficiency implications of corruption, the empirical literature has overlooked the distributional consequences of corruption.[2] In part, this reflects the belief that the rich or well-connected typically use bribes to be the first in line for a rationed government good or service, and the poor or individuals at the lower end of income distribution obtain the rationed good or service after waiting in line (Lui, 1985). In this way, bribes are assumed to clear the market because they reflect individuals' willingness to pay or their opportunity cost.[3] These views, similar to the early efficiency-enhancing views of corruption (Leff, 1964; Huntington, 1968), ignore that corruption may create permanent distortions from which some groups or individuals can benefit

---

[1]There are excellent reviews of the literature on the economic impact of corruption; see Rose-Ackerman (1997a, 1999), Tanzi (1998) and Wei (1999). This literature builds on earlier economic analyses of Rose-Ackerman (1978) and Klitgaard (1988).

[2]Exceptions include Tanzi (1995) and Rose-Ackerman (1997a, 1999). However, these studies are not empirical.

[3]The efficiency-enhancing theory of corruption does not seem to be supported by recent empirical evidence. For example, Kaufmann and Wei (1999) show that in a model in which government regulation and bureaucratic delays are endogenous, firms that pay more bribes are also likely to spend more, not less, time with bureaucrats negotiating regulations and face higher, not lower, cost of capital. They present evidence which corroborates this hypothesis.

more than others. They also ignore that individuals with high willingness to pay are not necessarily the intended beneficiaries of government programs. Moreover, the distributional consequences of corruption are likely to be more severe the more persistent the corruption, and the more entrenched the vested interests. The impact of corruption on income distribution is also a function of the government's involvement in allocating and financing scarce goods and services and may increase with the extent of government intervention.[4] Finally, empirical work on the distributional consequences of corruption has been hindered by a lack of consistent and reliable cross-country data on income inequality and poverty that only lately has been rectified (Deininger and Squire, 1996; Ravallion and Chen, 1997).

This paper is organized as follows. The next section lists arguments on how corruption may affect income inequality and poverty. Section 3 presents two models of income inequality and poverty. Section 4 documents the direct impact of corruption on income inequality and poverty. Due to possible endogeneity of corruption, Section 4 contains an exhaustive set of sensitivity analyses on the choice of instruments for corruption. Section 5 summarizes the results and policy implications of this paper's findings.

2. Corruption, Income Inequality, and Poverty

Corruption can affect income inequality and poverty through various channels, including overall growth, biased tax systems, and poor targeting of social programs as well as through its impact on asset ownership, human capital formation, education inequalities, and uncertainty in factor accumulation.

Growth

High corruption can lead to high poverty for two reasons. First, evidence suggests that a higher growth rate is associated with a higher rate of poverty reduction (Ravallion and Chen, 1997), and that corruption slows the rate of poverty reduction by reducing growth. Second, income inequality has been shown to be harmful to growth (Alesina and

---

[4]See Tanzi (1998) for a discussion of the political economy of corruption and the reform of the state.

Rodrik, 1994; Persson and Tabellini, 1994),[5] and if corruption increases income inequality, it will also reduce growth and thereby limit poverty reduction (Ravallion, 1997).[6]

Biased Tax Systems

Corruption can lead to tax evasion, poor tax administration, and exemptions that disproportionately favor the well-connected and wealthy population groups. This can reduce the tax base and the progressivity of the tax system, possibly leading to increased income inequality.

Poor Targeting of Social Programs

Corruption can affect the targeting of social programs to the truly needy. The use of government-funded programs to extend benefits to relatively wealthy population groups, or the siphoning of funds from poverty-alleviation programs by well-connected individuals, will diminish the impact of social programs on income distribution and poverty. Taxpayers and corrupt public officials can also divide the savings from taxes and duties, with the costs borne by poorer taxpayers with low ability to pay bribes, and reflected in lower provision of social services that are vital to the poor (Rose-Ackerman, 1999).

Asset Ownership

High concentration of asset ownership can influence public policy and increase income inequality. In a society where asset ownership is concentrated in a small elite, asset owners can use their wealth to lobby the government for favorable trade policies, including exchange rate, spending programs, and preferential tax treatment of their assets. These policies will result in higher returns to the assets owned by the wealthy and lower returns to the assets owned by the less well-to-do, thereby increasing income inequality. Furthermore, assets can be used

---

[5]Growth is harmed because high income inequality creates pressures either for populist programs, which reduce the overall productivity of public resources, or for postponing much needed adjustment to support the growth process (e.g., Alesina and Drazen, 1991; Laban and Struzenegger, 1994; and Alesina and others, 1996).

[6]It is possible for income inequality to be high enough that it results in rising poverty, despite high growth (Ravallion, 1997).

as collateral to borrow and invest; therefore, inequality in ownership of assets will limit the ability of the poor to borrow and increase their lifetime income and will perpetuate poverty and income inequality (Li, Squire, and Zou 1998; Birdsall and Londoño, 1997).

Human Capital Formation, Education Inequalities, and Social Spending

Corruption can affect income distribution and poverty via its impact on human capital formation and the distribution of human capital. First, corruption weakens tax administration and can lead to tax evasion and improper tax exemptions, as discussed above. Therefore, for a given tax system, the higher the level of corruption, the lower the tax revenue and the lower the resources available for funding public provision of certain services, including education.

Second, corruption increases the operating cost of government, and, therefore, reduces the resources available for other uses, including the financing of social spending that is crucial to the formation of human capital. In fact, higher corruption is found to be associated with lower education and health spending (Mauro, 1998).

Third, wealthy urban elites can lobby the government to bias social expenditure toward higher education and tertiary health, which tend to benefit high-income groups. Corruption can also increase expenditure on tertiary health because bribes can be more easily extracted from the building of hospitals and purchasing of state-of-the-art medical equipment than from expenditure on vaccinations.

Finally, corruption can increase the share of recurrent expenditure devoted to wages as opposed to operations and maintenance (Tanzi and Davoodi, 1997). This lowers the quality of education and health services and affects the ability of the state to improve educational attainment levels.

Uncertainty and Factor Accumulation

If the "rules of the game" in a corrupt country are unclear and biased toward the well-connected, the poor and the less-well-connected face an added risk premium in their investment decisions. This unequally distributed risk increases expected returns to any investment for the well-connected relative to the less-well-connected. Therefore, low income and poor groups—the less-well-connected—will be discouraged from investing in any resource—human, physical capital, or land—and income inequality and poverty will be perpetuated or accentuated.

3. Models

A. Corruption and Income Inequality

The empirical model of inequality used in this paper is in the spirit of Atkinson (1997).[7] It specifies the personal distribution of income in terms of factor endowments, distribution of factors of production, and government spending on social programs.[8] Specifically, the Gini coefficient is assumed to depend on the following variables:

- Initial distribution of assets (the initial Gini coefficient for land ownership);

- Education inequality (percent of adult population with no schooling expressed as a fraction of percent of adult population with completed secondary and higher education);[9]

- Education stock or educational attainment (average years of secondary education in population aged 15 and over);

- Capital stock-to-GDP ratio;

- Natural resource endowment (share of natural resources in total exports);

- Corruption;

- Social spending (various spending measures relative to GDP);

- Expenditure dummy—equals one when the Gini coefficient is expenditure-based and zero when it is income-based;

- Recipient dummy—equals one when the recipient of income or the spending unit is a person and zero when it is a household; and

- Net income dummy—equals one when the Gini coefficient is based on net income and zero when it is based on gross income.

---

[7] At present, there is no consensus about a proper model of income inequality.

[8] The models of Bourguignon and Morrisson (1990), Londoño and Székely (1997), and Spilimbergo, Londoño, and Székely (1999) are also based on the same underlying principle.

[9] Adult population is defined as population aged 15 years and over.

Distribution of income-generating assets has an impact on income distribution. Distribution of land is used as a proxy for asset distribution because data on the distribution of other income-generating assets, such as bonds and equity, are available for only a limited number of countries. Inequality in the distribution of land is expected to be positively correlated with income inequality for two reasons. First, the distribution of land has a direct impact on the distribution of income in a given time period, particularly in countries where income from land constitutes a large share of total income. Second, land can be used as collateral for borrowing and investing; therefore, inequitable land distribution limits the ability of the poor to borrow and increase their lifetime income.

Education inequality is expected to be positively correlated with income inequality (Tinbergen, 1975). A more egalitarian distribution of human capital will improve income distribution both by boosting the earning potential of the poor (Londoño and Székely, 1997) and by limiting the ability of the wealthy to lobby policymakers in their favor. In a similar vein, a higher educational endowment is expected to decrease inequality (Tinbergen, 1975).

A higher capital-output ratio or lower average productivity of capital is expected to be associated with higher income inequality. This may happen in developing economies where the most economic activity is concentrated in a traditional, low-productivity, unskilled labor sector, but also have islands of high-productivity and high-skilled labor. Similarly, a high natural resource endowment is expected to be associated with higher income inequality because of the high concentration of ownership and rent in this type of wealth as well as the high capital intensity and low complementarity between capital and labor in the natural resource sector.[10] As discussed, corruption is expected to increase income inequality.

Government transfers and spending on social services can constitute a major source of income in poor households. Well-targeted social programs (proxied here by different measures of social spending) are expected to lower income inequality.

Survey-type dummies are included as explanatory variables because differences in measured inequality can be due to differences in the type of survey data used. These dummies and the Gini coefficient data are taken from Deininger and Squire (1996). The dummies represent types

---

[10]See Leamer, Maul, Rodriguez, and Schott (1999) for additional arguments and evidence.

of cash flow (income versus expenditure), choice of recipient unit (household versus personal), and type of income (gross versus net of taxes). An income-based measure of inequality is expected to show higher inequality than an expenditure-based measure. This is consistent with aggregate consumption theories in which individuals can smooth their consumption via borrowing and lending while their income fluctuates. Furthermore, measurement errors for income may be higher than for consumption, particularly in developing countries, which tends to inflate measured income inequality. Individual-based Gini coefficients are expected to be higher than household-based ones. This is because poor households tend to be larger than rich ones, and because households are better able to make interpersonal and intertemporal adjustments in expenditure patterns than individuals. The Gini coefficient based on net income should be lower than one based on gross income if tax systems are progressive and redistribute income in favor of the poor.

B. Corruption and Poverty

The model of poverty used in this paper is a variation of models that determine overall income growth in the economy.[11] The model expresses the income growth of the bottom 20 percent of the population, a measure of change in poverty,[12] as a function of the following variables:

- Natural resource endowment (share of natural resources in total exports);
- Initial income of the poor (real income of the bottom 20 percent of the population in 1980 measured in purchasing power parity U.S. dollars);
- Initial secondary schooling (years of secondary education in population aged 15 and over in 1980);
- Education inequality (percent of adult population with no schooling, expressed as a fraction of percent of adult population with completed secondary and higher education);

---

[11]See Sala-i-Martin (1997) and Sachs and Warner (1997).

[12]This measure has been previously used by Deininger and Squire (1996) and Birdsall and Londoño (1997). Income growth of the bottom 20 percent of the population is defined as the average yearly growth rate in real per capita GDP of the bottom quintile of the population, measured in purchasing power parity-adjusted U.S. dollars.

- Initial distribution of assets (the initial Gini coefficient for land);
- Social spending (various measures relative to GDP); and
- Growth in corruption.

The rate of change of the income of the bottom 20 percent is chosen as the dependent variable because it is less prone to measurement errors than levels of poverty.[13] Another advantage of this formulation is that it is unaffected by country-specific factors that influence the level of poverty.

It has been argued that resource-rich countries grow less rapidly than resource-scarce countries (Sachs 1995, Sachs and Warner, 1997). Therefore, natural resource endowment is included in the model to examine if it affects income growth of the poor directly as well as indirectly through aggregate growth.

Initial income of the poor is included to account for diversity in initial conditions among countries. It is also intended to capture the extent to which the poor in one country are catching up with the poor in other countries. If there is a catch-up or convergence effect, the lower the initial income of the poor, the higher their income growth will be. Therefore, the coefficient on the initial income of the poor is expected to be negative.

Initial secondary schooling is included to measure the impact of human capital on the income growth of the poor. A positive coefficient is expected if human capital contributes positively to income growth of the poor. Two measures of distribution of factors of production are included: education inequality and the initial Gini coefficient for land. Each factor-distribution measure is expected to be negatively associated with the income growth of the poor.

Well-targeted social programs are believed to transfer relatively more income to the poor and reduce the incidence of poverty. In reality, it is quite conceivable that much of the benefits of social programs accrue to the middle- and higher-income groups.[14] To assess the impact of social spending on the income growth of the poor, three broad prox-

---

[13]Use of international poverty lines, such as the proportion of the population living on less than US$1 a day, will solve some but not all of the measurement problems. For example, sample size falls substantially as corruption data and less-than-a-dollar definition of poverty or other measures are not available for the same set of countries.

[14]For evidence on benefit incidence of social spending, see Tanzi (1974) and Alesina (1998).

ies for social spending are tried, all in relation to GDP; these are government spending on (1) social security and welfare, (2) education and health, and (3) the sum of spending items (1) and (2) plus housing and community amenities. Finally, in line with the model of income inequality, various indices of corruption are used to examine whether a higher growth rate of corruption reduces the income growth of the poor.

4. Empirical Results

A. Impact of Corruption on the Gini Coefficient

The models of income inequality and poverty are estimated using OLS and instrumental variable (IV) techniques on a cross-section of countries over the 1980–97 period. The IV technique would address endogeneity of the corruption variable. The income inequality regression is estimated using three specifications. In the first one, the Gini coefficient is regressed on a constant, three survey-type dummies, natural resource abundance, ratio of physical capital stock to GDP, education inequality, initial Gini coefficient for land, and a corruption index. In the second specification, education inequality is replaced with mean years of secondary schooling. The third specification includes both education variables to test for their relative impact on income inequality.

Table 1 reports the results for all three specifications for the OLS technique. The explanatory variables account for about 73 percent of cross-country variation in income inequality. In all three specifications, the survey-type dummies have the expected signs. Inequality is lower when the Gini coefficient is based on consumption rather than income, higher when the recipient unit is a person rather than a household, and lower when the coefficient is based on after-tax income than before-tax income.

The results also suggest that countries with high income inequality tend to have abundant natural resources, low capital productivity, high education inequality, low average secondary schooling, and unequal distribution of land. Distribution of education seems to matter more than its mean. Of the aforementioned five variables, abundance of natural resources and capital productivity are statistically more significant than others.

As regards the impact of corruption on income inequality, higher corruption is associated with higher income inequality using either

Table 1. Corruption and Income Inequality: OLS Estimates (Dependent Variable: The Gini Coefficient)

Independent Variables	(1)	(2)	(3)	(4)	(5)	(6)
Constant	27.56***	34.76***	30.11***	30.29***	34.53***	30.33***
	(4.30)	(6.55)	(4.72)	(4.93)	(5.95)	(4.86)
Expenditure dummy	−2.79	−1.37	−2.32	−3.99	−3.94	−3.97
	(−1.03)	(−0.57)	(−0.80)	(−1.44)	(−1.05)	(−1.11)
Recipient dummy	1.84	1.66	1.26	0.04	0.40	0.04
	(0.58)	(0.45)	(0.36)	(0.01)	(0.10)	(0.01)
Net income dummy	−6.91***	−7.10***	−6.85***	−6.79***	−6.86***	−6.80***
	(−3.25)	(−3.03)	(−3.16)	(−3.65)	(−3.49)	(−3.54)
Natural resource abundance	38.91**	34.77**	36.69**	27.32	23.92	27.37
	(2.38)	(2.18)	(2.36)	(1.61)	(1.29)	(1.50)
Capital stock–GDP ratio	0.05**	0.03	0.03*	0.04**	0.04	0.04*
	(2.28)	(1.40)	(1.81)	(2.41)	(1.56)	(1.85)
Education inequality	2.32*		1.79	1.49		1.49
	(1.97)		(1.46)	(1.24)		(1.19)
Secondary schooling		−2.12	−1.28		−0.45	−0.03
		(−1.45)	(−0.94)		(−0.21)	(−0.01)
Initital Gini coefficient for land	0.10	0.12	0.12	0.11	0.11	0.11
	(1.49)	(1.52)	(1.57)	(1.53)	(1.20)	(1.26)
Real per capita GDP ($\times 10^2$)				−0.05*	−0.06	−0.05
				(−1.93)	(1.63)	(−1.43)
Corruption	1.74***	1.62**	1.46**	0.94	1.01	0.94
	(3.01)	(2.61)	(2.54)	(1.46)	(1.44)	(1.40)
Adjusted R^2	0.73	0.72	0.73	0.75	0.73	0.74
Number of observations	38	38	38	37	37	37
F-statistic	13.80***	13.13***	12.32***	12.83***	12.06***	11.12***

Note: Estimation is by OLS. Numbers in parentheses are t-statistics based on White heteroscedasticity-consistent standard errors. A high value of the corruption index indicates a high level of corruption.

***Significant at 1 percent level; ** significant at 5 percent level; and * significant at 10 percent level.

one or two-tail tests at the one percent level. The magnitude of the effect of corruption on income inequality is considerable. A worsening in the corruption index of a country by one standard deviation (2.52 points on a scale of 0 to 10) is associated with an increase in the Gini coefficient of about 4.4 points (Table 1, column 1), the same increase in income inequality as a reduction in average secondary schooling of almost 2 years.[15]

B. Sensitivity Analysis of the Income Inequality Regression

Results reported in Table 1 (columns 1, 2 and 3) are robust to (i) use of other indices of corruption[16]; (ii) addition of social spending which may affect income inequality[17]; (iii) a measure of agricultural dualism, a statistically significant determinant of income inequality in models of Bourguignon and Morrisson (1998)[18]; (iv) addition of growth in real per capita GDP; and (v) presence of outliers. However, once real per capita GDP is added to the regression (Table 1, columns 4, 5, and 6) corruption ceases to be significant at the conventional statistical levels although its sign remains the same.

Real per capita GDP is often regarded as a proxy for the stage of economic development and many studies of income distribution often include this variable. However, real per capita GDP has also been regarded as a strong determinant of corruption (Treisman, 2000) which therefore reduces the explanatory power of corruption once it is included in the regression.[19] In addition, we found no evidence of a Kuznets curve, as the square of real per capita GDP is not statistically significant in regression which already includes the level of real per capita GDP. In the latter regressions, corruption has the expected sign but is not significant at the conventional statistical levels.

---

[15]This estimate is based on Table 1, column 2: (1.62 x 2.52) ÷ –2.12 = –1.9.

[16]Six other indicators are used. Four are compiled by Goettingen University and *Transparency International* (1997); the fifth one is taken from Tanzi and Davoodi (1997); and the sixth indicator is the so-called graft index that is constructed by Kaufmann, Kraay, and Zoido-Lobatón (1999a, 1999b). For example, using the graft index and rerunning regression in Table 1, column 1 produces a coefficient on the index that has the expected sign which is statistically significant at the 1 percent level. The resulting adjusted R-squared is even higher (0.77) than Table 1, column 1.

[17]Three measures of social spending are used as indicated in the previous section. Tanzi (1974) and Alesina (1998) have also found that social spending has no impact on income inequality.

[18]We thank a referee for pointing out this study.

[19]Countries with low levels of per capita GDP have, on average, higher levels of corruption. The simple correlation coefficient between real per capita GDP and the corruption index has a t-statistic of –12.

C. The IV Estimation of the Income Inequality Regression

The above regression results establish the existence of a statistically significant positive association between corruption and income inequality when real per capita GDP is not included in the regression. However, this association could stem from "reverse" causation, that is, high income inequality can lead to higher corruption and/or the observed association could be due to other factors affecting both. The instrumental variables (IV) technique can help address these problems. In this regard, choice of the instrument is important. A valid instrument for the corruption index has to be highly correlated with it, but not correlated with the error term in the income inequality regression or the income inequality itself (the Gini coefficient) other than its impact on the Gini coefficient through the corruption index. One such instrument is the extent of democracy in a country. Countries with a democratic tradition have established checks and balances and the rule of law, among other things, for effective monitoring of corruption and punishment of corrupt officials, particularly in the public sector. In fact, a variable measuring length of exposure to democracy has been found to be a robust determinant of corruption (Treisman, 2000). Governments in democratic societies use tax and expenditure/transfer policies to affect post-tax, post-transfer income distribution, but these policies are confined mainly to OECD countries (Atkinson, 2000; Chu, Davoodi, and Gupta, 2000) and to the extent that a democratic tradition has any impacts through this channel on income inequality, the dummy variable in the regression representing before- and after-tax Gini coefficient can account for this. In addition, democracy is not associated with income inequality, as demonstrated by Barro (1999). Therefore democracy seems to be a good instrument for corruption. The simple correlation coefficient between the democracy variable used in this paper (i.e., length of exposure to democracy taken from Treisman, 2000) and the corruption index is –0.75 with a t-ratio of –7, i.e., countries with long periods of democracy are perceived to be less corrupt.

The results of the IV technique using democracy as the instrument are shown in Table 2 for the same specification as in the OLS regression. Results are much stronger than the OLS version: significance and magnitude of the estimated coefficient on corruption increase even when real per capita GDP is included in the regression. In particular, the estimated coefficient when real per capita GDP is included in the regression is now significant at the 5 percent level, whereas it was not significant at the conventional statistical levels using the OLS techniques. The point estimate suggests that a worsening in the corruption index of a country by one standard deviation (2.52 points on a scale of 0 to 10) increases income inequality by 9 points (Table 2, column 1) or 11 points (Table 2, column 6). This is a significant increase given that the average value of the Gini coefficient in the sample is 39. An important reason for the increased significance of corruption in the IV regression is the fact that use of democracy as an instrument renders real per capita GDP insignificant in the regression.[20] Figure 1 shows the relationship between corruption and income inequality based on the IV regression result (Table 2, column 6). The fitted relationship shows that the results are not driven by any outliers.

We next test the sensitivity of the results in Table 2 to alternative choices of instrument. The set of instruments consists of the same democracy variable and one or two of the following six variables: initial real per capita income, country's latitude, ethnicity, initial corruption, ratio of public employment to labor force, and ratio of government spending to GDP. The first three variables have been used as instruments for corruption in previous studies of corruption (La Porta et al., 1998; Mauro, 1995, 1998; Hall and Jones, 1999; Treisman, 2000). Ratio of public employment to labor force and government spending to GDP are used as proxies for government intervention in the economy which may affect the extent of corruption.[21] Lastly initial corruption (in 1980) was used: it is predetermined relative to the future values of corruption, as the corruption variable is the average of the corruption data over the 1980–97 period. The attraction of using more than one instrument is that it generates overidentifying restrictions which allows us to test for the validity of such instruments. We use Sargan's test for this purpose which admittedly has low power in samples of the size we use in this paper. Therefore, results should be treated with caution in this respect.

The results are shown in Table 3 for eight sets of instruments. Of the eight regressions, the estimated coefficient on corruption is significant

---

[20]Barro (1999) provides evidence that real per capita GDP is a robust determinant of democracy. In our sample, the simple correlation coefficient between the democracy variable and real per capita GDP is 0.7 with a t-statistic of 6.4.

[21]We thank the editor of the journal for this suggestion. We also added the interaction between each measure of government size and corruption, another suggestion of the editor, on the assumption that impact of corruption may increase with the scale of government intervention in the economy. The interaction variable turned out to be insignificant. By contrast, the interaction variable was found to be significant in the poverty regression.

Table 2. Corruption and Income Inequality: Instrumental Variable Estimates (Dependent Variable: The Gini Coefficient)

Independent Variables	(1)	(2)	(3)	(4)	(5)	(6)
Constant	38.51***	39.34***	36.92***	39.03***	40.75***	38.26***
	(6.19)	(6.98)	(6.25)	(5.28)	(5.76)	(5.21)
Expenditure dummy	−5.35**	−5.28*	−5.77*	−5.18*	−5.74	−5.83
	(−1.96)	(−1.72)	(−1.89)	(−1.66)	(−1.49)	(−1.55)
Recipient dummy	−0.01	0.62	0.36	0.76	1.15	0.94
	(−0.00)	(0.17)	(0.10)	(0.22)	(0.32)	(0.26)
Net income dummy	−5.85**	−6.05**	−5.87**	−5.69*	−5.72*	−5.63*
	(−2.39)	(−2.39)	(−2.32)	(−1.83)	(−1.94)	(−1.87)
Natural resource abundance	41.02***	41.43**	42.75**	47.57*	43.44	46.47*
	(2.65)	(2.45)	(2.55)	(1.83)	(1.58)	(1.68)
Capital stock–GDP ratio	0.06**	0.06*	0.06**	0.05**	0.06*	0.06*
	(2.52)	(1.90)	(2.11)	(2.22)	(1.69)	(1.80)
Education inequality	0.66		1.00	0.82		0.97
	(0.45)		(0.76)	(0.57)		(0.71)
Secondary schooling		0.40	0.96		0.51	0.82
		(0.21)	(0.58)		(0.21)	(0.37)
Initial Gini coefficient for land	0.06	0.05	0.05	0.05	0.04	0.04
	(1.01)	(0.63)	(0.59)	(0.65)	(0.41)	(0.38)
Real per capita GDP ($\times 10^2$)				0.03	0.01	0.02
				(0.50)	(0.17)	(0.29)
Corruption	3.48***	3.74***	3.73***	4.21**	4.16**	4.25**
	(3.81)	(3.20)	(3.02)	(2.09)	(2.07)	(2.02)
Adjusted generalized R^2	0.76	0.74	0.76	0.77	0.75	0.76
Number of observations	38	38	38	37	37	37
P-value for Sargan's misspecification test	n.a.	n.a.	n.a.	n.a.	n.a.	n.a.

Note: Estimation is by instrumental variable techniques using democracy as the instrument for corruption. Other variables in the regression act as their own instruments. Numbers in parentheses are t-statistics based on White heteroscedasticity-consistent standard errors. The adjusted generalized R^2 is the measure of adjusted R^2 for regressions estimated by instrumental variable technique; see Pesaran and Smith (1994). Sargan's misspecification test is a test of validity of instruments. A high value of the corruption index indicates a high level of corruption.

***Significant at 1 percent level; ** significant at 5 percent level; and * significant at 10 percent level.

in three regressions at the 5 percent level and in one regression at the 10 percent level. The chosen instruments are valid at the conventional statistical levels in seven regressions as judged by Sargan's test. In all

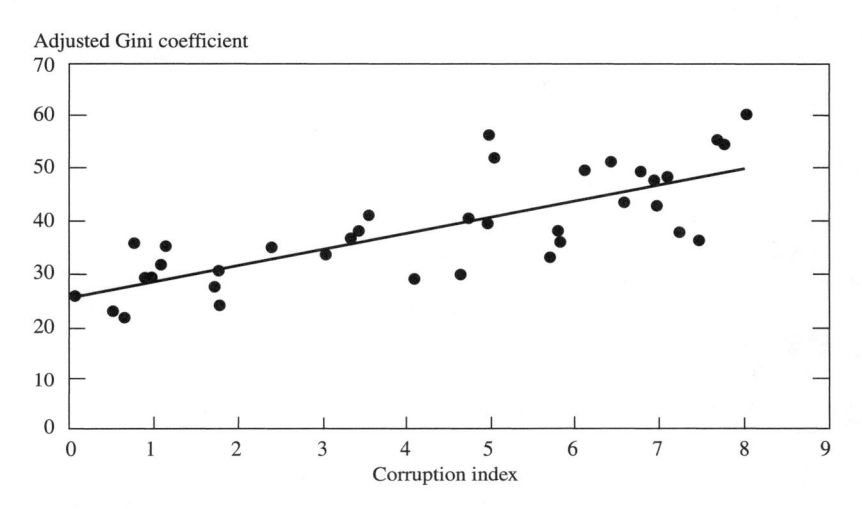

Figure 1. Corruption and Income Inequality

The Gini coefficient is adjusted using the regression in Table 2, column 6. A high value of the corruption index means the country has a high level of corruption.

regressions, the first stage R-squared is quite high, which suggests that the chosen instruments are highly correlated with corruption. The regression with the highest p-value for Sargan's test uses ratio of government spending to GDP and democracy as instruments which produces an estimated coefficient on corruption which is as high as the estimated coefficient when democracy was the only instrument.

D. Impact of Corruption on Poverty

The poverty regression is estimated using the OLS and the IV techniques and the specification given in Section 3.B. Table 4 shows the results of the OLS regression. All regressions contain the following variables: a constant, natural resource abundance, initial income of the poor, initial secondary schooling, and growth in corruption.[22] The three remaining variables (education inequality, initial Gini coefficient for land,

---

[22]Most of the variables included in the regression affect aggregate growth. Hence, aggregate growth is excluded in Table 4. Including it increases collinearity among the variables, which makes it difficult to distinguish the effect of each independent variable on the dependent variable. Nevertheless, adding aggregate growth produces results which are similar to Table 4, particularly with respect to the impact of corruption. Aggregate growth is significant only at the 10 percent level. These results are available from authors.

Table 3. Corruption and Income Inequality: Impact of Alternative Instruments (Dependent Variable: The Gini Coefficient)

Instruments	Coefficient	P-value	First Stage Adjusted R-squared
Democracy, initial income	3.12* (1.67)	0.02	0.73
Democracy, ethnicity	2.41 (1.52)	0.17	0.75
Democracy, ethnicity, initial corruption	1.34 (1.14)	0.15	0.77
Democracy, latitude, initial corruption	1.71 (1.56)	0.14	0.78
Democracy, latitude	2.95** (2.32)	0.40	0.76
Democracy, latitude, ethnicity	2.28** (1.99)	0.40	0.77
Ratio of government spending to GDP, democracy	3.95** (1.95)	0.58	0.73
Ratio of public employment to labor force, democracy	2.07 (1.39)	0.34	0.76

Notes: Entries in the second column show the estimated coefficient on the corruption index and its t-ratio (in parentheses) in specification (6) of Table 1. P-value is the probability value associated with test of validity of the chosen instruments. Adjusted first stage R-squared is the adjusted R-squared obtained from the first stage regression of the corruption on the instruments. A high value of the corruption index indicates a high level of corruption.

***Significant at 1 percent level; ** significant at 5 percent level; and * significant at 10 percent level.

and social spending) are entered one at a time and then all at once to see if the sign and significance of these variables—as well as that of corruption—change. In all these regressions, higher growth in corruption is associated with lower income growth of the poor, with the coefficient significant in four regressions at the conventional statistical levels. The estimated coefficient on the corruption index is most significant (at the 1 percent level) when the regression includes social spending (column 4). The results also show that the impact of corruption on poverty is quantitatively important. An increase of one standard deviation in the growth rate of corruption (a deterioration of 0.78 percentage points) is associated with a decline in income growth of the bottom 20 percent of the population of 1.6 percentage points per year (Table 4, column 4).

Table 4. Corruption and Poverty: OLS Estimates (Dependent Variable: Income Growth of the Bottom 20 Percent)

Independent Variables	(1)	(2)	(3)	(4)	(5)
Constant	0.01 (0.91)	0.00 (0.27)	0.05 (1.51)	–0.00 (–0.01)	0.00 (0.00)
Natural resource abundance	–0.09 (–0.94)	–0.08 (–0.79)	–0.09 (–0.99)	–0.15 (–1.49)	–0.12 (–1.33)
Initial income of the bottom 20 percent (x10^3)	–0.04 (–1.26)	–0.04 (–1.14)	–0.05 (–1.56)	–0.09** (–2.36)	–0.09** (–2.34)
Initial secondary schooling	0.01 (1.13)	0.01 (1.13)	0.01 (1.25)	0.01 (1.33)	0.02 (1.52)
Education inequality (x10)		0.05 (0.51)			0.14 (1.36)
Initial gini coefficient for land (x10^2)			–0.06 (–1.12)		–0.03 (–0.73)
Social spending (x10)				0.03** (2.43)	0.03** (2.38)
Corruption	–0.02** (–2.17)	–0.02** (–2.19)	–0.01 (–1.24)	–0.02*** (–2.57)	–0.02* (2.05)
Adjusted R^2	0.13	0.10	0.14	0.29	0.28
Number of observations	31	31	31	31	31
F-statistic	2.19*	1.71	1.96	3.56**	2.69**

Notes: Estimation is by OLS. Numbers in parentheses are t-statistics based on White heteroscedasticity-consistent standard errors. Social spending is sum of spending on education, health, social security, welfare, housing, and community amenities. The corruption index is multiplied by –1 so that a high value of growth in the index indicates a high growth rate of corruption.

***Significant at 1 percent level; ** significant at 5 percent level; and * significant at 10 percent level.

The results also show that income growth of the poor is high in countries with poor natural resources, low levels of initial income, higher initial schooling, low land inequality, and high level of social spending. Surprisingly, income growth of the poor is high when education inequality is high although the latter is not statistically significant.

E. Sensitivity Analysis and the IV Estimation of the Poverty Regression

The OLS regression is robust to addition of aggregate growth, allowing for the sample size to vary across various specifications in Table 4 and presence of outliers.[23] Sample size varies depending on data availability for each specification.[24] The OLS regression results establish association at best and not causality. The association could be due to high poverty causing high corruption or due to other variables. As in the analysis of corruption and income inequality, instrumental variable estimation is used to address these concerns, using initial corruption as the instrument. Initial corruption is predetermined with respect to growth in corruption over the 1980–95 period. Initial corruption turns out to be a powerful predictor for growth in corruption in the subsequent periods. The simple correlation coefficient between the two variables is –0.55 with a t-statistic of –3.84, suggesting that countries which were perceived to be highly corrupt at the start of the 1980s were perceived to have become less corrupt over the subsequent 15 years.

The results are shown in Table 5. Statistical significance and magnitude of the corruption index increases in the IV regression relative to the OLS regression. Corruption is now statistically significant at the 1 percent level in two specifications (columns 4 and 5) and at 5 and 10 percent level as before in the remaining specifications.

The effect of corruption on poverty is quantitatively important. A one-standard deviation increase in the growth rate of corruption (a deterioration of 0.78 percentage points) reduces income growth of the bottom 20 percent of the population by 4.7 percentage points per year (Table 5, column 4) which is considerable given the average income growth of 0.6 percent a year.[25] Figure 2 shows the relationship between growth in corruption and income growth of the poor based on the IV regression result (Table 5, column 5). The fitted relationship shows that the results are not driven by any outliers. This is also confirmed by deleting from the sample observations with extreme values (e.g., countries with largest reduction in corruption and largest improvement in income growth of the poor).

---

[23]Sample size would vary depending on data availability. These results, not reported, produce identical results to Table 4. Additional sensitivity analyses are not conducted since the specification follows the baseline specification in the growth literature.

[24]We could not experiment with different measures of corruption since there are not enough time series data on corruption for the available sample except for the corruption measure reported in Tanzi and Davoodi (1997).

[25]In the sample, there are countries in which income growth of the poor has increased dramatically (e.g., Thailand, 10 percent a year) and countries in which income growth had decreased substantially (Dominican Republic with 4 percent per year) and those with almost zero growth (e.g., United States, Sweden) over the 1980–97 period.

Table 5. Corruption and Poverty: Instrumental Variable Estimates (Dependent Variable: Income Growth of the Bottom 20 Percent)

Independent Variables	(1)	(2)	(3)	(4)	(5)
Constant	−0.00 (−0.08)	−0.01 (−0.38)	−0.00 (−0.12)	−0.02 (−1.02)	−0.08 (−1.28)
Natural resource abundance	−0.07 (−0.76)	−0.06 (−0.57)	−0.07 (−0.80)	−0.14* (−1.65)	−0.12 (−1.39)
Initial income of the bottom 20 percent (x10^3)	−0.03 (−1.01)	−0.02 (−0.78)	−0.03 (−0.90)	−0.09** (−2.52)	−0.07** (−2.25)
Initial secondary schooling	0.01 (1.50)	0.02 (1.51)	0.01 (1.54)	0.02* (1.77)	0.02* (1.87)
Education inequality (x10)		0.07 (0.77)			0.01 (1.60)
Initial Gini coefficient for land (x10^2)			0.01 (0.13)		0.05 (0.79)
Social spending (x10)				0.04*** (2.71)	0.04*** (2.85)
Corruption	−0.04** (−2.01)	−0.04* (−1.94)	−0.04** (−2.31)	−0.06*** (−2.87)	−0.06*** (3.31)
Adjusted generalized R^2	0.13	0.09	0.22	0.29	0.38
Number of observations	31	31	31	31	31
P-value for Sargan's misspecification test	n.a.	n.a.	n.a.	n.a.	n.a.

Notes: Estimation is by IV. Numbers in parentheses are t-statistics based on White heteroscedasticity-consistent standard errors. The adjusted generalized R^2 is the measure of adjusted R^2 for regressions estimated by instrumental variable technique; see Pesaran and Smith (1994). Sargan's misspecification test is a test of validity of instruments. The instrument is initial corruption. Other variables in the regression act as their own instrument. Social spending is sum of spending on education, health, social security, welfare, housing, and community amenities. The corruption index is multiplied by −1 so that a high value of growth in the index indicates a high growth rate of corruption.

***Significant at 1 percent level; ** significant at 5 percent level; and * significant at 10 percent level.

Additional sensitivity analyses are conducted using eight sets of instruments, similar to the sets used in the income inequality regression.[26] The results are shown in Table 6. In all cases, Sargan's test does not reject the hypothesis that the chosen instruments are valid. Corruption

---

[26]The rationale for the choice of these instruments is the same.

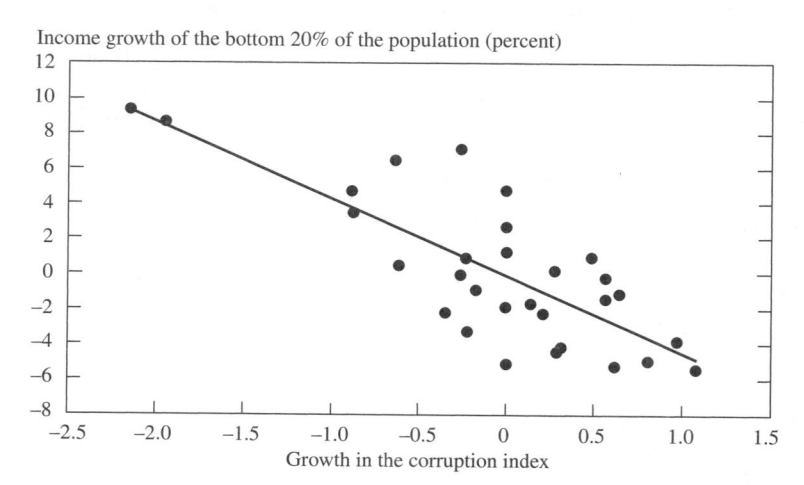

Figure 2. Corruption and Income Growth of the Poor

Income growth of the bottom 20% of the population (percent)

[Scatter plot with x-axis "Growth in the corruption index" ranging from -2.5 to 1.5, showing a negative linear trend]

The figure is based on the regression in Table 5, column 5. A high growth in the corruption index means the country has a higher growth rate of corruption.

has the same sign as before and is statistically significant at the 1 percent level in all but three regressions. Therefore, one may conclude that higher corruption leads to higher poverty.

5. Conclusions and Policy Implications

Corruption interferes with the traditional core functions of government: allocation of resources, stabilization of the economy, and redistribution of income. These functions influence income distribution and poverty in varying degrees, both directly and indirectly.

The budget is the principal vehicle through which any government conducts its core functions. Previous studies have demonstrated that corruption affects the revenue and expenditure side of the budget (Mauro, 1998, Tanzi and Davoodi, 2001) and impairs efficiency and growth (Mauro, 1995, 1998). The empirical evidence presented in this paper shows that corruption has significant distributional consequences as well and interferes with redistribution function of the government.

The paper finds that the impact of corruption on income inequality and poverty is considerable. A worsening in the corruption index of a country by one standard deviation (2.52 points on a scale of 0 to 10) in-

Table 6. Corruption and Poverty: Impact of Alternative Instruments (Dependent Variable: Income Growth of the Bottom 20 Percent)

Instruments	Coefficient	P-value	First Stage Adjusted R-squared
Initial corruption, initial income	−0.05*** (−3.42)	0.65	0.46
Initial corruption, latitude	−0.06*** (−3.34)	0.97	0.44
Democracy, ethnicity, initial corruption	−0.06*** (−3.18)	0.16	0.41
Democracy, latitude, initial corruption	−0.06*** (−3.12)	0.95	0.42
Democracy, latitude	−0.06* (−1.81)	0.84	0.30
Democracy, latitude, ethnicity	−0.07* (−1.86)	0.24	0.26
Ratio of public employment to population, initial corruption	−0.04*** (−2.60)	0.75	0.15
Ratio of public employment to labor force, initital corruption	−0.04** (−2.47)	0.40	0.48

Notes: Entries in the second column show the estimated coefficient on the corruption index and its t-ratio (in parentheses) in specification (5) of Table 4. P-value is the probability value associated with test of validity of the chosen instruments. Adjusted first stage R-squared is the adjusted R-squared obtained from the first stage regression of the corruption on the instruments. The corruption index is multiplied by −1 so that a high value of growth in the index indicates a high growth rate of corruption.

***Significant at 1 percent level; ** significant at 5 percent level; and * significant at 10 percent level.

creases the Gini coefficient by 11 points which is significant, given the average Gini value of 39. A one-standard deviation increase in the growth rate of corruption (a deterioration of 0.78 percentage points) reduces income growth of the poor by 4.7 percentage points per year which is considerable given the average income growth of 0.6 percent a year.

The paper's findings suggest that the adverse distributional consequences of corruption can, however, be mitigated by: (1) sound management of natural resources; (2) broad-based, labor-intensive growth; (3) efficient spending on education and health; (4) effective targeting of social programs; and (5) a low level of inequality in the access to education.

A central message of this paper is that corruption increases inequality and, given its negative efficiency implications established already in the literature, should be considered harmful to both growth and equity. Policies that reduce corruption will most likely reduce income inequality and poverty. The evidence gives support to political economy considerations that benefits of corruption and bribing public officials are captured primarily by the rich and better-connected individuals. There are many other mechanisms through which corruption can affect poverty and inequality, some of which were presented in the paper. Future research can focus on these channels and provide rigorous theoretical models of corruption, income inequality, poverty while working with a larger sample size than the one used in this paper.

Data Appendix

The Gini Coefficient and Quintile Income Shares

Data on the Gini coefficient and quintile income shares are taken from Deininger and Squire's (1996) "high quality" data set. This data set includes observations on the Gini coefficient that fulfill three key requirements for reliability: they must be based on household survey data, the survey coverage must be national, and the surveys must include all income sources.

Natural Resource Endowment

The proxy for natural resource endowment is the share of natural resource exports in total exports in 1970 (Sachs and Warner, 1997).

Physical Capital Endowment

The physical capital endowment is the average ratio of the stock of physical capital to GDP, both measured in constant 1987 prices in local currency, between 1980 and 1990 (Nehru and Dhareshwar, 1993).

Human Capital Endowment

The proxy for human capital endowment is the average years of secondary education in the population aged 15 and over between 1980 and 1995 (Barro and Lee, 1996).

Land Distribution

The proxy for the distribution of land is the Gini coefficient for land (circa 1980). It is based on the land rental market and was used by Deininger and Squire (1996).[27]

---

[27]Klaus Deininger kindly provided the data.

Education Inequality

Education inequality is proxied by the 1980–95 average ratio of the percent of population, aged 15 and over, with no schooling expressed as a fraction of percent of population, aged 15 and over, with completed secondary and higher education (Barro and Lee, 1996).

Corruption

Six indices of corruption are used. One measure taken from Tanzi and Davoodi (1997) is from the *International Country Risk Guide (ICRG)* and the Business International *(BI)*. The latter is reported in Mauro (1995) and is averaged between 1980 and 1995. The ICRG index reflects the assessment of foreign investors on the degree of corruption in an economy. Investors are asked whether high government officials are likely to demand special payments and whether illegal payments are generally expected throughout lower levels of government as bribes connected with import and export licenses, exchange controls, tax assessment, police protection, or loans. The ICRG index has been rescaled and spliced with the BI index so that the combined index ranges from 0 (most corrupt) to 10 (least corrupt).

Other five indexes are from the *Transparency International* corruption perception indices for 1995, 1996, 1997, an expanded 1997 index (Lambsdorff), and a historical corruption index averaged over the 1988–92 period. The expanded 1997 corruption index was constructed by Johann Lambsdorff (forthcoming) by applying the same technique as *Transparency International*, but includes countries for which a minimum of two survey sources were available. The rationale for their exclusion from the *Transparency International* indexes was the requirement of a minimum of four survey sources on every country to enhance the reliability of the data. By enlarging the number of observations available (from 52 to 101), however, the expanded 1997 corruption perception index compensates for the increased margin of error incurred by using data based on fewer surveys. Results from this measure are reported in the income inequality regression.

Real Per Capita GDP

The data on nominal purchasing power parity per capita GDP denominated in U.S. dollars have been converted to real data using the U.S. GDP deflator (International Monetary Fund, *World Economic Outlook*, 1997).

Social Spending

Three measures of social spending are used; these are government spending on: (1) social security and welfare, (2) education and health, and (3) the sum of spending items (1) and (2) plus housing and community amenities. These data have been expressed as fractions of GDP, both in local currency, and are from the same source (International Monetary Fund, *Government Finance Statistics,* 1997).

Democracy

This variable measures whether a country has been democratic for the past 46 years (Treisman, 2000).

Latitude

Latitude is a country's distance from the equator (Hall and Jones, 1999). This variable is measured as the absolute value of latitude in degrees divided by 90 to place it on a 0-to-1 scale.

Ethnicity

The proxy for ethnicity is an index of ethnolinguistic fractionalization for 1960 (Taylor and Hudson, 1972). It measures the probability that two randomly selected persons from a given country will not belong to the same ethnolinguistic group.

References

Abed, G.T., Ebrill, L., Gupta, S., Clements, B., McMorran, R., Pellechio, A., Schiff, J., Verhoeven, M. (1998) *Fiscal Reforms in Low-Income Countries: Experience Under IMF-Supported Programs,* IMF Occasional Paper No. 160 (Washington: International Monetary Fund).

Alesina, A. (1998) The Political Economy of Stabilizations and Income Inequality: Myths and Reality. In: *Income Distribution and High-Quality Growth,* ed. by Vito Tanzi and Ke-young Chu (Cambridge, Massachusetts: MIT Press).

Alesina, A., Drazen, A. (1991) Why Are Stabilizations Delayed? *American Economic Review,* Vol. 81 (December), No. 5, 1170–88.

Alesina, A., Ozler, S., Roubini, N., Swagel, P. (1996) Political Instability and Economic Growth. *Journal of Economic Growth,* Vol. 1 (June), 189–212.

Alesina, A., Rodrik, D. (1994) Distributive Politics and Economic Growth. *Quarterly Journal of Economics,* Vol. 109, 465–90.

Atkinson, A.B. (1997) Bringing Income Distribution in from the Cold. *Economic Journal: The Journal of the Royal Economic Society,* Vol. 107 (March), 297–321.

Atkinson, A.B. (2000) Increased Income Inequality in OECD Countries and Redistributive Impact of the Government Budget. *WIDER Working Paper* No. 202 (Helsinki: United Nations University World Institute for Development Economics Research).

Barro, R., Lee, J.-W. (1996) International Measures of Schooling Years and Schooling Quality. *American Economic Review, Papers and Proceedings*, Vol. 86 (May), No. 2: 218–23.

Barro, R.J. (1999) Determinants of Democracy. *Journal of Political Economy*, No. 6, S158–S83.

Bénabou, R. (1996) Inequality and Growth. In: *National Bureau of Economic Research Macroeconomics Annual*, 11–74, ed. by Bernanke, B.S. and Rotemberg, J.J. (Cambridge, Massachusetts: MIT Press).

Birdsall, N., Londoño, J.L. (1997) Asset Inequality Matters: An Assessment of the World Bank's Approach to Poverty Reduction. *American Economic Review, Papers and Proceedings*, Vol. 87 (May), No. 2: 32–37.

Bourguignon, F., Morrisson, C. (1990) Income Distribution, Development and Foreign Trade: A Cross-Sectional Analysis. *European Economic Review*, Vol. 34 (September), 1113–32.

Bourguignon, F., Morrisson, C. (1998) Inequality and Development. *Journal of Development Economics*, Vol. 57, No. 2: 233–257.

Business International Corporation (1984) *Introduction to the Country Assessment Service* (New York: Business International Corporation).

Chu, K.-Y., Davoodi, H.R., Gupta, S. (2000) Income Distribution and Tax and Government Social Spending Policies in Developing Countries. IMF Working Paper WP/00/62 (Washington D.C: International Monetary Fund).

Deininger, K., Squire, L. (1996) *New Ways of Looking at Old Issues: Inequality and Growth* (unpublished; Washington: World Bank).

Deininger, K., Squire, L. (1996) A New Data Set Measuring Income Inequality. *World Bank Economic Review*, Vol. 10 (September), No. 3: 565–91.

Elliott, K. A. (ed.) (1997) *Corruption and the Global Economy* (Washington: Institute for International Economics).

Goettingen University and Transparency International (1997) Corruption Perception Index. Available via Internet: http://www.gwdg.de/~uwvw/icr.htm.

Hall, R. E., Jones, C.I. (1999) Why Do Some Countries Produce So Much More Output Per Worker Than Others? *Quarterly Journal of Economics*, Vol. 114, No. 1: 82–116.

Huntington, S. P. (1968) *Political Order in Changing Societies* (New Haven: Yale University Press).

International Monetary Fund (1997) *Government Finance Statistics Database* (Washington).

International Monetary Fund (1997) *World Economic Outlook Database* (Washington).

International Country Risk Guide (1996) *Political Risk Services* (New York: Political Risk Services).

Kaufmann, D., Kraay, A., Zoido-Lobatón, P. (1999a) Aggregating Governance Indicators. World Bank Working Paper No. 2195 (Washington: World Bank).

Kaufmann, D., Kraay, A., Zoido-Lobatón, P. (1999b) Governance Matters. World Bank Working Paper No. 2196 (Washington: World Bank).

Kaufmann, D., Wei, S.-J. (1999) Does Grease Money Speed up the Wheels of Commerce? World Bank Working Paper Series No. 2254 (Washington: World Bank).

Klitgaard, R. (1988) *Controlling Corruption.* (Berkeley, Ca: University of California Press).

Knack, S., Keefer, P. (1996) Institutions and Economic Performance: Cross-Country Tests Using Alternative Institutional Measures. *Economics and Politics*, Vol. 7 (November), No. 3: 207–27.

La Porta, R., Lopez-de-Silanes, F., Shleifer, A., Vishny, R. (1998) The Quality of Government. NBER Working Paper Series No. 6727.

Laban, R., Sturzenegger, F. (1994) Distributional Conflict, Financial Adaptation, and Delayed Stabilizations. *Economics and Politics,* Vol. 6 (November), 257–76.

Lambsdorff, J. (1998) Corruption in Comparative Perception. In: *The Economics of Corruption*, (ed.) by Arvind Jain (Dordrecht: Kluwer Academic Publishing).

Leamer, E.E., Maul, H., Rodriguez, S., Schott, P.K. (1999) Does Natural Resource Abundance Increase Latin American Income Inequality? *Journal of Development Economics*, Vol. 59, 3–42.

Leff, N. H. (1964) Economic Development Through Bureaucratic Corruption. *American Behavioral Scientist,* Vol. 8 (November), 8–14.

Li, H., Squire, L., Zou, H.-F. (1998) Explaining International and Intertemporal Variations in Income Inequality. *Economic Journal*, Vol. 108 (January), No. 446: 26–43.

Londoño, J.L., Székely, M. (1997) *Distributional Surprises After a Decade of Reforms: Latin America in the Nineties* (unpublished; Washington: Inter-American Development Bank).

Lui, F. (1985) An Equilibrium Queuing Model of Bribery. *Journal of Political Economy*, 93, August, 760–781.

Mauro, P. (1995) Corruption and Growth. *Quarterly Journal of Economics,* Vol. 110 (August), No. 3: 681–712.

Mauro, P. (1998) Corruption and the Composition of Government Expenditure. *Journal of Public Economics,* Vol. 69, 263–279. [Reproduced as Chapter 9 in this volume—ED.]

Musgrave, R.A. (1959) *The Theory of Public Finance: A Study in Public Economy* (New York: McGraw-Hill).

Nehru, V., Dhareshwar, A. (1993) A New Database on Physical Capital Stock: Sources, Methodology and Results. *Revista de Análisis Económico*, Vol. 8 (June), 37–59.

Persson, T., Tabellini, G. (1994) Is Inequality Harmful for Growth? *American Economic Review,* Vol. 84 (June), 600–621.

Pesaran, M.H., Smith, R.J. (1994) A Generalized R^2 Criterion for Regression Models Estimated by the Instrumental Variables Method. *Econometrica*, Vol. 62, 705–10.

Ravallion, M. (1997) Can High-Inequality Developing Countries Escape Absolute Poverty? *Economics Letters*, Vol. 56 (September), 51–57.

Ravallion, M., Chen, S. (1997) What Can New Survey Data Tell Us About Recent Changes in Distribution and Poverty? *World Bank Economic Review*, Vol. 11 (May), No. 2: 357–382.

Rose-Ackerman, S. (1978) *Corruption: A Study in Political Economy* (New York: Academic Press).

Rose-Ackerman, S. (1997a) *Corruption and Good Governance*, UNDP Discussion Paper Series No. 3 (New York: United Nations Development Program).

Rose-Ackerman, S. (1997b) "The Political Economy of Corruption. In: *Corruption and the Global Economy*, (ed.) by Elliott, K.A. (Washington: Institute for International Economics).

Rose-Ackerman, S. (1999) *Corruption and Government: Causes, Consequences, and Reform* (London: Cambridge University Press).

Sachs, J.D. (1995) Natural Resource Abundance and Economic Growth. Discussion Paper No. 517a (Cambridge, Massachusetts: Harvard Institute for International Development).

Sachs, J.D., Warner, A.M. (1997) Fundamental Sources of Long-Run Growth. *American Economic Review, Papers and Proceedings*, Vol. 87 (May), No. 2: 184–88.

Sala-i-Martin, X.X. (1997) I Just Ran Two Million Regressions. *American Economic Review, Papers and Proceedings*, Vol. 87 (May), No. 2: 178–183.

Sarel, M. (1997) How Macroeconomic Factors Affect Income Distribution: The Cross-Country Evidence. IMF Working Paper 97/152 (Washington: International Monetary Fund).

Shleifer, A., Vishny, R.W. (1993) Corruption. *Quarterly Journal of Economics*, Vol. 108 (August), 599–617.

Spilimbergo, A., Londoño, J.L., Székely, M. (1999) Income Distribution, Factor Endowments, and Trade Openness. *Journal of Development Economics*, Vol. 59, 77–101.

Székely, M. (1997) Policy Options for Poverty Alleviation. Working Paper No. 342 (Washington: Inter-American Development Bank).

Tanzi, V. (1974) Redistributing Income Through the Budget in Latin America. *Banca Nazionale del Lavoro Quarterly Review*, Vol. 27 (March), No. 108, 65–87.

Tanzi, V. (1995) Corruption: Arm's-Length Relationships and Markets. In: *The Economics of Organized Crime*, (ed.) by Gianluca Fiorentini and Sam Peltzman (Cambridge, England: Cambridge University Press).

Tanzi, V. (1997a) Corruption in the Public Finances. paper presented at the Eighth International Anti-Corruption Conference, Lima, Peru, September 7–11 (unpublished; Washington: International Monetary Fund).

Tanzi, V. (1997b) The Changing Role of Fiscal Policy in Fund's Policy Advice. (unpublished).

Tanzi, V. (1998) Corruption Around the World: Causes, Consequences, Scope, and Cures. *Staff Papers*, International Monetary Fund, Vol. 45, 559–94. [Reproduced as Chapter 2 in this volume—ED.]

Tanzi, V., Davoodi, H.R. (2001) Corruption, Growth and Public Finances. In: (ed.) Jain, A.J. *The Political Economy of Corruption* (London: Routledge). [Reproduced as Chapter 8 in this volume—ED.]

Tanzi, V., Chu, K.-Y. (eds.) (1998) *Income Distribution and High-Quality Growth* (Cambridge, Massachusetts: MIT Press).

Tanzi, V., Davoodi, H.R. (1997) Corruption, Public Investment, and Growth. IMF Working Paper 97/139 (Washington: International Monetary Fund). [Revised version reproduced as Chapter 11 in this volume—ED.]

Tanzi, V., Kroll, J. (1997) Comments. In: *Corruption and the Global Economy*, (ed.) by Elliott, K.A. (Washington: Institute for International Economics).

Taylor, C. L., Hudson, M.C. (1972) *World Handbook of Political and Social Indicators* (New Haven and London, Yale University Press).

Tinbergen, J. (1975) *Income Distribution: Analysis and Policies* (Amsterdam: North-Holland Publishing Company).

Treisman, D. (2000) The Causes of Corruption: A Cross-National Study. *Journal of Public Economics*, 76: 399–457.

United Nations Development Programme (1997) *Human Development Report* (Oxford: Oxford University Press for UNDP).

Wei, S.-J. (1997) How Taxing is Corruption on International Investors? NBER Working Paper No. 6030 (Cambridge, Massachusetts: National Bureau of Economic Research).

Wei, S.-J. (1999) Corruption in Economic Development: Beneficial Grease, Minor Annoyance, or Major Obstacle? World Bank Discussion Paper No. 2048 (Washington: World Bank).

Part V

Corruption and Transition Economies

18

Corruption, Structural Reforms, and Economic Performance in the Transition Economies

George T. Abed and Hamid R. Davoodi

> *Cross-country empirical work has confirmed the negative impact of corruption on growth and productivity, but it is of little use in designing anticorruption strategies.*
> —Susan Rose-Ackerman (1999, p. 3)

> *The fight against corruption often cannot proceed independently from the reform of the state. In many ways, it is the same fight.*
> —Vito Tanzi (Chapter 2, p. 53)

I. Introduction

The literature on corruption is growing rapidly. Until recently, corruption was mostly a subject for sociologists, political scientists, and

---

The authors wish to thank Vito Tanzi, Michael Keen, Sanjeev Gupta, Lorenzo Figliuoli, Gabriela Inchauste, Mark Flanagan, and Karen Swiderski for helpful comments, and Randa Sab and Solita Wakefield for their computational assistance.

public administrators.[1] Increasingly, economists have sought to apply the tools of economic analysis to this phenomenon, building on the pioneering work of Becker (1968), Rose-Ackerman (1978), Klitgaard (1988), and Tanzi (1995). Economists have generally highlighted the adverse impact of corruption on economic performance while providing insights into its origins, manifestations, and possible remedies.[2] However, few studies have sought to examine the causes of corruption,[3] whereas fewer still have succeeded in linking the causes to possible remedies in a satisfactory analytical framework. This is partly due to the complexity and diversity of the underlying factors that give rise to corruption, many of which lie beyond the traditional domain of economics. More important, perhaps, is that greater effort has been made to "measure" corruption[4] than the more complex structural or institutional distortions that may underlie corrupt behavior. With the wider availability of "indices of perceived corruption" for an increasing number of countries, it is not surprising that economists have begun to examine the possible relationship between "corruption" and economic performance.[5]

This paper views corruption largely as a symptom of weaknesses in economic structures and institutions,[6] considered to be the origin of much of what is perceived as corruption in the public sector.[7] Further-

---

[1] See Weber (1947); Myrdal (1968); Leff (1964); Huntington (1968); and Heidenheimer, Johnston, and LeVine (1989).

[2] See, for example, Kaufman, Kraay, and Zoido-Lobatón (1999a, 1999b), who pull together 300 indicators of governance from numerous sources from which the authors then construct six basic governance concepts. Others have offered useful typologies (Rose-Ackerman, 1999, and Tanzi, Chapter 2 in this volume) or instructive case studies (Klitgaard, 1988), while seeking a better understanding of the phenomenon. On the impact of corruption on measures of economic and social performance, see, for example, Mauro (1995); Wei (1997a, 1999a); Tanzi and Davoodi (Chapter 11 in this volume); and Gupta, Davoodi, and Alonso-Terme (Chapter 17 in this volume).

[3] Among these are the papers by Ades and Di Tella (1999); Rauch and Evans (2000); and Treisman (2000).

[4] "Corruption" has been measured by constructing indices of "perception of corruption" derived from surveys of businessmen, public officials, and possibly others. See Tanzi (Chapter 2 in this volume) and Wei (1999a) for a discussion of some of these indices.

[5] Some studies have used data on conviction of publicly elected officials as a measure of corruption where the major source of conviction has been the violation of the public office by the elected or appointed official; see Goel and Nelson (1998) for an example.

[6] Although corruption itself may contribute to institutional weaknesses and structural distortions, this paper's hypothesis is that the causality is largely in the other direction. See Section IV.

[7] See Tanzi (2000) on the importance of public institutions and role of the state.

more, the paper finds that once these weaknesses are defined and somehow "measured," they tend to provide a stronger link to economic performance than do measures of real or perceived corruption. Thus although corrupt behavior should always be addressed head-on by administrative means, the design of economic policies to deal with the phenomenon called "corruption" is best pursued through structural and institutional reform. Accordingly, our main hypothesis, to be tested empirically in this paper, is that once structural reforms are taken into account, the corruption variables tend to lose their explanatory power in the analysis of macroeconomic performance.

Although we are of the view that this analytical framework may have wide applicability, we apply it to 25 transition economies for the period 1994–98. Conceptually, the choice of this group of countries derives from the wide attention given to the role of corruption in influencing the transition process in these economies,[8] and from the intensity of the structural and institutional change that has marked the transformation of these economies since the early 1990s. On a more practical level, comprehensive measures of structural and institutional reforms have become available for these countries since 1994.[9]

Section II of this paper sets out a simple analytical framework and applies it to the case of transition economies. Section III provides an empirical test of the paper's main hypothesis, using four indicators of macroeconomic performance that have been widely used in the literature on transition economies: growth, inflation, the fiscal balance, and foreign direct investment. Section IV provides evidence as to whether the structural reform index is a determinant of corruption, given other determinants of corruption in transition economies. Section V presents the conclusions.

II. Corruption as a Symptom of Lagging Reforms

Corruption, of course, is not an exclusively economic phenomenon. It manifests itself in the political process (e.g., rigging elections, trading votes within legislative bodies for self-serving gains); in the judicial system (e.g., tampering with juries, bribing judges); and in other, per-

---

[8]See Shleifer and Vishny (1993); Johnson, Kaufmann, and Shleifer (1997); Rose-Ackerman (1999); and EBRD (1999b).

[9]A narrower set of measures exist prior to 1994 (de Melo, Denizer, and Gelb, 1996).

haps less visible, spheres. Economists, however, focus on corruption as a public economic policy issue, because corruption undermines the state's capacity to carry out its designated functions in the economy (e.g., as a supplier of public goods and services, a regulator of markets, or an agent for implementing society's redistributive goals).

In this context, it is not difficult to see that economic policy distortions and weak state institutions provide an environment that is conducive to corruption. For example, where the demarcation lines between the state and the market are not clear and are not properly regulated, distinctions between what is public and what is private are obscured and corrupt behavior may ensue. Similarly, regulations that are pervasive, obscure, and applied capriciously invite economic agents to find ways, including bribing public officials, to secure favorable interpretations. Exchange and trade restrictions also tend to breed informal, often corrupt, channels for market-induced transactions.

In this sense, statements that link corruption to economic performance are essentially statements about the link between structural or policy distortions and economic performance. Corruption is, for the most part, a manifestation of these distortions,[10] and analyses dealing with the effects of corruption on macroeconomic performance may, therefore, only be dealing with the symptoms. As such, they may not be very helpful in suggesting remedial policies as they beg such questions as what economic conditions may have brought about the phenomenon of corruption in the first place and what economic policies are needed to combat it. Identifying these conditions is essential to our understanding of why corruption occurs and what economic policies would be most effective to combat it.

Anticorruption Strategies

In general, anticorruption strategies have employed a combination of direct actions against corrupt behavior while pursuing reforms of policies and institutions. Such strategies may be broadly classified as belonging to one or more of the following three approaches:

- One approach emphasizes *administrative and legal remedies* designed essentially to limit the discretion of public officials, for example, through carefully crafted rules and regulations. These are

---

[10]See Rauch and Evans (2000).

intended to increase the probability of detection of corrupt behavior through strengthened monitoring and enforcement, and to ensure speedy and stiff punishment of proven wrongdoers.[11] This approach might include the establishment of internal monitoring units in bureaucracies (e.g., investigation bureaus in tax and customs administrations), the protection of the role of whistleblowers, and, more generally, the creation of anticorruption commissions (pioneered in Hong Kong SAR and Singapore, and now established in a number of other economies).

- Another approach, often pursued in conjunction with other policies, relies on the promotion of good governance through adherence to *transparency and standards* in the conduct of the public's business.[12] Among the benefits of this approach is the strengthened accountability of public officials, hence reduced corruption.[13] Actions to improve governance may be initiated within the political process itself (e.g., by legislatures or the court system), by a more demanding donor community, or by the media and civil society. For such an approach to be effective, however, it must be supplemented by adequate follow-up and enforcement mechanisms—such as a competent and independent judiciary, external audit mechanisms, and vigilant legislative bodies—as well as a free press and an alert civil society.[14]

- The third approach, and in our view the most effective over the long run, is based on *fundamental economic reforms*, whose objective is to remove the conditions that give rise to corruption in

---

[11]This approach dominates the writings of policy analysts, public administrators, as well as economists. See, for example, Becker (1968); Wade (1982); Klitgaard (1988, 1997); Hines (1995); and Rose-Ackerman (1978, 1999). Hines (1995), for example, points to the impact of penalties inherent in the U.S. Foreign Corrupt Practices Act of 1977 on trade with other countries.

[12]See Ofosu-Amaah, Soopramanien, and Uprety (1999) for a comparative review of codes of conduct of public officials in different countries.

[13]This approach has been prominent in the fiscal reforms of Australia and New Zealand and in the IMF's promotion of the codes on fiscal and monetary transparency; for the latter, see on the IMF's website "Code of Good Practices on Fiscal Transparency," http://www.imf.org/external/np/fad/trans/code.htm, and "Code of Good Practices on Transparency in Monetary and Financial Policies," http://www.imf.org/external/np/mae/mft/index.htm. The work of Transparency International is a notable effort in this regard, representing an initiative originating in civil society; see Pope (1999a, 1999b).

[14]For empirical evidence that countries with free press are perceived to have lower corruption, see Brunetti and Weder (1999).

the first place. Such reforms seek to address weaknesses in economic policies and institutions by, inter alia, introducing into governmental activities greater reliance on economic incentives through civil service reform;[15] simplifying the tax system and reforming tax and customs administrations;[16] reforming public expenditure management systems;[17] introducing more internal competition among government agencies;[18] or commercializing or privatizing those activities of government that can no longer be justified as a public responsibility.[19] Similarly, where corruption is embedded in the supply of government goods and services (e.g., price support, subsidies), this approach would call for phasing out such programs in favor of greater reliance on the market through price liberalization; the substitution of market-based, self-enforcing mechanisms; or better targeting.

Although this paper focuses on the economic approach to curbing corruption, a few words may be in order concerning the other two approaches and the manner in which all three may be related or may be combined to combat corruption. Clearly, none of the three approaches is likely to be sufficient by itself. An effective anticorruption strategy needs to employ all three approaches, perhaps with differing emphases depending on the circumstances of the country. Indeed, most countries where the incidence of corruption is perceived to be very low (e.g., the Scandinavian countries, New Zealand, Canada, and the Netherlands) are generally seen to have well-developed administrative and legal systems, greater transparency and accountability of government, as well as sound economic institutions and policy fundamentals. In the final analysis, all three approaches have to come together to achieve an optimal outcome.[20]

---

[15]See Van Rijckeghem and Weder (Chapter 3 in this volume) and Rauch and Evans (2000) for the impact of civil service pay and meritocratic recruitment, respectively, on corruption; for a more general approach to civil service reform, see Klitgaard (1997) and Rose-Ackerman (1999, Chapter 5).

[16]See Crotty (1997); and Hindriks, Keen, and Muthoo (Chapter 15 in this volume).

[17]See Garamfalvi (1997).

[18]See Shleifer and Vishny (1993) and Rose-Ackerman (1999).

[19]See Shleifer and Vishny (1993) and Rose-Ackerman (1999).

[20]One such approach has been embedded in the so-called National Integrity Systems, which was developed by the President of Transparency International—Tanzania. See Langseth, Stapenhurst, and Pope (1999) for details; see also Wolf and Gürgen (Chapter 19 in this volume).

One merit of the fundamental economic reform approach is that by linking anticorruption strategies to the reform of economic policies and institutions, the fight against corruption can be defined as an issue in economic policy. Steady economic reforms aimed at reducing policy distortions and strengthening economic institutions are bound to reduce the opportunities for corruption, whereas progress in establishing effective administrative and legal systems and in creating a more open society is likely to improve detection of corrupt behavior and raise the cost to those who may engage in it. Ultimately, anticorruption strategies are related to the reform of state institutions.

In the case of the transition economies, the reform of the state has been associated with a reduction in the size of the public sector and, more important, with a fundamental shift in its role from one implying owning or controlling most productive resources to one that is more narrowly defined around essential state functions. In this process of transformation, greater emphasis has been placed on the state's role in securing the necessary conditions for the efficient operation of markets. These conditions are often related to the establishment of safeguards for the protection of basic rights (including civil and property rights) and to an effective operation of a rule-based regulatory environment.

Countries in transition have generally undertaken reforms in some or all of these areas and have achieved varying degrees of progress.[21] The hypothesis of this paper is that countries that have progressed the most in implementing these reforms have also had the greatest success in reducing opportunities for illicit rent seeking, arbitrary rule, and monopolistic behavior. The reforming countries' relatively superior economic performance, according to this hypothesis, is related fundamentally to the achievement of these structural and institutional reforms and only incidentally to the degree to which corruption may have been reduced. Indeed, this paper claims that corruption per se (as measured by the widely used corruption perception indices) has much weaker explanatory power than variables measuring structural and institutional reforms.

Measuring Structural Reforms and Corruption

In contrast to the variety of sources that exist for measuring corruption in transition economies (see below), the European Bank for Recon-

---

[21]See EBRD (1999a) for a detailed account of the progress over the last ten years.

struction and Development (EBRD) is the sole agency that has consistently quantified measures of structural reforms every year since 1994. Table 1 provides these measures, based on 1998 data, of the progress achieved in the 25 transition economies in eight types of reforms, referred to as transition indicators, corresponding to the following three broad categories:

- *rationalizing state functions* through restructuring of enterprises and privatization of small- and large-scale businesses;

- *increasing the reliance on market-based pricing* through the liberalization of price, exchange, and trade systems, and the establishment of competition policy; and

- *creating a sound regulatory environment*, especially for the financial sector, through the reform of the banking system and other financial institutions.

Concerning the rationalization of state functions, and hence the corresponding growth in the private sector, in 16 of the 25 countries the share of the private sector was less than 50 percent in 1994, compared with 6 countries in 1998; in only 1 country the share of the private sector stood at 60 percent or higher in 1994 (Table 1), compared with as many as 13 countries in 1998. It may thus be assumed that in all these economies, the size of the public sector has been reduced—in some cases, dramatically. The data for 1998 also suggest a strong correlation between the growth of private sector activity and EBRD measures of privatization and restructuring of the state enterprise sector, with the correlation coefficients ranging from 0.73 to 0.87.[22]

The broad category of "market-based pricing" includes measures aimed at price liberalization, freeing of the trade and exchange systems, and the development of effective competition policies. Figure 1 displays the degree of progress achieved in each of the eight transition indicators during 1994–98. The figure clearly indicates that progress has been considerable in fostering a market-based economy through small- and large-scale privatization, and in reforming the trade and foreign exchange systems; progress has been slow in the area of price liberalization. Progress has been much slower in creating a sound regulatory environment. The latter is measured only with respect to

---

[22]Correlation has actually increased over time. In 1994, for example, the correlation coefficients ranged from 0.61 to 0.73.

Table 1. Progress in Structural Reforms in Transition Economies, 1998[1]

	Private Sector Share of GDP (In percent)	Enterprises Large-scale privatization	Enterprises Small-scale privatization	Enterprises Governance and enterprise restructuring	Markets and Trade Price liberalization	Markets and Trade Trade and foreign exchange system	Markets and Trade Competition policy	Financial Markets Banking reform and interest rate liberalization	Financial Markets Securities markets and nonbank financial institutions
Albania	75	2.0	4.0	2.0	3.0	4.0	2.0	2.0	1.8
Armenia	60	3.0	3.0	2.0	3.0	4.0	2.0	2.3	2.0
Azerbaijan	45	2.0	3.0	2.0	3.0	3.0	1.0	2.0	1.8
Belarus	20	1.0	2.0	1.0	2.0	1.0	2.0	1.0	2.0
Bulgaria	50	3.0	3.0	2.3	3.0	4.0	2.0	2.8	2.0
Croatia	55	3.0	4.3	2.8	3.0	4.0	2.0	2.8	2.3
Czech Republic	75	4.0	4.3	3.0	3.0	4.3	3.0	3.0	3.0
Estonia	70	4.0	4.3	3.0	3.0	4.0	2.8	3.3	3.0
Macedonia, FYR	55	3.0	4.0	2.0	3.0	4.0	1.0	3.0	1.8
Georgia	60	3.3	4.0	2.0	3.0	4.0	2.0	2.3	1.0
Hungary	80	4.0	4.3	3.3	3.3	4.3	3.0	4.0	3.3
Kazakhstan	55	3.0	4.0	2.0	3.0	4.0	2.0	2.3	2.0
Kyrgyz Republic	60	3.0	4.0	2.0	3.0	4.0	2.0	2.8	2.0
Latvia	60	3.0	4.0	2.8	3.0	4.0	2.8	2.8	2.3
Lithuania	70	3.0	4.0	2.8	3.0	4.0	2.3	3.0	2.3

Table 1 (*concluded*)

	Private Sector Share of GDP (In percent)	Enterprises			Markets and Trade				Financial Markets	
		Large-scale privatization	Small-scale privatization	Governance and enterprise restructuring	Price liberalization	Trade and foreign exchange system	Competition policy		Banking reform and interest rate liberalization	Securities markets and nonbank financial institutions
Moldova	45	3.0	3.3	2.0	3.0	4.0	2.0		2.3	2.0
Poland	65	3.3	4.3	3.0	3.3	4.3	3.0		3.3	3.3
Romania	60	2.8	3.3	2.0	3.0	4.0	2.0		2.3	2.0
Russia	70	3.3	4.0	2.0	2.8	2.3	2.3		2.0	1.8
Slovak Republic	75	4.0	4.3	2.8	3.0	4.3	3.0		2.8	2.3
Slovenia	55	3.3	4.3	2.8	3.0	4.3	2.0		3.0	3.0
Tajikistan	30	2.0	2.3	1.8	3.0	2.8	1.0		1.0	1.0
Turkmenistan	25	1.8	2.0	1.8	2.0	1.0	1.0		1.0	1.0
Ukraine	55	2.3	3.3	2.0	3.0	2.8	2.0		2.0	2.0
Uzbekistan	45	2.8	3.0	2.0	2.0	1.8	2.0		1.8	2.0

Source: EBRD (1999b).
[1]Scale of 0 to 4 (0 = low progress; 4 = high progress). Data with "+" and "-" in EBRD (1999b) have been increased and reduced, respectively, by 0.25.

Figure 1. Average Annual EBRD Transition Indicators by Dimension, 1994–98

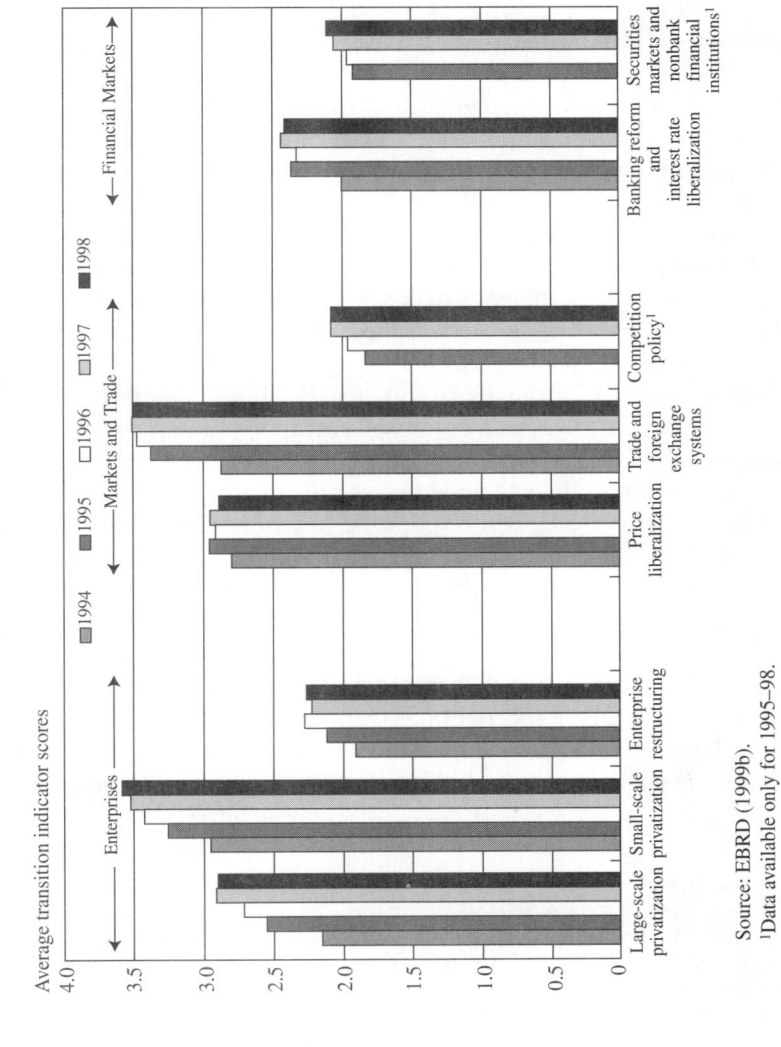

Source: EBRD (1999b).
[1]Data available only for 1995–98.

financial markets and is reflected in the reform of the banking and securities sectors.

Table 2 shows reform trends in these 25 countries through a simple average of the eight transition indicators, henceforth referred to as the structural reform index, for each year during 1994–98.[23] The averages reported in Table 2 mask the heterogeneity indicated above, but they nevertheless provide a general picture of progress by advanced and slow reformers and the overall trend in structural reforms. The table shows that although some countries have made more progress than others, the gap between the advanced and slow reformers has been narrowing somewhat. Overall, structural reforms as measured by the EBRD are trending upward.

Considering the role of corruption in transition economies, we have assembled a comprehensive data set on the evolution of corruption in the 25 transition economies over the period 1994–98. The data, shown in Table 3, are drawn from six surveys of perception of corruption. The index of corruption ranges from 0 to 10 where higher values of the index represent lower perception of corruption. Keeping in mind the qualifications that attach to any data based on surveys seeking to measure perceptions, the data nonetheless illustrate several points:[24] (1) on average, corruption is perceived to be low in advanced reformers and high in slow reformers; (2) although data for the earlier years are somewhat less reliable, corruption is perceived to be increasing in the advanced reformers and decreasing in slow reformers, but not enough to overturn the previous finding; and (3) the perception of corruption is highly persistent, a fact that is consistent with evidence from a large group of nontransition economies.[25]

To test for the relative importance of structural and institutional reforms vis-à-vis corruption in explaining differences in performance

---

[23]Throughout this paper, the simple average of indicators is used, as any weighting scheme is likely to involve additional judgments.

[24]Because corruption perception indices are based on surveys, the data for any one year are probably more meaningful than the trends implied by the year-to-year data. Changes in the underlying surveys over time (e.g., composition of countries) and varying number of surveys can create different indices for a country. Therefore, the data have been averaged whenever multiple surveys are available for a country in any year.

[25]See Tanzi (Chapter 2 in this volume). In fact, the correlation coefficient for 19 transition economies that have data in both 1995 and 1998 is about 0.75, suggesting that although perception of corruption does change, it does not change enough to radically reverse countries' relative rankings.

Table 2. Structural Reform Index in Transition Economies

	1994	1995	1996	1997	1998	1994–98[1]
Advanced reformers[2, 3]						
Croatia	3.2	2.8	3.0	3.0	3.0	3.0
Czech Republic	3.5	3.4	3.3	3.4	3.4	3.4
Estonia	3.3	3.3	3.3	3.4	3.4	3.3
Hungary	3.3	3.4	3.4	3.6	3.7	3.5
Latvia	3.3	3.4	3.4	3.6	3.7	3.5
Lithuania	3.0	2.9	3.0	3.0	3.0	3.0
Poland	3.3	3.3	3.3	3.4	3.4	3.4
Slovak Republic	3.3	3.3	3.3	3.3	3.3	3.3
Slovenia	3.2	3.2	3.2	3.2	3.2	3.2
Average	3.3	3.2	3.3	3.3	3.3	3.3
Less-advanced reformers[2, 3]						
Albania	2.5	2.4	2.6	2.6	2.6	2.5
Armenia	1.8	2.1	2.4	2.5	2.7	2.3
Azerbaijan	1.3	1.6	1.8	2.0	2.2	1.8
Belarus	1.7	2.1	1.9	1.6	1.5	1.8
Bulgaria	2.7	2.5	2.4	2.8	2.8	2.6
Macedonia, FYR	2.8	2.5	2.6	2.6	2.7	2.7
Georgia	1.3	2.0	2.5	2.7	2.7	2.2
Kazakhstan	1.7	2.1	2.6	2.7	2.8	2.4
Kyrgyz Republic	2.8	2.9	2.8	2.8	2.8	2.8
Moldova	2.2	2.6	2.6	2.6	2.7	2.5
Romania	2.7	2.5	2.5	2.7	2.7	2.6
Russia	2.7	2.6	2.9	3.0	2.5	2.7
Tajikistan	1.7	1.6	1.6	1.6	1.8	1.7
Turkmenistan	1.2	1.1	1.1	1.5	1.4	1.3
Ukraine	1.3	2.3	2.4	2.4	2.4	2.2
Uzbekistan	2.0	2.4	2.4	2.3	2.2	2.2
Average	2.0	2.2	2.3	2.4	2.4	2.3
Average, all countries[1]	2.5	2.6	2.7	2.7	2.7	2.6
Average, 19 countries[1, 4]	2.6	2.7	2.8	2.9	2.9	2.8

Source: EBRD (1999b).
[1]Unweighted average.
[2]Scale of 0 to 4 (0 = low progress; 4 = high progress).
[3]Data with "+" and "–" in EBRD (1999b) have been increased and reduced, respectively by 0.25.
[4]Consisting of 19 countries that match the corruption perception data in Table 3.

among the transition economies, we employ the transition indicators as measures of structural reforms and institution building. We then provide a test of the hypothesis that these indicators, as summarized

Table 3. Corruption Perception Ranking in Transition Economies[1]

	1994[2]	1995[3]	1996[4]	1997[5]	1998[6]	1994–98[7]
Advanced reformers						
Croatia	...	6.0	...	5.9	3.3	5.1
Czech Republic	7.5	8.6	6.0	6.6	5.7	6.9
Estonia	...	7.1	...	7.0	7.0	7.0
Hungary	8.3	8.8	6.6	7.2	6.7	7.5
Latvia	...	6.6	...	5.4	3.9	5.3
Lithuania	...	6.8	...	6.0	5.0	5.9
Poland	8.3	8.6	7.0	6.9	6.5	7.4
Slovak Republic	7.5	6.6	5.0	4.5	5.3	5.8
Slovenia	...	9.3	...	8.6	6.7	8.2
Average	7.9	7.6	6.1	6.5	5.6	6.6
Less-advanced reformers						
Albania	6.7	4.3	3.3	3.2	5.0	4.5
Armenia	...	3.0	...	3.7	3.3	3.3
Azerbaijan	...	2.4	...	2.5	3.3	2.7
Belarus	...	3.1	...	3.0	5.3	3.8
Bulgaria	7.5	5.6	6.7	4.6	4.8	5.8
Macedonia, FYR	...	4.6	...	5.6	...	5.1
Georgia	...	1.6	...	3.4	...	2.5
Kazakhstan	...	2.9	...	3.7	5.0	3.9
Kyrgyz Republic	...	3.3	...	3.7	...	3.5
Moldova	...	3.5	...	3.9	3.3	3.6
Romania	...	5.0	5.0	4.6	4.0	4.7
Russia	5.0	2.3	3.0	3.5	2.9	3.3
Tajikistan	...	1.4	...	1.3	...	1.4
Turkmenistan	...	2.9	...	1.7	...	2.3
Ukraine	...	2.5	...	3.3	3.9	3.2
Uzbekistan	...	2.0	...	2.8	...	2.4
Average	6.4	3.2	4.5	3.4	4.1	3.5
Average, all countries[7]	7.3	4.8	5.3	4.5	4.8	4.6
Average 19 countries[7,8]	...	5.4	...	...	4.8	5.2

Sources: See footnotes below.

[1]Scale of 0 to 10 (0 = highly corrupt; 10 = highly clean).
[2]Tanzi and Davoodi (Chapter 11 in this volume).
[3]*Central European Economic Review*, 1995–96.
[4]Transparency International (TI) and World Bank (1997).
[5]Political Risk Services; *Central European Economic Review*, 1997–98; World Bank (1997); and Lambsdorff (1998).
[6]Political Risk Services and TI.
[7]Unweighted average.
[8]Consisting of 19 countries that match the structural reform index in Table 2.

in the structural reform index, give a better explanation than the index of corruption for the observed variation in economic performance (growth, inflation, the fiscal balance, and foreign direct investment).

The case for the hypothesis that structural reforms lead to an improvement in economic performance is straightforward. A reduction in the size and scope of state functions, especially if effected through orderly privatization and effective devolution to market, is a necessary first step in creating the conditions for a private sector to emerge. Such a development is likely to enhance the efficiency of the economy as a whole through a more effective operation of incentives and the price mechanism. Furthermore, to the extent that such devolution is supplemented by liberalization measures, opening up the economy to external trade and to capital flows, and by a strengthened regulatory environment, it is likely to lead to higher private-sector-led investment and growth. Similarly, to the extent that reduced government spending for a given tax effort reduces the public sector deficit, crowding out of the private sector is reduced while macroeconomic stability is enhanced (and may be reflected in reduced rates of inflation), especially if accompanied by an amelioration in price and cost distortions through price liberalization.[26]

Thus, the connection linking structural and policy reforms to economic performance is rather direct and is in conformity with traditional economic analysis.[27] Although corruption may, if viewed as a tax, impede investment and growth directly, the link between corruption and economic performance is generally of an indirect nature, operating essentially through weaknesses in institutions, policies, and incentive systems.[28] Corruption indices may, therefore, be thought of as summary indicators of the extent to which institutional and policy reforms have been undertaken. They, however, are not likely to provide an explanation of such performance.

---

[26] Additional motivations on the impact of structural reforms and corruption are provided in the next section for each indicator of economic performance.

[27] A similar analysis of structural reforms, corruption, and economic performance in the Baltic and Commonwealth of Independent States countries has recently been undertaken with reference to reforms included in IMF-supported adjustment programs. See Wolf and Gürgen (Chapter 19 in this volume).

[28] The role of incentives in the corruption-growth relationship has recently been given a rigorous theoretical treatment (Ehrlich and Lui, 1999).

III. Explaining Economic Performance: Corruption or Structural Reforms

To investigate the relative importance of corruption and structural reforms in influencing macroeconomic performance, we use regression and decomposition analyses.[29] The following methodology is used throughout this analysis when reporting results. First, each indicator of macroeconomic performance is regressed on a corruption index and control variables. This is essentially the approach that has been adopted in the empirical literature on the economic impact of corruption (e.g., Mauro, 1995; Tanzi and Davoodi, Chapter 11 in this volume). By drawing on an extensive data set of corruption indices in transition economies (described in the previous section), this regression can also inform us if the previous findings on the economic impact of corruption that were based largely on nontransition economies also extend to transition economies. Second, each indicator of macroeconomic performance is regressed on an index of structural reforms and the same control variables. This approach has been used extensively in studies of the economic impact of structural reforms in transition economies (e.g., de Melo, Denizer, and Gelb, 1996; Berg and others, 1999), where the focus has been limited to structural reforms and did not include corruption.

Finally, the novelty of this paper is to integrate the previous two approaches into a frame of analysis that includes both the corruption index and the structural reform index as independent variables while allowing for the same control variables as in the previous two regressions.[30] This approach allows us to test the hypothesis that structural reforms are statistically and economically more significant than corruption in explaining economic performance. According to this hypothesis, the fit of the estimated regression, as judged by the adjusted R-squared, should also improve when the corruption index is replaced by the structural reform index. Using panel and cross-sectional data for the transition economies, we apply this methodology to each of the following indicators of macroeconomic performance as the dependent

---

[29]The decomposition analysis follows the standard approach used in the empirical literature on economic growth; see Easterly and Levine (1997) for a cross-country approach, and Berg and others (1999) for an application to transition economies.

[30]Because of the potential endogeneity problem, initial values of control variables rather than current values are included in all the regressions.

variable: growth, inflation, the fiscal balance, and foreign direct investment. Important not only in gauging economic performance, these indicators have been widely used in the analysis of the impact of corruption on such performance in transition economies.

For purposes of the regression analysis, the existing data on corruption indices restrict the choice of the start of the sample period to 1994. Thus, the sample period for all regressions in this paper starts in 1994 and ends in 1998.[31] The shorter sample period, in contrast to previous studies of growth in transition economies, therefore, excludes the so-called transition recession period (1990–93). As a result, the regressions used in this paper essentially apply to the upward-sloping part of the now familiar U-shaped curve, present in many indicators of macroeconomic performance in transition economies. Given the short time span and the limited number of observations, one cannot allow for rich dynamics between indicators of macroeconomic performance and other economic factors found in previous studies of transition economies (e.g., Berg and others, 1999). The only source of dynamics in the regressions reported in this paper, therefore, is the set of variables representing initial conditions, which may refer to 1993 or earlier, depending on the regression and data availability. However, it turns out that the results reported in this paper are generally consistent with those reported in previous studies of transition economies (of course, those studies did not assess the relative importance of structural reforms and corruption in influencing macroeconomic performance).

Growth

Against this background, specification of the growth regression follows the standard approach in the growth literature (Sala-i-Martin, 1997), but is augmented with other variables used in a growing number of studies of growth in the transition economies.[32] The dependent variable is the real per capita GDP growth rate. The right-hand side comprises six variables: a corruption index; a structural re-

---

[31]All the data used in the paper are taken from EBRD (1999b) unless otherwise indicated. Although EBRD (1999a and 1999b) provides data on 26 transition countries, only 25 countries are included in this paper, because of the lack of data on corruption for one of the countries.

[32]There are at least 20 econometric studies of growth in transition economies. To our knowledge, no study attempts to ascertain the robustness of the different variables used in these studies. This would be a good area for additional work.

form index;[33] initial real per capita GDP in U.S. dollars (a measure of convergence and other initial conditions); initial life expectancy (a measure of human capital);[34] the ratio of fiscal balance to GDP (a measure of macrofiscal stability); and the inflation rate. This specification thus allows for initial conditions, structural reforms, as well as macroeconomic stabilization policies to affect the growth rate. Additional control variables are then added to this regression; these include the choice of fixed exchange rate regime, a measure of natural resource wealth, the number of years a country lived under a central planning system, the initial Gini coefficient, the ratio of trade to GDP, the ratio of broad money to GDP, and the ratio of investment to GDP.[35] These variables have been used extensively in the empirical growth literature and in studies of growth in transition countries.[36]

Results are shown in Table 4.[37] They indicate that higher growth is associated with higher initial life expectancy, lower initial income (i.e.,

---

[33]This is defined as the simple average of eight transition indicators constructed by the EBRD. These are (1) large-scale privatization, (2) small-scale privatization, (3) enterprise restructuring, (4) price liberalization, (5) trade and foreign exchange systems, (6) competition policy, (7) banking reform and interest rate liberalization, and (8) securities markets and nonbank financial institutions.

[34]The data on school enrollment rates, another measure of human capital, are sketchy for most transition economies; in some cases, data are available only from 1995, and, therefore, cannot be used as initial conditions. Data on life expectancy, available for many countries, are from the World Bank (1999).

[35]Another strand of literature has also investigated the impact of compliance with IMF programs on growth; see Havrylyshyn and others (1999) and Mercer-Blackman and Unigovskaya (2000).

[36]Previous studies of growth in transition economies allowed for a richer set of initial conditions than used in this paper, but these studies mostly excluded the variables that are always included in cross-country growth regressions, such as initial per capita GDP and initial life expectancy (Sala-i-Martin, 1997). The choice of the sample period (i.e., the post-1993 period) used in this paper makes transition economies look somewhat like the nontransition economies used in many large cross-country growth studies and calls for including the same initial conditions in growth regressions as in nontransition economies (i.e., initial per capita GDP and initial life expectancy). In addition, many studies of transition economies have found the role of initial conditions to decline over time (e.g., de Melo and others, 1997; Berg and others, 1999; and Havrylyshyn and van Rooden, 2000). Therefore, initial per capita GDP and initial life expectancy are good proxies for many types of initial conditions used previously in studies of transition economies.

[37]The control variables mentioned earlier were also tried, but did not change the qualitative and quantitative importance of the two indices reported in Table 1. For example, a flexible exchange rate regime, abundant natural resource wealth, and higher initial inequality are all associated with lower growth rate, but these variables are no longer significant once the regression controls for the variables included in Table 1.

Table 4. Dependent Variable: Real Per Capita Growth Rate

Independent Variables	Panel (1)	Panel (2)	Panel (3)	Cross Section (4)	Cross Section (5)	Cross Section (6)
Constant	−187.92*** (−2.44)	−280.31*** (−4.11)	−184.20 (−2.59)	−261.95*** (−2.59)	−301.15*** (−3.37)	259.46*** (−2.95)
Corruption index	1.86*** (2.98)		1.35*** (2.77)	2.64*** (3.21)		1.06 (1.32)
Structural reform index		7.59*** (3.10)	4.79* (1.74)		7.14*** (4.60)	5.46** (2.49)
Initial real per capita GDP	−3.77*** (−3.78)	−3.54** (−3.61)	−4.80*** (−3.87)	−3.10** (−2.15)	−2.57*** (−2.78)	−3.12*** (−3.22)
Initial life expectancy	49.17*** (2.68)	67.73*** (4.15)	47.47*** (2.82)	63.79*** (2.63)	70.99*** (3.35)	61.83*** (2.98)
Fiscal balance– GDP ratio	0.35* (1.74)	0.58*** (2.91)	0.42** (2.23)	0.08 (0.31)	0.33 (1.00)	0.28 (0.88)
Inflation	−0.02** (−2.31)	−0.12[1] (−0.34)	−0.01** (−2.29)	0.03[1] (0.23)	0.66[2] (0.05)	0.04[1] (0.41)
Number of observations	80	113	80	25	25	25
Adjusted R-squared	0.49	0.39	0.54	0.60	0.67	0.67

Source: IMF staff estimates.
Note: Estimation is by OLS; t-statistics are in parentheses and are based on heteroscedastic-consistent standard errors. Initial per capita GDP and initial life expectancy are in logs. A "+" is a surplus for fiscal balance, a "−" is a deficit. ***, **, and * denote significance at 1 percent, 5 percent, and 10 percent levels, respectively.
[1]Multiplied by 100.
[2]Multiplied by 10,000.

the convergence effect), lower corruption, better track record on structural reforms, higher fiscal surplus, and lower inflation. Therefore, structural reforms, macroeconomic policies, and initial conditions are all important to the growth process.

These findings are generally consistent with other studies of growth in transition economies. The fitted regressions that include all of the six variables account for 54 percent of growth variation in the panel data and for 67 percent in the cross-sectional data. In the cross-sectional data, the regression with the structural reform index has a better fit, as judged by the higher adjusted R-squared of 67 percent (column 5), than with the corruption index, whose adjusted R-squared is 60 percent (column 4). However, this ranking is reversed in the panel data, where the regression with the corruption index accounts for 49 percent of the growth variation (column 1), compared with 39 percent for the structural reform index (column 2).[38]

Fiscal balance and inflation are statistically significant at the 5 percent level in panel data (column 3), but are insignificant in the cross-sectional regressions, indicating that time averaging of the data has eliminated the dynamic relationship between growth and these two variables present in the panel data. Initial real per capita GDP and life expectancy are highly significant (1 percent level) in all the regressions, indicating the importance of these measures of initial conditions. In this respect, transition economies over the period 1994–98 are no different from nontransition economies.

As for the two indices of corruption and structural reforms, each index is significant at the 1 percent level when the other index is excluded from the regression. However, when both are included, the structural reform index continues to be statistically significant whereas the corruption index becomes insignificant (Table 4, column 6).

The above results suggest that structural reforms may be the driving force behind the strong impact of corruption on growth found in previous studies that excluded a measure of structural reforms (e.g., Brunetti, Kisunko, and Weder, 1997). However, these results do not indicate by themselves the relative (economic) importance of each variable in accounting for growth. To gauge the importance of each variable, two types of decompositions are carried out, using the estimated growth regressions that contain both indices (Table 4, columns 3 and 6). One decomposition shows how much of the growth differential between advanced reformers and slow reformers is due to differences in the two indices and differences in other variables.[39] This

---

[38]One explanation for this finding has to do with the fact that the correlation between the corruption index and inflation is much smaller (0.41) than the correlation between the structural reform index and inflation (0.56). Therefore, in the panel data, when the structural reform index is replaced by the corruption index, inflation is statistically significant, which increases the adjusted R-squared, whereas when the corruption index is replaced by the structural reform index, inflation loses its significance and adjusted R-squared falls subsequently. Results of inflation regressions are consistent with this interpretation.

[39]Classification of countries into advanced and slow reformers has been used in many studies of transition economies and is used in this paper as well. See, among others, de Melo, Denizer, and Gelb (1996); and Abed (1998). This is the same classification as in Tables 2 and 3.

type of decomposition is useful as advanced reformers tend to have better performance than slow reformers as characterized by higher growth rates, longer life expectancy, better track record on structural reforms, lower perception of corruption, higher real per capita GDP, lower fiscal balances, and lower inflation rates. The second decomposition indicates how much of the growth can be accounted for, on average, by each index and other variables. This decomposition shows the average behavior of a transition economy and, therefore, does not rely on any a priori country classification. These decompositions are then carried out for both data sets. Results are shown in Tables 5 and 6.

The first decomposition based on the cross-sectional regression (Table 5, column 2) shows that of the 6.3 percent explained growth differential between advanced reformers and slow reformers, 3.3 percent is due to differences in corruption rankings, 5.2 percent due to differences in structural reforms, −4.8 percent due to differences in initial per capita GDP, 1.8 percent due to differences in initial life expectancy, 1 percent due to differences in fiscal balance, and −0.2 percent due to differences in inflation.[40] The large negative contribution for initial per capita GDP (−4.8 percent) reflects the importance of the convergence effect (e.g., that slow reformers would have grown 4.8 percent faster than advanced reformers purely on account of their lower initial per capita GDP). However, there are obviously other factors (those included in the regression and in the decomposition) that tend to widen the gap in per capita income between advanced reformers and slow reformers. The decomposition results based on the panel regression (Table 5, column 1) show that structural reforms are also more important than corruption, although not by as much as the cross-sectional results would indicate. Taken together, corruption and structural reforms are more important than initial conditions and macroeconomic policies. The superiority of structural reforms over macroeconomic policies indicated by this analysis is consistent with that of Berg and others (1999).

The second decomposition shows that structural reforms are two to three times as important as corruption in accounting for average growth performance in 25 transition countries (Table 6). The two decompositions lend support to the main hypothesis of the paper: struc-

---

[40]The negative entry for inflation is due to the negative sign on inflation in Table 4, column 6.

Table 5. Explaining Growth Differential Between Advanced Reformers and Slow Reformers[1]
(In percent)

	Panel (1)	Cross Section (2)
Growth differential (actual)	5.14	6.76
Growth differential (fitted)	5.17	6.28
Due to		
Corruption index	3.94	3.26
Structural reform	4.06	5.21
Initial real per capita GDP	−7.02	−4.80
Initial life expectancy	1.42	1.84
Fiscal balance-GDP ratio	1.42	0.98
Inflation	1.35	−0.21
Residual	−0.03	0.48

Source: IMF staff estimates.
[1]Based on regressions (3) and (6) in Table 4, and the average value of each variable within each country group.

tural reforms are economically more important than corruption in accounting for growth.[41]

Inflation

The literature on the determinants of inflation in transition economies has generally emphasized cross-country studies of inflation (e.g., Campillo and Miron, 1996), while incorporating features that are unique to transition economies.[42] In this paper, we follow the lead of Fischer, Sahay, and Végh (1998), who specify inflation as a function of the choice of the exchange rate regime, fiscal balance, and structural reform indices as compiled by de Melo, Denizer, and Gelb (1996) and EBRD (1999a), and a dummy variable representing trade disruptions

---

[41]To the extent that corruption is a symptom of poor institutions, the finding that lower corruption is associated with higher growth is consistent with the findings on the importance of institutions in transition economies. See, for example, Brunetti, Kisunko, and Weder (1997); and Havrylyshyn and van Rooden (2000).

[42]Some studies use changes in inflation rate as the dependent variable; see Cottarelli, Griffiths, and Moghadam (1998). As in most studies, we use inflation rate as the dependent variable.

Table 6. Growth Decomposition Based on All Data[1]
(In percent)

	Panel (1)	Cross Section (2)
Growth (actual)	1.58	−0.14
Growth (fitted)	1.58	−0.14
Due to		
Constant	−184.20	−259.46
Corruption index	6.85	4.87
Structural reform	13.30	14.27
Initial real per capita GDP	−32.92	−20.74
Initial life expectancy	201.36	262.02
Fiscal balance-GDP ratio	−1.83	−1.24
Inflation	−0.98	0.14
Residual	0.00	0.00

Source: IMF staff estimates.
[1]Based on regressions (3) and (6) in Table 4, and the average value of each variable.

following the collapse of the Council on Mutual Economic Assistance (CMEA) and the breakup of the Soviet Union in January 1992.

The specification of the inflation regression is based on the idea that both structural reforms and macroeconomic policies are important determinants of inflation. A fixed exchange rate regime is expected to result in lower inflation, as it is often seen as a nominal anchor that imposes discipline on both monetary and fiscal policy (Obstfeld, 1985).[43] Structural reforms are expected to result in lower inflation as liberalization of prices, introduction of profit-oriented incentives in enterprises, and the development of a private market tend to reduce cost and price distortions, increase competitiveness, and enhance productivity.[44] Higher corruption may be associated with higher inflation, because (1) corruption can lead to capital flight and tax evasion, which shrink the tax base, thereby increasing government's desire to resort to seigniorage (Al-Marhubi, 2000); (2) businesses may respond to corruption by going

---

[43]It is important to note that without conditioning on any other variable, transition economies that have a fixed exchange rate regime tend to have, on average, lower inflation, lower monetary growth, and lower deficit.

[44]Structural reforms can lead to higher prices, at least for a period, as such reforms involve the lifting of price controls and removing the suppressed inflation of the planning era.

underground, thereby increasing reliance on inflation tax (Al-Marhubi, 2000);[45] and (3) high and variable inflation can increase information problems in a principal-agent framework (Braun and Di Tella, 2000).[46] Higher deficits are expected to be associated with higher inflation, as they increase aggregate demand pressures and may induce monetary accommodation.[47] Thus, the baseline specification includes initial fiscal balance and a dummy variable for the choice of the exchange rate regime. To test the main hypothesis of this paper, indices of corruption and structural reforms are then added to the baseline specification.

Results are shown in Table 7 for panel and for cross-sectional data over the period 1994–98. The fit of the regressions, as judged by the adjusted R-squared, is much higher when the structural reform index—rather than the corruption index—is included in the regression. For instance, the regressions that include the structural reform index, but not the corruption index, account for 40 percent and 64 percent of the inflation variation in the panel and cross-sectional data, respectively, compared with 14 and 55 percent, respectively, when the regression includes the corruption index, but not the structural reform index. The results further indicate that in the regressions that include only one of the indices, each index is statistically significant (at the 1 percent level). However, when both indices are included (Table 7, columns 3 and 6), it is only the structural reform index that is statistically significant (at the 1 percent level); the corruption index is not significant, even at the 20 percent level.

As for the signs of each variable, results indicate that lower corruption and deeper structural reforms are associated with lower inflation. The results on the fixed exchange rate regime and the fiscal balance variables are not as strong. While the cross-sectional results show that lower

---

[45]Al-Marhubi (2000) provides evidence of a positive relationship between corruption and inflation.

[46]Braun and Di Tella (2000) show that countries with higher inflation volatility tend to have higher corruption, but do not find level of corruption to be related to inflation.

[47]We use all these variables—except for the dummy variable, as our sample starts in 1994—whereas that of Fischer, Sahay, and Végh (1998) starts in 1992, the year of the collapse of CMEA. Although the breakup may have lasting inflation effects, we proxy this effect by using initial values of other variables that may matter to inflation, such as the number of years under central planning, initial inflation rate, lagged inflation rate, and initial real per capita GDP. It is worth noting that adding these variables did not affect the reported results. Lagged inflation rate was the only variable found to be significant (with a positive sign, as expected), but this finding did not affect either the significance or the sign of the structural reform index.

Table 7. Dependent Variable: Inflation

Independent Variables	Panel (1)	Panel (2)	Panel (3)	Cross Section (4)	Cross Section (5)	Cross Section (6)
Constant	1.04*** (4.62)	3.05*** (7.02)	2.03*** (4.86)	2.12*** (4.75)	3.20*** (8.36)	3.17*** (7.42)
Corruption index	−0.12*** (−3.50)		−0.70[1] (−0.22)	−0.27*** (−3.91)		−0.02 (−0.14)
Structural reform index		−0.95*** (−6.69)	−0.57*** (−3.50)		−0.93*** (−7.24)	−0.89*** (−2.86)
Initial fiscal surplus–GDP ratio	0.27[1] (0.48)	−0.14[1] (−0.14)	0.34 (0.73)	−0.02* (−1.93)	−0.03*** (−2.68)	−0.02*** (−3.21)
Exchange rate regime	0.04 (0.26)	0.15 (1.12)	0.06 (0.39)	−0.36 (−1.56)	−0.24 (−1.14)	−0.24 (−1.13)
Number of observations	82	120	82	24	24	24
Adjusted R-squared	0.14	0.40	0.29	0.55	0.64	0.62

Source: IMF staff estimates.
Note: Estimation is by OLS; t-statistics are in parentheses and are based on heteroscedastic-consistent standard errors. Dependent variable is in logs. ***, **, and * indicate significance at the 1 percent, 5 percent, and 10 percent levels, respectively.
[1]Multiplied by 100.

inflation is associated with lower government deficit (significant at the 1 percent level) and a fixed exchange rate regime (statistically insignificant at the conventional levels), the panel data results indicate that neither of these variables is significant nor do they have the expected signs. The latter finding is not consistent with results obtained by Fischer, Sahay, and Végh (1998). There are at least two reasons that may account for this inconsistency: the choice of the sample period, as these authors use a longer sample during which annual inflation rates fell from over 1,000 percent to below 20 percent, and the choice of the fixed exchange rate regime, which may have mattered more in the early years of the transition in moderating imported inflation rates, given the absence of credible monetary institutions and policies (Wagner, 1998).[48] The mixed

---

[48]In 1994, eight transition economies were on a fixed exchange rate regime, compared with five in 1998. This is consistent with the observation that many developing countries in the 1990s opted for a more flexible exchange rate arrangement; see Caramazza and Aziz (1998).

evidence on the fixed exchange rate regime variable is consistent with arguments and evidence in the theoretical as well as empirical literature. The decomposition of the estimated regressions reveals the relative quantitative significance of the structural reforms versus corruption. Of the approximately 131 percent explained inflation differential between advanced reformers and slow reformers, 88 percent is due to differences in structural reforms, whereas only 5 percent is due to differences in corruption rankings; 28 percent is due to fiscal surplus and 10 percent to the choice of the fixed exchange rate regime (Table 8).[49] The second decomposition shows that structural reforms are 30 to 50 times as important as corruption in accounting for the average behavior of inflation (Table 9).

Fiscal Balance

Unlike the numerous econometric studies of inflation and growth in transition economies, there are no econometric studies—to our knowledge—of the determinants of fiscal balance across the 25 transition economies.[50] On the other hand, there are many descriptive studies of the evolution of fiscal balance in transition economies and of factors affecting either the expenditure side or the revenue side of the budget.[51] However, given the importance of the fiscal balance in underpinning macroeconomic stability, an important factor itself in improving overall economic performance, we examine the behavior of this indicator in the same manner.

The specification of the fiscal balance regression adopted in this paper follows the analysis of Alesina and others (1999), but is modified to take into account features of the transition economies. The regression specifies the ratio of the fiscal balance to GDP[52] as a function

---

[49]The percentages are approximations, because the dependent variable is defined as the logarithm of [1+ (inflation)/100]; this transformation is used in many studies of inflation in transition economies.

[50]An exception is Pirttila (2000).

[51]See Tanzi (1993); de Melo, Denizer, and Gelb (1996); Cheasty and Davis (1996); Barbone and Polackova (1996); Abed (1998); and EBRD (1999a). Tanzi and Tsibouris (2001) provide exhaustive analyses of fiscal reforms in the past ten years in transition economies.

[52]Fiscal balance, as reported in EBRD (1999b), is used as the measure of fiscal balance; limited data prevented us from using primary balance as another measure of fiscal balance. The attraction of this measure is that a surplus on primary balance can be used to pay off interest payments on debt.

Table 8. Explaining Inflation Differential Between Advanced Reformers and Slow Reformers[1]
(In percent)

	Panel (1)	Cross Section (2)
Inflation differential (actual)	−49.3	−126.5
Inflation differential (fitted)	−47.9	−131.3
Due to		
Corruption index	−2.0	−4.9
Structural reform	−51.4	−87.9
Initial fiscal surplus-GDP ratio	3.5	−28.3
Exchange rate regime	2.0	−10.2
Residual	−1.4	4.8

Source: IMF staff estimates.
[1]Based on regressions (3) and (6) in Table 7, and the average value of each variable within each country group.

Table 9. Inflation Rate Decomposition Based on All Data[1]
(In percent)

	Panel (1)	Cross Section (2)
Inflation (actual)	40.8	95.9
Inflation (fitted)	40.7	96.1
Due to		
Constant	203.0	317.0
Corruption index	−3.5	−7.4
Structural reform	−157.3	−231.0
Initial fiscal surplus-GDP ratio	−3.0	23.9
Exchange rate regime	1.5	−6.3
Residual	0.2	−0.2

Source: IMF staff estimates.
[1]Based on regressions (3) and (6) in Table 7, and the average value of each variable.

of real per capita GDP growth (a measure of the cyclicality of general economic conditions), the share of agriculture in GDP (a measure of hard-to-tax sectors), the number of years a country lived under a central planning system (a proxy for initial conditions, such as commitment to reform and a reduced role for government), the initial value of the ratio of external debt to GDP (a proxy for past debt obligations of the country),[53] and the choice of the fixed exchange rate regime (a measure of commitment to maintain fiscal discipline to defend the exchange rate). To this regression, we then add indices of corruption and structural reform, one at a time and then jointly, to investigate their relative importance.

Results are shown in Table 10 for both panel and cross-sectional data. Most of the control variables have the expected signs and all are statistically significant at the 1 percent level, except for the corruption index. The fitted regressions explain 63 percent and 81 percent of the variation in the fiscal balance for the panel and cross-sectional data, respectively. The results show that a higher deficit is associated with a lower real per capita GDP growth rate, a higher share of agriculture in GDP, longer years spent under a central planning system, a higher ratio of initial external debt to GDP, a flexible exchange rate regime, and deeper structural reforms. The corruption index has different signs in the panel and cross-sectional regressions. Each of these associations requires an explanation.[54]

The finding that lower growth is associated with higher deficits is consistent with the tax-smoothing argument *and* acyclical government spending pattern,[55] that is, countries tend to build surpluses during booms and run deficits during downturns. The finding that deficit increases with the share of agriculture in GDP is consistent with cross-country empirical models of tax structure where the presence of agriculture (a hard-to-tax sector) constrains the ability of governments to raise revenues (Tanzi, 1987; Stotsky and WoldeMariam, 1997).[56] The results further indicate that the longer a country lived under a central planning system, the higher its subsequent deficit. This result reflects the difficulties faced by a country with an entrenched command econ-

---

[53]Ideally, a measure of government debt (domestic as well as external) is more satisfactory, but domestic data are not available for many transition economies.

[54]Adding measures of urbanization, age dependency ratio (a proxy for demand for government services and pension commitments), and a measure of natural resource wealth does not change the reported results; in fact, all these variables were found to be statistically insignificant.

[55]Acyclicality is indeed true in the panel and cross-sectional data used in this paper.

[56]On average, agriculture represents about 18 percent of GDP in transition economies during 1994–98. Slovenia has the lowest share (4 percent) and Albania has the highest (57 percent). Albania happens to be a country with the highest deficit and the highest share of agriculture in GDP. The reported results do not change when the regressions are estimated on a sample that excludes either or both of these countries.

Table 10. Dependent Variable: Ratio of Fiscal Balance to GDP
(In percent)

Independent Variables	Panel (1)	Panel (2)	Panel (3)	Cross Section (4)	Cross Section (5)	Cross Section (6)
Constant	5.86* (1.84)	8.73*** (2.83)	14.11*** (3.11)	5.86 (1.21)	13.74*** (5.66)	13.17*** (3.78)
Corruption index	−0.67** (−2.31)		−0.47* (−1.90)	−0.62 (−1.32)		0.10 (0.24)
Structural reform index		−2.37*** (−3.51)	−2.58*** (−2.98)		−3.54*** (−6.58)	−3.65*** (−6.03)
Real per capita GDP growth	0.10 (1.43)	0.16*** (4.12)	0.15*** (2.50)	0.08 (0.69)	0.18*** (3.17)	0.17*** (2.63)
Agriculture share of GDP	−0.16*** (−5.72)	−0.16*** (−7.67)	−0.18*** (−6.40)	−0.18*** (−4.70)	−0.18*** (−11.36)	−0.18*** (−7.96)
Years under central planning	−0.06* (−1.80)	−0.05** (−2.29)	−0.09*** (−2.74)	−0.06 (−1.30)	−0.08*** (−3.52)	−0.08** (−2.43)
Initial external debt-GDP ratio	−0.04*** (−3.03)	−0.04*** (−3.26)	−0.04*** (−3.06)	−0.03** (−2.19)	−0.03*** (−4.61)	−0.03*** (−4.82)
Exchange rate regime	2.63*** (3.84)	1.86*** (3.15)	2.46*** (3.60)	1.49 (1.17)	1.49 (1.56)	1.53 (1.46)
Number of observations	72	106	72	25	25	25
Adjusted R-squared	0.57	0.60	0.63	0.68	0.82	0.81

Source: IMF staff estimates.

Note: Estimation is by OLS; *t*-statistics are in parentheses and are based on heteroscedastic-consistent standard errors. Exchange rate regime is a dummy variable, which takes on a value of one when exchange rate regime is fixed and zero otherwise. ***, **, and * denote significance at the 1 percent, 5 percent, and 10 percent levels, respectively.

omy to either reduce the role of the state by devolving spending or to raise revenues through a modern tax system. The results show that the general government deficit of an advanced reformer would have been higher, on average, by about 1.5 percent of GDP had it lived under a central planning system for as long as a slow-reforming country.[57] This clearly shows an important aspect of initial conditions in transition economies that has not been documented before.

---

[57]On average, slow reformers spent 17 more years under a central planning system than advanced reformers. The estimate is obtained by multiplying 17 by the estimated parameter on "years under central planning" in Table 10, column 3.

The finding that countries with higher initial external debt tend to have subsequently higher deficits runs counter to the expectation that countries need to run higher (primary) surpluses (lower deficits) in order to service their debts.[58] However, as the measure of fiscal balance used in the paper includes interest payments on external debt, the finding may simply reflect the inability or unwillingness of the country to undertake fiscal consolidation to reduce the debt burden, hence continuing on a vicious cycle of higher initial debt service leading to higher deficits and, absent fiscal reforms, requiring further borrowing and so on. The finding that progress on structural reforms is associated with a higher deficit is consistent with the notion that several aspects of structural reform may work on both sides of the budget to increase the deficit.[59] These aspects are the persistent presence of soft budget constraints[60] (e.g., soft government loans to state-owned enterprises, tax offsets, in-kind collection of social contributions), governments shouldering the costs of restructuring of state-owned enterprises arising from payment of severance pay and unemployment benefits; state takeover of social services previously provided by enterprises; payment of subsidies (as social safety nets) to mitigate the burden of higher prices due to price liberalization; and replacement of secure budget transfers from the enterprise sector with a modern tax system whose revenue performance improves only with a lag.[61] In fact, many observers had anticipated that deficits in transition economies would rise with structural reforms, at least for a period. This outcome is attributed to difficulties in reducing government spending combined with revenue shortfalls in the transition to a market-oriented tax system.[62] In fact, the available data indicate that progress on tax reforms and structural reforms go hand in hand. The simple correlation coefficient between a tax reform index and the EBRD structural reform index for a sample of 15 transition economies

---

[58]Alesina and others (1999) find a similar result for a group of Latin American countries.

[59]Previous studies of deficit in transition economies have found the opposite result—namely, that progress on structural reforms is associated with lower deficit (e.g., de Melo, Denizer, and Gelb, 1996; and EBRD, 1999a)—but this finding was based solely on the simple correlation coefficient or association between these two variables. In fact, this is exactly the result that we find if we do not condition on other determinants of the fiscal balance.

[60]See Kornai (1986, 1998) and EBRD (1999a).

[61]Using a different specification, Pirttila (2000) also finds that structural reforms, as measured by the EBRD indices, increase deficits.

[62]See Tanzi (1993, 1996) and Aghion and Blanchard (1994); for a recent assessment, see Tanzi and Tsibouris (2001).

is quite high (a coefficient of 0.72, with a t-statistic of 3.7).[63] The pickup in revenue performance as a result of these reforms, however, is evident only with a lag.

Higher corruption levels might also be expected to be associated with higher deficits (the cross-sectional regression result confirms the association, but is found to be not statistically significant), as corruption on both sides of tax collection and tax payment may reduce government revenues[64] and as rent-seeking individuals have an incentive to solicit budgetary subsidies and prevent the hardening of soft budget constraints. This is indeed the result one obtains if one simply looks at the correlation coefficient between corruption and the fiscal balance. However, the regression results reported in Table 10 show that the adverse impact of corruption on the fiscal balance disappears once allowance is made for the impact of structural reforms and other determinants of fiscal balance.

As in the previous regressions, decomposition analysis of the estimated regressions reveals the relative importance of corruption and structural reforms in explaining the fiscal balance. The results are shown in Tables 11 and 12. Advanced reformers have lower deficits than slow reformers, with a differential of about 3.5 percent of GDP.[65] Given this background and the regression results, the decomposition, based on the panel data regression (Table 11, column 1), shows that progress on structural reforms decreases the differential in fiscal balance between advanced reformers and slow reformers by about 2.3 percent of GDP. The contribution of corruption is much smaller (about 1.5 percent of the differential) and is lower than the contribution of the variable "years under central planning." The relative importance of structural reforms increases further in the decomposition based on the cross-sectional regression (Table 11, column 2), to about 3.5 percent, whereas the importance of corruption decreases substantially, to about 0.3 percent. Share of agriculture in GDP accounts for 3 percent of the

---

[63]The tax reform index is taken from Ebrill and Havrylyshyn (1999).

[64]See Ul Haque and Sahay (1996); Tanzi and Davoodi (Chapter 11 in this volume); and Johnson, Kaufmann, and Zoido-Lobatón (1999).

[65]Other notable features of the two groups of countries, important to the interpretation of decomposition results, are as follows. For advanced reformers as a group, corruption ranking, share of agriculture in GDP, years under central planning, and ratio of initial external debt to GDP are all below the averages of slow reformers, whereas structural reform rankings and growth are above the average of slow reformers; in addition, advanced reformers, on average, tend to maintain a fixed exchange rate regime relative to slow reformers.

Table 11. Explaining Fiscal Balance Differential Between Advanced Reformers and Slow Reformers[1]
(In percent)

	Panel (1)	Cross Section (2)
Fiscal balance differential (actual)	3.50	3.48
Fiscal balance differential (fitted)	3.04	3.39
Due to		
Corruption index	−1.50	0.31
Structural reform index	−2.29	−3.48
Real per capita GDP growth	0.86	1.15
Agriculture share of GDP	3.07	3.07
Years under central planning	1.58	1.42
Initial external debt-GDP ratio	0.45	0.27
Exchange rate regime	0.87	0.66
Residual	0.46	0.08

Source: IMF staff estimates.
[1]Based on regressions in (3) and (6) in Table 10, and the average value of each variable within each country group. Exchange rate regime is a dummy variable, which takes on a value of one when the exchange rate regime is fixed and zero otherwise.

differential between the two groups of countries.[66] The remaining variables taken together account for about 3.5 percent of the differential.

The decomposition based on the average behavior of each variable is shown in Table 12. Results show that structural reforms are, on average, the most important factor in accounting for the average behavior of the deficit in the 25 transition economies, followed by "years under central planning," and share of agriculture in GDP.[67]

Foreign Direct Investment

Explaining the pattern of capital flows, particularly foreign direct investment in transition economies, is a complicated task as there are numerous economic, institutional, legal, and political factors that affect

---

[66]Share of agriculture in GDP increases the differential fiscal balance, because advanced reformers have a lower share than slow reformers and because agriculture has a positive impact on deficit.

[67]Recall that the impact of structural reforms on deficit can vary by year and country. The reported results are simply averages across countries and over time.

Table 12. Fiscal Balance Decomposition Based on All Data[1]
(In percent)

	Panel (1)	Cross Section (2)
Fiscal balance (actual)	−4.41	−4.41
Fiscal balance (fitted)	−4.41	−4.41
Due to		
Constant	14.11	13.17
Corruption index	−2.30	0.44
Structural reform index	−6.96	−9.56
Real per capita GDP growth	0.12	−0.02
Agriculture share of GDP	−3.14	−3.27
Years under central planning	−5.22	−4.47
Initial external debt-GDP ratio	−1.56	−1.09
Exchange rate regime	0.55	0.39
Residual	0.00	0.00

Source: IMF staff estimates.

[1]Based on regressions in (3) and (6) in Table 10, and the average value of each variable. Exchange rate regime is a dummy variable, which takes on a value of one when the exchange rate regime is fixed and zero otherwise.

investors' choice of countries as well as the volume and timing of their investment. As in the case of the fiscal balance regression, there are no econometric studies of foreign direct investment covering the 25 transition economies, although there are numerous country case studies (e.g., Brock (1998) on Russia and Floyd (1996) on Poland) and many descriptive studies of the likely factors behind the flow of foreign direct investment (e.g., Lankes and Venables, 1996; EBRD, 1999a).

The approach adopted in this paper builds on Wei (1997a, 1997b, 1999b), who conducted a cross-country study of foreign direct investment with corruption as one explanatory variable, but the specification of the regression in this paper is tailored to take into account specific features of the transition economies. The regression specifies per capita (net) foreign direct investment as a function of natural resource wealth, wage inflation, secondary school enrollment rate, and population. To this regression, the two indices of corruption and structural reforms are added.

Countries with richer natural resource endowments are likely to attract higher flows of foreign direct investment. In the case of transition economies, these countries are primarily Azerbaijan, Kazakhstan, Russia, and Turkmenistan. Wage inflation is included to reflect the cost of labor inputs or more general macrostability factors; therefore, a higher wage inflation is expected to dampen the flow of foreign direct investment. Secondary school enrollment rate is a measure of human capital; a positive coefficient is expected for this variable, as countries with richer human capital are likely to have the complementary skills to work with imported foreign capital. Corruption is expected to deter foreign investment, as in Wei (1997a, 1997b, 1999b), where it serves as an additional tax on foreign investors. Finally, progress on structural reforms is expected to be associated with higher foreign direct investment. The positive impact of structural reforms on foreign direct investment can be justified on many grounds, ranging from structural reforms providing the necessary conditions for the operation of a market-oriented economy, the needed safeguards for the protection of property rights to a sound regulatory environment, and a liberal trade and exchange regime.

The regression results are shown in Table 13. The fitted regressions account for 35 percent and 56 percent of the variation in per capita foreign direct investment in the panel and cross-sectional data, respectively. The sign of each variable generally conforms to prior expectations. Countries with higher per capita foreign direct investment tend to be less corrupt, more advanced on structural reforms, and better endowed with natural resources; they also tend to have lower wage inflation, a higher secondary school enrollment rate, and a lower population size.[68]

Natural resource wealth, secondary school enrollment rate, and population size are statistically significant at the conventional levels in all regressions. The structural reform index is significant in the panel data at the 1 percent level, but the corruption index is not significant in either the panel or cross-sectional regressions when the structural reform index is also included. These results thus indicate that structural reforms are more important than reduced corruption in attracting foreign direct investment.

The decomposition results are shown in Tables 14 and 15. Of the explained $85 per capita foreign direct investment differential between

---

[68]These results do not change when the regression also controls for real per capita GDP, years under central planning system, real GDP growth, and GDP as another measure of size. We also added top marginal corporate income tax rate, which was found to be associated with lower foreign direct investment, as in Wei (1997a, 1997b), but these results are tentative because there were few observations on the tax rate variable.

Table 13. Dependent Variable: Per Capita Foreign Direct Investment
(In U.S. dollars per capita)

Independent Variables	Panel (1)	Panel (2)	Panel (3)	Cross Section (4)	Cross Section (5)	Cross Section (6)
Constant	−470.92***	−453.46***	−459.70***	−402.91**	−455.48***	−424.28**
	(−4.19)	(−4.85)	(−4.80)	(−2.13)	(−2.64)	(−2.27)
Corruption index	13.57**		5.07	21.37***		14.12
	(2.30)		(0.77)	(3.53)		(1.47)
Structural reform index		65.27***	71.66***		71.09***	34.52
		(5.86)	(3.83)		(3.73)	(1.21)
Natural resource wealth	63.55***	59.60***	72.80***	53.06***	61.28**	58.80**
	(3.55)	(4.57)	(3.59)	(2.84)	(2.33)	(2.35)
Initial wage inflation	−15.74**	−7.45*	−2.48	−4.86	−5.49	−1.55
	(−2.36)	(−1.62)	(−0.35)	(−0.63)	(−0.74)	(−0.20)
Initial secondary enrollment rate	112.59***	79.64***	71.22***	83.44*	75.96**	74.28*
	(4.45)	(3.97)	(3.36)	(1.97)	(2.00)	(1.84)
Population	−0.68***	−0.74***	−0.88***	−0.52***	−0.76***	−0.64***
	(−4.25)	(−5.79)	(−4.81)	(−2.82)	(−3.73)	(−2.95)
Number of observations	82	120	82	24	24	24
Adjusted R-squared	0.29	0.37	0.35	0.56	0.53	0.56

Source: IMF staff estimates.

Note: Estimation is by OLS; t-statistics are in parentheses and are based on heteroscedastic-consistent standard errors. Initial wage inflation and initial secondary enrollment rate are in logs. Natural resource wealth is a dummy variable, which takes on a value of one for Azerbaijan, Kazakhstan, Russia, and Turkmenistan, and zero otherwise. ***, **, and * denote significance at the 1 percent, 5 percent, and 10 percent levels, respectively.

advanced reformers and slow reformers (Table 14, column 1), $14 is due to differences in corruption, $59 due to differences in structural reforms, −$17 due to differences in natural resource wealth,[69] $3 due to differences in wage inflation, $11 due to differences in secondary school enrollment rates, and $14 due to differences in population size. By comparison, the decomposition results based on cross-sectional regression (Table 14, column 2) show that corruption is more important

---

[69]The negative contribution reflects the notion that advanced reformers are not endowed with rich natural resources; therefore, slow reformers tend to attract $17 per capita more than advanced reformers merely because they have a richer natural resource wealth.

Table 14. Explaining Per Capita Foreign Direct Investment Differential Between Advanced Reformers and Slow Reformers[1]
(In U.S. dollars per capita)

	Panel (1)	Cross Section (2)
Actual differential	95.09	89.41
Fitted differential	85.08	79.81
Due to		
Corruption index	14.50	42.32
Structural reform index	59.47	30.62
Natural resource wealth	−17.04	−11.76
Initial wage inflation	2.94	1.90
Initial secondary enrollment rate	11.05	8.85
Population	14.16	7.88
Residual	10.01	9.60

Source: IMF staff estimates.

[1] Based on regressions in (3) and (6) in Table 13, and the average value of each variable within each country group. Natural resource wealth is a dummy variable, which takes on a value of one for Azerbaijan, Kazakhstan, Russia, and Turkmenistan, and zero otherwise.

Table 15. Decompostion of Per Capita Foreign Direct Investment Based on All Data[1]
(In U.S. dollars per capita)

	Panel (1)	Cross Section (2)
Actual	68.46	56.83
Fitted	68.46	56.83
Due to		
Constant	−459.70	−424.28
Corruption index	25.41	66.36
Structural reform index	199.53	92.17
Natural resource wealth	9.77	7.35
Initial wage inflation	−3.18	−2.29
Initial secondary enrollment rate	313.99	328.03
Population	−17.35	−10.50
Residual	0.00	0.00

Source: IMF staff estimates.

[1] Based on regressions in (3) and (6) in Table 13, and the average value of each variable.

than structural reforms ($42 versus $31), although the estimated parameter for either index is not statistically significant in the regression. The decomposition results based on average data are shown in Table 15. These results indicate that progress on structural reforms, on average, contributes more to foreign direct investment than reducing corruption—about 1.4 to 8 times as important as corruption.

IV. Determinants of Corruption

The evidence presented so far indicates that (1) the statistical significance of corruption is reduced substantially once the structural reform index is added to the regression, (2) the fit of the regression for various measures of economic performance is generally higher with the structural reform index than with the corruption perception index, and (3) structural reforms are economically more important than corruption when both are included in the regression. These results are indirect evidence that structural reforms may be the driving force behind the influence of corruption.

In this section, more direct evidence is provided on whether the structural reform index is indeed a possible determinant of corruption, given other factors. Figure 2 shows the fitted cross-sectional regression of the corruption index on the structural reform index. The fitted regression indicates that 74 percent of the cross-country variation in the corruption perception index may be explained by variations in the structural reform index. Furthermore, the figure indicates that countries that are perceived to be less corrupt tend to have made more progress on structural reforms.[70]

The fitted regression, however, does not control for other factors that may affect corruption. The intention of this section is not to carry out a systematic investigation of the determinants of corruption in transition economies, because this would go beyond the scope of this study; instead, we simply regress the corruption perception index on the structural reform index and five other variables that can be regarded as potential determinants of corruption. This regression is estimated over the period 1994–98, the same sample as in the previous regressions. The five variables are (1) years lived under central planning prior to beginning the reform; (2) per capita GDP; (3) a measure of natural re-

---

[70]Results are the same if a separate figure is prepared for each year.

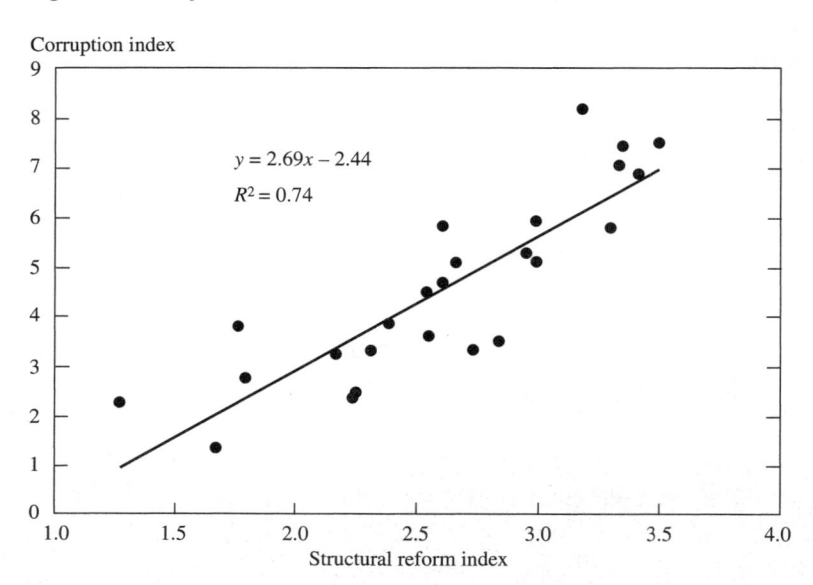

Figure 2. Corruption and Structural Reforms

Corruption index

$y = 2.69x - 2.44$

$R^2 = 0.74$

Structural reform index

Source: See text.
Note: Higher values in the "corruption index" indicate "cleaner government" or reduced corruption.

source wealth; (4) a measure of the decentralized form of government (referred to as "state" below); and (5) the ratio of imports to GDP.[71]

To reduce the problem of simultaneity, we use initial value of all the variables (1994 or earlier), including that of the structural reform index. Thus, all variables are predetermined with respect to the future evolution of corruption. The choice of included variables has been motivated by the recent research on the causes of corruption (Ades and Di Tella, 1999; and Treisman, 2000) and our reading of factors specific to transition economies. For example, the number of years that a country lived under a central planning system is a reasonable proxy for an environment that is conducive to corruption and the presence of illicit rent-seeking activities. Therefore, we expect corruption to be higher in countries that lived

---

[71]Treisman (2000) provides an exhaustive analysis of causes of corruption and uses additional indicators beyond those listed above; however, sufficient data for these indicators are not available for the transition economies.

longer under a central planning system.[72] This variable is likely to determine the pace of structural reforms as well; so its inclusion makes sure that one does not attribute a stronger role to structural reforms than is warranted. Previous research (Ades and Di Tella, 1999; and Treisman, 2000) found that countries with lower corruption tend to have a higher per capita income, a higher ratio of imports to GDP (a proxy for competition with domestic producers), a natural resource–poor economy, and a nonfederal form of government. A natural question of interest is whether similar results are also obtained for the transition economies.

The results of the regression for various specifications are shown in Table 16. Column (1) regresses corruption on the structural reform index, years under a central planning system, and initial per capita GDP. Column (2) adds three more variables: a measure of natural resource wealth, "state," and ratio of imports to GDP. Columns (3) and (4) are the same as (1) and (2) except that initial value of the structural reform index is used instead of its current value. These results are then reported for both panel and cross-sectional data.

The results show that corruption perception index is higher in countries that lived longer under a central planning system,[73] have a lower per capita GDP, and have made slow progress on structural reforms. These variables alone account for about 69 percent and 86 percent of variation in corruption rankings for the panel and cross-sectional data, respectively.[74] The estimated coefficients on each of these variables are all statistically significant at the 1 percent level for either panel data or cross-sectional data. These conclusions still hold when the current value of the structural reform index is replaced with its value at the beginning of the reform.[75] The structural reform index is quantitatively

---

[72]This variable may also be a reasonable proxy for the "exposure-to-democracy" variable used by Treisman (2000).

[73]This variable is quantitatively important as well. Slow reformers lived, on average, 17 years longer under a central planning system. This translates, given the regression results, into a higher corruption ranking of slow reformers by 0.85 points, large enough to equalize the difference in average corruption rankings between advanced reformers and slow reformers in 1998; see Table 3.

[74]Thus, the addition of just two other variables—years under central planning and initial per capita GDP—to the regression (depicted in Figure 2) increases the adjusted R-squared from 74 percent to 86 percent.

[75]As regards other variables, corruption is higher in countries with rich natural resources, although the effect is not statistically significant. The other two variables, state and ratio of imports to GDP, have no relation to corruption and have signs that are different from previous studies.

Table 16. Determinants of Corruption

Independent Variables	Panel (1)	Panel (2)	Panel (3)	Panel (4)	Cross Section (5)	Cross Section (6)	Cross Section (7)	Cross Section (8)
Constant	4.40*** (3.38)	4.39*** (2.85)	4.46*** (3.21)	4.81*** (3.15)	3.03* (1.99)	3.43 (1.22)	4.04** (2.34)	5.01* (1.97)
Structural reform index	1.05*** (3.16)	1.02*** (2.89)			1.36*** (3.55)	1.32*** (2.62)		
Initial structural reform index			0.87*** (3.07)	0.86*** (2.99)			0.97*** (2.67)	0.92** (2.19)
Years under central planning	−0.05*** (−4.81)	−0.05*** (−3.32)	−0.05*** (−3.05)	−0.04** (−2.41)	−0.04*** (−3.26)	−0.05* (−1.91)	−0.04** (−2.29)	−0.05** (−1.78)
Initial per capita GDP[1]	0.44*** (3.60)	0.45*** (3.45)	0.46*** (3.89)	0.48*** (3.91)	0.42*** (4.69)	0.42*** (3.83)	0.46*** (5.43)	0.47*** (5.37)
Natural resource wealth		−0.29 (−0.77)		−0.41 (−1.04)		0.03 (0.07)		−0.19 (−0.37)
State[2]		0.87 (0.04)		−0.10 (−0.49)		−0.05 (−0.15)		−0.20 (−0.58)
Ratio of imports to GDP[2]		−0.36 (−0.54)		−0.81 (−1.40)		−0.20 (−0.11)		−0.89 (−0.56)
Number of observations	84	84	84	84	25	25	25	25
Adjusted R-squared	0.69	0.68	0.68	0.67	0.86	0.84	0.83	0.82

Source: IMF staff estimates.
Note: Estimation is by OLS; t-statistics are in parentheses and are based on heteroscedastic-consistent standard errors. The variable "state" is a categorical variable and takes on a value of two if a country was an independent state at the beginning of the reform, one if a country was a member of a decentralized federal state (Yugoslav Republics) or was the core state of a centralized federal state (Russia, the Czech Republic) and zero otherwise (de Melo and others, 1997). Natural resource wealth is a dummy variable, which takes on a value of one for Azerbaijan, Kazakhstan, Russia, and Turkmenistan and zero otherwise. ***, **, and * denote significance at the 1 percent, 5 percent, and 10 percent levels, respectively.
[1]Coefficients are multiplied by 1,000.
[2]Coefficients are multiplied by 100.

important as well, because one-half of the difference in corruption ranking between advanced and slow reformers is due to differences in structural reforms.[76]

The above results show that progress in structural reforms reduces corruption, and the regression results in Section III have shown that lower corruption in general tends to improve economic performance, although not as much as structural reforms. We can now calculate the indirect impact of structural reforms (through corruption given in Table 16), and compare the results with its direct impact for each measure of economic performance as measured in Section III.[77] Following the main theme of the paper, the idea is to ascertain if the indirect impact is as quantitatively significant as the direct impact.[78] The indirect contribution combines the information from the regression results in Section IV with those in Section III.

The combined direct and indirect impact is calculated assuming that the structural reform index would increase by 0.25. This value seems to be reasonable since it represents the average increase in the structural reform index for slow reformers over the period 1994–98 and the average value of the standard deviation of slow reformers. In a sense, we are assuming that slow reformers on average maintain their recent pace of structural reforms. The results of this exercise are shown in Table 17. They indicate that the indirect contribution of structural reforms is economically significant for two variables: growth and foreign direct investment. Real per capita GDP growth would be higher on average by about 0.35 percentage points, a significant result, given the slow reformers' average real per capita GDP growth of –2.57 percent. In addition, per capita foreign direct investment of slow reformers would be higher by $5, a significant increase given their average per capita foreign direct investment of $23.

---

[76]This is based on point estimate of the structural reform index given in Table 16, column (5), and on average values of corruption and structural reform indices given in Tables 2 and 3.

[77]The indirect impact is calculated by multiplying the coefficient on the structural reform index in Table 16 by 0.25 and by the coefficient on the corruption index for each regression in Tables 4, 7, 10, and 13.

[78]This analysis holds other variables constant and does not take account of the indirect effects of structural reforms through these variables. Allowing for these additional factors will tend to increase the indirect contribution of structural reforms, given the results in Section III.

Table 17. Direct and Indirect Contributions of Structural Reforms to Economic Performance

Measure of Economic Performance	Panel Direct[1]	Panel Indirect[2]	Panel Total[3]	Cross Section Direct[1]	Cross Section Indirect[2]	Cross Section Total[3]
Real per capita GDP growth rate (percent)	1.20	0.35	1.55	1.37	0.36	1.73
Inflation (percent)	–0.14	0.00	–0.14	–0.22	–0.01	–0.23
Fiscal balance (percent of GDP)	–0.65	–0.12	–0.77	–0.91	0.03	–0.88
Foreign direct investment (U.S. dollars per capita)	17.92	1.33	19.25	8.63	4.80	13.43

Source: IMF staff estimates.
Note: The estimates in the table show the impact of improving the structural reform index by 0.25.
[1] From Tables 4, 7, 10, and 13.
[2] From Tables 4, 7, 10, 13, and 16.
[3] Sum of direct and indirect contributions.

V. Conclusion

With reference to the various studies that have shown the adverse impact of corruption on economic performance, this paper has sought to probe deeper by identifying the underlying conditions that give rise to corruption in transition economies. The paper considers corruption to be mostly, but not entirely, a symptom of underlying policy distortions and weak economic institutions, thereby anchoring anticorruption strategies firmly in the context of structural and institutional reforms. Indeed, when the importance of corruption is tested against that of structural reforms in explaining economic performance, at least for the transition economies, the explanatory power of corruption, as measured by the widely used corruption perception indices, is found to be relatively minor. Relying both on regression and decomposition analyses, this paper finds that progress on structural reforms—defined broadly to comprise the rationalization of state functions, reliance on market-based pricing, and the establishment of a sound regulatory environment—is both statistically more significant and economically more important than corruption in explaining differences in economic performance as reflected in growth, inflation, the fiscal balance, and foreign direct investment. Furthermore, this paper provides direct evidence that structural reform is an important factor in lowering corruption levels, given other factors that influence corruption. By reducing corruption, structural reforms are also shown to significantly increase economic growth and foreign direct investment above and beyond any direct effects.

Clearly, the increased attention to corruption and its adverse impact on economic performance has been helpful in stimulating a broader discussion of economic reform. However, to enhance the usefulness of recent studies of corruption in the formulation of economic policy, these studies would need to probe deeper into the link between corruption and the underlying weaknesses in policies and institutions. By shedding more light on the mechanisms by which such weaknesses create opportunities for illicit rent seeking and abuse of authority, the study of corruption can lead to the design of specific institutional and structural reform measures to underpin a credible anticorruption strategy. This paper has sought to probe this vital link, and, although the analysis is applied to the transition economies, the validity of the results is likely to hold in a wider context and merits further study.

If structural reforms are indeed more important to economic performance than reducing corruption, why have they received less attention in recent studies? And, more important, why have these reforms not been undertaken more vigorously in the transition and other economies even though great interest has been shown in the fight against corruption? Regarding the first question, it may be that the study of "corruption" is more appealing as a topic of analysis or public discourse than "structural reforms." It may also be that the wider availability of corruption perception indices for an increasing number of countries has stimulated economists' interest in studying the relationship between corruption and economic performance. One implication of this analysis would be to call for greater effort toward assessing and measuring structural reforms.[79]

The answer to the second question must lie, at least in part, in a political economy argument. Implementation of structural reforms tends to be slow and difficult, in part because the vested interests associated with the status quo are usually stronger and more vocal than those allied with a reformed, if yet untested, state of affairs. It is important to emphasize, however, that once these reforms are initiated and sustained, they tend to reduce opportunities for corruption and increase

---

[79]Bredenkamp and Schadler (1998) construct a structural reform index for 30 low-income countries participating in the IMF's Enhanced Structural Adjustment Facility.

prospects for better economic performance. Much has been written on the political economy of embracing structural reforms, the role of a committed leadership in spearheading such reforms, and the influence of international institutions. Further analysis of these issues is certainly called for, at least in the context of transition economies. However, such probing would go beyond the scope of this paper.

References

Abed, George, 1998, "Governance and the Transition Economies," paper presented at the conference sponsored by the Kyrgyz Republic and the IMF on "Challenges to the Economies in Transition: Stabilization, Growth, and Governance," Bishkek, Kyrgyz Republic, May.

Ades, Alberto, and Rafael Di Tella, 1999, "Rents, Competition, and Corruption," *American Economic Review*, Vol. 89 (September), pp. 982–93.

Aghion, Philippe, and Olivier Blanchard, 1994, "On the Speed of Transition in Central Europe," in *NBER Macroeconomics Annual*, Vol. 9, ed. by S. Fischer and J. Rotemberg (Cambridge, Massachusetts: MIT Press).

Alesina, Alberto, Ricardo Hausmann, Rudolf Hommes, and Ernesto Stein, 1999, "Budget Institutions and Fiscal Performance in Latin America," *Journal of Development Economics*, Vol. 59 (August), pp. 253–73.

Al-Marhubi, Fahim, 2000, "Corruption and Inflation," *Economics Letters*, Vol. 66 (February), pp. 199–202.

Barbone, Luca, and Hana Polackova, 1996, "Public Finances and Economic Transition," *MOCT-Most: Economic Policy in Transitional Economies*, Vol. 6, No. 3, pp. 35–61.

Becker, Gary S., 1968, "Crime and Punishment: An Economic Approach," *Journal of Political Economy*, Vol. 76 (March/April), pp. 169–217.

Berg, Andrew, Eduardo Borensztein, Ratna Sahay, and Jeromin Zettelmeyer, 1999, "The Evolution of Output in Transition Economies: Explaining the Differences," IMF Working Paper No. 99/73 (Washington: International Monetary Fund).

Braun, Miguel, and Rafael Di Tella, 2000, "Inflation and Corruption" (unpublished; Cambridge, Massachusetts: Harvard University).

Bredenkamp, Hugh, and Susan Schadler, 1998, eds., *Economic Adjustment and Reform in Low-Income Countries: Studies by the Staff of the International Monetary Fund* (Washington: International Monetary Fund).

Brock, Gregory J., 1998, "Foreign Direct Investment in Russia's Regions, 1993–95: Why So Little and Where Has it Gone?" *Economics of Transition*, Vol. 6 (November), pp. 349–60.

Brunetti, Aymo, Gregory Kisunko, and Beatrice Weder, 1997, "Institutions in Transition: Reliability of Rules and Economic Performance in Former Socialist Countries," World Bank Policy Research Working Paper No. 1809 (Washington: World Bank).

———, 1998, "Credibility of Rules and Economic Growth: Evidence from a Worldwide Survey of the Private Sector," *World Bank Economic Review*, Vol. 12 (September), pp. 353–84.

Brunetti, Aymo, and Beatrice Weder, 1999, "A Free Press Is Bad News for Corruption," Discussion Paper No. 9809 (Basel: University of Basel).

Campillo, Marta, and Jeffrey Miron, 1996, "Why Does Inflation Differ Across Countries?" NBER Working Paper No. 5540 (Cambridge, Massachusetts: National Bureau of Economic Research).

Caramazza, Francisco, and Jahangir Aziz, 1998, *Fixed or Flexible? Getting the Exchange Rate Right in the 1990s*, Economic Issues, No. 13 (Washington: International Monetary Fund).

Central European Economic Review, 1995–96, "The Great Growth Race," Vol. 3 (December–January), pp. 8–14.

———, 1997–98, "Welcome to the World," Vol. 5, pp. 14–21.

Cheasty, Adrienne, and Jeffrey M. Davis, 1996, "Fiscal Transition in Countries of the Former Soviet Union: An Interim Assessment," *MOCT-Most: Economic Policy in Transition*, Vol. 6, pp. 7–34.

Cottarelli, Carlo, Mark Griffiths, and Reza Moghadam, 1998, "The Nonmonetary Determinants of Inflation: A Panel Data Study," IMF Working Paper 98/23 (Washington: International Monetary Fund).

Crotty, John, 1997, "Measures to Address Corruption Problems in Tax and Customs Administrations," paper presented at the Eighth International Anti-Corruption Conference, Lima, Peru, September.

de Melo, Martha, Cevdet Denizer, and Alan Gelb, 1996, "Patterns of Transition: From Plan to Market," *World Bank Economic Review*, Vol. 10 (September), pp. 397–424.

———, and Stoyan Tenev, 1997, "Circumstance and Choice: The Role of Initial Conditions and Policies in Transition Economies," World Bank Policy Research Working Paper No. 1866 (Washington: World Bank).

Easterly, William, and Ross Levine, 1997, "Africa's Growth Tragedy: Policies and Ethnic Divisions," *Quarterly Journal of Economics*, Vol. 112 (November), pp. 1203–50.

Ebrill, Liam, and Oleh Havrylyshyn, 1999, *Tax Reform in the Baltics, Russia, and Other Countries of the Former Soviet Union*, IMF Occasional Paper No. 182 (Washington: International Monetary Fund).

Ehrlich, Isaac, and Francis T. Lui, 1999, "Bureaucratic Corruption and Endogenous Growth," *Journal of Political Economy*, Vol. 107 (December), pp. S270–93.

European Bank for Reconstruction and Development (EBRD), 1999a, *Transition Report* (London).

———, 1999b, *Transition Report Update* (London).

Fischer, Stanley, and Ratna Sahay, 2000, "The Transition Economies After Ten Years," IMF Working Paper 00/30 (Washington: International Monetary Fund).

———, and Carlos A. Végh, 1998, "From Transition to Market: Evidence and Growth Prospects," IMF Working Paper 98/52 (Washington: International Monetary Fund).

Floyd, David, 1996, "Foreign Direct Investment in Poland: Is Low Cost Labour Really the Sole Determinant?" *Economic Issues*, Vol. 1 (September), pp. 29–39.

Garamfalvi, Laszlo, 1997, "Corruption in the Public Expenditure Management Process," paper presented at the Eighth International Anti-Corruption Conference in Lima, Peru, September.

Goel, Rajeev K., and Michael A. Nelson, 1998, "Corruption and Government Size: A Disaggregated Analysis," *Public Choice*, Vol. 97 (October), pp. 107–20.

Havrylyshyn, Oleh, Ivailo Izvorski, and Ron van Rooden, 1998, "Recovery and Growth in Transition Economies, 1990–97: A Stylized Regression Analysis," IMF Working Paper No. 98/141 (Washington: International Monetary Fund).

Havrylyshyn, Oleh, and others, 1999, *Growth Experience in Transition Countries, 1990–98*, IMF Occasional Paper No. 184 (Washington: International Monetary Fund).

Havrylyshyn, Oleh, and Ron van Rooden, 2000, "Institutions Matter in Transition, But So Do Policies," IMF Working Paper No. 00/70 (Washington: International Monetary Fund).

Heidenheimer, Arnold J., Michael Johnston, and Victor T. LeVine, eds., 1989, *Political Corruption: A Handbook* (New Brunswick, New Jersey, and London: Transaction Publishers).

Hernandez-Cata, Ernesto, 1997, "Liberalization and the Behavior of Output During the Transition from Plan to Market," *Staff Papers*, International Monetary Fund, Vol. 44 (December), pp. 405–29.

Hines, James R., Jr., 1995, "Forbidden Payment: Foreign Bribery and American Business After 1997," NBER Working Paper No. 5266 (Cambridge, Massachusetts: National Bureau of Economic Research).

Huntington, Samuel, 1968, *Political Order in Changing Societies* (New Haven, Connecticut: Yale University Press).

Johnson, Simon, Daniel Kaufmann, and Andrei Shleifer, 1997, "The Unofficial Economy in Transition," *Brookings Papers on Economic Activity: 2*, Brookings Institution, pp. 159–239.

Johnson, Simon, Daniel Kaufmann, and Pablo Zoido-Lobatón, 1999, "Corruption, Public Finances and the Unofficial Economy," World Bank Policy Research Working Paper Series No. 2169 (Washington: World Bank).

Kaufmann, Daniel, Aart Kraay, and Pablo Zoido-Lobatón, 1999a, "Aggregating Governance Indicators," World Bank Policy Research Working Paper No. 2195 (Washington: World Bank).

———, 1999b, "Governance Matters," World Bank Policy Research Working Paper No. 2196 (Washington: World Bank).

Klitgaard, Robert, 1988, *Controlling Corruption* (Berkeley: University of California Press).

———, 1997, "Cleaning Up and Invigorating the Civil Service," *Public Administration and Development*, Vol. 17 (December), pp. 487–509.

Kornai, János, 1986, "The Soft Budget Constraint," *Kyklos*, Vol. 39, pp. 3–30.

———, 1998, "The Place of the Soft Budget Constraint Syndrome in Economic Theory," *Journal of Comparative Economics*, Vol. 26 (March), pp. 11–17.

Lambsdorff, J.G., 1998, "Corruption in Comparative Perception," in *Economics of Corruption*, ed. by Arvind K. Jain (Boston: Kluwer Academic Publishers).

Langseth, Petter, Rick Stapenhurst, and Jeremy Pope, 1999, "National Integrity Systems," in *Curbing Corruption: Toward a Model for Building National Integrity,* ed. by Rick Stapenhurst and Sahr J. Kpundeh (Washington: World Bank).

Lankes, Hans-Peter, and A. J. Venables, 1996, "Foreign Direct Investment in Economic Transition: The Changing Pattern of Investments," *Economics of Transition*, Vol. 4 (October), pp. 331–47.

Leff, Nathaniel, 1964, "Economic Development Through Bureaucratic Corruption," *American Behavioral Scientist*, Vol. 8 (November), pp. 8–14.

Mauro, Paulo, 1995, "Corruption and Growth," *Quarterly Journal of Economics*, Vol. 110 (August), pp. 681–712.

Mercer-Blackman, Valerie, and Anna Unigovskaya, 2000, "Compliance with IMF Program Indicators and Growth in Transition Economies," IMF Working Paper No. 00/47 (Washington: International Monetary Fund).

Myrdal, Gunnar, 1968, *Asian Drama: An Inquiry into the Poverty of Nations* (New York: Pantheon).

Obstfeld, Maurice, 1985, "Floating Exchange Rates: Experience and Prospects," *Brookings Papers on Economic Activity: 2*, Brookings Institution, pp. 369–450.

Ofosu-Amaah, W. Paatii, Raj Soopramanien, and Kishor Uprety, 1999, *Combating Corruption: A Comparative Review of Selected Legal Aspects of State Practices and Major International Initiatives* (Washington: World Bank).

Pirttilä, Jukka, 2000, "Fiscal Policy and Structural Reforms in Transition Economies: An Empirical Analysis," Bofit Discussion Papers, No. 5 (Helsinki: Bank of Finland, Institute for Economies in Transition).

Political Risk Services Group, *International Country Risk Guide* (CD-ROM version).

Pope, Jeremy, 1999a, "Elements of a Successful Anticorruption Strategy," in *Curbing Corruption: Toward a Model for Building National Integrity*, ed. by Rick Stapenhurst and Sahr J. Kpundeh (Washington: World Bank).

———, 1999b, "Enhancing Accountability and Ethics in the Public Sector," in *Curbing Corruption: Toward a Model for Building National Integrity*, ed. by Rick Stapenhurst and Sahr J. Kpundeh (Washington: World Bank).

Rauch, James E., and Peter B. Evans, 2000, "Bureaucratic Structure and Bureaucratic Performance in Less Developed Countries," *Journal of Public Economics*, Vol. 75 (January), pp. 49–71.

Rose-Ackerman, Susan, 1978, *Corruption: A Study in Political Economy* (New York: Academic Press).

———, 1999, *Corruption and Government: Causes, Consequences, and Reform* (Cambridge, England; New York: Cambridge University Press).

Sala-i-Martin, Xavier X., 1997, "I Just Ran Two Million Regressions," *American Economic Review, Papers and Proceedings*, Vol. 87 (May), pp. 178–83.

Shleifer, Andrei, and Robert Vishny, 1993, "Corruption," *Quarterly Journal Of Economics*, Vol. 108 (August), pp. 599–617.

Stotsky, Janet, and Asegedech WoldeMariam, 1997, "Tax Effort in Sub-Saharan Africa," IMF Working Paper 97/107 (Washington: International Monetary Fund).

Tanzi, Vito, 1987, "Quantitative Characteristics of the Tax Systems of Developing Countries," in *The Theory of Taxation for Developing Countries*, ed. by David M.G. Newbery and Nicholas Herbert Stern (New York: Oxford University Press).

———, 1993, "The Budget Deficit in Transition," *Staff Papers*, International Monetary Fund, Vol. 40 (September), pp. 697–707.

———, 1995, "Corruption: Arm's-Length Relationships and Markets," in *The Economics of Organised Crime*, ed. by Gianluca Fiorentini and Sam Peltzman (Cambridge, England: Cambridge University Press).

———, 1996, "Fiscal Developments: An Overview," *MOCT-Most, Economic Policy in Transitional Economies*, Vol. 6, No. 3, pp. 1–5.

———, 2000, "The Role of the State and the Quality of the Public Sector" (unpublished; Washington: International Monetary Fund).

Tanzi, Vito, and George Tsibouris, 2001, "Les réformes des finances publiques en dix années de transition," *Revue d'Économie Financière*, Numéro hors-série—Dix ans de transition en Europe de l'est: Bilan et perspectives (Paris: Association d'Économie Financière). ["Fiscal Reform Over Ten Years of Transition," *Revue d'Économie Financière*, Special Issue—Ten Years of Transition in Eastern European Countries: Achievements and Challenges (Paris: Association d'Économie Financière).]

Transparency International, "Corruption Perception Indices," available via Internet, http://www.transparency.de.

Treisman, Daniel, 2000, "The Causes of Corruption: A Cross-National Study," *Journal of Public Economics*, Vol. 76 (June), pp. 399–457.

Ul Haque, Nadeem, and Ratna Sahay, 1996, "Do Government Wage Cuts Close Budget Deficits? Costs of Corruption," *Staff Papers*, International Monetary Fund, Vol. 43 (December), pp. 754–78.

Wade, Robert, 1982, "The System of Administrative and Political Corruption: Canal Irrigation in South India," *Journal of Development Studies*, Vol. 18 (April), pp. 287–328.

Wagner, Helmut, 1998, "Central Banking in Transition Economies," IMF Working Paper No. 98/126 (Washington: International Monetary Fund).

Weber, Max, 1947, *The Theory of Social and Economic Organization* (London: Free Press of Glencoe).

Wei, Shang-jin, 1997a, "How Taxing Is Corruption on International Investors?" NBER Working Paper No. 6030 (Cambridge, Massachusetts: National Bureau of Economic Research).

———, 1997b, "Why Is Corruption So Much More Taxing Than Tax? Arbitrariness Kills," NBER Working Paper No. 6255 (Cambridge, Massachusetts: National Bureau of Economic Research).

———, 1999a, "Corruption in Economic Development: Beneficial Grease, Minor Annoyance, or Major Obstacle," World Bank Policy Research Working Paper No. 2048 (Washington: World Bank).

———, 1999b, "Does Corruption Relieve Foreign Investors of the Burden of Taxes and Capital Controls?" World Bank Policy Research Working Paper No. 2209 (Washington: World Bank).

World Bank, 1997, *World Development Report 1997: The State in a Changing World* (NewYork: Oxford University Press).

———, 1999, World Development Indicators Database.

19

Improving Governance and Fighting Corruption in the Baltic and CIS Countries: The Role of the IMF

Thomas Wolf and Emine Gürgen

I. Introduction

Among all the transition economies, perhaps nowhere has the need to improve governance and reduce corruption been more evident than in the 15 independent states that emerged from the dissolution of the former Soviet Union. These societies, which were under communist rule for up to 70 years, were characterized by a lack of government transparency and rule of law for generations; moreover, severe governance and corruption problems were endemic in most areas of the far-flung Russian empire even before the Bolshevik revolution. Under central planning, the

---

This paper was prepared for the Second Annual Meeting of the Anti-Corruption Network for Transition Economies, held at the OECD Center for Private Sector Development in Istanbul, Turkey, on November 2–3, 1999. The authors are grateful to John Odling-Smee, Jorge Márquez-Ruarte, and Oleh Havrylyshyn, as well as to colleagues from the External Relations, Fiscal Affairs, and Policy Development and Review Departments of the IMF, for helpful suggestions, and to Anna Unigovskaya for research assistance.

countries in question were influenced both by the economic system in place and by corruption. While the changes introduced after independence focused on correcting the systemic distortions, there was insufficient recognition of the equally compelling need to overcome corruption. This important aspect of the challenges faced by these countries has only gradually begun to receive the attention that it deserves.

This paper examines the indirect role that the IMF plays in combating corruption in the Baltic and Commonwealth of Independent States (CIS) countries[1] by promoting structural reforms that help improve economic governance and reduce the opportunities for rent-seeking behavior. Drawing on recent examples of corruption in the region, the paper analyzes the relationship between governance and corruption, and notes that poor governance generally creates opportunities and incentives for corruption. It points out that corruption tends to exacerbate distortions in resource allocation, lead to a relatively skewed distribution of income and wealth, and negatively affect growth and living standards. The discussion focuses on three broad weaknesses in economic governance: (1) excessive government intervention in economic activity; (2) lapses in government transparency, accountability, and economic management; and (3) absence of a stable, rule-based, and competitive environment.

The paper surveys the policy content of IMF-supported economic programs in the Baltic and CIS countries during 1992–99 to determine the extent to which weaknesses in economic governance were addressed. It notes that while the IMF's direct involvement in this area has been limited, and the words "governance" and "corruption" have seldom appeared in the language of IMF-supported economic programs, many of the specific measures that the IMF has urged governments to adopt have at least indirectly tried to address these concerns. For example, while such measures as the elimination of price subsidies and tax exemptions were included in these programs for fiscal and general economic welfare reasons, they also contributed to good governance and may have lessened the opportunities for corruption. Notably beyond the initial years, when reducing the very high rates of inflation received priority, programs in the region have typically included corrective measures in the three areas outlined above, with some shift of

---

[1]The Baltic countries are Estonia, Latvia, and Lithuania; the CIS countries are Armenia, Azerbaijan, Belarus, Georgia, Kazakhstan, the Kyrgyz Republic, Moldova, Russia, Tajikistan, Turkmenistan, Ukraine, and Uzbekistan.

emphasis in recent years to the second and third areas. The paper also examines the experiences of selected countries in the region in meeting structural conditionality under recent IMF arrangements, and concludes that, despite considerable progress to date (including through IMF technical assistance), much remains to be accomplished.

In the final section, the paper notes that the IMF will continue its work to help curtail opportunities for corruption in member countries by supporting measures to liberalize the economy, improve the management of public resources, promote accountability, and establish a transparent and stable regulatory environment. The paper concludes by outlining the key structural areas that are likely to receive emphasis in the IMF's future policy advice in the region, stressing that success in reducing corruption will depend ultimately on the determination with which countries recognize and address this serious problem.

II. The Relationship Between Governance and Corruption

As commonly used, the term "governance" refers to the manner in which governments discharge their responsibilities; that is, are governments effective, are their operations transparent, are they accountable, and do they conform to internationally accepted good practices?[2] Thus, governance covers a whole range of government activities, and is a broader concept than corruption. Corruption may be thought of as the abuse of authority or trust for private benefit,[3] and is a temptation indulged in not only by public officials but also by those in positions of trust or authority in private enterprises or nonprofit organizations. The bulk of this paper focuses on public corruption and its deleterious effects.

While corruption undoubtedly will always be with us to some extent, regardless of the success in improving governance, it is also clear that poor governance generally creates greater incentives and possibilities for corruption. Hence, while toughening the legal strictures against and punishments for corruption is important, it is essential to tackle the underlying governance problems that may encourage corruption. Indeed, a fundamental assumption underlying

---

[2] See Abed (1998) for a more detailed discussion of these issues.
[3] Tanzi (see Chapter 2 in this volume) provides several definitions of corruption and discusses factors that promote corruption.

IMF conditionality in programs with the Baltic and CIS countries has been that by seeking to improve governance—particularly in areas of economic policy—the IMF can also contribute to the fight against corruption.

Excessive Government Intervention, Regulation, and Discretion in the Economy

Economic governance may be seen as having three broad dimensions, although there is some overlap among them. First, poor governance is reflected in excessive government intervention and discretion relating to economic activity, including excessive regulation of private entities and adoption of preferential schemes. Some specific examples would be foreign exchange and trade restrictions, price controls, directed credits, and tax exemptions. These create incentives for rent seeking, including temptations for officials to use whatever discretion they have in the administration of state enterprises or the implementation of regulations to elicit bribes or kickbacks from those who would benefit from preferential treatment.

Although most countries in the region have substantially liberalized their economies, the problem of excessive intervention persists, either directly through state ownership, or through excessive regulation of economic activity and preferential schemes, as well as their discretionary application. Recent instances of corruption in the CIS countries related to this dimension of governance include (1) the abuse of tax-free status and preferential trading rights granted to so-called charitable institutions (e.g., the national sports foundation in one case); (2) the refusal to grant permits to foreign firms to build hotels to protect monopoly interests of local firms, and the delays in completion of foreign-built hotels in the capital cities of more than one CIS country due to the demand by local officials for bribes; (3) the demand by foreign trade officials in one country for bribes for import contract "registration," charged by the page (very short contracts are simply rejected out of hand); (4) the levy of individualized surcharges on the foreign exchange sold to foreign-owned companies in the context of a tightly controlled exchange market; (5) the creation, in one country, of a state energy company (headed by a close relative of a very senior official) responsible for licensing all oil imports by private companies; and (6) the sale, in another country, of a large public utility at an absurdly low price to an investor with connections to government officials who negotiated the deal.

In other cases, including in the Baltic countries, informally directed credits or government guarantees—at the instigation of government officials—have made possible low-interest bank credits to dubious borrowers. Failures to repay these credits have helped precipitate banking crises. While these cases may or may not have involved corruption as such, they clearly were instances of poor governance that weakened those economies. However, since economic liberalization has progressed quite far in most of the countries in the region, these types of governance problems tend to be less frequently encountered, although the scale of the bribes and rents involved can still be quite considerable.

Lack of Government Transparency and Accountability and Poor Management

A second dimension of economic governance involves transparency, accountability, and good economic and financial management by the state in those areas under its direct control. Hence, it is important in transition economies to maintain arm's-length relations between the government and the rest of the economy, including privatized enterprises; avoid conflicts of interest on the part of government officials; provide an efficient and well-paid civil service; institute an open budgetary process and strong expenditure controls; establish an efficient tax administration; avoid budgetary arrears; and generally maintain transparent government and central bank operations. Lapses in many of these areas provide a breeding ground for corruption.

Conflict of interest continues to be a major problem in many CIS countries. For example, officials in the customs administration and/or other government organs, in more than one country, engage in smuggling operations to undercut the marketing efforts and profitability of domestically established companies (and in some cases joint ventures) in domestic markets for alcoholic beverages and tobacco products. In one country, all enterprises in an important industry producing construction materials have nominally been privatized, but the resulting enterprises are all controlled by close relatives of a senior politician and the result, effectively, is a cartel with strong government support. In another country, a local manufacturer of building materials borrowed heavily from a commercial bank to provide supplies for a project being constructed by a close relative of a senior official. Following delivery, the manufacturer was never paid but was reluctant to press a legal case due to the status of the owner. As a result, the company went bankrupt and the local bank was stuck with a large bad loan.

Uses of the proceeds from humanitarian aid programs also open up lucrative possibilities for corruption. In one case in a CIS country, the government bought wheat on the basis of a concessional loan and, in turn, sold it at a price below the import parity price to a well-connected trader, who reaped substantial profits. Another case of poor governance involves the construction in one country of state-owned textile plants at significantly inflated costs, reflecting the absence of transparent procurement criteria. In another case, supposedly higher competing bids for a procurement contract under a World Bank loan program were found out later to have been forged by the authorities.

An underpaid and overstaffed government bureaucracy tends to encourage participation in the above-noted types of corruption, as well as in the more obvious cases of bribery noted in this section. An important contribution to reducing conflicts of interest and outright economic crimes by officials would be to promote transparency and accountability through the greater use of independent outside audits of government and financial operations, and the accounts of central banks in these countries (as has recently been the case, for example, in Russia). Achieving greater transparency and accountability in the privatization processes under way would also be essential.

Creation of an Effective Environment for Efficient Market Activities

The third area of economic governance involves the creation of a stable, rule-based, and competitive environment for the efficient operation of market activities. This requires a clear commitment by the authorities to the rule of law; enforcement of the sanctity of contracts and of property rights; a strong court system; effective bankruptcy procedures; a stable, fair, and transparent tax system; effective bank supervision; and the strict enforcement of bank prudential regulations. Such an environment will not only help reduce corruption but also stimulate saving and investment—including foreign direct investment—and thereby help provide the basis for sustainable growth.

Unfortunately, discretionary and unstable legal and regulatory environments probably remain the rule rather than the exception in the CIS region, with adverse consequences for corporate governance. For example, in one country the licenses of several foreign-owned financial service companies were recently revoked following the passage of new legislation requiring all such entities to be joint ventures with local partners; this happened despite the fact that an earlier law on the protection of investment had been intended to effectively grandfather all such investments. The dilution of "outsider" shareholdings by the issuance of additional shares of privatized companies and their assignment to dominant local shareholding groups, often at below fair market value, is a frequent occurrence in a number of CIS countries. Another common practice, in the context of mass privatization programs, has been to confer special advantages to domestic "investment funds" which are given a first call on shares in privatization at the expense of potential foreign investors. In several countries, lax bank supervision and weak enforcement of prudential regulations have enabled banks to lend primarily to their own shareholders, or to engage in otherwise risky lending, which has significantly weakened the banking system.

III. The Negative Economic Effects of Corruption

Aside from reducing the moral authority of and confidence in government, and tending to create an environment that is generally disillusioning for productive economic activity, corruption has other, more concrete negative effects on resource allocation, income distribution, and economic growth.

Corruption is likely to exacerbate distortions in the allocation of resources, because the officials benefiting from corruption will be less likely to press for the reduction or elimination of regulations or various distortions or exemptions that encourage corruption in the first place. Moreover, a thriving culture of corruption may encourage officials to increase the range of regulations and license procedures, hoping for even more bribes. Corruption may also exacerbate income inequalities and poverty, as it may help perpetuate an unequal distribution of wealth and access to education and other means to increase human capital.[4]

---

[4] A study by Gupta, Davoodi, and Alonso-Terme (Chapter 17 in this volume) has found a strong correlation between corruption and an increase in income inequality.

There is considerable empirical evidence that corruption has a negative effect on economic growth.[5] Since corruption constitutes a kind of tax on enterprises, it increases costs[6] and reduces incentives to invest. Pervasive corruption may also encourage many of the more talented individuals in society to engage in rent seeking rather than productive or innovative activity, with adverse consequences for economic growth.[7] Corruption, moreover, tends to discourage the formation and development of potentially dynamic small and medium-sized enterprises, since smaller entities frequently do not have the human or monetary resources to deal effectively and persistently with corrupt officials. There is also evidence that corruption tends to shift government spending away from social areas (such as health and education) and from the provision of high-quality physical infrastructure toward the construction of unneeded "white elephant" projects or lower-quality investments in infrastructure.

As noted in Section II, many of the corrupt practices documented in the CIS countries are either specifically aimed at, or at least have the practical effect of discriminating against, the foreign business community. This derives essentially from the closer contacts to be expected between government officials and the local business community, but also from the basic lack of transparency involved in most acts of corruption. IMF resident representatives in many of the CIS countries report that, in several instances, corruption has discouraged foreign direct investment and, in some instances, has led erstwhile investors to pull out of a country entirely.

Corruption can also be expected to have a negative effect on domestic savings and investment, and to stimulate capital flight, as it tends to weaken the domestic banking system. Moreover, most savers and investors hesitate to commit to an economic environment in which considerable official discretion and secrecy, together with corruption, create a high degree of uncertainty. This uncertainty will only be compounded

---

[5]See, for example, Mauro (Chapter 9 in this volume) and the references therein.

[6]A survey by a resident representative office of the IMF in a CIS country suggested that "informal payments" to various officials accounted, on average, for almost 40 percent of total enterprise expenses during the first year of operation.

[7]See also Gray and Kaufmann (1998), who refute the argument that corruption and bribery can "lubricate" a rigid administration by illustrating that where corruption is high, firms' managers spend more time with government bureaucrats, as corruption fuels the growth of excessive and discretionary regulations.

by the corrosion of the moral authority of any state that tolerates widespread corruption.

In short, corruption can be considered as one of the most important factors inhibiting investment and growth and thereby lowering living standards in many of the transition economies reviewed. Finally, and as suggested by the example provided in Section II, pervasive corruption will likely discourage the effectiveness of aid flows to low-income transition countries. This, in turn, could discourage donors from providing more aid, which could also have a negative impact on growth.

IV. Addressing Governance and Corruption Issues under IMF Arrangements

The IMF provides financial assistance to its member countries under different types of arrangements, varying in duration and the kinds of policy measures that countries are encouraged to adopt. Typically, in supporting member countries' macroeconomic adjustment and reform programs, IMF advice has focused on correcting macroeconomic imbalances, reducing inflation, and promoting trade, exchange, and other market reforms in order to achieve financial stability and lasting economic growth. More recently, in growing recognition of the adverse impact of poor governance (and ensuing corruption) on economic efficiency and growth, the IMF has turned its attention to a broader range of institutional reforms and governance issues in the programs that it supports. This shift—which is in line with the increased emphasis on governance issues in member countries—is reflected in the guidelines issued by the IMF's Executive Board in mid-1997 on "The Role of the IMF in Governance Issues."[8] The guidelines seek to enhance the IMF's role in this area, in particular through:

- A more comprehensive treatment, in the context of both the IMF's regular consultations to member countries and consultations related to IMF-supported programs, of those governance issues within the IMF's mandate and expertise;

- A more proactive approach in advocating policies and the development of institutions and administrative systems that eliminate

---
[8]See International Monetary Fund (1997).

the opportunity for bribery, corruption, and fraudulent activity in the management of public resources;[9]

- An evenhanded treatment of governance issues in all member countries; and
- Enhanced collaboration with other multilateral institutions, in particular the World Bank, to make better use of complementary areas of expertise.

These principles have also been guiding the IMF's work in the Baltic and CIS countries.[10] In addition to its surveillance and technical assistance activities, the IMF has entered into financial arrangements with each of these countries (except Turkmenistan). In most countries, this involvement began with the IMF's Systemic Transformation Facility—designed specifically to gradually ease transition economies into a heavy reform agenda—followed by Stand-By Arrangements and, more recently, by three-year Extended Arrangements or support under the Enhanced Structural Adjustment Facility (for low-income countries). Although many reforms advocated by the IMF were aimed at eliminating price distortions, improving the fiscal position, and other basic macroeconomic objectives, they frequently had the effect as well of promoting good governance through liberalizing the economy, improving the management of public resources, and supporting the development and maintenance of a transparent and stable economic and regulatory environment.

As illustrated in Tables 1 and 2, IMF-supported economic stabilization and reform programs in the Baltic and CIS countries have contained measures in all three of the dimensions of economic governance discussed in Section II, namely government regulation of economic activity and preferential schemes; government transparency, accountability, and good economic management; and creation of a stable and rule-based competitive environment for the efficient operation of market activities. The entries in the tables indicate the frequencies with which specific measures in each of these three broad policy areas were included in IMF-supported programs in the region during 1992–99. The

---

[9]For a discussion on ways for reducing the incentives for corruption, see Kaufmann (1998).

[10]The IMF's work in the transition economies of Central and Eastern Europe is not covered in this paper.

Table 1. Key Measures in IMF Arrangements to Improve Economic Governance, 1992–95[1]

A. Liberalization, Deregulation, and Privatization

	Elimination of tax exemptions	Phasing out government guarantees on lending	Elimination of price subsidies	Elimination of subsidized lending	Unification of reserve requirements	Exchange liberalization	Phasing out export surrender requirements	Trade liberalization	Deregulation	Demonopolization and regulation of natural monopolies	Privatization
Armenia	2	1	1								
Azerbaijan	1	1	3	1		1		1		1	4
Belarus		2	3	1	1		1	1		1	1
Estonia											
Georgia	1	2	1	1					1		1
Kazakhstan	1	2	2	2			1	2			5
Kyrgyz Republic											
Latvia	1	4	2	1		1		1	1	1	4
Lithuania	1	2	2	1		3	1	3			
Moldova		1	3	1	1	1	1	4			2
Russia	2		1								
Tajikistan											
Ukraine		1	4			1		3	1	1	3
Uzbekistan		2	5	1	1	1	1	6	2	1	1
Total	9	18	27	10	2	8	5	22	5	6	21

548

B. Government Transparency, Accountability, and Good Economic Management

	Improvement of expenditure control and creation of a treasury	Establishment of independent central bank and banking system	Strengthening of tax administration	Elimination of budgetary arrears	Reform of civil service	Improvement in quality and reporting of fiscal statistics, adoption of an open budgetary process	Public enterprise restructuring
Armenia	2	1					
Azerbaijan	1	3			1		
Belarus				1			
Estonia						1	1
Georgia	2	2	3	2	3		2
Kazakhstan		2					5
Kyrgyz Republic	3	3					2
Latvia		1					
Lithuania		2					
Moldova		1					2
Russia			1				
Tajikistan							
Ukraine	3	1					1
Uzbekistan							
Total	11	16	4	3	4	1	13

C. Establishment of a Stable, Rule-Based, and Competitive Environment

	Legal reforms[2]	Introduction of international accounting standards for enterprises	Strengthening of bank supervision and prudential regulations	Improvement in accounting and reporting in the banking system
Armenia	1		1	
Azerbaijan			2	
Belarus	4	1		
Estonia				
Georgia	2			
Kazakhstan	3		1	1
Kyrgyz Republic	2		3	
Latvia			1	
Lithuania			1	
Moldova	2			
Russia				
Tajikistan				
Ukraine	2		2	
Uzbekistan				1
Total	16	1	11	2

[1]Measures that constitute prior actions, performance criteria, and structural benchmarks in Stand-By, Enhanced Structural Adjustment Facility, and Extended Fund Facility arrangements.
[2]Including adoption of laws on bankruptcy, property protection, foreign investment, and taxation.

Table 2. Key Measures in IMF Arrangements to Improve Economic Governance, 1996–99[1]

A. Liberalization, Deregulation, and Privatization

	Elimination of tax exemptions	Phasing out government guarantees on lending	Elimination of price subsidies	Elimination of subsidized lending	Unification of reserve requirements	Exchange liberalization	Phasing out export surrender requirements	Trade liberalization	Deregulation	Demonopolization and regulation of natural monopolies	Privatization
Armenia	1	4	2	1		1					1
Azerbaijan		2	1	2		2		1			9
Belarus											
Estonia		2									1
Georgia	1	3	2				1	3			4
Kazakhstan	2	3	6					3			5
Kyrgyz Republic	1	2				1					2
Latvia		1									3
Lithuania	1		1		1			3			2
Moldova		4	4	1		1		4			4
Russia	3		6	5	1	1		3			2
Tajikistan		3	4	1		3	1	3		2	11
Ukraine	4	1	11			2	1	12	3		10
Uzbekistan									3		
Total	13	25	37	10	2	10	3	32	3	4	54

B. Government Transparency, Accountability, and Good Economic Management

	Improvement of expenditure control and creation of a treasury	Establishment of independent central bank and banking system	Strengthening of tax administration	Elimination of budgetary arrears	Reform of civil service	Improvement in quality and reporting of fiscal statistics, adoption of an open budgetary process	Public enterprise restructuring
Armenia	3	2	3	3	2	2	
Azerbaijan	6		4	1	8	1	3
Belarus							
Estonia	1		1				
Georgia	6	2	11	3	2		
Kazakhstan	2		12	2	1	1	3
Kyrgyz Republic	3		3	2	2	1	2
Latvia			1		1		
Lithuania	3						1
Moldova	2		1	2	1		1
Russia	5	1	6	1	1	3	1
Tajikistan	1	1	5	4			1
Ukraine	8	2	2	2	5		1
Uzbekistan							
Total	40	8	49	20	23	8	13

C. Establishment of a Stable, Rule-Based, and Competitive Environment

	Legal reforms[2]	Introduction of international accounting standards for enterprises	Strengthening of bank supervision and prudential regulations	Improvement in accounting and reporting in the banking system
Armenia	3		6	
Azerbaijan	9		7	1
Belarus				
Estonia	4		4	
Georgia	3		7	
Kazakhstan	2		3	
Kyrgyz Republic	1		1	1
Latvia				
Lithuania	7		1	
Moldova	6	2	1	
Russia	1		2	4
Tajikistan	4		3	1
Ukraine			6	1
Uzbekistan				
Total	40	2	41	8

[1] Measures that constitute prior actions, performance criteria, and structural benchmarks in Stand-By, Enhanced Structural Adjustment Facility, and Extended Fund Facility arrangements.

[2] Including adoption of laws on bankruptcy, property protection, foreign investment, and taxation.

Table 3. Summary of Key Measures in IMF Arrangements to Improve Economic Governance, 1992–99[1]

	1992–95		1996–99	
	Number	In percent	Number	In percent
A. Liberalization, deregulation, and privatization	133	61.9	193	43.4
B. Government transparency, accountability, and good economic management	52	24.2	161	36.2
C. Establishment of a stable, rule-based, and competitive environment	30	14.0	91	20.4
Total	215	100.0	445	100.0

[1]Measures that constitute prior actions, performance criteria, and structural benchmarks in Stand-By, Enhanced Structural Adjustment Facility, and Extended Fund Facility arrangements.

data show that all programs contained fairly similar policy actions, although there was a great deal of variation among countries in the sequencing and frequency of measures during the period in question, reflecting differences in initial economic conditions, the political will to reform, external factors, and so on.[11] Variations over time (before and after 1996) in the types of measures reflect mainly the different stages of transformation, with the policy emphasis shifting from macroeconomic stabilization and liberalization in the initial years to deeper and more diversified structural reforms more recently. Table 3 summarizes this development, with measures in the second and third broad areas of governance (i.e., those related to transparency, accountability, and sound economic management; and to building a stable environment) clearly gaining weight in the more recent period. This shift indicates not only the emphasis in earlier years on liberalizing economic activity and eliminating the initial very high rates of inflation but also the growing recognition that progress with structural reforms and good

---

[11]Frequency should be interpreted cautiously. For example, a high figure in a given policy area may indicate the repetition of unimplemented measures in successive programs.

governance are essential to sustain the stabilization gains and support the recoveries under way.

To better understand how IMF involvement might have a bearing on governance and corruption, it is useful to take a closer look at some of the economic reform programs in the Baltic and CIS countries. For this purpose, five representative countries were selected and IMF conditionality examined for each in the context of their recent IMF arrangements.[12] By way of illustration, Appendixes I–III provide information on three of the countries selected.[13] Only those measures that were thought to have an important bearing on governance and corruption were reviewed. It should be noted, however, that program content typically extends far beyond measures captured under IMF conditionality and covers a broad range of other policy actions adopted by governments. However, since the IMF exerts its most visible influence through agreed conditionality—noncompliance with which normally interrupts IMF financing and other linked lending—the discussion here is confined to the experience with conditionality. For the sake of simplicity, the period covered by each IMF arrangement is taken in its entirety, with no attempt made to distinguish between different annual arrangements under multiyear programs, nor between program reviews. For example, the "prior actions" listed lump together those imposed at different points in time, and measures in other categories of conditionality are similarly aggregated over time. The objective is to broadly capture policy conditionality and implementation over the life of the program.

Appendixes I–III show that, notwithstanding some differences among programs in the rigor with which conditionality was incorporated in similar policy areas (with "prior actions" being the most binding and "structural benchmarks" the least), all programs included measures to

- *Liberalize the economy.* Measures in this area mostly related to lifting price controls on goods and services; opening up the trade

---

[12]IMF programs typically contain the following types of conditionality: *prior actions*, which need to be in place for the program to be approved by the IMF's Executive Board; *quantitative macroeconomic performance criteria*, which call for compliance with quantitative targets for selected variables on specified dates; and *structural performance criteria* or *benchmarks*, which specify a timetable for the implementation of structural measures.

[13]To preserve confidentiality, countries are identified by letters rather than by name.

system by phasing out tariffs and taxes and registration requirements on foreign trade; and eliminating exchange controls on current transactions, including through the modification of foreign exchange surrender requirements.

- *Strengthen the budgetary process and the treasury system.* Measures ranged from strengthening revenue collection (including through the removal of tax exemptions) and streamlining government spending (including through the elimination of subsidies) to bringing extrabudgetary government funds on budget and extending treasury coverage.

- *Eliminate wage, pension, and social benefit arrears.* In all the cases reviewed, quantitative performance criteria (i.e., quarterly limits) were imposed on the government's domestic expenditure arrears, notably in the above categories, to ensure an orderly phasing out of such arrears.[14]

- *Reform the banking system.* Measures focused on establishing central bank independence, introducing a new chart of accounts, adopting effective prudential regulations, and strengthening bank supervision.

- *Privatize, restructure, or liquidate public enterprises.* The IMF sought sustained progress in these areas, with specific intermediate program targets to be met, and advocated the effective implementation of bankruptcy laws where called for.

- *Improve legal, accounting, and statistical frameworks.* Action in this area entailed adopting laws (e.g., banking laws, tax codes, customs codes, laws on natural monopolies, and so on), accounting frameworks, and macroeconomic data compilation and presentation practices that are compatible with international standards.

The final columns in Appendixes I–III show the status of implementation of the conditionality on structural reforms under the selected IMF-supported programs. By their very nature, prior actions were fully implemented, with one or two exceptions where there was

---

[14]The budgetary arrears problem was also tackled through the evolution of fiscal programming practices, as arrears often reflected unrealistic budgets, which contained overoptimistic revenue forecasts and spending obligations that could not be financed.

a delay or a waiver was granted for a required action. Performance in meeting quantitative and structural performance criteria was likewise generally good, with only minor slippages. However, compliance with structural benchmarks—the violation of which would not necessarily disrupt IMF disbursements—was more uneven, with some benchmarks delayed or postponed, although a fair amount of progress was usually made toward attaining the missed targets. The failure to meet structural benchmarks generally reflected the longer-than-anticipated time it took to obtain political consensus on the benchmark and the complexity of the measures, or the lack of supporting institutions, or both. Also, at times, structural benchmarks (as opposed to performance criteria) were deliberately used when, given the nature of the reform measure and the uncertainties relating to its precise timing, a more flexible approach was called for. In some cases, to ensure implementation, a missed structural benchmark was made a prior action in a later program review or a succeeding arrangement. In other cases, benchmarks were modified in light of changed circumstances or shifted to a subsequent test date, provided that the program was otherwise mostly on track.

Unfortunately, definitive conclusions cannot be drawn about whether the successful implementation of these programs actually lowered corruption, particularly in the absence of a reliable measure of corruption in these countries. Also, notwithstanding the progress to date, a heavy reform agenda still remains for the Baltic and especially the CIS countries. For example, although there is considerable empirical evidence of a strong negative relationship between the level of public sector wages and corruption,[15] not all programs in these countries contain measures, other than the elimination of government wage arrears noted above, to address incentive-driven corruption. Civil service reforms are only just beginning in most countries. Some of the measures introduced (including those to strengthen transparency), moreover, may take much longer to make their full impact. Nevertheless, one way of getting an approximate idea about the effectiveness of economic reforms in curbing corruption might be to compare the corruption levels in transition economies that are at different stages of

---

[15]See Ul Haque and Sahay (1996) and the references therein.

Table 4. Reform and Corruption Indicators for Selected Transition Economies, 1997–99

	Reform Indicators EBRD[1] 1998	Corruption Indicators Transparency International[2] 1999	Freedom House[3] 1997–98
Hungary	3.7	5.2	A
Estonia	3.5	5.7	B
Czech Republic	3.5	4.6	B
Poland	3.4	4.2	A
Slovak Republic	3.3	3.7	C
Slovenia	3.2	6.0	A
Latvia	3.1	3.4	B
Lithuania	3.1	3.8	B
Bulgaria	2.8	3.3	C
Kyrgyz Republic	2.8	2.2	D
Romania	2.8	3.3	C
Kazakhstan	2.7	1.3	D
Georgia	2.7	2.3	C
Moldova	2.7	2.6	C
Armenia	2.7	2.5	D
Albania	2.6	2.3	D
Russia	2.5	2.4	D
Ukraine	2.4	2.6	D
Azerbaijan	2.2	1.7	D
Uzbekistan	2.1	1.8	D
Tajikistan	2.0	. . .	D
Belarus	1.5	3.4	C
Turkmenistan	1.4	. . .	D

Sources: European Bank for Reconstruction and Development (EBRD), *Transition Report 1999*; Transparency International; and Freedom House.

[1]Simple average of EBRD transition indicators covering enterprise reform, financial sector reform, and market and trade reform. The indicator ranges from 1 (least reformed) to 4 (most reformed).

[2]The index refers to perception of corruption ranging from 10 (highly clean) to 0 (highly corrupt).

[3]Corruption indicators ranging from A (least corrupt) to D (most corrupt); the period covered is from January 1997 through March 1998.

economic reforms. Such an exercise, while heavily constrained by the difficulties in measuring corruption and the usual caveats for cross-country comparisons, suggests that countries that are at a more advanced stage of economic reform tend to display lower levels of corruption (see Table 4).[16]

To summarize, while IMF-supported programs have not directly tackled corruption in the Baltic and CIS countries, they have generally played an indirect role in helping to address these issues through economic and structural reforms aimed at improving economic governance. In particular, policies to promote deregulation, liberalization, and privatization have aimed at creating an environment less conducive to corruption. The IMF's technical assistance and training programs—focusing primarily on designing and implementing fiscal and monetary policies;[17] institution building (such as the development of central banks, treasuries, and tax and customs administrations); collecting and processing statistical data; and drafting and reviewing financial legislation—have been effective in complementing its surveillance and financing activities in these countries. Nevertheless, as many of the ongoing episodes of corruption suggest, much still needs to be accomplished to address this serious problem.

V. Future Areas of IMF Emphasis in Fighting Corruption

Turning to the future, the IMF will continue its work in helping to curtail opportunities for corruption in member countries by supporting reforms in economic policies and institutions, while intensifying efforts to promote transparency and accountability. A number of general initiatives are already under way in the context of strengthening the "architecture" of the international monetary and financial system. The IMF has drafted, and is actively encouraging member countries

---

[16]For example, two separate sets of corruption indicators (outlined in Table 4) developed by Transparency International and the Freedom House, respectively, generally show lower levels of corruption for those transition economies in Central and Eastern Europe and the former Soviet Union that began their economic reforms earlier and made greater progress, although the relationship is less apparent for the CIS countries, where reforms have generally had a shorter history.

[17]In the area of tax policy, for example, IMF technical assistance has generally aimed at simplifying, increasing the efficiency, and reducing the discretionary elements of tax systems to limit the scope for corruption.

to adopt, codes of good practices in fiscal and monetary management.[18] In several countries, the IMF is preparing, with the cooperation of the authorities, experimental reports on observance of standards and codes to help identify areas where transparency can be enhanced and to contribute to informed lending and investment decisions by revealing the extent to which countries observe internationally recognized standards. The IMF has also encouraged country self-assessments and provided technical assistance to help in this process. Finally, it has launched and recently expanded a standard of sound practices for countries to follow in providing economic and financial statistics to the public.[19]

Within this broader institutional framework, a great deal of thought is presently being given to determining the future areas of priority in fighting corruption in the Baltic and CIS countries. Clearly, despite the progress to date, much remains to be done to find a better balance between the roles of the state and the market, and to limit the conditions that breed corruption. IMF staff teams working on the countries in question will be guided by the initiatives noted above. The recent shift in emphasis toward strengthening government transparency, accountability, sound economic management, and creating a rule-based, competitive environment will gain considerable momentum in the period ahead. While specific policy advice will need to be tailored to the circumstances of each country, the following areas are certain to receive further attention:

- Acceleration of public sector reforms and downsizing of the government;

- A clearer specification of what constitutes government activity;

- Improvements in the management and oversight of the use of public funds;

- Integration of all extrabudgetary government activity into the budget framework;

---

[18]The "Code of Good Practices on Fiscal Transparency" and the "Code of Good Practices on Transparency in Monetary and Financial Policies" are available through the IMF's external website. See http://www.imf.org/external/np/fad/trans/code.htm and http://www.imf.org/external/np/mae/mft/index.htm, respectively.

[19]Referred to as the Special Data Dissemination Standard (SDDS). See http://dsbb.imf.org/sddsindex.htm.

- Elimination of offsets in the government budget;[20]
- Phasing out of barter arrangements in foreign trade;
- Clarification of central banking functions to exclude treasury operations;
- Adoption of codes of good practices in the conduct of fiscal and monetary policy;
- Adoption of tax codes, and reform of tax and customs administrations;
- Further progress with privatization and public enterprise restructuring;
- Regulatory reforms, including further reductions in business activity regulations;
- Reforms in the legal system,[21] including in the enforcement of legislation;
- Further progress with civil service reforms;[22]
- Independent audits of central and state banks and government and enterprise operations;
- Strengthening of and adherence to public procurement regulations;
- Adoption of laws and rules on asset declaration and conflict of interest; and
- Increasing the coverage, frequency, and timely publication of economic statistics.

Continued progress in the areas listed above can be expected to reduce the opportunities and scope for corruption. Stricter enforcement of sanctions on corrupt practices will also help, notably through its demonstration effect. However, one has to bear in mind that corruption

---

[20]"Offsets" refer to the offsetting of tax arrears against expenditure arrears.

[21]Notably, the further strengthening of bankruptcy laws and procedures; enforcement of contracts; protection of shareholder rights; improvements in (and better adherence to) the legal and regulatory framework for foreign investment; and promotion of an independent judiciary and court system.

[22]Including downsizing, strengthening incentives, building administrative capacity, and reforming institutions to increase accountability and reduce arbitrary practices.

has a long history in many of these countries and is strongly ingrained in their day-to-day existence. It often reaches all the way to the top, and the absence in some cases of a free press, a truly independent judiciary, and an effective political opposition makes it difficult to expose and challenge corrupt practices.

In the light of these considerations, care should be taken not to exaggerate what can be accomplished in reducing corruption through additional emphasis in IMF conditionality on improving economic governance. It is essential that corruption at the highest levels be minimized, because of both its stifling impact on growth (see Section III) and its corrosive effect on society in general, since the highest authorities fundamentally set the moral tone for the rest of society. It is equally important to increase public awareness of the detrimental effects of corruption, as these are often not clearly understood. There is, moreover, frequently a lack of conviction on the part of policymakers, the parliament, and civil society that effective measures to fight corruption can make a difference. These are issues of a social and political nature that go beyond the scope of IMF-supported economic programs, and will take much longer to resolve. Nevertheless, the close involvement of the international community can be expected to help bring about the needed changes.

The IMF will continue its efforts to improve governance and fight corruption in the region, and collaborate closely with other international organizations, particularly the World Bank, to ensure the delivery of effective, consistent, and timely advice. Insofar as IMF conditionality in the area of governance is concerned, it will generally be limited to measures, or groups of measures, that are critical for achieving the macroeconomic objectives of an IMF-supported program.

Finally, corruption is a "dynamic" phenomenon that tends to adapt quickly to changes in circumstances. Hence, the IMF will maintain close contacts with nongovernmental organizations and the private sector to keep abreast of the impact of measures to fight corruption and the further policy adaptations that may be called for to tackle this serious problem.

Appendixes

Appendix I. Selected Measures Affecting Corruption in IMF Arrangements: Country A—Stand-By Arrangement, 1997

Conditionality	Program Measures	Implementation
Prior actions	Eliminate most value added-tax and enterprise profit tax exemptions	Completed
	Improve loan classification system for banks	Completed
	Include extrabudgetary funds administered by the treasury in the budget	Completed
	Phase out enterprise contributions to extrabudgetary funds and reciprocal benefits	Completed
	Submit to parliament a new customs code consistent with international standards	Completed
	Progress with price liberalization (four measures)	Completed
	Progress with trade liberalization (six measures)	Completed
	Eliminate selected exchange restrictions	Completed
	Submit to parliament a new central bank law	Completed
	Initiate full international accounting standards audit of the savings bank	Completed
	Eliminate licensing for foreign borrowing	Completed
	Abolish excess wage tax	Completed
	Progress with privatization (three measures)	Completed
	Adopt measures to discourage barter in payments for electricity	Completed
	Move toward competitive gas market with an appropriate regulatory body	Completed
Quantitative performance criteria	Ceiling on budgetary arrears on wages, pensions, and benefits	Observed
	Indicative target on the accumulation of gas payments arrears by the central government and state budget–financed institutions	Observed
Structural benchmarks	Parliament approval of the new central bank law	Not done
	Progress with privatization (two measures)	Partially completed
	Phase out and simplify business licensing	Completed
	Ensure full passthrough of electricity wholesale to retail prices	Partially completed
	Adopt a pension reform program	Not done
	Make further progress with trade liberalization	Not done

Appendix II. Selected Measures Affecting Corruption in IMF Arrangements: Country B—Extended Arrangement, 1996–98

Conditionality	Program Measures	Implementation
Prior actions	Implement measures to raise and rationalize government revenue (14 measures specified)	Completed
	Eliminate mandatory registration of export contracts (private) at commodity exchange	Completed
	Resubmit to parliament the laws on unfair competition and on natural monopolies	Completed
Quantitative performance criteria	Ceiling on arrears of the pension fund	Observed
	Ceiling on other arrears of the general government	Observed
Structural benchmarks	Submit legislation for modification of natural resource taxation	Completed
	Introduce the classification system of the IMF's *Government Finance Statistics Yearbook* for government expenditure	Completed
	Elaborate sector-specific action plans for privatization	In progress
	Adjust utility tariffs (with two exceptions) to fully cover costs	Completed
	Progress with banking reforms (two measures)	Mostly completed
	Complete a review of the effectiveness of the new bankruptcy law	In progress
	Discontinue budgetary support to selected budget-financed organizations	Completed
	Design and implement a mechanism to deal with expenditure arrears in budgetary organizations	In progress
	Strengthen tax administration (two measures)	In progress
	Design a stable system of revenue sharing and expenditure among different levels of government	In progress
	Submit law on protection of consumer rights	Completed
	Publicize cases of seizure and bankruptcy to alert taxpayers	Completed
	Reduce government employment by 10,000 positions	In progress

Appendix III. Selected Measures Affecting Corruption in IMF Arrangements: Country C—Enhanced Structural Adjustment Facility Arrangement, 1997–99

Conditionality	Program Measures	Implementation
Prior actions	Eliminate selected wage and pension arrears	Completed
	Schedule repayments of budget loans by key debtor companies and ministries	Completed
Quantitative performance criteria	Observe continuous ceiling on outstanding stock of external arrears	Observed
	Observe ceiling on outstanding stock of wage and pension arrears	Waiver granted
Structural performance criteria	Remove certain discretionary tax exemptions by a specified date	Completed
Structural benchmarks	Set up budget commission to periodically review the budget	Completed
	Finalize organizational structure and regulations of the treasury	Completed
	Introduce new chart of accounts for the central bank	Completed
	Adopt and start implementing new chart of accounts for banks (based on international accounting standards)	Mostly completed
	Progress with enterprise restructuring (three measures)	Completed
	Progress with mass privatization program (details given)	Completed
	Submit revised law on principles of the budget to parliament	Completed
	Adopt action plan for civil service reforms	Completed
	Begin replacing scheduled indirect subsidies by direct subsidies	Completed with delay
	Submit to parliament the Code of Good Conduct for Civil Servants	Completed
	Provide State Tax Inspectorate with complete data on export and import declarations[1]	Completed with delay
	Adopt by a specified date certain measures on privatization	Completed

[1] As part of a broader benchmark to enhance cooperation between State Customs and State Tax Inspectorate.

References

Abed, George T., 1998, "Governance and the Transition Economies," paper presented at the conference cosponsored by the Kyrgyz Republic and the IMF on "Challenges to Economies in Transition: Stabilization, Growth, and Governance," Bishkek, May.

Gray, Cheryl W., and Daniel Kaufmann, 1998, "Corruption and Development", *Finance & Development* (March), pp. 7–10.

International Monetary Fund, 1997, *Good Governance: The IMF's Role* (Washington).

Kaufmann, Daniel, 1998, "Revisiting Anti-Corruption Strategies: Tilt Towards Incentive-Driven Approaches," in *Corruption: Integrity Improvement Initiatives in Developing Countries* (Paris: OECD Development Center, Organization for Economic Cooperation and Development).

Kopits, George, and Jon Craig, 1998, *Transparency in Government Operations*, IMF Occasional Paper No. 158 (Washington: International Monetary Fund).

Ul Haque, Nadeem, and Ratna Sahay, 1996, "Do Government Wage Cuts Close Budget Deficits? Costs of Corruption," *IMF Staff Papers*, International Monetary Fund, Vol. 43 (December), pp. 754–78.